Lancashire
County Council

ALSO BY MICHAEL FEENEY CALLAN

BIOGRAPHY

Anthony Hopkins

Richard Harris

Sean Connery

Julie Christie

FICTION

Did You Miss Me?

Lovers and Dancers

POETRY

Fifty Fingers

Robert Redford

MICHAEL FEENEY CALLAN

Robert

Redford

THE BIOGRAPHY

SIMON & SCHUSTER

London · New York · Sydney · Toronto · New Delhi

A CBS COMPANY

First published in Great Britain in 2011 by Simon & Schuster UK Ltd
This edition published in Great Britain in 2012 by Simon & Schuster UK Ltd
A CBS COMPANY

1 3 5 7 9 10 8 6 4 2

Simon & Schuster UK Ltd
1st Floor
222 Gray's Inn Road
London
WC1X 8HB

www.simonandschuster.co.uk

Simon & Schuster Australia, Sydney
Simon & Schuster India, New Delhi

Portions of this work were previously published in Vanity Fair

A CIP catalogue copy for this book is available
from the British Library.

ISBN 978-1-84739-898-7

JK) Ltd, Croydon, CR0 4YY

To

Corey, Paris and Ree

with love and thanks—

true journey-work of the stars

What is become of the horseman, the cow-puncher, the last romantic figure upon our soil? For he was romantic. Whatever he did, he did with his might. The bread that he earned was earned hard, the wages that he squandered were squandered hard. . . . Well, he will be here among us always, invisible, waiting his chance to live and play as he would like. His wild kind has been among us always, since the beginning: a young man with his temptations, a hero without wings.

Owen Wister, *The Virginian*

Contents

PART FOUR *Canyon Keeper*

Introduction

America Is the Girl

> Rocks, trees, wind on our cheeks! the *solid* earth! the *actual* world! the *common sense! Contact! Contact! Who* are we? *where* are we?
>
> Henry David Thoreau, *The Maine Woods*

It's Brigadoon, really, on a summer's day. You drive an hour south out of Salt Lake City on the I-15, turn east at the signposts for the Uinta National Park and catch the Provo Canyon Road as it wends along a river once famous for trout as populous as cobblestones. Then you head north again along the Alpine Loop road, and in a vee of aspens you find it: a modest trunk road to a circle of timber cabins, a ski lift or two beyond, and above, the breathtaking elegance of the glacial Mount Timpanogos, towering almost twelve thousand feet above sea level. Apart from the few small-signage properties, and the spidery frames of the lifts, it's as it was two centuries before, when the Ute Indians lived here. It is still the home of ground squirrels and four types of snakes. Golden eagles still overfly it. Mountain lions have been sighted. Deer numbered in the thousands until the particularly ferocious winter of 1990 wiped out 90 percent of them. Now the elk are back in numbers. It possesses, it seems, some powerful organic mechanism of renewal.

When you step out of your car (the only way to get here), the air has the minty intensity of the Alps. You breathe deeply, because at this elevation—more than six thousand feet—the air is thinner. Visitors get nosebleeds. It seems a place of enormousness. Huge sky. Huge mountains. Huge contradictions. Henry David Thoreau got lost on Mount Katahdin and in *The Maine Woods* expressed both the beauty and the concurrent threat of nature. It's a place to take pause.

Robert Redford discovered this canyon more than fifty years ago. Originally it was squatters' land, purchased from the government by a Scottish family in 1900 for $1.25 an acre under the terms of the 1877 Desert Land Act and granddaddied for sheep farming thereafter. By the 1950s the wool market was dead and the lands all but derelict. In 1961 Redford and his wife bought two acres and built a home. In 1968, flush with Hollywood success, he purchased several thousand adjoining acres and later called it Sundance in recognition of his movie breakthrough. In 1980 he set up an arts colony to promote young filmmakers. "I'd seen small movies like *Heartland* [directed by Richard Pearce], and saw passion that was going nowhere. There was no infrastructure to support these films. Hollywood in the seventies was only interested in blockbusters." His remedy was an arts commune, based in part on the artists' colony Yaddo and on the theory of the assembly line that would address scriptwriting, script filming and, eventually, product selling. He asked friends like actor Karl Malden, writer Waldo Salt and cinematographer László Kovács to assist. They came to the canyon and set the wheels in motion. Seventeen new filmmakers were invited that first season, and the results were immediate. Enthusiasm was defined by the work ethic; people labored seventeen hours a day. Short movies were shot, edited, debated, reshot, finessed. Aspirant filmmakers who came with nothing more than an idea left with the bones of a professional screenplay. A few thousand dollars were spent that first summer. Within two years the sponsors were rolling in and millions were being directed toward what was essentially an alternative filmmaking industry. In popular perception, Robert Redford had invented independent cinema.

Redford's initiative came on the heels of a stream of eco-activism and Indian rights pursuits. Its principle, says Redford, was conciliatory. He recognized the importance of business in Hollywood as much as he recognized the frustration of the independents. But a sense of exclusion, he felt, repressed emerging talent. Apropos of his environmental activism, he wrote in the *Harvard Business Review* that "people need the chance to see how much agreement is possible." Fostering independents, he felt, could only enhance Hollywood. But there were inherent contradictions. He disliked the overintrusion of Hollywood and only reluctantly allowed a studio presence in the Sundance boardroom. He wanted a clear demarcation zone. The bullishness raised hackles. Journalists visited and observed his brand of altruism as suspect. There was about it, one wrote, indulgence. The rebellious seventies had made him a star and a wealthy man: "This rustic Xanadu and the ideals behind [it] are his way of keeping that decade alive in all its skepticism and sincerity." Some accused him of "granola" filmmaking. But Redford stood his ground with ferocity, even against the advice of his lawyers when they told him he couldn't afford the mortgages and overheads that amounted to several hundred thousand dollars a year.

Redford maneuvered to keep his vision alive. He had in place already a mom-and-pop ski resort that comprised a ski lift and a basic restaurant. In 1985 he commercialized the operation, endorsing an expansion plan for accommodations around the estate that included two multiunit condominiums and a hundred houses, all of which, in keeping with his passion for maximum conservation, were built below the tree line. In 1989 he introduced a trading catalog, selling western apparel. Combined, these enterprises effectively underwrote the arts labs. But the labs, he felt, needed an evolutionary nudge. Filmmakers were being trained and projects honed, but there was nowhere for these projects to be seen. The showcasing required a festival forum, and he had it on his doorstep with the Salt Lake City–based United States Film and Video Festival. In 1985, he annexed it and relocated it in Park City, thirty miles up the road. Henceforth, the Sundance lab projects were one step closer to Hollywood.

In 1989, the film festival liberated Sundance. One movie—Steven Soderbergh's *sex, lies, and videotape*—broke out and won a huge Hollywood distribution deal. Its global recognition shone a light on the first principle of the Sundance Institute, which was to allow new artists the unconditional chance to express themselves. Sundance now had a cultivating laboratory and a marketplace. Redford had realized his vision in stubbornness. He had not gone to Hollywood. Hollywood had come to him. What followed was a decade of growth, before entropy set in and the business flanks of Sundance, designed to commercially buttress the arts institute, gave way. Sundance wobbled, but it didn't fall. Redford was forced to step back from much of his business, but not his dream. As the business wars raged, attendance at the film festivals grew exponentially. The summer labs—the place it all began—continued to thrive, with yearly script submissions now numbering in the thousands.

Redford's achievement has always been shadowed by skepticism. "Opportunism" was the most commonly offered obloquy, though it was hard to see precisely what self-service beyond the enhancement of a winter vacation resort might be at play. Certainly, by the time he initiated the Sundance Institute, Redford was a made man. His stardom, which began in the sixties, was rock solid, and successes like *Butch Cassidy and the Sun-*

dance Kid, The Way We Were and *The Sting* had lifted him to iconic status. And it was impossible to accuse him of stagnation in 1980. The year he planned the Sundance labs was also the year he set out as a director, winning an Academy Award for *Ordinary People* and establishing a determined second strand to his cinema career. What, then, were his deepest motives? And why was the voice of independence so important to him that it prompted what might accurately be described as empire building in the remotest and unlikeliest of places, the Wasatch Mountains of Utah?

Understanding the obsession that created Sundance necessitates understanding Robert Redford and his journey. Out of such an impulse—to better understand the making of this resilient new arts generator in the heartland of America—this book began.

I first met Redford at a taping for the Bravo television series *Inside the Actors Studio* at the New School in Manhattan in March 1995. I knew I had my work cut out. I admired him and thought much of his work was undervalued and that key thematic connections in his directorial films were unexplored. I also knew he disliked no-holds-barred interviews and that while he cherished the past in a curatorial sense as reflected in his movies like *A River Runs Through It* and *Quiz Show,* the personal past left him cold. But I asked for his cooperation, and I got it.

Once we agreed upon a biographical collaboration, the project immediately stalled. He was legendary for being late ("Call the book *The Late Robert Redford,*" Paul Newman advised me), and I immediately felt the full brunt of it. I flew halfway across the world for meetings that never happened or were largely unproductive because of distractions. I thought of Sartre on Alexandre Dumas's *Kean,* the story of an actor: "He is his own victim, never knowing who he really is, whether he's acting or not." Was this Redford's core character—a professional self-investigator, as good actors are, dulled by his skill for circumvention? Was he, like Jay Gatsby, whom he told me he so admired, lost?

Very quickly I learned that contradictions and paradoxes defined him. Throughout his movies, whether he is tackling politics, family or "the system," there is always the prevalent dominance of one man and his actions. Even at the height of his romantic idol career in the seventies, when women were mailing him their underwear, sagacious journalists were weeding out some underlying contradictory truth. He was, for one, "a subtle blend of Owen Wister's Trampas, a man who knows that words are deadly and final, and Sartre's Orestes, who knows that actions are the only true description of a man."

I labored on. I called him on his disregard for punctuality, which Sydney Pollack, his lifelong friend, had told me was anything but amusing. George Roy Hill, in the last days of his life, fumed about Redford's lateness during the filming of *Butch Cassidy;* Barry Levinson told me the habit cost almost $100,000 in the making of *The Natural.* Redford waved it away. And yet elsewhere there was generous accountability: for neglect of his marriage, incompetence in friendship, failed partnerships, failed businesses.

The paradoxical nature of his relationship with the past resurfaced after the events of 9/11. He was always active in the political shadows with the League of Conservation Voters, and his direct comments about the attacks on New York were few, but pointed. The crisis, he opined, was the result of America's failure to fully understand the world it shared. He stated that America, being a young country, was just spoiled enough not to have to think about the big picture. "We're sort of shallow. . . . We don't look to the past for any clues about our future; we don't look to history. If you look at the Bush administration's way of operating and thinking, you'd be led to believe they've no use for history. It's probably one of the reasons they've bungled everything so badly. What they've set in motion really has a horrible future."

By the time of 9/11 I had been working on the project for more than five years, pursuing Carl Jung's dictum that the truth is only available from the concert of many voices; I attempted to interview all and anyone who knew him. I was close to Redford, regularly lunching and supping with him in Ireland and America, but I felt his spirit was still evasive, and I still had uncertainties about the core philosophy of Sundance.

Reading his reflections on American foreign policy, I remembered a conversation I'd had with his daughter Shauna. Everything of value that she learned about her father, she told me, came in transit: in cars, while skiing, trail riding, on long walks. That reminded me of a key moment in *The Horse Whisperer.* He is courting Kristin Scott Thomas, the East Coast interloper, and she cannot come to grips with him. She is verbally dexterous; he is silent in the Native American way. He leads her on horseback to a high precipice above Big Sky Montana and shows her the land. The moment nudged me, because I'd shared that view precisely in my first experience of Redford out west. The location was different. It was Sundance, Utah, not Montana. But all else was the same: he was expressing himself in a view of America.

Very shortly afterward, I opened another bundle of files sent by Sundance. These included reams of his own notes and sketches over the years, together with his copious correspondence with luminaries in the arts and politics. One letter that got my attention came from the humorist Mort Sahl. Having enjoyed *Havana,* a movie in which many who knew Redford saw encoded autobiographical references, Sahl felt compelled to express his admiration. After a lifetime of bewilderment about the real Robert Redford, wrote Sahl, "I finally get it. America is the Girl."

To all who know the quotidian Robert Redford, there's no surprise in his fixation with the land. He fell in love with America, he says, when he first encountered Yosemite as a teenager in the company of his mother. The "sacredness" of the pristine environment overwhelmed him, and in the years that followed, with successive epiphanies in Texas and on Navajo reservations, he committed himself to some type of stewardship. When he found Provo Canyon in the fifties, he felt a call to set down permanent roots. Once he settled there, he bought up as much of the surrounding land as he could to block development and used it as a base for his activism against what he saw as the mismanagement of the national park system and such legislative loopholes as the 1872 mining act that effectively allowed the devastation of lands bordering the parks.

Recognizing this unconditional determination to protect land became the first key to a fruitful understanding of Redford. Then came the arts labs. One project from the very first Sundance lab, Gregory Nava's *El Norte,* made it to the big screen. In *El Norte,* a Mayan brother and sister, Enrique and Rosa, are tormented in their homeland of Guatemala and flee to Mexico, then to the United States. They are looking for "home." This central focus—"the pursuit of a sense of place," Redford calls it—permeated all the projects of that first Sundance lab and has woven in and out of everything Sundance has done since. Its importance cannot be overstated. Over the years, Redford has strived to encapsulate Sundance in a phrase: It's a place of experiment. A place of risk. Of diversity. This welter of branding somehow obfuscates the point. As flagged by *El Norte* and repeated ceaselessly since, the Sundance arts aspiration is toward an inclusive statement of Americanism.

Like Sundance, Robert Redford bestrides two worlds. He is the product of two very different and disparate families, one part New England settler, one part western. His life has been peripatetic. He has engaged careers on the East Coast and West. It may not be a coincidence that his arts laboratory—his "great experiment"—is not too many miles from Promontory Summit, where, in 1869, the golden spike was hammered that joined the East Coast and West on the transcontinental railroad. It may be that Redford's fugacious nature is not so mysterious, that it is studded in the artwork of the labs and the very stones of Sundance. It may be that Redford's journey is the same as Enrique and Rosa's: toward the integration of personal understanding and the harmony of home.

MICHAEL FEENEY CALLAN
Dublin
January 2011

PART ONE

California Role

For our country here at the west of things
Is pregnant of dreams; and west of the west
I have lived.

Robinson Jeffers, "Epilogue"

1

West

America bloomed on a dream, consolidated in the pages of the *Democratic Review* in 1845 when journalist John O'Sullivan wrote that it was "our Manifest Destiny to overspread the continent allotted by Providence for the free development of our yearly multiplying millions." Prior to then, "America" existed in a huddle of sparsely populated states that were outgrowths of the East Coast Dutch and British settlements. Across the Appalachian divide was limbo, and the travelers who first set out on the Oregon Trail wrote wistfully of "going home to America." Within two centuries, the wilderness was taken from the Native Americans, but its settlement was mythologized in blithe imaginings wrought by the stories of Owen Wister and the paintings of Frederic Remington. In truth, there were few cowboys, fewer than ten thousand at their peak, and the pioneers who trekked west traveled not in Conestoga wagons, but on draylike prairie schooners hauled by oxen. Fantasies are inherent in human nature, and much of the American landscape, unchanged for millennia until the great drive west in the nineteenth century, provoked heaven and hell.

California, especially, inspired heaven. It was huge, its very geography offering a multitude of opportunities for exploitation. Gold had been sprinkled there by the gods. Starting in 1849, the influx began, filling the twin ramshackle metropolises of San Francisco and Los Angeles with their various dreamers. In 1800 the California population measured a few thousand. By 1853, after the gold rush was finished, the population was a quarter of a million. The entrepreneurial energies of great financiers, including Leland Stanford, Mark Hopkins and Charles Crocker, made San Francisco the Paris of the West. Los Angeles, in competition, boomed by nurturing its reputation for blue skies and perfect, balmy breezes. The mission Spaniards, set on sanctifying paradise, persevered with Spanish orange and Portuguese lemon crops, which took hold when the early cattle kings dispersed. These Californian delicacies caught on back east and gave the environs of Los Angeles a bedrock export economy.

Still, California was no easy sell. To the recent immigrants settled on the East Coast—Scots-Irish folk like Redford's maternal great-grandfather, John Hart—the industrial options of the more established towns were more desirable. As the gold rush subsided and the Civil War ran its course, the fledgling Los Angeles chamber of commerce commissioned books like Charles Nordhoff's *California,* which sold the southern part of the state-to-be as a sanitarium. "California college girls are larger by most every dimension than are the college girls of Massachusetts," wrote naturalist David Starr Jordan in an act of shameless boosterism. But it was William Mulholland's extraordinary irrigation scheme at the start of the twentieth century that finally put Los Angeles on the map. Greenery suddenly spread out to envelop the San Fernando Valley, and the city was repackaged as a year-round tourist destination. The succeeding tourist boom fueled helter-skelter residential growth from Santa Monica to Van Nuys and, ultimately, nourished the invention of a dream factory called Hollywood.

Robert Redford was a first-generation Californian, born in Los Angeles as the citrus era ebbed and Hollywood hit flood tide. In the mid-1930s realities clashed as the Dust Bowl casualties came west, only to be stopped at the gates of the city by local police patrols while Angelenos hosted Greta Garbo and Gary Cooper. The Redfords were within the city limits, but poor; neighborhood friends hanged themselves in the Depression. Still, proximity to dream weaving, and the perfect climate, provided powerful distraction. Across the country, movie theaters saw their best business during the Depression years: such was the potency of the dream. For Redford, as for many of his childhood friends, the division between reality and fantasy was blurred. It wasn't unusual, if you were born within five miles of Sunset Boulevard, to see Charlie Chaplin or Betty Grable on your street, or at a store, or driving by. When Redford was a baby, the first person to hold him was the actor Robert Young, a cousin of his mother's; Cesar Romero carpooled him to school; John Steinbeck courted his future wife Elaine before his eyes in a neighbor's home; Redford played on the lawns of Metro-Goldwyn-Mayer executives.

Redford remembers that for a child of five, with a stressed father working fourteen-hour shifts as a milkman, Los Angeles was a place of magic, fragrant with night-scented jasmine. "There was this ritual," he recalls. "At dusk I would cycle to the very edge of the sidewalk and roll the lead wheel onto the curbstone, balancing it, as if I were poised on a chasm; I was told I couldn't go into the street so I was pushing it as far as I could. From there I'd wait for the sunset—and the air was so clear in L.A. at that time that those sunsets were amazing. I'd watch the dark come up from the east. And then, bit by bit, the stars appeared. It was mesmerizing just to contemplate it. The hugeness of this sky. The beauty. What could it mean? Where did it begin?" Redford loves this first childhood recollection: it represents for him the incessant curiosity that has ensured him a life of movement.

Los Angeles was a doddle from his birth until Pearl Harbor, but it was populated, he decided, with faces and personalities that didn't belong in the idyll of the endless summer. There was Grandma Sallie Hart, a faded southern belle with the troubles of the world etched in her beauty. And vaguely behind her was Grandpa Hart, a prairie pirate who lived "down south." Back east there was Grandpa Redford, a ghost whom Redford's father alternately grumbled and laughed about. And then the mysterious Grandmother Redford, who wrote to her son almost daily, with a tone of foreboding. Who were these people? Like Uncle David, his dad's bright-eyed, military-uniformed brother who blew in and blew out, none of them belonged to Los Angeles. In 1944, Redford started asking questions about his family origins; at Grandpa Redford's deathbed in 1964 he was still asking. "I never got answers," says Redford. "We were all just horse dealers, dope addicts and dropouts. None of my grandparents wanted questions and answers. But they were all storytellers. Who was my dad's dad? Just some failed musician, I was told. Who was my mom's dad? When I visited, he was more interested in teaching me to hunt than in talking about the past. To me, he was just a frontiersman. Only later did I make the connections to a big, rich story of several different cultures blending into one life in L.A."

The story that fed both branches of the family, the Redfords and the Harts, was one of rebels and outcasts. The factions arrived in the eighteenth and nineteenth centuries and clung to the East Coast and the ideals of pluralism and liberal democracy that had been established there. Freedom was the quest of both families. By the late fourteenth century the Redfords, Saxon in origin, had split into branches centered in Berkshire and Manchester. Prominent in the Berkshire branch was Henry Redford, a merchant who became Speaker of the House of Commons. He was to be the last celebrated Redford for six hundred years. The other branch, predominantly Catholics, fared less well in Manchester, striving to establish themselves as farmers just as the Church of England Tudors laid siege on Catholic power. Through the 1600s the Catholic Redfords lost their lands, intermarried with the Scots and became reformist Presbyterians at war with the Crown. In 1849, Presbyterian Elisha Redford married Irish Catholic Mary-Ann McCreery in Manchester Cathedral and signed his occupation as "unemployed spinner," meaning a garment industry worker. Other Redfords had already made the journey to Massachusetts under the Puritan flag, and apparently seeking to improve their lot, Elisha and his bride sailed for New York in the summer of 1849. Elisha and Mary-Ann immediately settled in the seaport trading town of Stonington, Connecticut, on the point of land that juts into Little Narragansett Bay. Elisha was a "jickey," the name ascribed to the many Englishmen who came every year to labor at the loom, and he worked hard in constant employment, striving to improve his family in a house shared with two other families. In 1851 the first of the American Redfords arrived when Mary-Ann gave birth to Charles, Redford's great-grandfather. Charles was educated to grade school level, and in adolescence opted to work as a barber in the heart of Pawcatuck, a census-designated section of Stonington then known for its poverty. As a teenager, Charles quickly showed a flair for entertainment and formed a singing quartet to entertain customers. He took up the mandolin, the musical rage of the time, and was suddenly in demand for local recitals. By the 1870s, his virtuosity had seduced a Scots Episcopalian girl from Aberdeen, Jane Archie, ten years his junior, who became his wife. They settled not far from his parents, who, though no more than modestly secure, financially helped Charles to leave Pawcatuck and invest in a barbershop partnership, Hepworth and Redford, across the river in upmarket Westerly.

Charles and Jane's first child, Charles Elijah, born in December 1880, would become Robert Redford's grandfather. Twin sisters, Grace and Claribel, followed. The family was close-knit and restive. The girls were intelligent, and Charles Elijah, even before his teens, evinced a musical skill that surpassed his father's. He mastered cello, bass and piano, but his instrument of choice was the violin, on which, at twelve, he excelled.

By century's end, Elisha was not much better off. He was still in a clapboard house in Stonington, still laboring as a spinner. If he dreamed of a better life for his children, there must have been fulfillment in his son Charles's joy with his barbershop and his music. Charles's children, too, seemed intent on moving up. Like his father, Charles Elijah longed for a career in music. And the sisters Grace and Claribel had brains to burn. The only shadow on Elisha's vision of their future was the apparent rebelliousness his grandchildren displayed. Charles Elijah wanted faraway shores, and though the girls planned on solid careers in education, they, too, were restless and difficult. In Claribel he found an obstinate, politically minded reactionary, and in Grace a freethinker who embraced communism.

Robert Redford's early life was dominated by women. They were not the women of New England, but women of the West. His mother, Martha Hart Redford, was, he says, the center of his universe. She taught him to drive when he was eight, taught him to draw, to role-play in games. She connected him with the past, introducing him to Native Americans on Navajo reservations in Arizona and to Yosemite. These conjunctions came naturally to her, because she was the stuff of the West, descended from Texans who were, in spirit, the polar opposite of the Redfords. A century before, the Harts and Greens of the maternal family line lived a frontier life along the Mississippi Valley, religiously random, indulgent, drifting. The Harts were Galway-Irish, the Greens Scots-Irish, and both families came to America through the southern colonies in the mid-eighteenth century. The Harts followed the frontier to Missouri; the Greens followed the money to Boston. While the Harts drifted, the Greens built one of the first large-scale printing presses in Boston in 1790. When a similarly ambitious undertaking in Arkansas failed, George Green set out with his family by wagon train in the late 1700s to settle lands near Austin, Texas. Along with three partners, he founded a new town called San Marcos. In no time George, a slave owner, had established mining interests and a loan company. His son, Edwin Jeremiah, known to all as Ed, was twelve when they set up in Texas. By the age of twenty he had expanded the family's businesses into every variety of service provision for miners across the region. He also built Green's Anglican Church next door to the family bank. During his service in the Confederate army, young Ed's wife died and he married her sister, Eliza Jane, who bore him six children, including Eugene, Robert Redford's maternal great-grandfather. As San Marcos's fortunes grew during Reconstruction, Ed became a legendary figure, a titan of the local business world. Among his social circle was another celebrated ex–Confederate officer, Zachariah P. Bugg, the sheriff of a Tennessee township. Zach's daughter Mattie married Eugene in 1891. Out of this union came Sallie Pate Green, Robert Redford's grandmother.

Sallie Pate's childhood was one of privilege and tragedy. Eugene Green followed his father into mining and banking, but died suddenly at twenty, when his daughter was just months old. Shortly after, his teenage widow, Mattie, died of typhoid. Ed became de facto father to Sallie and rechristened her Mattie, in memory of her mother. She was the apple of his eye. In 1896, when Sallie was three, Ed's wife passed away. Shortly afterward he married Alice Young Bohan, a recently widowed sister of his former wives. Alice was affectionate but not maternal, and Ed was sixty-five; it was Sallie's good fortune that the black wet nurse, Nicey, a Green household fixture since her own childhood, became an affectionate substitute mother.

In 1909, as Sallie turned sixteen, America's fascination with the new automotive culture, started ten years before by Henry Ford, was peaking. That fall, Sallie attended a county fair advertising a race for custom roadsters, one of dozens held across the country. The race was won by the Bluebird, the handiwork of a shoe salesman turned inventor/mechanic, recently arrived from El Paso, named Tot Hart. Having won the attention of Sallie and the rest of the Green family, he was invited by them to dinner.

Archibald "Tot" Hart was, like the Greens, of a western cut. His father, John Gabriel, was a traveling salesman from Spotsylvania, Virginia, who married an Ohioan, Ida Woodruff, in Missouri in 1885. In 1897, when Tot was eight, his father succumbed to cirrhosis, dying at the side of the road, and two years later his mother lay on her deathbed, urging her sons to pledges of temperance. Foster homes were found for Tot and his brother. Tot was small, but he had the energy of a terrier and liked the notion of risk. As with his father before him, the frontier beckoned. He headed south with nothing but the clothes he walked in, he later told Redford.

In the years that followed, Tot learned the survival skills he would ultimately pass on to Robert Redford. "He was a modern mountain man," Redford recalls. "He was a child when he hit the road, but it was do or die. He took work wherever he could find it, and learned to live off the land, hunting small game and harvesting berries. He loved the outdoors, but he also possessed a great gift with mechanical devices. Because he had to, he learned to build. He could build anything: furniture, boats, guns, even automobiles from scratch. He followed fifty trades, whatever paid for a crust of bread."

Tot fell for Sallie. It was the unlikeliest of marriages. Tot was dwarfish beside the mannequin figure of Sallie. His coloring was mousy and weather-beaten; hers, a pampered tan. He had no education; she had good schooling behind her. He was quiet; she was talkative, vain, sociable. But their common bond was ambition. Surviving on the edge, Tot had become foxy and tenacious. Years of traveling and scheming had honed his ambition: to build houses and cities on the edge of the frontier. The Greens and their connections afforded him a supreme opportunity. Sallie understood this. Rooted in Texas after their 1913 marriage, Tot began to build. With Ed's help, Tot constructed a Prairie-style home on the shores of Lake Austin at Travis Heights that became the blueprint for a community of homes by the lake built over the next ten years.

On April 12, 1914, Sallie gave birth to their only child, Martha, and their fortunes seemed secure. But almost immediately, through bad partnerships and failing health, Ed Green's empire began to slide. The properties Tot labored over failed to sell. Sallie began to drink. By the 1920s she was all but incapacitated as an alcoholic, and Tot was seeking comfort in the company of other women. Ed Green's death in 1924 devastated Sallie, but it was nothing compared with the humiliation of Tot's relationship with Mary P. Robinson, a well-heeled neighbor who flaunted their affair.

In the midst of her alcoholic despair Sallie experienced a religious conversion. "The doctor said, 'That's it, there's nothing anyone can do for her,' " Redford recalls his mother telling him. "Then, at the last minute, someone recommended this Christian Science woman doctor down the street who could work miracles. This woman was summoned, and gave Sallie the literature that changed her world. It was like a light switch. Sallie got out of bed, stopped drinking and swore never to touch liquor again, and she never did."

After six months' separation, Tot and Sallie were divorced in June 1928. In search of a new beginning, Sallie daringly decided on the faraway pastures of California, where some cousins lived. Armed with telephone numbers and a few hundred dollars from the settlement, Sallie and thirteen-year-old Martha headed west.

The Redfords, meanwhile, had also begun the move west. Ten years before, Elisha's granddaughter Grace, disenchanted with the increasingly anarchist movement headed by her hero Emma Goldman, landed a teaching post in Los Angeles, leaving her sister teaching in the dull confines of a ramshackle school in the heart of the most impoverished area. Elisha was dead by then, but the fabric of security he had sought to weave was rapidly coming undone. Charles had become a deadbeat, preferring his music, or a day at the bar, to barbering. Eventually he would become an insurance salesman. Charles Elijah had drifted into vaudeville. Redford remembers Charles Elijah as "Tiger," a wry moniker derived from his sandy complexion and grumbling persona. They grew close late in Tiger's life, and Redford viewed the old man as a stubborn introvert whose emotions never surfaced. For Tiger, Redford believes, vaudeville was not an indulgence, but an escape to a rosier life. Business and industry had variables, but given its scope, vaudeville seemed a sure thing. All across the East, theaters were flourishing. Composers, lyricists and music publishers were rolling in dough. Tin Pan Alley was a boomtown, and the talent-packaging houses of William Morris, Klaw and Erlanger and Keith-Albee could hardly keep pace with audience demand. Tiger's violin skills were such that a wealthy Westerly patron had offered him sponsorship for the Conservatoire in Vienna, but vaudeville seemed to him like the better bet. "I have a picture in my head," says Redford, "of the terrible drabness of life for immigrants from Europe, the financial struggles, the political and religious tensions. And then vaudeville comes to town in the painted tent. Suddenly there are people with greasepaint faces and funny hats. Suddenly there is laughter! I have an image of Tiger on his knees, lifting the edge of some circus tarpaulin, peeping into a happier world. No more struggle. No more stress. Freedom!" Tiger easily found a place in the orchestral pits of the B. F. Keith circuit, where he earned $7.50 a week in 1910, the year the Marx Brothers, then billed as the Marks Brothers, set forth on the same circuit.

In 1911 Tiger married Cornish-born textile worker Lena Taylor, whose grandmother came from Kircubbin, County Down, in Ireland. She was six feet tall, a good eight inches more than Tiger, and had a loud Irish manner and a booming voice. But she was no match for Tiger's stubbornness. The newlyweds settled into a rented wooden home in the Irish-Italian section of neighboring Westerly, across the Pawcatuck River. On November 19, 1914, a son, once again named Charles, was born, followed by David George on March 5, 1918. Now Tiger struggled to keep up. Big-time success evaded him, and he was an increasingly absent husband and father, chasing the expanding Keith circuit through the Midwest, eking out a few bucks in the pits while a jokey fiddle player named Ben Kubelsky—soon to be rechristened Jack Benny—burned up the center stage, earning $350 a week. When he was at home, his wife's severe rheumatoid arthritis complicated matters. Travel took its toll, too. In his memoirs Jack Benny described the Keith treadmill as "constant getting on a train, getting off a train, carrying your bags to the cheapest hotel or boardinghouse, running to the theater, running, playing three, four, five shows a day, smiling when you faced the audience, taking your bow and fighting all the time for a better place on the bill." Sometime in the mid-twenties, a couple of years before the end of vaudeville, Tiger retired to part-time violin teaching and occasional silent movie accompaniments at the Garde and Capitol theaters in New London, Connecticut. Five years later he unstrung his fiddles, carefully draped them with burial sheets and never touched them again.

Under Lena's influence Tiger assumed a Fenian sensibility, humming "Danny Boy" and sharing Lena's oft-repeated tales of the heroic emergence of the Irish Free State. Much of his neighborhood, however, was immersed in Italian ways. Since the 1890s, floods of indigent Italians from Calabria and Sicily had populated ghettos that overspread the well-established Irish communities. Tiger was happy among the Italians, but he also sought out the Irish drinking community and was at home among the old guard. "Once he settled, all the family became Republican Irish," says Redford. "I think it was a progression of his personal inbuilt rebelliousness." Rebellion was certainly apparent in the next generation of Redfords. The young boys, Charlie and David, were good students, but they were intoxicated by the Jazz Age. They stayed out too late too often and were punished for it. David made adjustments, finally kowtowing to a disciplined school life. But Charlie stayed wild, reveling in his natural athleticism and a rapier wit like Tiger's. In many ways the boys were unalike. David was tall and black haired like Lena; Charlie was smaller and sandy haired. David seemed to make peace with himself early on; Charlie remained irascible. Tiger foresaw trouble, and it wasn't long in coming. At fourteen Charlie started a relationship with an Italian bargirl that caused controversy in the neighborhood and embarrassment for Lena, who was now wheelchair-bound. Tiger wrote in desperation to his sister in Los Angeles. The only option, he said, was to get Charlie out of town. Grace, now living and teaching at Morocco Junction, just five miles from Hollywood, agreed. Charlie Redford was going west.

On a hot spring Sunday in 1928, fourteen-year-old George Menard, a transplanted Chicagoan, grew bored with morning services at the Fourth Street Christian Science Church in Santa Monica and sneaked out. He spotted a parked Model T on fire, grabbed a garden hose, lifted the hood and doused the engine. "A couple of minutes later," remembered Menard, "church let out and this dark apparition sailed toward me, about thirteen or fourteen years old, with an older lady by her side. It was their automobile I'd rescued, and they were grateful and so began a great friendship." The pretty girl that Menard admired was Martha Hart, and the woman was her mother, Sallie, just arrived from Texas. Martha had enrolled at University High School in West Los Angeles. Menard's sister Poofie had enrolled at the same school and would shortly become Martha's best school friend. George, operating in a different social circle, would coincidentally become best friends with a new arrival from the East Coast named Charlie Redford, who also attended Uni High. "But at that moment I wasn't thinking what a great match she'd make for someone else," said Menard. "I was thinking I'd like her for myself."

In later years, Redford learned from his mother about her smooth transition into Californian life. "When Texas came to California, it was a big deal," he says. "Sallie had renewed her health, and she was determined to reinvent herself as a social butterfly. My mother was naturally fun loving and extroverted, so they were on the right wavelength and in the right place." Sallie contacted her cousins, the Wards and the Giesens—old San Marcos settler families—who were well-heeled regulars in the society columns. Sallie's uncle Phil, a transplanted Chicagoan who had the Packard dealership in Beverly Hills, became a surrogate father to Martha. Phil's wife, Marge, was the sister of up-and-coming Hollywood actor Robert Young.

Though Tot sent money and maintained a strangely passionate commitment to both mother and daughter, Sallie had met Nelson Bengston, a man who exuded an aura of calm and reserve, the apparent antithesis of Tot. Bengston had turned from defense work to real estate during the Depression, but he was, says Robert Redford, a frustrated artist who was also a recovering alcoholic. The couple met at the Christian Science church: a shared belief in the curative power of religion bonded them, and, says Redford, their harmonious relationship allowed Martha's confidence to grow.

At Uni High, Martha thrived. She joined the glee club, the drama society, the writers' club. Judging by her school reports and the memories of those who knew her, she didn't so much rise to popularity as to reverence. She had the face and figure of a movie star and reminded people of Gene Tierney. She loved poetry and singing. She kept scrupulous scrapbooks, which reveal page after page of theatrical cartoons, jokey clippings about Will Rogers, lists of her many favorite popular songs ("Sweetheart Darling," "Secondhand Store," "Cabin in the Pines"), quotes from Keats and Shelley and her own poetry, bright as Pollyanna. Obviously she had withstood adversity well, surviving economic hardship, the dissolution of her parents' marriage and relocation. She remained attached to her father, but the strength of her mother seemed her greatest advantage. She laughed her way, say friends, through the Depression.

After high school graduation, Martha enrolled at Santa Monica Junior College, a transitional education institution hugely popular with well-off Angelenos. Her diaries show her popularity: boys were attracted to her like flies. Her first teenage love had been Zachary Scott, a fellow Texan who'd headed to England as she left for Los Angeles and was now making headway in regional theater. There was no shortage of substitutes. George Menard recalled that "most boys chased Martha from the day she arrived in L.A." But her eye was on Charlie Redford, who had also transferred to Santa Monica Junior College. According to Menard, Charlie, too, was a magnet for suitors. "They were really both spectacular creatures," said Menard, "but they were temperamentally totally unalike. Charlie stuttered. She was cheeky. He adored sports but she preferred to read Carl Sandburg. And of course he was a Yankee and she a Confederate."

"Still, from the moment they met, they were close, like twins," says another close college friend, Marcella Scott. "Charlie was living at the corner house on Bundy and Wilshire with his aunt Grace, who taught at Uni High, but he was restless. He was going through big changes. You detected this terrible insecurity in his stutter and also in his anger a lot of the time. Maybe it was embarrassment about the failures of his family and the poverty back east, which contrasted with the comforts of Los Angeles." Menard remembered the comforts of Grace's home, her intelligence, her warmth and her "historic" Boston bean soup. Most of all he remembers the wall-to-wall bookcases. "When Charlie and I weren't playing football or baseball, we were reading. The atmosphere in Grace's home was perfect for it, and for Charlie it became a mission of self-improvement." Menard was almost jealous of his friend's nimble progress. Charlie was chosen for the prestigious student body commission, then became the leading sportswriter on the college quarterly, *The Samojac.* The literary spurt, says Scott, was more Martha's influence than Grace's. It was Martha the A student who drove him. "Let's give credit where it's due: he owed a lot to Martha," says Scott.

In the winter of 1934, as Martha angled for a career by starting secretarial studies at Westwood's Sawyer Business School, Charlie's choices seemed few. Grace worked hard to support him, but she had just a schoolteacher's pay and a rented home. "It was still the Depression," said Menard, "and we were, metaphorically, on a very limited playing field." The options were low-paid work with the Civilian Conservation Corps (CCC) or the military. Through the winter, said Menard, Charlie was "bothered" about his future. At the same time, he was buoyant in his growing romance with Martha. At Christmas he sent her a card depicting old-timers on a pony cart with a funny caption suggestive of their close relationship: "We can't go on like this, Martha. We're just playing with fire!" Martha laughingly showed the card to her friends, then stuck it in her scrapbook beside the playbill for *Romeo and Juliet,* which they had seen that summer.

Charlie and Menard decided to join the CCC, digging on the Roosevelt (later Pacific Coast) Highway for $30 a month. After a few weeks Charlie converted his junior college academic results—straight A's in business—into a part-time clerical job at the stock exchange, working for E. F. Hutton of Beverly Hills. In the tight privacy of their relationship, says Marcella Scott, Martha and Charlie never seemed happier. Then, in February, Martha fell ill with a blood disorder. A critical complication was that she was several weeks pregnant. Christian Science, formerly a tower of strength, became a liability. Under the restrictions of her religion, blood transfusions were not allowed. Martha's condition worsened. She showed signs of escalating pernicious anemia and it was feared she was dying of blood poisoning.

Beyond Charlie and the doctors, no one knew of Martha's pregnancy. "There was a sudden change of atmosphere," says Scott, who was then Martha's closest friend. "One moment Martha was the footloose fun lover who was everywhere, then she had vanished like a ghost. We had no idea of the severity of this crisis. Looking back, in the context of her health and the judgmental ways of that era, the predicament must have been sheer hell for both of them."

When Sallie found out, she was torn between her religious convictions and her daughter's life. The best blood specialist was consulted. Martha entered Santa Monica Hospital, and an obstetrician was called in to supervise the baby's expected delivery in September. The crisis lasted months, but gradually Martha's anemia was brought under control. The pregnancy, however, remained in doubt. In July, Lena sent Martha a warmly reassuring card, signed "from Charles' mother, father and brother." Martha was keen on marriage, says Scott, but Charlie initially hesitated. He was genuinely in love, Scott insists, "but had a complete lack of confidence, based on his family's experience, of his ability to create a stable, prosperous home." In August, six weeks before her due date, Martha, who had been released from the hospital and was at home muddling through a heat wave while keeping up with the Berlin Olympics on the radio, was rushed back to start a long, difficult labor.

On the evening of August 18 in her third-floor room, Martha delivered a seven-pound, thirteen-ounce boy. Charles Robert Redford Jr., the name Martha had already decided on, was a blue baby, rushed immediately to intensive care. "My mother said it was touch-and-go," Redford recalls. "There was a serious lack of oxygen in her blood often associated with congenital heart defects. None of this was ever properly diagnosed, because of the background religious conditioning and the restrictions of treatment and medication. It didn't look like I'd make it. With the medical care available then, very few blue babies survived. She was in the grip of a terrible distress." After three days the baby stabilized. Martha, ever the resilient fighter, quickly regained her strength and pride. There was no longer any point in covering up. To the Redford and Hart families, she sent out frilled blue cards announcing: "A welcome guest has come to stay. We thought you'd like to know the name, the weight, the day." The cards were signed "Mr. & Mrs. Charles Redford." When Martha was released from the hospital, Sallie and Nelson took the baby while the couple drove south to Nogales, Arizona. On November 20, unknown to their closest friends, they tied the knot at a pueblo chapel. Soon after, they were living in suburbia, a pair of happy young marrieds with a bungalow and a baby.

2

Two Americas

At the time of Robert Redford's birth, the work programs of the New Deal had reactivated the economy. President Roosevelt had created six million new jobs and improved national income by 20 percent in three years. But, in the words of FDR's second inaugural speech in January 1937, there was still a considerable proportion of the population "denied education, recreation, and the opportunity to better their lot." There was work to be done, but there was measurable national unity and a prevalent sense of hope.

The first months of Redford's childhood were spent in sunny Santa Monica, the coastal adjunct of western Los Angeles that was like a fiefdom apart. The pleasure piers, stretching from Venice in the south to the Roosevelt Highway at its northern border, featured the unparalleled Zip roller coaster, any number of beach clubs, an Orpheum-circuit vaudeville hall and the La Monica Ballroom, a Byzantine-domed colossus, then the largest ballroom in the world. Offshore gambling, illegal elsewhere, was available in the floating casino off Catalina Island, frequented by the denizens of Hollywood. Cary Grant, Greta Garbo, Mae West, Douglas Fairbanks, Louis B. Mayer, Samuel Goldwyn, Jean Paul Getty and William Randolph Hearst all had properties in and around Santa Monica, pushing beachfront prices past $20,000 a foot, the highest real estate values in the United States.

But for Charlie, Martha and the baby, economic security was knife-edge. Sallie's resources were diminished to the point where she was often dependent on Tot, whose finances waxed and waned. Grace's schooldays support was a thing of the past and the onus fell squarely on Charlie, whose worsening stutter lost him his job at the stock exchange. The rental bungalow was suddenly unaffordable. Woody Knudson, the husband of a friend of Martha's, was manager of Edgemar Dairies, the biggest business outside of recreation in Santa Monica. With Martha's intercession, Woody offered Charlie work as a milkman on the wholesale route of West Los Angeles, yielding commissions that averaged $50 a month. Once in regular employment, Charlie allowed Martha a dollar a day for housekeeping.

Charlie was determined to improve their lot and applied himself with a dedication that Vivian, Woody's wife, admired. "The milkmen worked six days a week, lugging massive urns. If someone was sick, they worked seven days. They got up at 2:00 a.m. to begin their working day, then came home at six in the evening. They'd fall asleep during dinner from sheer exhaustion. Charlie and Woody had to catch four hours' sleep to get ready for the next shift. It was like a chain gang."

Though single-minded, Martha embraced Santa Monica's publicized commitment to the Moral Rearmament Organization, which saw a woman's place as solely in the home. She was domestically dutiful but spent much of her free time with her girlfriends and their children at nearby Crystal Beach. Redford clearly remembers those beach idylls: "It was just women, women. And the sand, the surf, and the vast expanses of horizon." Martha fussed endlessly over the baby (who was also called Charlie in his early life), Vivian Knudson recalls, while Charlie seemed indifferent. In fairness, the remorseless Edgemar schedules, exacerbated by the back pain Charlie suffered as a result of an injury on his first day, brewed frustration and bad temper. Redford remembers only his father's absence: "When I conjure those beginnings, I see my mother. He was just not there."

Many friends found it remarkable that Charlie and Martha's relationship survived the first year after Robert Redford's birth. "Charlie was never an easy man, probably because he was the underdog who had to rise to Martha's middle-class status," says Marcella Scott. "He was dominant by nature. Unfortunately, she was also a very assertive individual. So it was ripe for strife. But they got over it because they shared a goal of re-creating the good life their grandparents once had."

By 1939, Charlie could afford a $3,000 mortgage. As war broke out in Europe, the Redfords bought a brick bungalow on Tennessee Street in Sawtelle, a low-income area two miles south of Santa Monica. This was clearly a step down. Tennessee Street was bordered by the crowded Hispanic developments along Pico Boulevard. Having grown up with farmhand Hispanics, Martha was very comfortable in Sawtelle, a comfort she conveyed to her son. The austerity didn't matter at all to Charlie. He had found the first place he felt truly at home.

Marcella Scott insists Robert Redford quickly developed into "the most verbal two-year-old you could ever imagine." Vivian Knudson believes he was "an introvert—you could never get through to him." Redford himself only remembers the movies. His first vague memory is of sitting in the Aero Theater at Fifth and Santa Monica Boulevard, switching between his father's and mother's laps: "I slid off her knee in the dark and made for the light. I made it as far as the projection stage, and the management stopped the movie to sort the commotion."

Vivian was "vaguely scandalized" by the family's devotion to movies, the national palliative against economic privations. In the Redfords' case, though, it was something more. What began as a casual interest, says Vivian, became Martha's social staple, gradually drawing in Charlie. "She never stopped talking movies, and I saw the effect on Bobby from infancy." Vivian remembers coffee mornings at Tennessee with baby Bobby obsessively doodling "cowboys, cowboys, cowboys, almost before he could walk."

Martha was her son's role model, and her poise was distinctively romantic. "Broke or not," says Vivian, "she affected Hollywood elegance. She wore well-tailored clothes beautifully because she was broad shouldered and very slim hipped." She talked less about literature now; instead Hollywood comings and goings filled her diary. Early in 1937, six months after the birth of her son, Martha visited the MGM studios in Culver City to see Robert Young, who was playing the lead in a comedy called *Married Before Breakfast.* "She loved being on that set," says Vivian, "and took every opportunity to connect with the movie world after that." Movies were also about family bonding. Redford fondly remembers Hopalong Cassidy, Roy Rogers, Buck Rogers, Flash Gordon, Tarzan, most of all Disney. "Those Saturday matinees elevated everything. They gave us distraction and joyfulness. But they were also a shared interest, a glue that united us."

Life in Sawtelle for Redford was outdoorsy and sociable. Most of his friends living in the cookie-cutter, brick-and-timber houses of Tennessee Street were Mexican, some black. This was a Public Works Administration building site, and there was a sense of unified experience, of neighborly sharing. Martha, however, wanted to secure a better social status for her son. In 1942 she enrolled him at Brentwood Grammar, a swanky school "across the tracks" at the edge of Beverly Hills that Sallie strongly favored. Despite his age, Redford felt the change of tenor: "I suddenly had one foot in high society and one on the street."

From the start, Brentwood was a disaster. On his first day, Redford took an aversion to a teacher's wig and her garish makeup, and decided to leave. He was found and returned to class. After several similar incidents *two* hall monitors were assigned to keep an eye on him. He ran away three times in all. Finally they had to call his father off his milk route.

Redford hated school and its rigidly imposed discipline, but it didn't bother him at all that some of his classmates came from the wealthiest homes, nor that he was poor by comparison. "I was impervious," he recalls. "I was instinctively more interested in the individual than the dress. I was unimpressed by show. I was instead drawn by humor or originality of any kind." His advantage, clearly, was that he had already been exposed to a wide range of people from varying social standing because of his parents' backgrounds.

Martha had taken her son to visit Tot in Texas for the first time the previous summer. She took the wheel of the '36 family coupe and drove all the way, stopping briefly at Gallup, New Mexico, where Redford first caught sight of Navajos and Zunis on the reservation. By the time he arrived at Tot's impressive pile on the shore of Lake Austin, he was living a storybook.

Tot, to his delight, was as active and daring as any Roy Rogers. Under cathedral skies, in the dense forests around the lake, the precocious five-year-old was handed fishing rod and gun and initiated into the ways of the wilderness. The bizarre exposure of so small a child to guns and hunting seemed of little account to Martha or Tot, but Redford interprets this as a throwback to old southern values. Tot's impact was profound, especially given Charlie's absences: "He was the manifestation of everything I'd heard about frontiersmen-heroes multiplied a thousand times," Redford recalls. "The house was spacious and magnificent, and he'd built it with his own hands. He knew the names of every bird, fish and snake and could hunt for his own dinner every day." Tot adored his grandson, bounced him on his knee for cowboy sing-alongs, slung him on his back for the hunt and dumped him into the freezing waters of Barton Springs to learn to swim, exactly as he'd taught Martha when she was a baby. Redford loved Tot, and the gentle paternalism of Tot's Mexican "man," Gil Husauras, who shared Hispanic cusses with him, like the neighbors on Tennessee Street.

Six months later Charlie introduced his son to the East Coast. The experience, by contrast, was funereal. New London, Connecticut, where Tiger had moved, was gray skied. "On Spring Street where my grandparents lived the driveway was choked with weeds," says Redford. "There was my grandmother Lena, seated alone in the angled front window of a gray house, incapacitated by arthritis, propped in pillows, radiating an atmosphere of gloom." Charlie was rigid with anxiety, returning from exile. Lena screamed when she saw him. There was no open affection, only propriety. Redford recalls sitting nervously in a stiff chair while Charlie took charge of reorganizing furniture and dumping trash before Tiger returned from his new day job as a maintenance fitter for General Dynamics Electric Boat. With hindsight, Redford came to recognize Charlie's embarrassment at revealing the depth of the family poverty. Unlike Martha, who genuinely loved her parents, Charlie was awkward with and resentful of his. There was a willingness to heal scars, but laughter was in short supply. "New London was everything Texas wasn't," Redford recalls. "The rooms were small and claustrophobic. No one moved much. My grandfather hardly spoke. Lena terrified me. She had a spooky aura. All she did was listen to Arthur Godfrey on the radio and ramble on in a strange Irish accent, telling ominous tales of the old country. I couldn't wait to get out of there."

Perhaps, as director Alan Pakula believed, it was Redford's early cross-country travels and the sharp contrasts of culture he experienced that seeded his restlessness. At Brentwood, conformity was grudging, his motion constant. "He wasn't an exceptional-looking kid," says his classmate Tissie Keissig, "but he was a natural class leader because he had a *go-go-go* that grabbed your attention." While his grades lapsed, he became a fanatical athletic competitor. "I was the undisputed track champion," says Betty Webb, another classmate, "and then suddenly I noticed this cute, redheaded, freckle-face kid who came out of nowhere fixed on the idea of beating me at everything. The next couple of years were a tussle between Bobby and me, trying to outdo each other at track." Betty liked him "because he was a little arrogant, and ferocious in pursuit of whatever interested him. Kids like that kind of confidence."

The arrogance was a swaggering emulation of the new heroes in his life, of Tot and especially Charlie's brother, David, who was in the army, stationed at Fort Leavenworth, and visiting often. Three and a half years younger than Charlie, David excelled at sports in high school, receiving an offer to play baseball in the St. Louis Browns organization. He enrolled at Brown instead, where his aptitude for languages won him a Rhodes scholarship to Oxford. David enlisted in the military when the war began. Studying accountancy part-time at the University of Southern California and exhausted by his day job, Charlie had become bookish and subdued. David, by contrast, retained the smiling, generous flamboyance that made him instantly likable to all who met him. Bobby regarded him as a god.

David taught Bobby the rules of baseball and elaborated the parlor games Martha devised. He often agitated Charlie with his swagger, but he was also a bonding force within the family. "It was really only David who got Dad out of his shell," says Redford. "The uniform, for example, naturally inspired all sorts of war games. In my mind I can see David and Dad like kids, rolling over the furniture, competing with each other to entertain me with my favorite shooting games. I loved to do the big dying thing, and when I was 'killed,' it was the highest drama. I took an hour to lie down. Those rare moments of Dad's relaxation, when he would let his hair down long enough to have a laugh, are the ones that stick."

Sometimes, though, David pushed Charlie over the edge. Redford remembers David accompanying his parents to a live radio broadcast in the early forties. Bobby sat at home with Sallie, listening in awe as David answered a quiz question to win the top prize of a not-insubstantial $50. There were whoops of delight in the house as young Bobby awaited his hero's return. An hour later, as Bobby lay in bed, doors were suddenly slamming and anger swept the house. Charlie, it seemed, had thrown David out. David was in the garage, from where Bobby could hear him playing a trombone. David had insisted on buying the trombone on the spot with the $50. "Dad called that outrageous squandering," says Redford. "Everyone was short of money—and then this extravagance!"

Redford's bond with David was in some ways divisive. Looking back, Redford recognizes the difficulties of his father's position. David had had a stable home life, careful parenting, the good looks, the academic results, the musical skills, the athletic skills, the humor, now the uniform. Charlie had been abruptly uprooted in his teens and exiled to L.A. Poverty always shadowed him, even in his happy relationship with Martha. Time and circumstances seemed always against him. Even when he tried to enlist after Pearl Harbor, he was rejected because of his bad back. "He was devastated," said George Menard, who accompanied him to the recruitment center. "But in some ways, the bad back was a kindness. He was a patriot, whose hero was Nathan Hale, but he was also a pacifist. The idea of open conflict, of having to kill someone, would literally have destroyed Charlie. He was a very soft, gentle soul." While David fought the war, Charlie graduated to a desk job at the El Segundo refinery offices of Standard Oil.

Redford saw his father bend under the pressures of survival. To his credit, his dedication was to improving his family's lot, but the toll was high. "He was constantly on edge. He could cuss the house down when the mood took him. Standard Oil was the compromise, the moment he chose his course, and it was my belief that he took the wrong road. At the time, the great middle-class pressure was to become 'the organization man' and he settled for that. He missed his niche. From his junior college days he had a talent for sportswriting. The evidence was in his letters, till the end of his life. He was a terrific storyteller, with an acerbic wit that shone through. I felt resentment toward him for many years: that he'd discouraged me, suppressed my individualism. But that, I now feel, was my misunderstanding. My father made sacrifices for us."

At Brentwood, meanwhile, Redford continued his hyperactive ways. Nothing calmed him, but one teacher's passionate readings from *Farmer Boy* and *Little House on the Prairie* finally got him interested in books. "It was soothing," says Redford. "Like a drug." Charlie had started a midweek routine of taking the family to the Santa Monica Public Library, an alternative to movie nights. "Something strange happened to me," Redford recalls. "I was magnetized to the mythology section. It was suddenly the be-all of my world. I couldn't wait for Wednesdays, to go through the doors of that library. My parents would turn left for the adult section, and I'd make straight for Perseus, Zeus and *The Odyssey.* Even when I couldn't really read, I'd pick out a word, 'Perseus,' and conjure the story from the illustrations. These monsters and myths became living realities. None of my friends were interested in ancient myth, and I often wondered why. I think my interest originated with the way information was handed down to me as a small boy. It came encoded. And the big themes of mythology decoded it and made sense of a lot I didn't otherwise understand." The literary precocity also made Redford open to whimsy: "Blame my dad. My mom was the games player in the living room, but Dad was the bedtime-story teller. Sometimes he'd read to me; more often he'd tell a tale out of thin air. One night he gave me the history of the Redford clan, tracing it back to Ireland and Scotland and demonstrating how I was related to Robin Hood." Redford's contribution to the next day's show-and-tell was the announcement that he was Robin Hood's cousin.

Betty Webb saw Bobby Redford as a loner. They attended the same Christian Science church in Beverly Hills. She was keen on him. "It was the attraction of the enigma, no doubt. There was also that crazy competitiveness. He just could not lose! Maybe his uncle David was influential—this great, distinguished winner!—but his dad pushed him very hard athletically. As a consequence, he was really good at track, and he became known as a very able softball player. Martha played some tennis, so he excelled at tennis, too. I tried to keep up with all this. We had a lot more in common than anyone else, so I was way out front in the dating stakes." Redford and Betty's first date was a chaperoned doubles match at the public tennis courts, followed by a drive to the Santa Monica Pier. "He didn't talk much," says Betty. "I remember his silence."

Redford didn't talk, he says, because he was lost in the world, confused by the wide divisions he perceived in his family. "It was really a response to noncommunication—that I now see. My father's way was silence." Redford got to like observing from afar. He started surreptitiously drawing, studying faces, expressions and gestures. He loved to go under the kitchen table, from where, hidden by the tablecloth, he would draw the feet and legs of those gathered for supper or a card game. "I drew the world as I saw it at floor level. It was fascinating, watching the shoes people wore, their posture, the relaxation of their feet, or the tap-tapping nervous feet." Redford progressed to drawing arms, hands and faces. Avoiding homework, he would entertain himself copying faces from *Life* magazine. Marcella Scott, still close with Martha, had become a sought-after artist, and Martha posed for her. On these occasions, says Scott, Redford sat close by, studying her.

"But I never broke through with Bobby," says Betty Webb, "no matter how much we talked. I felt he was absorbed in this inner dialogue. There was some escapism that worked for him, and he stayed inside that magic circle."

The magic circle encompassed the ongoing weekly visits to the library and the movies. He saw *Bambi* twenty-three times, loved *Fantasia, Pinocchio,* the Three Stooges. But he found Charlie Chaplin cold and somehow compassionless. "I suppose I found greater comfort in animals, cartoon and otherwise," says Redford. "It was a yearning for uncomplicated friends that left a mark and has lingered through my adult life." A devotion to dogs—which would be lifelong—started when he fostered a series of strays. "Mom was always compliant, but Dad would fume." He nurtured his first find, a scraggy mongrel, day and night for months. It was hit by a truck on Tennessee Street and killed: "My first collision with mortality. *Pow!* I loved that mutt like my best friend. Its death wiped me out."

There was not much time for moping. Throughout 1942 and 1943 Japanese bombing scares kept the foghorn atop Santa Monica City Hall busy. Blimps from Airship Squadron 32 dotted the skies. Blackouts began, and the colorful electric trolleys, recently displaced by dull but too-well-lit municipal buses, came back into service. Redford loved the excitement. Uncle David's visits became irregular, but more highly charged. He was now always in uniform, and the drama of war hung about him. They often went to the movies together. "The one that stands out was *The Fallen Sparrow* with John Garfield," Redford recalls. "It was dark and spooky for a kid, totally beyond my years. But that was Uncle David. He was all for taking it to the edge. I loved him for that, and I've loved every John Garfield movie since."

Redford understood little about the war in Europe. "For a kid, it just meant rationing, wastepaper drives and FDR's fireside talks. I certainly didn't connect any risk for Uncle David with the seriousness of this conflict that everyone was talking about." David was a sergeant in the Third Army. In early 1944 he sailed from New York on the *Ile de France.* He followed the first wave of the Normandy invasion and landed on Utah Beach with Forward Echelon Group X, an elite scouting party designed to penetrate the retreating enemy lines. An interpreter, he was ordered to go to the front to assist with the interrogation of prisoners. On January 1, 1945, as part of a small team on a top secret mission involving the Saarlautern bridgehead in Germany, he was killed by sniper fire.

It took a week for the news to filter home. When the telegram arrived, eight-year-old Bobby was fetched from school. An army major arrived with the details. "It upended everything," says Redford, "because it brought me face-to-face not only with the issue of human mortality, but with the issue of truth. Dad was a profoundly, hurtfully honest man. This was the primary contrast between him and my mother. The 'Redford trait' was a kind of darkness. Life was all trials and troubles. Mom was the opposite. She was positive. She would tell it like it is, but she was also the one who kept the tooth fairy and Santa alive. Every Christmas she'd get cotton wool and lay it along the windowsills to make Californian snow. Then she'd stand outside my bedroom door shaking sleigh bells, whispering, 'Here he comes!' But on Christmas morning Dad would say, 'Santa? There's no darn Santa. Have you any idea how much sweat it takes to earn those toys?' He blew it for me with the cold facts. But when it came to the death of David, when I was old enough to understand, there was this terrible conspiracy of silence. It was as if it didn't happen. My grandmother Sallie just said, 'He's passed,' without the slightest elaboration. I said, 'Passed? What the hell does that mean?' But I got no answers. And Dad drew up the bridge, refused to talk at all. So here was this gap: honest, tenacious people with a gaping hole where the *real truth* was. But I wanted the full picture."

In the face of David's mysterious death, the contradictions of religion and spirituality irritated Redford. There was no value at all, he felt, in vague, otherwordly promises. "I was precocious in that regard. Something broke in me. Sallie would give me the lectures about the peace to come and my guarantee of salvation, and my mom would give me some, a little less convincingly. But I didn't buy into it. It wasn't that I didn't believe in God or Spirit, but Christian Science seemed an excuse for Republicans to get together, and my father's inclination toward Catholicism didn't do it for me, either. When Uncle David died, I started questioning institutional thinking. I couldn't have expressed that then, obviously. I was a kid, but a process started that has never stopped."

3

Krazy in Brentwood

Robert Redford's parents were apolitical in the tradition of their upbringing, but they fully understood the changes the war wrought. Charlie particularly was wary of national paranoia, reflected in the public tolerance for witch hunts against Japanese and Jews, and the activities of the House Un-American Activities Committee, established in 1938 as an anti-Nazi program. In his storytelling Charlie attempted to convey to his son that the kind of American homogeneity that was being extolled was as unsavory as Aryanism. It flew in the face of decency and betrayed the pluralist foundations on which American greatness was built.

As a boy of ten Redford was oblivious to the big picture, but he witnessed the changes on Tennessee Street as the war ended. Overnight, congenial neighborliness was gone and identity clashes accelerated. Previously marginalized groups whose members fought in the war wanted their fair share back home. Local grievances became national debates. "But all I knew was I lost friends," says Redford. "There was no longer the ease with my Mexican buddies. It was 'us and them.' "

A Hispanic gang, the Pachucks, began to terrorize the environs. Redford got punched around because he was small. "There was a kid called Felix who picked on me, probably because I went to a good school, I was good at track and popular with the girls, and he beat up on me. I toughened up fast, borrowing from Tot's philosophy, which was, 'Be ready to look out for yourself.' " At one point, Redford was bullied onto a rooftop and prompted to jump to prove his manhood. He did, and almost killed himself. "Facing down fears hit home early, and I attribute my survival to my mother and Tot. You have two choices, it seemed to me. You can be led by your fears, or you can overcome them. I chose Tot's way."

The changes were everywhere, even in the landscape. Douglas aircraft manufacturing had boomed during the war, bringing copious employment and thousands of newcomers to West Los Angeles. Now the GI Bill launched a new building drive. Sallie's new husband, the real estate agent Nelson Bengston, was suddenly busier than ever, working the markets of the new, vast acreages of cheap tract houses that spread out through the chaparral between Sepulveda Boulevard and the coast. Redford hated these changes. "When I'd drive with my parents in the forties through Orange County, it was just that: a country of citrus groves. That started to fade fast. Even on my route to school, it was different. Once, it had been fields of gold. Now it was gray tract housing. I lived through that moment when Los Angeles traded its rural soul to a smog-spewing industry machine, and it made me very sad."

It also exacerbated a growing resentment of "fitting in." Standard Oil was expanding, and Charlie's income improved. There was, marginally, more time for the social conventions, for the soirées and card games and Sunday brunches Sallie and Martha so loved. Redford balked. "Mom made every effort to turn me into a version of Dad," he remembers. "He had the Irish trait of dressing up to cover his poverty, so an attempt was made to smarten me. Dad was always perfectly groomed, with neat hair, a polished face and the smell of Old Spice. Mom tried a kind of axle grease called Waveset in my hair to control the cowlicks, but still it stood up in fifty directions. She starched my shirts every week, put me in stiff collars. I rebelled. I'd get to the end of the street, and I would strip off my shirt, throw it on the ground and stomp the starch out of it."

The rebellion against parental control intensified. At every juncture, it seemed, Bobby clashed with his father. It began with an argument about music. Redford felt—still feels—that he had music in him. Uncle David's stories of playing one night with Count Basie thrilled him. He loved to hear his parents sing along to Woody Herman and Bing Crosby on the radio. He, too, loved to sing. When a door-to-door guitar tutor offered cheap lessons, he jumped at it. Charlie, remembering his own father's failure as a musician, would not hear of music studies. Redford was furious.

They clashed about sports, too. Spurred by the athleticism of girls like Betty, Redford had made it up to a good American Legion junior team sponsored by Huntington, a sporting goods company. He also played tennis for his school and swam competitively at the Bantam Club on San Vincente. But problems arose when Bobby failed to meet Charlie's expectations. "I hated it when my parents came to see me play because Dad was *always* critical," says Redford. "I was never the best player, but I had stamina, I hung in. The trouble was, even when I was taking the medals for tennis and swimming, it was never good enough for him. It was an unfixable situation, because I discovered that it wasn't me he was assessing, but himself. Bit by bit I learned that he had been a great ballplayer, but he never had the chance to develop it. That frustration burned a hole inside him."

Redford had other things to keep him busy—like sex. "I was impatient," he says. "I didn't know what it was, but I wanted it, as much as I could get." Shopping with his mother in Westwood one day, he was surprised when a handsome, unshaven man in Bermuda shorts grabbed her in his arms. "She called out 'Zach!' with a great gush of passion. I had no idea this was Zachary Scott, the actor, nor that my mother and he had had a close friendship, or a love affair, back in Texas. I went home and blurted it to Dad: 'Hey, Dad. Mom met up with Zach Scott!' It bent him out of shape." Scott, Redford learned, was married, with a daughter called Waverly who also attended Brentwood Grammar, in the class ahead of his. Over the next months, despite Charlie's reservations, Martha befriended Zach's wife, Elaine, and Waverly became the object of Bobby's pubescent fantasies. "I loved the exotic world the Scotts lived in," says Redford. "This was another frontier for me, this great, elegant house with a gilded spiral staircase in the Hollywood Hills. This was a mythical palace compared with Sawtelle. In our house you just had to open the front door to walk into your neighbors' lives. The Scotts' *rooms* were bigger than our house."

Zachary Scott became part of the school-day carpool, often driving Bobby and Waverly to Brentwood Grammar. Though Waverly was just a year older, Redford relished the idea of the "mature" girlfriend. "She was constantly teasing me, and we played all those mischievous hide-and-seek games in that big house with minimum chaperonage, testing each other's boundaries." And then one day, playing on the landing, the two kids heard strange noises downstairs. "We peered over the banister and saw what was going on. It was Elaine, her mom, making love with a stranger. I didn't know who he was, but later on he became a player on the family scene. He started coming around a lot more. He started to carpool us. I didn't realize I was witnessing the end of Zach—who we later learned was a closet homosexual—and the start of Elaine's big relationship with John Steinbeck."

In the spring of 1946, Charlie's labors paid off in the joint purchase with Nelson and Sallie of a substantial duplex on Homedale Avenue, across Sepulveda from Brentwood. It was a marginal but significant move upward. Today, the area has a Beverly Hills character, but in the forties, before the construction of the San Diego Freeway, Homedale sat in a vast, bland development, devoid of trees, partly designed by Nelson as cheap housing for returning GIs. Still, Charlie and Martha had salvaged Bobby from the ethnic battlefield of Sawtelle. "I didn't want to leave," says Redford. "The good feeling in the street was dead, but I still felt I belonged in that multicultural setting." Facing total immersion in the snazzy Brentwood set, Redford was, he says, depressed: "I preferred that old world."

Late the following spring Redford woke one day with his eyelids encrusted and his limbs dead. He couldn't move. No one told him for weeks, but he had polio. "The previous day was excruciatingly hot," he says. "I had been down at the beach, in the ocean on a paddleboat with a friend. There was an allotted area to pedal in near Santa Monica Pier, but given my restlessness, I was way past confinement. I pedaled out too far and got dehydrated. I barely made it back to shore. I became ill, and then polio was diagnosed."

Redford remembers the worries about mortality and the guilt he felt at overdoing things. "I was in terrible discomfort, physically and mentally. When I woke every day, Mom sat by the bed with wet cloths and swabbed my eyes to open them. She kept me going. When I could sit up, I drew. I owe that mostly to my junior school art teacher, Miss Huff. She believed I had an artist inside me, and she had begun to encourage me. That was the branch I reached out for." By August he could walk again. Soon afterward Martha, who had been pregnant with twins, lost the children shortly after birth. Now Martha clung closer to her only child. As a treat as they both recovered, she organized a two-day campout at Yosemite Valley. "It stands as a moment of real awakening in my life, and it seems magical now," says Redford. "We'd been driving for hours, leaving the tract houses and orange groves, and suddenly we were in the High Sierras inside a womblike tunnel, maybe a mile long, unlike anything I'd ever encountered. When we came out the other side, onto Glacier Point Road, there it lay before me: El Capitan, Bridalveil Fall, Half Dome, wilderness. I'd seen a lot of America as a kid, but nothing on this scale of sheer majesty."

Redford has said that, despite the tedium of schooling, the loss of David, the loss of his siblings and his father's demands, he loved his childhood. It was all due to Martha. "I owed everything to my mother for opening me up to the willingness to *experience.* When I went through that tunnel and first laid eyes on Half Dome and the view from Glacier Point, I remember thinking: I have to be part of this."

At twelve, Redford transferred to Emerson Junior High School in Westwood. There he came to fancy Kathleen "Kitty" Andrews, the dark-blond daughter of a well-to-do furniture manufacturer whose home on Bundy Drive was the hub of Emerson social life. They had briefly known each other at Brentwood. Now Kitty stood tall among the Trim, Neat and Terrifics, the girl buddy group whose sweaters, with the yellow logo TNT, became premium Emerson status symbols.

Redford quickly stormed the TNTs. He had worked hard to become a great dancer—"waltz, foxtrot, samba, Charleston, the lot"—at the local hot spot, the Cotillion on Santa Monica Pier, and, says Betty Webb, who continued to be his official "date," seemed suddenly widely sought after by the girls. "He was the funniest person alive," says Kitty, "not in joke telling, but in his mannerisms. He was the kind of kid who'd walk down the street and make a major drama of it, dodging behind trees, vanishing, reappearing, doing a flip like Buster Keaton. The key to his attractiveness was his athleticism. He *moved* like a dancer." Janna and Sheila, Kitty's sisters, were equally attracted to him.

Redford's success with the girls elicited jealousy from his male peers, but that scarcely discouraged him. Steve Bernhardt, the son of a movie director, saw Redford as strategically inventive: "He chose his allegiances carefully. For example, he courted Jill Schary, who was the daughter of the MGM chief, Dore Schary. He also hung out with Bill Chertok, whose father coproduced *The Lone Ranger* for ABC. These guys had great properties. Schary had a mansion in Beverly Glen, and the Chertoks a terrific weekend retreat at Shelter Cove, in Lake Arrowhead, with a Chris-Craft, butlers and maids." Redford agrees he was strategic, but so was everyone else, says Jan Holman, another of the TNT blondes who shared summer outings to Lake Arrowhead with Redford: "He was a gentleman. I understood why the guys were jealous of him, because he was naturally adept. He had a physicality that was unusual, even among healthy, outdoorsy boys. Stripped to the waist, he was a beautiful specimen, like some Scandinavian god, with a fine blond down across his body."

Redford concentrated on the new blooming romance with Kitty that displaced Betty. "He was very generous as a boyfriend, always attentive," says Kitty, who still has the rolled gold charm bracelet he gave her that first Christmas. "I felt I saw things in Bobby that other people missed. His writing, when he wrote to me, was advanced beyond his years. His artwork was also exceptional. I think the boys were envious of him with good cause."

Redford adored Kitty but was also attracted to Sheila, with whom he formed a close and open friendship. "You can oversubscribe to childhood angst, but Bobby was in a real turmoil," says Sheila. "Much of it had to do with heritage. He was a first-generation Angeleno, remember, and he was unsure of his place in the world. There was poverty in his background, and a kind of taunting wealth. He really didn't understand his background at all, and he was like a kid pressing his nose against the windowpane of other people's lives, wondering, What's going on in there?"

Redford also developed a good friendship with Carol Rossen. Her father, Robert Rossen, was a Warner Bros. screenwriter turned director. The previous year, HUAC had forced Rossen to renounce his Communist Party membership, and though he continued to work, he also continued to host political parties with blacklisted writers like Dalton Trumbo and Albert Maltz. Carol fancied Bobby Redford, too: "In my case, we had in common a curiosity about the real world, though we found it hard to talk openly about it because we were brought up in silence. Neither Communism nor Jewishness was openly discussed in my home, and it bothered me. I was Jewish, but my only understanding of Judaism came in the casual observance of Passover and Hanukkah we shared with my grandmother. That seemed like a terrible waste of heritage, and some part of me was in rebellion to this imposition. Bobby and I were joined, because we were on a private quest to get out of this phony world and into the sunlight."

Carol hid her Jewishness. She fit in with the Bundy set, she says, because she was redheaded, desirable and smart, with creativity and money in her background. "The scene was very racist, very WASPy and extremely politically right-wing," says Carol. "But I wasn't about to rock the boat."

Redford, however, was. With increasing maturity came unlimited confidence; with an increasing sense of being boxed in came recklessness. He started spending time with a wilder group and organizing exploratory midnight rituals. "I'd get up in the small hours," Redford recalls, "sneak out my bedroom window, follow the road past the Veterans Hospital and assemble the team, like the Pied Piper of Hamelin. Then we'd set out to investigate the darkest recesses of the neighborhood by night." He climbed fences to swim in neighbors' pools. He "borrowed" beer from friends' unattended storerooms. Dodging the late-night police patrols electrified proceedings.

Gradually the stakes grew higher: breaking and entering and annexing vacated properties for all-night drinking sessions became the main game.

Redford's main coconspirator was Bill Coomber. To Dave Stein, a mutual acquaintance, Coomber was the force that released the sleeping tiger in Redford. "It was waiting to happen," recalls Stein. "Bob was a very repressed individual. Bill gave vent to the anger in him. Bill wasn't so much Bob's passport to escape the stuffiness of the Brentwood set as his tutor in crime. Bill had the kind of privileges the Andrews girls had. The girls didn't question their privileges. Bill did. He questioned by abusing them, by testing their limits: he kicked back. There was a real element of Butch Cassidy and the Sundance Kid in Bob and Bill. For a time they were criminals. Lovable, but criminals."

For Redford, though, Coomber was a liberator. "My relationship with Bill was, literally, life sustaining," says Redford. "He became like the brother I didn't have."

Coomber remembers their first meeting, at Emerson. They talked, and Redford invited Coomber to the UCLA sports field for an informal Saturday football game. "Bill was a mixer," says Redford, "a very relaxed and loud personality with no inhibitions—and I wanted that for myself."

Like Redford, Coomber had no siblings. The center of his life was his mother, Helen Brady Coomber, a three-time divorcée with independent wealth and a mansion on Denslow Avenue. Her fortune came from her father, the nationally syndicated medical columnist William Brady. As a young girl, Helen had started training as an actress at the American Academy of Dramatic Arts in New York, where her family lived, and had moved successfully into theater and radio. Then, when her father's asthma necessitated a move to the West Coast, she abandoned her acting dream and relocated, too. Upon her father's death, the considerable inheritance facilitated "blazing adventures," according to her sister, Lala. Helen married "impulsively" several times, her union to Frederick Van Coomber yielding her one son, Bill. "When Mr. Coomber moved on," said Lala, "Helen treated Bill as the man of the house. She showered him with gifts, money, everything, and Bill was an adult at thirteen."

Redford liked Helen. She was kind to a fault, had humor like his mother and was constantly reading, according to Lala—"everything from Erich Fromm to Proust." Redford remembers that "she wasn't a storyteller. She was gushing, but she had a drama about her, a kind of Norma Desmond quality. Just talking to her, you knew her life was diverse and big."

In the Emerson school newspaper in the fall of 1949, Redford had been identified as "Krazy" and likened in personality to Milton Berle. It noted that he took to the stage in a playlet called *Time Out for Ginger,* a boy-meets-girl farce to which MGM sent talent scouts in hopes of finding a replacement for the aging Mickey Rooney. Redford doesn't remember this—"which shows how much interest in acting I had." But the next spring he was in the school play, *Wilbur Faces Facts.* Helen applauded him afterward, though Redford remembers more the enthusiasm of some schoolgirl friends. "That was a weird experience," says Redford. "It wasn't like sports or work. I wasn't trying. I was up there goofing off and people were laughing. The girls came up. 'You're good,' they said, and so I thought twice about it."

Coomber saw no support for the whimsical side of Redford at Homedale. "I thought Charlie was really rough on his son," he says, "always getting him to do endless thankless chores, like mowing the lawn week after week, whether it needed mowing or not." Redford grew more and more angry about Charlie's rules. "All I ever heard was, 'You gotta improve those high school grades. You gotta make it to Dartmouth or Stanford.' I realize now that those colleges represented the Gates to Heaven for him, because everyone he knew who succeeded in business had the right degrees. He wanted that kind of stability for me, but I didn't want it at all the older I got and the more of the world I experienced."

Redford's interest was absorbed by Coomber's obsessions: magic and general derring-do. "It was," says Coomber, "like a secret life. I had 'normality,' school and home, and then I had all these sidelines." Occasionally he performed magic shows—for tips—at a Westwood club. More often he was driving without a permit, boozing beyond reason and shoplifting petty items. He also loved climbing the high-rise buildings around Westwood Village after dark, and Redford joined him, scaling the sheer tower of the imposing Fox Village Theater.

There were shared football games, sleepovers, campouts and horseback-riding sessions in Will Rogers State Park, where Redford's love of riding began. "It was never open competition," says Coomber, "but we were always pushing each other. When we were riding, I was the experienced one. But Bob had to ride faster. There was never any admission of weakness from Bob—ever. It was always take it to the limit."

When the boys were just fifteen, they decided to tackle serious mountaineering outside Palm Springs. "Bob wanted to do it," says Coomber, "because it took him back to the wilderness. As soon as we could get our hands on an automobile—illegally, of course, since we were underage—we were off to Palm Springs."

Climbing the ten-thousand-foot Mount San Jacinto, Coomber and Redford overreached. "It was dumb and it was my fault," says Redford. "We started out with a party of friends on a bitter cold weekend. We camped, climbed, camped again. No one was stupid enough to want to try for the summit, except me. We knew the temperatures fell by forty degrees at night. Bill said, 'Okay, we'll give it a shot.' We had no sleeping bags, no more rations, just some cheap street gloves that started to shred. Suddenly it was so dark we couldn't distinguish the black ice. We were up very high, disoriented, lost."

The friends lit a fire from tinder in a snowbound cave. Exhausted, they took turns sleeping, constantly stoking the fire to stave off freezing to death. Coomber felt they wouldn't make it down alive. At first light they found a way down. They gorged at the Mountain Diner, then slept in a sand trap at the local golf course. They had been gone for days, but when Redford returned home, no questions were asked. "It had got to the point where my parents were sick of asking questions," says Redford.

At home, Redford was expressing himself more and daring to argue openly—"usually about nothing at all"—with Charlie. The family had acquired its first television set, an eleven-inch Philco, and, led by Bobby's dinnertime talk, embraced the wider world—the fall of Joe Louis, the rise of Milton Berle, Truman's policies, the collapse of the American Communist Party. Redford was drawn to politics but frustrated by Charlie's arcane communication. "He was highly intelligent but so polluted by *his* family's failure to stand up and be counted, so most of it was buried in dismissive wit. It was a pity, because when he let his feelings and opinions air, his insights were amazing."

In 1950, as Congressman Richard Nixon prepared for a Senate run in California, Charlie's reticence was breached. Kenny Chotiner, a classmate of Bob's at Emerson, was the son of Murray Chotiner, a key Nixon aide. From carpooling, Martha was friendly with Chotiner's wife, Phyllis. Charlie tolerated the friendship until Nixon developed his campaign as a character assassination, lambasting his Democrat opponent, Helen Gahagan Douglas, as a pinko. The Chotiners became the subject of screaming dinnertime debate. Charlie railed against the Nixon camp's ethics; Martha emotionally supported her friend. When Nixon won his seat, Charlie never forgave him. "Here was another instance, the *character* of leadership, like the persistent issue of racism, that my father was sharp to, but much too muted about," says Redford. "Those Chotiner arguments stuck in my mind because of these great instincts my father had. He resented bullshit. And he predicted before anyone I knew that Nixon meant trouble."

Increasingly intrigued as he was by social politics, the fate of Carol Rossen, whose family life was upended by the HUAC campaign against her father, stimulated Redford. "It drove me nuts when her family was effectively exiled from the area," says Redford. "I wasn't aware of the finer points of HUAC, that Trumbo and Maltz had gone to jail, and big-profile people like Gary Cooper, John Wayne and Walt Disney were trying to weed out these pinkos."

Given his rebellious nature, a life of insouciance would not last.

4

East of Eden

Redford's last year at junior high coincided with a career shift for Charlie. Standard Oil had opened a district office at Van Nuys in the San Fernando Valley, and Charlie was to be a divisional accountant based there. For Redford, the Valley represented an inland desert, a wasteland. But he objected in vain.

Before the move, the family made another cross-country journey to see Tiger and Lena back east. It was a mistake: the antagonism between father and son had become corrosive. On the way home, driving through Colorado, Redford jumped ship. He took a summer job tending horses in the stables at Estes Park, sixty-five miles northwest of Denver, a declaration of independence that seems significant in hindsight: already he was opting for fresh country air in preference to the tense, oppressive claustrophobia of Los Angeles.

Back home the adventuring with Coomber that had been excusable as tomfoolery became delinquency. Redford had transferred to University High, Coomber's new school, which proved a mistake. "The problems got out of hand at Uni High," says Coomber. Both became members of the legendary boys' club, the Barons. "We were a street gang," says Coomber, "there's no other name for it. The Barons became our camouflage for all kinds of petty theft." During the previous fall, Redford had been detained for breaking into a local girls' school after dark. Now Coomber was arrested and charged with grand theft for purloining the five-foot brass propeller at the naval memorial in Ocean Park. Shortly after, Redford was arrested for borrowing an automobile that had stolen jewelry in its trunk. Helen and Charlie interceded, and charges were dropped against Coomber and Redford. Redford was abruptly removed from Uni High and temporarily ensconced in the Catholic Notre Dame High School.

"You could say Bob was a spoiled brat reacting to his toys being taken from him," says Steve Bernhardt. "In Westwood, he had a good love life, a stable family, wealthy friends. All this was being displaced with this family move to the desert."

In November the Redfords moved to the Valley, to a barnlike bungalow at 5637 Buffalo Avenue, a mile from Van Nuys High School, into which Redford transferred. Sallie and Nelson were left behind, as were so many friends. He was distraught: "It was worse than I imagined. We had moved into an oven. There was no culture, no air, no sea, just badly tended orange groves and some awful movie star dude ranches. It was a very western place, but primitive. Our house was a cracker box with a barbecue in the small yard. It was a *Twilight Zone* version of suburbia."

Redford stopped attending school. He hitched instead to Hermosa Beach, the surfers' hangout, where Coomber and friends from Emerson hung out. They drank, waxed surfboards, listened to the jocks of radio station KMPC. At four every afternoon, he would hitch back across the hills to Buffalo Avenue and pretend he'd been to class.

The deception lasted a month. When Charlie learned the truth from a truant officer, he exploded. Redford promised to mend his ways, returning to school and taking an evening job at a local pharmacy. Within a week he and his new friend Dave Brockman were supplying stolen Cadillac hubcaps to a fence who managed the liquor store down the street.

Kitty knew Redford was slipping away from her. She visited him in the Valley and saw the changes. Barred from seeing Coomber and the Emerson friends, he was building a new life and forming new friendships. Hotrodding was his new pastime, shared mostly with Brockman, the son of a judge. "I didn't think Bobby had become delinquent," says Kitty, "but he was struggling to keep life in perspective. We were kids, but we'd had a special, very mature bond, and that bond was slipping, partly because of the geographical separation, partly because of the changes in both of us."

The relationship with Kitty ended that year when her family moved east, but Redford had already romantically moved on, acquiring a new girlfriend named Pat Lyons. Redford was not yet seventeen; Pat was twenty. "I sought out an older girl," says Redford, "because I was hungry for experience. Less and less I wanted what my parents had." Lyons introduced him to smoky L.A. jazz clubs like the Haig, the Oasis and Howard Rumsey's Lighthouse, to the world of cool jazz, Chet Baker and Gerry Mulligan. This was about as far as he could get from the pleasantries of Santa Monica's big-band ballrooms, and he was thrilled. "I loved the profanity, the booze, the blue-lit, hazy rooms. Most of all I went for this terrific discordancy in the music. It wasn't polite. The world I was stuck in was all polite. But this was expressive and completely free."

One weekend his parents took off for a four-day trip to San Diego, leaving the family Chevy at home. Redford drove it to San Francisco, in search of more jazz. He had no permit, so was obliged to dodge the highway police, taking the scenic Route 101 past Malibu toward Big Sur. The sense of liberation evoked by wild, untamed nature once again kicked in. "On that journey I realized I hated L.A. for its compromises," says Redford. "I decided that somehow I must get out of it permanently."

In San Francisco, Redford and his friends stumbled on a party at Lawrence Ferlinghetti's newly opened City Lights Bookstore in North Beach. The hosts were the forward guard of the Beats: Gregory Corso, Allen Ginsberg, Gary Snyder, Kenneth Rexroth, Michael Mclure. The poets took turns reading their work. Jack Kerouac collected donations in a hat. "This was years before [Ginsberg's] *Howl,*" says Redford, "but there was a sense of manifesto. I had never experienced what you might call an alternative communal vision, but this was it. These guys were obviously doped. But they had a track on something honest that made absolute sense to me. It was a mind-blowing evening."

The previous summer, the summer of 1952, a *Life* magazine survey listed the national teen idols as Roy Rogers, Joe DiMaggio, Vera-Ellen, Louisa May Alcott, General Douglas MacArthur and Doris Day, none of whom, with the exception of DiMaggio, Redford connected with. Instead, his natural affiliations were with the rebels, with Kerouac, then wrestling with *On the Road,* with Miles Davis's improvisational jazz, with Alan Watts and radio station KPFA prompting the Bay Area toward Eastern thinking. Coomber had prophesied to friends that Redford was facing some major, life-altering change. "I told them either he'll break through in some important career or he'll end up in the gutter like a bum. There'd be no middle way," says Coomber. Redford experienced a new focus with the Beats. "The music I was listening to and those guys in North Beach opened my eyes," he says. "One perfect example was a night with Pat at the Haig, watching Gerry Mulligan play to the room, and everyone, except one smooching couple, was enraptured. So Mulligan went over to their table and leaned in with his sax and blew them into orbit. That was an education for me: That jazz wasn't just entertainment. That it was a weapon, an onslaught on convention. That art, or however you phrase it, had the power to change things fundamentally."

Charlie continued to believe his son's redemption lay in sports. In his first fall at Van Nuys High, Redford made the football team. But he quit. He still loved the Red Sox, and had fantasies about being the next Ted Williams—"the only public figure I ever idolized"—but now he avoided baseball as well.

Redford tried marijuana and hashish, spent weekends "rumbling" hot rods on dirt tracks in the Simi Hills and romanced Pat's friends when he could get away with it. Coomber was absent, but Redford didn't need the prompting of his friend's wildness. En route to a drag trial in Santa Barbara, he lost control of a souped-up coupe and crashed at ninety miles an hour. Lucky to be alive, he was ferried home, dazed. Charlie was outraged. Redford says, "All I remember was the look of absolute hopelessness on his face, looking at me and saying, 'Who are you?' "

In the spring of 1954 Redford graduated from Van Nuys High. "If you'd asked me on that day of graduation, 'What do you want to do with your life?' my answer would have been, 'Get as far away from Van Nuys High as I can, period.' " As the names of graduates were read out, Redford sat at the back of the assembly hall, reading *Mad* magazine.

Given his grades, his college options were restricted. The University of Colorado at Boulder, though, offered the possibility of an eventual sports scholarship. Faded though its allure was, Redford thought he might resume his baseball. "So it was a no-brainer. Colorado was baseball. And, more important, the mountains. Escape."

Redford started out brooding and isolated. He focused on the arts at Boulder, and baseball was quickly abandoned. Jack Brendlinger, a senior, four years older, took him under his wing. They first met during fraternity rush week by the moat in front of the Kappa Sigma house. Brendlinger was drawn to Redford, he says, because he looked so out of place: "Our frat house was 90 percent well-heeled, well-tailored students from Chicago's North Shore, and here was a depressed-looking bum in an Irish tweed jacket with his hair styled in a ducktail. I sat beside him and the first thing he said was, 'Man, this just isn't for me.' " Brendlinger invited Redford to join him for a round of golf. After Redford shot a blistering nine, Brendlinger decided he belonged in Kappa Sigma. "Bob was unfazed during the hazing. For him, it was masochistic competition," says Brendlinger. "He was a strange guy."

Redford's insularity swung to extroversion. He befriended Dave Barr from Glendale and a Minnesotan called Hugh Hall, and moved off campus to share an apartment with them. He resumed his drawing and started what would be a lifetime habit of diary keeping, filling notebooks with spontaneous observations. The Kappa Sigma Chicagoans, in particular, became the templates of the North Shore folk whom he would essay twenty-five years later in *Ordinary People.* "You shouldn't generalize, I know, but my observation was of advantaged Americans besotted, as my father was, with the vision of the organization man," says Redford. "These were Eisenhower's people. Everything came secondary to the ultimate career, and education was limited to the streamlined agenda that served that career. It was a narrow, elitist view, and, like Brentwood, it had no introspective, self-analytical tendency nor much interest in human communication." In compensation, Redford gravitated toward a group of Jewish students whom he called "this reverse cabal," because of their humor and their constant questioning of the status quo.

Within months Redford had become beloved in the drinking circles but was regarded as a loose cannon. He was the most relaxed with Hugh Hall, the son of evangelistic Baptist parents, because he was spontaneous. They enjoyed the same literature (Willa Cather, Sinclair Lewis) and the same music (George Shearing, Chet Baker), and equally enjoyed attacking convention. Hall was a part-time disc jockey at the local radio station, KBOL, who delighted in mocking his audience with filthy, erudite innuendo. "He was so smart," says Redford, "he could fund himself writing overnight term papers for students. He could also recite the *Kama Sutra* on the radio without anyone knowing what he was talking about." Together they subverted game shows to win Redford prizes and staged outrageous doublespeak phone-ins. Once, Redford burst into the studio while Hall was broadcasting and pretended it was an armed holdup. It almost cost Hall his job, but he went on to a career in regional broadcasting, changing his name to Sam Hall.

Redford's new romantic fixation was Wanda Shannon, an old Westwood flame who had gone to Vegas to become a dancer in one of the big hotel floor shows. During spring break in April 1955, Redford and five friends decided they'd visit Wanda. When they arrived, they learned that Elvis was in town. "I'd already discovered black music with Big Jay McNeely at the Blue Sax in North Hollywood and made the blues-jazz connections, so I wanted to experience this Elvis thing," says Redford. The Elvis show was a support act to Freddy Martin at the Frontier, a fancy supper club that Redford's group couldn't afford. "So I persuaded the guys to pool cash and we came up with $10, then charmed a waitress to let us dine on rolls while we watched the show." From the moment Presley started with "Hound Dog,"

Redford was a convert. "It was electrifying, a validation, to see these stuffed-shirt socialites who'd come to see Freddy Martin clamp up in reverence. I thought, Hey, a kid with nothing, from nowheresville, can do *this*!"

Sinatra was at the Sands. His theatricality riveted Redford: "We sat at the back in darkness. Then, from the shadows, emerged this liquid, velvet voice: '*You see a pair of laughing eyes. . . .*' I realized he was a storyteller. He was introducing a new version of himself with 'Wee Small Hours in the Morning.' Later on I learned how he perfected his phrasing by emulating Tommy Dorsey's breath control with the trombone. The combined effect was huge artistry.

"I went to Vegas expecting razzmatazz and status quo. Instead, I found artists at work. It was a different kind of artistry than the Beat scene, but it was no less radical. I expected to be cynical. I wasn't. Vegas encouraged me to be more eclectic in my tastes, to move away from the knee-jerk rebellious response—to grow up, maybe."

He'd bought an old car and now started traveling, establishing a peripatetic pattern that would last all his life. Aside from the regular drives between Colorado and home, he motored to New Mexico, Utah, Nebraska and Wyoming.

"The love of movement reflected the fact that, apart from art history, the only classes at CU that interested me were geomorphology and anthropology," he says. "Geomorphology fed this curiosity about landscape. I relished those drives home to L.A. and started alternating routes. In winter, I'd drive the southern route via Gallup and Albuquerque; in summer, the northern route via Vegas and Salt Lake City. I got fired up on sedimentology to the point where I was reading books about it voluntarily. I'd bore everyone at home with detailed descriptions of schisms and alluvial fans. The Rockies and the desert became vital for me: they were the fossilized history of the world. And then anthropology kicked in. The human culture element breathed life into it all. The man who opened this up for me was one of the best teachers at CU, Omer Stewart."

Driving toward Salt Lake City once to pick up the two-lane Highway 91 home, Redford diverted at Ogden, turned for Heber City and stopped at a riverside diner called the Chalet. He had lunch and then surveyed the area: "The river, the snow on the mountains, the cladding of screw pines and aspens, it all had what I'd now call a European character. I found a little side road called the Alpine Loop and drove up the hill, which was the north fork draw of Provo Canyon, until the road ran out. It was so beautiful that I couldn't pull myself away. The mountain, Timpanogos, was to me like Everest. It was Yosemite on a different scale. Spiritually, it was fascinating. When I left, I couldn't shake it off. I lay in bed and thought about it. And whenever I had the chance to go back, I did. It became my favorite *long* shortcut, the only way to go home. I have a clear recollection of thinking, Someday I'd like to put a stake down here." The canyon that attracted him was called Timp Haven, destined to become the Sundance village from which he would build his personal cultural vision. It was also, ironically, owned by Omer Stewart's family.

Martha's health, meanwhile, had begun to decline. At the time of the loss of her twins in 1947, Redford remembered hearing through a closed door someone saying, "It's either her or the twins." The fact that she had a weak heart and a chronic congenital blood disorder was skipped over, partly, Redford believes, because of religious preconditioning. She'd recovered, but not totally. "She was so full of optimism, she had such a bright, loving smile, that I thought she was immortal," says Redford. And then he noticed her wane. "I'd come back home in the middle of the day, and she'd be wearing her dressing gown, which seemed so unlike her. When I'd question it, she'd just say, 'Oh, I was tired.' " Martha put on weight and her skin took on a blue hue. Redford knew she was in pain, and observed that she could only find relief getting in the car and going for drives out to the desert. Redford was happy to take her driving. "After all, she taught me, when I was about eight. In those days, when Dad was working in El Segundo, we'd drive out on the back roads to collect him late at night. Mom used to put me on her lap and work the pedals while I steered. Now she sat in silence while we drove in circles."

At CU, Redford distracted himself with his art. "I looked around Boulder to try to find the arts community, but there was none," he recalls. Richard Dudley, the fine arts professor, advised him the community would be of his own making. Dudley was a wild man, a transplanted New Yorker. "Art is about you and your vision," Dudley told him. At Van Nuys, Redford had won a Scholastic Gold Key for drawing and, as part of the prize, had been offered summer work as an apprentice, cleaning cels for the lead animators at Disney Studios in Burbank. He'd visited but disliked the assembly line labor. Instead, on the advice of a kind technician, he walked up the block to UPA, the tiny independent studio run by Faith and John Hubley, which made the Gerald McBoing-Boing shorts that launched Mr. Magoo. "I didn't have any sort of plan then," says Redford. "I just loved those cartoons and thought my own sketches were kind of similar." The Hubleys, operating from a shack behind a restaurant, welcomed the young Redford into their workshop and showed him their designs. "They were just amenable folk excited by what they were doing and patiently making ten-year projections of each character's development. It was great down-home enthusiasm, and I loved the fact that they cherished the individual artist." Redford asked for a job and was told to "go find experience—anywhere—and come back to us."

Redford first saw Dudley's CU program as a prep course for a possible career in animation but soon found his horizons expanding. A committed modernist, Dudley promoted the deconstructive principles of expressionism and denigrated the stubborn teaching formula that centered on Hellenic form. His idol was Paul Klee, the Blaue Reiter transcendentalist whose famous contribution to abstract art was the narrative use of symbols and numbers within mosaics. Klee searched for spirituality in his art, and Dudley tried to convey some of the attraction of intellectual surrender to his mostly female class. Redford jumped at the invitation to free expression but found himself "a stroke behind all this; I needed a few years to catch up with the emotional release of expressionism." But the bond with Dudley was inspirational. "He wasn't an admirer of the fauves, and I was anticolor at the start, so we talked the same language," says Redford. "He was also gripped by a raging frustration, lost in the backwater of Boulder, and consequently anarchic, which felt familiar. I was confident in my style because I had been sketching for so long. I was ready to experiment. Other students were stuck in theory, and that drove Dudley nuts. One girl labored over a very detailed Florentine nude, which inflamed him because he wanted all of us to let the tiger out. He approached her, took her inkwell and upended it over the drawing. Then he grabbed her hand and scrawled through the ink, smearing it everywhere. *'Let it go! Let it go!'* I found that stimulating." Nonetheless, Redford's grades were awful.

In May 1955, Martha died of complications arising from the recurrent septicemia she had been suffering from since her difficult pregnancy. Charlie called his son, who caught the next plane from Denver. "I'll never forget his meeting me at the airport," says Redford. "I'd never seen him as a vulnerable man, and the balance of power had always been one-sided. I'd raised hell, but he was always boss. At the airport it was completely different. He fell to pieces. I told him to get out of the driver's seat and I took the wheel. Everything changed when my mother died. His world fell down. Mine seemed to also."

5

Behind the Mirror

Photographs of Redford taken soon after his mother's death are revealing. He looks like a punch-drunk boxer, shoulders hunched, collar upturned, tie askew. In Los Angeles, family friend Vivian Knudson found him "disoriented and angry." Coomber observed him "torn apart. He was devastated by her loss, and it pushed him far inside himself at exactly the time he had the chance to grow outward."

For the next eighteen months he consoled himself with girls and books. All direction disappeared. He was submissive. When Charlie insisted on summer field work, loading boxcars and cleaning oil drums at the El Segundo refinery, he acceded. George Menard insisted that while Charlie recovered from Martha's passing, "Bobby was seriously screwed up. He mumbled about vague career plans in art or design, but Charlie said it was all nonsense, that his future must be something more substantial."

More convulsions followed. In November, Lena died in New London. At the same time Hugh Hall, his friend from CU, signed for two years in the military. Redford searched for comfort in literature, devouring Thomas Wolfe, Sinclair Lewis and Thomas Mann. Each struck chords that would resurface explicitly and implicitly in his later work: Wolfe the egotist, filled with spiritual wonder, the hunger for self-realization and chronic alienation in equal parts; Lewis, dissecting American smugness and philistinism in *Main Street* and *Babbitt;* Mann, probing Western civilization. All engrossed Redford; all left a sense of want.

Finally, in Henry Miller, Redford found what he was searching for. A fellow student loaned him the slim, European-published *Nights of Love and Laughter.* This was Miller at his most raucous and profane. Redford loved it. "No one I'd found was so frank about tackling the hypocrisies of society. Yes, he talked about hunger and anger and sexual voracity. But it was all in the spirit of saying, 'Let's just lay it out here. Let's be honest about human beings.' It was frank, direct human communication, and that was a rare commodity in my life."

Late in the spring of 1956 he decided abruptly to go to Europe. Dudley, as much as Miller, was behind the decision. "It was also what John Hubley had said: get experience." The University of Colorado had made it clear that he wasn't welcome back. His home life also suddenly became unbearably complicated. True to form, there had been no analytical discussion of Martha's passing, just silence. Now Charlie announced in a letter that he was planning to marry Helen Coomber. Even today both sides of the family express bewilderment at this overnight romance. According to Lala Brady, the family friendship had deepened significantly in the weeks preceding Martha's death, but neither she nor anyone else had any inkling of wedding bells.

For Redford a long-distance exile became a necessity: "Domestically it was too much to deal with. The job prospects at home were terrible. Plus, I really wanted art in my life, that much I now knew. Expressionism was the big scene in the United States, but I preferred the Europeans like Utrillo, Modigliani, and especially Gauguin, and the postimpressionists, who were immensely exciting for me." In Europe, Redford reasoned, he would be closer to the wellsprings and might escape the American cultural inertia that Miller disdained.

Brendlinger and Redford had drifted apart over the last year, but Redford approached his old supporter. "I was contemplating the summer ahead and the obligations I had for the Naval Reserve," says Brendlinger, "when Bob comes up and blurts, 'I've decided to go to Europe.' " It was agreed they would join up for a while over there in search of adventure. In France, Brendlinger could take language courses at the Sorbonne and maybe be a ski bum in Switzerland, while Redford, with an introductory letter from Dudley, would enroll at the École des Beaux-Arts in Paris.

Charlie thought of his son's new plan as a lark, but was met with the usual bullish stubbornness. "*I* knew what my father wanted me to be," says Redford. "The problem was, he didn't know who I was. If I didn't get out of there then, I believe I'd have continued a serious downward slide."

Early in September, Redford hitched to Denver, from where he and Brendlinger drove a Lincoln Continental to New York, providing a vehicle-delivery service for a rental agency. In Manhattan, they bought round-trip tourist-class tickets to France aboard the USS *United States* for $300 apiece, almost half their money. Then Redford splurged on a farewell gift to himself—a Broadway ticket to see Jason Robards in Eugene O'Neill's *Long Day's Journey into Night.* It brought him to tears with the eloquence of its language and the echoes of grandfather Tiger's New London.

At the time of Redford's arrival in France in 1956, the cold war was raging. Earlier in the year Polish riots against Soviet occupation had filled American headlines. In November, Hungary would launch its five-day rebellion. Redford arrived in the gap between the two. "I was open for political conversion," he says. "I'd had the full American education, which amounted to conservatism, social torpor and an absolute lack of understanding of other cultures. France, to me, was Hemingway and Gertrude Stein. Of course, in some circles there was a better perspective, but the popular understanding was negligible. I arrived in Europe an innocent, but with a metaphorical, and literal, notebook in my hand."

Charlie had reluctantly agreed to send $100 a month. "Bob would spend his month's money in a week," says Brendlinger, "and then live off mine. I think he was almost in debt from the time we arrived." They had made no arrangements for accommodation in Paris, and since it was auto show week, no hotel rooms could be found. At the last minute a clerk at American Express found an old lady with rooms on the Right Bank. One week's board ate up a month's budget. "We were off to a very bad start," recalls Brendlinger.

Redford, however, was uncowed. This was the world he wanted: edgy, overstretched, extreme. He hung out in the university district and sought to meet some French women. It was no easy chore. "They just didn't like Americans," says Redford, "and coming from my uninformed place, it was hard for me to judge how much of their rudeness was personal." Redford started a crash course in recent French history, learning about de Gaulle, the war in Indochina, the warring factions in Algeria. "My exposure to pre-Gaullist France," says Redford, "was the start of coherent political awareness because I had to apply myself to understand why it was hard for us to fit in there. It was valuable for making me reevaluate America, too. I started reading Walter Lippmann and Art Buchwald for the better perspective. And I understood for the first time the colossal role America was playing all over the world. Because of out-of-control French inflation and the strength of the dollar, Americans were like visiting conquerors. And that's how it was across many parts of the world. We had influence: in money, in military strength, in the movies. We touched other people's cultures in extraordinary ways in the twentieth century."

Day courses at the Beaux-Arts did not commence until October, so Redford and Brendlinger decided to leave town. On the advice of a German they met at a jazz club, they set off for Majorca. There, for $40, they rented a Moorish villa belonging to the Catholic Church at Can Pastilla, south of Palma. They were in sight of the sea and surrounded by white walls draped in bougainvillea. But Redford did not enjoy the blissful isolation for long. "He would sit at these open-air bistros all day long and sketch the customers," remembers Brendlinger. "All the faces he chose were the sad ones. All of this work was very moving and evocative, and I saw a side to him that was new. This wasn't the flake from CU. This was some troubled kid." Brendlinger, whose father had died when he was very young, wondered if Redford wasn't struggling with the grief of losing his mother. "I gathered she was the heart of his self-esteem. But I think it was more than that. He had a creative urge bursting to break out, and it had been suppressed. I began to understand that Europe was do or die for him, secretly.

"We got to talking about our after-college destinies, and how the business world would kill both of us. Bob talked about his love for art and wondered where art and movies might intersect. The movie industry, we decided, offered lots of perks, like travel, long resting spells between jobs, et cetera. Bob was a vain kid, but his ego wasn't so big that he was imagining himself as an actor. I said to him: 'What about acting?' But he was thinking only of art. I said, 'After this is over, we can go back to L.A. and make a great life for ourselves conning our way through the movie industry.' He seemed amused by the thought." But all Redford was interested in, he says, was getting to the Beaux-Arts.

In October the friends returned to Paris and took a room for $1.50 a night at the Hôtel Notre-Dame on the Quai Saint-Michel. Redford started at the Beaux-Arts. The school's emphasis had recently shifted from painting and sculpting to architecture. For day students, the first two years were couched in classicism and Renaissance studies. Redford slumped: "This was the school where Delacroix, Ingres, Renoir, Degas and Monet trained. It was supposed to be the ultimate communal school that valued experiment. But the environment I found was academic and very self-serious. It was everything that made me uncomfortable. All I did was sit in a courtyard and learn about Alberti's mathematical theories and the principles of aerial perspective and chiaroscuro."

After four weeks he transferred to the recently accredited modernist Académie Charpentier. Here informality inspired Redford. "I finally started to forget academic study and experiment. It was the first time in my life that I could work in unself-conscious freedom, try things and fail or succeed, and build a portfolio. I changed fundamentally. When I first arrived in Paris I was wearing a bateau-collared shirt and beret I'd stolen from a Beverly Hills store. I was playing at being Gene Kelly in Paris. By the time I was at the academy's little third-floor atelier, the phoniness was gone. I was painting in oils, every day. I particularly loved to paint pregnant women, for their fullness in any pose. Up till then my ambitious artwork was dark, like Franz Klein's. Now it was full of blazing color." Modigliani became his new, cherished template, as much for his history of wildness as for his art: Modigliani was an uninhibited, glorious drunk, indulging the most dangerous *affaires,* stealing stone from municipal building sites, defying everyone, a persona that felt comfortably familiar.

Brimming with new energy, Redford joined with student radicals organizing street demonstrations against the Soviet suppression in Hungary. Curiosity put him in the middle of the action, though his political education was very much a work in progress. In a police baton charge in the university district, he was clubbed and injured. "It wasn't what drove me out of Paris," says Redford, "but it contributed. It wasn't just antistudent at that rally, it was anti-American. I was beginning to understand I had a lot more to learn."

At the start of December, Redford and Brendlinger rejoined and hit the road. Redford wanted to go to Italy. He had decided he would draw and paint on the streets and earn his way. They hitched, following a youth hostel map that took them first to Capri and then to Rome for Christmas. "It was excruciating," says Brendlinger. "We always seemed to miss a hostel bed and end up sleeping in the dirt. It was also an intensely cold winter, colder than Colorado." In an often published account of the trip, Redford is reported to have copied a trick from a Jack London story and buried himself in cow dung for warmth. "It's true," says Redford, "ridiculous, but true." By the time they reached Rome in mid-December, both were almost out of cash and subsisting on cheese and water. They hurried through the Roman sights—the Piazza Venezia, the Roman Forum, the Colosseum—then hitched to Naples and cadged a ferry ride to spend Christmas in Anacapri. Back in Rome on New Year's Eve they gate-crashed Bricktops, the haunt of the glitterati, where Redford joined a jostling pack of revelers stealing kisses at midnight from Ava Gardner.

When they reached Florence, Redford made a decision. "No disrespect to Jack, but I wanted this solitary trip. It was partly masochistic. I wanted to be alone with the grief I had and the difficulty I had with my personal identity. More than anything, I wanted to go on a journey with my art. Was it any good? How far would it take me? Could I survive with it, and it alone?" Brendlinger departed for the ski resort of Zürs, and the friends agreed to meet again in Munich in March.

Redford began a rapid slide. It was as if the true trough of his depression revealed itself once constant companionship was removed. The photographs Brendlinger took throughout the Europe trip speak for themselves: at the start Redford looks chubby and comfortable; by the time he's in Florence, he is gaunt and stripped of expression. "I lost forty-two pounds," says Redford. "Nervous tension and the constant movement burned the weight off me. What was I nervous about? Failing, and having to go back to resume a Los Angeles life. It was bad in Paris. It became unbearable in Florence." Speaking no Italian, bereft of friends, he took a room with a family called the Barbieris and enrolled for classes at a dingy, private *scuola* supervised by tutors from the Accademia di Belle Arti. The Orphean descent began. "Because the Barbieris spoke no English, there was almost no communication, just like at home," says Redford. "I hardly saw them because I lived by night and slept half the day. It was the dead of winter, fifteen Celsius below, and I slept in my gray wool overcoat for the heat. Staying warm became the big deal. And staying sane. And working. Just these three things: warmth, sanity, work. I smoked cut in half Alfa cigarettes to stay warm."

Each afternoon, when not attending classes, Redford lived a military routine: "It was always very late when I'd rise. I'd eat a small plate of penne or ravioli and take a coffee at the railway station, then go walk the Ponte Vecchio. I walked and walked and walked, looking and sketching. I had a large sketchbook in which on the left facing page I wrote my thoughts and on the right I drew." One of the *scuola* tutors, Tony Reeves, a Canadian from the American arts program at the academy, offered encouragement. Very much in mind of Picasso's contention that abstract art is worthless unless its concept is rooted in recognizable reality, Redford studied himself. "I started examining my own face in the solitary three-quarter-length mirror on the washstand in the corner of my room. Just sitting on a chair, staring and staring, deconstructing my features. I was trying to disassemble the human form and find out who I was at the same time." In his isolation Redford became obsessive-compulsive. "I became convinced that if I filled the room with smoke, I'd make it warmer. So I cut up my cigarettes in the belief that they'd last longer. I smoked for twenty hours a day. The room was airless. It got so that I couldn't breathe. My head was spinning. I wasn't eating anymore. I started losing weight by the day. Growing more and more inward. I didn't want to talk, didn't want to make a sound, to sleep. Didn't want to do anything except keep an eye on that fellow in that mirror over the washbowl."

On a February night so cold that ice formed in the water jug on the nightstand, Redford says he began to crack up. "Staring in the mirror, I saw someone I didn't recognize at all. I began to hallucinate. I couldn't see flesh or bones, but I saw through the skin into some indescribable new entity."

He broke down. Florence was the cathedral of highest art, the home of Leonardo, Michelangelo and Giotto, and he couldn't make it there. "I was thinking all the time, If I can only hang on here, then maybe . . . ? But I knew I was a goner. I started to laugh and then I started to cry and I couldn't stop. It was the weirdest thing. My old self was gone. Dead. I was not the same person after that night in Florence."

He now roamed the streets of Florence for days, panicked by the extent of his failure. He felt he had lived an inauthentic life until then, which qualified him for only one thing: role-playing. Tony Reeves saw he was indigent, took pity on him and organized a small gallery showing of his work that earned a couple of thousand lire and funded the passage north. He would meet Brendlinger in Munich as planned and head home.

When Brendlinger saw him again, he was concerned about his friend's weight loss. "He looked very frail, with a beard and a general disheveled appearance," says Brendlinger. "But it wasn't much different from nights on the road. I had the impression he'd been sleeping in some ditch somewhere." Redford felt himself "wasted and shaky but hanging in."

They arrived back in the United States on March 14, 1957. Redford parted company with Brendlinger after an overnight stop at a Brooklyn hotel and embarked on a solo cross-country journey, exactly as Henry Miller did when he returned from postwar exile, notebook in hand, to reevaluate his homeland. On his first sight of New York, the returning Miller wrote: "Back in the rat trap. I try to hide away from my old friends;

I don't want to relive the past with them." This was exactly Redford's mind-set. Still upset by the Florence experience, he hitchhiked from New London (where he visited Tiger and borrowed $35 "for the Greyhound west"), through Illinois, Oklahoma and Tennessee, to Tot's home on Lake Austin. He longed for some of Tot's upbeat wisdom, but during the winter Tot had fallen off the roof and was a virtual invalid. Seeing him shuffle around in a steel back brace like an infirm old man was almost too much to bear: "He was only sixty-eight—a young sixty-eight—and seeing him so damaged and jaded destroyed me. I thought, All the good stuff is gone."

After a few days, Redford called Charlie and asked him to pick him up at the bus depot. Charlie didn't recognize his son. "I was waiting by the curb but he drove past," recalls Redford, "then drove past again until I finally flagged him down. He couldn't find words to express his shock at how I looked, and I certainly hadn't the words to express what I'd gone through. We drove home in complete silence."

Home was now Helen's lavish house. Her son, Bill Coomber, was living there, having transferred to UCLA. Redford embraced him, but was impatient to be away from the situation. There were some who believed he was angry at Charlie and Coomber for the new closeness they'd developed. Redford denies it: "I didn't feel resentment. In fact, I felt good for Bill, that the madness in him was gone, and he was at peace. For Dad, I think he'd found a safe haven. For so many years he'd had adversity and struggle. I don't believe he'd got over the big displacement of his childhood, being sent away from Connecticut and more or less abandoned. I think he was hungry for a settled life, and Helen had the resources to provide that."

At loose ends, Redford agreed to another summer of work at the refinery oil fields. He had agreed to rent an apartment with Brendlinger in Los Angeles for the summer. They did, in Varwood, an apartment complex above Hollywood and Vine. Here, instantly, Redford's mood changed. He was in the bohemian world he craved, and in his Milleresque notebook, he recorded every detail. Nearby Sunset Boulevard, where he lunched many days, was "a façade, only this." The streets were paved with "shoulder pads, falsies, elevator shoes and toupees of the many and various fonts of banality." But he loved Varwood's grotesquerie. Setting up his "easel of good will" while Brendlinger dreamed of sugar mamas in ermine, he befriended all the residents: the loudmouthed landlords, "Tel Aviv's version of Ma and Pa Kettle, who exercise by running from each other's shadows"; the Allens, he homesick Scottish, she "sometimes auburn"; Morey, the Spanish-Hawaiian-French Canadian opera singer; Sam, the Capitol Records rep "who plays and duets off-key nightly with a vinyl Sinatra." Four attractive Mormon girls from Utah also resided in Varwood. They became instant friends: "In the days that followed, our apartment became a Grand Central Station filled with unfolded maps of Europe, watermelon seeds and the constant chatter that accompanies new acquaintanceships. The fabric of the fertile bohemians sufficiently aired, we finally lent ourselves to being natural once again."

All of the girls were first-year students at Brigham Young University. A chemistry had ignited between Redford and seventeen-year-old Lola Van Wagenen. She was "a world apart," says Redford, "from the women I'd been with in Europe." The four girls had come to Los Angeles from the rural town of Provo, consistent with the proselytizing policy of the Mormon mission, to engage the outside world. Lola seemed the most sophisticated. She had been a beauty pageant winner at Provo High, had appeared onstage in her school's production of Thornton Wilder's *Our Town* and was a member of a doo-wop sextet, the Downbeats, which had toured the Northwest and won radio and television spots in Washington.

Redford found much to share with her. "She would come and talk to me while I painted," he wrote in his diary. "We would go for walks, up and down the celestial thoroughfares, through backwaters and parking lots, all the while discussing innocent issues ranging from moods people suffer to tales of past experience. I found her charming, more than pleasant, and most of all a good companion." They went to see Harry Belafonte at the Hollywood Bowl and visited the observatory in Griffith Park. They went bowling and to the movies. Lola had "an extraordinary effect" on Redford, recalls Brendlinger. "She just slowed down that emotional spin. She was ridiculously right for him. They were total opposites, but they fit like hand in glove."

"Our relationship got off to a better start because we were honest with each other," Lola told a Utah newspaper years later. "All that stuff that comes from dating wasn't there. When you date, you want the guy to think you're neat . . . and you don't get to know each other because you're too busy doing your number. Bob and I talked our way into love."

Redford believes that Lola saved his life. "It was about honesty. I felt I couldn't be real within my own family—even with Jack—but I could be frank about my needs with her. She approved, and that was a blessing." The discipline of her Mormonism even appealed to him, though he knew nothing about the religion. "What she told me I found fascinating. I was open to it. Sallie had started me off with her emphasis on religious salvation, and I was seeking resolution. In my eyes, my life at that time was muddy, uncouth. Lola, and Mormonism, represented something healthy and redemptive, which I needed."

In July, Redford persuaded Lola to spend "a honeymoon weekend" with him in Monterey. One of the Provo roommates didn't approve, and word reached Lola's parents of their daughter's dalliance with a Beat bum. The parents immediately sent cousins to L.A. to investigate. By then, says Redford, he and Lola had crossed the river. "We were in love. We thought, We have too much in common to let it go. Neither of us was conformist. We liked challenges. So we ignored them and started making plans."

In fact, Redford had been exploring new options since his return. During his time in New York he had picked up a prospectus for the Pratt Institute in Brooklyn, the highly regarded art and design school cartoonist John Hubley had attended. He had also, spontaneously, collected literature about the various drama and actor-training groups in Manhattan. Though Helen Coomber had trained at the American Academy of Dramatic Arts, he focused on that institution simply because its advertisement in *Variety* was the biggest and most distinguished-looking. On May 3, he had written off for AADA application forms. "There was no great intuition at play," says Redford, "it was simply a Plan B for escape. I was primarily thinking about animation and possibly stage design, and thinking I should go back to New York, find gainful employment, study a little and make it back to Europe to paint. Lola's arrival, of course, skewed that plan a little."

Redford and Brendlinger were evicted from Varwood at the end of July. Redford had saved some money for New York while working at El Segundo, and was optimistic. On August 1, he persuaded Helen to write a letter on his behalf to support his application to AADA. "Kindly look with favor upon my stepson, Robert Redford," Helen wrote. "Because I once graduated from the academy I feel able to say that he can benefit from Academy training."

On September 1 he mailed the requested check for $160 to AADA, as a deposit. In mid-September he packed a bag and flew to New York. He soon learned he was wrong about the entry process, that he would have to audition before any decision about acceptance was made. "I suddenly had to perfect a couple of pieces," Redford remembers. He chose a lament by Branwell Brontë and a monologue from Philip Barry's play *The Youngest,* which he would present in front of a selection committee. Frances Fuller, protégée of the great acting teacher Charles Jehlinger and the academy's current director, personally oversaw the interview. Redford was infuriated by the inattention of the main interviewer: "It was, I later learned, just the standard audition," says Redford. "But I had a chip on my shoulder, and I resented the fact that it was a cattle call. I was facing a table at which these interviewers sat, with Frances Fuller to one side and this man in the middle. His body language, his dismissiveness, offended me, and I started shouting. The Philip Barry piece was supposed to be an angry tirade, so I personally directed it at him." Redford wondered there and then whether he'd blown his chances, but Fuller curtly told him to return the next day. That was a gesture of bureaucracy. Within the academy, she was already telling the staff they had made a remarkable find.

PART TWO

Bonfaccio

In dreams begins responsibility.
William Butler Yeats, *Responsibilities*

6

At the Academy

The American Academy of Dramatic Arts was as bad a choice as Redford could have made for theater studies. Given his nonconformist attitude, the cutting-edge options might have been better for him: the Neighborhood Playhouse, the American Theatre Wing, the Actors Studio. The academy was, literally, old-school.

Situated in a fin de siècle three-story building on West Fifty-second Street in Manhattan, recently relocated from Carnegie Hall, it creaked like a galleon under the weight of a fifty-year-old syllabus honed by Charles "Jelly" Jehlinger, the Edwardian dean of American theater theory. The graduate course was a two-year program, with qualifying exams after the first year. The classes were conducted each weekday morning. The yearly complement was three hundred students, reduced to one hundred in the second year. Classes were structured as Jehlinger decreed in the 1920s, to cover dance, mime, voice, fencing (a staple for so many costume dramas), costume and makeup. Shakespeare studies also featured prominently. Richard Altman, one of Redford's first instructors, noted that the school was also "compromised by the costs of that huge building. We took students willy-nilly, and that was not the best way. I constantly begged Frances Fuller, 'We need less students and more discernment!' But it had to be a cattle market to keep it going."

Redford started in October 1957. Frances Fuller, diminutive, clear-headed and married to the television impresario Worthington Miner, told Redford later that his audition rant had reminded her of AADA alumnus Spencer Tracy, who also spat through his teeth. "What they got was anger, not acting," says Redford. "I was repelled by the atmosphere. It was condescending, like we were the rabble and this was the 1600s. The situation was complicated by the fact that I didn't want to be an actor. I wanted to be Modigliani. I wanted to study theater because someone somewhere said, 'You can go out in summer stock and paint backdrops.' So I could be an artist, at last!"

His work commitment, however, was real because he and Lola—who was back at her studies in Utah—had made a firm decision to build toward a life together in New York as soon as possible. But it was a struggle to keep disciplined. After weeks of apartment-hopping, he settled finally in a third-floor room on Columbus Avenue that was a cramped ten feet square. His next decision was to widen his theatrical social circle, by drinking at watering holes like Charlie's Bar on West Fifty-second Street, which many AADA students frequented. Almost immediately he befriended Ginny Burns, a New Yorker whose mother ran a children's theater group in Barrington, Rhode Island. Ginny noticed him as "someone apart," though, she says, it was hard not to. The first week, at a vocal assessment class tutored by June Burgess, the new students were asked to bring along a favored song to show off their vocal capacities. "Everyone did," says Ginny. "Bob didn't. When it came to his turn, he stood up with immense intensity, as if he was preparing to jump out the window. Then, in a smoldering voice, he dove into Edgar Allan Poe's 'The Raven,' which he claimed appropriate because it was lyrical. He didn't merely recite it. He hollered it like an opera, jumping from one window ledge to the next, caroming around the room, stunning Burgess. I thought it was the single most amazing piece of theater I'd ever seen. I adored him, just for this soul baring."

"Firstly, I loved Poe," says Redford, explaining his choice. "And, secondly, there's a supreme musicality in all his poems. But then there was the theme of madness, and that felt apt to where I was at. I'd been insane. I was still loopy."

At AADA, Ginny and Redford grew close. Ginny remembers that they "played tennis in Central Park and hung out at the Park Avenue apartment of Nikki Lubitsch, the movie director's daughter, who was also an AADA student. We drank a lot of Nikki's scotch and listened to Sinatra, which Bob liked to sing along to. What we also had in common was a *gradually developing* interest in acting. Let's face it: we were not actors, and certainly Bob didn't have much inclination to be one when we commenced."

If Redford had any modicum of actorly leaning, it was toward theater. But the great flowering of serious American theater that came with the social changes of the Depression and yielded Arthur Miller, Clifford

Odets and Tennessee Williams was past. More representative of fifties theater were musicals like *Flower Drum Song* and *My Fair Lady.* Innovative work was still in progress at the Neighborhood Playhouse and the Actors Studio with Lee Strasberg, but Redford was not inquisitive at that point. "I was fairly indifferent to contemporary theater," he says now. "In film I'd seen Fred Zinnemann's *The Men,* which was Brando's debut and which I liked very much. But I was not scrambling to work out Marlon Brando's screen technique or understand the differences between movie and stage acting."

Through his teens, movies had lost their fascination for him. "I'd always had a problem with authenticity," says Redford. "When I was very small, my dad would project 8 mm films of Tom Mix on a sheet in the living room. I bought into all of it. But when I got older, it bothered me that Gene Autry couldn't walk right and John Wayne couldn't ride right. The worst letdown was Disney's *Song of the South,* because it was phony, because you could see the wires. I couldn't abide this. If you're giving me a fantasy, give me *Scaramouche, Captain Blood*—the kind of full-on stuff Rafael Sabatini created, not the half-baked version."

But, during AADA, classic movies he rediscovered from the forties stimulated his interest. In John Ford's *My Darling Clementine* the legendary showdown between the Earps and the Clantons of Tombstone is presented in the imagery of *Paradise Lost* and *Paradise Regained,* where Henry Fonda's Wyatt oversees the consecration of the town's new chapel against evil opposition. In John Huston's *The Treasure of the Sierra Madre,* Humphrey Bogart is the adventurer succumbing to the terrible elemental forces of the desert and his own greed. It was the texture as much as the content of these films that galvanized Redford. "They had a resonant truth like those myths I loved as a child." In them he saw the appeal of movies as an art form, and, incrementally, felt challenged.

But in the eyes of AADA not all was running smoothly. Francis Lettin, the senior rehearsal instructor who had recently staged a Broadway reworking of Chekhov's *The Seagull* with Montgomery Clift, remarked in his early notes that Redford was "standoffish." Sandor Nagy, who taught fencing, judged Redford "awkward." Harry Mastrogeorge, the radio actor turned tutor who would become a leading supporter, wrote that Redford "seems to have some desire [to act], but as a person I don't think he has found himself yet. He is possibly a little unstable as a human being."

Redford continued to work hard, at last focusing on the modern American stage classics, including *Bus Stop* and *A Streetcar Named Desire,* and, for the first time in his life, making studious notes with enthusiasm. In a Tennessee Williams workshop conducted by Broadway director and academy senior Ezra Stone, Redford was asked to read the role of Stanley in *Streetcar.* Stone was stunned by the result. "He's a master at cold reading," Stone told Mastrogeorge. "I tried to stump him again and again, but it was undoable. He has no nerves. He's made for the stage." Redford liked the Stanley role because "it was tough, in your face, and its starkness I could connect with." He learned he preferred modern pieces with an edge. Only later did he apply himself to the value of the speech and movement. "At the start I rejected technique," he says. "I just didn't want to ponce around."

Though Lola and Redford remained in frequent touch by mail and phone, he discovered her absence intensified his feelings for her. He was sociable and finding enjoyment in his studies, but there existed, he says, "a hole" in his being. His feelings were muddled, says Redford, but he was reaching for some sort of spiritual elevation that would calm him and make sense of his fragmented life. Ginny Burns and another close friend, Bob Curtis, who would become a priest, saw the fireside conversation at yet another new apartment on Seventy-third Street turn toward faith. Ginny and Curtis attended church service daily; Redford avoided church. But Redford was clearly processing a new discovery brought to him by Lola: Mormonism. "He was suddenly committed to great changes in his life," says Ginny, "and they involved spiritual choices."

Lola guided Redford to a study of Mormonism. He began reading obsessively, devouring the Book of Mormon and the history of Joseph Smith's American vision. "I'd had religion pushed on me since I was a kid," says Redford. "But after Mom died, I felt betrayed by God. There was an abhorrence of religion, and yet I was still searching. Mormonism interested me as a story. The Mormons built a magnificent empire. Looking back, it sits less comfortably. Really, they stole the trick from Catholicism: they just set up a copycat Vatican. And their beliefs had a kind of voodoo logic. That's the unattractive bit. The positive part, as I got to know Mormons personally, was their decency. I also admired the ordered life they led. I wanted a sane life, so Mormonism found me willing, temporarily."

Lola's background made involvement unavoidable. Both sides of her family, the Dutch Van Wagenens and the Scots-English Barkers, converted in the middle of the nineteenth century and made their way to the hub of Mormonism, in Salt Lake City. The intermarried Van Wagenens and Barkers spread throughout Utah and produced many significant bishops and fund-raisers for the Church. By the 1950s, the Van Wagenens had become one of the most respected families of the Provo ward.

In 1957, just past his twenty-first birthday, Redford was homesick as Christmas approached. Charlie had shown his son little affection of late, so Redford decided to go west to meet the Van Wagenens. Redford was welcomed in Provo warmly but warily: "There was grace, but there was resistance, and taking my past history into account, who can blame them? Frank, Lola's father, was very generous and mannerly, so he was quickest to accept me. Phyllis, her mother, on the other hand, had a mother's defense mechanism."

Still, Redford loved the Christmas warmth and unity. According to Lola's youngest brother, Wayne, "Bob immediately fit in with Dad because of his tremendous curiosity. My father was attracted to the inquiring mind. Bob was always up for new experiences, so they met in the middle." The Mormon weekly ritual of "family home evening," where everyone sits down formally to dinner and engages in exchange, was a balm for Redford. "I couldn't believe this family's enthusiasm for talk," says Redford. "It was a novelty to me." But the tensions remained, and the hints of marriage were stubbornly ignored.

Redford gloomily returned to New York after Christmas. His unease was made worse by continued mixed reviews. The speech teacher insisted he couldn't speak well; the rehearsals supervisor noted his "trouble with projection." Another instructor complained that "Redford is lowering the characters of Shakespeare to suit his own modern mannerisms." But Edward De Roo, marking Redford's portrayal of John Proctor in the post-Christmas *The Crucible,* scribbled on his sheet: "Leading man material." Harry Mastrogeorge was inclined to agree: "I observed a continuation of serious personal issues in him, the main one of which was his hard-headed refusal to 'do it the company way.' But he also showed a growth of originality in his approach that made you say, Wait a minute . . . !" Mike Thoma and Richard Altman, two influential figures on the Broadway casting circuit, were also starting to pay attention, though Altman worried about Redford's arrogance. "He lacked *physical* release," says Altman. "I wrote in my reports that I believed this would come in time—that acting was more than important for him, it had become *critical.* But the trouble was, he feigned nonchalance, and that arrogant attitude, I believed, was a problem that could have finished him off as an actor."

Redford acknowledges the importance of Altman's insight. "Bit by bit I was beginning to feel that acting might allow me the self-expression I sought. Was it 'critical' at that time? Maybe not. But it is true that I was nonchalant, though that mask was slipping."

Redford continued to cling to his fine arts interests and told Ginny he wanted to maintain his painting. She was absorbed in the creation of *Americada,* AADA's first newsletter. On her invitation he became its art director, sketching actress Thelma Ritter for the inaugural issue and illustrating the following five. "I was aware he was in a rut emotionally," says Ginny. "He'd leaped forward in his skill as an actor, I felt, but suddenly he seemed to hit a wall, which I feel had less to do with performance skill than with heartache." Walking by the lake in Central Park in April, Ginny confronted him: "He was talking about Lola incessantly, so I stopped and took out a handful of change and gave it to him. He looked at me like I had two heads. 'What's this?' he said. And I told him, 'She's all that matters now. Face it. Call her.' "

Redford called from a pay phone at the corner of the park. "Ginny nudged, but I was heading that way," he says. "I just said, 'Come on, let's do it.' " Lola hesitated. "Her academic life at BYU was taking shape and I was asking her to abandon all that. She was highly intelligent and knew the risk. More than anything, she was going against her parents' wishes." Redford wanted them to elope, avoiding a Mormon wedding. Lola offered a compromise: she would secure her parents' approval and agree to a double ceremony, one informal, one Mormon.

Summer was coming, and Redford contacted Charlie, requesting more work at the El Segundo refinery to fund his imminent marriage. Charlie's response was compliance—and anger. Martha's old friend Marcella Scott encountered Charlie driving down Sepulveda in a white-faced rage. "We pulled over and talked. All he wanted to do was vent steam about Bobby and the mess he was making of his life: 'Now he wants to get married, damn him!' was all he was saying, ranting."

On August 9, a few days before his twenty-second birthday, Redford married nineteen-year-old Lola in a five-minute service at the Heather on the Hill, a walk-in chapel on the Strip in Vegas. They had eloped. Bill Coomber was his best man. They returned to Monterey for the honeymoon. Five weeks later the formal Mormon ceremony took place at Lola's grandmother's home. Charlie and Helen attended—the sole representatives of the Redford family—along with fifty Van Wagenens. "I stopped short of the Mormon baptism that was expected of me," says Redford. In time, all but one of the children of the marriage would be baptized into the faith, though none would retain it.

Thanks to the work Charlie grudgingly got him at El Segundo, Redford and Lola had amassed $300 in savings over the summer. Much of it went on the marriage services. Within forty-eight hours of the Provo ceremony, they exchanged their gold rings for $150 and paid their fare back to New York.

Lola was every bit as edgy as Redford in New York. She entered the fall of 1958 with trepidation, she said, "facing what [Bob and I] knew would be a winter of hardship." Redford says, "I knew nothing at all, and I carried a terrible sense of guilt. I was asking someone to believe in me when I didn't believe in myself. Yes, I wanted to change the world. But so did every Joe in the street. The bottom line was, I didn't have a dime to my name. And that's all that matters when you are a couple starting out."

For his second year of theater studies, thanks to good exam results, Redford had the assistance of an AADA scholarship. Financially, though, things remained tight. In the fall Lola found work as a bank teller for $55 a week, and Redford enrolled at the Pratt Institute, taking night courses in set design, "because I still thought I'd probably end up painting scenery." Redford says Pratt "just wasn't right for me. It had a famous architectural department, but it seemed too concentrated on technical drawing, which always left me cold. It wasn't the school's fault. It was mine." He also found part-time work as a clerk at a store on Seventh Avenue and served nights as a janitor at the ANTA Theatre for a combined personal income of $93 a week. "It was exhausting to the point of stupor," says Redford. "But there was an advantage beyond funding a marriage. Spending more time at the ANTA meant I could watch more plays and understand more about the profession of acting."

Among the new friends at the Mormon Manhattan ward functions Lola and Redford attended was Provo-born Stan Collins, who was two years older than Redford and studying business at Columbia. Collins found Redford intent on personal growth. "Redford's charm," says Collins, "was not the common variety, but that gift from God you encounter once every fifty years. Both of us had just got married, and money was the main source of our insecurity. But with Bob there was also huge, electric determination about direction. He put so much verbal emphasis on art. He wasn't painting at all—he had no time for it—but it was all he seemed impassioned about, and you knew somehow, someway, he'd make it in the world of creative endeavor."

By Christmas, Lola was pregnant. The discovery triggered some understandable economic anxiety—and also a breakthrough. Watching Redford rehearse a piece on the ANTA stage one afternoon in December, the instructor Richard Altman saw "a suddenness, like an exhalation of breath. Bob had been struggling for eighteen months. But it stopped abruptly. It was a revelation. He wasn't fighting himself anymore. Exceptional stress can inspire exceptional art."

The transformation, says Redford, occurred in a workshop for Arthur Miller's *All My Sons.* Altman had assigned Redford the role of the son, and a much older man named Harry was to play the father. Altman sent both to the greenroom to rehearse the last scene of the second act, when the son confronts the father about manufacturing shoddy aircraft parts that caused the death of his brother. "Harry had all the lines and was so full of nervous tics and orders about how to proceed," says Redford. "I had just a few words, where I scream at the father, 'Don't you live in the world? Where do you live all day!'—and then I pound him back into his chair. At that point, Harry instructed me to be careful of his suit, because he had to go back to his day job after the workshop." When they started performing, Redford focused on what Harry had warned him about: *Be careful, don't damage my suit.* "When the time came for me to pound him into his chair," says Redford, "I leaped at him, grabbed him by the neck and flung him across the stage. He crumpled up under a table. I felt instant remorse and shame. And Altman said, 'All right, thank you. Who do we have next?' " Backstage, Harry confronted Redford in tears, accusing him of inexcusable behavior. "I told him, 'You're right, I apologize, it was inexcusable,' and I thought at that moment that acting was finished for me. I was ready to walk out of the theater and never look back. But Altman called me aside and said, 'Don't apologize. I think I know where you are going with this, and we'll talk more tomorrow. Just keep going with it.' "

Two school plays were to be performed after Christmas, Chekhov's *The Seagull* and Jean Anouilh's *Antigone.* In *The Seagull* Redford was cast as Konstantin Treplev, and he was not keen on director Francis Lettin's interpretation of the role. The drama starts with a play within a play, when Treplev stages a dense symbolist show to impress his mother, the famous actress Arkadina. She laughs at him, and he storms off. "Lettin saw my character as a wounded, soft, desiccated boy," Redford remembers. "I disagreed. This was a radical work, designed to knock down the barriers of melodrama. I saw in Treplev insanity, passion and anger. Most of all, I saw incestuous desire. This is a young man who secretly wants to take his mother to bed, to win her affection. All this anger and physicality was comfortable to me, and I started playing Treplev that way, which Lettin didn't like at all. I was physical, I stomped around the stage, I was a caged animal, stifled by my incestuous thoughts."

Redford rehearsed in Central Park, walking down Broadway, riding in cars—"never at home. I needed emotional isolation to brew the part, and I did it in a state of purposeful agitated movement, working up steam." When he was primed, Redford rehearsed with another student, Ellen Siccama, concentrating on sexual chemistry, but both Frances Fuller and Lettin opposed him. "Lettin kept calling me to a halt. 'Why are you moving around there? What is that supposed to achieve?' And then, at the last minute, he did an amazing thing. He did a full turnaround. 'I'm confusing you, aren't I?' he said. And I, of course, said yes. And Lettin said, 'Look, I had a precooked idea, and now I'm standing in the way of something fresh. I'm wrong. Do it your way.' That took great humility and it taught me a lot. He stood back as a director and he freed me up."

Opening night saw Redford performing before the first large audience of his career, at Finch College. It also marked the first time Lola saw her husband perform onstage. The fact that it was a success, that the audience approved and the fellow cast members congratulated him for his originality of interpretation, was disorienting. More confusing was what Redford calls "the bizarre sexual attention" focused on him in the after-show party. He was aware of the advantage of his looks and his charm with women, but was surprised by the intensity of the new attention. "I didn't discuss it with Lola. I think I only see it now, with the perspective of time. I'd taken a risk and broken down some invisible barrier. Women were looking at me in a very interesting new way. I thought it odd but invigorating at the same time, but after a drink or two I just wanted to be out of there." Before he left, Francis Lettin cornered him. "He said, 'Every now and then you see an actor who you think could really play Hamlet. I've been in this business thirty years and I've seen actors come and go. But you are the first I've seen who could *really* do it. It's entirely up to you now.' "

Antigone followed a month later. Redford played Creon in a classicist style light-years from the Chekhov. Once again, the effect of independent thinking, risk and experiment produced the tumultuous audience response. Redford exulted in the intoxicant of applause. "After *The Seagull,* every opening night, every stage play, was something new. Till that point, I'd been dealing with AADA formula. With *The Seagull,* everything altered."

7
Graduation

Several of the AADA tutors continued to question a behavioral smugness, but Redford puts it down to stubborn personal confusion. The writer David Rayfiel, who would come to know Redford through his collaborations with mutual friend Sydney Pollack, explained it well. "When we appreciate Cézanne's apples, we see first of all the simplicity. But that's not what knocks you over. It is, as Willa Cather said, the *anxiety* of the apples—and that comes from an existential unease, from something suppressed. I always felt that about Bob. He was outwardly supremely confident, but underneath there was always the doubt."

On the walls inside AADA were photos of the esteemed alumni who had gone to the top—among them Grace Kelly and Kirk Douglas—but Redford insists he had no "instinct" for them. "I recognized how iconography worked, how John Wayne became representative of the frontier heartland, but I hated the caricature that came with repetitiveness. The actors who appealed to me were the characters who were usually lost down the playbill. People like Franklin Pangborn, Billy De Wolfe, Van Heflin. No one had much to say about their technique, but I learned more from them than I did from Kirk Douglas."

With graduation looming, Redford was itchy to break out. The Actors Studio suddenly seemed like a good idea, "because that's where they broke the rules." It was at the radical Group Theatre of the thirties that Konstantin Stanislavski's "Method" was first taught in America. Stella Adler adapted it, and Lee Strasberg refined the technique for the Actors Studio. It attracted Paul Newman, James Dean, Eli Wallach and Geraldine Page and gained notoriety as the new and insightful way to act, though its techniques only dented the dominant melodramas of the fifties. "Whether we were AADA proponents or radicals," says Harry Mastrogeorge, "we all thought people like Strasberg were onto something psychologically valuable in terms of freeing up the actor." Redford and classmate Ellen Siccama decided to study with Strasberg after they graduated from AADA. They rehearsed a few scenes from William Saroyan's *The Time of Your Life* and performed it at an open audition at the Studio's home in the Seventh Associate Presbyterian Church, in a stark, clinical room with blazing spotlights. Redford hated the atmosphere. "I presume the idea was to strip you naked and reveal your primitive self," he says. "For me, it felt just as contrived as AADA."

Richard Altman, like Mastrogeorge, believed Redford could have found little of value at the Actors Studio: "He was past the point of tricks. The kind of acting breakthrough he made with *The Seagull* has to do with self-realization. Years later I watched him play a scene with Michelle Pfeiffer in the movie *Up Close and Personal,* and I was blown away again by his *honesty.* Superficially, one might reduce the key acting element to composure. But that's understatement. There is a place beyond that where all great players go, which is just *truth.* Bob hit on that at AADA; others learned it at the Actors Studio."

The Actors Studio might not have been an option, but opportunities were opening up for him nonetheless. A few days after his performance of *The Seagull,* he received a cable from MCA, the leading actors' agency, proposing a meeting with a view to representation. Redford says he had never heard of MCA.

MCA started as a modest Chicago management company in 1924 under the directorship of a former eye doctor, Jules Stein. By the 1950s it had become a business phenomenon within the emerging television world. Led by Stein's lieutenant Lew Wasserman, the agency had sidled from artist representation into television packaging, delivering to producers an all-inclusive package of creative talent, including writer, director and star. From there, it was a short step to launching a television production company, MCA TV. MCA thrived, acquiring the Universal Studios lot in 1958 and, later, Paramount's movie library. Most significantly, it had been responsible for breaking the studio salary mold and obtaining for actors a percentage of movie profits. The deal brokered by Wasserman for James Stewart when the actor quit his MGM contract in 1944 still resounded through the industry and lured clients to MCA. At the time Maynard Morris, a senior executive at MCA, cabled Redford, the agency's client roster extended to more than five hundred Hollywood actors and three hundred Broadway performers.

It was one of AADA's instructors, Mike Thoma, who set the ball rolling for Redford with MCA. In a term report, Thoma, who was also directing and producing on Broadway, had noted that "Redford shows a flair for comedy." So impressed had he been, he recommended to MCA agent Stark Hesseltine, a friend, that he see *The Seagull.* It was Hesseltine who had advised Morris that Redford was a desirable client.

Redford approached this important opportunity naïvely. His friend George Oakes, an AADA classmate who was already working on Broadway, told Redford that MCA would pay him $140 a week, whether he was working or not. "I badly needed cash, and I believed him. So when I sat down with Hesseltine and Morris, that's what I asked for." Redford would later re-create the scene that unfolded in *Quiz Show,* where the network suits put the squeeze on Columbia professor Charles Van Doren (played by Ralph Fiennes), bullying him into accepting their questionable operating principles. Redford had done some homework and knew that Maynard Morris had discovered Charlton Heston, Gregory Peck, Lee Van Cleef and Marlon Brando. Morris was clearly a good talent assessor, but he was also used to getting his way. "I was a babe in the woods, knowing nothing about the rules," says Redford. "What I depicted in *Quiz Show* is how it went for me. These guys were slick. Very slow, like a choreographed pitch, Stark got up from his table in the corner and sat at the edge of Maynard's desk. Maynard came around to perch on the other side, all very smooth. I was the lamb in the middle. Right away I said, 'So, wait a second. You will rep me, but you won't place me on a retainer and you cannot guarantee me work? Well, that's a weird scenario. I'll have to sleep on it.' But Stark wasn't about to quit. He told me flat, 'You don't have a choice, kid. MCA is where it's at. You walk out of here, you walk out of a career.' "

Redford signed on. The rumor at AADA was that Hesseltine was gay and was wildly attracted to him. Redford says that was beside the point: "He treated me with brotherly respect. He looked after me. In time, he became a guest at my home, and when we ran into a crisis, he loaned me money. He was a good guy."

Around this time, Mike Thoma also recommended him to director Herman Shumlin for a last-minute walk-on role in his production of Julius Epstein's breezy *Tall Story* at the Belasco Theatre. Redford accepted $82 a week gratefully and found himself for the first time, at twenty-two, on the professional stage, albeit in a distinctly background role.

In no time, though, MCA was proving its worth. He was backstage one afternoon when he got a call from Eleanor Kilgallen, MCA's New York television agent, offering him a part in an *Armstrong Circle Theatre* episode. Redford enjoyed the few television shows he watched—*The Honeymooners,* Sid Caesar's show—but felt he was better set up for theater. Then Kilgallen told him the salary was $360 for a couple of rehearsals and a live transmission and he was overjoyed.

He wasn't entirely new to television. Several months before, in March, he had made a humiliating appearance on Merv Griffin's *Play Your Hunch* game show, an invitation accepted more in jest than with any career objective. "In the greenroom, when they'd ask me what I did," says Redford, "I told them I was an actor. Their response was, 'That won't work at all. What else do you do?' So I told them I was also a painter, and they said, 'Okay, better. Let's go with that. You're an artist down on his luck. The audience will buy that.' " The scandal of the rival, fixed show *Twenty One* and the congressional hearings that would reveal Van Doren's complicity in "winning" $129,000 were still six months away. "I'd already seen *Twenty One* and sensed it was a setup, and now I was playing the same game. I did what I was told to do, and when I took a dive, I put out my hand for the $75 fee they promised me. Instead, they gave me $75 worth of Abercrombie and Fitch fishing tackle. I was hardly going to feed Lola and furnish a room with that."

Armstrong Circle Theatre was television of substance, in the style of CBS's seminal docudrama *You Are There,* seen by millions live in the New York area and later broadcast in what was called a hot kine, a tape of the live broadcast. Redford's episode was called "Berlin: City with a Short Fuse" and presented the tensions surrounding the 350-day blockade of Berlin by the Soviet Union. Redford was to play a southern soldier, Benjamin Peebles; he had a substantial forty lines. Also cast were Keir Dullea, playing the lead, and AADA classmate Johnny Carlin, who was already forging a career for himself in afternoon soaps. Douglas Edwards introduced the story, in grand Walter Cronkite style, then each soldier walked up to the camera and recited his name, rank and serial number before the drama commenced. As Private Peebles, Redford was supposed to be light relief, but at rehearsals he got big laughs as he milked the jokes. The producer complained, saying the laughter was too distracting. The process of chipping away Peebles's lines began. "My forty lines became ten lines, then five, then four lousy lines. I became so invisible in the script that they had to invent a line that went, 'Where's Peebles?' Some other guy had to answer, 'Aw, he's out back eating.' I remember telling the producer, 'So Peebles is eating again? You should have hired a fat actor.' "

After two days of rehearsals the show went on. As Redford prepared for his first line, Johnny Carlin moved up behind him. "He whispered, 'See the red light on that camera? As soon as it comes on, you will have twenty million people waiting for you to screw up.' " Redford says he barely made it through. "But the adrenaline rush was something else. Forget mountain climbing! I had to do that again."

In April, shortly before the broadcast, Sallie died in Los Angeles, and on May 29 Tot died. Redford flew to Texas to sort out his grandfather's affairs. "It was the end of an era," says Redford. "Mom was gone, now Sallie and Tot. I felt a bond with the West cut, and I was not prepared to let it go. I loved New York, I loved my life with Lola. But I wasn't prepared to say goodbye to everything I'd got from my grandfather." In material terms, little was left of Tot's labors. All Redford took from the estate was a 1949 jalopy that he drove back to New York and then found he couldn't afford to keep. He gave it instead to Johnny Carlin.

Redford's AADA graduation took place soon afterward. But he was dismayed that, despite his A-plus standing, the best Hesseltine could find for him was summer stock in Bucks County, Pennsylvania. At first, Redford said no. "To me," he says, "summer stock was play school. Stark said I was wrong, that summer stock was the farmyard for Broadway. You made your way either by apprenticeship dog work behind the scenes or in the good stock companies, preferably close to New York, where the casting people could come down and see what you had. And Bucks County was the top of the pile, he told me."

Carol Rossen had also become a client of Hesseltine's. In her view, Hesseltine's "deceptive gentlemanliness" was a double-edged sword: "He was literary, elegant, apparently a humane academic, not much older than either Bob or I. When you met him, you were swayed by his beautiful, lilting Boston accent, which sounded like one of the Kennedys. He also stuttered, and he had exquisite manners. But he was also a mean bastard with tunnel vision. When he saw something in you, it was *that and that alone* he nurtured, and you'd better buy into it. You didn't want to get on the wrong side of him, because he had a capacity for bitterness that was unparalleled. I always believed, when he died, he'd die by a bullet fired by a disaffected actor."

Redford gave in to Hesseltine. In July he met with Mike Ellis, the Bucks County producer of Anouilh's *Tiger at the Gates.* Ellis offered Redford the co-lead role of Paris. "But then he said, 'All these classical types had curly hair. So get yours curled.' " Redford's reaction was to refuse the play again. "It all felt wrong. There was a basic problem with the creative thinking, I felt. Certainly I didn't want a boring translation of an old text. That kind of conventionality did nothing for me. But neither did I want what seemed to me crassness. Ellis wanted the wigs, but what he was really after was a circus, not the Anouilh classic by any means. On the surface, he appeared well set up. He had a Shakespearean actor, Herb Hatfield, in the lead, and Louise Fletcher, all the way from Hollywood. But it was cockeyed, a Felliniesque concept." A major row with Hesseltine ensued. "Finally, I looked at Lola and the financial situation we were in, and I said, 'All right. But you've got to buy me a hat.' " Redford never got over his distaste for the production. Still, it marked his first leading role on the professional stage.

He was consoled almost immediately by an echo of the past. Dore Schary, author of *Boys Town* and onetime MGM wunderkind, had gone from strength to strength over the last year on Broadway. His hit play *Sunrise at Campobello* had won five Tonys. Now he was preparing a potentially controversial follow-up, *The Highest Tree.* Redford had been friendly with Schary's daughter Jill in Brentwood, though he hardly knew Dore well. The connection was irrelevant, however, since it was casting director Ruth Frankenstein's decision to offer him a key part in the new play.

The Highest Tree explored the conscience of a dying nuclear physicist, played by Kenneth MacKenna, trying to come to peace with his contribution to the parlous division of ideologies in the world. Redford had just a dozen lines as the son of a friend of the physicist. Elizabeth Ashley was the female lead, though she was then called Elizabeth Cole. From the start of rehearsals in August, Redford felt uneasy with Schary's high-minded direction, which was in conflict with the relaxed, improvisational style he was honing for himself. "It was potentially presumptuous to be standing there as a new actor, saying to this great man, 'Hey, I think you have this wrong.' But I was thinking that a lot of the time." Playwright Garson Kanin observed the problem: "Schary never lost the desire to stage-manage every breath everyone took," he said. "That was his handicap." Cast member Natalie Schaefer remembered Redford as being nervous and insecure, and blamed Schary entirely. "Because he wasn't really a director. [Schary] kept harping on about Bob's [poor] projection and nervous aspects of his performance. Bob wasn't sure enough of himself at that point to argue."

On September 1, while the show was previewing out of town, Lola gave birth to a son, Scott Anthony. Redford took a day out to celebrate and was, he says, "elated, spinning, really." He always enjoyed the company of children and, despite the disappointments of his own childhood, looked forward to building a family. Lola's brother Wayne, who was a small child when he first met Redford, recalls his natural facility with kids. "Mormon houses are kid oriented, and Bob loved that. He was playful, that's the thing. Given the choice of hanging out with the old folk or the kids, it was no contest. I know my family was skeptical about the marriage, but when I look back, no one had any doubts about one thing: he was always going to be a good dad."

On November 4 the play opened at the Longacre, but the reviews were uniformly appalling. As it staggered onward, playing to half-empty houses, catastrophe struck at home. The Redfords had recently moved to a marginally bigger apartment at 180 West Ninety-third Street. There, baby Scott died, the victim of crib death. Redford felt total despair. Ginny recalls the anguish, the questions, the reverberating shock that reduced everyone to monosyllabic mumbles.

The funeral service was attended only by Bob, Lola, Ginny and Hesseltine. Redford dropped out of *The Highest Tree* for several days. He did what he always did at times of turmoil: he started moving. For three days he and Lola drove aimlessly around Pennsylvania and Maryland. "It was an unspeakable pain for us," says Redford. "For myself, the gothic part of my nature came down on me. I know it sounds self-absorbed, and in hindsight it was, but it felt like retribution. I had rejected common sense to pursue this reckless life. My father had told me I was irresponsible. The Van Wagenens told me I was irresponsible. This, I felt, was a disaster entirely of *my* creation."

In the last week of November *The Highest Tree* closed after just twenty-seven performances. The cast took up a collection to help fund the Redfords in crisis, and the money was used for a trip to Los Angeles to distance themselves from the tragedy. "It's what you do," says Redford, "when you face the unsurvivable." In New York little progress was being made with theater offers for Redford, so MCA focused on television. Close to 80 percent of all homes had television now, so production was copious, and there were acting opportunities aplenty that might easily lead to movie work.

Hesseltine introduced Redford to Monique James, who handled MCA's West Coast TV operation. James liked him. "It was the era of George Peppard," said James. "All I ever heard from producers was, 'Get me George

Peppard.' When I met Bob, I immediately saw a similarity. A little more sandy or red haired, maybe, but that general look. I also liked his manner, which was very open and direct and unaffected. I saw he was grieving and vulnerable, but he had strength, too. I wanted to help. I told him, 'It may work well for you here.' " James worked fast, securing him parts in *Perry Mason, Rescue 8* and *Maverick.* When the new year arrived, to their own surprise, the Redfords were still in Los Angeles.

Michael Ritchie, the director who would partner Redford's independent movie breakout in the late sixties, became aware of Redford's screen presence in these first hesitant efforts. "But he meant nothing," said Ritchie, "because television was hemorrhaging product and you couldn't keep up. It was just wall-to-wall entertainment and, even then, through overproduction, the standards were starting to slip." Two years later, Kennedy's Federal Communications Commission would characterize TV as "a vast wasteland." "It was all Madison Avenue cowboys," said Ritchie, "and that was the world Bob risked sliding into."

But Redford saw West Coast television as a learning lab. "From a technical point of view, it was great," he says. "Television moved very quickly from live transmissions to tape, then film. My timing was good from that point of view. Because, the truth is, there is no difference between, say, a filmed episode of *Maverick* and a big Hollywood movie, other than the obvious: budget. The geography of the set is the same. A gaffer is a gaffer, and a grip is a grip."

The Redfords rented a two-room apartment on the pier at Malibu as soon as the television earnings allowed it. Life became calm again.

Within MCA, however, Redford was seen as an increasingly attractive property. "Stark rather selfishly wanted Bob back in New York, in theater," said Monique James. "That was his fantasy. I challenged that, and I wanted to prove him in television. Bob could be a funny guy, a cutup, but he was also very, very tough. He was impervious to the humiliations of the business. He had the tenacity for the casting trail. Because of all that, I knew he'd never get stuck in *Rescue 8.* So I pushed for better roles for him."

NBC offered Redford a part in "Captain Brassbound's Conversion," an adaptation of George Bernard Shaw's play for the estimable *Hallmark Hall of Fame.* The role was small but, significantly, alongside two great Hollywood players, Christopher Plummer and Greer Garson. Redford saw irony in this. Since childhood he had fancied Greer Garson and, while working as a janitor at the ANTA Theatre, had often watched while Plummer rehearsed. He was thrilled to be sharing a soundstage with acting legends. "It's not always the size of a part, but the connections involved that are important," said Monique James. "Neither of us wanted to bed down in *Maverick,* and this was a turning point."

In the Shaw play, Redford's part was just six lines as a soldier called Blue Jacket, who shows Greer Garson into a cabin. "Somehow I impressed her," says Redford, "probably because I so obviously relished every second of being around her. She took to me like I was her little puppy. Finally I got her to myself in her dressing room and told her how much I admired her. She was sitting regally in a flowing, frothy pink gown, looking like all I'd romantically dreamed her to be. She responded with such grace: 'My dear, dear, dear, *dear Blue Jacket* . . . !' Her kindness made me weak at the knees. Now, I thought to myself, if only I could play opposite Maureen O'Hara."

In May, as Redford was rehearsing "Captain Brassbound's Conversion," Lola discovered she was pregnant again. That seemed like the cue to leave Los Angeles. "I didn't want the baby to be born there, and I'd had enough of shows like *Maverick.* So when the Shaw play was done, I was done." The Redfords were literally filling the trunk of their Chrysler when another call came from Monique James. Redford remembers, "She told me, 'You simply cannot miss this one, Bob. This is *Playhouse 90.* This is gold.' "

James had fought to keep Redford in L.A. She recalled: "Ethel Winant, the casting director for *Playhouse 90,* told me emphatically she didn't want a newcomer for this particular big role because this was a historically important show. It was a Nazi war story, said Ethel, and it called for George [Peppard] because he had the best Aryan look. She also wanted a heavyweight actor, not some have-a-go fellow. I lied to her, telling her George didn't want the part. All I was doing was trying to create an opportunity for Bob. I gave Ethel no choice: she had to check out Redford."

Playhouse 90, which had been running on CBS since 1948, was regarded as the apogee of TV drama. In the mid-fifties, producer Hubbell Robinson refined its format to provide a kind of social debate forum for America's leading television writers. Although it was among the most Emmy-awarded shows, CBS announced its end in the summer of 1960. Rod Serling's "In the Presence of Mine Enemies," about the uprising in the Warsaw ghetto during Nazi occupation, would be its grand finale.

Redford read twice for the role of a young Bavarian Nazi, Sergeant Lott. The part was big, interwoven throughout the script. Fielder Cook, the director, stopped him in midsentence during the second audition and told him the part was his. He also mentioned that Redford would be playing alongside Charles Laughton, who was to portray the terrorized rabbi of the ghetto. Arthur Kennedy was also in the cast.

Redford found Serling's script the most thought-provoking of any he had worked on since *The Seagull.* As a decent young "soldier of the soil," Redford's George Lott vacillates between detachment and concern for the five hundred thousand Jews trapped in the ghetto. He becomes attached to the rabbi and tries to defend him when the rabbi avenges a rape. Bit by bit, the rabbi gently tries to convert and transform Lott.

"It was among my most nerve-racking experiences because of Laughton," says Redford. "Part of it was his sheer physicality, which was as commanding as his legend. He was also intense and introspective. I had to make the emotional adjustment to play a co-lead with this legend." At one point, as the rabbi insults the Nazi commander, Lott is instructed to strike him. In rehearsals, Cook insisted Redford mime the assault. Redford felt increased apprehension as the broadcast night, May 18, approached. "Just a few minutes before we went on air, Laughton came up to me," says Redford. "He announced, very authoritatively, 'Do not under any circumstances hit me. I cannot tolerate it. Fake it, do something, anything . . . just do *not, I mean do not,* touch me.' " Redford tried to consult Cook, but with seconds till air, Cook couldn't be bothered. When the moment came, Redford smacked Laughton hard across the face. "He looked absolutely horrified, and I felt terrible. When the show was over, I went to him and apologized. You did what you had to do, he said. And he was right. Dramatically it worked. It was honest. That scene reminded me that it was only authenticity that counted."

"In the Presence of Mine Enemies" was Redford's first unmitigated success, finally winning him the attention of the media. He "stole the show," wrote the *Hollywood Reporter.* Jack Gould in *The New York Times* praised "an exceptional contribution in his depiction of a man trying to reconcile a personal code with military brutality." The play was controversial because it acknowledged the humanity of Nazis like Lott who empathized with the Jews. But thousands of callers clogged the switchboard at CBS, demanding apologies. Leon Uris publicly condemned Serling. But Redford felt it was "a courageous work" and he was privileged to be associated with it.

In June the Redfords returned to New York, apprehensive about the second pregnancy, but excited by the renewed enthusiasm of MCA. The success of *Playhouse 90* had hiked theatrical interest, and Hesseltine was already dangling a carrot. It seemed as if the days of sideline performances were over. In the offing was a major role in an important television version of a play by the matchless Eugene O'Neill.

8

The New Frontier

New York was electric. This was the run-up to the Kennedy era, the year of the election, with a breeze of newness in the streets. It was also, for Redford, a bounteous time—he had scored ten roles on television in just eight months, including, in his last days in L.A., a good part in NBC's first coast-to-coast color broadcast, an episode of the thriller series *Moment of Fear,* called "The Golden Deed," opposite Macdonald Carey. The excitement of significant progress had gone some way toward assuaging the pain of Scott's loss, and Redford was feeling serene.

He was also looking good. Too good. He had a golden tan after spending long days at Malibu, clearly evident as he played a slick psychopath opposite Carey. The problem was that Sidney Lumet, in the midst of casting his television production of *The Iceman Cometh* for the National Network, a precursor of PBS, could not abide the notion of Parritt, a neurotic and thin character in the play, as a surf dude. Lumet liked what he'd seen of Redford in *Playhouse 90* but disliked the tan. Lumet's casting director, Marion Dougherty, met with Redford nonetheless. "I can do it," Redford said to her. "I will bring myself to the requirement." She was won over: "I knew the text, and *The Iceman Cometh* is all about subsurface," says Dougherty. "Appreciating Bob's looks was easy. But listening to what was underneath is what convinced me. He had a lot to say for himself. He was sensitive and probing and intelligent. I called Sidney and asked him to rethink. He finally said okay."

An O'Neill role was, for Redford, a walk into Tiger's past. Once, in a casual conversation, Tiger had told him that Doc Gainey's, O'Neill's favorite pub, was also one of his. "Did you know him?" Redford asked. Tiger chewed his cigar, scratched his head and said, "His brother was a bum." Redford's frequent visits with Tiger in the cramped, dark rooms of New London would now serve the young actor well.

Sidney Lumet, Redford well knew, was the ultimate actors' director, having started in the Yiddish Art Theatre at the age of four and having appeared on Broadway often since the 1930s. In 1947 he'd set up a rival acting group with disaffected members of the Actors Studio (among them Eli Wallach and Yul Brynner) and had ten years' experience directing more than 150 episodes of crime series for CBS television. The regard in which he was held was evidenced by Henry Fonda's insistence that Lumet direct *Twelve Angry Men,* which became Lumet's movie debut in 1957 and garnered three Oscar nominations. "I was more anxious to please him than any director I'd encountered," said Redford.

The four-hour, four-act production of *Iceman* was to be an exact re-creation of the 1956 Circle in the Square stage production, directed by José Quintero, which was regarded as the definitive version and consecrated Jason Robards as O'Neill's signature actor. Robards was back in the lead role of Hickey, the bar bum philosopher, as were several members of the 1956 cast. The play was to be taped over several days in October, for transmission in November.

Set in 1912, *Iceman* deals with salesman Hickey's arrival at his regular haunt to harangue his old drinking friends about their habitual despair. His apparent conversion throws the gathering into turmoil, but his posturing covers up the fact that he is traumatized because he cannot come to terms with the fact that he has murdered his wife. Essentially a work that posits a dark confusion in the center of the American psyche, *The Iceman Cometh* is often described as O'Neill's most autobiographical work. O'Neill himself insisted to his friend, the writer Dudley Nichols, that it was not pessimistic. "[O'Neill] did not feel that the fact that we live by illusion is sad," said Nichols. "The important thing, he felt, is to [recognize] that we do."

Redford's Parritt urges Hickey to abandon delusion by choosing suicide. Redford understood the centrality of the role and wrestled for weeks with text and subtext. "My Parritt came from a place of intuition, accessed from my own contradictions. What was marvelous about Sidney was that he allowed intuition. He had a Method reputation, but he didn't do the Stanislavski thing. There was no heavy analysis. Instead, it was organic development. Drawing on the actor's instinct made absolute sense to me."

Jason Robards coached Redford more than Lumet did. "We got on right off the bat," Redford would write in his eulogy for *Time* after Robards's death in January 2001. "He was extremely generous to me. In the play, when his character meets mine, he says, 'We're members of the same lodge in some way.' Because of our personal connection he invested that moment pretty heavily, and I'll never forget that line." Redford was aware of Robards's reputation as the peerless O'Neill interpreter. "So it was critical for me to pay attention to him. He wasn't preachy about acting, but he was an encyclopedia. I learned more watching his nuances than I did from any stage actor."

The insights of the play left a mark on Redford. In his diary he jotted down a few of Hickey's searing lines: "The history of the world proves that truth has no bearing on anything" and "Men don't want to be saved from themselves because then they'd have to give up greed . . . and they don't want to pay that price for liberty." Redford underlined the last speech. "It summarized what I felt about American life as I knew it growing up. We were all looking for the good life, but we didn't want to probe too deeply. It was a life of illusions and noncommunication, and that had always felt wrong. O'Neill was about reaching for understanding, and working that text made me comfortable for the first time about this life I'd found myself in. I wasn't yet an actor, but I was in a state of becoming."

Before *Iceman* aired, Hesseltine finally found Redford work in theater again, in another Hibernian drama, James Costigan's stage version of his Emmy-winning television play, *Little Moon of Alban.* Harryetta Peterka, a friend from AADA, remembered Herman Shumlin, the director of *Little Moon,* who had also directed Redford's walk-on in *Tall Story,* voicing uncertainty about his own decision to cast Redford. "He'd seen Bob in an episode of *The Deputy* and was unimpressed. He said, 'Frances Fuller keeps saying he's shaping up like Spencer Tracy. I can't see it. He's too glib.' But then he liked the *Playhouse 90* and Hesseltine convinced him to take a chance with him in the Costigan play."

Redford had seen the NBC version of *Little Moon of Alban* and loved Costigan's dark musicality. It reminded him of all Lena's old Fenian stories. The play is set in Ireland at the time of the 1916 rebellion and revolves around the conflict of an Irish nurse from a Republican family, Brigid Mary, forced to tend to a British army lieutenant, Kenneth Boyd, who is responsible for the death of her lover, the IRA gunman Dennis Walsh. Brigid Mary, despite herself, falls for Boyd as she urges him to fight for life in the face of death. Redford would have preferred the Boyd role but happily took on Walsh. "Walsh's last big speech, just before he's killed, is spectacular," says Redford. "He walks onto a Liffey bridge and recites a lament about Irish martyrdom. I knew I could knock that down so well. I only had to tune back in to Lena."

Experienced actors—John Justin as Boyd and Julie Harris as Brigid

Mary—surrounded Redford. But Shumlin's direction, Redford now feels, weakened the production. "He was no Sidney Lumet, though he did try to expand the historical content of the play, which was a plus. But he was from the old school, like Jehlinger, bossy, rigid and backward-looking, and he succumbed to the temptation to simply re-create what had been done before in the television version.

"It absolutely killed me to see what Shumlin allowed Justin and Julie to do with those sensitive scenes Costigan wrote. Brigid Mary resolves her problem by deciding to become a nun. I remember sitting at the read-throughs watching this beautiful finale Costigan had written where Boyd accepts his personal concession to *faith* and walks away, kissing Brigid Mary one last time with the words, 'I shan't say goodbye, it seems mundane. I shall simply say this: that I kiss your mouth, *most humbly and gratefully*.' I would have sold my soul to deliver those lines. But they played them sentimentally and threw it away."

Among those filling the IRA roles in the play were the Clancy brothers, on the brink of an international career as a folk group. "Redford was one of the lads," said Liam Clancy, "and as comfortable in his Irishness as I am in mine. But there was a problem. We drank together, and he told me all his concerns about the play, and all he wished it to be. He had all the focus of a serious stage actor, but I sensed he was being pulled away. Most of the young actors like me among the cast were struggling. Redford was around my age, but he was different already. He had big, important champions in his corner: MCA, casting people that brought fear to young thespians. I felt he was fighting to keep focus and not get lured into the falsehood of stardom. I also felt he was at his best talking about the character in the text, not show business."

During the previews of *Little Moon of Alban* in Washington, D.C., *The Iceman Cometh* aired on the National Network on November 14. It was just a week after the election of John F. Kennedy as president, and the air was charged with excitement. As Redford was preparing makeup, the call came from New York that Lola had gone into premature labor. He left the theater and took the night train, arriving just in time for the birth of a daughter, Shauna. "The death of a child can destroy a couple," says Provo friend Stan Collins. "In their case, I believe it did put a distance between them. But Shauna's arrival reversed the damage. They were no longer absorbed in what might have been. They finally had a family to pull together for."

Little Moon of Alban opened at the Longacre in December. The *New York Post, Variety, Newsday* and other periodicals praised Redford's performance, but the play closed, to Redford's dismay, after just twenty performances.

The compensation was a sudden influx of TV parts. "For the rest of us struggling thesps," said Liam Clancy, "a failed play means poverty. But, in that regard, Bob was way ahead of us all." In a Reginald Rose *Play of the Week* he was the murderous son of a senator. Memorably for all who saw it, he then played a psychotic neo-Nazi in a particularly nasty episode of ABC's *Naked City.* "I'm not sure what made Bob happier," says Stan Collins, "the acting or his home life. But it seemed very critical to him to measure himself in acting progress." Redford concurs: "I felt acutely compelled to prove my worth. But that should not detract from the fact that Shauna and family life were hugely satisfying then."

In a bravura gesture Redford decided to rent a Cadillac and visit Tiger to show off the new baby. Tiger was now a resident at a nursing home in New London. Charlie had once told his son that when Tiger was informed of Redford's artistic ambitions, he'd said, "Tell the kid he can't eat art." During the visit with Lola and the baby, it was clear Tiger's opinion had changed. "I was sitting drinking coffee," says Redford, "and he shuffled across the floor in his big wool overcoat and threw down a copy of *TV Guide.* I looked, and there was the listing for *Perry Mason,* costarring me. It was his silent way of acknowledging what I was doing."

At Christmas, Redford and Lola decided to return to Los Angeles in part to introduce Shauna to Charlie and Helen and in part to reconnect with Monique James since, clearly, television was the meal ticket. "The Shumlin experience left a lousy feeling about New York theater," says Redford. "An incident during *Little Moon* summed up my problem. It was my central scene, where I'm shot by the Black and Tans and dragged into Brigid Mary's kitchen. I lie dying in her arms. This was hard for me, because I was finding it difficult to connect with Julie Harris. Just as I hit my stride, Shumlin grabbed my wrist, saying, 'Don't cover the face, dear boy. Hold your hand this high, not that high. No, lower, lower, lower.' I could not handle that mechanical way. I thought, There's no art in this. If this is acting, I cannot be an actor." Redford now found himself brooding, wondering if his altered domestic setup and the trip west were not some terminus.

Lola flew on with Shauna, while Redford took the train, wanting time alone to contemplate his future. The train stopped to take on water in

Gallup, New Mexico. "Since Florence when I was depressed, I'd perfected a kind of meditation, a self-hypnosis that tuned out the world and reoriented me. At Gallup, while meditating, something bizarre happened. I was locked inside myself, and suddenly there was an Indian face at the window. This apparition cut in and whipped me to some other consciousness. You can rationalize this however you want: the urban guy, jaded with the buzz of Manhattan, suddenly blasted into the bleakness of the desert world, whatever. But for me, in the way it happened, it was a transcendent experience. In simple terms, it yanked me backward, to the forties, to driving with my mother and encountering this native culture, upon which modern Americans are parasites. But it was not memory or nostalgia. It was a feeling of being sucked into timelessness. I was bogged down in the business of a career, asking myself, Should I choose this, or decide that? And that face at the window just pushed me into a feeling of, *Just be.* It was an unexpected Zen moment that alters you in some way."

Transformed—hardened, he says—Redford arrived in L.A. determined to press Monique James for parts akin to the one in *Iceman.* She complied, finding him roles in an episode of the series *Bus Stop,* directed by Robert Altman, an *Alfred Hitchcock Presents* and a showcase *Twilight Zone* with Gladys Cooper, in which he played Death in the guise of a friendly neighborhood policeman knocking on the door of a smart old-timer. "He suddenly drove me hard," said James. "My specialization wasn't movies, but I had a soft spot for Bob. There were lots of pretty boys around, but not so many who made you think twice the way he did. He was driven. He was also the kind of guy, when he left the room, you looked after him and said, I wonder what's really going on inside that lovely head? What's the dark secret that makes him so determined?"

"I was not into shared soul-searching," says Redford. "In that regard I was, and remain, a loner. I like to face the issues alone. Similarly, in deciding the direction I wanted to go in as an actor, I mostly engaged that dialogue with myself. Why did I want to persevere? Vanity is the easy explanation, but I now knew it was more than that. The nearest I can come to explaining the drive is something Jack Kerouac said about the problem facing the American artist. There are many voices in America, he said, so the best solution is to write one story in the bum dialect, another in the Indian dialect and so on. I liked that. I had a very broad sense of America, or the parallel Americas, and I knew I wanted to study the differences. I wanted the power of witness. Then I wanted to turn it into some performance truth. You have to be careful of overstatement, but I suppose I had some intuition or observation about America or Americans that I wanted to essay."

James stretched, getting him tryouts for a few movies, but he consistently failed. "That taught me a lot about the business," says Redford. "Slowly this tapestry unfolded: that show business—even art—was *gladiatorial.* I had to work harder."

With new antitrust laws, MCA, which was ever expanding into movie production and had now acquired a record label, was under pressure to restructure. James urged Redford to retain a Beverly Hills lawyer, Alexander Tucker, and he signed a new movie agent contract with Citron and Park, the high-profile MCA spin-off. But he refused to sever contact with Stark Hesseltine. "I saw how one could become soulless in the pursuit of success, and I would not allow that to start happening. Stark had been loyal to me, and I felt I should reciprocate. He knew nothing about movies, but he was a decent human being, so I decided I would stick with him as my overall agent and adviser as long as I could."

The fidelity facilitated the most productive and long-lasting friendship of Redford's life. Sydney Pollack, a young actor from South Bend, Indiana, was also an MCA client, and met Redford during readings for a small-time movie called *War Hunt.* "It was Stark Hesseltine who got me interested in Redford," Pollack recalled. "All I ever heard from Stark were stories about this young blond surf god who was such a great guy. That got me interested to know Bob." Pollack had left home at seventeen, abandoning "the usual bourgeois expectations" of his shopkeeper father, first to join the army, then to study acting at the Neighborhood Playhouse under Sandy Meisner. Resistant, like Meisner, to the literal Method, he made his Broadway debut at twenty-one in 1955; he also became Meisner's paid assistant. John Frankenheimer, one of television's most prolific young directors, introduced Pollack to Burt Lancaster, Frankenheimer's production partner on *The Young Savages.* Pollack became dialogue coach to the street punks in the movie, and his work so impressed Lancaster that he convinced MCA's Lew Wasserman to represent him. Under the patronage of Lancaster, Pollack headed west in 1960, first to coach actors for Frankenheimer, then to direct episodes of CBS's courtroom drama series *The Defenders* and ABC's medical series *Ben Casey.* When he met Redford, he was recently married to the actress Claire Griswold and taking time out from *Ben Casey* to return to his first love, acting.

Pollack remembered being struck by Redford's "command" when they met in an audition room. Much of this, Pollack admitted, was superficial accoutrements. With his recent good television earnings, Redford was living at the Hotel Bel-Air; he had also acquired a Porsche 350 series speedster, the first of twenty he would own over the years. "I understood these markers," said Pollack. "This is a business where appearance and reality vie with each other. But you quickly get the knack of looking beyond. And what I saw in Bob, as Stark said, was a man of quality."

Very shortly, the two actors were hanging out, drinking vodka and talking long into the nights. "We were very different physically," said Pollack. "Bob was Mr. Sports. I was never into the jock thing; I never held a tennis racket in my life. But Bob's competitiveness was infectious. And though he was always into sports, always checking the sports results, the competitiveness was much broader and healthier than that. It came from his gut and it came from the spirit of the times, the Kennedy spirit. Even if you weren't political, and Bob was only marginally then, it was impossible not to be revved up by all the changes that were going down in 1961. Bob was hot-wired, and that made him a very attractive guy to be with."

Redford "loved Sydney from the get-go" and concedes his own political soft-focus. Still, he says, it was impossible to remain indifferent to Camelot: to Kennedy's brain trust, the exhortations to young people, the fact that the White House itself was now a culture and arts center. "I wasn't paying close attention, but it seeped in," says Redford. "Later, looking back from the stance of supporting liberal politics, I saw that the fifties-sixties changeover was the pivot of everything that redefined America as a global force. I wasn't a contributor, but I was lucky to be alive at a time when the notion of America *as a concept* came back into question, and people looked objectively, without the pressure of a world war, at the capacity of our role in world affairs. It was a time of open questioning, which I cherished and enjoyed discussing with Sydney."

Redford and Pollack's friendship took off during *War Hunt,* Redford's first—albeit small-scale—movie, which he still regards affectionately. During *Little Moon of Alban,* two young film enthusiasts, Terry and Denis Sanders, had come backstage with a script they'd developed with Stanford Whitmore about the Korean War. Redford liked them before he read the script: "They were of Turkish extraction, very quirky and cutting-edge." The brothers were UCLA film school graduates whose cinema verité short about the Civil War, *A Time Out of War,* had won an Academy Award. Because of that success, Universal had given them $250,000 to make their first feature, this modest *War Hunt.*

The script dealt with the spiritual abyss of war, examined in the erosion of sanity on the battlefield, where Private Raymond Endore, an exhausted reconnaissance man desensitized to slaughter, attempts to abduct his young ward, a Korean child called Charlie, and take him from the killing fields to the freedom in the hills. Other major roles were those of Private Roy Loomis, a man of reason and conscience, and the straight-ahead, unquestioning Sergeant Owen Van Dorn.

When Redford read the script, the role of Endore jumped out at him. "I thought, Oh, I get it. They've seen me do the psychos on TV, and now I'm going to be this neurotic wild guy." Terry Sanders, the producer, told Redford that John Saxon, the longtime Universal contract player, would be his main costar. "Given John's status, I assumed he'd play the heroic Roy Loomis. But I was wrong. I could not believe it when Denis, who was directing, told me to learn Loomis's lines. Saxon would be playing Endore! I could not believe that these guys saw me as a friendly face. I thought, *Finally!* I told Monique: 'What a relief! I was beginning to be typecast as a loony. Now these Sanders guys are opening it up. They see *the actor.*' "

When shooting began in Topanga Canyon, Redford encountered a crew top-heavy with talent. Apart from Saxon and Pollack (cast as Owen Van Dorn), there was John Houseman as UA's creative adviser, Francis Ford Coppola as gofer, Dean Stockwell in charge of the still photography and Ted McCord as the cameraman. "These guys were the second generation out of UCLA film school, following the so-called breakthrough guys like Stanley Kubrick, who'd just hit internationally with *The Killing,*" says Redford. "They were the American New Wave and people had high expectations for them. I was elated. Sydney and I thought, Whoa, this could be really inventive and great!"

Redford's fee for three weeks' work was to be $500, somewhat less than a comparable television fee. But Redford and Pollack were quickly concerned about the immaturity of the producers. "I looked around and saw great actors on the set," said Pollack. "There was no question about that. But there was a studenty feel about the Sanders boys, a feeling that they had many unresolved creative issues as we went along. I was experienced enough to know you simply have to have your plot worked out before you shoot a foot of film. You can't risk boardroom debates in the field, and that's what they were doing."

"Sydney and I were the kind of actors who avoided seeing the big productions like *Cleopatra* in favor of the new stuff the Europeans were doing," Redford recalls. "So we were supporting all the edgy stuff. But Denis seemed less sure every day of where we were going. In my opinion, he opened a door that allowed John [Saxon] to take over the movie. John was experienced. They were not. And that might have been a mistake."

Saxon disputes that he took over the movie but believed *War Hunt* was a classic in concept and execution. "In the context of the times, it was an original gem," he says. "It was a transition film, because the studio system had just shut down, Europe was happening and no one at the executive level knew where to go next. No decisions were being made in Hollywood, and this was the first moment that the independents stood out. In later life Bob would become the patron saint of the independents with Sundance, and I choose to believe this was his baptism. Had he come to movies at any other time, in any other way, he might not have found the inspiration. The Sanders brothers helped bring in the new era. We all benefited. And I believe Bob intuited the significance of what we'd all done even if he failed to process it at the time."

Saxon admits that he angled to "supervise" the postproduction, working closely with Denis Sanders. But when UA saw their version in the spring of 1962, a recut was ordered and effected. Saxon objected, personally confronting the senior UA executive in charge, David Picker. "I told him, 'You have to reinstate all the original Sanderses' footage, please. These guys have a vision of something very deep and meaningful about war and human nature, and you need to show it that way—the intimate, disturbing way.' " Picker wouldn't allow it. "UA had no time for metaphysics," says Saxon. "They cut it again and dumped *War Hunt* onto the market, where it was just another low-budget black-and-white war picture."

That may have seemed the case to Saxon, but the reviews didn't bear him out. Howard Thompson in *The New York Times* praised "one of the most honest and haunting war movies in years," in which Redford was "excellent." Bosley Crowther declared it "a stunning achievement, a kind of poetry," while the *New York Herald Tribune* and the *Hollywood Reporter* both singled out Redford's noteworthy movie debut. "We got away with it," said Pollack. "It was a combination effort: the Sanders brothers, UA—and some great acting chops. We didn't deserve it, none of us, but it turned into a nice little film."

After *War Hunt* had been completed, on a boozy night at Saxon's home in the Santa Monica hills, he and Redford discussed the future of the movie business: "My life within the studio system was over," says Saxon. "I was on my way to join Otto Preminger for a movie in Europe. I told Bob that all that remained in L.A. was television. I said the movie market was dead. He wouldn't have any of it. He was still a relative unknown, had no real power, but he was emphatic. 'There's plenty left to do,' he told me. I said, 'But the movies are finished out here,' and he just looked at me and shook his head. He was a stubborn critter."

This stubbornness now focused on his theater failures. "I suddenly thought, Wait a minute, I'm missing something here. Forget drama. Laughter has always been my truth. It's my personal sanity preserve. I decided I wanted to try comedy, and theater was rich in comedies at that time." Tom Skerritt, whom Redford had also befriended when he too acted on *War Hunt,* remembers Redford outlining this decision: "It made absolute sense, once you knew him. He was never a straight-line guy. He's an absurdist. He was also bizarrely ambitious. You could speculate forever on Freudian theories of alienation, of the artist's inability to reconcile or overcome his childhood needs, and how that void opens the path to creation. You could say Bob's alienation brought him to the higher ground. But however it happened, it happened. *War Hunt* was one piece of the mosaic. Comedy was the next piece."

Hesseltine was appalled. "He said I was foolish," says Redford. "He said I was already on my way in solid drama, that there was a momentum going since *Iceman.* He would not support me. He was, he said, grooming me for the classics. That, I felt, was his blind spot. He maintained some romantic vision of me as Paris in a skirt in *Antigone.* But that just wasn't me. I put my foot down. I told him I'd rather rot than be remembered for *Route 66.* If I failed trying, at least I tried."

In the middle of this debate, on an afternoon when he was visiting Monique James, Redford found a script on her desk whose author's name caught his eye: Norman Krasna. Krasna, recipient of an Academy Award for *Princess O'Rourke,* had a marathon career dating back to the thirties, when he'd collaborated with Groucho Marx. Krasna's wit was cornball and his style light-fingered. The script on James's desk was *Sunday in New York,* and Redford became excited when he saw the name of Garson Kanin, a literary giant in his view, appended as director. "To me, Garson represented the ultimate Hollywood comedy sophistication, because of all the great Hepburn-Tracy movies he'd written with his wife, Ruth Gordon. I thought, This is my navigator!"

Redford insisted Hesseltine approach the producer, David Merrick, a leviathan of Broadway, for a role in the play. But at first, Merrick refused to even audition him. Redford continued to pressure Hesseltine with hourly phone calls. Finally Hesseltine broke through with Mike Shurtleff, Merrick and Kanin's casting director, who had seen *The Iceman Cometh* and been impressed. On Shurtleff's recommendation, Merrick conceded to test Redford, provided the actor paid his own fare to New York to meet Kanin. Redford was told he would be reimbursed if he got the part. "So I took the red-eye to New York, and I read for Kanin and landed the part. But Merrick, the cheap bastard, never reimbursed me."

Crossbred from a wealth of George Cukor and Billy Wilder comedies, *Sunday in New York* benefited greatly from the participation of Kanin, who had directed a Krasna-written movie, *Bachelor Mother,* for RKO in 1939 but was, more importantly, Cukor's magical collaborator on the classics *Adam's Rib* and *Pat and Mike.* Having cut his teeth on RKO comedies, Kanin had, by his account, "fine-tuned a revolutionary comedy directing style" of his own. "I knew what worked and what didn't by trial and error over thirty years with some of the greatest light comedians and writers America has ever known." Admiring as he was of Krasna, however, something about *Sunday in New York* sat uneasily with Kanin. Perhaps, as the actress Sondra Lee, cast in a prominent role, observed, it was the "acrobatic, in-your-face sexuality of a plot on the brink of the Swingin' Sixties"—a will-she-or-won't-she-yield-her-virginity romp that bordered on the pornographic compared with Tracy-Hepburn—that stalled Kanin. Or perhaps, as Redford believed, it was the fault of the writing. The story line, to be sure, was familiar. Eileen Taylor, an ingénue from Albany, visits her airline pilot brother in his New York apartment, argues the principles of modern morality, goes out to see a movie, meets Mike Mitchell, a part-time art critic on the make, catches her brooch on his suit, agrees to meet for tea at Longchamps restaurant to discuss the $2 repair and, over the next six comedic scenes, falls for him. They end up gamboling in bed, "laughing hysterically," says the script, "which is an ideal way to begin a marriage." Redford liked the jokes, but "let's face it, this was not up to the standard of a Kanin-Gordon script."

Whatever its weaknesses, the play was transformed, said Kanin, by Redford's arrival. "I didn't intend to cast him in a lead role. We already had a major New York actor signed and sealed and in the wings. But then Bob came in to read for a lesser part, and I thought immediately that he *looked* like Spencer Tracy. He did his small piece and Merrick and I thanked him, but he said, very politely, that he would like to read for the lead. We were a little shocked, but we said go ahead. There was nothing to lose. He walked into the wings and reappeared in a few moments, in the same clothes, and proceeded to give a subtle, funny, original performance as Mike Mitchell, the main character. He was canny. He'd been holding back on the first reading, which wasn't terrific, because he believed he *was* the lead, and he was correct."

Redford stressed the edginess in *Sunday in New York* and, according to Kanin, brought the trendy sexuality to the fore. "We jumped forward with Bob, and that was his contribution, not ours." David Merrick avoided rehearsals, leaving Kanin in uncontested control. Kanin duly attacked Krasna's script, replacing pedestrian lines with his own witticisms. For Sondra Lee, the rehearsals took fire when Redford and Pat Stanley, playing the virginal Eileen, "hit their stride within two days." The entire play was dependent, says Lee, on sparks from that romantic chemistry. "And Bob and Pat delivered, big-time. They flirted. It was powerful. They were smooth as silk, and they made something from nothing very much."

The play opened at the Cort on Broadway on November 29 to mixed reviews, but the critics had only good things to say about Redford. Walter Kerr of the *New York Herald Tribune* said Redford "is really first-rate no matter what the evening is doing." And Richard Coe of *The Washington Post* deemed him "a marvelously skilled farceur." Redford was pleased. "But I knew it was a hairsbreadth success," he says. "And the truth was that just one review turned it around for all of us." Howard Taubman in *The New York Times* commended a play that "is inventive and chic [and] sparkles with freshness and humor." That review alone, says Redford, secured the play's survival and his first significant stage success.

Christmas of 1961 was heightened by Lola's new pregnancy, steady income and, for the first time, late-night appreciative crowds at the stage door. Redford felt validated, and Sondra Lee remembers him blissfully happy, even crossing Manhattan on foot in a snowstorm to deliver her holiday gift. "Of all of us, he came best out of that play," says Lee. "People were talking about him, not the play."

The ebullience was short-lived and the play closed in April. On May 5, Lola gave birth to a baby son, David James, seven weeks prematurely. The horrors of maternity crises of the past—of his mother's illnesses and the loss of his son—came crashing down. Mother and son fought to survive. The baby had the kind of extreme hyaline membrane disease that, says Redford, was life threatening. "The doctors gave Jamie just a 40-60 chance, but he hung in. Over a month his condition improved, and then he stabilized. It was a colossal relief for us."

Pollack knew the near loss of the baby had deeply unsettled Redford.

Pollack was still in Los Angeles, directing *Gunsmoke,* and urged his friend to come west, so that he and Lola could recover. Monique James also called, telling him about the many exciting offers for television work. "You almost lose a child, you reevaluate," says Redford. "So I sat down and restrategized my career." He told Hesseltine he wanted a break from theater. Simultaneously he instructed Monique James and the new movie agent she had recommended, Arthur Park, to concentrate primarily on big-screen work. He was straightforward about his aims: he wanted money to build a home in the mountains. "Family became the priority and I decided to concentrate on the most expeditious way of building a secure home."

In July the Redfords returned west, first to Provo, then to a rented apartment in Laurel Canyon, not far from the Pollacks' Mulholland Drive home. "Bob and I were always good for each other when we got together," said Pollack, "because we fired up each other's imaginations and fantasies. Neither of us skied then, but Bob suddenly started going on about this idyllic Rocky Mountain home he wanted to build, which would be hemmed in with snow half the year. I was thinking, He's out of his mind—it's all the stress of Jamie's birth and everything. But then he surprised us by declaring that he'd already bought a plot near Provo and was getting ready to build, cutting clearings and laying foundations with his own hands. It came out of nowhere. I was dumbfounded. I said, 'Wait a second! You want to work in movies and you want to live in the wilderness! How do you reconcile these two lifestyles?' I told him he was nuts."

The high-volume work, as he wanted it, rolled in: parts in *Dr. Kildare, Alfred Hitchcock Presents,* any number of TV westerns. Then Park called to say there was, finally, big movie interest. MGM had two promising projects: a movie version of *Sunday in New York,* which would be directed by Peter Tewksbury, and Tennessee Williams's *Period of Adjustment,* to be directed by George Roy Hill. "I was very hopeful," says Redford. "I thought both were right for me, but the readings did not go well."

Redford's problem, Monique James felt, might well have been his ubiquity on television. "It was always a balancing act," she said. "But I was encouraged all the time by the quality of what Bob was being offered. None were makeweight parts in TV, all had worth." Huge consolation came in his role in ABC's notable anthology series, *Alcoa Premiere,* hosted by Fred Astaire. Redford knew he was onto something: "Every so often you read a script and the part solidifies, living and breathing before you have the chance to apply yourself. This was my first experience of that."

The teleplay, by Halsted Welles, was called "The Voice of Charlie Pont," about a failed writer, George Laurents, married and settled and working as an "assistant to an assistant to the janitor" at a Boston bank, who is preyed upon by an old school buddy, the criminally opportunistic charmer of the title. What most pleased Redford was the fact that, as in *War Hunt,* he was being offered "the soft-guy role," and not the psycho. Redford was duly cast as the writer, and Bradford Dillman as the con man.

No production Redford had been involved with until that time had such audience impact. Among those who took notice was a newly emerging theater director, Mike Nichols. Nichols, in transition from his long-running comedy partnership with Elaine May, was preparing his directorial debut with Neil Simon for the 1963 Broadway season. "So I was on the lookout for talent," he remembers, "but not particularly looking to fill any role in Neil's play, which was to be called *Nobody Loves Me.* So, I'm casually watching this 'Charlie Pont,' watching the new blond guy whom I don't know, and I experienced that frisson you get when you're surprised by someone. It's the unexpected wave that catches the swimmer off guard. It wasn't a 'Gee, he was interesting'; it was more a 'Where the hell did he come from?' " Nichols took note of Redford's name. "I just thought, He's gonna crack it."

That fall there continued to be plenty of heated talk about his potential, but no clear breakthrough. He wanted more movie auditions, but he was suddenly advised by the Sanderses' company that he was committed to them exclusively for at least another film. "My mistake, but it was terrible because I really didn't like what they were offering," says Redford. In response to his rejections, the Sanders brothers were threatening to sue. At this point Carol Rossen reentered his life. That spring, by chance, he had found her photograph among Hesseltine's files. Surprised she was working as an actress around New York, he told Hesseltine to send her warm greetings. Now Hesseltine surprised the Redfords during a beach barbecue by bringing Carol along. Redford was delighted. "I'd cut off that part of my life, and in doing so I lost some good people. Carol was one of the good ones. Reconnecting with her was good, because it brought the past into perspective and allowed me to assess the distance I'd traveled."

But Carol observed that her old friend was on the edge: "He'd changed in one way: what had always been a fiery temperament had become a *very* short fuse. I was in admiration for all he was achieving, and I loved Lola and the kids. But he felt he was in the wrong place, not just in the entertainment industry, but in life. It exuded from his pores. Everything of worth was happening in Europe, he said, not here. In movies they had the nouvelle vague, and the British had the New Wave. We had Doris Day and Pat Boone. This was also the time of the Cuban missile crisis and the feeling that Kennedy's sociable foreign policy wasn't all it was cracked up to be. We were supposed to be living in Camelot, but you had youth revolts and that feeling of the powder keg. America hadn't got over McCarthy, and Bob was desperate to find a way *not* to be part of the status quo."

Carol was more accurate in her judgment of Redford on the edge than she knew. Shortly after, having disrupted family life with petty arguments that masked his true inner turmoil, he suddenly decided to take to the road again by himself. "I drove two hundred miles," he says, "through Big Sur to Morro Bay, and parked the car. I just knew, for everyone's sake, that I had to put a distance between me and the world. Big Sur was always a fabulous mystery to me, something that sat on the edge of my imagination, beckoning. It was a mystery I wanted to solve by being *in it.* So I decided to walk it." That November there were subzero temperatures and the coast road was closed because of landslides. Redford didn't care. He had a sleeping bag, writing materials, a sketchbook and a flashlight. "I was Kerouac walking back to face the demons at the cove in Big Sur. Of course, I was processing as I went, all the time questioning myself. Did I want to continue in the rat race? Was I letting Lola and the kids down?"

Over several days Redford walked ninety miles toward Monterey, finally stopping at Deetjen's Big Sur Inn, where he made a new friend in the Norwegian proprietor, a fanciful image of his darkest self. "Here was a man who'd come full circle in the journey of life. He'd come to America to build a better life. Somewhere he flipped and murdered a man. In consequence, he went to Alcatraz. From there he was out on a convict chain gang, digging the coastal highway during the Depression. And through that he ended up, like Miller at Big Sur, isolated from the world, free of self-contempt, managing an inn at the edge of nowhere. He was occupying a shack he had to build while a member of the convict road gang that built the Big Sur access road in the thirties."

For days the men talked in a drunken free association that revived Redford. "He'd get plastered and cuss the world: the social injustice, the bent hierarchy, the lack of mettle in the youth. He was volatile, but he had great wisdom. All the time, with this crazy talk and the wind rattling the windows, piano music was playing, day and night. Finally, I asked him what it was, because it was like the counterpoint of sanity, a Greek chorus to our yarns. And he told me it was Pachelbel, Canon in D, which I promised to get for myself when I got back to L.A. Then I forgot the name of the composer and, try as I might, I couldn't recall it." It would be fifteen years later, while renting a Big Sur property to work on the script for *The Electric Horseman* with Pollack, that Redford rediscovered Pachelbel: "Sydney and I decided to go for dinner, and at the last minute I remembered Deetjen's, so I said, 'Maybe it's still there. Let's go back.' " The old man was dead—but everything else remained, including the Pachelbel music gently flooding the dining room. At that time, Redford was planning to direct his first film, *Ordinary People.* The Pachelbel music suddenly framed this unshaped work in his mind. "I reflected on that later," he says. "It fit a pattern in my life of serendipitous moments. Those are the moments—the Big Sur walk and Deetjen's—that you feel you are not so much the navigator of your life as the object of some design."

Back in Laurel Canyon, emaciated and bearded as in his post-Europe days, Redford announced abruptly that he wanted to quit L.A. forever and concentrate his life in the mountains of Utah. He would resume theater, he said, and spend his working months in New York.

Then came news of an Emmy nomination for "The Voice of Charlie Pont." On the heels of that came an offer from Bing Crosby Productions for Redford to play the lead role in a new ABC summer series, *Breaking Point.* Redford said no. "Then the honey trap opens," he says. "The seductive talk starts. This would be groundbreaking drama, all about a psychiatrist running group therapy sessions. I would be the star counselor. I thought about that. I was twenty-four years old, and I was supposed to be counseling sick people? I told Monique James, 'How can I play this? It's *me* who needs the shrink.' "

Arthur Park came down hard on Redford: "Kid, I've been a lifetime in this business, so let me put you straight. Don't be a schmuck. Movies are great, but forget about them. They pay television stars in the top guest slots $3,500. They want to pay you $3,750 *a week, for thirteen weeks.* Nobody your age is getting that. Take it."

Redford still refused. "Lola stood by me at first, because she was keen to get back to Provo and build a homestead. Then the offer went up to *$6,000 a week,* which was unprecedented. She said, 'Wait a second . . . ?' and I thought, Gee, maybe I should rethink it."

Redford spent all night on the beach at Malibu, walking, getting his feet wet. "I became that kid of six on the bicycle in Sawtelle, looking for the answers in the stars. Lola and I had big debts. Stark had loaned me some money, and this house we wanted to build was obviously going to cost some. But I felt I'd already ransomed myself to the Sanderses' contract, and that felt bad, like I was an Indian who'd lost his spirit to a photograph. I didn't want any more of that, but I also had to think about the family."

When Redford returned home, there was another summons from Park. When he arrived at Park's office, the agent was shaking: "While you were out playing Hamlet on the beach, kid, Bing Crosby Productions upped the offer to *$10,000 a week*! I'm doing this job thirty years. Don't throw this back in my face. Let me retire with this one under my belt."

"Coming back from the beach, I was at the point of saying *maybe,*" says Redford. "But that decided it. Somewhere between the Sanders brothers and this horseflesh deal was my personal reality. I told Arthur, 'The offer is great, because it makes it easy for me. Let them offer me twenty thousand, or thirty, or forty. It just makes it easier to say no.' "

Redford had resolved his priorities. It wasn't money he wanted, it was roots.

9

Big Pictures

The two acres Redford had purchased for $500, a onetime chicken-coop plot at the north fork draw at Timp Haven on the flank of the hill facing Mount Timpanogos, would become the physical nucleus of Sundance. Incrementally, over the next five years, he would purchase six hundred more acres of wild lands from Justin Stewart to broaden his base. Redford insists "there was no long-term strategy." But a significant pattern was forming. With every peak of achievement came an act of withdrawal.

Lola and the children were housed in an apartment in town while Redford took to camping on-site, intent on constructing his house with only local builder Garn Phillips and his son to help. In 1961, Redford had seen Frank Lloyd Wright's Taliesin West, built in Arizona, in *Sunset* magazine. "That started my love affair with organic architecture, and also the organic notion of building." The highlight of Taliesin West for Redford was a unique stone-in-cement chimney. Redford wanted his A-frame built around this design, but both Phillips and Lee Knell, the Provo architect consulted in the planning, were stymied. Finally Redford found stonemason Jay Bown, a half-Cherokee Mormon based in Cash Valley on the Iowa border. "I drove 130 miles north to find this apparently hostile guy who met my plan with indifference. He was standing on his sixty-foot flatbed truck and wasn't impressed by the fact that I was this actor who wanted to do the impossible. Finally I said to him, 'Okay, I'm going to try it anyway. I just don't want to screw it up,' and he came around." The timber used was local; the granite shipped from nearby Deer Creek and Strawberry was so ancient it was studded with dinosaur-era fossils. They labored through the summer and fall. The house became an obsession for Redford. As it came together, it comprised fourteen timber A-frames, thirty-eight-foot-wide windows looking out to Timpanogos, an encircling pine deck, three bedrooms and a cathedral living space. "We had moose and deer, a mountain lion, bald eagles, every sort of wilderness creature—but no running water," he remembers. "When the winter snows came, we boiled water to cook and bathe with. When the snows were heaviest in January, the house was half buried, and we used sleds to trek from the canyon entrance. When the family came to stay, it took an hour to transport them, and the supplies, from the entrance to the house. It was nineteenth-century living."

As Redford labored in bliss, his future was being shaped by yet new advisers. Arthur Park had been replaced, by mutual agreement, by Meta Rosenberg of Rosenberg and Coryel, who had a plan to pay off the Sanderses from the proceeds of a possible movie deal with Columbia. Rosenberg already had that deal in hand, with producer Irving Allen, who wanted Redford for his Viking movie, *The Long Ships.* Ostensibly this was what Redford sought: good casting, alongside a major star—Richard Widmark—in a movie to be directed by the respected Jack Cardiff. But Redford dithered. Hesseltine was calling at the same time, telling him of Mike Nichols's interest in casting him in *Nobody Loves Me,* the follow-up to Simon's Tony-winning *Come Blow Your Horn.* "I was very flattered," says Redford, "because I obviously knew Neil's and Mike's reputations. And, of course, I'd always said I wanted good theater. But I was so at peace in Provo that I didn't want to get back in the race." After weeks of phone exchanges, Redford finally offered an equivocal agreement. Sticking to his word and choosing East Coast over West, he told Nichols he would accept the play, but strictly on the condition of his finding comfort in the project. "I was emphatic," says Redford. "I told Mike, 'I will do *the tryouts* in Bucks County. But I will not commit to Broadway.' I know it was half-assed, but it was the best I could do, given where I was at emotionally."

Redford accepted a fee of $110 a week, much to Rosenberg's dismay. "I know that was a time of reconsideration for the people professionally associated with me," says Redford. "My judgment was in question. It seemed unthinkable that an actor on the brink would turn down $10,000 a week to take a pittance. People started saying, 'He's unstable—watch out!' But the only appeal for leaving Provo was the old challenge of theater. That's all that got me moving again."

In April, Redford left the building site, more physically fit than ever, and drove his Porsche to New York. At producer Arnold Saint Subber's house, Nichols found him unapologetically reluctant to dive in. Nichols became alarmed, mostly because the play was loaded with importance for both him and Simon. "Neil needed the follow-up and I needed at least a professional show. After I split with Elaine [May], I was the leftover guy who didn't know what to do with his life. I needed some break, and Saint Subber had handed it to me. He was the guy who said, 'Direct!' and sent me this Neil Simon work in progress. I'd played prima donna at first. I said, 'Okay, I'll do it in summer stock if we can get that blond guy from "The Voice of Charlie Pont." ' Saint Subber could have told me there and then to go get lost, but he supported me. So I wanted to pay him back . . . and here was Bob, offering a halfhearted commitment."

Nobody Loves Me had the same romantic breeziness as *Sunday in New York.* It had the same occasional bumptious wit, too. It seemed to Redford very much a product of its time, about indolent young lovers playing out misunderstood affections. Simon, a fluid and prolific writer since his high school collaborations with his brother, Danny, had graduated, via the CBS radio writers' school, Catskills revues and Sid Caesar's shows, to the faultless *Sergeant Bilko.* He would later write in his autobiography that *Nobody Loves Me*—shortly to be retitled *Barefoot in the Park*—came in fits and starts over many years. As they convened at Saint Subber's, said Simon, he was still laboring.

Redford's role would be Simon's alter ego, Paul Bratter, a fastidious, newly married attorney. His wife, Corie, the whirling dervish of the piece, struggles to organize their ridiculously inappropriate newlyweds' apartment while sparring with the exotic, Tyrolean-hat-wearing upstairs neighbor, Victor Velasco. What ensues is Corie's conversion of uptight Paul to Victor's laid-back bohemianism:

> CORIE: You can't even walk into a candy store and ask the lady for a Tootsie Roll. You've got to walk up to the counter and point at it and say, "I'll have that thing in the brown and white wrapper."
>
> PAUL: That's ridiculous.
>
> CORIE: And you're not. That's the trouble. Like Thursday night. You wouldn't walk barefoot with me in Washington Square Park. Why not?
>
> PAUL: Very simple answer. It was seventeen degrees.

Nichols was pleased with his other casting: Elizabeth Ashley as Corie, Kurt Kasznar as Velasco, Mildred Natwick as Corie's mother and Herb Edelman as the telephone man. "I knew they were all solid, all good at getting 'the bounce' in the thing. If I had reservations at all, it was with Bob and Liz's mind-set at the beginning." Ashley, whom Redford had met on *The Highest Tree,* was the hottest property around, having just won a Tony for *Take Her, She's Mine* and having headlined Paramount's summer hit, *The Carpetbaggers,* playing opposite her new lover, George Peppard. The stresses caused by this relationship—Peppard was extricating himself from a ten-year marriage to move in with her—were known but, says Nichols, not fully understood. "I thought lack of enthusiasm was my problem. I had to find a spark to ignite these fine actors and shake off some ennui."

The laughs in rehearsals came slow. According to Neil Simon in his memoirs, "Once I heard a huge laugh coming from the rehearsal room. I couldn't resist. I ran in to hear what part of the play they were doing. They weren't. They had taken a break and Mike was regaling them with hysterical stories about his life."

Within a week, Nichols, and the production, perked up. "I saw what Bob was giving us. He had the farce experience from *Sunday in New York.* He could roll with the unexpected moments. And Bob was also a very funny guy when he was pissed, and he was pissed a lot in those days, so that was great electricity for Paul Bratter. Once Bob himself got those elements by the neck, he had the character, and he was off and running."

Redford, though, thought the prep time was insufficient. He felt unready when the show opened out of town at the Bucks County Playhouse. Ashley, emotionally spent from overwork and the complexities of her love life, was exhausted before the show started. No one saw the approaching nervous breakdown that would put her out of the show within three months, and ultimately out of show business for half a decade. But it was Simon who fell apart after the first night. "He just disintegrated," says Nichols. "As far as he was concerned, we had on our hands the worst play ever written. He actually asked the theater manager that very question: 'Is this the worst play you've ever had?' In my opinion, apart from the fact that the third act didn't work, we brought the house down. All the laughs came on cue, and I knew Bob was the center of it. He'd tightened up enormously and, for the performance, gave it everything. I learned he was the kind of actor who *inhabits* the role, and so it was perfectionism that lifted Paul Bratter. Neil wrote an uptight character. Bob's eccentricity made him someone lovable." Redford believes that Paul Bratter was unquestionably his most successful theater role.

After Bucks County, there was a hiatus before the play would begin its pre-Broadway tour, at New Haven, in the fall. Redford returned to the Utah building site and resumed what he calls his "soul work." By August, the house was finished. "My whole psychological framework changed," he says. "Simply, the day-to-day work, carving stone, digging, seeing this house grow like a flower in the landscape, touched me very deeply. I already felt I belonged in the canyon, that it had a hold on me. Now I felt that what I had just accomplished was far more important than Broadway." Stan Collins, who knew the area well from childhood hikes, was impressed by the beauty and craftsmanship of the finished house. He also saw something beyond pride of ownership. "Bob definitely sensed a mission. The house was amazing, but it was a little too far up the canyon, a little too off the road, a little too inaccessible. You got the impression that he had a hidden hand, that there was more to this idea of building a house in Utah than met the eye."

When Redford rejoined the play in New Haven, he "behaved badly. I did not want to be there, and I did not cooperate. It was really tough on Mike, on everyone, and today I feel ashamed of how I was." Neil Simon had fixed the technical problem, boosting the third act by adding a love affair between Velasco and Corie's mother. A jolting review brought Redford to attention, a local critic remarking that "the play was fine, except for Redford, who couldn't be heard past the first few rows." Redford says, "It was true—I was lying down. I was spiritually still in Utah, so you might say I was on my way out the door." Over dinner Nichols inadvertently saved the day. They talked of the characters, of the personalities of the actors, of Ashley's troubles. "And then," says Redford, "Mike said something that connected me once again with Bratter, whom I'd lost. He said, 'You have the secret'—meaning, the answers to the character rested with me. I suddenly saw the power of my choice, that Paul Bratter could be whoever I wanted him to be. There wasn't any analysis beyond that. I made some actor decisions. I went onstage, and I just kept silent. Elizabeth delivered her lines, and I just smiled and looked at her. And it worked! She looked at me, waiting for the line . . . and she had to look again, waiting. The tone between us sharpened. Freshness and power came back into Bratter, and I was connected with acting again. The show was back on the road."

Nichols felt the need to confront Redford on another matter. "I became fascinated by the fact that he had no interest in his beauty. It was depressing, because he wanted to plaster his hair down and play the nerd. He had come to like Bratter again, but he felt himself playing *against* Liz, and that confused him. She, after all, was supposed to be the object of desire." Once again over dinner the play was reenergized. Nichols says, "I told him, 'Look, I've had years of experience in a double act, and I've learned one thing: you cannot win the battle unless you accept that it's a battle.' Bob just nodded and we ended our meal. When we did the show that night, it was a completely different show. Liz became *invisible.* He pulled out every trick and knocked her off the planet. That's when we really took off."

Ashley's affair with Peppard, she later said, added to the burden of years of overwork and derailed her emotionally. "I felt like a failure," she wrote in her memoirs. "I had a lot of energy and flash and was as adorable as I could be. But I wasn't any good and I knew it. I could tell that Redford knew it too, and every time I went out onstage it compounded my sense of inadequacy. The more I acted the worse it seemed to get." Nichols disagrees. "Certainly, as we headed for Broadway, she didn't slacken in terms of commitment. Bob challenged her, and she gave him a run for his money."

When they played in Washington, Richard Rodgers deemed the play "irresistible." *Newsweek* declared it sublime. Redford, however, was in despair. He recalls, "What the reviews said to me was, This play is finished. It was done, it worked! So for me the work was over. I went to a bar to have a drink with Mike. He asked me what was wrong and I told him, 'I feel lonely onstage. It's the signal for me that something's wrong, that I'm not connecting.' I told him I couldn't go on with *Barefoot* because the critics had put the cap on it. He asked me to reconsider, and I told him honestly that I couldn't. And then he did a very smart thing. He said, 'All right, forget all that's been said tonight. Forget what the critics like. Forget that Richard Rodgers likes it. From now on it's a completely blank sheet of paper, it is no longer blocked out. Whatever we have is whatever *you* want to do. Just take it and go with it. You are Paul Bratter. Play it whatever damned way you feel.' "

Nichols remembers the conversation as stressful but invaluable, both in securing a friendship and in developing their respective careers. "Bob taught me something. I wanted a play set in stone. He didn't. He wanted a play that was evolving *every* night. Something that was always new. In my experience, very few actors would go that far. It's too energy consuming. That, I felt, was the mark of his integrity."

The results, momentarily, were disastrous. "It was a case of swinging too far to the left to counter the swing to the right," says Redford. "But it bonded us so tight and together we made the adjustments and straightened it all out."

The play became the toast of Broadway's fall 1963 season, opening on October 23 and garnering the biggest receipts of 1963–64 and a Tony for

Nichols. Over the next two years it would earn $50 million, a 500 percent return for its investors.

Redford, Simon and Nichols were elevated to a kind of national stardom with the enormousness of *Barefoot's* success; so was Ashley, who appeared on the cover of *Life* in November, the week before she was admitted to a psychiatric ward at Payne Whitney. For Simon, after years of laboring in television, fame was bewitching. Nichols found it exhilarating. For Redford, national attention was wonderfully confusing. "I was suddenly Mr. Focus. Eleanor Roosevelt and Noël Coward dropped by. Natalie Wood came backstage. Bette Davis summoned me to her suite at the Plaza. For me, the best was Ingrid Bergman, who came backstage. When she was leaving, I went after her to say, 'Miss Bergman, I just wanted to tell you how great I think you are.' She smiled with the greatest charm and said simply, 'Do only good work.' It came with such sincerity that it stopped me dead in my tracks, and it felt like the most positive result of the whole business."

On November 22, in the middle of the hysteria for *Barefoot,* Redford was being wined and dined at the Four Seasons by agents from William Morris, who were enthusiastically discussing movie possibilities. As he was sandwiched between them in a crosstown cab, the news came on the radio that Kennedy had been assassinated. Redford stopped the cab and went walking. "I walked for hours, in shock like everyone else, but also recording the public reaction like a journalist." The night's performance of *Barefoot* was canceled. The following night, and in the nights after, Redford noticed a strange phenomenon in the theater. "We'd had to adjust the text a little, to take out, for example, a jokey reference to me, Bratter, dying in the prime of my life. All that was understandable. But after a short period, I found the oddest thing. The sound of the audience laughter changed. It was subtle, but it was very marked. The laughter became raucous and harsh. And it never returned to the way it was before. It was as if innocence was gone from American audiences. At least, that's what it felt like." Redford, like many, later saw the assassination, and the following tragic deaths of Martin Luther King Jr. and Robert Kennedy, as representative of a ground shift in American attitudes. "It was a terrible erosion of the belief system that had been in place since the Civil War. These were serial deaths of a president and national leaders at the hands of fellow Americans. This poked a finger in the chest of every American alive, saying, 'This country isn't the *United* States. This is a coalition of interests, not all of which are in alignment. *Let's think this through* before it's too late.' "

Through late 1963 and into 1964, as *Barefoot* ran, Redford continued to appear on television in quality shows, his favorite of which was an episode of *The Virginian.* He rationalized this work simply: it paid the bills, the $6,000 for *The Virginian* coming in especially handy to help fund a new apartment on West Seventy-ninth Street. But he would only take parts he could learn from. "The criterion I applied was, What can I absorb from this? Who wrote it? Who's in it?" He accepted an episode of *The Virginian* called "The Evil That Men Do," written by Frank Chase and directed by Stuart Heisler, to work alongside Lee J. Cobb. "You couldn't go wrong studying him," says Redford. "Here was an actor who did it all, starting in the Group Theatre, doing stage, the classics, movies, and now he was in television. He'd had a heart attack and had obviously slowed down, but I was keen to learn from him." After a particularly intense scene, in which Redford found himself stretching to impress the great man, Cobb took him aside: "I know what you're looking for, son, but you won't get it from me. I've paid my dues, done my work, and now I just want to be comfortable."

Redford's television career was soon over. The decision was made, he says, by television, not by him. The fifties, as the film historian Leslie Halliwell has pointed out, was television's Elizabethan age, a time when the medium offered interpretations of O'Neill, Shakespeare and Molière and introduced the contemporary genius of playwrights like Reginald Rose (*Twelve Angry Men*) and Paddy Chayefsky (*Marty*). All that changed in the sixties when twenty-four-hour demand and sponsors' greed greatly diminished quality. What followed, said Halliwell, was "the age of the beer can, with America's anonymous network selection committees consciously gearing all their programs to the mentality of the fat little guy in the midwest who slumps in his armchair pouring Coors down his throat."

Redford wanted no part of it. Through the trials of the last five years and especially the ups and downs of *Barefoot in the Park,* he realized that acting per se truly interested him, that the attachment was honest and edifying. "But I wasn't sure that theater could sustain me, either. Like television, it was on the slide. The swing was toward the pop hit formula. I tried to look beyond Broadway for inspiration and found plenty to admire in actors like Richard Burton, Albert Finney and, especially, Paul Scofield, who enchanted me that year in *A Man for All Seasons.* But at that point, even in England, these great actors were being badly served. I felt, and still believe, that theater is the center of the universe for actors. It's intimate, and therefore it's a force for honesty. You sit and say to your audience, at arm's reach: 'Sit down, let me tell you my story. I am a salesman with a home and a family. . . .' You earn their trust one by one. But I was a realist as much as I was an idealist. I knew I wouldn't be able to feed my family on the scraps thrown to me by Arthur Miller or Edward Albee, and I knew Neil Simon wouldn't produce a *Barefoot* every season. So I had to move on."

The cinema, after his meditations on *The Treasure of the Sierra Madre,* was always the good option and by the summer, he had a workable movie offer. Paramount, excited by *Barefoot*'s success, proposed a good project, *Situation Hopeless . . . but Not Serious,* with Alec Guinness. In one fell swoop, Rosenberg resolved the Sanderses' contract and Redford was free to proceed as he wished. The Paramount movie would be shot in Europe. "I got excited," says Redford. "Europe had thrilled me and I wanted to go back, to get that stimulation. It was serendipity again."

In October 1964 Redford left *Barefoot* and flew to Munich with Lola and the kids. He started writing in his diary again, carefully logging the developing opportunity. The movie was based, he was pleased to record, on actor Robert Shaw's 1960 novel, *The Hiding Place,* "a wonderful work" that had already been twice adapted for television, most recently as a *Playhouse 90* episode with James Mason and Trevor Howard. It is the story of two American airmen, Captain Hank Wilson and Sergeant Lucky Finder (Englishmen in the book), from opposite ends of the social divide, who are incarcerated in a basement in Nazi Germany by a storekeeper, Frick, who enjoys their company so much that he refuses to tell them the war is over. Guinness would play Frick; Mike Connors, star of the police television series *Tightrope,* would be Finder; and Redford would play Wilson. The director was Gottfried Reinhardt, son of the famous Max. Reinhardt's wife, Silvia, was script consultant. "And there I had problems," says Redford, "because Shaw's original work was rock solid. Silvia danced around with it unnecessarily, as is the Hollywood custom, to validate her fee."

Silvia's main redevelopment was to further Americanize the story, something Robert Shaw was reluctant to agree to. The drama was tilted toward comedy or, as the work was routinely described around Paramount, satire. Shaw's novel was a wry, serious narrative that *The Times* of London had commended for its "high dramatic value." Redford's journal reveals fast-developing gloom. Ten days into shooting at the Bavaria Studios in suburban Munich, he wrote that the director was an overfunded boor, his wife a sexually playful attention seeker. Worse, Guinness was "cold in manner, overcontrolled, [a man who] does it all by numbers." Today Redford says, "It was my first experience of working with English actors, who appeared, at that time, more involved with craft than movies.

They worked 'out to in,' as opposed to 'in to out,' and that was hard for me. Alec was a good actor, but he had it all worked out for himself before he got to the set, which left nothing for the spontaneity I'd learned to love under Mike Nichols's direction. For me, as a new actor, the lack of opportunity to connect was demotivating."

Mike Connors believed the problem was with the Reinhardts and their failure to come to grips with the material. "This type of yarn was Guinness's perfect territory," says Connors. "The story of the cellar with these captive 'pets' was pure Ealing comedy. It was fun! Alec understood that, but they didn't. Gottfried's failing was that he was not authoritative, he had no control over Guinness or any of us, and Silvia's problem was that her writing was pedantic. So they combined to drag us down."

What is clear to all in hindsight is that *Situation Hopeless* failed to gel as a comedy. It was assembled awkwardly, with little accent on the rhythms of wit. The acting styles clash. In all the long, sedentary dialogue sequences Guinness indulges in circus mode, while Redford and Connors give stock performances. "But it wasn't one of those productions where you could actively contribute," says Connors. "It was more a case of, 'Stand here, say this.' "

While he socialized with Connors and his wife, Redford mostly preferred family evenings at the hotel in the Leopoldstrasse, playing with the kids. He would put them on each knee facing him and tell them the tale of the Three Little Pigs. In his diary he wrote, "During one of these [play] moments, time past came thundering into the present. I remember myself as a child, and my father, so vividly. I remember having the extraordinary ability to make him truly laugh. I knew his ticklish spot and hit it time and again. I could clearly again see him laughing till tears came into his eyes. This great bear who so dominated my childhood leaning back, his teeth bare to the gums, face contorted and beet red, nose bunched and wrinkled. And me pouring it on, going at it with such vigor and ham, all encouraged and feeling important. Those times were wonderful." They also provoked gloom, given the joyless "humor" of Silvia Reinhardt's script.

After the Christmas break, taken in Salzburg, Redford faced a few days of work to wrap the movie, then a return to New York. At Christmas, he says, he felt despondent. He had discovered a European tipple he liked too much—a juniper-flavored gin called Steinhäger. What faced him back home was a void. "He really had no hard plans," says Mike Connors. "He told me he had an understanding that he'd probably do the movie version of *Barefoot*—if, indeed, they ever got around to doing it. 'Beyond that,' he said, 'who knows?' "

Meanwhile, Nichols, for his part, had decided he did not want to make the movie of *Barefoot;* he was eager instead to make his film debut with a modern masterpiece, Edward Albee's *Who's Afraid of Virginia Woolf?* In December, as a Christmas gift, he couriered the script to Germany. Redford read it in Salzburg and disliked it. "I knew the play," says Redford. "I didn't like it when I saw it at the Billy Rose Theatre in 1962. I thought Albee was magnificent. I thought the George and Martha, husband and wife, roles were the best. But the role I was being offered, the younger professor, Nick, just died in the text. I felt he started powerfully, but the author didn't know what to do with the character, and so he trailed off after the first half. I didn't want that part."

Rosenberg was shocked by Redford's decision to refuse the movie, as was Nichols. "I thought he could have invested some real magic in that role," says Nichols. "I thought he made a mistake then, and I still think he made a mistake."

By January, Rosenberg had alternatives in place: one was a movie offer from producer Alan J. Pakula at Warner Bros., the other a three-picture deal at Paramount, inclusive of a big-screen version of *Barefoot in the Park.* "In principle," says Redford, "I should have been ecstatic. But I loved being on the road in Europe. I loved connecting with Shauna and Jamie and discovering their personalities." In his diary, Redford acknowledged his "risky" decision making, stubbornly insisting on an extended New Year's family vacation in Europe, despite Rosenberg's pressure. "I look forward to getting to Spain," he wrote, "and to renting a villa where, hopefully, it will all end, the sleepless hours and the push, the nerves and the needless anguish."

On December 4, 1964, Redford's last television performance, in an episode of *The Defenders* directed by Stuart Rosenberg and filmed during *Barefoot,* was aired on CBS. A month later he was in Majorca, family in tow, unemployed. "It was blissful as long as I could persuade myself that it would last," he remembers. During *Barefoot,* a full-page presentation of his paintings had appeared in the pages of the *New York Journal American.* Now he tried to resume his art but found it next to impossible. "Writing seemed easier, so I kept a log of what I was seeing and feeling, and it served as my personal analyst. It was a devil's advocate. It allowed me to question myself."

The family traveled to Can Pastilla in an attempt to reawaken what he describes in his diary as "the richest experience I have ever had." But the marble villa he once lived in was neglected and overgrown, with a Coca-Cola billboard blocking its sea view. The Redfords moved west and found a blue-and-white villa perched on the cliffs at Port d'Alcudia. In the shade of Mediterranean pines, surrounded by bougainvillea (his favorite shrub), Redford walked the cliffs and mocked himself for his yearnings for "a Beatnik-type freedom."

Within days, he wrote in the diary, Lola had observed a major change in him. For the first time since they'd met, he was relaxing, happy to sit and idle by the fire. He was reading Saroyan; she, Aldous Huxley. On January 4, T. S. Eliot died, and the newspaper articles about his passing, as well as the contemporaneous reports of Allen Ginsberg's street protest for the legalization of marijuana in New York, roused him. In his journal he wrote at length about American cultural values and his desire for a better understanding of what it is to be an American. T. S. Eliot represented "dignity and restraint" that had survived half a century—"He seems to have found the rare area between detachment and involvement"—while Ginsberg encapsulated everything that was wrong with the youth, "soaking his body in the Ganges, stalking the Far East" while becoming "confused, confusing and ridiculous." Redford says his viewpoint has changed: "I could not then hook into Ginsberg's work because, like him, it was too loudly desperate. It was about me, me, me. I preferred Gary Snyder or Robert Creeley. Ginsberg's was not the voice I was open to at that time."

Ginsberg's, though, was a critical new American voice at a time of ferment. Every American newspaper Redford got his hands on reported the convulsions at Berkeley, the Joan Baez rallies at Sproul Plaza, the helicopters teargassing students. It was, says Redford, a bewildering tapestry to unravel. On one hand, there was the clear progress of Johnson's Great Society with the landmark bills for civil rights and wilderness protection. On the other was military escalation in Vietnam and the Merry Pranksters. "I alternately felt that the place was in trouble or undergoing a terrific change. More than anything, the confused signals I was getting reflected the confusion inside myself. I had sympathy with the reformists, but I was involved with starting a career and raising a family, so I was, literally, elsewhere. On the other hand, this terrible ferment was a place of some attraction to me."

The day he read of T. S. Eliot's death, Redford also received a telegram from Meta Rosenberg summoning him home. In his diary, Redford recorded the "feeling of sickness in my stomach." Lola was eager to get back to New York so the kids could start school; he was not. In his diary he wrote hopefully of meetings in Paris with François Truffaut and Tony Richardson, both of whom had expressed interest in working with him. "But when I got down to it, I knew my fate was with Rosenberg and the Warners soundstage. I was the one who asked for that. I was the one who set those wheels in motion."

10

Child's Play

F*or we wrestle not against flesh and blood, but against powers, against the rulers of the darkness of this world. But don't worry. May we meet in the castle of lost souls, in the land of the black swan, otherwise known as the Prince of Darkness. Welcome, little captive, to the waterfall of sweet dreams."*

In the elegant faux-Grecian splendor of a Brentwood mansion, Redford has finished speaking and is sprawled drunkenly on a plump Empire bed, a half-full glass of brandy in one hand and Natalie Wood, one of the biggest stars in the world, at his feet. This introduction to the world of Daisy Clover, the wide-eyed teenager on the brink of stardom, is scintillating, Shakespearean even, and delivered with a panache that immediately secures the characterization of Wade Lewis, a rising actor uncomfortable in his skin. Alan Pakula, the young producer of *Inside Daisy Clover,* stood in the wings and watched Redford's true baptismal moment with sheer delight. "I thought, He's nailed it," said Pakula. "And he's pulled it off because he's just as uncomfortable as Wade Lewis."

The movie, written for Wood, who was coming off *West Side Story,* a winner of multiple Academy Awards, was a fable about the destructive power of showbiz, a cogent, less romanticized version of *A Star Is Born,* and it pivoted on Lewis. In the script, Daisy swaps carny life shared with her nutty mother for the cynical patronage of Raymond Swan, a Hollywood mogul. Swan promises to mold every move she makes—deciding even when she may cut her hair—to effect her stardom. But Lewis takes her off the rails with him instead, marrying her and ditching her.

Pakula had wondered about his partner Robert Mulligan's choice in casting Redford. "He wanted Bob more than I did, but when I saw this sinister side, I thought, He's perfect." The worry, said Pakula, was that this kid from Brentwood would play it like a spoiled brat. "But Bob had the smarts. He'd done the schoolwork, and he chewed up the faux Shakespeare like he'd seen it all, lived it all. As the scene moves on, as he asks Daisy if she would like to get drunk with him, and she says, 'Yes, on sweet sherry,' the savage arch of his brow, that sardonic double take, was the best cinema I'd seen all year."

Redford had met with Pakula and Mulligan, a hot partnership since their 1962 collaboration on *To Kill a Mockingbird,* backstage at the Biltmore the previous summer. They had the script from English critic Gavin Lambert, based on his own 1963 novel, and they had Wood, whom they'd recently collaborated with on *Love with the Proper Stranger.* Wood, a friend of Lambert's, dropped by at the Biltmore, too. Redford already knew her. They'd met at Van Nuys High, where the San Francisco–born actress, already established, was fulfilling California's legal educational requirement while caroming from movie to movie. "She said she wanted me to do *Daisy Clover,*" Redford recalls. "She saw what I was trying to do with Paul Bratter, and she saw that I was all about taking a chance. And when I read Lambert's script, *I* got it. Wade Lewis was gay, and I stalled. I told Pakula and Mulligan, 'No, I will not play this role, because I won't do it justice.' Natalie had the power after *West Side Story,* and she insisted they redraft it for me, to make it more interesting and easier for me to play. They did. So I said, 'Okay, I'll do it.' "

Many, including Pakula, believed Lambert's story was a commentary on the life of Norma Jean Mortenson, the naïf who became Marilyn Monroe. Lambert says the story was "fundamentally a woman's tale, about enchantment, exploitation and survival in Hollywood." For Lambert, whether Wade was gay or not was irrelevant. "What the story was about was how Daisy finds inner strength to overcome the abuses and regain herself, as she does in the end. Natalie was ideal for the character, because it was her life story. Daisy's mother didn't want her to be a star and Natalie's did, but otherwise it was similar."

Inside Daisy Clover, astonishingly Natalie Wood's thirty-eighth movie, was originally a Columbia project developed to follow *Love with the Proper Stranger.* Michael Callan, the Columbia contract actor, was the first choice for Wade Lewis, but then Warners contracted Wood to make *The Great Race* and bought out *Daisy Clover,* too. The switch allowed Wood to take control of new casting, and, apart from Redford, she chose Ruth Gordon to play her mother and Christopher Plummer for Swan. Rosenberg refused to entertain Redford's hesitation on this project. "She told me to get real," says Redford. A $6,500 fee was agreed on, small change compared with Wood's $33,000 a week, plus 5 percent of the gross.

Redford flew from Spain to New York at the beginning of February, saw the kids into nursery school, then traveled on to rehearsals in Los Angeles. On February 16 the first read-through took place at Lambert's Santa Monica home. Bronx-born Pakula, who had come to Hollywood via Yale, found much to talk about with Redford: "I'd been through Warners animation and produced theater plays and kissed ass to do some movie directing, so our experiences were similar in many regards. I also knew enough to recognize the outsider. I'd known Jimmy Dean quite well, double-dating Pier Angeli's sister while Jimmy courted Pier. I knew the Jimmy Dean edge when I saw it, and I saw it in Bob. Natalie was the one who spotted him first, but I'd seen him do the Schary play, where he hadn't a lot to say, but he kind of growled, demanding attention. I'd auditioned him and passed on him then. This time around I saw he could be the great outsider, like Tod Hackett awaiting the burning of Los Angeles in *Day of the Locust,* a guy with a big agenda. It's inside him, I thought. So, if he can get it out . . . ?"

Redford was disoriented by his homecoming. One moment, he says, he was barefoot in the Balearics, the next he was being fêted at the best suite at the Beverly Wilshire. "It was full-on Hollywood, a hint at a lifestyle I'd previously only observed as a very distant outsider growing up in the town. I was treated like royalty, by Warners' decree. The first morning, the room service guy came to serve me breakfast and laid it out and started giving me the weather report for the day—'Good morning, Mr. Redford. It is fifty-four degrees outside, but the forecast is fine. It will be eighty degrees by midday'—as if by rote. I said, 'Where are you from?' And he mumbled something, because my question wasn't in his 'script.' But I wanted to know where he was from. I didn't want bullshit, but I was going to get it. It took me ten minutes to get the details: that he was from Gary, Indiana. When I said I knew Gary, he just wanted to be out of there. I was overstepping. He had his role, and I had mine. I hated that game."

Lola and the kids flew out, and Redford rented an expensive family home on Rockingham for the duration, where Lola's brother and sister, Wayne and Betty, resided with them. "Bob was the new prince in town," says Wayne, who loved the nights out at Trader Vic's, the favored eatery. "They were on the learning curve themselves and found a lot of fun working out the dos and don'ts of etiquette." At one point, an invitation to a Richard Burton and Elizabeth Taylor party in Bel Air arrived. Wayne was excited, Lola noncommittal, Redford plain dismissive. "Work always preoccupied him," says Wayne. "Just work."

The movie was shot on the Warners lot, on location at Apple Valley and at the pier area of Santa Monica. "It was a milieu I knew like the back of my hand," says Redford, "and it should have been conducive to great work. As I saw him, Wade Lewis was mysterious, arrogant and charming, attractive to both sexes, but he could not be captured. Mulligan and Pakula seemed to buy into my vision of the character. But Gavin wasn't buying. I liked Gavin very much, and I was told he'd based Wade Lewis on Monty Clift. I knew enough by then to understand that a whole generation of actors like Rock Hudson lived the lie. But I did not want to go there. What I opted for was something sexually more subtle. I tried to depict an entirely different species: the insatiable hedonist, the guy who has the power and the appetite and uses them to screw men, women, dogs, cats, anything. A complete narcissist. A guy like Caligula, who doesn't care." Lambert insists Redford misread his, Pakula's and Mulligan's intentions: "I wrote Wade as a gay man. Apart from the one relationship he had with Melora, the wife of the studio boss, he was unwavering in his gayness. I thought that Bob had accepted that, and Mulligan and Pakula certainly went for those undercurrents." But Redford was emphatic: "I wanted to experiment. I wasn't aware about the waves I was raising. I was selfish in developing what I thought was a more complex character, and probably not respectful of the intentions of such a special, important writer. In ways, it was like my experience with Lettin and *The Seagull.* I was insisting on doing it my way, and maybe not the way the writer or director had interpreted it."

Wood clearly appreciated Redford's obduracy. In an interview she told *Photoplay:* "He's the most unbendable actor I know. He sticks to his principles when all about him are shedding theirs. He is unbribable by fame. He'd sooner starve than conform."

One incident during filming sealed the friendship between Wood and Redford. As they shot in a small boat off Santa Monica Pier, a sudden change in the wind direction cast them adrift in the Malibu current. Mulligan, on the unwieldy camera launch, attempted to leash the boat but snapped the retaining cables, breaking an assistant's leg. For twenty minutes Redford and Wood rode the squall, all the time moving farther out to sea. Wood, who hated the sea, panicked. Redford laughed her through it. "He was laughing so much, she surrendered and trusted him," said Mulligan. "Later, when he realized how precarious the situation really was, he sobered up. But that jock heroism impressed Natalie, and, as friends, they never looked back."

Rumors of an affair between them were rife on the set. Pakula observed "a natural connection that arose from mutual recognition of the rebel heart." According to Wood's personal assistant Howard Jeffrey, Natalie "fell head over heels for Redford" during the shoot, while accepting that "he not only looked like Jack Anderson, the all-American boy, but he lived like him as well." Redford admits to a great attraction to Wood and a closeness beyond friendship, "but I was aware very early on of the liabilities of intimacy with the women you act with. There are two industries: the film business and the parasite called the gossip industry, which can devour you. I loved Natalie's seriousness. She wasn't crazy like Monroe. She was the kind of girl who'd sit up all night writing notes: a trouper, the real thing. Nat and I became tight. When she married the agent Richard Gregson, I was her best man, and we stayed close until the end of her life" (with tragic irony, in a boating accident, off Catalina Island, in 1981).

Gavin Lambert, visiting the set, judged Redford, like Wood, an actor of instinct, not intellect. As the movie progressed, Lambert was surprised by Redford's intensity. Approaching a defining sequence, where Lewis interrogates himself in the dressing-room mirror before making love to Daisy, Redford sought out Lambert and insisted on his presence on the soundstage. "He felt it was critical to have me at hand," says Lambert, "undoubtedly because of the sexual plurality of what he was portraying. But he really didn't need me. He sailed through it, and I thought, My God, his comprehension is precocious. You'd expect it from someone who has made forty pictures, not someone who's made two. At the same time, his skill wasn't an intellectual one. It seemed more what we'd call a natural gift."

After seven weeks of filming, Redford was happy to be back in Provo for the first blaze of the spring flowers. In his diary he wrote that he was on the run again, hiding away on his hill, happy to be reunited with Lola and forgetting the calendar. In April, just before he left Los Angeles, Wood proposed a role for him in her next project, a Tennessee Williams adaptation for Seven Arts and Paramount called *This Property Is Condemned.* Redford met with Wood's producer, Ray Stark, and disliked him. "He had the character of the mercenary merchant who will say anything to get his way but can never be trusted. He lived like a Roman emperor merely because he lived beneath the Hollywood sign." The script, a leftover from an abandoned Taylor-Burton project, was poor. "The only appeal was Natalie. The script wasn't authentic Williams. It was a hundred pages blown up from a twenty-minute one-acter about two kids remembering the Depression that Williams himself didn't like. Ray Stark threw every writer he had at it, from John Huston to Francis Coppola, but none of them managed to get over the fact that it was a one-act play."

Rosenberg pressed Redford about maximizing his situation. Monique James reminded him that Louella Parsons was already formally announcing his arrival on the Hollywood star scene in the *New York Journal American.* His name, suddenly, was vying for space with Steve McQueen, Rock Hudson, Marlon Brando. The Brits were currently the toast of the town, with Sean Connery's James Bond and the Beatles dominating the media, but there was plenty of room for new Hollywood stars. Redford still dawdled. Then Wood informed him that she and Stark were in discussion with several interesting directors, among them Arthur Hiller, John Frankenheimer and Clive Donner, though none had been confirmed. Redford thought of his friend Sydney Pollack. Pollack had just completed his modest movie directorial debut, *The Slender Thread,* and had an option contract with Paramount.

Wood frowned. "Sydney Pollack? Who's he?"

"He's the new hot guy. You don't know about *The Slender Thread*? Have they been hiding him from you?"

Wood called in Pollack for an interview.

Pollack's progress in Los Angeles and New York had been as serpentine as Redford's, but he had won an Emmy for television directing, and *The Slender Thread,* a true-life story of a suicide hotline made for Warners, was gathering good notices. "We were butterflies emerging together," said Pollack. "There was this dark, depressive state we shared when we got together, and we were getting together a lot at that time. Night after night we drank and debated. We drove back and forth to Provo in his Porsche. We never stopped talking. A lot of the people around us were intellectuals. But we were autodidacts; we did it ourselves. We loved drama. We loved fantasy. We liked the idea of the Method but we hated the fad. For me, Kazan was king. But, like Bob, I hated all the pretentious existential heaviness. Basically we were on the same page and so all the time we shared seemed productive."

"Long before Sydney directed me," says Redford, "the director-actor dynamic was in play. It was a dialogue that could switch either way, real productive interactivity based on our curiosity about the world and a desire to put new spins on conventional platforms. Out of that bond came *This Property.*"

On Wood's say-so Pollack was assigned the job. While James Bridges labored on a new script and everyone waited, Rosenberg found the perfect project to fill the gap: Sam Spiegel, the producer of David Lean's hit *Lawrence of Arabia,* wanted Redford for Columbia's *The Chase,* to be directed by one of New York's most eminent emerging television directors, Arthur Penn. Spiegel, well educated in Europe and exiled by Hitler, was on his way to establishing his reputation as the world's most successful independent producer, maker of *On the Waterfront, The Bridge on the River Kwai* and *Suddenly, Last Summer.* Spiegel's reputation was founded on the literacy of his stories, his discernment in casting and the sheer size, ever growing in scale, of his productions. The script for *The Chase* was by Lillian Hellman, who had adapted Horton Foote's fifties play about mob rule. Redford read it and couldn't put it down. Superficially about a redneck murder hunt, it was layered with character insights and strong on metaphor. The story revolved around small-town Texan Sheriff Calder, under pressure in his community to find Bubber Reeves, who has escaped from prison. The oil-rich Val Rogers controls much of town life, and his son, Jake, is on edge because he has been having an affair with Anna, Reeves's wife. Calder attempts to bring Reeves in unharmed, against the will of Rogers as the scurrilous mob instincts rage.

Redford felt the script had the same power *The Treasure of the Sierra Madre* possessed. It was, clearly, less an entertainment than a commentary on human behavior. He was also stimulated by the extraordinary creative elements Spiegel had assembled. He had enjoyed Penn's prodigious *Playhouse 90* work and the string of stage triumphs that included *Two for the Seesaw* with Henry Fonda and *An Evening with Nichols and May,* and he was aware of Penn's movies, *The Left Handed Gun,* about Billy the Kid, and *The Miracle Worker,* about Helen Keller, both penetrating studies of parent-offspring relationships that examined the integral violence in human relationships. Most attractive was the casting: Robert Duvall, Angie Dickinson, Jane Fonda, E. G. Marshall and—best of all—Brando. "I was invigorated by the prospect of sharing screen time with Brando because I regarded him as an artist, like Robards," says Redford. "I was also open to whatever education he might give me by association."

The part on offer to Redford was Jake Rogers, the son of the oil magnate. Redford called Meta Rosenberg. "I'll do the film, but I want to play Bubber Reeves," he told her.

Rosenberg was shocked. "You're out of your mind," she told him. "That's the small part. That's the guy on the run who we hardly see till the end."

"But it was the better part," says Redford today. "It carried the movie, because Bubber's fate determines the moral values of the community. Bubber makes the movie's point. The role was also the renegade, done-down kid, and that was easy for me, since I'd considered myself an outsider to convention for a lot of my teens." Rosenberg reluctantly called Spiegel, who conceded and cast James Fox as Jake instead.

Arthur Penn had seen *Barefoot* on his friend Mike Nichols's recommendation. "Bob came to read at Sam's house," said Penn, "and he was super confident. I was wary because *Barefoot* left no impression on me. I was prejudiced, too, because the guys I preferred were the Actors Studio people. And I was also prejudiced because I thought he'd be better as Jake, despite what he wanted. But I was smitten. More than anything it was his physical impact. He was right. He automatically fulfilled the role of Bubber Reeves, the convict, because Bubber, for me, was a representational figure who symbolized the purity that was lost after Kennedy's assassination. He becomes a golden martyr. And Bob, the golden, confident guy, was exactly right for it."

In Foote's play, Reeves is a convict bent on revenge against the sheriff who locked him up. Lillian Hellman softened him, and Penn decided to introduce a strong parallel between Reeves's fate and the killing of Lee Harvey Oswald. "It seemed natural to me," he said. "There was a fortuitous intersection of recent events in American life and elements in Hellman's script. The murderer-patsy, the Texan locale and the statewide bloodlust hooked in my mind with the national paranoia after Dallas. I thought about how Oswald had never been legally tried, that it was the court of public opinion that got him. Then *The Chase* became a commentary on our gun culture. Reeves is someone who's been abused and fallen off the edge of society. When he escapes from the state prison farm and a man is accidentally killed, the small-town community that bred him wants him dead because he's the target for their life rage. That became very poignant to me." Hellman's final script disappointed Penn, however, "because it seemed more obsessed with the fetish behavior of too many minor characters—though it was still laden with potential."

Jane Fonda, cast as Bubber's wife, Anna, was curious about Redford and keen to work with him. She was a year younger than he, and her own relationship with acting had been bumpy. She had reluctantly tried it at Vassar before deciding, like Redford, instead to study art in Paris. The passion to act finally took hold when she played alongside her father in a production of *The Country Girl* in his hometown, Omaha. She was still, she says today, "pathologically hesitant," until Lee Strasberg persuaded her into the Actors

Studio and onto Broadway in a couple of so-so plays. Henry Fonda's friendship with Josh Logan led to her being cast in the movie version of *Tall Story,* her debut, but it took another few movies, among them *Sunday in New York,* before Stanley Kauffman in *The New Republic* was acknowledging her skill and "the hum of magnetism." A hit in France followed, with René Clément's *Les Félins,* before she met director Roger Vadim on the set of his *La Ronde* and returned to America in iconic splendor, "the American girl gone to sex," in Sheila Graham's famous description. Fonda was, she says, "awkward" about the sexual identification. "It always felt contrived, and so I was very open to directors like Arthur and earthy roles like Bubber Reeves's wife." *Cat Ballou,* a comedy western she had just completed, was a hit nominated for multiple Academy Awards that Fonda saw as a step onto the higher ground. *The Chase,* she felt, would be a worthy follow-up, "though, I have to say, I was about to settle into my marriage [with Vadim] and was emotionally compromised by debilitating personal insecurities as we began."

Spiegel told Fonda he'd chosen Redford because of his effect on women: "He was cast, Sam said, because of the reaction of women in the studio offices. They went all atwitter when he came in, and Sam judged that as the audience litmus. It was a fair criterion because I saw it myself. There are attractive people everywhere, but then there is that thing called charismatic attractiveness, which Bob had. A couple of years later, when we were making *The Electric Horseman* together, I witnessed it full force. A woman approached him at Caesars Palace in Vegas and said, 'Hello,' and then *literally fainted at his feet.* That kind of power is rare. Elvis had it, and Rudolph Valentino, and very few others."

Fonda, who previously only knew Redford as a face on the audition trail, found herself in thrall. "I didn't expect to fall so much under his spell. Looks apart, the first attraction was his humor. I was too much into myself to relax, and he drew me out because he was funny. Beyond that, I found echoes of myself in his darkness. The nature of the script, of whom we were portraying, also pushed us into deep waters. Like the characters in the script, we both had awkward childhoods. I had the same complicated relationship with my father that he had with his. I'd learned about how stardom happens, and my feeling was that he was bound for stardom. At the same time I saw a schizophrenic side: that he wanted this acting life while all the time resenting it, which is what I felt. Neither of us analyzed too openly, which was another thing we had in common. But the undercurrents of understanding were there, and they helped keep me going because, despite outward appearance, I was so personally very unsettled."

Redford was keen to work with Fonda, keener still to work with actors he admired who'd had Method training in New York. The role, however, was a fragmented one that meant a lot of prisoner-on-the-run physical movement, directed by the second unit, along the Russian River in northern California, with only a couple of dialogue scenes. Penn's shooting schedule was five months; Redford worked just five weeks, only two of which were in the company of Brando, Fox and Fonda. "To some extent," says Penn, "his was the most challenged role, because while he's on the run in the early part, he's a cipher. The action is like a chess game with the people in the town and their responses to the fugitive. Then in the last act, the last forty minutes of the film where Bubber returns to his hometown to face the mob, he is there in your face, explaining himself and his raison d'être, very suddenly and dramatically. Brando has dominated the picture till that point, then Bob is on equal airtime."

In the first act, the town's moral dissipation is counterbalanced by Brando's Calder, the Socratic sheriff who refuses to kowtow to either the feudal power brokering of E. G. Marshall's Val Rogers or the bloodlust of the mob. He holds the moral center, convinced that Bubber is a victim of circumstances. Then Bubber shows up, hiding out at the auto scrap yard by the wharf. When Anna comes to Bubber, leading Calder in order to save Bubber from the mob, Bubber is forced to face what awaits him. The nighttime scene is effectively the movie's climax, and the underlying emotions are the most complex Redford had yet handled—the mob wants a scapegoat; his family finds him confusing and pitiful; his wife loves another man. Reflecting on his two years in prison for a crime he didn't commit, Bubber says he's spiritually finished. Hellman's dialogue, hitherto prolix, becomes brilliantly sparse: "I'm done with myself," Bubber tells Anna. "When you're ready to die, no one can take away your freedom."

Redford's work was shaping up as his best to date. Throughout production, Penn was delighted with the performance, as, he says, he was pleased with Fonda. Redford, for his part, wrote in his diary that Brando was the best, that he was "role model stuff." Contrasting Brando's approach to Natalie Wood's demanding attitude to detail, Redford felt Brando "drifted on the breeze." Momentarily, the acting grail Redford sought was found. "Great acting," he wrote, "is no more than child's play. What a joy it is to look at it that way, to enjoy an extension of the great part of childhood. Fully. Self-indulgence. Spontaneous reactions, guilelessness, full and free. If you're really good, you are still a kid. Brando is good because he's a kid. He's acting because it's easy and he can get his jollies and still be a kid. Always playing around. Always. Talks like a kid. He just takes it in front of the cameras with him. He's no genius. Nor is he brilliant or anything like that. He's just a kid who stayed a kid. Fellini—a kid. *8½*—a kid's dream. He's jacking off royally, with a whole load of charm. Wonderful! God bless him!" As a footnote on the same page, he added: "I am glad I am a kid still. The answer is in the kid's eyes."

Ironically, the very self-indulgence Redford was cheering wore down the production. The trouble started, it appeared, when Spiegel began contesting Penn's direction. Brando, once fun, became perverse. There were now long, showy standoffs, phone call distractions, no-shows. "Whether Marlon was doing this to challenge Sam is another matter," Redford says. "I had a little rethink about him, and his process. On reflection, some of that internalized stuff bothered me. I later thought it was selfish and mean-spirited, because it seriously affected Arthur." Jane Fonda concurred: Brando, for her, was a major disappointment.

During the shooting of the finale, where Bubber, Anna and Jake are cornered by the mob, Fonda found herself in the trunk of a car at midnight, really getting to know Redford. "We ended up bunched together like little kids," she says, "waiting for our filming cue, just talking about our lives. Night shooting induces intimacy, so we were ready to open up." Redford talked about his wild days in Westwood and Van Nuys, about climbing the tower of the Fox Village Theater, about how mountains always challenged him. "Out of that conversation came a really devoted, understanding friendship that has lasted over the years," says Fonda. "Who can say why it works? Similar values, really, and a similar outlook about the world and its problems."

Political activism was a part of *The Chase* coterie—a new experience for Redford, as much as for Fonda. For the duration, Penn was dwelling in Sammy Davis Jr.'s Beverly Hills home, where he threw weekend fundraising parties for CORE, the Congress of Racial Equality, with which he'd long been involved. Brando, a supporter of Native American rights, was a regular guest, but Redford and Fonda tended to shy away. Fonda says her noninvolvement was because she was "politically ignorant." As for Redford, "he just wasn't social; tact went right over his head," says Fonda.

"It took him fifteen years, until we made *The Electric Horseman,* to learn to play the games of professional diplomacy, and even then his attitude was conditional." Redford was inspired by other things. "We had endless talks about this miraculous A-frame, which was his personal experiment in alternative living," said Penn. "More than anything, I got the impression that he wanted to be away in the hills, but I never got the time to crack him, because I was too busy fighting my own fights."

According to Penn, he was satisfied when he wrapped the movie in August. He oversaw the first assembly, but while he was fulfilling a theatrical directing contract, Spiegel took the half-cut footage to London to reedit to his liking. Some of Penn's most beloved scenes were consigned to the floor. "I was devastated," said Penn, "not because he took the plot, or my work, in a different direction, because he didn't. The movie was already there. But he selected the wrong shots. There were so many instances where the take he went for was the bad take, the one I would never have used. Cumulatively, it was a disaster." The film, released in February 1966, was not well received, though *Variety* liked Redford. He himself felt it had good and bad things in it—"and fortunately the good outweighed the bad."

Just weeks before *The Chase* opened nationally, Paramount opened *Situation Hopeless* quietly. It was just as well. Redford was appalled to learn that Reinhardt, like Spiegel, had botched the editing. Mike Connors had seen the rough cut and liked it but was horrified with the finished film: "Either Silvia or Gottfried changed *the* vital scene where the airmen who have been incarcerated break out of Herr Frick's basement and stumble on a movie crew shooting a war movie. They run scared, because they think it's a real battle. That's how we, the actors, played it, and that scene played beautifully. What came out in the end was something else entirely, where the airmen realize it's a movie and laugh it off. It became utterly meaningless, and it busted the movie."

This Property Is Condemned, meanwhile, was in development hell. Pollack was standing by, but Ray Stark had now brought in John Houseman to rescue the ailing script. Redford saw disaster coming and wanted to avoid it. He wrote in his diary, "I think that if Natalie gets nervous enough, she will say, 'Hold it!' and walk, she being a million-dollar property with the million-dollar career who really doesn't want to blow it. And that will be my out! If she goes, then I'm free."

In September, before *The Chase* was released, Redford lashed out. He had been informed that filming would begin in New Orleans in three weeks, but he had yet to see a usable screenplay. Summoned to Stark's office to review Houseman's latest version, he railed: "There is no character for me to play!" As a result, James Bridges started yet another rewrite, churning out twenty-five new pages a day, while Charles Eastman, a friend of Wood's, developed a parallel new script for her. Redford's diary records the chaos: "Natalie arrives, is furious. *She thinks.* She wants to know why her character, Alva, has been changed (she hasn't), why my part is now bigger, why Simone Signoret hasn't been cast as the mother (she is wrong for the part), or Vivien Leigh (she thinks the movie is a piece of shit) and why Charles Eastman hasn't been signed as the main writer."

Pollack stepped in as mediator: "I'd been through enough script crises on *Ben Casey.* I knew that it's usually a case of the more writers, the more mess. My feeling was we had to slough off these writers." Good-paying work on *The Fugitive,* another long-running series, had rewarded Pollack with a much-loved toy, a single-engine Cessna airplane. He flew to San Jose and locked himself in a motel room with two packing cases of scripts. "I threw out all the furniture except the bed and littered the floor with what we had, which was *fourteen* scripts. I took scissors, glue and a staple gun and assembled a matrix, which I then delivered to Bridges." During *The Slender Thread* he'd engaged the television playwright David Rayfiel to produce a literate script that would keep his stars, Sidney Poitier and Anne Bancroft, happy. Now he asked Rayfiel to save *This Property Is Condemned.* "David had the task of taking all the elements—mine, Natalie's and Bridges's—and blending them with dialogue *that worked.*" Pollack gave Rayfiel cash from his own pocket. Henceforth they would be lifelong collaborators, frequently fine-tuning Redford's projects.

Ray Stark, meanwhile, deliberated, calling endless meetings with Natalie, using extravagant home soirées as ersatz think tanks. Redford hated these afternoons chez Stark, peopled with odious glitterati served by liveried butlers, where Stark invariably referred to him as Sydney or Jim. On September 9, Redford bolted for Utah, where, in a phone call to Meta Rosenberg, he issued an ultimatum: "Either Stark shoots the movie Sydney Pollack's way *now,* or they can go sue my ass."

"It was down to Bob and me in the end," said Pollack. "Bob trusted me, just me, and we developed that mother together till we found something that was shootable. Not necessarily Tennessee Williams, but shootable."

This Property Is Condemned is set in Dodson, Mississippi, in the grip of the Depression. Owen Legate, played by Redford, is a railroad agent who arrives to lay off workers. Staying at a local boardinghouse, he begins an affair with Alva (Wood), the proprietor's daughter, a flirt who is also seeing laborer J. J. Nichols, played by Charles Bronson.

Filming started in October in New Orleans. If, as is often suggested, Pollack molded Redford's romantic iconography, the process began here. *This Property Is Condemned* had all the components of Williams—anguished hearts, gothic gloom, vivid backdrops, vibrant exchange—but there was much else besides. Henry Jamesian restraint, moody camera work and poignant music were the evolving Pollack staples, and they were used, unremittingly, to power up the romance. And it was, undeniably, romance that held the film together—subtle, substantial romance that drew force when counterpointed against grander-scale social conflict, a device that Pollack and Redford would return to in *The Way We Were, The Electric Horseman, Out of Africa* and *Havana.* "I had the feeling Bob and I were starting something," said Pollack, "because the uniqueness of the way we worked was something else. We were like composers, the music writer and the lyricist, putting together an effect, and that was what we set up there on the screen with *This Property.*"

Despite all its problems, despite the fact that Tennessee Williams insisted on removing his credit, *This Property Is Condemned* succeeded in many areas. It came in on time and just dimes over budget. Though Stark was equivocal, Pollack was satisfied and Redford and Wood liked it. Audiences, too, seemed to like it. However, *Newsday* called it "a horrendous soap opera" and *The New Yorker* blamed Wood. But *Variety* praised Redford's "total acting [through] voice, expression and movement," and in the New York *Daily News* Kathleen Carroll concluded: "[Redford] can't help but succeed now in the romantic leading man category."

Nothing would come so easily. During the shooting in New Orleans, John Frankenheimer, Pollack's friend, had visited, having just seen an early assembly of *Inside Daisy Clover.* "Frankenheimer said it was extremely daring of me to do what I did," says Redford, "but I hadn't seen the finished film and didn't know what he was talking about. I asked him and he said, 'Well, it takes guts for a start-out guy like you to play a flagrant gay character.' I told him that I didn't play a gay. I played Wade Lewis, the narcissist. And he said, 'You'd better take a look at what they have on release.' "

Redford was furious about what he saw as out-and-out perfidy. He told his tale to anyone who would listen. Mike Nichols listened, and agreed that Pakula and Mulligan "really fucked him over royally. Nothing to do with Bob's homophobia or lack of it. What he created on-screen they corrupted. They took out parts of the story as he'd filmed them and stuck on a voice-over telephone scene where some character tells Natalie in plain English, 'Didn't you know Wade is gay?' It was a complete turnaround for the story in his mind, and it upset him deeply."

By Christmas, Redford was wrestling with other problems. He had returned from Germany hopeful of career and family stability. But for half of 1965 the family was in Utah or New York while he was stuck in Los Angeles. There were long separations, stubborn, widening gossip about an affair with Natalie Wood and too many awkward, apologetic late-night phone calls. The talk of romance with Wood put the greatest pressure on his marriage. "It struck me that I was starting to 'go Hollywood' without noticing," says Redford. "I'd bought a flashy Lincoln Continental and started driving around like a head of state. It was ridiculous. After a couple of weeks I took it back to the dealer and told him to take it off my hands. I suppose I was succumbing to the temptations like everyone before me. It was stress, and compensation. I drank too much, spent too much; everything was as phony as the statues in Ray Stark's garden. I knew if I went on like that, my marriage, or I, would be dead inside a year."

On January 1, with no immediate movie commitment, the Redfords boarded an Italian liner bound for Gibraltar.

Paramount's start date for *Barefoot in the Park* was months away, so Redford had time to reorder his thoughts. Days before he left, he recorded in his diary the first stirrings to paint again, "watching Shauna, who is all the colors of the fall, a living Renoir." Europe, he wrote, was the place to do it, specifically Spain. This, his third European excursion, was different in every way from the previous adventures. Stan Collins, now managing investments at the Provo branch of stockbrokers Goodbody and Company, waved him goodbye "as if he were royalty. It wasn't like before. The first time, he had a suitcase. Now the family packed trunks." There were also influential theatrical and movie friends to bid them adieu. Richard Schickel, the critic for *Look* and *Show* magazines, came to the dock for the send-off. Schickel, who had been introduced to Redford by Carol Rossen, observed "a very courageous, or foolhardy, move, depending how you looked at it: here was a guy, the better part of ten years looking for a career, abandoning it as soon as it got moving. I thought he was nuts."

The family took up residence in Mijas, an hour from Gibraltar, in January 1966. Redford took to sitting on an iron chair in the garden of the rented villa, just staring. For almost a month he hardly talked. Lola and the kids, familiar with this isolation, concentrated on fashioning a new home for themselves. "I had no practical plan," says Redford. "I wanted to paint and read, that's all."

The Andalusian coast Redford opted for was hardly a primitive Eden. Mijas was part of the fast-developing Costa del Sol, haven for the privileged likes of Aristotle Onassis and the Duke and Duchess of Windsor, who had hideaway haciendas there. What had been, in the fifties, farmland dotted with fishermen's cottages and Arab forts was now prime real estate. The previous year, *Life* magazine's William Sansom extolled the best of what remained in a feature titled "The Great Game of Getting Away from It All": "Dress is heterodox. Anything goes, from a Hawaiian shirt to a black sombrero. Students, of course, look like students, and beats like beats"—and all of this against a fading backdrop of "an Arcadian agricultural scene where oxen pull the plow between groves of olives and almonds, and limes and lemons loom as large as boxing gloves."

Mijas was an olive growers' community the size of Greenwich Village, where the writer Robert Storey and Prince Bernadotte of Sweden lived. The Redfords' villa, outside the town, was sparse, white and capacious, with an empty swimming pool in the yard and the hills of Churriana beyond. The unique square bullring was a ten-minute walk along the switchback two-lane road that led to the coast. Redford took to walking this steep road daily, winding down among the olive terraces to the seaside village of Fuengirola for wine and provisions. Jamie's first clear memories of his father are of these days of decompression. "I was vaguely aware of my dad as a life force, but, for us, the home revolved around Mom," Jamie says. "Looking back, I realize he was fighting his demons. But he was a buoyant force. Once he got moving, he was never inactive. There was a drama about him, and that affected all of us."

Shauna had enrolled at the Dalton School in Manhattan and Jamie was due to begin there that spring, but the trip upended the plan. In later life, Jamie and Shauna would both observe that education was a priority in their father's eyes. "But at that time," says Jamie, "he truly felt there was more to be learned traveling than studying." Jamie has hazy but happy memories of these Spanish days. "I enjoyed it, except for the Semana Santa Easter festival. It was a crucifixion scenario, where the faithful parade through the streets reenacted the journey to Calvary. But this wasn't play-acting. It was extreme self-mortification. There was blood everywhere, and the person playing Christ was actually nailed to the cross. It was upsetting for a kid of four to endure, but Dad thought it was okay, that it was honest cultural exposure, which I guess it was." Jamie is less sure of the outing to the local butcher's shop, in preparation for Sunday lunch: "Right before my eyes, they slaughtered a lamb and cut it up. Okay by Dad, not okay by me. I hollered the place down." Redford himself saw this exposure as "my own reenactment of how I'd learned the rules from Tot and Gil in Texas. It was like my mom being thrown into Barton Springs to sink or swim. It was tough love, but I didn't feel it was excessive." He hesitates. "Well, maybe a little excessive."

The dreams of painting Shauna in all her Renoir colors disappeared in the dazzling distractions of summer. Like the French Riviera, the Costa del Sol doubled its population from May through September, and well-wishers came to the Redfords' villa with letters from mutual friends in New York and Los Angeles. Gradually the social whirl absorbed Redford, displacing the meditations on career and family. The writer Tom McGuane was one of many houseguests. "It was pleasant," says Redford, "but it was a diversion I didn't want. I began to understand that the community I was fantasizing about wasn't on the *costa.* It was really just a combination of Palm Springs and the dropout guys." Redford indulged, but became frustrated when he encountered the partner of Lorenzo Semple Jr., the Hollywood screenwriter, on a pathway one day. The men conversed, and it emerged that Lorenzo was living down the road, writing *Batman* scripts that were then sent by overnight courier to ABC in Los Angeles. "I thought, That's it! This is just another Hollywood-on-location. Time to get out of here."

The family made for Crete instead. Here he mimicked Henry Miller again, settling down on the island's north shore. Jamie and Shauna loved the fantasy tour and the high spirits. "It all stepped up a gear," says Jamie. "Suddenly it was lectures about myths and monsters, and they all scared me stiff. Dad lived for this storytelling. I can see myself sitting on some beach, and him telling me about the Cyclops that lived in the cave there." The family stayed in Iráklion, exploring the coastal sweep from Chania to Sitia and the long, winding hiking trails of Europe's longest gorge, the ten-mile Samaria, flanked on one side by the White Mountains and on the other by the cypress forests of Mount Volikas. Bit by bit the diary, and the conceit of bohemian living, were lost to the joys of what Redford calls "a simple extended family vacation with a little bit of social research thrown in." He knew now that he had outgrown the part of Beat bum, that he was a family man with duties and gifts to give. "The days in Irák-

Grandmother Lena Taylor Redford in New London, Connecticut, circa 1950. She was the source of Irish yarns and embodied the austerity of working-class New London. *(Courtesy of Robert Redford)*

Redford's father, Charles, in Los Angeles in 1934, shortly before his marriage to Martha Hart *(Courtesy of Robert Redford)*

David, Redford's uncle, around the time he enrolled at Brown University. A Rhodes scholar and war hero, he was the greatest adventuring influence on Redford's young life. He died in World War II. *(Courtesy of Robert Redford)*

Playtime with Uncle David, 1942.
"It was always games. He and Mom fired my imagination." *(Courtesy of Robert Redford)*

In Texas with Martha and Charlie in 1943. Redford felt he had "found a kind of frontier" on the shores of Lake Austin. *(Courtesy of Robert Redford)*

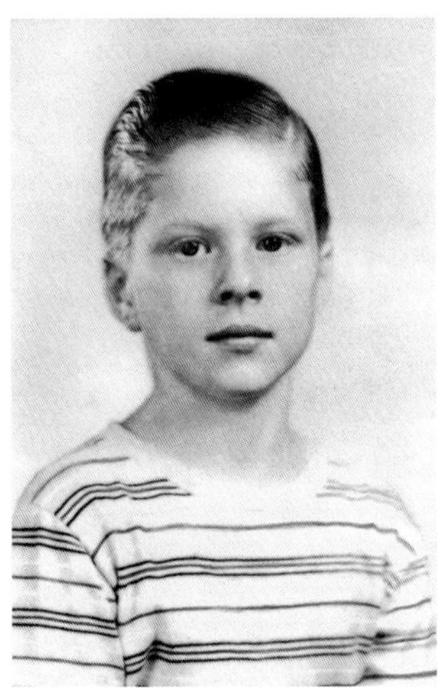

Redford at ten, 1946
(Courtesy of Robert Redford)

At the Bantam Club on San Vincente Boulevard, 1949.
Redford is in the front row, second from left.
(Courtesy of Kathleen Andrews)

With Bill Coomber *(far left)* and Chip Crosby, brother of David Crosby of the Byrds. Redford was aware he was pushing teenage rebellion toward delinquency. "We were out of control," says Coomber.
(Courtesy of Robert Redford)

Saying good-bye to Martha in the fall of 1954 as he leaves for Boulder, where he would enroll at the University of Colorado.
(Courtesy of Robert Redford)

Redford's artwork from Boulder.
"I had no interest then in American abstract art,
or the current movements.
I thought I might be a good animator."
(Courtesy of Robert Redford)

Scouring the art galleries of Paris, 1956.
Jack Brendlinger kept Redford company,
but he was happiest alone, quartering the city.
(Courtesy of Jack Brendlinger)

"By the time we got to Italy," says Brendlinger, "we were living on cheese and bread and whatever we could bum off anyone we met."
(Courtesy of Jack Brendlinger)

Cannes, winter 1956. Despite the glamorous pose, Redford was penniless. He slept on the beach in front of the Carlton Hotel. *(Courtesy of Jack Brendlinger)*

Redford with Frances Fuller, the director of the American Academy of Dramatic Arts in New York, who oversaw his admission to acting studies *(Courtesy of the American Academy of Dramatic Arts, New York)*

Rehearsing with fellow AADA student Ginny Burns. "I was in awe of his freedom," says Ginny. "When he recited 'The Raven' he literally flew around the room." *(Courtesy of Ginny Burns Kelly)*

Rehearsing scenes from Arthur Miller's *All My Sons* in an academy workshop, winter 1958 *(Courtesy of Robert Redford)*

With director Francis Lettin, who cast Redford in Chekhov's *The Seagull* and was impressed by the actor's determination to break the mold *(Courtesy of the American Academy of Dramatic Arts, New York)*

First publicity shot, 1962. "I was beginning to think I might like to be an actor." *(Courtesy of Robert Redford)*

lion were among the best, but I knew I had to come back, that it was important for me to build a future for my family."

In July, Stan Collins received a postcard from Crete in which Redford described his change of heart. Lola had suffered enough waiting for the career break; now, wrote Redford, "she's on the spending trail, cutting through Europe like a Mack." Redford recalls, "We did indulge ourselves. We overspent like crazy, but I was confident that I had a career to come back to and a check in the pipeline."

The check he was referring to was for the movie of *Barefoot in the Park,* this time costarring Jane Fonda, assigned to television director Gene Saks when Nichols turned it down. Redford was refreshed by his sabbatical and, in a more profound way, renewed. Stan Collins believes the trip had "sorted out his marriage and his family and got his discipline back in order." Shauna, too, felt the Mediterranean trip had sharpened his perspective. "He had something to work out of his system, relating to his place in acting and, maybe more importantly, to his place in a marriage," she says. "When he came back, it was new ideas and new energy."

Upon his return from Crete in early fall, committed though he was to *Barefoot,* he went to see Mike Nichols, who was in the middle of preparing a movie adaptation of Charles Webb's novel *The Graduate.* Redford immediately pushed, says Nichols, to audition for the role of Benjamin, the sexual innocent seduced by the middle-aged Mrs. Robinson. In October, just days before the scheduled start of *Barefoot,* Nichols, against his instincts, conceded to a screen test. In the screen test, shot with Candice Bergen, Nichols was troubled by Redford's robust, suntanned presence. "I told him he was wrong for it," says Nichols, "but he wouldn't let it go. I was living in Brentwood and he came for supper and we shot some snooker and he went on and on about his ability to play the part. He said he perfectly understood the character, who was a social misfit. I finally said to him, 'Bob, you're a vastly talented man. But be honest with yourself. Look in the mirror. Do it. And then tell me: Can you honestly imagine a guy like you having difficulty seducing a woman?' He couldn't answer me, because it was self-evident. A guy who looked like Dustin Hoffman could play Benjamin. A guy who looked like Redford would be a joke."

As the five-week shoot for *Barefoot* began, Fonda and Redford looked forward to reconnecting. "There was a certain amount of balancing to be done in the day-to-day rehearsals," says Fonda, "because I was the newcomer to this text and he had the role down pat. But he was a gentleman.

He let Gene do what he had to do, and he made room. He never preached, and anytime I needed redirection he contributed caringly. He would take Gene aside and make the point in private, then Gene would coach me." Redford had been worried about staleness with the Bratter character. "It's something I knew could get in the way," he says, "so I pushed to get through that barrier." He joyfully renewed friendships with the members of the Broadway cast. "I'd forgotten how much I'd enjoyed Milly Natwick and Herb Edelman. Herb was my type of guy, the court jester who bought people little gifts and tried to make them laugh all the time. That was great, because moviemaking gets boring."

For Gene Saks, a veteran of *Armstrong Circle* and *Kraft Theater* live broadcasts and an old friend of Neil Simon's, the most important task was overcoming Redford's boredom. Saks recalls: "Bob wanted to remind everyone every day that he wasn't as starchy and uptight as Bratter. So whenever I called, 'Cut!' he threw off the suit and tie and loafed." Redford agrees that "boredom" was the key challenge. "I'd taken Bratter everywhere I could, and the character was just hot air compared with, say, Parritt in *The Iceman Cometh* or the stuff I'd done with Sydney on *This Property Is Condemned.*" Neil Simon, only just embarking on his movie writing with the concurrent Peter Sellers movie, *After the Fox,* had adapted his own play, adding little more than the obvious outdoors expansion, where Bratter finally gets to actually walk barefoot in Washington Square Park. "What gets interesting, in those circumstances, is the chance to break down the mechanism," says Redford. "You have done the play as an organic whole; now you are assembling the collage in film style and you get to see some new things. You say, 'Hey, I could do this just with my eyes' or 'Hey, I could do this sotto voce.' Gene helped. He was adaptable and he knew he'd get the best from me by letting me take it wherever I could."

Fonda was happy with the outcome. "It was light entertainment," she says. "Neither Bob nor I saw it as a career movie. It was marking time, a movie with a nice script and a nice director. Sometimes that's enough."

During days off, Redford spent time with his Van Nuys High School buddy Dave Brockman. Brockman, who had shared a hot-rod fanaticism with the teenage Redford, had always suffered from depression; now Redford noticed a sharp decline. As Thanksgiving approached, he invited Brockman to visit Utah for the holiday. "I had a sense that it might be important for him to get away, and I looked forward to reconnecting and finding out what was wrong." But the production schedule necessitated an overnight trip to New York to shoot the Washington Square Park exteriors the day after Thanksgiving. The Redfords had to withdraw the invitation to Brockman. Over the weekend Brockman gassed himself to death in the garage of his home in the Valley. Redford was devastated. "I felt responsible. I always had this thing that death was on my shoulder, 24/7. My dogs, as a kid. My uncle. My mom. My firstborn. A darkness right on top of me."

Redford headed west when *Barefoot* wrapped, resuming the Provo–Los Angeles circuit, driving his new stripped-down 904 racing Porsche like a maniac, disappearing for days on end. Peer Oppenheimer, a journalist he'd met in Spain, reported a gathering storm in a piece written for *Family Weekly* titled "The Hide-and-Seek Life of Robert Redford." "The danger of success," Redford told Oppenheimer, "is that it forces you into a mold. I prefer independence." In fact, what he was seeking was a purpose beyond movies. "I was aware that all this spiritual shit was a nightmare for the family," Redford now says. "I had anger management issues; there were a lot of unresolved conflicts." For succor he turned to Utah, to Mormon conviviality and the mountains. In a copartnership with Stan Collins, he put up $8,000 to purchase Hoover's Clothing Store, a fifteen-thousand-square-foot property in Provo that specialized in ski gear. The venture failed, with only the ladies' fashion basement, which Lola managed, showing a profit. "I thought it would be a lark, but it was a burden. At the end of the day, it was just a store, just money. It meant nothing."

What he was really searching for, Redford says, was peace of mind. Nothing could calm him. "I'd replaced the booze with pills. Stan introduced me to a diet pill that was supposed to keep me in shape, but it fried my brains. I took Seconal for sleep, but I was wired and yet tired all the time."

Talk of westerns filled his evenings. He had, he told Pollack, a new regard for them. Gene Saks had observed that, during *Barefoot,* whenever he was relaxing, Redford would "strip off Bratter's suit and opt to wear a Stetson and boots to let us know who he really was." *The Virginian,* Redford told Pollack, was one of his best experiences, "because of the story values and the character authenticity." Pollack was at work on a gritty western for Burt Lancaster, United Artists' *The Scalphunters,* about a trapper at war with the Indians who steal his hides. Pollack had come to it excitedly, having learned the western ropes from his TV years. "Like most Americans, Bob and I shared the experience of growing up on a diet of John Ford and John Sturges," said Pollack. "It was a secondary education, this western thing, a birthright information source. We were also equally irritated by the phoniness of it. For *The Scalphunters,* I discussed it with Burt and we made a conscious decision to deglamorize it. Same with Bob. We started talking about creating a movie like *My Darling Clementine.* We'd say, 'If we get the chance, we'll break some ground, we'll do it different.' "

Now, as the third movie in Redford's three-picture contract, Paramount offered him *Blue,* a script by television writer Ronald Cohen set in the disputed no-man's-land between Mexico and Texas in the 1850s. The story was a gritty romance about a Mexican bandit who falls for a Texan, to the chagrin of his family. Redford felt an immediate attachment: here was the borderland, Tot's territory. For a few weeks he researched the background enthusiastically. Then, in a planning meeting, the executive overseeing his contract at Paramount, Bob Evans, casually informed him he'd also signed Silvio Narizzano, the Canadian director riding high on the current British pop hit *Georgy Girl.* Redford winced. "I thought this was wrong. In my view, *Blue* would only work as a movie of historical reverence, never as a pop film."

During the early discussions about *Blue,* Redford experienced a clear understanding of the limitations of defining himself solely, or even principally, in movie terms. "Movie stardom was never going to do it for me. Neither was Hoover's retail store, or diet pills," he says. "Many of my Mormon friends, like Stan, saw my struggle as a religious crisis. And then the pressures for conversion came on, very kindly, very committed, very determined. I was courted, I was given Mormon literature, and though they tried, I was not blessed. The more they pushed me to commit to the Church, the more I pulled away."

After Christmas, Stan Collins and his wife, Mary Alice, invited the Redfords on a driving trip to Lake Powell, one of the country's biggest man-made reservoirs, in southern Utah. The couples stopped at Gallup, New Mexico, and Redford rambled around on the Navajo reservation. It was five years since his Pacific-bound train had stopped for water at Gallup and the face at the window incited a healing Zen moment. "This time around I took my time. I explored and really lost myself in the culture," he says. "It blew me away. I felt at peace and at home, with the faces, the postures, everything." Redford talked to the traders, sat in the dirt to play with face-painted kids. "Some drunken Navajo called me Bonfaccio, and it stuck. From then on, to myself, I was Bonfaccio, the white interloper. Bonfaccio became a moniker and it was the name I wrote on the clapper slate when I first signed myself as director of *Ordinary People.*"

Since his preteens he'd been reaching for a bridge of understanding between the two contrasting Americas of his parental origins: the frontier Texas of Tot and the urban East Coast world of Tiger. During *The Chase,* the activism of Brando, Penn and CORE had teased his awareness of Native American and minority issues, and in November, as he finished *Barefoot,* the eruption of youth politics in the Sunset Strip riots, where a coalition of liberals protested the overdevelopment of L.A., further focused him. At Lake Powell, contemplating *Blue,* he believed he had achieved some liberating clarity.

Purchasing Timp, he reflected, was about reconciliation. It seemed fated, even, for it was close by in 1869 that the golden spike was driven into the ground at Promontory Summit, to mark the joining of railroads from east and west. He was attracted to Indian culture, he decided, because it was the root of *all* Americas. Redford calls this the moment of awareness that presaged his sense of stewardship about the canyon and also his commitment to explore the diversity of American culture, which would later be foundational in his creation of the Sundance Institute. "There's always a key moment," he says. "That was mine."

Soon afterward, a silversmith Hopi called Fred Kapote made Redford the ring he still wears today. It depicts a turtle, representing patience and endurance—two staples that would be well tested in the days ahead. In the spring, he was ready to face Bob Evans and the fight for a role beyond stardom.

11

Toward Concord

Barefoot in the Park opened at Radio City Music Hall in the summer of 1967. It earned $9 million, five times its budget, in the first six weeks, a resounding success. But Redford had an appetite for change, and change was in the air. America was agitated. Disillusioned by the Bay of Pigs fiasco, anxious because of the missile crisis, the death of Kennedy and the war in Vietnam, Americans everywhere were reappraising core values. This was the year Brian Wilson retired the Beach Boys' California Dream and the Beatles metamorphosed from mop-topped innocents to Sgt. Pepper's Lonely Hearts Club Band. It was also the year Andy Warhol brought his avant-garde movies to the marketplace at Cannes. Change was everywhere.

Redford listened to *Sgt. Pepper's,* grew his hair, explored magic mushrooms as an alternative to hash. "There's no question that a fresh wind was blowing," he says. "People were impatient for answers, for newness. But new and good don't necessarily correspond. This was at the center of my thinking when I saw what Paramount was attempting with *Blue.*"

After several contentious script meetings at which Redford felt "the wrong sensibilities entirely" were being imposed on a western story, a date was finally agreed for production of *Blue* to commence. Redford was troubled because he had found Narizzano evasive and he didn't trust Evans in his promise of a new script. He set out, however, by train from New York to join the production. "Halfway to Arizona," he says, "I got off and rang Meta. I told her it wasn't going to happen. I'd been promised sight of a final draft of the script but it was withheld from me. I said, 'I'm sorry. I think this is going to be a very different movie from the one I signed up for. So I'm out.' "

Paramount's wrath seemed inevitable. The company had just come through a corporate takeover and the biggest reshuffle in its fifty-year existence. The previous October, Gulf + Western Industries, a conglomerate encompassing mining, manufacturing and finance companies and founded by entrepreneur Charles Bluhdorn in 1957, offered Paramount's embattled shareholders an acquisition deal for 10 percent more than the market price. Since its creation by Adolph Zukor, Paramount's fortunes had risen and fallen. It was, of course, one of the Big Five that dominated Hollywood, and its star roster was unmatched. Valentino, William S. Hart, Mae West, the Marx Brothers, Humphrey Bogart, Gary Cooper, Bing Crosby and Grace Kelly had all been contract players, and the studio had made classic works like *Sunset Boulevard* and *The Ten Commandments.* But in the forties an antitrust initiative required that Zukor sell off his theaters. Then television began making its mark. The record profits of $20 million in 1949 fell to $6 million in 1950. But Bluhdorn envisioned a fusion with other entertainment media and decided to take a chance. His area of specialization was the Caribbean sugar industry, but he was hot for Hollywood. Bluhdorn's bid for Paramount was accepted by the shareholders, and he quickly proved his worth by establishing the Leisure Time umbrella, comprising Paramount, the publisher Simon and Schuster and New York's Madison Square Garden. As movie ticket sales, in decline since the mid-fifties, started an upswing in the late sixties, there were those who regarded Bluhdorn as a visionary as well as a good businessman. His passion, he told everyone, was making Paramount the industry leader.

To Redford, Bluhdorn, who was just seven years older than he was, at first seemed fatherly. "He was this nice, silver-haired, big-smile guy who just shook my hand with enthusiasm and said, 'Gee, this is a great moment for me. You're the first movie star I've ever met.' " Three months later, after Redford had balked at *Blue,* Bluhdorn was launching a $250,000 lawsuit against him.

Redford's assets amounted to not much more than $100,000, and his personal debts topped $50,000. He had no contracts in hand, and no clear picture of the direction of his acting career. On top of this, Paramount was enjoining him from working until a settlement was reached. Redford's response was knee-jerk. He changed agents, lawyers and business partners. Meta Rosenberg, who challenged his reasoning on *Blue,* was replaced by Natalie Wood's new boyfriend, the former London International Artists' agent Richard Gregson, who had come to Los Angeles to find talent for new British films. Gregson moved quickly from agent to production partner. The priority, though, was legal advice. Redford felt he had been badly served: "One of the great lessons of the movies in the sixties was the need for *inventive* legal support. The situation might be likened to environmental law, which didn't exist in the sixties. In movies, the studios had been so all-controlling that personal lawyers were weaklings. Now it was the new era, and I needed someone more imaginative than lawyers who were old-school studio-serving guys." At the Dalton School, Shauna and Jamie were friends with the Frankfurt kids, whose father, Steve, was Redford's age and the youngest president ever of Young and Rubicam, the global ad agency. During social evenings, Steve introduced Redford to his brother Mike, a partner in a small law firm. The trio bonded. "Their whole family attitude was can-do," says Redford. "It was amazingly refreshing after the narrowness of L.A. movie lawyers." Bronx-born, the Frankfurts had humble beginnings but saw their father claw his way to prosperity. "Our father was an original," says Mike Frankfurt, "a small-time lawyer who made a great life for his family by high-risk rolling. His motto was, 'If we go to the poorhouse, we take a cab,' and that was the principle I built my own legal practice on, and the one that attracted Bob."

Mike Frankfurt was a pragmatist who immediately saw that Redford's great asset was the popularity engendered by *Barefoot.* "I saw that he had a lot going for him," says Frankfurt, "but I also saw how the dice were loaded. Paramount had a good case. The fact that Bob's concerns about *Blue* weren't game playing but genuine creative concerns was almost incidental. One sympathized with Bluhdorn, who was looking for good news for the Paramount shareholders. He didn't need troublemakers. From my perspective, it was a simple issue of utilizing Bob's popularity and going in hard to meet in the middle. There was nothing to be gained for anyone by standing their ground and calling each other names. We needed them, and they needed us. So we must compromise, forgive, deal and move on."

In the end, Paramount dropped the injunction in return for Redford's agreement to make two movies for a combined fee of $65,000, followed by three further films. Redford was not happy about the arrangement but was mollified by Mike Frankfurt's creation of a far better boilerplate for all future contracts. "I worked closely with Gregson," says Frankfurt. "Richard would use his European contacts to drum up some business. Contractually, from now on, we'd market Bob on the assumption that he had broken through. We needed to rewrite the rule book. Henceforth, we would require a percentage of the gross, and Bob would have script approval and casting approval written into all deals, like Natalie Wood and every other big star."

Early on it seemed the two films Redford would make to fulfill his initial commitment would be Abraham Polonsky's *Tell Them Willie Boy Is Here,* a Universal western based on true events that Paramount was happy to loan him out for, and an adaptation of Oakley Hall's novel *The Downhill Racers,* to be directed by Roman Polanski. Robert Evans, now studio vice president, had brought Polanski over from Europe specifically to make a movie about skiing, which was the director's favorite pastime, though *Rosemary's Baby,* another pet project, had taken precedence. Earlier, in the planning stages of *Rosemary's Baby,* Redford had met with Polanski. In his memoirs, Polanski wrote that he wanted Redford for the lead in his horror movie, but the meeting went awry when Redford arrived in a wig and a false beard to deflect legal servers, only to be cornered by a lawyer. Polanski claimed, somewhat bizarrely, that the information had been leaked by Evans, who wanted to dampen a Redford-Polanski friendship. The legal papers, Redford explains, arose from an incident at a restaurant where he had punched a paparazzo. "I don't believe Evans was opposed to me working with Roman," he says.

Soon after, Polanski was in trouble with Evans because he was running late on *Rosemary's Baby* and incurring heavy costs. Rumor had it that Evans was on the point of dumping the ski project. Redford saw an opportunity. "I believe that I was screwed by Evans and the makers of *Blue,*" says Redford, "and I wanted Bluhdorn to know what really occurred. I bided my time. I knew I had to wait till the lawsuit was settled, but then I went to him and told him in detail the promises that were made, and how I was let down. He was most understanding. He said, 'That's bad. I had no idea. I hope Paramount can make it up to you.' " Redford made his proposal there and then to Bluhdorn. If Evans ditched Polanski, Redford wanted to step in and take over the ski movie, maybe set it up as a flagship project for the production company he was in talks with Gregson and Frankfurt about. "Charlie was very decent," says Redford. "He didn't mess around. 'Okay,' he said. 'Here's the deal. If you can make this skiing movie for less than $2 million, it's yours to do.' "

It was an exhilarating moment—for Frankfurt, Gregson and Redford. "We knew we had an opportunity par excellence," says Frankfurt. "The way I saw it, Bob had managed to turn a terrible, career-compromising lawsuit into a production company!"

Redford had only just begun to ski. He also lacked production experience, as did Gregson and Frankfurt. "But I knew it was my best option," says Redford. "Firstly, it represented autonomy. If I could crack it with my own production company, I had choices beyond the studio or the agent. Secondly, I would in principle be in a situation where I could control the integrity of a production. As a producer, I could have my say in what appeared on-screen, like Spiegel did." Indeed, Redford's first decision was that the skiing movie would be shot in Europe. "For me, Europe was still the big tease. I'd seen the mountains of Italy and Switzerland. I knew it would all be extraordinary on film. But I also knew the cost would be twice what Charlie was offering if we went the Europe route. It didn't worry me. It was a chance to build my own film for the first time."

Redford's team named their production company Wildwood, after a fork in the road leading to Timp Haven. It was to operate out of the West Los Angeles office of Richard Gregson. "Bob's confrontation with Bluhdorn took balls," says Frankfurt. "But this was the sixties, remember, and we took chances. It wasn't just Bob, it was everyone." Redford's courage was fed, says Frankfurt, by the new social circles in which he was moving: "New York was his power pack. He'd begun to hang around with some smart, motivated people. And it struck me that he was quite tactical about these friendships." Among the Redfords' new friends were Ilene Goldman and her husband, Bill, a novelist and recent screenwriter, who was just finishing a big speculative script called "The Sundance Kid and Butch Cassidy," based on folklore surrounding two of the Wild West's most controversial bandits. Redford also befriended the new liberal mayor of New York, John Lindsay, a friend of Steve Frankfurt's. "Those were dynamic days," says Frankfurt. "So much was happening with youth culture, the Brit invasion, black actors like Sidney Poitier finally making the mainstream, Bobby Kennedy championing the poor. There was a feeling of real cultural rebirth, and all our conversations were filled with massive ideas of all the great changes that *could be.* Bob was at the head of the pack, thinking *big.*"

Before the ink was dry on the Wildwood shareholding papers, Redford astonished Frankfurt with the audacity of another, grander scheme. Timp had begun to obsess him. It was more than a family hideaway. It was a place of history. Redford told Frankfurt he had become "soul-bound" to the canyon, which to him was "a slice of John Muir's America." Lola and the kids used the A-frame during summers and through the holidays. "But for Bob," says Frankfurt, "it was much more than a vacation home." The bordering lands were all owned by the Scottish Stewarts, who had staked their claim in 1900 under the terms of the Desert Land Act and displaced the remnants of the roving Ute Indian tribe. The Stewarts first started a sheep farm, then in the fifties the brothers Ray and Paul Stewart developed the mountainside opposite into a Tyrol-styled ski resort that attracted hundreds of locals all through the winter. Timp Haven, as the resort was called, was on its last legs when Redford started buying acreage around the old sheep pasture. What remained was a Polynesian-themed timber refreshment hut called Ki-Te-Kai ("Come and get it" in Maori), an old T-bar lift and a grassy slope. Redford loved visiting. The winter skiing had become a social highlight of his year, and the Lindsays, the Schickels, the Goldmans and the Frankfurts joined in for seasonal weekends on the slopes.

Sitting on the perimeter fence of the homestead one day, admiring Timpanogos with Frankfurt, Redford said, "I'd like to own it all, Mike."

Frankfurt smiled. "What? A mountain? You'd like to own the entire canyon?"

"Yep. I'd like to make sure no one screws it up. I mean it. Could we afford it?"

Frankfurt remembers thinking, He doesn't have the cash to own it, but he'd make the perfect custodian. Redford explained that a few days earlier Stan Collins had informed him that the Stewarts were negotiating a sale to two rival property developers. "Their plan was for tract housing," says Frankfurt. "Clear the screw pines, dig into the ski slopes, build, build, build." Frankfurt recalls that Redford was upset by the plan. "He said, 'Can you imagine why anyone would just ditch this beautiful place for money?' It was so heartfelt that I was moved. I told him, 'Okay, you want the whole canyon? The answer is no—you cannot afford it. But let's give it a shot anyway. There are tax breaks for second properties. We can leverage. We can be inventive. It might work.' "

At that moment, says Redford, the notion of an arts sanctuary was not in his thoughts: "I wanted to preserve the land, that was all." Stephanie Phillips, an agent who had begun working with Redford, recalls it differently: "I know Bob says that, but in my memory he already had more than a hunch about what this property could eventually be used for. We were in the middle of a cultural revolution in America. So much was changing, with the counterculture, with entertainment. Bob was onto it. Even then, at the very start of his expansion in the canyon, the idea was fermenting. Here, he thought, can be a haven for the arts, an experimental place. New York and Los Angeles were the centers, of course, but he was pondering how he could bring this virgin hinterland into the equation."

Frankfurt turned to a friend, the Los Angeles lawyer Gary Hendler, for advice on acquiring a substantial acreage from the Stewarts. Hendler's advice was to use the 1966 tax break for second-home purchases to obtain credit. He agreed with Frankfurt that the lands could then be sustained by expanding the recreation facilities, while holding development in check. Accordingly, two separate plots were purchased that defined a large family estate for the Redfords north of the ski area and, on the opposite side of the Alpine Loop road, the nascent resort itself. The family estate amounted to 1,179 acres; the resort, 2,200 acres. The cost, almost entirely leveraged, including the resort's assets, was $1.6 million.

On August 5, 1968, in a press conference at the Utah Travel Council in Salt Lake City, the deal was announced. Wildwood Developments, a company composed of Redford, Frankfurt, Bob Gottschalk (Frankfurt's business partner), Boston banker Hans Estin and Stan Collins, would relaunch Timp Haven as a year-round public recreation venue. From the podium, Frankfurt said the business objective was to double current facilities "while still maintaining the present beauty of the area." To ensure year-round business, there would be a snowmaker installed and a lodge built to draw the vacationers who usually gravitated to Colorado. Eventually, said Frankfurt, a Swiss-type village would be erected, "with architecture strictly controlled to maintain uniformity and harmony with the natural surroundings." Redford then took center stage, emphasizing that "the new enterprise will be geared toward family recreation," emphasizing camping, fishing and riding. "As a business plan it looked okay," Frankfurt remembers. "But there were disadvantages, the biggest being Bob. Yes, he wanted to preserve the canyon and he was prepared to operate a ski resort to fund it all. But truly, he wanted it all for himself. He didn't want snowmakers and hospitality lodges. He wanted a fiefdom that he would invest *himself* in. And he wanted to personalize it with a name that was dear to him."

Frankfurt was about to turn in late one night in New York when Redford called from Utah. "I got the magic name," he said. "I want to call it Bougainvillea."

Frankfurt said, "Forget it, Bob. Not only will no one remember the name, they'll never be able to spell it. Think of something else."

Ever since Lewis and Clark ventured west, settlers had struggled with the parallel joys and dangers of the New World. James Fenimore Cooper's Leatherstocking Tales condensed the experience, introducing Natty Bumppo, the adventurer, and his alter ego, the native Chingachgook, each inhabiting a wilderness of extraordinary contradictions. The dime novels published by Beadle and Adams half a century later brought the scout, the cowboy and the outlaw into American life. Thereafter, actors like William S. Hart and movies like *The Great Train Robbery* in 1903 rounded off a stratified universe where Indian attacks, cattle rustling and mail robberies defined survival. By 1940, of the 477 movies released that year, 30 percent were westerns. Of the 178 movies produced in 1967, just 11 percent were westerns. What remained of the western fantasy was a bloodbath in the hands of Sam Peckinpah and Sergio Leone. Choreographed violence dominated; nuance of cultural or historical exploration was rare.

Still, Redford's interest was historical investigation: "I knew I was ignorant. I had a clear picture of myself as an undereducated American. What I'd learned from Tot was the tradition of the mountain man, of self-sufficiency. What I'd educated myself about was the arrogance of easterners settling the West. As the years went on, I developed a need to understand the Native American dispossession. Curiosity drove me to seek out ethnic projects at that time, and I narrated the *Blue Lake* documentary about developer exploitation of Navajo resources. But I wasn't an activist. I felt maybe I could contribute something by trying to find western movies of insight."

Tell Them Willie Boy Is Here was promising. It was based on Harry Lawton's carefully documented 1960 novel, *Willie Boy: A Desert Manhunt,* the theme of which was the victimization of the Native American, explored in the true story of a Las Vegas Paiute, Willie Boy, who "captures" for marriage a Chemehuevi girl. In 1909 the real-life tribal dispute became a national scandal when Willie Boy shot dead the father of his bride-to-be and went on the run, pursued by Sheriff Wilson, Constable Ben de Crevecoeur and a posse dedicated to the idea, prevalent at the time, that "a good Indian is a dead Indian." The story's significance, as Harry Lawton wrote, was "not just in the fact that this was the last great manhunt in the Western tradition, but in the nature of the Paiute, who was the protagonist of the hunt." The Paiute tribe's problem, Lawton stated, was its refusal to conform to modern American life.

Writer-director Abe Polonsky, like Carol Rossen's father, had suffered badly at the hands of McCarthyism. A committed Socialist harassed into exile, he continued to ghostwrite Hollywood scripts, none of which matched his 1947 masterpiece for John Garfield, the boxing story *Body and Soul.* During the sixties he lived in France, spending almost five years developing *Willie Boy.* In the mid-sixties a liberal-minded executive at Universal, the former agent Jennings Lang, was intent on green-lighting blacklistees' projects. Polonsky's Native American drama accordingly became a personal mission that finally took wing with the Paramount loan-out.

Polonsky's original plan was to faithfully reenact the 1909 incident with Native Americans. Universal management flatly refused. Later Polonsky said in interviews that he got what he wanted, casting Redford as Coop (a fictionalized composite deputy sheriff, named in tribute to Gary Cooper), Robert Blake as Willie Boy and Katharine Ross as the girl. Redford recalls it differently: "Universal would not support authenticity. In fact, they ignored Abe completely and offered me the role of Willie Boy. I thought that was absurd. Since the studio wouldn't even entertain the notion of casting honestly, I recommended a friend, Bobby Blake, whom I'd admired in *This Property Is Condemned.* I said I would play the sheriff."

Redford liked Polonsky, but he believed the years in the wilderness had ground down his confidence. An article in *Variety* criticized Polonsky's approach to movies: "He is not a director who works through his actors. Thesps are simple tools to his vision . . . their presences more than their abilities are used." Redford agreed: "There was plenty of interchange of ideas but there was no improvisation. Connie Hall, who was Katharine Ross's husband, was a very experienced cinematographer, but he was also an artist with a heavy authorial viewpoint. He saw Abe stumbling and he stole the movie from under him. I loved the script. I loved what the movie aspired to, but it evolved outside [Abe's] control into something else."

It was a pity, because so much of the movie was earnest and ambitious. Setting it on the real-life Morongo Indian Reservation, Polonsky clearly portrayed the separate, competing communities ravaged by prejudice. Coop, the law enforcer played by Redford, courts the compliant government superintendent Dr. Elizabeth Arnold, played by Susan Clark. This affair parallels Willie Boy's forbidden courtship till Willie Boy kills his girl's father. Coop is then swept into a crazed posse hunt and, in the end, is obliged to go alone after Willie Boy in hopes of saving him.

The similarities to *The Chase* drove Redford's enthusiasm. "The last forty minutes were *the reason* I chose to do the movie," says Redford. "There were only a few lines of dialogue in that last act, because it was all about *the hunt.* It had real tension, like [Fred] Zinnemann's final showdown between Gary Cooper's marshal and the villain Frank Miller in *High Noon.* It was totally original. Then Universal panicked: Who would watch forty minutes of mime? So, exactly as happened with Arthur Penn and Spiegel, they took the edit away from Abe and pared down the final act to eight minutes and redid the ending. In the screenplay, the tension resolved in the exhaustion of the protagonist and antagonist: they have hit the wall; they are burned out. Coop finally respects Willie Boy's tenacity and won't kill him. Willie Boy fatalistically accepts Coop's right to kill him. It was a powerful impasse, a brilliant ending, but the studio wanted a Jeff Chandler black-and-white shoot-out, so that's the way it was done. When I saw it, I was shattered. It was spoiled. I just had to let it go."

In the run-up to *Willie Boy,* Redford started preparing his skiing movie, which was now called *Downhill Racer.* "What I hoped for with *Willie Boy* and *Downhill* were movies that illuminated the human condition. For *Downhill,* the first thing was to get rid of Oakley Hall's source novel, which was après-ski stuff. I decided I wanted to examine the illusion of greatness in winning at all costs. I like the gray area, the bit where the duality of human nature shows through." At Wildwood, a series of long, late-night script meetings addressed every aspect of the movie-to-be. Redford deliberated awhile before choosing writer James Salter, whose short fiction he admired, to develop his concept. "It became a grand-scale thing in increments. I decided it would be a social commentary about competitive sports. Then I decided it would be part of a trilogy that looked at American life. After the skiing movie, we would make a movie about political life, and then a movie about big business. All with the same theme: the Pyrrhic victory of winning."

The trickiest part of getting *Downhill* going was outmaneuvering Bluhdorn, who was determined to see his golden boy back as a romantic pinup. In February, as Redford prepared to go to France on a $20,000 Paramount budget to secure footage from the 1967 Winter Olympics, Bluhdorn confronted him with the suggestion of a musical remake of the Gregory Peck and Audrey Hepburn classic, *Roman Holiday.* "My attitude was, Oh, please! But I couldn't say a word. I went along with him." Franco

Zeffirelli and Dino De Laurentiis were in partnership for the *Roman Holiday* remake, so Bluhdorn arranged a first-class ticket to Rome to meet with them. Redford took the ticket, then traded it for economy tickets for the Wildwood team to Grenoble, France. "I thought, It'll serve the same end: Paramount will get a great movie out of this."

For background research, Salter moved to Grasse, not far from Grenoble in southern France, where the Olympic teams were based. Redford gave Dick Barrymore, a young ski photographer, the job of shooting the crucially important Olympic footage. Then he asked sportswriter Dan Jenkins, a neighbor in the Redfords' Manhattan apartment building, for assistance in soliciting the support of the American Olympic skiing team. Jenkins persuaded the national skiing coach, Bob Beattie, to allow inside access at the off-limits areas of the Olympic Village. "This footage was, in reality, 'test footage,' to show Bluhdorn we could do it," says Redford. "So it had to be excellent. We gave $18,000 to Barrymore and $2,000 to Salter."

It started well. Beattie was a gentleman; the Olympic team was generous with time and advice. But then, three-quarters of the way through filming, Barrymore left for other projects, presenting Redford and Gregson with twenty thousand feet of 16 mm film. "Suddenly it was chaos," says Redford. "In order to get the movie green-lighted for the fall, we had to present our footage to Bluhdorn urgently." Redford reorganized his schedule, taking time out from *Willie Boy* and editing the footage himself. "Then I saw a problem. We had lots of shots of slopes and snow and skiers. But we had no shots of me in this show reel. By now it was high summer in L.A. and suddenly I was obliged to create a winter ski scene. That became the first directorial challenge of my life."

Redford went to Shelby's Sporting Goods store in Westwood, where he'd worked briefly in his teens, and borrowed a motorcycle helmet, silver duct tape, a Windbreaker and goggles. A replacement cameraman, John Bailey, was summoned. Bailey was twenty-three, a recent college graduate whose ambition was to make big movies. Together they drove to Mulholland Drive, with a couple of wooden boxes as props. Mulholland is in the hills, with a high skyline that overlooks Los Angeles. Bailey set up his camera while Redford pulled on the phony ski gear. "We'd painted stars and stripes on the helmet, and that was all we needed. John lay down in the grass to shoot skyward, like I was the skier in action. I kept taking drags of a cigarette, the smoke of which replicated my breathing in icy weather. It worked. Cut into the Grenoble stuff, it looked authentic."

In July, Redford showed Bluhdorn eighteen minutes of tightly edited film. "It was all straightforward after that. He liked it. He trusted me. We had our green light to start shooting after *Willie Boy.*"

Redford found a newcomer, Michael Ritchie, to direct on the strength of an NBC television pilot, *The Outsider.* It starred Darren McGavin in a Dashiell Hammett takeoff, full of moody grayness and long silences. "I wanted an iconoclast, so I called him. We met. We had a meeting of minds, and I said, 'Let's go!' "

Tying down the script became the central focus. Revisions at Wildwood were daily affairs. Everyone contributed, even Natalie Wood, who was now Richard Gregson's constant companion. The main problem was establishing the nature of the central character, the jock David Chappellet. Redford emphatically did not want an old-style hero. Salter had thought the American ski champion Billy Kidd would be the perfect template. "He was tough—from a poor part of town, I imagined, honed by years on the icy runs of the East," Salter later explained in his memoirs.

One night over dinner in Grenoble, surrounded by the ski team, Redford pointed across the room. "The racer he was interested in was at another table," wrote Salter. "I looked. Golden, unimpressible, a bit like Redford himself—which of course should have marked him from the first—sat a little-known team member named Spider Sabich. What there was of his reputation seemed to be based on his having broken his leg six or seven times. 'Him?' I said. 'Sabich?' Yes, said Redford; when he was that age he had been just like him—vain, rough edged, with a bit of arrogance, and a daredevil."

Salter's treatment, dated September 1967, proposed the protagonist as a twenty-one-year-old Vermonter, "like the young Dempsey, hard and not as big as one would expect." The best of it was the acerbic coach-jock relationship, deftly lifted from Oakley Hall's novel. And, beyond that, Salter's poetry: "And now over a sequence that is almost entirely close shots, shots like yesterday's newspapers, last week's, last year's shots that are like Lorca's *Lament for Ignacio Sanchez Mejias,* like the white Madrid infirmaries of *Death in the Afternoon,* a virtually silent sequence of a badly injured man being carried into x-ray, his clothing cut away. . . ."

"I thought, If we can blend Salter's eloquence with Ritchie's quirkiness, we're really onto something," says Redford. "It seemed a good process: Salter, Ritchie, then me, all contributing differing elements. What we all decided we wanted was something that had a semidocumentary feel, that seemed real."

Money was a problem. And though foreign location work was more expensive, Redford was adamant that only Europe would do for the location. Gregson flew back to Europe and found the perfect locale at Wengen, alongside the Jungfrau, the highest mountain in Switzerland. The choice was dictated by the Fédération Internationale de Ski races, which were staged on the nearby Lauberhorn and which would form the background of the action. The cost projections soared beyond the allotted $1.6 million.

"On the face of it," says Mike Frankfurt, "Bob was in clover. It had taken a year, but he had overcome the animosity with Bluhdorn. He had formed his own production company. He had a major movie in *Willie Boy.* We had even managed to buy the Stewart lands at Timp and set in motion a little recreation industry. But those were the surface realities. In truth, he hadn't consolidated. The self-produced Paramount picture was potentially an unaffordable juggernaut. Whether he and Ritchie could actually pull off an independent movie—because that's what it really was—was up in the air. And, also, Universal was not happy with *Willie Boy.* It was done, but it was languishing on a shelf. He was in clover, but he had a lot to prove."

His frame of mind was changing, too. In April, Martin Luther King Jr. was assassinated. In June, Bobby Kennedy was killed. By August, when the Democrats' presidential convention in Chicago turned into a bloodbath, America seemed an alien place. "If you had any moral sensibilities," says Redford, "you were reeling. Personally, as I'm sure for most Americans, it was a time of utter confusion. There was a frantic feeling of, What to do?" Absorption in work seemed the best medicine, and he pushed himself to perfect his skiing on the longest pro skis, 220 downhills. At the same time, in the spirit of a new commitment to social involvement, he raised funds for the Salt Lake Native Culture Center.

"In New York, Bob and Lola attracted influential people," says Mike Frankfurt, "and they utilized this as a political tool. Both had a clear picture of the divisions in American life, the rich and poor, black and white. They also had a clear picture of the Republican silent majority, and the divisions in the Democrats between the supporters of Eugene McCarthy and McGovern and Humphrey. More than that, they also had a clear understanding of the power of celebrity. They understood there was a direct correlation between the size of the media profile and the audience that could be commanded. They weren't charging at political life, but there was an impulse. The initial activism came in fits and starts. But the tone of it changed around the time Nixon got elected [in 1968]."

Redford had actively supported McCarthy until his landslide loss to Humphrey during the 1968 convention. "Maybe I was naïve to think he could pull it off," says Redford. "But he was a lot better, in prospect, than Nixon's gang." In Frankfurt's view, Nixon's dramatic election victory that year sharpened Redford's focus. "He wanted to engage debate. He had no vision of himself as a frontline politician, but the events of 1968 made *Downhill Racer* and commentary on American life more important to him. He wanted to make movies that got people talking. And he knew, of course, that he also needed to nurture the stardom that would give him the power."

As *Downhill Racer* slowly brewed, Redford engaged Creative Management Associates to find him those new starring roles. It should have been Gregson's job, but he was preoccupied in Europe. CMA was an outgrowth of MCA headed by Freddie Fields and David Begelman. Fields took over Redford's management but assigned day-to-day business to his assistant, Stephanie Phillips. Phillips had established herself molding careers for character actresses, including Joan Hackett. She had also worked closely with Begelman in the management of Henry Fonda, Peter Sellers and director George Roy Hill. In fact, it had been Phillips who was responsible for Redford's joining with MCA to begin with. She became a fan after having seen him onstage in *Barefoot.* "Joan Hackett introduced us," says Phillips. "And from then on I just kept whispering in his ear. I thought he was exceptional, for his looks, his swagger, his wit. I wanted to represent him from the start." Her wish come true, Phillips immediately looked at the roster of available films and singled out Hill's production in planning for Fox, called "The Sundance Kid and Butch Cassidy." "I had a particularly good rapport with George since he did *The World of Henry Orient* in 1964," says Phillips, "so I pressed Bob on him, and he was receptive. But we had obstacles. Paul Newman, we knew, was Fox's first choice to star. So we had to knock Brando, Beatty and James Coburn out of the picture to get the role for Bob, which I felt we could do."

Richard Zanuck, Darryl's son and recent head of Twentieth Century–Fox, wasn't amenable. Fox's fortunes had waned in the fifties, until Darryl Zanuck overthrew his former associate Spyros Skouras. Now they were riding high on the enormous success of *The Sound of Music* and, in the spirit of Darryl's philosophy of three-ring entertainments, were keen on a glamorous western. Big stars were needed for the roles of Sundance and Butch. And in Zanuck's view, the jury was still out on Robert Redford. Phillips pushed, but Zanuck preferred Warren Beatty by far.

The dilemma fell in the lap of George Roy Hill. A graduate of Yale in 1944, Hill had served as a marine pilot in World War II and pursued graduate studies at Trinity College in Dublin before working in the Gate and Abbey theaters. He was an Emmy winner for television writing and directing in New York in the mid-fifties and moved into movies with adaptations of Tennessee Williams's *Period of Adjustment* and Lillian Hellman's *Toys in the Attic* in the sixties. Hill was forty when he started in movies and always contended that it was maturity that impressed on him the centrality of the actor. Paul Newman, in his view, was the epitome of film art. "I knew Newman's genius, which was a genius of understatement," said Hill. "No matter how good the story, no matter how dexterous the cameraman, no matter how smart the director, you simply cannot achieve an effective motion picture without an immensely skilled screen actor." Newman's commitment to the Fox western was, said Hill, half the battle. "And then when Steffie pushed for Redford, I thought, Yes, that might be interesting. Only that."

Hill met Redford for a drink at Joe Allen's bar on Forty-sixth Street. "Since I liked the script," says Redford, "I really wanted to get in. But the understanding was that Paul would be Sundance, since the title led off with that name, and Butch was the costar. George assumed I wanted to be Butch Cassidy, but I said, 'To be honest, I've read it and I think I'd be better as Sundance. It's the part that interests me.' And from there the talk progressed, and George became intrigued by this notion. I learned that he felt Paul was really more like Butch anyway. George said that the role Paul played in *Hud* was really not him. Paul was full of nervous energy, and funny. And the more we talked, the more George came around to the idea that I should be the Sundance Kid."

"After that I decided I wanted him for Sundance," Hill recalled. "It was that simple. You'll read press pieces about me wanting Marlon and all the rest, but it's garbage. Fox wanted Beatty. Paul wanted Jack Lemmon. But I wanted Bob. Then I had to go to Paul's apartment and set about winning him over."

Newman had little or no interest in Redford's progress: "I'd seen him onstage in *Barefoot,* and I'd seen *Inside Daisy Clover,* but I had yet to be convinced." Personally, Newman said, he felt a sense of "ownership" with the Butch Cassidy film, since it had first been proposed to him in the fall of 1966, ironically, by Redford's friend and neighbor, Bill Goldman. "He flew all the way down to Tucson, where I was filming, and dished it all to me, this marvelous story about the real Wild Bunch gang he was developing on spec. He said, 'This is going to be the best cowboy picture ever made.' Then he disappeared, and the next I knew, [Steve] McQueen called me and said we should make this thing called 'The Sundance Kid and Butch Cassidy' that somebody had shown him. I collected the script from McQueen's house and read it overnight, and the next day I called Steve and suggested that the two of us should buy it outright from Goldman. He said no deal was available because Goldman's agent was playing the auction game. So that was the end of it for McQueen and me. I forgot about it. Then, out of the blue, Dick Zanuck had it and Hill was offering it to me, with no Steve attached."

Newman had no problem relinquishing the role of Sundance. Hill informed him that the movie's title could easily be reversed and, anyway, the character of Butch was a perfect fit for him. Despite the ongoing grumbling from the studio, Hill took Redford to meet Newman and Newman was won over. "George was probably right," said Newman. "I'd wanted Lemmon as the costar to return a favor. But he hated horses and said no. When I met Bob, I liked him. After that, you go by instinct, and you go with the flow. It was an exceptional piece of writing anyway and, under George's direction, I knew it would be a fine movie. So when George said, 'Trust me, it's Redford as the Sundance Kid,' I said, 'What the hell.' "

Advised of Newman's blessing, Fox agreed to Redford as Sundance. "It was humbling," says Redford, "because Paul and George were obvious artists. I was the kid, and they went to bat for me with Zanuck. Was I sure the movie was something special? Yes. It was rich with humor and texture. I liked Goldman's work, though I thought the script had too many jokes. I had the highest admiration for George. When I was told I got it, it was a relief because I felt, Okay, if I make a mess of *Downhill*, I might still have a career. It was Paul who made the decision. I will always be indebted to him for that—taking a chance on a comparative unknown."

Late in August, still preparing for *Downhill Racer*, Redford joined some Broadway friends—Penny Fuller, an understudy from *Barefoot*, and production manager Bill Craver—for a weekend of sitting in the sauna and riding at Timp. On the first evening, says Fuller, he was preoccupied with "the immensity of the changes going down with the purchase of the canyon lands and the contradictory objectives of all these new movies." They played jazz and sat late into the night under the tall windows of the

A-frame. Redford outlined his plans. He would preserve the canyon for posterity. He would protect it from commercial exploitation. His own developments would be arts based. An on-site children's theater would be the start of a program he'd yet to work out. He had toyed, he said, with various names for this mountain fastness, but now he had the best name. It evoked an Indian ritual of growth through pain. He would call it Sundance.

Redford joined Paul Newman, Katharine Ross (again), Bill Goldman and Hill at Fox for two weeks of rehearsals in September. Hill reminded Redford of his uncle David. He was convivial, a sharp-as-a-pin military man with a perverse sense of fun. "It was easy to talk with George," says Redford, "because it felt familiar." In Hill's view, "Redford had layers. He had a Celtic wildness that shone through the laid-back dude. Zanuck called him a playboy. But he made a mistake: that was just *the look.*"

Marcella Scott, Martha's friend from childhood, worked as a studio secretary assigned to Hill and sat in on the earliest meetings for *Butch Cassidy and the Sundance Kid.* She was impressed by Hill. "He was a loudmouth in the nicest sense, a stage Irishman. He wore tennies everywhere, hated ties—just like Bob—hated rules. But he was fastidious beyond belief within his own universe. I've never known a man to read so much and work so hard, and he *demanded,* usually in a roar, that everyone around him contribute the same energy. He was the kind of man who'd suddenly realize at midnight that he had been remiss in not replying to some obscure memo, and he would think, I am not being professional, and sacrifice a night's sleep to dictate something generous and unnecessary. Bob and he were made for each other, because Bob, too, had energy beyond everyone else."

Erudition spilled naturally from Hill, a man who drew heavily on his Irish temperament (both sets of grandparents were Dublin Irish) while, unlike John Ford, shying away from romanticizing his Irishness. Pauline Kael viewed Hill's work as "implacably impersonal," which Hill manfully construed as a compliment, since "restraint" was his personal byword. But film historian Andrew Horton, later evaluating his oeuvre, concluded the director deployed "Voltaire's traits of the master storyteller who frames a serious view of life in a comic-ironic vein, manipulating genres for his own purposes." Redford appreciated Horton's analysis. "George was chronically underrated on account of his eclecticism. He was not a 'straight-line' director, in that he did not obsess about one style or one subject. When I see directors like Marty Scorsese being so celebrated for excellence and George so ignored, it upsets me. Marty is brilliant as a stylist, but George was an immense storyteller and he had the gift to jump genres and never let you down. In my movie experience till then, George was the first *real* storyteller I'd met. His approach was analytical *and* lyrical, and consequently comprehensive."

For Newman, Hill's specialty was his genius with actors: "George's preference was New York theater actors, people like Cloris Leachman, whom he loved. They were trained with improvisational skills, which he relished. Add to that his deep respect for *the art* of acting, which came from his being an actor in Ireland, and you got the magic. He didn't slow you down when you were hot; he rolled with it. On the other hand, when you stumbled, he stepped in to help in the blink of an eye. That's a very rare attribute for a director: understanding acting. In my opinion, on *Butch Cassidy,* Redford and I might have been any two decent actors. What George did from the rehearsals onward was allow us to run with the script, to just go nuts, then nurse the whole shebang in the direction he wanted, which was original and visionary."

Humor, on which the simple, linear story of the demise of Butch and Sundance at the end of the outlaw era was built, also oiled the day-to-day production, which began in Durango, Colorado, on September 16. Newman, who loved auto racing, showed up in his souped-up Volkswagen and immediately taunted Redford in his cherished Porsche 904, one of only 103 ever made, specially designed for the Sebring race of 1964. Francis Feighan, Fox's publicity man, saw "two overgrown kids on separate sides of a dusty track, revving their engines like gladiators getting ready for the fray. You knew it was all in jest, but the testosterone in the air was overpowering."

Jamie, just settling into Dalton, was given eight weeks off, as was Shauna, who joined Lola and Joanne Woodward on location. This family camaraderie—"incessant talk, gags and laughs," says Jamie—helped a twelve-week shoot hampered by the kind of stunt accidents and injuries that might be expected from a reenactment of the dying days of the Wild West. "There was a feeling of unusual intensity from the start," said Feighan. "The legend of Hill's dedication preceded him. He'd knocked *Hawaii,* which was a sprawling three-hour movie, into shape when Fred Zinnemann couldn't. And he was sure as hell going to make a silk purse out of Goldman's script. He worked sixteen hours a day from the first week in June of 1968, when he called Goldman to Fox to discuss the script, till the end of the final edit in June 1969. He even worked from a stretcher for ten days when he put his back out. And later on he got studio dispensation to sleep in a dressing-room loft beside the edit suite." Redford says he found this degree of application inspiring. He also loved the locations—"among my favorite scenery anywhere in the world: Silverton, Colorado, Virgin and St. George in Utah, and the Mexican desert."

From the first days of shooting there was a brotherliness in the partnership of Newman and Redford that had Hill, said his assistant, Bob Crawford, "hopping around like a four-year-old who's finally cracked the candy jar." Stephanie Phillips, though, remembered a nervous start. There had been controversy about Redford's bandito mustache. Phillips disliked it, and Redford was reminded of the story of Darryl Zanuck returning from Europe halfway through the shoot for *The Gunfighter,* where Gregory Peck wore a mustache. "That facial hair is going to cost me $2 million," said Zanuck. "Given Stephanie's commercial instinct," says Redford, "the mustache was in trouble. But I was emphatic it stayed, because that was the way those bandits looked at the turn of the century. It was authentic. And George agreed, so it stayed put." Hill enjoyed Redford's cheekiness. "Bob was a little rougher and less mature than Paul," he recalled. "So there was a definite experience discrepancy. Paul played on that, which created some fine moments that weren't in Goldman's script. Paul was Actors Studio, Redford was 'the other side'—that was another pretense for rivalry. That's all good stuff, but it can slide out of control. It can become too much fun for the actors, and lose the point. At the end of the day it's the director's job to make *a characterful relationship* out of all this. I had to rein them in at times."

"We got it up on its feet real quick," Newman remembered. "Redford worked different to me, a bit faster. But Method fades as soon as you face the movie camera. The technology of the film set works against Stanislavski, and good film actors know it. I once asked Elia Kazan how often one should rely on sense memory, and he said sense memory never worked for him. So you take what works for you, which was what I did, and it varies with the definition of each production. Orson Welles complained that he'd made *The Long, Hot Summer* with Tony Franciosa and Lee Remick and Joanne [Woodward], who were all Method trained, and it was like trying to cycle a bicycle through a barrel of molasses. I was always conscious of that, so I didn't bring Stanislavski to the set. I brought a Porsche-engined Volks."

In real life, Butch Cassidy's Wild Bunch, renamed the Hole in the Wall Gang to avoid confusion with Sam Peckinpah's movie of that name, were serial bank robbers and murderous postfrontier thugs. Harry "Sundance" Longabaugh was a dangerous Pennsylvania-born gun for hire. Goldman proposed an alternative, Robin Hood version of villainy. "I always loved Bill's writing," says Redford. "*Temple of Gold* and *Boys and Girls Together*, his novels, seemed very much like J. D. Salinger to me. He had the ability to capture and emulate a style. In this movie he wanted to emulate *Gunga Din.* But in some of his writing his wit and imitative style became overblown and reduced what might have been. George was aware of this with *Butch Cassidy and the Sundance Kid.* So he took out many jokes and reordered it to allow the scenes to breathe. He was very ruthless in a discriminating way." Hill said, "I was always aware that we were exaggerating history. In our movie, Butch and Sundance are lovable because they are polite, despite their mania for bank robberies and their complete incompetence. They fuck up all the time but come back with aplomb. I played off Newman's history and Redford's newness. Up till then, Paul was known as the hard rebel loner of *Hud* or *Cool Hand Luke.* Bob was a blank sheet of paper. For the movie we made them goofballs, and because that was so fresh in context of what we were doing, it won over the audience."

Where, though, was the *Darling Clementine* earnestness or the western veracity Pollack and Redford aspired to? For Hill, the validity was in the symbolism. "The movie was about Vietnam. Not literally, of course, but it symbolized a whole contingent of society that was bailing out. It was, I suppose, in sympathy with the dissenting voice, maybe even supporting it." Redford preferred to see core truths in the depiction of banditry. "George asked me at one point, 'What is your motivation for playing Sundance?' And I said, 'He's a killer, a psychotic. So when I'm looking at some guy, all the time I'm thinking, Will I kill him?' " Within that subtextual hardness, says Redford, the movie retained a quasi reality that gave it worth.

The movie's triumph, though, was its wit, concentrating on the dynamic contrast of characters: Newman's Butch is the thinker, fast and calculating; Redford's Sundance the traditional, silent westerner. They don't take their lives seriously, but now and then they show moments of perception that hint at the inevitability of a tragic demise (they die in Bolivia). "Damn it, why is everything we're good at illegal?" Butch asks. Such self-referential irony both softens and enriches, and even the most casual, throwaway exchanges are joyfully charged: During the chase, Butch says to Sundance, "I think we lost 'em. Do you think we lost 'em?" Sundance says no, to which Butch replies, "Neither do I."

Hill credited "the magic" between Newman and Redford with the movie's success; Redford says it was Hill who made it tick. "None of us felt we were making the landmark western of the late sixties. But the ground did move. It wasn't like *Willie Boy,* where there was a feeling of emotional disengagement between actors and director. George kept us tight. On *Butch Cassidy,* I remember laughing a lot and thinking, This is just too much fun, which means it's either shit or gold."

Mike Frankfurt and Stephanie Phillips had collaborated on Redford's Fox contract, which was for a flat fee of $150,000, considerably less than a quarter of Newman's fee with percentage, but still the best of his career. They had hoped for a back-end percentage—a cut of the profits—but Redford was happy. "He had other fish to fry," says Phillips.

At Thanksgiving, while Redford was dubbing in Los Angeles, Lola and Ilene Goldman discussed establishing a health and consumer activist group. Their talk arose from a chance comment by Suzanna, the Goldmans' five-year-old daughter, about "the bad air" in Manhattan. On the phone, Redford supported the decision to set up a biweekly roundtable discussion forum at their Seventy-ninth Street apartment. Businesswoman Cynthia Burke and Carlin Masterson, the actress wife of theater actor and director Pete Masterson, joined to formulate the first team, whose task it would be to research health and consumer issues. Twenty other friends, mostly women, also joined, and the group named itself Consumer Action Now (CAN) and pledged to establish a portfolio to tie in with the first Earth Day, scheduled for April 22, 1970, by activist Dennis Hayes. The initial action, partially funded by Redford, was to compile a research paper on food additives that would be published in a widely circulated ecology newsletter, edited by Lola.

Redford supported CAN but concentrated on different group activism. With Stephanie Phillips's husband, Richard Friedberg, Mike Frankfurt, producer Gene Stavis and businessmen Charles Saltzman and Marty Keltz, he helped fund a new organization called Education, Youth, and Recreation (EYR). Its purpose was to promote "alternative film" through the university campuses of North America. Redford says, "Stavis was the organizer, Friedberg the theoretician, Keltz the salesman. But the impulse was mine. I loved the nouvelle vague. I loved what was happening in Europe, not so much Swinging Britain, which was just consuming itself in self-parody, but with directors like Fellini, Truffaut and of course

Bergman who were giving us another view of the human experience. I wanted to encourage a comparable independent artistry in American film and started it there with EYR."

The idea was profound. For many, 1967 and 1968 represented a pivotal era in American cinema, as in American life. The Oscar successes of radical works such as Arthur Penn's *Bonnie and Clyde* and Mike Nichols's *The Graduate* marked a fundamental change in the institutional view of filmmaking, and Sidney Poitier's achievement in hits like *In the Heat of the Night* and *Guess Who's Coming to Dinner* and in becoming 1967's top box office star signified the progress of civil rights. This seemed to be the fruition of a decade of liberal theorizing that had taken hold among educated youth on the campuses and soaked into mainstream culture. For Redford, the change was an inevitable and desirable social evolution. "I thought we, as a people, were insular and hyperconservative. I thought what Kennedy and those other liberal mold breakers were about was the essential therapy of self-reevaluation. We needed to broaden our knowledge and outlook. We needed social inclusion and attention to the poor, the blacks, the dispossessed. And in our movies we needed the lateral view. It was no good regurgitating Dean Martin comedy action movies forever. We had to have the marginal voices on-screen, so that we could understand how the other half lives. My feeling was that we must explore diversity in our culture and we must find an audience willing to listen."

The university campus, Redford believed, was a good place to begin. Here were the kids who became the staffers and fund-raisers for Eugene McCarthy and Robert Kennedy, and they were now under fire as President Nixon took office. Redford hit the road with EYR. "When I swung a free weekend or two from postproduction on *Butch Cassidy,* I went out to Berkeley, or wherever I was invited, and pushed the concept. Keltz covered the other bases. The notion was to grab the neglected movies, movies like Billy Friedkin's *The Birthday Party,* and offer screening packages from Wednesday night to Sunday night for $450. We had two guiding principles: to promote a different type of cinema and also, as a sideline, to locate and sponsor new talent. I wanted to offer polemic in film in the most democratic, accessible way. What Peter Fonda and Nicholson and Hopper were doing was one way of changing the zeitgeist. I wanted another tack."

Through Stavis's efforts, a handful of fledgling filmmakers were funded from EYR's finance pool, among them Martin Scorsese and Sam Shepard. Scorsese's NYU short *The Big Shave* was acquired and distributed, and Shepard, whose play *The Unseen Hand* Redford had admired at the Yale

School of Drama, was personally handed $10,000 to develop a new short. "That wasn't the best investment I ever made," says Redford, "because he disappeared to Paris and blew the cash living the émigré life. I didn't see him for a long time, but he eventually apologized and sent the money back."

New ground was crossed. Jean-Luc Godard's *Le Gai Savoir* was acquired, along with the notable shorts *King, Murray* and *Lions Love* and Bob Crawford's fly-on-the-wall documentary about the making of *Butch Cassidy and the Sundance Kid.*

"But in the end it didn't work," says Redford. "We misread the campus spirit and got no further than the package we distributed to the University of Pennsylvania. At face value, Tom Hayden, Abbie Hoffman and those Chicago Seven guys were winning the war against Vietnam and right-wingism. What we saw was the weeklong takeover of the Columbia campus, and the antiwar rallies. But Nixon was smart and he was lucky. He fought back, and the triumphalism that came with America winning the space race and putting a man on the moon helped him no end. The pendulum was swinging and the appetite for counterculture was uncertain. It surprised me, but the students didn't want radical film. They wanted to see *Doctor Zhivago* like everyone else. They were *conditioned* to want *Doctor Zhivago.* EYR lasted seven months and lost $250,000. Mike Frankfurt had told me, 'Don't worry, at least it's a good tax-deductible investment.' It wasn't even that. But it started something rolling."

PART THREE

Life on the Mountain

> To get to art, one leaves experience—the simple *living* of life, the following of one's nature. . . . Art [. . .] is a journey into thin air, a walk into whiteness, where you lose everything but yourself.
>
> Joan Acocella, *Willa Cather and the Politics of Criticism*

12

Fame

In January, while *Butch Cassidy* was in postproduction, *Downhill Racer* started shooting. Briefly, it felt cursed. Redford was tired, after twelve weeks in the saddle on *Butch,* and unfocused. While attempting a shortcut at the resort, riding over a ridge on a snowmobile, he crashed. His knee went into the motor and was sliced up. He was hospitalized, and it suddenly looked like he wouldn't be able to do the ski sequences in Switzerland. "In the movie I look uncomfortable in those early scenes because I was in agony," he recalls. "But I had no time for recovery. It had come to a point where there was no turning back."

Michael Ritchie, who felt he was just getting to know Redford, carefully watched him work. Ritchie, Harvard educated and a magpie for literature, found a friend in Redford. "But the intellectual rationalizations peter out," said Ritchie. "We were at the point where I had to step up with the proverbial bullhorn and say, 'Act!' And when that happened, I was surprised. I'd seen Bob's work on TV and film. I felt I knew his technique. But I saw that he had changed post–*Butch Cassidy.* He was a different actor."

It was true. Prior to *Willie Boy,* a rhythmic theatricality informed Redford's performances; playing Coop he introduced laconic understatement, and playing Sundance refined it. "Bob rolled that on into *Downhill Racer,*" said Ritchie. "He found something in the spatial power of silence, and that became his reference point for Chappellet. I'd take something Salter had written and say, 'Hey, Bob, you know what we could do here?' And Bob would say, 'We do nothing.' I'd say, 'Maybe we could use some effects or music,' and he'd say, 'No, nothing.' The end result, with Chappellet as with the Sundance Kid, was that audiences had to *reach out* to find Bob."

Redford's theory about Chappellet, honed with Salter, was that he was a *team* skier in name only; in fact, dazed by the hunger for personal victory, Chappellet is disconnected from the world, from his father, his coach, his life. Ritchie thought this brave, that Redford was disdainfully anatomizing the sacred place of the jock in society. Redford felt impelled: "I'd been sold on the wondrous jock since childhood. Sports was *the* glory business. But in my lifetime it changed. The way the old guys conducted themselves—Jack Dempsey, Joe DiMaggio—was a whole lot different from the guys of the sixties. The outspokenness started with Muhammad Ali. And by the seventies, the bad behavior of guys like [Olympic swimming gold medalist] Mark Spitz became de rigueur. It was cool to be a jerk. Winning was everything, bad behavior now excused. That was what I wanted to plumb: Chappellet the asshole. He isn't nice to the coach because he doesn't have to be. That's the privilege of the sportsman now, good or bad: he can conduct himself however he feels. I thought, This is not a good role model marker for the way we, as a society, are going."

Frankfurt, Gregson, Lola and the kids moved to Wengen for the duration of the shoot, which lent it a pleasant air of a family vacation. Redford continued to work the script. "But we were under the gun," said Ritchie. "Time was always the enemy. When I'd first met with Gregson and Bob at the Hotel Bel-Air, I was offered the deal of $30,000 in hand, no perks, which I accepted. But that meeting was it in terms of planning. There was hard work from Bob and Salter on the script, but the rest—the structuring of a production—was left to me." Gregson's preparation, said Ritchie, left something to be desired. The main race scenes were scheduled to be shot around the Lauberhorn, but no one mentioned that a James Bond extravaganza, *On Her Majesty's Secret Service,* was being filmed on the Schilthorn, the mountain opposite. Ritchie now realized getting a first-rate crew would be impossible. "The Bond people paid better; they were a big boom-time production," said Ritchie. "So we got the leftovers." Moreover, Redford had assumed the availability of Willy Bogner Jr., the Olympic contender turned cameraman and the only accomplished ski photographer working in film; his 1965 documentary, *Fascination with Skiing,* had won prizes and he knew the European slopes intimately. But Bogner had signed for the Bond picture. At the last minute, Joe Jay Jalbert, a skier from Washington University who worked on the Olympic B team contenders, signed up to shoot the ski action. "We had to train him to use the camera real fast," said Ritchie. "It sounds simple, but this wasn't vacation snaps. Joe Jay had to learn to handle a fifteen-pound Arriflex while skiing downhill at full speed. It took forever to get a single, steady, usable shot."

Gene Hackman and Camilla Sparv were cast in the prominent roles of the team coach and the object of Redford's affection. "That casting was critical," said Ritchie, "because, firstly, Gene has no star ego and doesn't care how you photograph him. And Camilla, like Bob, has classic beauty that you simply couldn't shoot badly. It was so important because, with the budget we had and the style I wanted, there would be no time for complicated lighting setups. My attitude was, We are making a documentary; we are cutting for reality. There were no read-throughs, and what we were doing every day was a kind of cinema verité."

The film followed Olympic downhill races over three seasons, as America closes in on its first big ski medals. Chappellet is seeded eighty-eighth at the start, progresses to twentieth and finally, in the third season, wins. But he is undisciplined. "Bob's way of playing Chappellet was to push up his own nature," said Ritchie. "Everything he'd been as a kid, the uncompromising flunk out, the reluctant jock—all of it went into Chappellet. Dialogue disappeared all over the place. Several times I asked him, 'Where's the goddamn line?' And his answer was a shrug. His constant nervous mannerism of chewing gum drove me insane. I'd call a cut just to get him to spit out the gum. And then I understood this was Chappellet being Bob. This was Chappellet telling Hackman the coach to fuck off."

Despite a directive from Paramount's legal department to the contrary, Redford insisted on doing most of his own skiing, to Hackman's dismay. "Gene liked Redford," said Ritchie. "But he was appalled by the skiing. He said, 'Does that idiot know about insurance liabilities? If he falls, we're all on our way home.' " Walter Coblenz, Ritchie's production manager, was given the unenviable task of monitoring Redford's excesses, a nightmare task, says Coblenz, "because you really don't tell Bob what to do. You politely request, and then hope."

By the summer, everyone was optimistic. Side by side in separate studios, *Butch Cassidy* and *Downhill Racer* were in editing and progressing well. "From Bob's point of view," said Ritchie, "it was a fantastic prospect. There was a lot of buzz and expectation about George's picture, and a lot of curiosity, more than anything, about ours. So Bob, as an actor dependent on the limelight, was well placed. Nervous, but well placed."

In September, *Downhill Racer* previewed first. Redford and Ritchie were horrified. Paramount's marketing people had promised Gregson that the unheralded movie would not be shown after a major feature. They reneged, screening the movie after *Midnight Cowboy* at a Santa Barbara cinema. "How wrong can you get?" says Redford. "Santa Barbara is a sunshine retirement haven for easterners and the U.S. military. People come to get away from snow. In ten minutes I saw the audience wanted out. People began leaving." Ali MacGraw, who was attending with her husband, Robert Evans, comforted Ritchie: "She told me it was a great movie, an innovative movie, so fuck 'em all. I took heart from her, because she was a lady of discernment." Evans, representing Paramount, slapped Redford's shoulder and told him, "I thought it played very well." Redford found no comfort in this, since three-quarters of the audience had already bolted the theater. A half hour later, in the restaurant next door, Evans brought in the audience response cards. He was frowning.

"All right. They're bad."

"How bad?" Redford asked.

"You can take a look if you want, but they're all bad."

Ritchie and Redford set about reediting the film from scratch, taking out the music track and liberally reinstating a "wild track" of natural ambient sounds to enhance the documentary atmosphere. The movie was, says Redford, vastly improved, but the distribution delay suggested a failure from which, receiptswise, the film would never recover.

Meanwhile, the journey to completing *Butch Cassidy* had been bumpy. The back injury at the end of filming had laid Hill low, and he was forced to edit lying down. But he persevered, delivering a quirky, original movie, laced with sepia-tinged stop frames and stand-apart pop music. The music, all twelve minutes of it, which seemed to amplify the humor, had been an afterthought. At the first rough cut screening in April, the music was a utility sound track, borrowed from existing movies. John Foreman, Paul Newman's producing partner, had suggested the pop song interlude that accompanies the bicycle montage in which Butch befriends Sundance's girl, Etta. In April, Simon and Garfunkel's "59th Street Bridge Song (Feelin' Groovy)" decorated the scene. After the rough cut, Burt Bacharach was summoned and he came up with "Raindrops Keep Fallin' on My Head," which bewildered Redford: "I did not know what it was doing there. I knew George wanted to beef up the relationship between Butch and Etta but . . . a song like that? First of all, it wasn't raining in the scene. And then, what had any of it to do with their relationship?" Zanuck suggested the song be dropped. Hill refused. The whole editing phase, said Hill, was a firefight.

A pre-premiere screening was held under the auspices of the film society at Yale, Hill and Newman's alma mater. Redford attended with low expectations. "I wasn't focused on it. George was, because it was his baby. Bill Goldman was the most excited, because he was obsessed with all the promotional aspects of the business as much as filmmaking itself." Among the guests was Barbra Streisand, meeting Redford for the first time. "We drove up in a limo with George and there was this milling crowd," says Redford. "I assumed they were students doing the studenty thing. But when we got out, it was terrifying. Pushing, shoving, screaming. The bleachers were overturned. Joanne [Woodward] was knocked to the ground, and Paul was seriously pissed. Barbra's dress was almost torn off her body, and I had the feeling we could have been hurt. It was the first time I'd been scared by a crowd. But I also thought it might be a good omen."

The "star power" of the opening night, with Newman, especially, in attendance, was the intoxicant. But after the screening, when the students voiced their response, the enthusiasm was even wilder. Hill, the veteran, was shocked. "I got to thinking that maybe it *was* remarkable," he said, "so I began to look forward to the reviews."

The first media preview in San Francisco, as Goldman described in his memoirs, was "disastrous." Then came the nationwide opening later in September. "It was the strangest opening I ever experienced," said Hill, "because it started really 'up' at Yale, and then it plunged down. It didn't go to plan. Goldman and I went to a midtown Manhattan theater to watch, and the audience yawned. I told Bill, 'Well, we tried.' And I did my best to forget it, which was tough, because I had thrown everything into it."

The print reviews mostly were poor. In *The New Yorker,* Pauline Kael's lambasting review was titled, "The Bottom of the Pit." Hill was deeply offended and wrote personally to her, in a letter that began, "Listen, you fucking cunt." "I thought she was unkind," said Hill. "Her way was to be snide when she personally disliked you, and it's unfortunate, but a lot of very smart people get away with appalling crudity because they're articulate and witty. I especially hated self-serving wit, so I answered her with the crudity and tastelessness she commanded."

Audiences nationwide rejected the critics' consensus. Within months box office receipts exceeded $40 million. The movie had cost just $6.5 million. "It moved by great word of mouth," says Redford. "People saw it and told their friends. It was an instance where the critics meant little. The audiences made up their own minds." Hill was stunned, "because I'd decided, Okay, it didn't work." Newman was more phlegmatic. "Movies are like kids. They're always surprising. *Butch Cassidy* was just one of those brats that races past anything you hoped for." Redford believed inserting the Bacharach song made a huge difference. "How bad can a guy's judgment be? I hated the song, and suddenly, for the next six months, I had to listen to it everywhere I went. I mean everywhere: cabs, restaurants, stores. There was nowhere to go to get away from it, and it was at the top of the music charts for half a year."

The effects of *Butch Cassidy* were far-reaching for Redford. In February 1968 he had been sleeping in hotel hallways in Grenoble with James Salter to save money. Two years later, in February 1970, he was a national icon on the cover of *Life* magazine, labeled "New Star Robert Redford: A Real Sundance Kid." The magnitude of the hit, believed Michael Ritchie, helped the recut of *Downhill Racer.* "We were sometimes a little down about recutting, and I think it helped, if only to remind us how great an actor Bob was and how good his instincts were."

Universal, too, was encouraged and finally released *Willie Boy,* which had been sitting on a shelf, a month after *Butch Cassidy.* Eight weeks later Paramount officially released *Downhill Racer.*

"I really cared about *Downhill Racer,*" says Redford, "but Paramount distribution threw it away. First, they wanted to open it big, like another *Butch Cassidy.* I, of course, resisted. I said, 'It's a small film, not a blockbuster.' So they said, 'Okay, we'll change tack.' But they opened it, of all places, in Kitzbühel, Austria, playing it like an après-ski treat. I later learned what really happened. Charlie Bluhdorn had moved back to his sugarcane operation. The honeymoon was over in terms of his intercession, so we were back in the hands of the so-called distribution pros. I learned they used small movies like *Downhill Racer* as an expenses dump. People ran up lunch expenses on other productions and attributed them to costs for our promotion." Redford earned not a dime—not even a salary—from *Downhill Racer.* But the sad fate of the film did nothing to diminish the level of stardom he had now achieved. By year's end he was a daily staple in the gossip columns in newspapers, and the networks were rescheduling the forgotten TV shows he starred in. Richard Schickel, who knew him well, wrote a long feature on him in *Time* magazine in December. Lorillard, the tobacco company, launched a Redford cigarette, with a face that looked remarkably like his on the promotional packs handed out to sales reps.

"There we had to draw the line," says Redford. "I called up my lawyers and we hit Lorillard with a lawsuit. They fought back, but it cost them half a million dollars in the end." Redford was pleased, then amused when Martin Garbus, the civil rights lawyer who presented the case on his behalf, gave him a token gift of one of Lorillard's promotional packs, with his pseudoface beaming out. Redford took the packet home and placed it in a glass display case. A week later, he came home to find his kids had breached the case and smoked the cigarettes.

Redford took pride in his business sense. He took pride in the fact that he built his A-frame for $14,000 and spent just $20,000 for the first-phase development of the Sundance acreage (the money was borrowed against his *Willie Boy* contract). But almost immediately the partnership founded by Frankfurt started to disintegrate. "None of us had real money to begin with," says Stan Collins, who was responsible for the financial management of this new, amorphous business. "We were all to pitch in $20,000. Bob did his bit. But I didn't have $20,000, so I gave my services in lieu. Mike Frankfurt provided his legal services. Which meant that, apart from Bob, only Gottschalk and Hans Estin put hard cash up." Gary Hendler, a tax management expert, had structured the deal with the less experienced Frankfurt, but Redford took the bulk of the risk, and it was Redford who first spotted the defects in the partnership. The 98 percent mortgage was signed in his name, with repayments amounting to $360,000 a year. "At first, I didn't notice it. Everything moved so fast, and all I cared about was securing the canyon. To do that I had to keep working, to keep solvent, and I was working so intently I wasn't taking care," says Redford.

There was progress, though. Redford assigned Wayne, Lola's brother, to build a new guesthouse, the Mouse House, beside the A-frame. On the resort side, a second chairlift was installed at a cost of $200,000. The new lift system spanned over a mile to an elevation of fifty-two hundred feet above the base camp, complementing the existing Poma lifts, which took novice skiers to an elevation twenty-six hundred feet above camp. The objective of all this, says Frankfurt, was to compete with Alta, Utah's only major ski resort, just thirty miles away.

Despite the progress, Redford was nervous: "It became pretty evident that the promises made were not going to be kept," he recalls. "There was no money. And I began to worry that no one was sincerely committed." Hendler, who was slowly taking over from Frankfurt, was ostensibly following the boss's orders, but Redford was concerned about him, too.

Hendler had been skeptical about the purchase of the canyon lands to begin with, but had come around to Frankfurt's idea of developing the resort as a nationally advertised vacation spot. Redford saw the conundrum: Hendler's appetite was for building, but his, essentially, was for preservation.

Hendler was Brooklyn born and Harvard educated. Despite being short, he had become a star varsity basketball player, an achievement, Redford opines, that reflected his determined stubbornness. While others preferred to take weekends off, he worked nonstop. Hesitant at first, he had seen the opportunities afforded by the property boom of 1970 and surrendered to Sundance. "Prior to Gary," says Frankfurt, "our setup in New York was hand-to-mouth. With EYR, we were always begging for the loan of office space. We found Bob a hole in the wall on East Fifty-fifth Street and that was our business base in its entirety. Gary wasn't interested in any of this small-time panhandling. He saw the big picture. The economy was booming and the property market was on the up. People had disposable income. It was a good time for vacation properties. Gary came to see the light and he wanted Bob to benefit."

Hendler moved fast. First, a number of half-acre plots were sold at $10,000 each to a pool of friends assembled by Frankfurt and Hendler, including Steve Frankfurt, Universal's Lew Wasserman, producer Dan Melnick and Sydney Pollack. The idea was for them to build vacation homes adhering to controlled architectural guidelines. A search was then begun for venture capital partners for a major expansion, led by Hendler and his mentor from Harvard, Larry Fleischer, who managed sports stars. Fleischer had managed the basketball careers of New York Knicks Dave DeBusschere and Bill Bradley. Frankfurt, like Redford, was comfortable in these circles, but less comfortable with the business operations of Fleischer. "No one was saying yet that this would be the arts center of the Southwest," says Frankfurt, "but it was clearly going to be arts connected, and I worried that Bob's art vision and Fleischer's business would clash. We all accepted that the facilities had to be expanded, and Gary said Fleischer would involve Restaurant Associates, the restaurant and catering enterprise he was heading up, and they would buy into the resort and invest seed capital. We all hung on for this deal, but nothing happened."

Some began to believe the new setup was a ready-made disaster. Brent Beck, who joined as resort manager at the end of the first Sundance season, found "low morale among the few staffers and a feeling that this so-called new resort was operating beyond itself." For Jerry Hill, who had worked in the canyon since he was fifteen, the early scenario was "nightmarish—it was a race to the bank in Provo every Friday to get in first and make sure the darn check didn't bounce."

Some investors introduced to Redford were less than desirable. There was the Utah tourism executive who proposed the training and sponsoring of America's first all-black Olympic ski team as a novelty draw. There was the executive of an NBC division interested in cashing in on the current second-home tax break advantages for staffers. And then there was the southern businessman who saw great potential in a cowboy-themed mountain park that would be accessed from the Alpine Loop by motorists driving under a Disney-like hundred-foot-high billboard depicting a smiling Redford as the Sundance Kid.

When they started out, Hendler was a junior partner in the Los Angeles law firm of Irell and Minella. Within a year he was in partnership with Art Armstrong and handling the legal affairs of star clients like Ella Fitzgerald and, later, Sean Connery, Pollack and Streisand. "That's where the real trouble started," says Redford. "Gary was clever, and he made money for these people. I did not want to be dragged into the territory of, 'You must do this picture for X cash, because we need X cash.' Everything I'd done till that point was about *avoiding* that trap. But Gary would sit me down and say, 'Sean [Connery] is doing three movies a year. You can be like Sean. He's financially far better off than you. You can use this money for the resort.' I would say to Gary: 'Who made the world? An accountant? No, it was made from chaos, and creativity led the way out of the chaos, *so for God's sake let us focus on the creativity*.' " Later, Redford would say that Hendler had his best interests at heart, but that down deep Hendler really conceived of Sundance as little more than a tax write-off.

Redford had also become uneasy about Gregson, now an equal partner. Too many projects Redford expressed interest in were sidelined, and the easy communication between the men had lapsed. "I felt affection for him," says Redford. "He was a smart man. But I never knew exactly the truth of how Wildwood was being run. I was never told. When he set it up, he insisted on structuring it as a Bermuda-based company, for tax reduction purposes. It was legal and impressive on paper, but it was far too complicated and maybe compromising for my liking. And then, like Gary, his vision and mine diverged. I discovered his ambition for Wildwood was an empire. He wanted an alliance with a major entertainment music company, and he put the wheels in motion to start that without consulting me. We were thinking differently, so I saw separation as the best option. We stayed friends, but I told Dick, 'No, this Wildwood isn't for me,' and I shook his hand. It cost me $25,000 that I didn't have to buy out his share, but it was a price I was happy to pay."

The underlying dilemma, however, was about the essence of his acting career. Gregson, like Paramount, saw a big future for Redford as a glamour attraction, making headline movies with the likes of Paul Newman and earning big paychecks to underwrite Sundance or whatever extracurricular notion appealed to him. Redford was more considered. *Butch Cassidy and the Sundance Kid* was a joyous experience, but he was realistic about it: it might be a fluke. He also didn't want to base his decision making on Hollywood mores. He wanted independence and experiment. "The trouble was, his obligation to Paramount meant they had some control over his direction," says Mike Frankfurt. "He liked the experience of the small-time movie with Ritchie so much that he wanted more. But Paramount now had a positive sense of what Robert Redford should be. He was a romantic adventure boy, and that's how they'd pitch him from now on."

Redford rejected the first half-dozen scripts Paramount offered, but accepted *Little Fauss and Big Halsy,* which had an edginess that smacked of the emergent alternative cinema. That Hollywood was changing under the weight of foreign influences and youth power was unquestionable. The Brits were here in force, evidenced in movies like John Schlesinger's *Midnight Cowboy,* an essay in social agitation. Elsewhere, the piss and vinegar of youthful experiment was flowing in *Woodstock*, *M*A*S*H* and *Five Easy Pieces.* This "adventurous disinhibition," in Redford's words, was also in *Little Fauss.* The script was written by bit-part actor and playwright Charles Eastman. Eastman, whose family served in the technical and secretarial departments of various Hollywood studios, had worked for three uncredited months on *This Property Is Condemned.* As a writer he'd become legendary for holding on to the screenplays he wrote. One of his unproduced works, "Honey Bear, I Think I Love You," was cited by Robert Towne, the screenwriter of *Chinatown,* as highly influential. His breakthrough, such as it was, was his self-directed *The All-American Boy,* a six-part meditation on human fallibility, couched in the profile of a boxer, played by Jon Voight. The movie languished on the shelf for years, and was only released in 1973, following Voight's success with *Deliverance.* Eastman's next project was *Little Fauss,* which new producers Brad Dexter and Al Ruddy sold to Paramount.

A trailer-park-trash story about two dirt-track-bike-racing enthusiasts, the unctuous Fauss and his manipulative, sexually insatiable buddy, Halsy, the new script was distinguished mainly by its insistence on glorifying losers. This Milleresque cynicism was the appeal of the proffered role of Halsy. Michael Ritchie felt the choice was "plain ornery, just Bob's way of flipping the bird at convention in general." But Redford says, "It was the great writing that got me. It wasn't Henry Miller, but it was sweet and iconoclastic. Plus it did exactly what we tried to do with *Downhill Racer*, which was deflate false myths."

Sidney J. Furie, a Canadian whose career began directing Cliff Richard, the British equivalent of Elvis, in travelogue musicals, was the unlikely director. Redford didn't know his early work, but Gregson had introduced him to Furie's quasi–James Bond movie, *The Ipcress File,* starring Michael Caine, and the recent Frank Sinatra vehicle, *The Naked Runner,* which Redford liked. He was stimulated, too, by the proposed costars. Michael J. Pollard, the New Jersey–born actor who started in television and was nominated as best supporting actor for Arthur Penn's *Bonnie and Clyde,* would play Little Fauss, and Lauren Hutton, the leading Revlon model, would play Halsy's girl, Rita Nebraska.

Shot in three different western states through the summer of 1970, *Little Fauss* tested Redford's physical and emotional stamina. The bike racing, filmed at the Willow Springs Raceway outside Los Angeles, at the Manzanita Speedway in Phoenix, and at Sears Point in Sonoma County, in the sweltering heat of June, was the easiest part. But Furie and Pollard made the going tough. "Furie was one of the dictatorial, do-it-my-way-and-don't-ask-questions brigade," says Redford, "and that works with a lot of actors; in fact, they crave it. But it wasn't for me. The trouble was, I knew this Halsy character. He was the kind of self-serving bum I'd known in my younger days, and that was an interesting psychology in the context of where America was going in the early seventies. But Furie wasn't up for that." Pollard, another of Stark Hesseltine's finds, was moody and introverted. Redford made several attempts to discuss the deeper levels of the script, but gave up. He found Furie entrenched and Pollard "a self-absorbed, freewheeling Actors Studio anarchist" who had no patience with revision. No friendships were formed.

That the end result was eccentric was no great surprise. Jamie, Redford's son, later regarded *Little Fauss* as a personal favorite because he felt it captured his father's essential rebelliousness. Alan Pakula regarded it as the last unself-conscious revelation of the actor's real-life "edge." These revelations, however, struggled against a thinly plotted script that was remarkable for its repetitiveness. Longueurs apart, Redford's Halsy might be seen as a metaphor for the blind self-centeredness of rebellion: he uses women like Kleenex and compulsively manipulates the hero worship of Little Fauss for his own purposes. Beyond the generalities, the plot plods: Halsy sweet-talks Little Fauss into joining him on the race circuit, causes the accident that breaks Little Fauss's leg, abandons him, then borrows his name, license and bike to compete elsewhere. The biker groupie, Rita, the object of contention for both, gets pregnant, but neither her pregnancy nor Little Fauss's being drafted affects Halsy at all. At the end, the men drive to another race at Sears Point and disappear among the faceless competitors. The mood in turns is darkly comic, then wildly self-referential, then finally nihilistic.

The epilogue of Eastman's original draft, the draft he and Redford cherished, contained this sentence: "Somewhere is Halsy, somewhere is Little, but they are lost in the crowd for they are not winners but rather among those who make no significant mark and leave no permanent trace." Redford loved this subtle observation of a crucial social lie. "Because we are in a remedial society that actually isn't about remedies at all. It's a lie. And people like Halsy do their thing and vanish. Their lives have no consequence."

In the end, Redford felt keenly that the movie was a lost opportunity. He described it to *Rolling Stone* as "a fucked movie." But he remains fond of it. "I thought the underlying sentiment was an expression of what was truly at risk in the sixties fallout: loss of faith. It was about the condition that makes losers. Furie didn't get that. There were so many moments when he told me to do it one way, and I just couldn't. I *knew* the truth of these people, but he couldn't go there."

Redford's displeasure with Paramount grew. Since the studio had done nothing to push *Downhill Racer,* he instructed CMA to seek reversion of its nontheatrical rights to Wildwood. The request was received unsympathetically. Paramount had invested in him over the years and seemed offended that he was not keen to return the commitment. During the production of *Little Fauss,* Paramount learned that Redford was preparing a movie for Warners with Sydney Pollack. Stanley Jaffe, the new vice president working with Robert Evans, was allegedly offended, disappointed, doubtless, that his star was moving away from the studio just as he had hit the big time. In the fall of 1970, Paramount complained formally about Redford's "contempt" for the legal settlement of 1968. The terms of that agreement had specified the actor's availability for three movies before

September 1971, for a fee of $150,000 per movie. That agreement, said Paramount, had not been honored. Jaffe informed Hendler he was "sick of hearing Redford moan"; that Redford had spurned the offers of substantial scripts like *Murphy's War,* to be directed by Peter Yates; that the studio in fact lost $1 million to date on *Downhill Racer,* which had gone $600,000 over budget; that the studio also lost $5 million on *Blue* (which was finally made starring Terence Stamp).

Redford was outraged by the misrepresentations. "I cared about Charlie Bluhdorn because I liked him," says Redford. "I did not care about Paramount. As far as I was concerned, the onus was on them to come up with the good scripts, and they didn't, so I moved on. They had no allegiance to me. They paid me a lousy $60,000 for *Barefoot* and $90,000 for *Little Fauss.* So I felt as though I owed them nothing at all."

The heat of Paramount's fury reflected Redford's new importance. He was now a hugely valuable commodity.

13

Two and a Half Careers

As Redford became a star, Sydney Pollack was hitting his stride. Burt Lancaster's patronage and friendship proved their worth on *The Scalphunters,* the gritty, mature western that made its money back in six months and served as the movie breakthrough Pollack longed for. Lancaster then offered him *Castle Keep,* a war movie funded by Columbia, to be shot in Yugoslavia. While Pollack worked on *Castle Keep* with Columbia's assigned producer, John Calley, he was also preparing an independent project that Charlie Chaplin's company had been floating for years, Horace McCoy's *They Shoot Horses, Don't They?* a brooding social essay about Depression-era excess starring Jane Fonda that would go on to earn nine Academy Award nominations, including one for Pollack as best director.

For Redford, his friendship with Pollack was more than ever a haven. They sought out each other's company, kept in constant touch by phone and solicited advice and jokes. "Bob was never 'work' in my mind," said Pollack. "We were coconspirators, really, trying to make sense of Hollywood together. He would share his woes with me, and I with him. I was there for him with advice on *Downhill;* he was there for me on my movies."

As scripts piled up at Wildwood, Redford singled out two submitted by the agent Joe Wizan, a friend of Gregson's from his London International agency days who was trying to become a producer and packager. The projects were "Apocalypse Now" and "Liver-Eating Johnson: The Legend of the Crow Killer," both written by Wizan's new discovery, John Milius, a Missouri-born film school graduate from the University of Southern California who had won an award for a short film. Wizan told Redford, "Pick which one you'd like. I can set either up, no problem." Redford read and liked both scripts. Each had a primal starkness that was revelatory of a raw, frontier Americanism that interested Redford. Over a couple of days, he reflected on both submissions and decided "Liver-Eating Johnson," a western, was exactly what he'd been looking for. He phoned Pollack and suggested they do it together.

For Pollack, the timing was perfect: "I was in the position to get it moving because I'd made *They Shoot Horses, Don't They?* and there was a great industry buzz about it. I'd also come in on budget with *Castle Keep,* so John Calley was happy. And then, just by luck, John was appointed head of production at Warners and he and Ted Ashley, Warners' president, started looking for something original they could call the next big thing."

Milius was a lifelong admirer of Teddy Roosevelt's and a champion of what he calls "the warrior culture." His early writing had a barbarous intensity, projecting a world where humanity and sanity are constantly assaulted and heroism is ambiguous. Pollack loved Milius's script, which he described as "a stylish, literary piece about a Paul Bunyan type who ate trees: weird!" But he agreed with Redford that in its present form it was unshootable. Redford turned to Milius's source novel, Vardis Fisher's *Mountain Man,* and decided the gold was in the original. "It was the story of an authentic mountain man," he says, "based on well-documented facts and closer to the real West than anything I'd ever read or seen. I made some simple connections: the Rockies, where I lived, wilderness, authenticity, the men who cracked the frontier, truth. I told Sydney, 'We can do this *the authentic way.* There's no other option. Let's go.' "

With Wizan as producer and Warners' backing, work started. Edward Anhalt, who had won several Academy Awards throughout the fifties, was assigned the rewrite, and contracts were signed all around. Redford accepted an up-front $200,000 against his best-yet fee of $500,000. Pollack's fee was $220,000, a 20 percent improvement on *Castle Keep.*

Pollack and Calley decided to shoot the film in southern Spain. Redford was shocked. He had been adamant from the outset: this movie should be made in the best, authentic setting—his own front yard. "I had an acute sense of location. The script was the unsensationalized life of a Rocky Mountain trapper. John Johnson, the original mountain man, lived in these canyons around Sundance 120 years ago. That was one good reason to do it here. There was also a budgetary advantage in the Utah right-to-work law. It made financial sense. There was no way I was going to go along with Sydney if he wished to make this on a Warners' lot with pickups in Spain."

Pollack insisted that the movie could not be made entirely on location for its budget of $4 million. But Redford dug his heels in. "He had a stubborn streak a mile wide," said Pollack. "I argued. I begged. I reckoned, We'll go through hell on this one, but he'll get his way." Redford did. A month after *Little Fauss* wrapped, the newly titled *Jeremiah Johnson* started shooting with autumnal pickups in Sundance's Alpine Meadows, at Mirror Lake, on the flank of Timpanogos and along the ridges of Provo Canyon. "It turned into a mess," said Pollack. "We simply were not ready for production. As soon as we started, I knew for sure we could not do it for the $4 million agreed. Bob was a very expensive actor by now. And Calley was worried because the numbers didn't add up. He said, 'Bob is too costly, and these locations of his are too awkward. It will never work. You will run out of money.' But Bob continued to be insistent: 'We can shoot in Utah,' he said."

According to Pollack, Ted Ashley, backed by Warners' legal executive Frank Wells, pulled the plug in Utah. Warners then announced that the movie would be shot on the back lot, with the second unit doing some background shooting around Lake Arrowhead.

Redford would have none of it. He flew to Los Angeles with Hendler, Begelman and Fields for a showdown with Warners. Begelman advised Ashley, Calley and Wells that their star might become unavailable because of "illness." Threats and counterthreats flew. When things calmed down, it was agreed that Ashley, Calley and Wells would deposit $4 million in Zions Bank in Provo, which would represent their total contribution to the production. If the costs ran over, they would have to be covered by director and actor. A lien would be put on Pollack's production company as collateral.

Pollack was not at the meeting and felt this proposal was hardest on him. "It wasn't an easy decision for me to accept," he said, "because I was only just establishing myself and my company. I thought about getting out at that point, but I couldn't because Bob had already spent his $200,000." And it was true that Redford was financially stretched to the limit that summer. Nevertheless, Redford insists he was as exposed in the deal as his friend. "It was wrong of me to agree to the $4 million in Sydney's absence, and I did apologize eventually. But I deferred part of my fee, because of the risk. I was sharing this with Sydney, and I wanted to be fair."

For a while Pollack refused to return Redford's calls. "I was pissed," says Redford. "It was clear this wasn't going to be an easy film to make, and he was getting cold feet. But we had made promises to each other. I got him on the phone and told him, 'Don't fuck me around, Sydney. You know we *have to* do this picture.' It was tense and drawn out, but finally loyalty carried the day."

David Rayfiel received a sudden frantic summons from Pollack: "He said, 'Forget you were born in Brooklyn. We have a story about liver-eating frontier savages. Milius has done some good work, Anhalt has done some work, Redford has done some. But I need you to fix it.' "

Milius's script had been gutted by Anhalt, Redford and Pollack and now revolved around the clash of value systems on the frontier between the white man and the Indian. Johnson's battle against the elements—at the forefront in Milius's script—was now background. In search of personal freedom, Johnson, an ex-soldier, leaves civilization to pit his wits against the Rockies. Along the way he befriends the regional tribes, the Blackfoot, Flathead and Crow, adopts an orphan boy and wins a gift bride from the Flathead, before inadvertently offending the Crow by helping a team of army scouts traverse their sacred lands. His new family is slaughtered in revenge and Johnson's harmony with the wilderness ends.

"I never saw movies as theatrical three-acters," says Rayfiel. "For me, a movie is narrative, like a novel. So what I gave was a clarity of flow and, hopefully, some character-illuminating dialogue that pointed up Johnson's nature and how he responds to his loss." As part of his revision, Rayfiel gave Pollack and Redford a five-page essay concerning Johnson's relationship with his Flathead bride. Pollack found this invaluable. "Some juice in that liberated a lot of the story line for Bob and I," said Pollack. "That human element was missing in Milius. There was no humanized contact. It was formerly just enmity all the way. But David's notes turned it around for us. Finally we found a shootable script."

Pollack's screenplay file for *Jeremiah Johnson* is the fattest and most revealing in his script library. It shows what underlay his and Redford's teamwork. "I was not a front-row political artist any more than I was a visual stylist," said Pollack. "But I always believed every speck of research was crucial, and the smallest detail must be finessed. Bob was not like that. He had to have a central reality that he could hold on to, and work from there. He was overview, I was detail." Starting on January 12, 1970, three weeks after the opening of *They Shoot Horses, Don't They?* Pollack recorded his conceptual notes for creating the character of frontiersman Johnson with Redford. He concluded with a quote from a *Newsweek* article about Redford: "A new movie hero has emerged, often a surrogate [of] the director himself, outside society, alienated by mainstream American values, searching for his identity as he moves across the face of America. These new heroes are often losers whose heroism is measured not in their ability to triumph, but to survive."

Thereafter, over the next twelve months, Pollack recorded page after page of conversations, source references and ideas, all focused on reducing the gap between Redford and Johnson. Carol Rossen, who was a friend of Pollack's as well, believes that *Jeremiah Johnson* "was the fusion of Bob and Sydney and the interdependency of their creativity. Many people have remarked that Sydney really wanted to *be* Bob, that all he lacked was the blond mane. And there's truth in that, because, after all, he was an actor, with an actor's training. But it was also a spiritual transference. They made seven movies together because they were mirror images of each other. The bottom line is, they saw life in very similar ways."

Uninterrupted filming of *Jeremiah Johnson* finally began in January 1971. But Pollack and his cinematographer, Duke Callaghan, agonized as the schedule swung with the vagaries of weather: "The snows of St. George in southern Utah were terrible," said Pollack, "and we were using Cinemobiles [mobile ministudios] as the lifelines. There was no way I was going to let it overrun, and Bob was a superb partner in keeping us tight. In the end it was the greatest way to learn production, because I was playing with my own money. And it worked to my advantage: I beat the clock and brought it in at $3.1 million. The deal I'd made gave me 50 percent of the first $100,000 under budget and 25 percent of the second $100,000 and so forth, so I made an extra $100,000-plus by coming in $900,000 under budget." Pollack and Redford split the reward fifty-fifty.

Redford's satisfaction with the movie was spiritual, but others extrapolated different values. There seemed, many said, a concentration of acting technique. The writer Robert Pirsig has observed that Redford's appeal to the public, like Gary Cooper's, is the "inscrutable silence," as portrayed in the Sundance Kid. This, says Pirsig, reflects a Native American demeanor lost to the culture. In *Jeremiah Johnson* Pollack observed a finessed focus: "He surprised me. He was running around with me, doing all the production things, riding snowmobiles and digging us out and laboring. But then the shooting started, and he retreated inside himself. So much of it was mime. And to mime, you need some extraordinary composure because if you are going to be self-conscious, this is where it will show. I got the impression he was here in the canyon for all the right reasons, and the relaxation, that honesty, took him to this very, very calm place. Everything became minimalist, very contained. I did not direct that pacing. He did. For me, he became another kind of actor on that picture, a far more internal actor, and I always tried afterward to tap into that place."

Much credit, too, is Pollack's, since it was he who assembled the visual collage surrounding Redford's inward journey, most striking in the sequence, not long after the movie's intermission (it was presented as a two-part movie in theaters), when Johnson, having led the soldiers through the Crow lands, returns alone, homeward-bound. Duke Callaghan's camera, alternating vast panoramas with microscopic close-ups, animates Johnson's fear of the consequence of his tribal transgression and his smallness against wilderness. "Finally, you don't 'act' a movie like *Jeremiah Johnson,*" says Redford. "It becomes an experience, into which you fit and flow. It was grueling and I was changed by it, no question. We re-created a way of life that real people lived in these real mountains, the same now as they were then. You learn by immersing yourself in their reality."

As postproduction finished, Lola and the kids, with the help of Sundance caretakers Mike Shinderling and Jerry Hill, marked Redford's thirty-fourth birthday by building him a mud and wood hideaway like Johnson's on the meadow trail to North Point, high above the A-frame. This retreat—where he could sleep on a mud dais, cook over a hole in the floor and watch the stars beyond the glacial peak of Timpanogos through the loose pine slats—deeply touched him, and it has become a place of reflection and solace over the years.

On October 22, 1970, a day after the release of *Little Fauss and Big Halsy,* Lola gave birth to a daughter, Amy, a full ten years after Shauna's arrival. Redford welcomed the domestic celebration as an invitation to reprioritize his life. Film work had consumed him for five years and, given his new success, looked likely to accelerate. He felt the need to address his other interests, and, he says, "fill out the palette" of his life.

Activism was the main issue. The Goldmans' apartment at 815 Madison Avenue became unofficial operational headquarters while the Redfords decorated their new apartment, at the corner of Fifth Avenue and Ninety-fourth Street. While Lola, Ilene and the circle of friends campaigned for research into the use of phosphates and detergents, Redford encouraged the picketing of supermarkets. Cynthia Burke, a principal CAN administrator, saw Redford as a major asset—especially given his new celebrity—but expected no long-term involvement from him. "He was really too strikingly individualistic to be absorbed into the CAN team," she says.

The direction of Redford's activism was clarified by *Jeremiah Johnson,* turning him permanently to wilderness preservation and environmentalism. During *Jeremiah,* at the behest of the American Museum of Natural History, he had recorded a wildlife conservation album, *The Language and Music of the Wolves,* which became a national best seller for Columbia Records and inspired wide debate about depleted wilderness species. This satisfied him more than much he had done over the last few years. More and more he found himself absorbed by environmental study. He read Rachel Carson's influential *Silent Spring,* a clarion call against the earth's degradation, and former interior secretary Stewart Udall's *The Quiet Crisis,* which traced the route from Indian stewardship to the technological rape of the land. It intrigued him that, after the first Earth Day, *The New Republic* had mocked the concept of eco-activism, yet six months later a full issue was devoted to the subject. Shortly after, in December 1970, the Environmental Protection Agency (EPA) had come into being. Redford interpreted all these movements as signs of a national willingness to assess neglected, critical issues. He was proud of CAN and Lola's work but he sought something closer to wilderness for his own focus and found it almost immediately, literally in his own backyard.

For months he had been observing the buildup of heavy machinery at the mouth of the Provo Canyon Road. There had long been a plan to expand the two-lane highway into a wider cross-state conduit, which he had spoken out against. Now it appeared to be under way. Redford understood that a widened road would deface the landscape, but he only grasped the full extent of the potential impact when the local chapter of Trout Unlimited asked him to become formally involved. The Provo River, one of the great trout rivers of the West, was under threat. Redford researched the proposed road and discovered the extent of the vested interests: elected officials and transport department executives who owned sand quarries and gravel supply companies. On the group's behalf, Redford visited Utah governor Calvin Rampton. Redford had been good for business in Utah: he had created many jobs and ensured prominent western premieres of *Butch Cassidy* and *Downhill Racer* at Provo and Orem. But Rampton gave him the brush-off. "I sat and listened to all the old chestnuts about due process," says Redford. "What he meant was the vested interests would continue to control the process. I suddenly saw that this was the ancient issue, the old-style abuse of Indian lands all over. What I was dealing with, I quickly learned, was the tip of the iceberg in the West. In the preceding decade, no fewer than six major power plants had been sited in the Four Corners. No one in New York or L.A. minded much. But they were causing the kind of doomsday pollution scenario Rachel Carson prophesied. I decided there and then it was time to get off my ass and do something, even if it meant making an enemy of Rampton."

Redford helped combine the three local activist groups into one. Then he organized groups of sixth-grade and junior high school students to form a human chain march on the governor's mansion. "It achieved no more than a holding action on the highway dispute," says Redford, "but it got people talking in an enlightened way." Lola advised her husband that the war might best be fought on several fronts. CAN was making itself known in Washington and making friends like Dick Ayres, who was raising funds for the new legal regulatory watchdog, the Natural Resources Defense Council (NRDC). Redford followed this trail and introduced himself to a number of key movers and shakers with conservationist leanings, among them Wayne Owens, the administrative secretary to the progressive Democratic senator from Utah, Frank Moss, who himself had formulated an environmental platform for a run at Congress. These new relationships, says Redford, fed an urge to engage with society in ways other than moviemaking.

"He opened up another part-time career," said Sydney Pollack. "I used to say to him, 'Bob, this is specialized work; this will drain your energies.' But he just had to do it. It was a compulsion connected to the landscape." Michael Ritchie, who had fallen out of touch since *Downhill Racer,* was fascinated by the stories of Redford's multitasking. "One minute I'd hear he was recording some conservation album, the next he was back in Europe skiing, or down in the Caribbean. He'd promised me we'd do another movie from that trilogy he envisioned, that he was fired up by the experience of working with me, but nothing gelled. I'd hear from somebody that he was planning something with Peter Yates or George Hill, that he wanted to move on. But the overall impression was that he was spinning like a top."

Redford refocused again. Hendler and Frankfurt were polishing their plans to expand the Sundance business model, but suddenly he stopped showing up for meetings. Calls went unanswered, letters ignored. Stan Collins saw panic among the partners: "They wanted a business planner, a practical guy. He went artsy. There was an arena on the Sundance property that was an open-air theater. He decided that would become the children's theater, and that's what he gave his attention to. He didn't want to talk about condo building or new potential partners with cash. He only wanted to talk about the obstacles to creating an arts community."

By 1971, Redford had slowed down the expansion of the Hendler-Frankfurt venture partnership. "It came to a head," says Redford, "because I saw that the bottom-line philosophy from the partners was, 'Let's sell the hell out of Sundance.' Gary said, 'Let's put in water, power and development and cultivate a small city. We can take $15 million out of this in three years.' I, of course, wouldn't have that, so they all got to rethink and became magnanimous about saying, 'Well, you have the vision, so maybe we should sell back our shares.' And they were saying that because they saw the danger of their exposure. Then there was the problem of the alternative sidebar investments they wanted. I could not be involved in investments that were not *emotionally* led. Finally, their message to me was, 'The way we see Sundance is different from you. You see some airy-fairy preserve.' Gary's message to me was, 'Don't push your version of Sundance. It's a diseased dog.' But to my thinking, I was just starting. I didn't care how diseased it appeared: I was going to nurture it. I realized something had ended, that Sundance wouldn't succeed the way Gary's business group was headed. So I bought out everyone except Stan, whom I kept in for 10 percent, because he was a longtime buddy."

Frankfurt was not surprised by Redford's U-turn: "I sensed that the sole architect of Sundance's future would be Bob. Only Bob. The mom-and-pop aspect of developing the canyon was always more attractive to him than the corporate version. I knew where he was going, and for the next seven years, nominally supported by Collins and I, it was really just Bob cutting the course."

Few of the studio offers coming in now inspired Redford. There were several in the brew—projects in development with Francis Ford Coppola, Steven Spielberg, Brian De Palma, Arthur Penn—but the movies currently dominating cinema fare were potboilers. He especially hated the "yearbook" disaster films, so called because of the strips of star photos flanking the promotional posters. Stephanie Phillips believed he saw himself essentially as a hero figure, but Redford contests this: "No, I did not. People on the outside might have made assumptions on those lines, but I was interested in the individual who is overcome by outside forces, the suppressed or flawed individual. I did not want one-dimensional heroism, and that is why I avoided those blockbuster movies."

Some tantalizing, worthy projects came close. George Roy Hill was keen to adapt J. P. Donleavy's novel *The Ginger Man,* then playing on Broadway. Hill had befriended Donleavy and the real-life Ginger Man, Gainor Crist, in the fifties in Dublin and introduced writer and actor. Redford made several walks around Woodlawn Cemetery with Donleavy, but little substantial progress toward a film was made. He loved the writer's eccentricity but, like Hill, lost interest in what Hill called "the gigs and reels." Otto Preminger stepped in, but he failed to find studio interest.

Another contender was *Serpico,* based on the true story of a Manhattan cop's fight against police corruption. Redford liked Frank Serpico but hesitated when Serpico secured an agent. "That's when all the nonsense of deal making and points positioning took over. It was a shame, because I was interested in Frank as a human being, and his story of the little guy against the institution was exactly what I loved."

Fred Zinnemann wanted him for Universal's *The Day of the Jackal,* based on Frederick Forsyth's novel about a plot to kill Charles de Gaulle. Redford thought not. "Freddie Fields said I was crazy, because it was Zinnemann, the surefire box office hit. But I couldn't accept it. There was no depth to the story. I needed a journey into the character's psyche and motivation. It wasn't there. He was just a psychotic killer, and the story described his maneuvers to try to kill de Gaulle. It had a 'So what?' feeling for me."

Redford found what he wanted in a project written by Bill Goldman, *The Hot Rock.* On the face of it, it's hard to see why this makeweight movie appealed. But the fee—$400,000 from Fox—explained much. "The real reasons were domestic," says Redford. "Amy was new in our lives. I wanted to be in Manhattan for the summer, close to Lola and the baby. I wanted to get my bearings because the feeling I had was similar to the aftermath of that first Hollywood spell, after *This Property Is Condemned,* where I sensed I was spending too much time away from home."

Peter Yates, the project's director, was a Royal Court stage-trained Englishman, who, like Sidney Furie, had worked on Cliff Richard musicals. Three years before, he'd made his brilliant transition to American cinema with Warners' *Bullitt,* a model police thriller laced with action scenes that made San Francisco seem like an arcade game. Yates saw Redford as "one of the great cinema treasures, like Clark Gable. It's a matter of science, that kind of screen beauty, something to do with ratios and millimeters, like the Mona Lisa's smile." The men liked each other, though Redford was aware of a cross-cultural chasm: "In the middle sixties everything

English was good. But that presented many problems, because the cultural essences and the patois are different. By the 1970s, people were beginning to think twice about this Brit invasion."

Goldman's script, based on Donald E. Westlake's novel of the same name, was a tall tale of a crack team of thieves, led by ex-con Dortmunder, who are commissioned to steal from a museum a diamond of importance to an African potentate. It had been written primarily for George Segal, who would play the locksmith Kelp, second in command to his brother-in-law, Dortmunder, the role offered to Redford. Pakula thought this was "the worst possible thing Bob could have done at that moment, because the eyes of the world were on him, and that plot was just the sort of facile garbage you see on television every week." But Redford—a George Segal fan—was keen: "The story was about a gang of thieves, emphasis on *gang*, so there was the joy of playing in an ensemble team for the first time since the American Academy. I enjoyed that camaraderie," he says.

Structure, Goldman wrote in his memoirs, is all, and indeed structure, and Quincy Jones's jazz track, was all that held the movie together. The rest was a repetitive (four attempts to steal the diamond) *Pink Panther*-esque muddle lightened by the casting of Zero Mostel and Paul Sand. In an apparent attempt to recapture the magic of *The Sundance Kid*, Goldman's script piled on the witty lines: surveying the explosive devices needed to blow their way into the museum, fellow conspirator Sand offers Redford an unusual Molotov cocktail. "It's a kinda European type," he says. "I learned it at the Sorbonne." Demonstrating another kind of bomb, Sand tells him, "I learned this one at Berkeley." "You must like to study," Redford quips.

"I suspect Goldman was trying to outdo the Sundance Kid," says Redford, "but this was an altogether lighter piece, so the jokes didn't work so well. And Peter did have that difficulty of assimilating American humor. It's a tough task for a non-American, and I think he struggled."

Ted Zachary, who was Yates's first assistant, defends both Yates's and Redford's work on the movie. "Whatever the script deficiencies, Peter was adept. He'd done *Robbery* in Britain, which was sharp as anything, and then the in-between American picture, *John and Mary*, which was sensitive. So he had a wide understanding of drama, and of actors. He never once crossed with Bob. In fact, their relationship was the most harmonious I've ever experienced. Then again, Bob was the most *ready* actor I've worked with. I never remember him with a script in his hands. He knew what Goldman had written inside out, and he never missed his mark. For me, he was an education in perfectionism."

There was an education for Zachary, too, in the kind of stardom that hung about Redford. At East Meadow, Long Island, Yates, Segal and Redford were rehearsing a scene at an abandoned prison. Frank Serpico was visiting and hanging out with Redford in his motor home dressing room nearby. "My job was to control the location," says Zachary, "but I got no forewarning of mob behavior. I'd never seen it, unless it was on television, watching the kids go crazy for the Beatles. But suddenly these *Sundance Kid* fans found out Bob was in there, and they laid siege on the motor home. They surrounded it and started trying to rock it off its wheels to get him out. Serpico was horrified. We all panicked. It was a cut-and-run scenario."

Redford's image by now was in the hands of the grinders of the media mill. Six years before, Louella Parsons had allowed him a modest quote or two in her columns. By 1971 his opinions were being solicited on everything from lasting marriage to eggs Benedict. He acknowledges his complicity in this image building but says he regretted it even as it happened. The photo images that flooded magazine stands stirred the hysteria. Not since Sean Connery bounded onto the scene in *Dr. No* a decade earlier had thespian beefcake been so brazenly peddled. These ubiquitous images—usually from *Little Fauss*—perfectly bridged the gap between the coiffed pinup and the counterculture. In them, Redford is tanned and tufty, a bare-chested, tight-jeaned lothario with a louche, even menacing, gaze. Laurence Luckinbill, writing for *Esquire,* hinted at the turmoil beneath this gilded exterior. Hanging around at the Redfords' apartment and chatting about every subject under the sun for several hours, Luckinbill deduced that the actor's real passion was not for icons, but for losers. The journalist asked what's next. "And my question lies there like a discarded sock," wrote Luckinbill. Redford then confronted the interviewer "with the measured concentration of a pole-vaulter. 'What's next?' he repeats. 'Nothing, just nothing.' "

"In reality," says Redford today, "I was conflicted. On one hand, it was the most amazing time. I was young, celebrated, with plenty of work. On the other hand, it was a Faustian deal. No matter how you try, you are commodified. Whether you are a competent actor, or an artist, is incidental. The main business is, you are product. I had a hard time steadying myself against that stuff."

It was also hard to stabilize against the vicissitudes of Hollywood business. As *The Hot Rock* was completed, Redford looked forward to the parallel release of *Jeremiah Johnson.* Side by side, he felt, these very different movies would demonstrate his substance. It wasn't to be. Exactly as happened with Paramount and *Downhill Racer,* Warners' distribution showed contempt for the finished *Jeremiah Johnson,* which was ready for release late in 1971 but was left on the shelf. The following spring, to Warners' surprise, the movie was invited to feature out of competition at the Cannes Film Festival. The stir it raised prompted Warners to finally release the film properly in cinemas nationwide in December 1972.

Redford was hurt by Warners' lack of confidence in the film, but the hurt only hardened his resolve to do better. In Gregson's absence, Wildwood was now a one-man operation, and he decided emphatically that this must be the epicenter of his art. Michael Ritchie contended that this was the enclave where the "secret" Robert Redford lived. "He was really an author. His writing credit wasn't on *Downhill* or *Jeremiah Johnson* but he really was an author as much as David Rayfiel, or even Salter. I always felt that was denied him, but he was in a no-win situation, because he had all this luminous stardom and neither the public nor critics have much patience for author-stars."

It was at Wildwood throughout 1971 that Redford honed what was to become *The Candidate.* The first inklings of it came to him as he sat with a can of Coors in his hand, watching a televised fund-raiser for President Nixon moderated by Oklahoma football coach Bud Wilkinson in October 1968. Redford was outraged that Nixon had refused to debate the Democratic candidate, Hubert Humphrey, because there was a third candidate, George Wallace. "It was incomprehensible arrogance in the face of a country in such turmoil," says Redford. "To anyone with a brain in his head, there was a huge division between 'old politics' and 'the politics of joy' that Humphrey was attempting to present. A hundred cities across the country were in flames on racial issues; half the nation was calling for a stop to the bombing in Vietnam. The youth, the poor, the blacks wanted a voice, and those who might have spoken for them—Kennedy and McCarthy—were out of the picture. And here was this car salesman monopolizing the airwaves and selling us snake oil for a reelection. I thought, It's not about substance, it's about presentation, about perception of reality, which allows for manipulation."

Incensed, Redford commissioned *Village Voice* journalist Pete Hamill to tackle "a script about character, national politics and the vested interest." Thereafter, in the snatches between movies and star interviews, he embarked on a research campaign, befriending political columnists like Mike Barnicle, exploring CAN's senatorial contacts, visiting the Kennedy archive. *McCall's* reported Redford frequently in the company of former light heavyweight boxing champion turned activist José Torres and Hamill, haunting the corridors of the campaign offices of gubernatorial and senate candidates in the New York State elections. In fact, says Redford, this research proved much more edifying than the tedium of the movie promotional circus. More and more, he sought the company of political, rather than business, associates. Basketball star Bill Bradley, himself nourishing political ambitions, was among the most stimulating dinner companions. In such company, says Redford, he felt intellectually stimulated in a profound new way. "The forties were the war years. The fifties were the boom years. The sixties was the revolution. And the seventies offered the payoff. All those long-haired hippies and yippies divided into two groups. There were those who'd doped themselves into oblivion. Then there were the guys who went to the Ivy League colleges, and Stanford and Berkeley, and pulled out the stops when McCarthy and the Democrats let them down. They took it upon themselves to rewrite the rule book. They were lawyers, like John Adams of the Natural Resources Defense Council, who took on the system surreptitiously. While Nixon was over in China working his realpolitik, these guys slid in underneath and were the brains behind the National Environmental Policy Act, the Energy Production and Recovery Act, everything that matters in calling a country a country. From 1972 onward the cream of the rebels rose to the surface: Tom Harkin, Pat Schroeder, Gary Hart, Jerry Brown—great political minds who concentrated on working the system against itself while Nixon was busy getting us involved in Cambodia. I was excited by this, that I was working at potentially the greatest time in American political life, when this vast swell of educated kids was taking on those profound issues raised by Udall and Carson, and I wanted to be part of it."

Hamill's script didn't work out. It was too much like Edwin O'Connor's *The Last Hurrah*. "This was not Pete's fault, because I hadn't sufficiently enunciated the kind of satire I wanted. I wanted a snipe at the fallibility of government when it's based on personality." When Redford told Bradley of the script problem, Bradley recommended Eugene McCarthy's speechwriter, Jeremy Larner. Redford learned that Larner—like Michael Ritchie—was steeped in politics. New York–born, Midwest-raised, Brandeis-educated, he was the speechwriter who allegedly pushed

McCarthy most to the left. Redford liked the notion and flew to Canada, where Ritchie was shooting *Prime Cut* with Lee Marvin, to sound out his willingness to direct the as-yet-unnamed project. With Ritchie aboard, Redford summoned Larner to the Wildwood office in the West Fifties, just before *The Hot Rock* commenced shooting.

Larner approached the meeting, he says, wearing his "alienated novelist" hat. His first novel, *Drive, He Said,* had been written in 1960, when he was twenty-three. It took him four years to find a publisher for it. A career in sports and political journalism followed, then a first venture in filmmaking with Jack Nicholson and Bob Rafelson, coscripting the movie of his novel, which Nicholson directed. In between came the work with McCarthy and a friendship with Kennedy aide Richard Goodwin that opened up a yearlong teaching post at the Institute of Politics, housed within the John F. Kennedy School of Government at Harvard. "But I wasn't professorial," says Larner, "and I took pride in my storytelling, so I faced Redford and Ritchie as I faced Jack Nicholson, as a story maker, with the attitude of, 'I bet this is just another Hollywood crock-of-shit offer.' "

Redford's response, he says, was, "Relax, Jeremy. Just say what you feel like saying."

According to Larner, Ritchie then told him: "We have about ten guys to consider for this writing job, and we have to start shooting in November. If we miss that window, Bob isn't available."

"That kind of straightened me out," Larner recalls, "and I remember replying, 'I write fast.' "

Redford explained his story line: he wanted to make a film about a liberal California senatorial candidate, the son of a respected former governor, who sets out simply to upset the front-running conservative candidate, then gets drawn into the battle and sells out.

Larner immediately challenged the concept. He told Redford, "In my experience, they don't sell out. They get carried away. It's like McCarthy, it's like Nicholson, who are interchangeable. They fix on a belief and are confronted by the Niagara Falls of reality. They hear the sound of the rushing water but don't see it. Then, before they know it, they are over the falls, and they evolve into something else."

Redford was not happy with the response.

Larner felt he had not told Redford what he wanted to hear. "I learned quickly that Bob likes to control conversations. Ultimately, I gave in, because it is too disturbing not to. But there and then, at that first Wildwood meeting, I was talking turkey, in effect saying, 'The problem with you guys—Nicholson, McCarthy, Redford, whoever—is that you fictionalize your own existence. It becomes tough for you to know when you have, in fact, gone over the falls.' "

The clash was momentary. In Larner's view, "Redford got it. I looked into his eyes and saw that he could conceivably be insulted by me, but he wasn't. He was challenged personally by my concept of celebrity corruption and it did not offend him. He could objectify. That was enough to engage me. And with that sparky energy, we began."

California governor Jerry Brown came to believe *The Candidate*'s central character, Bill McKay, was based on him. Others would claim Larner and Redford had satirized Bobby Kennedy or McCarthy, and that the campaign manager, Marvin Lucas, was Dick Goodwin or the Los Angeles lawyer Nelson Rising, an aide to California senator John Tunney. None of this, says Larner, is true, though elements drawn from real life were incorporated. For Redford, some real-life templates were close at hand. Jamie and Shauna were close friends with John Lindsay's children, and the Lindsays regularly skied at Sundance. In fact, not long before, Lindsay had chosen Sundance as the venue to announce a shifted allegiance from the Liberal Party to the Democratic Party, with Redford by his side for the photo op. Redford denies Lindsay was reflected in McKay's character; Larner wasn't so sure. "I think something of the post-JFK noblesse oblige brand of altruism that Lindsay represented slipped into every conversation we had about the film," says Larner. "But it's true that Lindsay's 'arc' was completely different. That is, different in every way, except one: Lindsay's failure demonstrates the failure of political humanism, which is precisely the moral we tried to project in McKay's success."

Redford early on employed spin doctor David Garth, a Lindsay ally, as technical consultant. Larner immediately saw a central character in his fiction come to life. Klein, the head of Bill McKay's media campaign, he decided, would be a version of Dave Garth. "Klein/Garth was vital in my story," says Larner, "because he would be the Greek chorus in the whole fictional campaign. He would be credibility. He was the guy who would say, 'You are X points behind in the polls and you need to do such and such.' I knew this breed of hustler—like Dick Goodwin also—who believe they can direct history as much as any candidate." Larner's first meeting with Garth was electric. "He told us that he was personally going to see to it that John Lindsay became the next president of the United States. He said he knew how to do it, that he would send Lindsay out in the primaries to do it the folksy way, the non-Republican way, by staying in people's houses and not the big hotels. I thought this was horseshit, because in my time with McCarthy I'd heard all this magic elixir stuff from every type of hustler—including myself—and most of it was nothing. It was horseshit but it was sensational because I thought, If we can base our media hustler on Dave Garth, and then give a little of Lindsay to Robert Redford's McKay, we'll get attention and get our point across."

Within days, Redford called to say Garth had had words with his lawyer and had withdrawn from the film, "in case it impinged on his legitimate political work." He had wanted $200,000 to advise.

No matter. Larner still wanted to "keep it real." Redford, however, seemed keener on the poetry than real-life role models. The men verbally sparred, says Larner, and he realized that despite the triumph of the *Sundance Kid,* Redford still didn't have the clout to drive the movie as radically as he wished. "His power with the studios was fragile, and he was still beholden to *the deal.* Maybe that's the grand illusion of Hollywood star power. Maybe it always comes with a begging bowl."

As for the deal, it was Redford's good fortune that Richard Zanuck, riding high on *Butch Cassidy,* had moved to Warners. Redford was yet to experience the annoyance of Warners' lame distribution of *Jeremiah Johnson* and was content to make a deal that was as lean as *Downhill Racer.* The budget, drawn up by Ritchie and production manager Walter Coblenz, was agreed to at a rock-bottom $1.5 million, with no off-the-top fee for Redford. "I accepted because I wanted to get on with it, and Mike and I decided we'd do it tight and in documentary style, with the camera frame jumping around." Redford was also amenable because he liked the new regime at Warners, with Zanuck in the driver's seat and Frank Wells serving as production chief. "It was a brand-new dawn for them. They were up against it as a working enterprise, and suddenly hungry for risk. We had a lot in common; we were idealists and we made good partners at that time."

The scriptwriting for *The Candidate* was unlike what Redford calls his "fireside collaborations" with Pollack. To begin, Larner and Redford created index cards on which were written pertinent headlines concerning the campaign as Redford envisioned it: The cards said "Fund-raiser" and "Environment" and "Hotel Room Service." These were laid out like a puzzle and placed in order of good "beats" for the screenplay. "Once we had that," says Redford, "it was down to Jeremy to create the people."

While Redford worked on *The Hot Rock* through the summer, he and

Larner jogged or played tennis when they could in Central Park, all the time massaging the script. When Redford's shoot wrapped, they holed up at Larner's home in Massachusetts. The first of what would be seven drafts of *The Candidate* was finished by summer's end. Redford found it "delightful, but too windy" and set about fierce editing. Larner, at first, took offense.

"He wouldn't allow the dialogue I'd written for Bill McKay's mistress," says Larner. "He told me his public would not accept the mistress *as a personality.* I questioned this, the historical reality, the Kennedy brothers' mistresses, all that. I was stunned by his concept of his personal image. It was annoying, I suppose, but you had to credit his clarity."

As the movie came together, Ritchie delighted in what he saw as "another Pyrrhic arc" story line, similar to *Downhill Racer,* where an objective is sought at huge personal cost, the war is won and the audience is left to meditate on the putative rewards. When we first encounter McKay, he is consulting with autoworkers, sleeves rolled up, a high-minded lawyer without guile or venality. Then he is manipulated by his campaign manager, Marvin Lucas, into tackling the incumbent senator, Crocker Jarmon. McKay agrees because it allows him a podium from which to state what he truly feels about social problems. When McKay's openness elicits a strong response from the electorate, the party pros step in to repackage him. To his astonishment, McKay, the rank outsider, ends up winning the senatorial campaign. When Chappellet wins on the ski slopes in *Downhill Racer,* a reporter asks him, "What will you do now?" to which he mumblingly replies, "I don't know." At the end of *The Candidate,* McKay faces the same conundrum, asking his campaign manager, "What do we do now?"

Ritchie, whose capacity for intellectual theorizing was impressive, believed that form followed function in film. His prize example was Hitchcock, who thematically loaded interwar movies like *The 39 Steps* and *The Lady Vanishes* with national paranoia but never lost sight of paced storytelling. In *The Candidate,* said Ritchie, the trick was reversed. "I know it might be said of me, in my earlier days, that I was a 'form' director. But that's not how I approached it. I was a story guy. So was Larner. But it was to Bob's eternal credit that the form, the theme, if you like, of this movie was the center. Very few productions I've been involved with developed with such evaluative power. I remember reading what Larner and Bob came up with and saying, 'If we get the beats right, we really have something amazing.' "

Unlike Pollack's, Ritchie's career had hardly leaped forward in the last few years. His current film with Lee Marvin, produced by Joe Wizan, was another studio-less production, but Ritchie was comfortable. "I liked finding the oddball script. I liked finding unknown actors. I liked being the outside guy. And this fit in with the radical Bob. I often thought we were like fugitives on the run. It put great pressure, in a good way, on the imaginative process because, in every department—design, costume, all of it—we were always improvising."

In choosing actors, Redford and Ritchie collaborated closely. Peter Boyle was selected for Lucas, Don Porter for Senator Jarmon, Allen Garfield for Klein and for Nancy, McKay's wife, Karen Carlson, a twenty-seven-year-old Louisiana-born Miss America runner-up. Natalie Wood and Bill Bradley had walk-ons. "Those were impromptu situations," said Ritchie. "Someone would drop by the day we were shooting, and Bob'd say, 'Okay, you're in.' " Natalie Wood became a McKay fan in a jostling crowd; Bradley a bus driver. Actual ABC and NBC anchormen covered McKay's campaign in the film.

The most exciting casting for Redford was Melvyn Douglas, a frontline victim of McCarthyism who was "graylisted" in the fifties for his support of liberal Democratic causes. It was Douglas's wife, Helen Gahagan Douglas, who had fallen afoul of Nixon in the bitterly contested 1960 Senate race, when Nixon labeled her "a pinko right down to her underwear." Gahagan Douglas, in response, christened Nixon "Tricky Dick" and went on to fill the post of treasury secretary in Kennedy's administration. Redford recalled how his father had stood up for Gahagan Douglas all those years ago, and took great pride in offering her husband the role of McKay's father, a former governor of California, who attempts to call his son to task in the film.

The Candidate started shooting in November 1971, a studio film in name only, based in offices at Mill Valley in Marin County, not far from Charlie and Helen's new home, on San Francisco Bay at Tiburon. It was shot over forty-one twelve-hour days, wrapping shortly after Christmas. Logistically, it was a massive undertaking, spanning media events, campaign speeches and endless traveling scenes. Said Ritchie, "We were constantly hustling for favors from department stores, cabs, everybody we crossed. Someone loaned a limo, someone else had a radio show crew who were willing to drop by. Our ticker tape parade was the classic example. There was no way we could fund a proper street parade. So we cashed in on the fact that there was a New Year's Eve tradition in San Francisco where, at 1:00 p.m., office workers opened their windows and threw out the shreds of last year's calendar. 'Okay,' we said, 'here's our parade!' So we staged McKay's drive-through and everybody participated. They clustered at the windows to see the great Robert Redford! And that became a very expensive-looking campaign parade on film." The improvisations stretched to the final hours of filming when, on a United flight home to Los Angeles, an extra scene with McKay and his fellow travelers was shuffled together.

For Ritchie, the biggest disappointment was Karen Carlson, who, he said, "became besotted" with Redford as production progressed. "I didn't like that, because she became emotionally involved. I tried to intervene, but it's impossible when you are dealing with real people, with real obsessions. I spoke to Bob and he was helpful but, I think, also concerned. Her role was the dutiful wife. It often felt like *Fatal Attraction.*" Carlson herself admitted to "schizophrenic" feelings, confessing to writer Bruce Bahrenburg during production that McKay/Redford's dallying in the wings with an attractive extra upset her: "I didn't know whether it was [the wife] Nancy reacting to McKay or myself to Bob Redford," said Carlson. "But I knew that it was time to try to separate my feelings. I had a long talk with Bob about them."

As *The Candidate* drew to a close, Michael Daves, the assistant director, observed Larner as "a permanent fixture in Bob's life, working under horrendous pressure to draft, redraft, find a new scene, lose a new scene, find an angle, stick in a commercial, take out a name or a face or a place." In the end, perhaps, this very closeness overwhelmed the friendship. Redford liked Larner, found him hugely gifted, but one incident sounded the death knell for Larner. "I wanted to write a scene based on a true-life experience, where the candidate goes onto an Indian reservation and pumps the flesh," says Larner. "The chief adorns him with a headdress that doesn't fit, and the scene, visually and verbally, has all the imagery of the humiliating phoniness of what candidacy truly is. I wrote it but Bob said he couldn't play it, that his relationship with the Indian community was too precious to him. I defended my scene, saying, 'This is just a movie, Bob, and McKay, the character, loses his integrity here.' But Mike Ritchie took me aside and warned me to drop it. He told me, 'You won't get Bob to do what Bob doesn't want to do. This isn't a matter of negotiation, so please spare all of us the trouble.' "

Robert Penn Warren once wrote of Hemingway's *A Farewell to Arms* that its triumph was the summing-up of "the inner meaning" of its era, not in historical overview but because "it cut back to the beginning of the process." Ritchie believed the same held true for *The Candidate:* "When I looked at the finished cut, I knew we had made a statement. McKay wasn't Robert Kennedy or Tunney or anyone the media claimed he was. The way Bob conceived it, he was the encapsulation of 'the moment' just after Eisenhower. He was a reduction of all of the innocence and naïveté that drove the youth revolt of the sixties. The suits were the corruption. McKay was every kid who ever burned a flag on a campus or stuck a flower in the barrel of a gun. He was Bob: the guy who believed an individual can change the system. But then gets eaten by the system once in it."

In the recent past, Redford's family life had changed. In 1968 Tiger died of heart failure in Waterford, Connecticut, his son at his bedside. The distractions of travel, of maintaining a life in New York and Utah and Los Angeles, had created wide, empty spaces in family life. Shauna, Jamie and Amy all strove to keep their relationships with their father, and all suffered the strain of his fame as much as his absence. Jamie remembers the early seventies as "the time of the crazies." There was the well-circulated magazine report about the woman who claimed she married Redford in secret in Mexico in 1956; the frequent anonymous calls to the Redfords' unlisted numbers; and the stalkers, hustlers and paparazzi who seemed to tag along everywhere. The family struggled to maintain normalcy and unity. They continued to spend holidays together, and constantly stayed in touch by phone. But an erosion was taking place. Jamie and Shauna insisted on walking the few blocks to the Dalton School each day, but this simple pleasure was often denied them. "From time to time security guards came into the picture," says Jamie. "We absolutely hated the idea of it, but the escalation of my father's fame was beyond Bill McKay in *The Candidate*. It was so extreme that we were made aware of the risks just by opening a newspaper. We worried about him because he was so visible. At that time he was everywhere, like Hershey bars. We wondered, Will he endure? Will the family endure?"

14

Idols

Over Labor Day weekend of 1971, while Redford worked with Larner in the living room of the writer's Cambridge, Massachusetts, apartment, he was unaware that the first act of the Watergate drama was unfolding in the kitchen. Larner had offered refuge to Daniel Ellsberg, the former marine officer turned RAND defense analyst. Ellsberg had purloined seven thousand pages of documents about the American government's secret policy on Vietnam, the so-called Pentagon Papers. Having failed to engage congressional interest in a public exposé, he had given them to *The New York Times,* which had published them in June. Attorney General John Mitchell had imposed an immediate restraint order, but the Supreme Court had overruled him, and damning new excerpts of the papers were published to widening public outrage. They established that the government knowingly lied about the facts of the Gulf of Tonkin incident as a pretext for accelerating the Vietnam War. By the end of the summer of 1971, Ellsberg was on the run from agents of the Nixon government who, allegedly, wanted to silence him.

"I knew Jeremy was sincere, well connected, anti-Vietnam," says Redford, "but it was all very James Bond–ish. We'd be sitting at the table shuffling the script, and there'd be a noise back there and Jeremy would say, 'Quiet, Dan! Take it easy now.' " These incidents passed without further discussion.

Redford's mind was as much on money for the moment as politics. He had earned about $3 million since his career began, and all of it was spent. The best money he had made, for *The Hot Rock,* was quickly absorbed in the various resort maintenance issues at Sundance, which was now more or less entirely his baby. With not much optimism for the box office success of *The Hot Rock* and low commercial expectations for *The Candidate,* he knew he had to look more into mainstream films. There were two possibilities in advanced stages, both George Roy Hill projects. One, a movie about Hill's great passion for biplanes, had been commissioned from Goldman and was still in the writing. The other, *The Sting,* was almost set to go. But after *The Candidate* he was emotionally burned out. He called Hill and said he needed to take a break. Hill was supportive and told him to "go somewhere and forget all this gold mining."

Redford had one unavoidable obligation: to attend the Cannes screening of *Jeremiah Johnson* with Pollack. Disappointed with the fate of this movie in America and the implications of Warners' commitment for the upcoming *Candidate* release, he was buoyed by the European enthusiasm. "I went for a vacation, but suddenly Sydney was waylaying me with a new script called *The Way We Were.*"

Redford told Pollack no. "Ray Stark was the man behind it, and I told him it sounded to me like another Ray Stark ego trip. I didn't even want to read it."

"I would not let him off the hook," said Pollack. "I said, 'You've got it wrong. This isn't a fuzzy piece for Barbra Streisand. This is substantial, and—what do you know—it's political. I pressured and pressured him all summer as soon as we got back from Cannes." Getting nowhere, Pollack decided to camp out in the foyer of Wildwood in New York. "It was the process of attrition," said Pollack. "He did it with me on *Jeremiah.* It was payback time."

The Way We Were began with Stark, who was looking for a *Sound of Music*–type vehicle for Streisand. His association with her dated back to Broadway in the early sixties, when he had cast her as Fanny Brice in *Funny Girl.* In 1968 he produced the movie version, which won Streisand an Academy Award. Stark had, said Pollack, "an ownership thing" about Streisand and, accordingly, envisioned another huge musical film, which he felt she owed him.

Stark commissioned an original script from Arthur Laurents, whose career spanned *Lux Radio Theater* and work with Hitchcock on *Rope.* But Laurents objected to the "absurd" notion of another musical and came up with the alternative of a romantic parable based on the lives of some of his personal friends caught up in the HUAC-era blacklisting, particularly Frances Price and Jigee Viertel. Laurents subsequently wrote a 125-page essay featuring Katie Morosky, a Marxist agitator at Cornell in the thirties who falls in love with an apolitical novelist, Hubbell Gardner. Stark liked the idea but hated Laurents's suggestion for Sydney Pollack as director.

Laurents, impressed by *They Shoot Horses, Don't They?,* persisted and won the support of Streisand, who tried to sway Stark.

"I was under no illusions," said Pollack. "Barbra was smart. She liked my Sandy Meisner connections because she was ambitious, as an actress, to learn. Same with Jane Fonda on *They Shoot Horses.* Jane said, 'Thank you, Sydney, because no one ever treats me as an artist. I am never requested to act. Just to "star in." ' Barbra wanted to push out, and she saw with *They Shoot Horses* that I could handle social issues, that I would give weight to it." Pollack found it hard to contain his enthusiasm for the story concept. "I called Arthur right at the start and said, 'You know what you're proposing here? This is dynamite. This will be the first-ever blacklist movie, the first one to show how it was.' "

Pollack's role was still up in the air when the script was handed to Streisand and her lover, Ryan O'Neal, who was offered the role of Hubbell. Around that time, *What's Up, Doc?,* a Streisand-O'Neal comedy, opened and failed and, says Laurents, ended the romance between the stars. Stark and Streisand now began talking about Redford as Hubbell.

Redford, unsurprisingly, supported Pollack. "The truth is," says Redford, "Stark had no affection for *This Property Is Condemned,* which he sold to Warners as part of his portfolio, and really dumped. To him, Sydney did not smell good. I pushed. I said, 'If you want to even consider me for *The Way We Were,* it has to be Sydney developing it.' So I made this noose for myself because Stark gave in and suddenly I had an outline written up for me that I hated." It was reported at the time that Redford was unhappy with his role's being secondary to Streisand's Katie. Redford says he was distressed because his part was a symbol, not a character.

"What I was really worried about was the whole concept of basing a movie on Barbra as a serious actress," says Redford. "She had never been tested. I told Sydney, 'Her reputation is as a very controlling person. She will direct herself. It'll never work.' " Laurents claims he had difficulty understanding the concerns, since Pollack blocked him from communicating with Redford. Agent Steffie Phillips believed this was "an escalating problem of Sydney's insecurity on top of Redford's insecurity on top of Barbra's inexperience."

In his memoirs Laurents reports his first clash with Pollack at Ray Stark's condo in Sun Valley, Idaho. Pollack donned his usual script doctor's hat, hacking out ideas on his own manual typewriter, a proprietary, authorial posture that set Laurents on edge. Pollack then upset the writer by saying, "You don't know how everybody in Hollywood is amazed by you? Because you've written the best love story in years, and you're a homosexual." "What do you say to a man like that?" wondered Laurents. "Do you attack him? Do you attempt to educate him? Or do you just say to yourself, What an asshole!" Pollack's insensitivity tilted the odds against productive partnership, said Laurents, but he hung in.

Pollack saw events differently. Laurents was composing his characters from a diversity of bits, a little of Jigee Viertel, a nuance of someone else. The consequent fragmented psychology made the romantic story line "too unbelievable by half." Worst of all, said Pollack, Laurents had not resolved the political story. "It was about a relationship complicated by HUAC, but those vivid subtexts were lost. It's not that he didn't understand HUAC, but he didn't contextualize it properly. There had to be a kind of education curve for the audience, and Arthur was bad at that."

To fix it, Pollack employed *eleven* writers, among them Alvin Sargent, Paddy Chayefsky, David Rayfiel and Dalton Trumbo. Offended, Laurents left the production (though he was later rehired).

Trumbo proved to be Pollack's ace in the hole. He was one of the jailed members of HUAC's notorious Hollywood Ten, and his prolificacy was dented by the witch hunt, but he recovered in the sixties, writing screenplays for *Exodus, The Sandpiper* and *Hawaii.* In a detailed correspondence, Trumbo analyzed Laurents's story and suggested alternative real-life identities for the characters. He saw one character, Rhea, as a version of Meta Rosenberg, Redford's former agent "who behaved like most informers when called before HUAC: she gave the names of communists she probably did not like, and withheld the names of communists she probably did like, my name among others, though I was in jail when she testified." He saw Hubbell as "a good guy who is trapped by the committee into becoming an informer and thereby destroyed." He could not, however, connect Hubbell with any actual person he knew. Pollack called Trumbo's attention to the actor Sterling Hayden's book *Wanderer,* which dramatized Hayden's guilt over naming names to HUAC: "The reason I have been so hung up on Hayden's book," wrote Pollack, "is that I keep finding tiny character clues within it that seem like starting points for Hubbell. I think the blacklist should be dead center to the drama rather than keeping it to one side. This in turn makes the political material less talky and more dramatic immediately. Secondly, it fulfills the metaphor of Hubbell as America. And, thirdly, it gives him something *to do,*" which had been Redford's concern to begin with.

"I was hung up on Dalton's views," said Pollack, "because I felt that historical veracity was the way to persuade Bob into playing the role. I thought that this was a huge story—a love story, yes, but so much more in the representation of Morosky as the do-or-die Marxist and Hubbell as the jock-novelist who *doesn't need* to face the moral issues but is faced with the demands imposed by love and the compromises that come with love. Stark wasn't as impressed by the HUAC stuff as I was, but we needed it, if only to beef up Hubbell. I did not alter Laurents's story line 'manipulatively,' as Arthur accused. I did it because I had a hunch Bob and Barbra would be magical together, and I knew I had to engage Bob's intelligence."

But Pollack's dilemma was that Fox had already indicated its refusal to support a political movie. "So we compromised, and what we had, however diminished, was good. I did know, though, that people were angry with me. Blacklisting was only fifteen years before, and it was fresh in people's memory. People were thinking, At last! Finally, we get a movie that confronts this ghastly thing. And so they wanted more than Fox was prepared to support. But I was signed by Ray Stark to deliver a vehicle for Streisand, and that was the first principle I served. Dealing with Bob was another matter."

Streisand was elated when Redford came aboard. Sue Mengers, another of her agents, sent a confirming two-word cable: "Barbra Redford?" "Barbra was delighted because she had a crush on him," said Pollack, "even before we started. It was hard for women not to have a fixation, because he was everywhere, like Elvis. He was the golden boy long before Hubbell came along."

On September 17, after more than a year's preparation, filming started on *The Way We Were*. It had been delayed slightly when Redford, vacationing on Lake Powell with Dick Cavett, was bitten by a bat and had to endure seventeen days of the famously agonizing stomach injections against rabies. In the first weeks, location work jumped from Union College in Schenectady, New York, to the University of Southern California campus, Marion Davies's Beverly Hills home, Harry Cohen's old Columbia offices and the gated Malibu Colony. All the time, said Pollack, Redford grumbled. "I knew how uncomfortable he was with Hubbell, but I also knew a great persona would emerge. He wasn't cruising, and he responded very well to the prodding I gave, which was a lot."

Redford agrees that Pollack pushed him hard: "I give full credit to Sydney. And he did honorably respond to my script concerns. An important last-minute addition came. Alvin Sargent and Rayfiel wrote Hubbell up finally as someone with a point of view. Until then, he was Katie's stooge, the guy who won't either support her Communism or name names."

In a new scene toward the end of the script, Hubbell meets Katie at Union Station at the height of the furor about naming names. Bissinger, the movie director to whom Hubbell is in thrall, pays lip service to the "martyrs" who brought the trouble down on themselves. Hubbell stays silent, but Katie rails against the immoral witch hunt. A riot breaks out, and a fight involving Hubbell, and the police are forced to throw Hubbell and Katie into a waiting room, where lines are finally drawn:

KATIE: Doesn't it make you angry listening to Bissinger ridicule those men? Calling them martyrs first because they have guts, which he doesn't, to fight for their principles, to fight for their Bill of Rights, his Bill of Rights, and yours?

HUBBELL: Bill of Rights? What Bill of Rights? We don't have any Bill of Rights. We don't have free speech in this country. We never will have.

KATIE: We never will if people aren't willing to take a stand for what's right.

HUBBELL: We never will because people are scared. This isn't college. This is grown-up politics, and it's stupid and dangerous.

KATIE: Hubbell, you are telling me to close my eyes and to watch people being destroyed.

HUBBELL: I'm telling you that people are more important than any goddamn witch hunt. You and me. Not causes. Not principles.

KATIE: Hubbell, people are their principles.

"Hubbell isn't a victim anymore," says Redford. "He's his own man. And that strength gave him a weight in the romance that made the final split with Katie dramatic. The questionable nature of true free speech was a provocative notion, and I attached to that. It also reflected some of the polemic of *The Candidate.*"

Streisand and Redford became close from the outset. "I think we'd both have preferred a more political Dalton Trumbo–type script," says Redford. "But finally Sydney came down on the side of the love story. He said, 'This is first and foremost a love affair,' and we conceded that. We trusted his instincts, and he was right. *The Way We Were* became a success because

Sydney controlled the project with his point of view, which was not easy given Ray's behavior and interference."

Word from the set was that Streisand and Redford were igniting extraordinary personal chemistry. An observer on the set saw this as "useful, because it was obvious that Barbra was just too, too crazy about Bob. She had a hard time controlling her emotions, and when she played scenes with him, like the fireside courtship scene at Malibu, she was drooling. But Bob was very tactful."

Streisand looks back on the experience as a high-water mark. "I just loved working with him," she says. "Every day was an exciting adventure. We played well together—in the moment, slightly different, slightly unknowing, always interesting. He's a man of depth who has what it takes to be a great movie star: mystery behind the eyes. You wonder, What is he *really* thinking?" Redford in turn found her very attractive. "When we started on *The Way We Were,* she wanted me *to be* Hubbell. That was how she conceived me. And then, as the shoot went on, she saw I was not that man, not in any way. So she reoriented herself, and the professional took over. But afterward I wondered, Did she return to that banal concept of me? Was I—am I—a Hubbell figure in her mind? I never fully sorted that out, and some of that tension made our chemistry on-screen."

Pollack dealt with other tensions: "Each of them was a pain in the ass from time to time because they both knew how they liked to be presented; Barbra knew about camera positions and editors' options and all that. So I directed, but they would challenge it. At Malibu, we went on for hours because she had a favorite profile, and I had to play around it to satisfy both."

Redford bit the bullet: "Yes, it was troublesome. I was dancing with her, and I was in my place, doing just fine. But she wasn't dancing; it was awkward. Then Sydney pulled me aside and whispered, 'Come on, man, she's uncomfortable.' Apparently *she* had a side she favored, right or left. A discomfort about her nose from one or the other angle. Fine by me. I acknowledge that kind of thing, when it affects that actor's confidence. I said, 'Okay, whatever works.' "

Of no dispute was Redford's utter inability to do the same take twice, a given, Redford admits, with most good actors. "He could not do it," said Pollack. "It made hell for me and it made hell for the editor to match continuity. Over the years with Bob, I learned to make adjustments. Like running five angles on a scene to cover my ass so that it will cut in the editing.

Like not showing my anger when he showed up late, which is normal for him, dishing some bullshit excuse. I kept my anger in check until the scene was in the can, till the weekend, when I could say outright, 'You son of a bitch' without messing up his mind for the scenes he needed to play."

But *The Way We Were* helped engender a deeper mutual respect. Redford had started resentfully. By the end he was laughing. Pollack slapped his back at the finish and said, "Man, that was some hot stuff. You know what this is going to do to your box office?"

All summer Redford was absorbed with the slow-burning Watergate story. In June 1972 there was the break-in at the Democratic National Committee offices, followed by the launch of a lawsuit by the Democrats against the Republican Committee to Re-elect the President (CREEP). On a promotional junket for *The Candidate* in August he was aware of "a buzz" among the many journalists traveling with him. "There was obviously some big story brewing," he says, "because I kept hearing the words 'Nixon' and 'scandal' and 'burglaries.' I started trying to fit a picture together." Shortly after, for the first time, he became aware of Bob Woodward and Carl Bernstein's investigative reporting. "I noted their names, and the fact that the story was so bizarre. I thought, This is something beyond a thriller." On October 25, *The Washington Post* published the first of Woodward and Bernstein's revelatory features, reporting testimony to the grand jury naming Nixon aide Bob Haldeman as the so-far-unnamed fifth person controlling CREEP's political espionage. "That got me," says Redford. "I immediately called Lois Smith [his publicist] and asked her to get in touch with Woodward or Bernstein. I was interested in these guys."

In November, as *The Way We Were* was being filmed, Nixon was reelected in a landslide. The blow for Redford was softened somewhat by his friend Wayne Owens's congressional victory, but he still felt agitated. "I really hated Nixon. It went back to that 'pinko' incident with Gahagan Douglas. I felt he was a dirty fighter, and we didn't need him in high office." In December, Lois Smith called to say Woodward would meet Redford, not formally, but at a Democratic Party fund-raiser at the Motion Picture Association hall in Washington, D.C.

The meeting seemed secretive, "with Woodward hiding in the shadows and giving me snatches of information." It emerged that he and Bernstein had a book deal with Simon and Schuster and were about to embark on writing their account of Watergate. "I told him I wasn't interested in any book. But I was interested in them, and in what was unfolding on the national stage. I said, 'There's a movie in this.' He said maybe—maybe he'd be interested in taking that further—and then he disappeared."

The idea of a strategic political follow-up to *The Candidate,* an assumption many make about Redford's Watergate project, was not the prime motivation. What appealed, in the first instance, was a commentary on the state of journalism. Not much more than a hundred years before, Thoreau had queried the essential worth of communication from one village to the next. What is edifying for us to know? The question was lost in the nineteenth century when press objectivity was diluted by advocacy journalism. The selective view, the vested interest, became prominent in American publishing. Radical changes in the twentieth century fundamentally changed the Fourth Estate. Investigative journalism, its worth proved by Ida Tarbell and Upton Sinclair, took precedence throughout the media and made stars of journalists. The emergence of New Journalism, and the literary elevation of news, further complicated the transmission of printed information to a point, Redford believed, where it was often impossible to unravel the value of the "straight news" story. Since Redford himself was being regularly interviewed and evaluated in print, the notion of interpreting the interpreter was very provocative to him. "I was asking, Who were Woodward and Bernstein? What motivated them? Had *The Washington Post* board decided to take down Nixon? Who was the front-runner here?"

These issues of anatomizing principles were on his mind as he addressed a dilemma facing Sundance. As part of an incremental growth plan, he had now commissioned an on-site cinema and more recreation annexes. Was it possible to keep extending—indeed, to even hold on to—this vast acreage with only the small income generated by a short ski season and a restaurant with twenty tables? The simple answer was no. His earnings were increasing—he got $400,000 with a 12.5 percent deferred slice of the net profits for *The Way We Were*—but the money was being gobbled up faster than it came in. "I knew it wasn't sustainable, and I knew my lifestyle was so peripatetic that Sundance often seemed a luxury, but it still boiled down to the question, Am I prepared to see this canyon go to tract house development? And the answer was no." Brent Beck, the resort manager, saw disaster looming in the collision of Redford's possessiveness with business reality. "We, the staff, thought he was crazy. He walked away from more than one potential investor with sound business expansion plans. We thought, How can there be long-term survival without a compromise? Okay, we don't want this to be Disneyland, but we need new investors—fast." Mike Frankfurt saw this as a moment to bow out. "I couldn't keep up," he says. "I was in Manhattan; Bob was mostly in L.A. It made sense that Gary Hendler, who was geographically closer, should fully take over the head contracts and supervise the deals he needed to make with Freddie [Fields] and Steffie [Phillips] to keep the cash flow going. As I saw it, Bob had set his course: he was going to make Hollywood movies to pay for Sundance, and he was going to utilize Sundance primarily as a base for his other operations in independent movies and environmental politicking."

Hurrying for cash, Redford resumed the work in planning his next movie, which was now many months late, with George Roy Hill. *The Sting,* their new project, is a film with a history almost as convoluted as its plot. It had started in October 1970, when David Ward, a young writer contracted to actor-producer Tony Bill, taped a ten-minute synopsis of an original concept inspired by the writings of Nelson Algren. Bill sent the tape to Redford, who liked it and arranged a three-way meeting in New York. Ward admits he was "kind of surprised by Tony's choice of Redford, because the part of Hooker, the con man around whom the plot resolves, I had in mind for a young guy. But I was immensely impressed by this new notion of the wily Sundance Kid playing the very wily Hooker." Ward had written just one movie for Tony Bill—the critically, if not financially, successful *Steelyard Blues*—and had, he says, a desire to do something in his favorite territory, "among the lowlifes of Algren and Steinbeck and in the era when you could best idealize criminal life, which was the twenties." At the meeting, Redford was encouraging, says Ward, but unwilling to commit. The story, though, he liked. It was about two fast-talking Prohibition hustlers, Hooker and Gondorff, who scam and double-scam with the objective of taking down a murderous thug. Already tagged to play Gondorff was Peter Boyle. "I liked Ward," says Redford. "But he was very inexperienced, and I wasn't even sure I had a place in this. I told him, 'Do a great script, and I'll see what I can do to support you.' "

Ward worked in the converted garage of his rented Topanga Canyon home, writing with a pencil on a yellow legal pad. He produced several drafts over twelve months before submitting a final one to Redford. Hill, who had been drawn in by Tony Bill, also received the script. Hill liked it immediately. "But I felt he'd made a mistake in the tenor of the dialogue," said Hill. "It was too modern, not at all of the period, and that was its weakness. But, that said, David presented a fantastic script. It was so intricate that it needed no input from anyone, just dialogue adjustments." The attraction for Hill was the stun-the-audience twist at the end and, even more, the evocation of the bygone era. "Period was my soft spot," said Hill. "Nothing beats historical scene setting. That was what I liked about *Hawaii,* what I liked about *Butch Cassidy.* I used every trick and technology available to get the audience in. When I read *The Sting,* I imagined that old Universal art deco logo and sepia faces and Model Ts."

While Redford was absorbed on *The Way We Were,* Hill met with Tony Bill and his partners, Michael and Julia Phillips, made a deal and took the project to Richard Zanuck, who was now producing independently with David Brown. It was Zanuck and Brown, finally, who sealed the production with Universal. For Ward, the only moment of hesitation was when Dan Melnick, a former drama executive at ABC, suggested they cut loose from Hill and Zanuck to make the movie themselves, with Ward directing. "In the end," says Ward, "I knew I would be selling a great story short. The option was either a very-low-budget movie directed by me or the blockbuster directed by George. It was a no-brainer."

When Hill called Redford to tell him of the great new script he'd found, Redford laughed. He had already read it, and approved. "But the truth is, I didn't see it as the massive project it became. I saw it as a modest, tricky little thing," says Redford. Then Hill told Redford he wanted Paul Newman for the role of Gondorff. "I was surprised," says Redford, "because Peter Boyle was already there. So I said, 'Okay, I trust you. I love Paul, and if the studio will go with him . . . ?' " The problem, however, was that for Universal, Newman's star was on the wane. This shocked, then amused, Redford and Hill. For seven years through the sixties Newman had ranked in the top ten of box office earners. He had been nominated four times for an Academy Award. He had won a British Academy Award, for *The Hustler* in 1961, and a New York Film Critics Circle best director award for *Rachel, Rachel,* made just before *Butch Cassidy.* Hill thought the situation laughable. Freddie Fields called to propose a resolution: Redford was being offered $500,000, with 15 percent of the gross. Newman was being offered a fee, but with no points—a proposal he immediately refused. The only way Newman could be fit into the deal, said Fields, was if Redford conceded his percentage points to him. Redford was unhappy. "But I felt obligated to Paul, for what he had done in supporting me at the start of my career. I gave in. Paul got my points, and that turned into a considerable fortune of earnings, millions and millions of dollars. I told him later that it pissed me off, but I forgave him."

In Ward's story, Hooker steals illegal gambling money from Illinois mobster Doyle Lonnegan, who kills Hooker's partner and issues a death warrant. Hooker flees to Chicago, where he schemes with Gondorff, a friend of Hooker's dead partner, to lure Lonnegan to town and fleece him in a racetrack scam. When the Feds close in, it appears that the con will be curtailed, but Hooker and Gondorff conspire with the Feds to round off a coup.

For Newman all this was "just brilliant, really the best twist I'd ever read. It was also a better drama than *Butch Cassidy,* because of the equality between the characters of Gondorff and Hooker. There was no star role. That, in turn, brought out the best in Redford and me, because the invitation was there, and we were competing. But I won. I took the audience sitting down. Redford spent the whole movie running." Sure enough, Redford's sole complaint about *The Sting* was the physicality of the film. "I knew it the minute I read it. That movie starts with me and ends with me, and in between I'm the one on the run from the mobsters and the Feds. I'm the one carrying the plot to the audience and dodging around corners." In acknowledgment, Hill presented him with a plaque inscribed ROADRUNNER, which became his nickname for the duration.

In January, a week after *The Way We Were* wrapped, Redford and Newman were making *The Sting* on the Universal back lot. Just before shooting got under way, George Roy Hill stormed into the office of the Phillipses with press clippings of another Universal movie, *The Mack,* which appeared to have an identical story line. Michael Phillips remembers that Hill was frantic: " 'Let's can this,' he said. 'It's not worth the trouble if we're making a movie that's already been made. I don't want the grief, the injunctions, the lawsuits.' But I calmed him down. The other movie had a different background, a black cast; it was a whole other universe. I said, 'George, get a grip. We have Newman and Redford, an incredibly smart screenplay and the wittiest dialogue either of us has ever read.' I gave him a lot of warm reassurance, and so he went out on the soundstage and started working."

Hill first painstakingly rehearsed the movie, theater-style, then "let the actors go." On *Butch Cassidy,* said Hill, Redford never talked back. By now he'd learned the knack. "A couple or three times I had to tell him to shut it or I'd kill him," said Hill. Newman remembered only "sharp, theater-type ensemble work that seemed to go unusually well, in that there were no revisions, no callbacks, no second thoughts." David Ward was told not to speak with Newman. "George's reasoning was that Paul was a Method actor who loved to worry the character out. He needed to talk and talk and talk. So my engaging him would have slowed *The Sting* down. Bob's working style, on the other hand, was 'Let's get it over with.' The best part for George was that Bob didn't want to analyze. He would say, 'The script works, leave it alone.' And George was delighted for that cut and thrust that helped keep things moving fast."

The one glitch during the fifty-day schedule was a breach in studio security. Since 1967, Redford had been stalked by a fan, Nadine Davies, from San Francisco. It started with obsessive fan mail after *Barefoot in the Park,* then, during *Willie Boy,* intrusions. In the spring of 1968, Redford was filming at Universal Studios: "Suddenly [his friend from *War Hunt,* the actor] Tom Skerritt rushed up to me and said, 'Watch out, there's some weird woman going through stuff in your dressing room, and security is worried about her—she doesn't seem to be sane.' " The police were called and Davies was removed. Weeks later Redford was at the Hotel Bel-Air watching television when the report of Robert Kennedy's assassination at the Ambassador Hotel came on. In a stunned state, he was suddenly informed to stay in his room, because a stalker was in the bushes and the police were on their way. Davies was arrested outside his room, and later a California court issued a restraining order. Back at the same studio, the same lot, for *The Sting,* Nadine Davies was back, too. Redford was rehearsing a gambling scene opposite actor Ray Walston with Newman watching when, all of a sudden, Redford saw "absolute terror" in Newman's eyes. "I knew instantly that something wasn't right, and I swung to follow his line of vision. I can't say what was on her mind, but it wasn't good. Paul knew it; I knew it. Time froze. There was this awful suspended silence as I watched this woman bear down on me—rush at me—with a frantic, fixed stare. I've seen a million fans. This wasn't a fan. She was demented. Newman suddenly started hollering so hard he blew my ears out. He just yelled, *'Get her! Get that fucking woman out! Now!'* She got close—maybe fifteen feet away—then security jumped on her."

Though they hadn't many scenes together, closer friendship with Newman built over these weeks. Since *Butch Cassidy,* aspects of their journeys mirrored each other. Newman had set up his own independent production partnership, First Artists, with Streisand, Steve McQueen and Sidney Poitier. He had also made *WUSA,* a political allegory that was well received but failed at the box office. "I saw Bob had changed," said Newman. "He was more sure of himself, maybe a little more serious. The similarities between what Joanne and I were doing and what he was doing at

Wildwood and with his local politics gave us a zone to operate in. I'd gone out for McCarthy in '68 and worked for civil rights. When he made *The Candidate,* I think he was saying he wanted to do something more than dumb acting, too. We didn't make a deal about these things. We didn't sit around discussing where McGovern went wrong and how Lindsay screwed up. But it was there, in the dinner table gossip. Sometimes when I looked at him, I saw myself ten years earlier, saying to myself, This acting business is stupid. How do you plant a device that blows it up? By the time of *The Sting* he was beginning to formulate a direction."

When Hill wrapped *The Sting,* he had an inkling that some alchemy had been achieved. Newman said, "I believe it was a mosaic. We had Edith Head, the great costumer, who made us all look so good. We had Robert Shaw, who was the best villain. We had John Scarne, the Italian card shark, do the sleight-of-hand stuff. We had those *Saturday Evening Post* title boards for the different acts, and we had a great set and ragtime music. George was a master builder. He layered all that on, and he kept his distance. You see nothing show-offy in George's directing, ever. There's no 'Oh boy! What a shot!' fancy stuff. You are there to be told a story, and he tells you the story. All of that came together on that picture, and that's why it ended up with all those Academy Award nominations."

The movie, which Universal opened confidently on Christmas Day 1973 with simultaneous New York and Los Angeles premieres, garnered ten Academy Award nominations in most of the main categories, including for Redford as best actor. Oddly, Newman was not nominated, though Hill felt there was aptness to this. "Bob delivered a lot more. There was more on him, and he pulled it off." Redford himself was flattered, but fixed on avoiding the frills. "I just think the movie worked as an ensemble piece, so I took no special pride. Anyway, I always believed that no one participant really wins an Oscar. We're all in it together." In the seven winning categories, including for best picture, best original screenplay and best director, Hill certainly felt Redford won out. "His presence was right through it, really. I don't believe it would have happened without him." For the best actor award, Jack Lemmon's performance in *Save the Tiger* beat out Redford's.

Such a massive success inevitably drew the brickbats. Four lawsuits were launched against *The Sting,* mostly from academics who had written books on one aspect or another of Prohibition life, card games or FBI methodology. David Ward had been paid $300,000 to write the movie.

By 1979, Universal's lawyers were demanding the money back in settlement of a Kentucky lawsuit. "Bob, Paul and George came out for me," says Ward. "They called Universal's legal department and said, 'Get real. This guy has given you a huge moneymaker. You owe him. You don't penalize the good guys. You penalize villains.' "

Though Redford benefited enormously through his early career by good patronage—the support of Nichols, Pollack, Newman, Goldman and especially Hill—he remained resolutely his own man. Stephanie Phillips remembers that, despite the power of CMA and Freddie Fields, he was stubbornly autonomous: "He would listen very intently to your advice, then go do it his way." After *The Sting* he was once again perceived to be on a run. Both the rebooted *Jeremiah Johnson* and *The Way We Were* triumphed, each earning around $22 million. *The Sting* grossed a near-record $160 million. "There was a positive soar of support," said George Roy Hill. "I saw him grasp it. He had been viable, but now he had real power. It made it easier for me to plan bigger-budgeted pictures with him, and it made it possible for him to be choosy in what he did." It was, then, by the most comfortable serendipity that he would be able to sidestep a handful of half-hatched projects—a script about Henry Miller–esque bums by *Five Easy Pieces* writer Carole Eastman and a version of *Bury My Heart at Wounded Knee* that he wanted to produce—to submerge himself in a classic Jazz Age role he'd long coveted.

One of Hollywood's hottest recent stories was that Bob Evans had persuaded Scottie Smith, the daughter of Scott Fitzgerald, to release the rights to *The Great Gatsby* for a remake. For years Sam Spiegel and Ray Stark had chased the project. Pollack had made a bid, too. But Evans wanted to gift the famous role of Daisy, Gatsby's vaporous inspiration, to his wife, Ali MacGraw. The idea had come to Evans the year before, when MacGraw gave him a leather-bound, personally calligraphed copy of Fitzgerald's "Winter Dreams," a short story thematically linked to *Gatsby,* for Christmas. Evans's return gift came too late. During the making of *The Getaway,* MacGraw fell in love with costar Steve McQueen and decided to leave the marriage. The new movie, however, was too good an opportunity to pass by. Already Evans had partnered with Broadway's David Merrick to produce, and Truman Capote had been commissioned to write the screenplay. Evans had his work cut out. The first film version, by Herbert Brenon in 1926, was irretrievably lost, and the second, made in 1949 by Elliott Nugent and starring Alan Ladd, was rarely seen. Both had been overshadowed by the power and durability of the literary source. Evans himself was quoted as saying that pulling off a decent film version was "a mammoth task."

Early in the year, Redford discovered Evans was looking for a new Daisy and a Jay Gatsby. He asked Fields to call, but Evans turned him down flat. "He was no fan of mine. He wouldn't even consider me. Warren Beatty and Jack Nicholson were his preferences," says Redford. Undeterred, Redford asked for a meeting with Jack Clayton, Evans's chosen director. He met with a skeptical Clayton for ninety minutes in the terminal at Heathrow Airport in London. Clayton, who had been favoring Nicholson, was won over. He told his partner, Haya Harareet, "You can see the possibility of danger beneath that romantic WASP image." Still, Evans resisted, telling Clayton, "No, he's blond, Gatsby's dark haired." When Redford heard this, he exploded. "I began to think Evans never read the book. Sure, he liked the idea of doing a Fitzgerald, but he didn't know the text. Nowhere in it does Fitzgerald say Gatsby's hair is dark. He says, 'His hair was freshly barbered and smoothed back, and his skin was pulled tight over his face.' That's it. That's the description."

As negotiations commenced, Redford was in the process of splitting with CMA. Matters were complicated by the fact that Freddie Fields was also representing Ali MacGraw and Steve McQueen—both of whom David Merrick wanted in the movie regardless. Evans asked his mentor, Charlie Bluhdorn, who still held the presidency of Paramount but was no longer active in moviemaking decisions, to intervene. At a group viewing of the female screen tests in New York in December, Bluhdorn, Evans and Paramount's head of sales, Frank Yablans, joined Merrick and Jack Clayton to decide on either Mia Farrow, Katharine Ross, Candice Bergen or Faye Dunaway for Daisy. Merrick was stubborn. All the tests, he insisted, were inadequate. MacGraw remained the right casting for Daisy, he said, and Freddie Fields's suggestion of casting McQueen as Gatsby made the greatest sense, since Fields was proposing also to defer fees. Jack Clayton politely said he wanted Mia Farrow for Daisy. Evans, desperate, agreed with Clayton. When Merrick became apoplectic, Bluhdorn stood up and bluntly told him: "Ali MacGraw is not doing this picture. Is that clear? Paramount owns the rights. If anyone wants to walk, have a merry Christmas."

Evans might not have been a Redford fan, but Bluhdorn had never lost his soft spot. When Clayton called Redford to tell him the role was his, Redford was overjoyed. "I wanted it because I wanted to play a desperate

Redford marries Lola Van Wagenen in Provo, September 1958. It was their second ceremony. They had legally tied the knot five weeks earlier in Las Vegas. *(Courtesy of Robert Redford)*

On the Broadway stage in James Costigan's *Little Moon of Alban,* with Julie Harris *(center)* and Norah O'Mahony, December 1960 *(Courtesy of Robert Redford)*

Barefoot in the Park on Broadway, with *(from left)* Mildred Natwick, Elizabeth Ashley, and Kurt Kaszner. The Biltmore Theater, October 1963 *(Courtesy of Robert Redford)*

Backstage at the Biltmore with Ashley and visitor Ingrid Bergman *(Courtesy of Wayne Van Wagenen)*

With Patricia Blair in NBC-TV's *The Virginian,* 1963. Redford saw filmed episodic television as a training ground for movies. *(Courtesy of Robert Redford. Photograph: National Broadcasting Company)*

A visit with his children Jamie and Shauna to grandfather Tiger Redford in New London, 1964. *(Courtesy of Robert Redford)*

With Natalie Wood, 1966. "Our relationship was very close and trusting. She was an exceptional human being." *(Courtesy of Sydney Pollack)*

Redford's first meeting with Sydney Pollack, on the set of *War Hunt.* "We were friends from the get-go." *(Courtesy of Sydney Pollack)*

With Marlon Brando on location for *The Chase.* Redford's admiration for Brando was great. He recorded his observations of the actor's technique in his diary. *(Courtesy of Francis Feighan. Photograph: Columbia Pictures)*

A home in the hills. With Jamie at the A-frame in Provo Canyon that Redford had envisioned and built himself. *(Courtesy of Robert Redford)*

On location for *The Chase* in Northern California, with Jamie, Shauna, and Lola. "I felt that Hollywood was a dangerous place for family life. The distractions were too many." *(Courtesy of Wayne Van Wagenen)*

Natalie Wood and her soon-to-be husband Richard Gregson, who would be Redford's partner in his own production company, Wildwood. Wildwood was set up in 1968. *(Courtesy of Robert Redford/Wildwood Enterprises/Sundance archive)*

The war room at Creative Management Associates, Redford's agents in Los Angeles. Around the table *(from left)* are Stephanie Phillips, Freddie Fields, Redford, Mike Frankfurt, and *(back to camera)* David Begelman. *(Courtesy of Robert Redford/Wildwood Enterprises/Sundance archive)*

The family with lawyer and friend Mike Frankfurt, at Mürren in the Bernese Oberland, Switzerland, winter 1968 *(Courtesy of Mike Frankfurt)*

Timp Haven, Utah, in the 1950s, shortly before Redford purchased the canyon lands. A decade later it would become the Sundance resort.
(Courtesy of Robert Redford/Sundance archive)

Redford and the family with friend Stan Collins at the A-frame. "The house was always filled with music," says Shauna.
(Courtesy of Robert Redford)

The breakthrough: Redford as the Sundance Kid, 1969. Richard Zanuck, head of Fox, wanted him to lose the mustache. But Redford was adamant: "It was authentic. I got my way." *(Courtesy of Robert Redford. Photograph: Twentieth Century–Fox)*

Paul Newman, Katharine Ross, and Redford in *Butch Cassidy and the Sundance Kid,* 1969. "We had no idea we were on to something special." *(Courtesy of Robert Redford. Photograph: Twentieth Century–Fox)*

With Gene Hackman on *Downhill Racer,* 1969. "I wanted Hackman in it, because he was the best actor around."
(Courtesy of Robert Redford/Wildwood Enterprises)

New arrival: Lola holds baby Amy Hart Redford, Provo, spring 1971. *(Courtesy of Robert Redford)*

As Bill McKay in *The Candidate* (1972), a movie planned as part of a trilogy commenting on aspects of modern American life
(Courtesy of Robert Redford/Wildwood Enterprises)

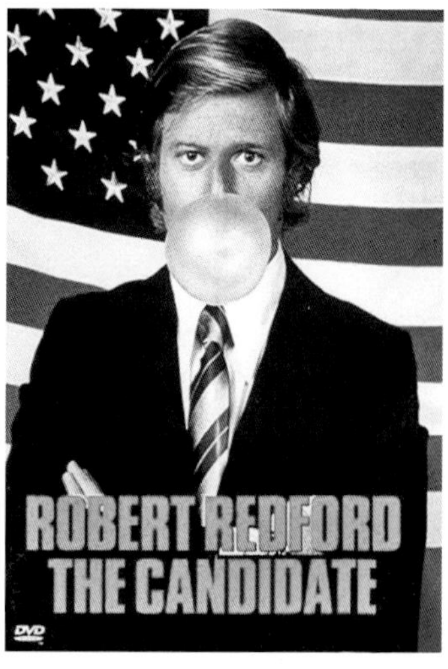

The wit of *The Candidate* suggested a voice of originality in contemporary cinema.
(Courtesy of Robert Redford/Wildwood Enterprises)

Joking with Paul Newman and director George Roy Hill during the making of *The Sting,* 1973

(Courtesy of George Roy Hill)

With Pollack and Barbra Streisand at Malibu during the making of *The Way We Were,* 1973. "All credit for that movie's success goes to Sydney."

(Courtesy of Sydney Pollack)

With Mia Farrow in *The Great Gatsby,* 1974

(Courtesy of Robert Redford. Photograph. Paramount Pictures)

With Dustin Hoffman in *All the President's Men,* 1976. "Dustin and I were like chalk and cheese, very different in every way. But that drove up the energy."

(Courtesy of Robert Redford/Wildwood Enterprises)

Returning to the American Academy of Dramatic Arts in Manhattan, where his favorite actor, Jason Robards Jr., a fellow graduate, was honored in 1978 *(Courtesy of the American Academy of Dramatic Arts, New York)*

The Electric Horseman, 1979. "It seemed to say a lot about integrity." *(Courtesy of Sydney Pollack. Photograph: Columbia Pictures)*

"*The Electric Horseman* was such a hard script to crack," said Sydney Pollack. "It finally came down to romantic chemistry. Bob and Jane [Fonda] could deliver Tracy and Hepburn any day." *(Courtesy of Sydney Pollack. Photograph: Columbia Pictures)*

man. I had never played a desperate man before, and I wanted to chart this bizarre new identity a man fabricates for himself to achieve his aim." When he'd first read the book, in college, he'd not considered it a great American novel. "It seemed florid. But when I went back to it, I saw it was something extraordinary, the depiction of human obsessions, and I felt some great screen work could come from it. It was American Gothic, a rarity and tantalizing."

Though Englishman Jack Clayton might have seemed an unlikely director for *Gatsby,* he came well prepared. A technician who had worked his way through the ranks since he started as a runner at Alexander Korda's Denham Studios in the 1930s, Clayton made his feature debut with *Room at the Top,* starring Laurence Harvey, a movie that was as much an indictment of the British class system as *Gatsby* was of America's. That was not his only qualification. In his twenties in the 1940s, Clayton himself had attempted to buy the rights to *Gatsby* from Fitzgerald's estate and had been, he said, fixated with the novel for thirty years. He consulted with Matthew J. Bruccoli, the Fitzgerald estate curator, and with Scottie; his research work was exhaustive. Clayton's vision for the movie was specific from the start, and though it deviated in part from the novel, it had Scottie's support. The tragedy of romantic idealism, he felt, was the center of the story. Clayton imagined the movie "with a golden look" and stylized in such a way that the two focused relationships—that of high-living Gatsby and Daisy alongside seedy Myrtle and George Wilson—were lit and dressed in strongly referential contrast to each other to emphasize the squalor of human passion.

The novel presents the mysterious Jay Gatsby through the eyes of the kindly patrician midwesterner Nick Carraway, who has come to live on Long Island alongside Gatsby's mansion and close to the home of socialites Tom and Daisy Buchanan. Carraway befriends the nouveau riche Gatsby, attends his extravagant parties and meets his New York cronies. The truth of Gatsby's origins remains unclear—was he a war hero or a bootlegger?—but it is clear that he is obsessed by Nick's cousin, Daisy, whom he fell in love with before the war and determines to seduce again. Gatsby clashes with Buchanan but he succeeds in reconnecting with Daisy. While driving in Gatsby's car, Daisy accidentally knocks down and kills Myrtle, her husband's mistress. As Gatsby tries to confront the crisis, Carraway advises him to get away from the community. He has made his judgment of his friend—"They're a rotten crowd. You're worth the whole bunch put together"—but Gatsby doesn't flee. In the end, Myrtle's husband, George, kills Gatsby in his swimming pool. This story arc is strong, but the novel's structure is loose, with long sections of dialogue and sudden melodrama studded with Fitzgerald's sidebar metaphors: Daisy's green light, the valley of ashes that divides the privileged enclaves from the urban Manhattan huddle, the all-seeing oculist. These varied elements, Clayton felt, made for a difficult screenplay adaptation.

Capote's script, when it arrived shortly after Christmas 1972, was disastrous. It was dialogue-heavy and cast Nick Carraway, the narrator, as a flamboyant gay. Clayton immediately wrote to Capote that it was unsuitable: "It's like a great fish that is all head and no tail." What in fact he was identifying was the problem he'd noticed in the novel itself: Daisy and Gatsby don't get together until the middle of the book, and only in the last third do plot and incident dramatically accelerate. Clayton's need, he said, was to truncate the first half, get Daisy and Gatsby together within twenty minutes, then widen and pace the ending. Capote had no stomach for this, so Francis Ford Coppola was brought in as a replacement by Evans.

Redford liked the Coppola script given him four months later. But while he was fine with the idea of expanding the "new" phase of the Gatsby-Daisy romance, he remained wary of many deviations from the novel dictated by Clayton. For example, all reference to Gatsby's beginnings, to the seafaring millionaire Dan Cody who apparently gives him his break, was removed. Through the spring, Redford went back to the novel. "I became concerned there might be a built-in problem with so mythologized a book. It seemed to overawe the adapter. Capote couldn't handle it. Coppola did better. But I wasn't sure Clayton grasped the heart of it."

Clayton's objective was twofold: apart from developing the modern-day relationship of Gatsby and Daisy, which Fitzgerald dismissively summarized in one line, he also wanted to create a David Lean–style romanticism that would heighten the otherworldly "impossible dream" of the story line, which, essentially, lambastes the class mentality that proscribes rich-poor unions. Above all, insisted Clayton, the tension within the story had to be tweaked in order to command its audience and drive home its point. Clayton wrote in his preparatory notes: "I intend in fact to keep throughout the film a constant feeling of extreme heat. I want people to perspire all the time and I want to see even stains on people's dresses. . . . As [*Gatsby*] is a story basically about obsession, it is absolutely necessary that the film has constantly a kind of mystery to it. Mystery, mystique and absolute touching sadness."

Overarching objectives apart, Redford needed a hook on which to hang his personal Gatsby. He found it not in discussion with the director, but in reading Scott Fitzgerald. Says Redford, "Fitzgerald wrote that Jay Gatsby was awkward when he said 'old sport'—it didn't come out of his mouth easily. I thought that was terrific. There's a whole encyclopedia right there, and it's from there I started to build up my own version."

Gatsby started shooting in Newport, Rhode Island, on June 11, 1973. Much of the action of the story takes place at Gatsby's mansion and Carraway's "eyesore" bungalow on the mansion's grounds. A Tudor home called Rosecliff, under the management of the Newport Preservation Society, was negotiated as the Gatsby property, while a construction crew under designer John Box, winner of four Academy Awards and the man who designed *Lawrence of Arabia,* built the Carraway bungalow from scratch. The only other major exterior location, Fitzgerald's symbolic valley of ashes, was constructed at Pinewood Studios in England. Along with Box, many of the leading crew members, including emerging cinematographer Douglas Slocombe and hairdresser Ramon Gow, were British, but, said Clayton, "an unmitigated, unprecedented effort was made to build Fitzgerald's American Jazz Age, which became a kind of surrealist-deco blend beyond any distinctive accuracy." Box famously described the awkwardness of pinning down Clayton's vision: "Call it [capturing] the quality of a butterfly or a bird."

There are many legends in the British film community about Redford's unpopular presence on the set of *Gatsby.* He was said to be uptight and unapproachable. Bruce Bahrenburg, a writer commissioned to keep a diary of the film for publication, spoke of his remoteness. One British newspaper went so far as to suggest that Mia Farrow had complained about Redford's insensitivity. She denied it, sued and was awarded damages.

There were several contributing factors for the bumpy ride. Farrow was pregnant. Merrick and Evans's decision to do half the production in England (where the budget could be pared back 20 percent, to $4 million) elicited criticism from several principal cast members because of "atmosphere" variations. Redford himself was struggling internally to grasp the amorphous soul of Gatsby and bridge the interpretative differences between Coppola, who wanted to remain faithful to Fitzgerald, and Clayton, who wanted something new. George Roy Hill had at first mocked the idea of Redford playing Gatsby. He had considered Alan Ladd wrong for the part all those years ago, and now, Redford. "I thought, for a start, it was one of the trickiest of all great American works. I thought that Gatsby is unknowable—that's the key—and I wondered how any director or actor would play that out." Then he thought about what he perceived as Redford's "fundamental loneliness." He said, "When I reflected on it, I could think of no one more apt for the role of Gatsby. Bob was the guy in the gray area. But when you got into the deep stuff with him, it was bottomless. And that's where he went for Gatsby."

The power of *The Great Gatsby* as a novel is the poetic proficiency that incited more contradictory critiques than any novel of the 1920s. Superficially it's a love story. But it is also a satire, in which Fitzgerald mocks the greed of the postwar, heroless Lost Generation. The strength resides, as critic Lionel Trilling pointed out, in the notion of Gatsby as the supreme metaphor for America. What exactly, the novel asks, is "great" about the average midwesterner Jimmy Gatz, who comes east to the Old World bridgehead of Long Island to conquer the beautiful Daisy? America's greats were not of the stature of Alexander the Great; instead the epithet "great" belonged to vaudevillians and the likes of Rudolph Valentino. Was that great enough? Metaphors apart, Fitzgerald's *Gatsby* was a significant literary mutt, steering away from the contemporary naturalistic trend of Stephen Crane and Frank Norris and back to the romanticism of John Keats. "Nobody really grasped that," says Redford. "Literature and Hollywood don't seem to mix well, and if we failed as we went along, we may have failed by overlooking some aspect of the poetry other than the visual style. The truth is, Hollywood wanted to make *The Great Gatsby* because it was a literary success, not because it was great literature. Enough time may not have been taken to work that one out."

Clayton and Redford got on well enough, but there remained a variation in conceptualization. Clayton's mistake, Redford felt, was that he often tried too hard to sustain the literal translation within a scene while, at the same time, striving for originality. Clayton's complaint was Redford's independence under direction: "If I had one issue with him, it was his refusal to do the same take twice," he said. "His reasoning was that he was in process of discovery, and the 'newness' of a spontaneous movement made it real. There was also the problem of the pace of his delivery. He was slow. Everyone else had a beat to their lines. He was out of sync a lot of the time, but, again, he reasoned it by saying people didn't react by rhythm. They were arrhythmic. They stalled and stumbled. Someone moaned to me that Redford never knew his lines. It became apparent that he was remote from us because he was inside Gatsby; he was resident in 1922 when we made that movie."

Redford insistently defends his "stumbling": "Gatsby is only comfortable with Nick Carraway. With Daisy and everyone else he is trying to be someone he is not. I was projecting that, and I feel it was misunderstood, especially by some of our English crew."

In Coppola's script, Carraway presents Gatsby as a mythic hero, "like an ecstatic patron of recurrent light." When finally he is killed in the swimming pool by George Wilson, there is a stronger sense of historic destiny than of moral rectitude. The closely observed cinematic symbolism—as when Gatsby and Daisy kiss and the camera tilts down to record their embrace reflected in the goldfish pond, signaling Gatsby's imminent end—speaks volumes about Clayton's skills, and yet the movie, when it hit the theaters, was generally considered a failure. Among the major reviewers who rejected it was Janet Maslin in *The New York Times,* who castigated Clayton for expanding the modern-day aspect of the romance, and disdained his "maverick stupidity." Coppola himself hated the movie and argued openly with Clayton, whom he insisted corrupted his faithful script. Coppola had told Clayton that this was a uniquely American story to which he personally related. Clayton disagreed; he felt the themes were universal: this broadening is what he set out to accomplish. Mia Farrow felt the fault lay not with Clayton, but with Merrick and the marketers at Paramount who positioned it as a successor to the previous year's *Love Story.* "Ultimately," said Farrow, "[it] was a victim of overhype. The market was flooded with tie-in promotions, from Ballantine scotch to Gatsby cookware, [and it was] blown into something it was never meant to be, and released as if it had been *Gone With the Wind.*" Scottie Smith said her father would have liked the finished film.

During the eighteen tense weeks of production, Redford's family had joined him on location. Throughout, says Jamie, Redford found daily escape in the day-to-day media speculations about Watergate, arising from the trial of the burglars and subsequent developments. In the spring and summer, the Senate hearings dominated national television broadcasting, achieving the highest audience ratings in history. Redford couldn't get enough of it. Says Jamie, "You'd go to chat with him in his dressing room and he'd be there with Mia, transfixed, watching the box, and he'd say,

'Hold on, Jamie, look at this. Can you believe Nixon ditched Haldeman and Ehrlichman? Can you believe what [John] Dean just said: that the burglary goes beyond [G. Gordon] Liddy and [James] McCord? Was Nixon behind all this personally? Have we got him in the net?' "

By 1974 and the publication of Woodward and Bernstein's *All the President's Men,* he had his answers.

15

Watergate

The evening Redford first encountered Bob Woodward in Washington, D.C., he also bumped into Ethel Kennedy, Bobby's widow, a woman he much admired. She had seen *The Candidate* and, responding to the McKay role, told Redford she was no fan of it. Her view of politics, she said, was that it represented the highest calling. Redford found this not upsetting, "because I felt that Bobby Kennedy proved that the system works best when it's challenged. We set out to do a little of that, and the urge to challenge is also what drove me to keep following Watergate."

The eighteen months from October 1973 through March 1975 was the most concentrated period of Redford's life in terms of movies. It started with the premiere of *The Way We Were.* Within ten days of completing *The Great Gatsby* at Pinewood, he was in Texas readying George Roy Hill's biplane barnstormer, *The Great Waldo Pepper.* Immediately after came *Three Days of the Condor,* the next big picture with Pollack.

All the while, Lola was making great advances with CAN, fighting for consumer rights and environmental protection. "The big difficulty was that Mom was going through huge life changes just as he hit his stride," says Jamie. "She was at the center of a circle of women who had shifted their power base from consumer awareness newsletters to Washington lobbying. They had a grant from the Department of Health, Education and Welfare to introduce a consumer-environment program into a pilot schools scheme in District 25 in Queens. Mom was no longer working from the apartment. She was flying to Washington a lot, and that put a strain on her, on us, on everyone."

CAN's progress, says administrator Cynthia Burke, was based on defining issues of state legislative neglect, like clean water management in Manhattan. Out of CAN came the specialist boards set up to tackle single issues, and it was on one such committee that Lola befriended Richard Ayres and John Adams, two of the six Yale lawyers in the process of cofounding the Natural Resources Defense Council. According to Adams, a recruit from the state's attorney's office who would become director, NRDC arose to fill the vacuum in federal legislation: "What we had till then were three bodies: the Wilderness Society, the Audubon Society and the Sierra Club, each with a separate and specific brief, and each scientifically weak. What NRDC set out to do was add science to the problems under review and establish a committee that would pull together the strands of each organization into one powerful lobbying group." Ayres especially admired Lola's drive. He got to know her well doing door-to-door fund-raising for clean water lobbying. "That was a nightmare concept," says Ayres, "since Manhattanites don't like people hammering down their apartment doors at night, even if it is for a great cause. It was also legally tricky. I admired Lola's courage, and when I got to know Bob, I saw his equal courage and I saw he had grassroots politics in him, too. Lola was a big asset, but we saw Bob in an entirely different way as a potential political figure for us."

In 1972, Adams asked Ayres, who was closest to Lola, to sound out Redford's interest in a formal working partnership removed from the women's group. Adams had read about Redford's interest in Native American issues and his local environmental work in Utah. "In one piece about the abuse of Utah's lands, he spoke of the desirability of an academy for the management of our natural resources. This was exactly our thinking at NRDC." Redford called Adams and told him he was interested. "I talked to him about 'the prevention of serious deterioration issue,' which is pollution law jargon for clean air," said Adams. "He was excited. He said yes, he would be interested in joining. We had what we wanted: a figurehead."

For years Redford had been swaying in and out of involvement with various Utah lobbies, the Environmental Defense Fund and other organizations. He had learned that the federal clean air and clean water acts in place since the mid-sixties were weak and operated basically by delegating everything to the level of state law, which was even weaker. The fact that NRDC had been to Washington and was fighting a proposal to build a power plant on the Hudson River was profoundly exciting, since Redford was already researching proposals to build massive new energy plants in southern Utah. "The thing they had above the EDF and others was that they were lawyers. All of the other lobbies had worth, but they didn't have the means to take these issues to the resolution they needed. The timing of this was perfect for me. I also thought, It's targeted in Washington, which is where I need to be."

That Redford had long been separating from Lola's organization was obvious to many people. Mike Frankfurt saw it as an inevitable result of divergent lives and Redford's new interests. "CAN's focus was the practical issues affecting Manhattan. That's where those women began, and that's where they psychologically remained. What really interested Bob was only the law and the Washington dimension. In that sense, at that moment they started to drift apart."

And, of course, Watergate was drawing him to Washington, too. As Redford was wrapping up *The Great Gatsby* in the fall of 1973, Richard Nixon was digging himself a deeper and deeper hole. In November the president proclaimed to a stunned meeting of Associated Press editors in Florida, "I am not a crook." By March, with the indictment of the Watergate Seven—the core group close to Nixon against whom the strongest evidence of dirty tricks had been amassed—the presidency was in peril. Shortly after, the House of Representatives commenced formal hearings on the possible impeachment of Nixon. Not long after that, Woodward and Bernstein's book about the 1972 burglaries and what preceded and followed them came close to completion. "Carl and I were pursuing the book our own way," says Bob Woodward, "but we'd been influenced by Redford in the way we compiled it. It was he who suggested we make it about the investigation, and not about the dirty tricks campaign. He had his movie idea. We had our book to be getting on with. But the two ran side by side."

"The film started to move after I'd first talked to Woodward," says Redford. "After the Washington meeting he came to my apartment. When I knew he and Carl were coming by, I told Bill Goldman, since we were friends. Bill said, 'Gee, I'd love to hear all this.' And so Bill was there with Bob, Carl and me. And, of course, the story was magical. It was tremendously important nationally, obviously. But I was also interested in Bob Woodward as a man. He was quirky. He had some odd mannerisms. I liked that. When he left, I said to Bill, 'There's the movie. These guys. Their personalities. The aspects of each that propel the other. The way the investigation was led by these personalities.' I made that observation to Bill as a general remark. I didn't mean to involve him in the project, and I wasn't commissioning him as the screenwriter."

The release of *The Way We Were, The Sting* and *The Great Gatsby* six months apart in the winter and spring of 1973–74 pushed Redford to unrivaled status as the world's number one box office star. George Roy Hill saw Redford struggle for balance. "It's a condition I well knew, though in Redford's case the fame was the most extreme kind. He was pulled in every direction. You could no longer have time in a public place with him. He was always looking over his shoulder. Always distracted."

This was exacerbated by Redford's "elastic perception of time," a perennial problem that caused many aggravating late arrivals on set. Hill was troubled as they began preparing to make a movie for Universal that had long been a fantasy of his, *The Great Waldo Pepper.* "I was a little annoyed, to be honest. He was never the easiest guy to stay in touch with, since he was so bad at punctuality and, with my marines background, it was an obsession of mine. There were a few instances where I didn't hear from him when he told me he'd call, and I said, 'Fuck 'im, he's doing this big-star thing.' But that wasn't his problem. His problem was some dismissal of authority he carried around, some unease with his own authority figures, maybe."

All Hill's fantasies, he said, were built around music and flying. He had learned to fly while still attending school in Minneapolis and earned a pilot's license at sixteen. Air shows fascinated him, and his favorite Saturday sport was attending the frequent rallies at his local airport and fields around the state. The tragedy of aviator Charles "Speed" Holman, a Northwest Airlines pioneer who crashed and died at the first Omaha air races in 1931, left a deep impression on Hill when he was just nine years old, and he spent his teens, he said, meticulously studying the escapades of the early stunt aviators and the technology of their planes. During the war, he was a transport pilot in the Pacific, and when he resumed civilian life, as a cub reporter in Texas, he made the decision to someday essay the life of Holman and his peers.

The Great Waldo Pepper, a period piece, was the fruition of that promise. "I couldn't have turned that one down even if I wanted to," says Redford, "because it was George's obsession and I was in his debt." Unlike Redford's relationship with Pollack in which "Sydney intellectually dissected things," his relationship with Hill, Redford says, was more intuitive. "The friendship was father-son in a most intersupportive way. I had the highest regard for his spirit. And when something was totally his, like *Waldo Pepper,* the joy of just being around him was contagious."

Like *Butch Cassidy, Waldo Pepper* dealt subtextually with the pathos of myth. By now, Hill, Redford and Bill Goldman had an almost family empathy, so it was no surprise that Hill chose Goldman to write his dream story. Though Goldman wrote the script, the concept, plot and resolution were Hill's. "I got a little of *Huck Finn* into it," said Hill, "and a little of Holman. I wanted to start it the way it starts, with the camera lovingly tracing over the scrapbooks of my childhood, my flying heroes, the great barnstormers, and showing their dates of birth and dates of death. And then the story of Waldo commences, the story of a man defining himself only against his self-set challenges, a man who connects with the dream, who can make a friendship, or make love, but who never touches the crowd. He is a circus freak. He entertains everyone. But he is alone inside a fantasy. And he will live and die like that, which is both his glory and his tragedy."

After a period of friction with Hill ("about Golman's inclination to talk too much," said Hill), Goldman delivered a script that Hill felt "had a lot of good things, though nothing too remarkable." The production was pressured into moving forward, however, by the brief window of Redford's winter availability.

Casting was coordinated by Bob Crawford. Scores of actors were interviewed, especially for the co-leads of Waldo's girlfriend, Mary Beth; his barnstorming rival, Axel Olsson; and his flying idol, the German wartime ace Ernst Kessler. For Hill, much of this casting was trickier than usual because he was measuring the aspirants against the heroes of his childhood, men like Ernst Udet, the second-ranking German ace after Manfred von Richthofen, who on numerous dogfights saluted and spared the lives of disabled airmen and who finally committed suicide when called up for service in Göring's Luftwaffe; or Jimmy Doolittle, the daredevil who first achieved the miraculous "outside loop" maneuver that Waldo attempts in the movie. "I felt some duty to those men," said Hill, "because they were like astronauts to me. They were the aviation pacemakers."

Hill's notebooks attest to great ambition in the casting. Among those considered to costar with Redford—"or to substitute [for] him if *Gatsby* runs ridiculously over as *The Way We Were* did"—were Jack Nicholson, George Segal, Donald Sutherland, Sam Waterston and Warren Oates. Bo Svenson and Bo Brundin were cast as Olsson and Kessler, with Susan Sarandon nudging out Patti D'Arbanville to play Mary Beth. "For the women the issue was the type," said Hill. "Here I wasn't affected by the history, but by the aerial movies I loved, like Bill Wellman's *Wings* or *Hell's Angels*. Those castings were spot-on, great chiseled faces so evocative of the era." Redford, too, was spot-on in Hill's book. "He had the Errol Flynn debonair look right out of my scrapbooks. No stretch of the imagination to see him in leathers, with a white scarf trailing in the wind. I wanted all the others to look 1920s, too. In the end, I settled for faces with character over acting experience. Which may have been a huge mistake."

Though the story was set in Nebraska, the Texas locations Hill chose, partly for sentimental reasons, around Elgin, Floresville and Lockhart were areas he knew well from his postwar flying, with second unit shooting in Florida and California. The choice of locations was further dictated by the winter sky profile: the kind of cumulus cloud cover so typical of Texas in February would enhance the illusion of death-defying speed in the many biplane flight sequences.

As Waldo, Redford portrays a gutsy individualist in the style of Charles Lindbergh, determined to live out his dream, which is to capture the kind of glory given to World War I pilots. Along the way he is demeaned—he even appears briefly in drag for a flying circus—but his goal is to be a real hero, unlike the silver screen Valentino whom Mary Beth so adores. The opportunity for undisputed greatness comes in attempting the allegedly impossible outside loop. He tries but is beaten to his goal by Kessler, the German ace glamour boy, and only settles the score by joining the Hollywood dream factory, where he finds employment as a stunt pilot in a war movie. Here, in a last-reel twist, he eventually outmaneuvers Kessler in a mock dogfight and wins the kudos.

Bob Crawford saw the venture as a home movie for Hill. "He had such fun doing it. He flew planes on location and directed scenes with the actor in the seat behind him. Most of the derring-do was either something he'd already flown or something he dreamed about. He'd done it all himself already. He'd crashed planes. He'd won races. Bob got to live out the bits in between."

Most famous of those bits was the wing walking, with minimal harnesses, at three thousand feet. Redford found this exhilarating. "I'm not sure what the insurance connotation was, but George wouldn't have cared. He would have lied to them. Risk came easy to him, as it did to me. It was scary, but I liked it." Bo Svenson did not. He refused to participate and was, accordingly, suspended by Hill, with the threat of dismissal. Svenson sued immediately, stating Hill's objectives put his life in peril. "I made a mistake in casting based on image," said Hill. "What I should have done was take each of them up in a barnstormer, done some loops and set them down, then said, 'Okay, now you fly it.' It wasn't a movie for blue screen [studio back-projected images]. It always lived and breathed for me as the real thing. And I loved how Redford served that."

Redford, however, never felt it was important work. He sensed it would not do well. In the end, the script downed the movie. In the story, Waldo's relationship with Mary Beth is carefully graphed in the first act and a half. Dialogue and wit are sharp, and Mary Beth emerges as a lovable, if overpossessive, supporter of Waldo's. "But then bang in the middle of the second act, she's inveigled into wing walking and she's killed. It was a disaster. We killed the movie there and then," said Hill. "If we'd cast Jack Nicholson, the audience would have accepted that level of despair and darkness. But Bob had taken on the role as our national glamour king. He was the sunny good-luck guy—even when he was playing a bandit—and the audience expected light around him. Dramatically, the decision to kill Mary Beth in itself wasn't bad. But in a Redford movie, in the vicarious way women were relating to him after *The Way We Were,* we were doomed because we were effectively killing *them* off. I recognized that problem only in the editing, but by then it was too late to fix."

Though the movie generated $20 million in receipts, its reception in the spring of 1975 was bleak, with Robert Lindsey in *The New York Times* pronouncing it a dud. Lindsey's comments provoked the often impulsive Hill to urge Universal to sue *The New York Times* over the review.

Redford's prolificacy was such that his Olympian position seemed untouchable. The sixteen-point addendum to his *Waldo* contract exemplified the power he now held: he had approval of director and all costars; he was covered for living expenses if he was more than fifty miles from home, charged at $1,000 a week; five first-class air tickets were to be supplied to him to travel to and from all locations; he had the use of chauffeured limousines throughout filming or related work; sole-star billing above the title was guaranteed, as was health insurance, the use of a personal makeup artist and costumer (Gary Liddiard and Bernie Pollack, Sydney's brother, respectively), Wildwood's right to approve all publicity images, and one 16 mm print of the movie for personal use. He also received a percentage of the gross box office earnings, without deducting costs.

With bristling confidence of his status, he moved on to the Watergate story. In June 1974, the previously unknown and totally incriminating tape of Nixon and Haldeman colluding against potential investigators was released, and the following month the House Judiciary Committee recommended the first article of impeachment against the president on the charge of obstruction of justice. The second and third articles, for abuse of power and contempt of Congress, were subsequently passed, and a few days later, on August 8, Nixon resigned.

Earlier, in April, on his return from *Waldo Pepper* location shooting in Texas, Redford had met up again with Woodward and Bernstein in Washington. Their book was near completion and he agreed to pay $450,000 for the film rights. Shortly afterward, due to a misunderstanding, Simon and Schuster, the publisher, sent the galley proofs of the book to Bill Goldman's agent, and before Redford knew it, Goldman was the screenwriter on the movie. "I was troubled from the beginning about Bill but friendship kept it going," says Redford. Woodward never doubted that Goldman would be the screenwriter. "He was there at the start," says Woodward, "and we spent a lot of time together. So I assumed . . ."

Redford recalls setting out his vision for the film to Goldman. "I told him I didn't want a thriller," he says. "This story was allegory, about a certain innocence that was corrupted by Watergate. Woodward and Bernstein personified the innocence. They were the old school, the journalists who investigated, extrapolated and worked to a standard. Because they were personally such a study in contrasts, I thought there was amazing psychological material to mine. Bill, I knew, was very skillful. But I had reservations about that. When he wrote his novels, it was homage to his favorite novelists. When it came to *Butch Cassidy,* it was homage to his favorite buddy movies, like *Gunga Din.* One admired him for it. But what troubled me on a personal level was the fact that his views were caustic. It was fun to be in his company and hear him, until you thought, What happens when this judgmental bit is turned on me? I became uncomfortable in some aspect of our friendship, and that should have warned me off."

In a very short time, Goldman turned in his screenplay, which no one liked. Woodward, Bernstein and Redford were dismayed, mostly because Goldman had not visited the *Washington Post* offices nor interviewed the key participants, like Ben Bradlee, the executive editor. "He put a lot of work into it," says Woodward. "There was no question of it. But it wasn't accurate to *The Post* or the way we worked." Nevertheless, Redford stayed loyal and sent out the script to a few directors he was interested in. When Elia Kazan and William Friedkin turned it down, he started to seriously rethink. "I got the impression that no one took it seriously. Bradlee felt it was glib, like another *Butch Cassidy,* and that was very worrying." For a while, Redford confided to friends that he thought he was losing the project. And then one day, with no prior notice, Carl Bernstein and his wife at the time, Nora Ephron, showed up with their own version of the screenplay. "They just took a shot at it," says Woodward, "because the other one was so wrong. But Bob hated it. He told Carl, 'Don't you know Errol Flynn is dead?' "

Goldman was offended that Bernstein had even attempted a script, and when Redford started to plead with him to rewrite his version, he resisted. "It was a predicament to be in, since we were losing ground, given the time frame of topicality," says Redford. By this stage, having briefly considered Michael Ritchie and Pollack as potential directorial collaborators, Redford had made a handshake deal with Alan Pakula, who was fresh off another journalistic conspiracy movie, *The Parallax View,* and whom, he says, he had "fully forgiven for any perfidy on *Daisy Clover.*" When finally Goldman handed his reluctantly reconstructed new script to Pakula, utter despair set in. "All hope was lost," says Redford. "Alan hated the script, and we immediately made arrangements to rewrite it ourselves, since we learned Bill was tied up already, writing *Marathon Man* for John Schlesinger. I was furious, but to what purpose? The friendship was gone—that made me sad—but there was a movie that had to be made." Redford booked rooms at the Madison hotel across from the *Post* offices for one month, and he and Pakula repaired there to redraft the screenplay. About one-tenth of Goldman's draft remained in the end. "Bill gave the start point and the ending," says Woodward, "and those never changed." Goldman would win an Academy Award for the script, but his participation was by now finished.

With the publication of their book, Woodward and Bernstein hit the promotion trail while Redford, in Washington, did additional research. He called on his CAN and NRDC contacts. The allies made in his previous fund-raising work for Wayne Owens and Tip O'Neill opened doors to congressional staffers with tales to tell. Joan Claybrook, the lawyer and lobbyist for Ralph Nader, served as a navigator. "Basically these people gave me insight into the universe of Washington—how it operated, who depended on whom, who knew the inner workings of whomever else." He also talked with reporters Mary McGrory, John Chancellor, Dan Rather and Sy Hersh—"all of whom had their own spin on what really happened with Watergate, why burglar James McCord blew the whistle, how Nixon masterminded the evasion, where the rot began. You couldn't talk to any of them without new insider information on Cox or Mitchell or Liddy raising its head," says Redford. "It had a snowball effect, which helped the fine detail of what Pakula and I were doing with the new screenplay."

In the weeks that followed, Redford and Pakula divided the background research objectives, with Pakula's finely detailed political research led by his Harvard graduate assistant Jon Boorstin, and Redford's taking the form of "character study," which was achieved by spending long hours driving around with Woodward and Bernstein as they continued their investigation of Chuck Colson, a Watergate conspirator who was not yet charged but in the process of plea-bargaining for his role in smearing Daniel Ellsberg. "This was exactly what I'd wanted Bill Goldman to do," says Redford. "We needed to get in there with those key figures, to dig into the life. Goldman did it before on other projects, but he wasn't there for this, which I knew would be one of the most tricky films I'd ever make."

The mood of the nation, sated on treachery, soaked fast into Hollywood. By 1974, there were several worthy conspiracy movies, including *The Conversation* and *Chinatown.* The monumental industry change of Steven Spielberg's all-out pop diversion *Jaws* was months away but, for a moment, a new, different, more discerning age seemed to be dawning. For Pakula, this was a crossroads moment in American cinema. With ten years of producing behind him, ranging from *To Kill a Mockingbird* to *Up the Down Staircase,* Pakula had long predicted a maturation of audience appetites. His own directing began in 1969 with *The Sterile Cuckoo,* a stagy, collegiate psychological study starring Liza Minnelli, and was followed by the thoughtful thriller *Klute,* for which Jane Fonda won an Academy Award. "My belief, based on my experiences, was that a vast market was not addressed. Audiences were impressed by the foreign imports, but very few American filmmakers experimented. American theater per se was similar. We had a disproportionate interest in diversion therapy and too little interest in discovery. What came upon us in the Watergate era after a decade of assassinations and dirty tricks was a kind of national enlightenment. Collectively we became cynical. I thought it was healthy. I also thought it was bound to affect entertainment culture, and I remember feeling then, more than at any time before or since, that we were onto our own 'New Wave.' Great movies were under way—things like Milos Forman's *One Flew Over the Cuckoo's Nest, Dog Day Afternoon, Network*—and we were suddenly looking for social discussion in film, and I thought this was a breakthrough. And this was my attitude in taking on *All the President's Men.*"

For Redford, there were glorious offers abounding—including roles in Stanley Kubrick's *Barry Lyndon* and in *Superman*—but he declined. He was sure he wanted to do something with weight. The meeting point between him and Pakula was their common view that accorded intellect and curiosity to the audience. "I knew Bob wanted Wildwood to gain distinction as a producer of quality films," said Pakula, "and he wanted signature, personal films. He used all his assets. He had great personal skills with agents. They liked him mostly because he was a money magnet, but also because he was earnest. He was the real deal. No one was going to get him into a Mel Brooks movie."

As research on the Watergate movie went on, Redford decided to fit in another acting role. With three strong successes behind them, Pollack was more eager than ever to make another movie with his old friend. The fact that Pollack had acquired a cabin at Sundance, ten minutes across the canyon, kept communication open and easy. "We talked about projects all the time," said Pollack. "We were on the phone daily, always saying, 'Maybe.' Then I saw an opportunity during that summer of 1974. I had a deal with Paramount; he had time. I thought, If we can hone the right one down fast, it's perfect."

For a while, the two men worked evenings on Robert Penn Warren's *A Place to Come To,* an epic, Joycean novel Redford loved. But a workable adaptation, it was agreed, would take years. They pledged to continue, but looked elsewhere. One evening in Utah as he was raking through Watergate research documents, Redford turned again to a script that had come to him with Peter Yates's name appended. It was written by the former *Batman* writer Lorenzo Semple Jr. and adapted from a slim, melodramatic novel by James Grady, a twenty-four-year-old assistant to Lee Metcalf, the U.S. Senator from Montana.

"To begin with," says Redford, "it was nothing I was interested in. It was a potboiler, all set in D.C., and the end had guys parachuting down with Sten guns and big cannons and heroin and the kind of stuff that didn't excite me personally. But in the middle was a great concept, about a guy struggling to deal with a situation he cannot understand. It was basically about paranoia, and that did grab me." This, at its heart, was a CIA story. With a simple shift of emphasis, Redford felt, Grady's book could be moved from potboiler to a postulation of the CIA's ambiguous morality. Form would then shift from thriller to commentary, the implication of which was a national security system fouled by its own principles, where individual objective and institutional aim were not often, or even necessarily, harmonious. This fit well with the Watergate zeitgeist. Redford pulled on a jacket and crossed the canyon by motorbike to knock on

Pollack's door. "I told him, 'This one has something. Read it and tell me if you think we can remodel it. I think we can.' "

Semple's redrafted script transformed the six days of the Condor—the duration of the chase in which the CIA agent code-named Condor attempts to dodge assassination as he unravels an internal coup designed to cover up a heroin-trading cabal—into three. Despite Semple's verbal dexterity—and his evident artistic growth in his recent adaptation of *Papillon,* combined with impressive work for Pakula on *The Parallax View*—he failed to produce the paranoia Redford hoped for. Pollack once again turned to David Rayfiel to layer the script. "Bob's instincts were spot-on," said Pollack. "It was a Russian dolls scenario, and it had this tremendous personal story of Joe Turner, the guy who trusts his organization, then wakes up one day to see that everything he believed in has turned on him and everyone's out to get him. The story then unfolds like a Hitchcock film, with the audience pulling for Joe as he moves through this bewildering world just one step ahead of a bullet in the back. All the time he's homing in on a criminal cover-up. But it was not an easy adaptation to film, and I saw Lorenzo's problem very quickly. The action, ironically, slowed it down. There needed to be a lot more humanity, and I saw that in terms of romantic engagement. I have been accused of playing that card too often, but I make no apologies because it engages people. How human beings connect, how they embrace and trust and love, engages people. And once you have that connection, the audience is paying attention and all the rest works." It was Rayfiel's ultimate job, said Pollack, to bring "breathing and feeling" into the story. Finally, after ten collaborations with Pollack, Rayfiel was on his way to earning his first formal screen credit. "A lot of the humanizing was in building up the girl role, Kathy Hale," says Rayfiel. "She's the innocent bystander, a photographer Turner kidnaps and holes up with and talks to. She becomes his dialogue with us, the audience, and with her we share his tension."

At the end of the summer, as they worked at a Connecticut house Redford rented close to Rayfiel's, important new elements were introduced by Redford, including substituting oil for the heroin cover-up in Grady's novel, which Redford thought more apt, especially in light of the environmental stance he was taking in Utah. It was also his idea that Turner, having exposed Atwood and Joubert, the CIA villains, should turn his information over in final retribution to *The New York Times,* a symbolic salute to the best of the Fourth Estate. "I worked hard on *Three Days of the*

Condor," says Redford, and Rayfiel attests to his "really vivid insights, not just lines of dialogue, but overview. I was impressed by his intuition for drama, for when a scene should start and how vulnerable the hero should seem—just so much, not too much. He had a writer's eye and ear more than any actor I ever worked with."

Redford also collaborated on the casting, approving Max von Sydow for Joubert, Addison Powell for Atwood, Cliff Robertson for Higgins, the CIA's deputy director, and Faye Dunaway for Kathy Hale. The movie was then relocated from the novel's Washington to New York, and a tight schedule was honed to facilitate the hoped-for winter start of the Woodward-Bernstein movie.

Redford felt he was focused; Pollack sometimes didn't. For him, too often, "Bob's attention was divided. He was into patrolling Washington with Hersh and McGrory a little too much. We started shooting in October, before we lost the light [of the early winter evenings], but it got quite stressed from time to time. I remember complaining to him, 'Excuse me, can I get five fucking minutes of your time, please?' I was also uptight because Dino [De Laurentiis, the executive producer] had a tough reputation, and *my* neck was on the line."

Redford feels that Pollack was unfair in his judgment, and also dismisses the crew rumors that he and Dunaway did not get on. He very much liked Dunaway, he says, though he felt at that time she "existed in a bubble emotionally" and seemed intensely distracted, perhaps by events in her personal life. "Those rumors might have originated from one incident, where she had to rail at me with some very rapid lines and she simply could not remember the words. So I left the room and Sydney stepped in and delivered her speeches to her line by line."

When Pollack previewed the first cut for De Laurentiis and friends, it proved a major disappointment. "Every part of it was awkward, every beat was off," he remembered. To fix it, he instructed Don Guidice, his editor, to "cut every scene. Take the heads off every shot. Take the tails off every shot. Take out reaction shots. Take out establishing shots. Reduce everything by half."

The effect, says Redford, was stunning. "Sydney had never made a film that moved as fast as a moving train and looked so tense. It was a new style of work for him, and it set the bar for all his later thrillers."

Pollack was proud. As contributions to paranoia movies go, he knew he had scored. It was now Pakula's turn.

Sundance, meanwhile, had taken a debilitating body blow. In 1973 serious competition arrived with the opening of Park City, a new resort funded by a California businessman, fifteen miles up the road at a higher elevation, with more organized accommodations and services. Redford's resort manager, Brent Beck, saw Sundance at a turning point. "We were on our knees by the time Park City opened. When the snows came, our business was limitless. In 1973 we had 122,000 day-pass skiers. But the problem was, the snow often didn't come till late January, sometimes even later. Hendler was goading me on because I was the chief executive with the responsibility of making it all viable, but the only extra revenue I could generate was from leasing acreage for sheep farming. That amounted to nickels and dimes. We charged $6 a head for sheep, and there weren't many sheep because Bob didn't want the area overfarmed. So income from farming was just $1,200 a month. As soon as Park City came on the scene, we knew we were going to the wall, that there was no way to survive unless we went a radical new route."

Redford had been routinely pumping in a minimum of $300,000 a year from his own pocket. Now it was apparent that not even this annual injection could keep the resort afloat. Compromises had to be made. Stan Collins brought in Bobby Davenport, the Kentucky Chicken King franchise owner, as coexecutive to manage a newly restructured resort. The first priority, with the help of Davenport's credit line, was to create more accommodations for overnight visitors. Beck went around the canyon to the existing plot holders, like Sydney Pollack, Steve Frankfurt and *Jeremiah Johnson* set designer Ted Haworth, and persuaded them to put their cabins into a rental pool. "These cabins were second homes for the residents," says Beck, "so I urged them to join the club. Their silver and tableware and linens weren't the best. I said, 'Look, you have to put something in to get something out. If we address this together, we can all make money and we can compete with Park City.' They went along with it, most of them. We created the rental pool, which Sundance then managed, and we had a chance finally to open year-round business opportunities."

Redford's support for Davenport, like for the business partners forced on him before, was never more than halfhearted. "What I didn't want to happen was covert sellout," says Redford. "No one was more sensitive than me to the burden of paying a mortgage in excess of a quarter of a million. But Park City becoming the pacemaker for redevelopment was the wrong way to go. Stan and Brent did well, but truthfully I believed we couldn't compete in the long term. It was an artificial objective we were chasing."

Beck was critical of Redford's ambivalence. "You could say Bob was part of the trouble. The environmental politics were getting in the way. Two Utah issues dominated his thinking: the state's on-off plans to expand the road along the Provo River, and Cal Edison's plan to build a power plant down the road to supply California's needs. Bob was no longer doing resort business when he came home, which was rare enough anyway. He was organizing town hall meetings, organizing busloads from Washington, organizing student protest bodies. At the same time he refused to let go of his personal fantasy, which was to own a ski haven in the Wasatch Mountains. I used to say to him, or to Lola, who was more practical, 'You will have a big price to pay for this luxury of owning a mountain.' The price, in my mind, was a kind of pollution, a price he was already paying. For a start, the mountain itself was permanently scarred by the ski runs he built there. I said to him, 'Bob, if you want to maintain this Alpine fantasy, you have to yield. The development of the Sundance business is not an option. It's a necessity.' When I'd say those things, his eyes would blank out and he'd mumble, 'Yeah, yeah,' but he was stubborn, so he was an enemy unto himself."

For Beck, the balancing act was harrowing. Committed as he personally was to supporting Redford's conservation instinct, unavoidable irritants rained down. "For example, our main summer scenic hike was to Stewart Falls, the most beautiful natural waterfall in the Southwest. I managed that trail and made little decorative plaques with all the important information about native flora and fauna. But then, because of the *Sundance Kid* connection, the Hollywood fans started pouring in and the trail became a souvenir trail. People weren't coming for the nature. They came to steal the plaques belonging to the Sundance Kid. When Bob was here, it was worse. The fans followed his every move, and when he arrived from L.A. or New York, they were here waiting—the gawkers, autograph hunters and hustlers looking for endorsements. We were caught all the time between the rock and the hard place."

Within weeks of Davenport's arrival, Redford argued with him about conservation and disengaged from the business partnership set up by Collins. "It was all a big mistake," Redford insists. "Davenport didn't have the influence or the money he said he had. I went back to where I started. Independence was the way forward. *I* needed to make the decisions, because no one else had the passion for the canyon. As time went on, my love affair with the place intensified. I wanted to ski there. But I wanted others to share that, too. And I wanted people to have access to the summer trails, as if it were a slice of the Uinta National Park. I changed in the seventies. As a younger man, since my grandfather Tot taught me, I was an enthusiastic hunter. I could ride and I was a good shot. But the canyon changed me. I stopped hunting when I saw a buck die at the A-frame. The canyon was full of deer and moose. At that time, it was open season hunting. Then, one afternoon, I was sitting in my living room and this animal came to the bank outside the window and sat there, badly wounded, dying. I went out to try to help, but it was past saving. There was nothing I could do. I sat there, watching it watching me; many, many minutes, maybe more than an hour. And then it glazed over and sank down dead. I was deeply moved. It was another of those Zen moments. That was, literally, the end of hunting for me. It seemed suddenly absurd to be killing for sport. I felt the same about the land. To be draining its resources simply to compete with Park City was immoral. On the other hand, to let it go to any old flake who wanted to build tract housing was equally wrong. So I had to keep drawing from the finances of my film work to fund it, until I could find a way to help it fund itself."

In November, Redford put the wheels in motion of preproduction on *All the President's Men.* Both Michael Ritchie and Jeremy Larner had expected involvement in the film and felt let down when that didn't pan out. Said Ritchie, "I thought *All the President's Men* would be number three in our trilogy: first sport, then politics and now the 'big business' of journalism. I tried to call Bob, but he was never available." Larner was philosophical: "Friendship and partnership, I learned with Bob, were variables. By *his* definition, and only his definition, it worked fine. You were involved if fate allowed. Otherwise . . . ?" But Redford defends his choices with *All the President's Men* as a drive for creative newness. "I had done a lot with Mike, and with Sydney Pollack. Jeremy won an Academy Award for *The Candidate,* which was well deserved. But personally I needed a fresh challenge, and I wanted to test myself, too."

Finally happy with their script since, crucially, "it made some affirmative statement and not another negative commentary about Watergate," Pakula and Redford sat down to cast the movie. Redford had several old friends he wanted to work with, among them Penny Fuller from *Barefoot in the Park,* Jane Alexander, another theater actress who had made the transition to film and had recently been nominated for an Academy

Award, and Hal Holbrook, Carol Rossen's husband, who would play the role of Deep Throat, the reporters' White House informer. Redford's initial concept had been a cinema verité black-and-white film in which he would not perform. But a distribution deal had been done with Warners, and Ted Ashley's concerns were primarily the commercial realities. "Ted didn't beat around the bush," Redford recalls. "He told us he needed to sell my name on the marquee, so the movie he was funding must have me in it." If he was to act, Redford felt the obvious role for him was that of Woodward. "I thought I could do something with those little nervous mannerisms, like his always shredding paper. I could make up an accurate picture because I'd spent weeks and weeks with him." For Bernstein, his first choice was Al Pacino, an actor he much admired. "But then I chewed it over, and for some reason Dustin Hoffman seemed more like Carl in my mind's eye, so I called Dustin and asked him if he was interested. That was a very short phone call."

Hoffman had, in fact, followed every facet of Watergate and knew about Redford's sessions with the journalists. Hoffman recalls: "While I was shooting *Papillon* in Jamaica, all the Watergate hysteria was unfolding. I did what Redford did. I kept tabs. My brother worked in the administration in Washington, and we were on the phone every single day, debating it. I always wanted 'in.' I only felt pissed that Bob got involved with the project before I did. If he hadn't gone after it, I would have."

Since his experience with Jason Robards in *The Iceman Cometh,* Redford had wanted to work with him again, if only to repay the kindnesses Robards showed him. In 1972, after years of alcohol problems, Robards was almost killed when he crashed his automobile into a roadside wall in California. He was badly disfigured in the accident and needed reconstructive facial surgery, which was carried out by a plastic surgeon who was a Mormon and a friend of fellow Utahan Gary Liddiard, Redford's makeup artist since *The Candidate.* Through Liddiard, Redford monitored Robards's recovery. Discovering he was on the mend, he offered him the role of Ben Bradlee, which was gratefully accepted.

The most important relationship for the producers was the one with the resident senior staff of *The Washington Post.* It was common knowledge that a general air of skepticism hung around the executive offices, but Pakula, a naturally sociable person, proved to be the production's best asset as he created relationships with Ben Bradlee and the paper's owner, publisher Katharine Graham. In their memoirs, both Bradlee and Graham speak with the glow of Hollywood awe about Redford's arrival on the scene. Bradlee was amenable, happy to show Redford off to his family and to converse with the production team led by coproducer Walter Coblenz. Graham, on the other hand, agreed to breakfast with the Redfords but wanted no part of the movie. "It's understandable," says Redford. "How could she know how we'd end up presenting *The Post*? She was cautious and protective, which was what you'd expect of a caring proprietor."

Redford wanted Geraldine Page to portray Graham in the film. Graham refused the offer, though she later regretted her decision and wrote a note of contrition to Redford. "Contrary to what's been written," says Redford, "she did not block us filming at *The Post.* We filmed for two weeks, but it went haywire." The reason the *Post* shoot was abandoned, says Redford, was that "the journalists and secretaries went crazy when Hollywood came in their midst. It was all giggling women and people doing their makeup and a general feeling of disorder. It was as bad for them as for us, and we knew we had to get out of there." The entire *Post* newsroom, desk by desk and filing cabinet by filing cabinet—"even down to the selfsame wastepaper baskets"—was built on a soundstage at Warners in Burbank.

As the cameras rolled on *All the President's Men,* late in the spring of 1975, Redford had the comfort of working with a team of top-notch creative technicians molded over several years by Pakula in his various executive and directing functions. Among them were production designer George Jenkins and cinematographer Gordon Willis. Both had worked on *Klute* and *The Parallax View* and here, with Pakula and Redford, conceptualized a visually unusual world, where the overlit, all-revealing glare of the newspaper office jars alongside the silent alleys and half-lit underground garages where the secrets unfold. Spatial design, said Pakula, was everything. "I believed this colossal story needed attention to size. We were dealing with something that could alter our view of investigative journalism *and* political office, so it had to feel big. It was therefore decided to use a lot of panorama shots, and when the journalists leave the cradle of the newsroom and go into municipal buildings, they are dwarfed by their surroundings. Gordon had a very novel approach to his lenses based on the notion that a good cinematographer always surprises the eye, and we were all of one mind that, since the information to be related was often complex, even tedious, we needed a very stylized look and, of course, dynamic performances."

For Redford, "finding" Woodward became the fun of the film. "I decided he wasn't who he said he was. He tried very hard to present himself as the most boring man in the universe, but I didn't buy it. The outward appearance was that Bernstein was the personality and Woodward the quiet one. That's how they presented themselves. But in fact Carl was the fuzzy, warm guy who tap-danced with his ego, while Bob was the hard man who went for the throat. The more I listened to them, the more I saw how they operated. Carl was the one who'd get angry and then he'd open the door for Bob, the reassuring good cop. But the secret was that the good guy was as hard—harder—than the other fellow. I was constantly trying to get Woodward to talk candidly, and what I did learn, from a story he told me about his misreading of a test at Yale, was that he was a workaholic. He'd taken a two-day exam and believed he'd studied appropriately, but got it wrong. He then told me, 'I realized I didn't know what good work was, and the rest of my life I've been redoubling my efforts to try to do good work.' " A key discovery for Redford also came in a chat with Woodward's assistant, Scott Armstrong. "Scott told me, 'He hides a lot within him, he's a hard worker, a workaholic, and, oh yes, he has this thing about fires. He's always poking at fires, always burning stuff.' Maybe, I reckoned, that had something to do with the nefarious process he's been through. Here's a guy, I decided, who is forever covering his tracks because he has to, to keep moving safely." At one point, Redford suggested adding some fire scenes to the movie. Pakula demurred. "It didn't matter," Redford says, "because those little observation handles were all I personally needed."

Hoffman, says Redford, had less trouble finding Bernstein: "Carl and Dustin had a lot in common. Both were radicals, uptight and loose at the same time. And, like Carl, Dustin had a very, very healthy ego. He required a lot of hand-holding, which is anathema to me. I don't need reassurance. But I loved Dustin's professionalism and the gifts he brought to a film that required committed intellect to steer it away from becoming a Mickey Spillane. Of the two of us, Dustin probably got closer to Alan. They, too, had a lot in common, and they both liked to talk an awful lot."

"The difference between Bob and Dustin is summed up in one comment," said Pakula. "We were dining during the film, and Bob was talking about his mountain in Utah. The more he talked, the more passionate he became. He told Dustin how he'd found that canyon in the fifties and just had to nest there. Dustin's response was, 'Gee, I love mountains, too, Bob. But I'm happy to look *at them.* I don't need to be *in them.*' "

But being "in" the movie, in the fullest sense of submersion, was what drove Redford. It was clear to Michael Ritchie that a process of quasi authorship was accelerating him ultimately toward directing. "His habit was to work very methodically, like a miniaturist. Some said he could be self-serving or overpowering. But my experience of him was of forensic detailing, then absolute trust. He was careful, a good team player, but he also had his own personal objective for the movie in sight all the time. In that way I think he was often frustrating for directors to work with." It was true that Redford and Pakula had a symbiotic closeness in *All the President's Men* beyond the usual director-actor relationship. Hal Holbrook and others spoke of an ambidextrous exchange that allowed both to move from one side of the camera to the other. But others speak of Pakula's chronic overanalysis, which often resulted in long delays as he attempted to make up his mind about a scene. In these instances, said Walter Coblenz, it was not Redford but Gordon Willis who stepped into the breach. Still, Pakula never felt personally challenged. "Bob and I both had a shared visual sense about the picture. I had done a lot of conceptual prep work with Jon [Boorstin]. As I saw it, we were blending templates. I grew up on [Elia] Kazan, really loved him. *On the Waterfront* was the most impressive movie from a performance point of view that I'd ever seen. Later I learned visual style from Hitchcock. For *All the President's Men* I wanted to blend both. Bob was in full agreement. We saw our first objective was atmosphere. We were trying to paint a picture, and so we were relying heavily on Gordon's camera work. Gordon was a very moody worker, especially when he had a drink too many. But he was an artist, not a craftsperson, and that was a big turn-on for Bob. So, yes, we did clash, all of us. But we were on the same page in conceptualization of a big, visually gorgeous film."

The only regular irritant for Pakula was what he called Redford's "hurry to be on the next page." All of the main actors—Hoffman, Holbrook, Robards, Martin Balsam, Jack Warden, Jane Alexander—were good conversationalists. "They were analysts, and they all wanted to debate the historical relevance of what they were doing. All, that is, except Bob. Which wasn't the best situation, because Dustin would slow down while Bob hotted up. 'Let's just get the fucking thing on its feet,' Bob would whisper, constantly, while Dustin was sitting, head in hands, in the corner."

Remembering the Redford he knew on *Inside Daisy Clover,* Pakula perceived a change in acting style. "My wife and I watched a screening of one of his movies [in the early seventies] and she turned and said to me, 'Blackglama,' which was a jolt. A commercial was running at the time for Blackglama furs. The point was, you put on this fur like a layer of glamour, that it was an aura you draped over yourself. She felt Bob's megastar thing had become a layer. On the set, he remained the perfectionist I'd got to know during *Daisy Clover.* He had a terrific memory for lines, his and others', and he was unusual in his overview. Even experienced actors like Harrison Ford will show a blind spot to background action. Redford never did. His peripheral vision was brilliant. But the edge that I remembered wasn't there. I wondered had something corrosive happened with the specific success of *The Way We Were*? *The Way We Were* made him as a romantic hero, which was largely Sydney's doing. On *Gatsby,* Bob copied the formula, and it was he who suggested that Clayton extend the Daisy-Gatsby love affair, though it didn't happen. I wondered if his success with Sydney had taken away the edge. That may have been his personal Faustian trade-off."

This gripe, Pakula conceded, was expressed by no one else. Robards, for one, was an ardent fan of Redford's, and vice versa. Pakula recalled, "Jason kept whispering to me, 'That kid has class. Dustin acts with his body. But Redford acts with his fingertips.' "

Getting permission to shoot at public buildings was difficult. "They just didn't want us in Washington, so every permission was a stranglehold," says Walter Coblenz, who had responsibility for such things. "I made a decision. I wanted to pull the shoot out as soon as possible because they were throwing obstacles at us. We shot at the Library of Congress, for example, and they just didn't want us. There was anger and denial all around. We were told that the incident portrayed in the book was inaccurate, that the library had never been involved. That drove Woodward mad, because he knew what was true, he *was there.*" Later, Coblenz had a meeting with Ron Nessen, Gerald Ford's press secretary, about staging a briefing scene at the White House. Nessen said there'd be no problem, that Ford understood the quality and purpose of the movie. "We scripted it in," says Coblenz, "but of course we were naïve. There was no way Ford would allow Redford to come to the White House to diss the previous president. We were suddenly told it was all off, that the administration didn't approve. It felt hugely ironic. It seemed like business as usual."

In the end, Pakula shot 300,000 feet of film, which would eventually be cut to 12,300 feet for a 2:18 movie. With a scheduled opening in April, Redford was astonished to get a call from Coblenz during the Christmas holidays. Redford had left the production three months before, assuming all was well. Coblenz told him, "Bob, you better get back to L.A. We've got all these rolls, and Alan is paralyzed. He is so immersed in it that he can't sort it out. We're screwed. We'll never make an opening." Redford knew Pakula's problem was often overanalysis and indecision. "There was also the fact that he would never work beyond 6:00 p.m. Soon as the clock chimed, he was out of there for his cocktail and his social night." Redford flew from Utah to L.A. and hunkered down with the editor—the sixth Pakula had employed—to wrap the movie. "And we just labored round the clock. We had the deadline, so it had to be done."

The budget, at the start, had been $6.5 million. By January the production was, admitted Pakula, "$2 million over budget and a month over time. On the other hand, we all remained friends, which was no small accomplishment. Kay Graham still had her doubts, but Bernstein and Woodward were okay and that seemed the right order of things." For Redford, Warners' support was welcome but equivocal. "We had a new champion there in Frank Wells, who was now president of the company. He didn't grumble too much about the overruns because he felt it was a noble endeavor. At the same time, Warners believed the movie would make no money. Watergate had been done to death on every TV show, every magazine cover, you name it."

Redford and Pakula argued about only one thing in the editing: the finale. Pakula wanted to show TV footage of Nixon's resignation and the famous defiant farewell wave on the steps of the helicopter on the White House lawn. Redford resisted. "I told Alan again and again, 'This isn't about Nixon. It's about journalism. I want to end with the guys just working away.' But I was overruled and so we settled on a compromise, which was the image of the teletype announcing Nixon's resignation. In retrospect, Alan was probably right. The movie *was* about the power of responsible journalism, but it was also about a historical political terminus. After Nixon's departure it was no longer un-American to question the morality of the chief executive. That moment of farewell was a big deal."

Warners' worries about poor returns proved groundless. *All the President's Men,* which opened with a benefit for the Fund for Investigative Journalism at the Kennedy Center for the Performing Arts in Washington on Sunday, April 4, 1976, and immediately after for a Natural Resources Defense Council benefit in New York, grossed $51 million, Redford's best box office since *The Sting* and considerably better than *Three Days of the Condor,* which was still playing across the country (grossing $41 million, almost twice the take of either *Gatsby* or *Waldo Pepper*). The volume of good reviews was impressive. For Frank Rich in the *New York Post* the movie was "a rare and classic example of what Hollywood can do when it's willing to bank on good taste, shrewd intelligence and deep personal conviction." Of greatest pleasure to Pakula and Redford was Vincent Canby's verdict in *The New York Times.* For Canby, the movie was "an unequivocal smash hit, the thinking man's *Jaws.*"

The release of *Jaws* on June 20, 1975, in the middle of production on *All the President's Men,* changed American cinema irreversibly, but not in the way Pakula had imagined. Sidney Sheinberg, then head of Universal, the movie production arm of MCA, had conceived of a new idea for the wide release for movies. Until now, movie distribution was a drawn-out process, where prints were sent to an assortment of towns and cities on a one-by-one basis, then screenings were extended if box office returns indicated audience approval. Sheinberg's plan was to amortize costs by sending hundreds of prints to all locations, coupled with a nationwide marketing campaign to raise awareness for the new movie. *Jaws* was the first true wide release, opening in 409 theaters simultaneously. The paradigm was proved by the receipts, which were in excess of $100 million, making it the most financially successful movie in thirty years (over its theatrical span, *Jaws* would earn $470 million). Two years later, employing the same now generally adopted strategy, *Star Wars* set a new record, establishing a precedent for a kind of box office competitiveness hitherto unknown.

Redford embraced the shift, but with reservations. Warners was happy to follow in Universal's footsteps, and Redford embarked on his first major tour, visiting six cities across the country in rapid succession. It was to be his last press junket for years. "I was concerned about the marketing aspect. Were we at the point where the packaging was as important as the content? *Jaws* was a good, populist movie. But it became the flagship for a campaign that overtook American movies. It became a very slick process, advertising directed, about selling popcorn and product placement. I thought the timing of *All the President's Men* very fortunate, because it was a very honest and unpolluted film. I'm not sure if we could have managed it in its purity a decade or two later."

Redford had been working nonstop in television and film for more than ten years. There was never a day, his daughter Shauna attests, when he hadn't a script or text for adaptation sitting on his lap. He was getting run down. "Somewhere around that time I experienced a panic attack," says Redford. "I was on the promotions circuit. I'd flown into La Guardia and went to catch a cab. It was a frantic time, all deadlines and media and legal documents and op-eds and all the drivel of celebrity raining down. I was alone, standing at the curb, when someone pulled into the space allotted for the cabs, and someone else got aggravated, and there was blaring of horns and shouting and all the rest. But it *sounded* different. And I looked around at the airport building: that huge rabbit warren of impersonal lights, faces at windows, the anonymous vastness of it all. I thought, Jesus, what if this cab doesn't hit the spot allotted to it? Does the whole universe unravel? And then I started sweating . . . and for a moment I slipped out of my body. *What if the system fails?* What if the center comes undone? Look at all the things that have to work in synchronicity just to turn a wheel! It became an out-and-out panic attack. Like, *How can anything work in this world!*

"I thought about the last five years. After *Butch Cassidy*, it was just one movie after another. Want to see the dailies? Sure. Want to have a script session? Sure. Want to view the location? Sure. Want to stand on the wing of a biplane? Sure. Want to go north, south, east, west? Sure, sure, sure. I'd hardly seen my family. The kids were growing up. Lola was working two weeks every month in Washington, and had moved there to try to stabilize family life while we were shooting in town. But Wildwood's offices were then on the Warners lot in Burbank, and I was there more than I was with her. Right after *All the President's Men* I stopped dead. I decided to wind it all down. I felt: Maybe I won't be an actor anymore. I thought: I've forgotten how to paint. Maybe I will write—poetry, short stories, maybe a screenplay. But I was exhausted, and I longed for the tranquillity of the West."

Tranquillity was the one thing Utah could not then provide.

16

Out of Acting

While working on *All the President's Men,* Redford visited Gerald Ford in the Oval Office. "We spoke about skiing, a lot of platitudes," says Redford. "Then he went out and made a speech about Cambodia. What did I learn? That the air ain't so rarefied up there. You don't have to be a Rhodes scholar to be president."

The entire experience of *All the President's Men* heightened Redford's confidence in his political possibilities. It was while researching the movie that he met Joan Claybrook, the public interest lobbyist then running Ralph Nader's organization, Congress Watch. Redford had always been mindful of the accomplishments of Nader's activism. He didn't need to read CAN's newsletters to know that it was through Nader's lobbying that car safety had improved, car emissions were controlled and literally millions of lives had been transformed. Grassroots politics, Nader reminded him, is where it all begins. But agitating and lobbying were different animals, he knew. Was he prepared for the committed discipline of lobbying?

It was over dinner with Claybrook that the gauntlet was thrown down. "Bob was whining about Ford's nomination of Stanley Hathaway, the former governor of Wyoming, as secretary of the interior," says Claybrook. "He stated what we all knew, that Hathaway was a promoter of overdevelopment of wilderness for mining. And I said, 'You know, Bob, I'm so tired of guys like you complaining about situations like this. You have fame, ergo you have power. You are opposed to this guy? Try and stop him, then.' He said, 'What do I need to do?' And so his formal political education began."

Claybrook found Redford keen to tackle Capitol Hill. "I told him he had to personally meet fifteen or so senators who were going to vote to see Hathaway in, and state the case. I made the appointments with all but two or three of the guys we knew would never vote with us, and put together the background files for him to hand out. I didn't think, with his movie commitment, that he'd be able to follow through, but he did. So we developed a little routine. We would meet at the corner of the Senate building and I'd hand him his notes and in he'd go, alone, with his rap down pat. I told him, 'You have to look in the guy's baby blues and ask him, 'Are you going to vote with us?'—and count every one of those votes on a handshake. If the senator says he'll think about it, it's not good enough. You tell him you will call tomorrow."

CAN contacts opened some doors; his celebrity some others. Senators Tip O'Neill, Chris Dodd and Ted Kennedy—a regular skier with his family at Sundance—were all helpful. Over the course of forty meetings, Claybrook and Redford finally had their majority. Redford was ecstatic, but Claybrook cautioned him about the hurdle to come. "Next, the committee will meet for their formal vote. And when they do that, you have to be there, sitting in the front row to look every one of them in the eye when the time comes."

On the day, Redford and Hoffman were filming until dawn. Claybrook was certain Redford would never make the committee meeting. "But, what do you know, he made it," she remembers. Claybrook saw the power Redford represented. "Since a Hollywood star was actively involved, there was extra press attention. The press had been digging and they'd come up with dirt. Stories were emerging about Hathaway's corrupt business practices. I grabbed what we had and told Bob to play the delay card by asking Senator Henry Jackson, who was chairing, to postpone the vote so that a proper investigation could be undertaken."

Jackson ordered the investigation but allowed the vote, and Redford, says Claybrook, "fell apart" when Hathaway won by four votes. "I had those bastards," Redford told Claybrook. "They promised me and they lied to my face." Claybrook told him not to be discouraged: "It's a game, and that's the ethic, that's how two-faced it is. Just remember, *You don't always lose.*" Redford used those words, verbatim, five years later in a scene about institutional corruption in the movie *Brubaker.*

Even today Redford winces at his naïveté. "I did not want to contemplate the extent of the vested interests on the Hill. Neither could I believe the level of bait switching and duplicity. Joan taught me about 'the yellow walk,' where the guy disappears to the bathroom just as the vote is called. On one hand, this was childish, kindergarten stuff. On the other, it was devastating because I realized how much the checks and balances are needed, how little we can trust." As it turned out, he and Claybrook were rewarded for their efforts when, four months after Ford appointed Hathaway, the investigative committee documented the malpractices in Wyoming. Soon afterward Hathaway suffered a breakdown and was forced to resign. "I was completely indebted to Joan for showing me how, in the cliché, power corrupts," says Redford.

The lessons in Washington fired him up for the power plant fight in Utah. Utah had been an easy target for developers servicing the ever-growing California. Southern California Edison—Cal Edison—had announced that its biggest single enterprise, the coal-burning Kaiparowits plant, would be built in eastern Kane County, an area of spectacular natural beauty ringed by the Bryce Canyon, Grand Canyon and Zion national parks. The *Southern Utah News,* the *Deseret News, The Salt Lake Tribune* and the regional television affiliates supported the plant, which, it was advertised, would render full employment at top dollar to traditionally underadvantaged towns like Kanab. Cal Edison had further joined with four other major energy providers in California, Utah and Arizona to plan for a total of eleven power plants throughout the West.

Applying what he'd learned from Claybrook and others, and with the support of NRDC and EDF, Redford went into battle, first forming a pressure group, Southwestern Energy Alliance, with a view to holding public hearings. When that failed, he accompanied Cal Edison's public relations man, Howard Allen, on a helicopter tour of the national parks in order to take the opportunity to press home the inevitable environmental losses. Simultaneously he locked horns with every journalist and Cal Edison surveyor who would face him. Two prime supporters joined him in the fray: former secretary of the interior Stewart Udall and Salt Lake City mayor Ted Wilson, the only local politician to get involved.

"It was my first major conservation issue," says Redford, "and what I discovered very quickly was the mass of ignorance out there. It's not just the greed of industrialists. It's a lack of fundamental awareness, a mind-set created over 150 years that says Manifest Destiny allows us to do what we will with the land. My passion came from the pages of Wallace Stegner, who prided himself on his attachment to the land. We flew over the Escalante Red Rocks, this paradise that has been untouched for millennia, and I thought about what Stegner has written: that here is a place where the silence allows you to hear the swish of falling stars. I told Howard, 'The last thing southern Utah needs is a behemoth to break the silence and pollute the water and the air.' "

But Allen was the least of Redford's obstacles. The people of Utah dismissed Redford's campaigning out of hand. "The problem was historical," says Brent Beck. "Take the example of Provo, which was the state's second-largest population center. It was Mormon and it was Republican. Cultural and business life revolved around the university and U.S. Steel: education and income, period. What Cal Edison represented for southern Utah was what U.S. Steel gave Provo—it was financial stability for a neglected area. The way those southerners saw it, they had a chance to make some money. Bob wanted to challenge that."

Redford knew he was making enemies among Utahans statewide. He took comfort from his role model, Wayne Owens, who had worked for Bobby Kennedy and had become the first liberal Mormon to win a seat in a state beloved of conservatives. "Wayne changed common perceptions the grassroots way, by walking around, by getting off the mediaspeak bandwagon and bringing it down to the level of the common man," says Redford. "Sure, a lot of right-leaning folk were unhappy. But enough people liked that Wayne was a guy from the sheepherding community who wanted new, egalitarian rules. They were tired of the status quo, with the bankers and rich businessmen owning the state." Ted Wilson, a former assistant to Owens, was elected, too, against the odds. For Redford these victories represented a beacon of opportunity. For decades, as he saw it, the country seesawed on a government of compromises—a Republican chief executive with a Democratic House and maybe Senate (or vice versa), held in balance by the political action committees (PACs) and specialist lobby groups shoring up House and Senate incumbents expecting payback. With people like Owens going to Washington, there was optimism that change could be made without constitutional challenges. The battle to block Kaiparowits, for Redford, was a brick in the wall.

Before the battle was fully engaged, and just seven days after completing principal photography on *All the President's Men,* Redford joined a group of adventurers to collaborate with *National Geographic* magazine on a three-week horseback expedition to measure the cost of changes in the West. Redford viewed this as a golden opportunity. During *Butch Cassidy and the Sundance Kid* he had befriended Lula Betenson, Butch's surviving sister. In conversation with her and with local historian Kerry Boren, he had been apprised of the fact that the trail ridden by the famous outlaws was gradually being eroded by an assortment of developments. While working with Pakula in Washington, he'd stopped by the *National Geographic* offices and proposed they produce a photo essay that might record how the West once was. Now, with Kaiparowits looming, the need seemed urgent. At first, the magazine was unsure, then Redford suggested he himself conduct a ride along the trail, with a group of historians and observers he would assemble. Ted Wilson saw this as a stroke of genius. "Anyone who spent time with Bob knew he was a poet. He'll talk about Willa Cather before he'll talk about Richard Nixon. The "outlaw trail" ride [as the *National Geographic* adventure was called] was his political style. It was glamorous, with lots of references to Butch Cassidy's gang and all the rest, but it was really a powerful tool for gathering votes."

Adrenaline, says Redford, drove him; but there was also the need to disengage from the airless offices of Cal Edison and the congressional staffers and reconnect with the land. Ostensibly, the *Geographic* project was a marathon survey ride, Pony Express fashion, around the bolt-holes employed in the 1880s and 1890s by the Wild Bunch, starting at Kaycee, Wyoming, and ending at Lake Powell. His old buddy Tom Skerritt saw it also as an emotional stabilizer. "That was the restatement of Bob the Outlaw, the loner who's most comfortable saddling a horse and disappearing on the mesa. It was a reminder that he was really nonpartisan, that his politics began with the 'We, the people' part of the Constitution."

The photographer Jonathan Blair, whose *Geographic* assignments ranged from Pacific Islands wildlife refuges to Turkish shipwrecks, photographed the trail over six months, with emphasis on the primordial nature of the landscape. The ride itself, which comprised a team of five men and three women, was managed by Boren, using fresh horses at well-spaced staging posts across the Continental Divide as well as occasional four-wheel drives to lug equipment. Among the riders, selected by Redford, were Oregon-born Dan Arensmeier, a former East Coast Xerox manager who had abandoned big-city life for the ways of the West, and his wife, Sherry; Terry Minger, a conservationist and town manager of Vail, Colorado; naturalist Ed Abbey; and Redford's Sundance-based friend Mary Whitesides, an artist. Redford, Boren, the Arensmeiers, and Blair and his wife and assistant, Arlinka, rode the first part of the trail from Barnum, a site east of the Wild Bunch's cliff-side Hole in the Wall hangout, through the Andrew Wyeth–like flats of Wyoming and across the Wind River Mountains to the mining town of Atlantic City, where they joined up with Minger. Ten days later, crossing the most difficult mountain terrain into Utah, they met up with Abbey and his wife and Whitesides.

National Geographic would publish a thirty-six-page feature on the ride in November 1976, and later a lavishly illustrated book. In both, Redford retold the Butch Cassidy tale, dressing it with the personal motivation for his current activism. Every phrase from the native cowboy's lips is relished—"Head out to that juniper, turn left, go west to the Rocky Mountains and may the Good Lord bless your skies"—and every opportunity is taken to acknowledge the dignity of the Indians, the lost stewards, and the cavalier governing of the Bureau of Land Management. Since the early seventies Redford had abandoned his diary keeping and replaced it with stapled-together notebook jottings titled "Redford Musings," which became the foundation for essay and book. In one notebook he scribbled: "Maybe it's because of our future rush, our need to expand and grow at any cost, but we have lost something, something vital, something of passion and romance."

"Everything I wrote I truly felt," he says now. "I was saying, 'Look at how fast it's slipping away.' What we did to the Native American was reprehensible. But it's not over. We've poisoned reservation lands in Arizona. Soon, if the energy companies have their way, we'll do the same in Utah. All so that Californians can enjoy hot tubs and neon lights. I came off that ride more determined than ever to kill Kaiparowits." Shortly after, he would write to Arensmeier about the emotional impact of the ride: "It was as if some supernatural force plucked us from our daily harness and gave us a glimpse of greener valleys."

Throughout the ride he was reminded of how tired he truly was. He had accidentally packed Jamie's sleeping bag, which was too small to cover him in the freezing nights: "Every morning I woke up feeling a track meet had taken place on top of me. It wasn't so much the physical hardship of the trip that wore me down. It was the background: the work overload."

But in the spring, it all seemed worthwhile. Shortly after the airing of a forceful segment of the CBS newsmagazine *60 Minutes* hosted by Dan Rather, which Redford had personally orchestrated, Cal Edison announced it was abandoning Kaiparowits in the face of environmental impact reports. Ted Wilson believed Redford deserved enormous credit for the victory: "Of course, there were many people involved, many voices. But it was because of him that Rather came south and the whole business became nightly news. No matter how you cut it, no one else in the locality—neither Wayne Owens nor I nor anyone—could have garnered that interest. Bob simply deserves the credit for mobilizing ordinary people and blocking Cal Ed from abusing this state."

The rewards weren't all sweet. On April 22, the *Southern Utah News* published an article headlined "Rally Ends in Hanging, Burning of Environmentalists," with accompanying pictures of effigies of Redford, Mayor

Wilson and a symbolic EPA hanging from a gallows alongside a coffin painted with the slogan KAIPAROWITS: STUDIED TO DEATH. In the view of John Nelson, chief engineer of the town of Kanab, "misinformation and inflation" that consumed over a million and a half man-hours and cost $20 million left Kaiparowits "a piece of wasteland that has no other use." The *News* pulled no punches, printing a half-page condemnation of "Skunk Man Redford" from the new-to-the-scene American League for Industry and Vital Energy, which itemized Redford's personal environmental misdeeds arising from his overdevelopment of his tourist resort.

"Of course there was economic fallout," says Dick Ayres, working with the NRDC. "But you have to measure it contextually. What do you do? Allow one generation to thrive at the cost of a loss to all future generations? The truth was, Cal Edison planned an 'oil by wire' monster that would have ruined the Grand Staircase–Escalante [national monument area] forever. That was an unacceptable loss, and Bob reversed it." Still, Redford felt empathy for those disappointed by the lost immediate financial advantages of Cal Edison investment: "There's no question that low-income folk suffered. But a quick fix that damaged our heritage was not the answer. As I saw it—and Ted, Stewart and many others—this was a one-issue case. We were certainly not dumping on Utahans. There were battles to be fought in Utah and elsewhere for fair educational opportunities, for jobs, for Indian rights, for species protection. We understood this. But this was about conservation. And one important thing emerged from all the furor about Kaiparowits: plain and simple, people understood very little about environmental threat."

It was the greatest irony that the Nixon administration could claim environmental achievements—it saw in the creation of the Environmental Protection Agency (pollution control) and the passage of the Environmental Quality Policy Act (monitoring impact statements), the National Air Quality Standards Act (monitoring auto emissions), the Resource Recovery Act (controlling recycling) and the Water Pollution Act. But Nixon certainly never deserved all the credit. Some of those achievements were the result of work by eco-activists in Congress and a handful of lobbyists like Nader and the scientist Barry Commoner. The Water Pollution Act, for example, survived Nixon's veto, and the first Clean Air Act in 1970, championed by Senator Edmund Muskie, only won Nixon's support as a political maneuver to counteract Muskie's rising popularity as a Democratic presidential candidate. Probing this deeper understanding of environmental politics horrified Redford. In 1970 Americans constituted less than 6 percent of the world's population but used 40 percent of the earth's resources while producing 50 percent of global pollution emissions. Cheap energy, almost half of which was imported oil, powered the rapid economic growth, but when OPEC embargoed oil in 1973 and sent prices soaring, the advocates of unrestricted domestic development for self-sufficiency—of massive strip mining, offshore oil drilling and relaxation of environmental regulations—took center stage. After Earth Day in 1969, the work of Barry Commoner and the NRDC dented public apathy by creating an awareness of imminent irreversible ecological damage and inspiring pockets of activism akin to the civil rights and antiwar movements of the sixties. But the sustainable development lobby was inconsistent at best and in danger of being lost under the economic exigencies of successive administrations dealing with recession and inflation.

"Education was the answer," says Dick Ayres. "But people have an extraordinary difficulty with the word 'education.' Too often it implies self-discipline or personal reform, and there's a natural resistance to such things." Redford believes, "The message was pure. We are in stewardship of the earth. We have a moral obligation. We accomplished something morally important at Kaiparowits and I had hoped it would advance a trend. I believed the country was ready for change. We finally had a liberal Democratic Congress that was becoming truly energized. Jimmy Carter was headed for office. The confluence of factors was telling us that for the first time in fifteen years we were ready for social reform."

In the run-up to the election Redford dedicated himself to study. He had aligned with the Utah Native American Consortium and dedicated a slice of his time to two PBS documentaries, *The New Indians* and *The Wolf Equation,* which were further ecological wake-up calls. All this work concentrated him on the battleground of wilderness preservation. In Ford's last days in office, Congress had ordered the Bureau of Land Management to survey all roadless areas to establish new wilderness designations in the Federal Lands Policy Management Act, an extension of the 1964 Wilderness Act. Redford saw this as a golden opportunity to widen debate about the environment. Addressing the use of land was critical because of the recent movement of the population. Over the last fifteen years, Americans had started migrating en masse to the Sun Belt of the South and southwestern states, where populations had doubled since 1960. Arizona, his next-door neighbor, had shown a population growth of 25 percent in five years. "Clearly resources were already strained, and the situation would worsen," he felt. "I thought this was a marvelous thumbnail to bring to the attention of the next administration to show how quickly we were losing ground to civilization changes and consequent mismanagement of what we had." Along with John Adams and NRDC, which was immersed in clean air initiatives, Redford prepared documentation to land on the next president's desk.

During the primaries, Carter summoned a number of study groups to his headquarters in Plains, Georgia. Redford visited, representing the Hollywood PAC contingent, with his land use documentation. "I was under no misapprehension of what he was looking for," says Redford. "It was power alliances. I liked his plain talking. He was interested in the same thing FDR was interested in: the voice of the common man." Redford, though, had learned his lessons from Joan Claybrook. In the final analysis, Carter was as unfocused on the issues that seemed critical—energy and the environment—as the Republicans before him. But Redford was not dissuaded. "I thought, He's looking for the Hollywood endorsement from me. So I'll look for something from him. I'll play by the rules of the game."

Two years before, the governor of Idaho, Cecil Andrus, a renowned environmentalist, had written a fan letter to Redford, inviting him to bring film business to the state. In his research Redford had discovered that Andrus had made conservation his main concern in Idaho, a state as fundamentally conservative as Utah. Like Redford, Andrus had tackled a major power plant—Pioneer, near Boise—and blocked strip mining in the White Cloud Mountains. A friendship developed and Andrus became, says Redford, part of his "education team." Now Redford decided to employ Andrus as a bargaining tool. Without guilt, he pressured Carter into considering Andrus for the job of secretary of the interior. "I don't think Carter had anyone in sight, but I knew Cecil's values, I knew we were both motivated by Earth Day concerns and I knew he would be a big asset for the country if Carter continued to be under pressure with rising oil prices and the moves to increase our own oil production."

When Carter was elected, Andrus got the Interior job. Joan Claybrook, too, took a post in the new administration. Redford thought the appointments were critical, since Carter "had no energy or environment policy to begin with." The overarching national energy crisis focused everyone. Nixon and Ford administration policy had been to counter oil price hikes by extending leases for drilling along the southeastern coast. Carter wanted retrenchment, initially with the emphasis on limiting leases. Andrus proved hugely influential, and his impact on the new policy was evident by April 1977 when, in a television speech, Carter cited the resolution of the energy crisis as having the importance of "the moral equivalent of war." But the continued high oil prices, exacerbated by the Iran crisis, weakened Andrus's hand and compromised his determination to apply conservation measures based on alternative energy sources. Elsewhere, he lost the fight to roll the Interior Department, the Forest Service and other resource agencies into one department of natural resources. Redford was disappointed. According to the timber industry, the scheme failed because the argument for unity was unclear; according to Andrus, it failed—despite Carter's open-mindedness—because of White House hubris. "Here in the West is example after example in which the administration wouldn't listen to experienced voices, or mismanaged a problem, and it turned people off," said Andrus, "The inside-the-Beltway crowd blew the one real chance they had to get some much needed rangeland reform."

John Adams and the NRDC continued to deploy legal arguments to force strong new provisions in a revised Clean Water Act, and in this, at least, there was success. Adams was very appreciative of Carter's and Andrus's support in this effort—but mostly of Redford's. "He was not properly credited with that achievement," says Adams. "Those revisions got voted through largely because of Bob's awareness campaign. He was here, there and everywhere at that time, writing letters to congressmen, pillorying people in business, taking meetings with Andrus, popping up on radio spots all over the nation, week after week." Adams calculates that Redford alone was responsible for increasing NRDC membership by a hundred thousand. "He became the face of clean air, but he was much more than that. Bob was an ideas generator, and though Andrus—and ultimately Carter—were frustrated in office by the events in the Middle East overtaking them, they always had Bob in their sight as a reformer. They always had room for him."

In an effort to bolster CAN, Redford launched another awareness program with the Environmental Defense Fund, this time to publicize cancer-causing agents in pervasive, nationwide pollution. He set up a spin-off, Citizens Action Now, a variation of Consumer Action Now, structured like the Business Roundtable, which raised $50 million a year to lobby for solar, geothermal and other alternative energy sources. NRDC did the heavy lifting, then Redford persuaded Ted Ashley at Warners to become involved. "This was two or three years before the nuclear meltdown at Three Mile Island," says Redford, "so we had no bad publicity from the energy sector working in our favor. But what it boiled down to was profile. We knew the Business Roundtable was powerful, but we also knew we could match their profile in the media. They were committed to more drilling, more strip mining, more nuclear excess. We were pledged to reduce all of it."

Warners arranged sixteen special premieres across the country to raise money for this "Hollywood CAN," and Redford flew to Nashville to drum up support from performers like Willie Nelson, Charlie Daniels, Waylon Jennings and Harry Chapin. An ambitious series of benefit concerts was planned, but ran out of steam after the premiere event with Daniels. In the end, says Redford, Hollywood CAN went the way of Carter's energy policy. "We were too uncoordinated, just like Carter's camp. We naïvely believed activists of the same stripe fight together. They don't. Ralph Nader is a great guy, but his first interest is Ralph Nader. We partnered with his Congress Watch on the basis of splitting the monies fifty-fifty. It's sad to admit that bureaucracy—including our own administrative slowness—bogged it all down." A decade later, such global initiatives as Bob Geldof's Live Aid would prove the curative value of high-profile music fund-raisers. Hollywood CAN, alas, raised little and lasted less than a year.

What Redford had achieved in a year of hunkering down with Andrus was a personal understanding of diplomacy. "There was no use in throwing stones. I began to understand that the sustainable development issue was a coming together of big business and special interest groups and legislators in goodwill, to shared ends. Today, in the twenty-first century, we see the undisputed problems with global warming. Thirty years ago, it was just a dim warning light flickering away. But we had to find a way to tackle it, and I believed this couldn't be resolved with a big stick. We needed camaraderie."

With Andrus, Redford sketched out a potential National Academy of Resources. In 1978 he laid it out for the *Los Angeles Herald Examiner.* The academy would be

> a specialized institution for the higher studies of our natural resources and wouldn't specialize only in environmental preservation. The academy would be all-inclusive in respect of the various disciplines that guide our use of resources, including biology, zoology, oceanography, geomorphology and environmental law. It would be a defense academy of our resources in much the same way that West Point, Annapolis, and the Air Force Academy exist for our armed defenses. The resource acad-

emy would be designed to educate people about the nature of our resources and to establish guidelines for which resources should be preserved intact, and which should be developed in the safest, cleanest, most efficient way. The academy would be funded by the Department of the Interior and therefore would be able to utilize its facilities around the country, such as the national parks.

The academy went down like Hollywood CAN. "It failed," says Redford, "partly because it had to get past Energy Secretary James R. Schlesinger, who was well intentioned but just about the worst person to take Carter's policies to the public. It really annoyed me, but I didn't quit."

If the government wouldn't produce the working model, he resolved to do it himself.

It was one thing to preach conservation and energy restraint, another to practice it.

After Redford decided on a sabbatical from film, two priorities took precedence beyond politics: family and reordering Sundance as a model of self-sufficient eco-friendliness. The previous fall he had started planning a radical new home just up the meadow from the A-frame that would encompass cutting-edge design techniques and energy-saving devices. To develop it, he sought out the innovative architect Abe Christensen, who was currently exploring uses of solar and alternative sources in design. Construction of the house, affectionately tagged the Big House, would serve as a model for a scheme Christensen and Redford agreed on to build moderately priced solar-heated homes throughout Utah. In tandem with the new house, Redford decided to expand Sundance business into farming and horse breeding, nonpolluting initiatives long native to the area that would help fund the ailing resort.

As building commenced, Redford sent out the word about suitable new farmland. Brent Beck found a fifty-six-acre farm called Spanish Fork at the mouth of the canyon and, on a cross-country flight, Redford told Gary Hendler he wanted to buy it. Hendler said it made no commercial sense. "That was a blessing," says Redford, "because I could then say to Gary, 'Okay, let's make changes: from now on you guide my tax affairs. I do not want guidance in my arts work or my businesses.' " The next day, Hendler called from Los Angeles to recommend a new adviser, his mild-mannered office manager, Reg Gipson. Gipson, a lawyer in his early thirties, was the Idaho-born son of a missionary who had reared his family in rural India. He recalls Hendler summoning him in some confusion: "Gary assumed that I'd have some agricultural experience, since I grew up on a mission settlement. I didn't. But I did know you don't buy a ranch from the comforts of an urban office. I flew to Utah to check out the water rights, sorted it and bought the ranch. So began Bob's next phase of experiment with Sundance."

Spanish Fork, rechristened Diamond Fork Ranch, became the base for breeding Arabian and quarter horses, an operation that ran for ten years until another farm, Charleston, replaced it and Redford started growing crops. Acres of corn, sugar beets, tomatoes and alfalfa were sown just a mile or two from Christensen's new homestead. Jerry Hill, officially the mountain manager, served as a general overseer and worried that Sundance had overstepped. "We were still the same small group of caretakers, but the lands we were supervising grew. The task list became bigger and bigger. I've been in this area since I was a kid, and it was weird to see the canyon become like a little town. It just kept growing and growing. I thought, It'll be real hard to keep up with all this. I also thought, A lot of the folk around here will resent Redford's determination to keep expanding."

Regardless of Redford's motivation, the very sight of new faces on the canyon roads, of builders and surveyors and flatbed trucks piled with newly quarried stone, incited new waves of fury. The American League for Industry and Vital Energy was quick to add to its list of offenses. Its well-circulated handout detailed every transgression: "Whereas, Mr. Redford has laid waste a great swath of timber lands in Provo Canyon for his own personal aggrandizement. Whereas, Mr. Redford delights in the unnecessary utilization of electric power for night skiing at his resort. Whereas, Mr. Redford has reputedly wasted a great deal of propane gas in the heating of his present home. Whereas, Mr. Redford is despoiling a beautiful meadow to build a new $600,000 home with an unsightly cyclone fence surrounding it. Whereas, Mr. Redford has supposedly secured a quarter-million-dollar grant from a federal agency to develop solar power for his new home. . . ."

Anguished, Redford chose not to respond. "We were sitting ducks," he says, "because Lola and I had affiliations outside the state that were not of the Utah tradition. The fact that CAN had established a lobbying office in Washington with a specific mandate for solar energy development didn't sit well with the Utah energy lobbyists. The fact that we were partnering with the Smithsonian to install educational solar displays in the Science and Technology Hall was considered some kind of scam. All these factors were twisted into presenting us as counterculture radicals who were crippling the state's economy. We were the villains in their midst."

It didn't help that all the Redfords had severed their Mormon links. Brent Beck, Jerry Hill, Stan Collins and most of the other resort supervisors remained active Mormons; much of the junior staff—the farmhands, restaurant waiters and ski attendants—came from Brigham Young University; many of the day-trippers were local Mormons. But the Redfords stood apart. "Since the early seventies Mom had lost interest in the church customs," says Shauna. "Dad wanted to distance himself, too. For him, it was more an ongoing tussle with the Mormon infrastructure—the day-to-day dealings with staff and businesspeople—than any religious disenchantment. From a spiritual point of view, he was on another path entirely."

Redford strove hard to recover domestic normality, though time and age had enforced a fragmentation. For Lola and the children life was still centered around schooling in New York, with summers in the canyon and skiing *en famille* with Tom Brokaw and his family, usually at Vail, Colorado, in the winters. Shauna cherished her father's determination to keep the family order going. "We'd all arrive in Utah in early June and break up on Labor Day—that became the hard-and-fast rule. When we were together, we did the normal things, though Dad's restlessness meant we were always in motion. He wasn't a sit-down-and-watch-TV dad. He liked to play tennis, take a sauna, swim, build a fence. He did it with all of us, but he and I made a special connection when we took out the horses. I valued my time on horseback with him. We discussed everything under the sun. I wanted to study art, and he was supportive. The fact that he'd not been encouraged as a child made him want to make up, I think." For Amy, who was five, the bright physicality of her father's presence was enough: "He was a movie star, so he was often absent. I took for granted that that's how life was. But when he was there, he was this vortex that came along and swept me into all kinds of sports and activities. I loved him for that child-energy."

Jamie, however, was struggling. He was prone to stomach ailments diagnosed as irritable bowel syndrome, and by his mid-teens his general health was unstable. At Dalton his grades were bad, and his only interest was drama: "But, like Dad, I'm superstitious. I read the signs. And the signs told me early on that acting was not for me." In fifth grade Jamie wrote a school adaptation of *The Iliad;* he was offered the lead but, true to his father's perverse nature, chose instead "the bad-ass bastard" Achilles. "Everything in that play informed me I would never be the next Robert Redford. First, my helmet didn't fit, so it was a struggle to hear the lines. Then, when Odysseus comes onstage to beg Achilles to join him in battle, I had my best lines, which ended, 'Forget it, I shall sit in my tent and wait till Agamemnon comes.' When I opened my mouth, out came, 'I shall shit in my tent.' "

Increasingly Jamie drifted toward music for self-expression and would soon become a fixture on the club scene, hanging out at Manhattan's Studio 54 until "the potentially lethal atmosphere for a kid with money and an association with fame drove me for cover." Utah, in the circumstances, was an escape, though Jamie, who had no interest in horses, related to it as a boyhood laboratory where he had learned to ski and discipline himself with hard labor. Now he preferred to strut the deck that faced Timpanogos, with his amp turned to the max, blaring Eric Clapton riffs across the canyon. "I saw that Dad was putting more time and energy into Utah, but I also saw Mom at the center of this strong group of CAN women that tugged at her time. It was a family situation where trouble lay ahead."

Christensen's eco-home, Redford hoped, would be the magnet to draw the family back together. But as the demands of the new farm and horse business grew, Redford was prematurely forced to contemplate Hollywood work again. "I never made a movie decision based on money," he says. "But that year was the exception." *All the President's Men* had proved a phenomenon throughout 1976, winning three New York Film Critics Circle awards and four Oscars, among them best supporting actor for Jason Robards and the one for Bill Goldman as screenwriter. The competing films that year included *Rocky* and *Taxi Driver,* movies that introduced new contenders to the Hollywood A-list in Stallone and De Niro. The following year brought *Star Wars* and the sweeping technology revolution. But Redford was still in demand. Prospective projects poured in. Even Hitchcock, preparing his swan song, *Family Plot,* expressed interest. Redford was "thinking differently. I knew acting per se was no longer enough. Directing now took center stage in my thinking. I knew nothing about the technicalities of cameras. All I knew was from observing great talents like Gordon Willis and Duke Callaghan. But I began to imagine some story I could visualize on-screen, with absolute control, like a painter." He asked Barbara Maltby, a CAN friend, to try to find some story "about behavior and feelings" and was surprised when she quickly gave him the galleys of a novel by Michigan-born Judith Guest, a great-niece of the poet laureate Edgar Guest, called *Ordinary People,* about a dysfunctional family's attempts to survive. "It hit me very profoundly. The point of contact for me with a script or story was always, Do I know these people? I did know the characters in *Ordinary People.* They were people I'd met at the university, wealthy North Shore Chicagoans who dealt in a specific way with issues of solution finding and communication. The book was about just that: communication. A family is in distress with the death of one son, and the mother can no longer relate to her remaining son or her husband. How do they communicate their inner feelings? How do they go forward?" Redford called the writer Alvin Sargent, and Wildwood commissioned a script. "But I had no idea where to start mounting such a production. Who would trust me to direct? I knew one thing: I wouldn't make money from it. It was a labor of love."

But money he needed, and a remarkable opportunity fell into his lap. The British actor-director Richard Attenborough had been trying for years to mount a film on Gandhi. When the project stumbled for the umpteenth time, a producer friend, Joe Levine, offered him an alternative. Levine was a onetime garment maker who started his Hollywood career distributing Italian musclemen movies before producing significant successes like *The Graduate* and *The Lion in Winter.* While neither as prolific nor as discerning as Sam Spiegel, Levine had sound instincts and was happy to package Fellini's *8½* for American distribution alongside Steve Reeves's *Hercules,* despite the fact that he personally considered Fellini "as phony as a glass eye." Whether the barons of established Hollywood yet took him seriously, Levine was undeniably a force in maverick moviemaking and was known for his clever marketplace footwork. He had earned more than $30 million from *The Graduate* and pushed much of it back into his company, Avco Embassy. When it stalled, he set about establishing a new venture, the Joseph E. Levine Presents company, whose flagship, he decided, would be a prestige classic.

During a conversation in a bar in Los Angeles, seventy-year-old Levine explained to Attenborough his passion for *A Bridge Too Far,* Cornelius Ryan's posthumously published book detailing the Allies' attempt to foreshorten the war in Europe in September 1944. Attenborough saw immediately that the project was as complex as any potential *Gandhi,* and that though Levine constantly invoked another Ryan opus, *The Longest Day,* which had been a triumph for Fox in 1962, the dramatic dynamics of the stories had little in common. *The Longest Day* concerned the success of D-Day. *A Bridge Too Far* was the account of Operation Market Garden, a story of failure. During the fated mission, nine thousand airborne troops had slipped behind enemy lines with the objective of taking the bridge across the Rhine at Arnhem; only six hundred survived to dig in and fight two elite panzer divisions with small arms. Unquestionably the event was laden with tales of individual heroism, but the campaign was defined by its gross mismanagement.

"You can fool all of the people all of the time," Joe Levine famously said, "if the advice is right and the budget is big enough." And he was ready to throw countless millions into *A Bridge Too Far.* Attenborough was impressed by Levine's stated desire to make a tribute to fallen heroes. "We've had three decades of lousy noisefests like *Midway,*" Levine told a journalist in 1977. "All those movies were self-congratulating. Operation Market Garden couldn't be like that. It had to be honest and compassionate because it was about the self-sacrifice of forgotten men." Attenborough was persuaded by the sentiment, the star-studded vision Levine had—and the $20 million budget, part pledged by United Artists, a company then cruising on its James Bond profits. UA was in for distribution, though only on condition that Levine could supply more than a dozen high-profile stars in the style of *The Longest Day.* Levine instructed Attenborough to go out and find the biggest names around. It was then agreed that Bill Goldman would be the screenwriter.

In a matter of weeks, and without a script yet, Attenborough had secured the services of Michael Caine, Sean Connery, Dirk Bogarde, Laurence Olivier and a number of other notable British stars, many of whom were friends of his. "Once we had that ring of quality," said Levine, "we went for Hollywood."

The offer to Redford came during the height of the excitement about *All the President's Men.* Attenborough was in Holland assembling a demi-army and wanted a name to fill the lead role of Major Julian Cook. Steve McQueen had been offered the part and was procrastinating. At first Redford demurred. He had made his commitment to lobbying, family and Sundance. Hendler, though, saw a golden moment. McQueen was driving the fee higher and higher, Levine was running out of time . . . and suddenly Redford, if he accepted the role, would be able to cover the extra costs incurred in developing his property. Hendler closed the deal, securing a record-breaking $2 million, with very lucrative penalty money for Redford if the movie overran.

Whereas at first the role seemed to Redford "like a name in a telephone directory," there was a sentimental dimension for him. Operation Market Garden was a prelude to the Third Army thrust during which his uncle David was killed. "In that way *A Bridge Too Far* was a kind of homage to Uncle David. I'd never been to the battlefield area where he died. The movie gave me a chance to visit his grave in Luxembourg and acknowledge him in a personal way."

Levine sweated like a workhorse, he said, to make his movie work. "Darryl Zanuck had the best advantage with *The Longest Day* because the heroes die in his movie. That makes for a dramatic audience experience. We were faced with the opposite. None of the leading guys died, and then the mission failed. Add to that all the different skirmishes, the airborne assault with gliders, the ground attacks, the planes, the boats, the tanks, the parachutes, and it was *War and Peace*. Dickie [Attenborough] worked harder than any director I have ever known just getting the military hardware right. He was having daily breakdowns trying to negotiate with the Dutch and the Brits and the Germans to borrow guns, tanks, trucks, and everything else we couldn't afford to build. I regarded that movie as a nightmare. Gratifying, but a nightmare."

Goldman overcame the inherent dramatic weakness by redefining the scenario simply as "a story about the cavalry that arrives too late." The roles of the lesser ranks who fought and died were beefed up. Redford liked the approach: "The risk with the story was always diffusion. It was a three-hour movie documenting parallel stories about the parachute assaults from the 1st British, the 82nd American and the 101st American Airborne Infantry paving the way for the main British thrust. That's a lot of moving targets, a lot of talking heads, a lot for the audience to comprehend and remember." Employing immediately recognizable faces—Ryan O'Neal, James Caan and Anthony Hopkins, among others—solved the problem. "I normally dislike movies that rely on star casting, but this time it seemed valid for plot clarity." There was also much to admire, he felt, in the sharp-focus roles written for Caan, playing a lowly sergeant who fights for his principles, and Anthony Hopkins, as Lieutenant Colonel John Frost, the tenacious frontline British commander. Redford came to love his own irascible character, Cook, who unwittingly led his men into a massacre while crossing the Waal River to back up the Arnhem bridge defenders. Among the most moving moments in a movie every bit as full of action and as noisy as *Midway* was Cook's conducting his men in the communal recitation of the Hail Mary as they dove into battle. "Bill gave me some good words to work with," says Redford. "That role could easily have been a cipher, but the choices that Attenborough and Goldman made gave it a great dignity."

Though *A Bridge Too Far* took six months to shoot, Redford was in Holland just four weeks. Throughout the shoot at Deventer, thirty miles north of Arnhem, he was hounded by the media as never before. When Costa-Gavras, the Greek director of *Z,* invited him to dine in Paris, he fled willingly. "I was trying to escape the craziness," says Redford, "because Europe was saturated with *All the President's Men,* and by association I was being connected with the downfall of Richard Nixon. I'd rarely had to use personal security guards, but the violations were freaky. One German newspaper sent a naked woman to my hotel room with a birthday cake, presumably to get a scandal story. The paparazzi were all over Deventer like flies. One New York guy even flew to Amsterdam, spending a fortune in time and dollars just to get one candid shot. I naïvely thought, If I get away from the production location, I'll be fine. Paris will be a break from all that madness."

Sanctuary turned into a circus. "It was worse," Redford recalls. "The crowds outside the restaurant were insane. Gavras's wife was knocked to the sidewalk and I tried to lift her up, but Alan Burry, a publicist present, shouted, 'Don't do it!' The paparazzi would just die to get that shot: Redford helping some broad to her feet. In the end we escaped through the kitchen and I had to run ten blocks back to the hotel." The next day, Burry summoned Century Security, an internationally recognized bodyguard agency. "The guy who ran it knew his stuff," says Redford, "and he chilled me to the bone. This wasn't just fan delirium, he said. Century did some digging to find there was a kidnap plot against me. You could have knocked me over with a feather. A plot *against me*? Why? Who could I have offended so badly? In fact, I had offended the right-wing contingent, the Nixonites. *All the President's Men* left a stink, and they had me on the hit list. When I was in Paris all those years before, it was predominantly left-wing. Now it was the other way, and the press had me as the Man Who Took Down Nixon. The security guy literally threw me in the back of a car and took off for the border like he was competing at Le Mans. I thought it was melodrama and, to be honest, I believed none of it. I was wrong. We later learned, from an independent investigation, that it was justified, that those people were real, and their order to get me was real. I read the reports, I saw the evidence and it horrified me."

A Bridge Too Far was released with great fanfare in June 1977. Redford had seen the rushes of the movie, thought it was fine, thought Hopkins was good, "but overall it was not as good as *The Longest Day.*"

Back tending to his horses in Utah, he surprised himself with the realization that he'd seen just four movies in a year. Only Buñuel's *Cet Obscur Objet du Désir* left a good impression. Woody Allen's *Annie Hall* was too parochial for his taste; others were just unmemorable. "I was also not touched by the big new movements in technological and disco films. They seemed hidebound, with nowhere to go in terms of substance."

With Pollack, he resumed work on the script for Robert Penn Warren's *A Place to Come To;* at Wildwood he continued to collaborate on Alvin Sargent's retooling of Judith Guest's novel. Pollack believed his friend was suffering burnout. "I knew him well enough to know when the fire was gone. He was a guy with such remarkable discipline. He was up and out jogging at 7:00 a.m. He was playing tennis in subzero temperatures. He was relentless. But when he was tired, he was ornery and not disciplined, and that's how he had become. We fought a lot over *A Place to Come To,* and that summed up the problem. He was juggling too many sidelines. He needed to stop."

Redford continued to blend art with activism. He collaborated with Saul Bass and Charles Eames on a Dalíesque animated short promoting alternative energy, called *The Solar Film.* Solar energy had become another battle cry of his. Over the weekend of May 3–6, 1978, to help increase awareness of it, CAN mounted Sun Day, launched with a tribal sunrise ceremony on the steps of the U.N. in New York. Barry Commoner, Margaret Mead, Bishop Paul Moore and Andrew Young were among the event leaders, lecturing and giving media interviews. "Earth Day identified the environmental problems," said Lola. "Sun Day identifies the solutions." Central among the solutions Redford expounded upon in an interview he gave to his friend Tom Brokaw on NBC's *Today* was a national commitment to exploring solar energy for industrial and domestic use along the lines of the Christensen experiment he had committed to at Sundance. This interview incited Mobil Oil to place a large advertisement in *The New*

York Times sniping at the principles of Sun Day and defending the practicality of fossil fuels. Herb Schmertz, vice president of Mobil, went so far as to rebuke Redford personally in a letter to the editor. Redford found this "a real victory for the cause, because the fact that they took note meant they were scared. It was the Ralph Nader principle at work again: think globally, act locally, and you shake up the big boys."

Depending on whom you asked, Redford's competition with Lola was either a spur or an omen. President Carter appointed her as EPA representative for the International Year of the Child, and she was now also on the boards of the National Audubon Society, the U.S. Committee for UNICEF, and the Chicago-based National Sudden Infant Death Syndrome Society. "I don't believe their competitiveness was a negative thing," says Stan Collins, "but it was real enough. Its basis wasn't vanity. It was results. They had their own goals within environmental politics, and they stuck the course." Jamie wasn't so certain. He knew his parents had started marriage counseling, and he feared the end of the marriage was near: "They also had a widening separation of interests. Mom was the great academic politician. Dad wasn't like that. He saw grand themes. Mom would target the fine detail of phosphate damage to crops and carcinogens in the food chain. Dad went for the wide sweep. He was arguing for heritage, tradition and cultural integrity. I admired him for his devotion to anthropology, but I admired him from afar. I was too ill to be of any help."

After years of being attended to by stomach specialists at the Utah Medical Center in Provo, during his senior year at Dalton, Jamie achieved a proactive breakthrough. Watching a PBS television special late one night, he learned about new endoscopy procedures in the GI tract. "Truthfully, I felt that no one had paid enough attention to getting me a proper diagnosis. The feeling always was, 'Hey, Jamie is freaking out again!' I don't blame Dad or Mom. But you can only push the problem on the back burner for so long. After the PBS special, I made the appointment independently and walked into the gastroenterologist's office in New York and handed over my files. The reaction was, 'Oh boy, you have a serious ulcerative colitis condition and you need radical treatment very urgently.' " Redford spotted Jamie's declining health—and the terminal crisis of his marriage—from the corner of his eye. "I was distracted," he admits, "and in error."

A Place to Come To had him fully engaged, more excited than he'd been about any story since the Woodward-Bernstein adventure. *Close Encounters of the Third Kind* may have been booming at the box office, but that wasn't his kind of film. Robert Penn Warren's epic is about Jed Tewksbury, a southerner whose beginnings remind one of Tot's history and whose resolution tackles the human need for meaning. Tormented by his choice of women, Jed feeds his wandering urge, distinguishes himself as a jock and scholar, fights against the Nazis and becomes a figure of world renown. In the end he addresses the emptiness he still feels in a pilgrimage to his mother's neglected grave: "I thought . . . maybe I might be able to weep. And if I could weep, something warm and blessed might happen. But I did not lie down. The trouble was, I was afraid that nothing might happen, and I was afraid to take the risk."

The poetry of Warren's writing, the metaphor, the subtext were what appealed to Redford. In years to come, the books he would choose for his own directorial adaptations would often be distinguished by metaphor and symbolism. "Yes, it was a story you had to reach for," he says. "But it was a terrific Everyman tale. I also thought Penn Warren was neglected, and that his stories were powerfully visual in a way no one explored. I had the highest hopes."

But in the summer of 1978 Pollack announced that the deal he'd been trying to set up with Warners was dead, and that the project was undoable. Redford agreed that the script they had in progress with David Rayfiel was inadequate, but he was "pissed" that Pollack pushed it aside in favor of a new project for Columbia. "I thought we didn't need to quit, and I told Sydney so. We argued some. In the end, the friendship was more important than the film."

In his notebook he records his feelings:

> Wildwood stationery lies fallow in the briefcase unused. Unnecessary. Accouterments of waste. The swarm of beehive activity is but the noise of anticipation. Nothing more. All is calm. No wind blows and no birds sing. Sitting here heavy headed beneath the enveloping shroud of depression and clarity. The clear eye I've waited for. The eye that sees what really is, and there is nothing. *Alice in Wonderland* is my book. Hollywood has paid me back in full for my disloyalty. Fear and trembling pass as business as usual. Lying, cheating, treading water, waste, anxiety, resentment, distortion, shallowness are the trade qualities and if you are so possessed—then—you are all right.

He was not all right, and he knew it. In a state of suppressed rage he agreed with Pollack to take on *The Electric Horseman* for Columbia. Anything but epic, yet mordantly resonant, it was a movie about a champion rodeo rider and a champion horse abused by commercialism and about to make a valiant escape to more honorable values. It had, for Redford, a poignant biographical ring.

17

Painted Frames

America had vastly altered over the last ten years, beginning with the deaths of Bobby Kennedy and Martin Luther King Jr., then with the debacles of Vietnam and Watergate. The dissidents who smoked pot in the Summer of Love became the graduate environmentalists and politicians who, too briefly, breathed hope into the seventies. But while politicians like Jerry Brown, Gary Hart and Jimmy Carter promised much and accomplished little, some significant spiritual ground shift was undeniable.

Redford's relationship with Pollack had also changed. Over the decade Pollack's career had been consistent. He had made half a dozen movies and enjoyed a stable married life with Claire Griswold and their three children. Redford's career was stellar. This was the decade that gave him superstardom beyond his wildest imaginings, where his name and image were so ubiquitous that even dictionaries listed him under words like "glamour" and "idol." He had acclaim, wealth and opportunity, but he also had a failed marriage. Now, when the men got together, they inclined toward argument. Three of Pollack's six movies that decade were Redford movies. In the same period Redford had made a dozen movies, of which *The Sting* and *All the President's Men,* movies unrelated to Pollack, garnered the most attention. When *All the President's Men* proved so successful, Redford felt Pollack was jealous. Pollack expressed "surprise" that the movie worked at all and told Redford wryly, "I should have done it." Pollack, for his part, found his friend less accommodating and kind.

John Saxon, who joined the cast of *The Electric Horseman,* saw Redford, fifteen years after they worked together on *War Hunt,* as a man divided. That his fame was "monolithic" Saxon found ironic: "Not least because I was once a studio contract star. I played by the rule book, the studio way, and saw my career terminated by studio decree. Bob did it the other way, by bucking the system. He was an emblem of the new style, where artists took control of their destinies. This was what the seventies were about, from Scorsese to Lucas, from Redford to Stallone." Redford was a decent man, Saxon says, a man who had secured his casting in the film without making any big deal of it: "But he wasn't an easy guy to say thank you to. There was a chasm, a distance he'd put between himself and the rest of the world. I thought, This is the price you pay for that kind of fame."

"I was aware of it," says Redford. "I knew I was facing a sea change. I knew what was coming and it probably made me a tough person to be around."

The Electric Horseman was very much a stopgap that facilitated continuity in the relationship between Pollack and Redford, which might otherwise have fractured irreparably. Its preproduction, according to Pollack's files, was a mess, commenced upon with no script, no coherent casting plan, no sensible scheduling. All they had, in fact, was an agreement to make a movie for Ray Stark's company, Rastar, to be distributed by Columbia. Part of the trouble, said Pollack, was that he had panicked when *A Place to Come To* failed to gel and had rummaged around Stark's optioned projects until he found this oddball outline from the mid-sixties that was sure to interest Redford. Redford had been speculating about making a rodeo movie for years; Pollack thought Shelly Burton's treatment was a perfect fit. Later Steve Bernhardt, Redford's old friend from the Emerson Junior High days, would contend it was he who, years before, sent *The Electric Horseman* to Redford. Redford believes Bernhardt may be right: "The seventies were awash with script submissions."

In the story, Sonny Steele, an ex–rodeo rider, is employed by a multinational corporation called Ampco to promote Ranch cereal, riding a doped show horse around at entertainment spots. Anesthetized with alcohol, Sonny goes AWOL. The original story went only as far as Sonny's flight from the venality of Las Vegas to the great outdoors and leaned heavily on symbolism. It then fell on Pollack to create and shape a full-length movie. "I saw we had problems even when I commissioned the first script," said Pollack. "The story ended after the first act. I scrambled around for more. I like that part, wringing out a film story. The redemption, I decided, must be in a romantic relationship. Sonny needed to be saved by love. And so we invented the character of Hallie Martin, a television journalist who has a good feeling about Sonny's integrity and follows him into oblivion to get his side of the story."

Pollack commissioned Bob Garland, a writer he knew from television, to develop the screenplay, but, Redford says, the resulting work was "spaghetti junction. It was just so many unresolved incidents sitting there. I thought it was ironic that Sydney abandoned the Robert Penn Warren because it was so tricky, and then we ended up with this mishmash."

They soldiered on. Redford requested that Jane Fonda take the co-lead when Pollack's first choice, Diane Keaton, was allegedly blocked from participating by her possessive boyfriend, Warren Beatty. "Quite simply, Warren wouldn't have Diane kissing Bob Redford, the most desirable star in the world," said Pollack. "He wasn't dumb. He wouldn't want the competition."

The previous year Fonda had lambasted Redford in an article in *The Village Voice.* "I've known two Robert Redfords," she'd said. "When we made *Barefoot in the Park* he was a young man full of interests, sensitive to the problems of the time, politically and socially involved. But now he's perfectly integrated, and an instrument of the star system. He is, and remains, a bourgeois in the worst sense of the word." Redford stayed silent. He was sensitive to the tumultuous changes she had been through. In 1966, when he'd last worked with her, Fonda was approaching what she calls "the psychological metamorphosis" that steered her toward the leftist campaigning that branded her Hanoi Jane. Her marriage to Roger Vadim ended and she turned to leftist activist Tom Hayden, head of Students for a Democratic Society and author of the "Port Huron Statement" (the group's manifesto calling for participatory democracy), who would become her husband and crusade partner through the seventies. Today, analyzing her espousal of extremist activism, she expresses regret for excesses. "Everyone now understands it: it was a transitional time for most thinking Americans, and for me personally it was a painful and exploratory time."

When they reconnected, Redford was pleased to find he still had much in common with Fonda. She had worked with Alan Pakula in *Klute,* for which she won an Academy Award, and was about to receive her second, for *Coming Home.* Hayden, who had been indicted with the Chicago Seven for disrupting the 1968 Democratic National Convention, had been appointed to the Solar Utilization Scheme of the Southwest Border Commission by California governor Jerry Brown. Hayden and Fonda's broad-issue group, the Campaign for Economic Democracy (CED), was also currently lobbying for rent control, government-sponsored child care, new police review boards and the public takeover of utilities. Fonda was pumping in $500,000 a year to CED. "You couldn't help but admire her," says Redford. "Jane liked to get her nose into things. That's how she ended up sitting on tanks and buddying up with the Vietcong. She was not a talker, she was a doer. If she was a dissident, she was the kind the country needed, because she made people think and she put her money where her mouth was."

Through the summer, Bob Garland, David Rayfiel and Alvin Sargent worked around the clock on the script, which Fonda had yet to see a page of. At one point, Rayfiel sent an ominous Churchillian note to Pollack: "Never has so much been written by so many for so little." Fonda, though, was not amused: "There were moments when I began to fret. It wasn't a normal scenario. It seemed to be a movie based on a lot of talk and no paperwork, which was something I'd never before encountered." On August 1, twelve weeks before filming, Redford wrote on his copy of the latest cobbled-together script: "The present version is too encumbered. Too much hardware, too much plot, too much 'necessity' to justify the size of it all. Too urban, as opposed to simple rural." Pollack and Redford continued to work very closely and amassed piles of videos to watch. "It was the start of the home video era," Pollack said, "and so we had easy access to the old Cary Grant movies, the Billy Wilders Bob loved and the Frank Capras I loved. Out of them we took the spirit of joy and brightness and put it into *The Electric Horseman.* All the time we knew we were dealing with a story about the cynicism of showbiz, about the exploitation of humans and animals that fall into the trap, about dark things. But we played with it until we found the upbeat story. We also had a wonderful bonus. The story became stronger with the history of these actors, of Jane and Bob. The hard-driving characters meet, clash and fall in love. What could be better? I'd developed a reputation, or so Jane told me, as the master of foreplay. She said, 'You're always leading the characters right up to the bedroom door, and that makes for a very sexy picture.' So that's what I built on: foreplay. Let the audience impose their fantasies on these characters. Let them play with the notion: Is Bob screwing Jane? Will it go that far?"

Though the script Fonda was given still only amounted to a scattering of action pages, some notes Pollack made to himself five days before production titled "Night Thoughts" finally defined characters intertwined by childlike romantic idealism. Pollack singled out one speech for Hallie: "When I was a kid, the prince was all in white. Nothing he did was ever wrong. He had justice and morality and ethics all on his side. It was loaded, really loaded. I guess like most fantasies." On the same page he summarized Redford's Sonny in a speech: "There are people in Africa or some damn place who believe that if someone takes their picture, they won't live as long. That you take something away from them. Well, maybe you just have so much to give out—like a light bulb—and if other people are taking it all the time, then there isn't much left for you."

"Once I had those speeches, I had the film," said Pollack. "From that point on we knew who these characters were, how they were attracted to each other and what they truly represented."

Redford condensed Pollack's theorizing into a simple trick: a walk. "There was too much development," he says. "In the end you could look at Sonny sixty ways. I wanted to see him as the guy who says, 'No more.' He has given it all to the point where he's *literally* bent out of shape. His back no longer works. He walks with a rick, like every step hurts. His story is in the walk." And the romance? "It made sense; it was organic in the story. And with Jane it was easy."

The Electric Horseman started location filming in November at Caesars Palace, the only casino in Vegas willing to trade gambling losses for Hollywood publicity (since gaming tables would be closed for long hours daily during production). Redford was glad to be moving at last, but impatient with the kind of intrusive photographers and crowds that had dogged him in Holland. According to Fonda, who had her own contingent of noisy fans, Redford was "prodded, tugged, felt, kissed and treated like one of those animal curiosities from Siegfried and Roy." In his off hours, Redford dined and drank in the privacy of his suite with Pollack and Fonda, or the country singer Willie Nelson, who was cast in his first dramatic role playing Sonny's manager, Wendell. Mostly, though, evenings were dedicated to work with Pollack on the script. "The thing that kept me concentrated," says Redford, "was the fear that the movie wouldn't hold together at all."

As Fonda spent her free time giving fitness lessons, based on routines she'd learned in Gilda Marx's Body Design gym, to crew members in her suite—a prelude to the Jane Fonda Workout industry to come—Redford enjoyed the horsemanship. Movie wrangler Kenny Lee had located for the movie a calm, disciplined five-year-old bay Thoroughbred, Let's Merge, at a dressage school in the San Fernando Valley. Redford and the horse hit it off. "Managing the horse kept me healthy," says Redford. "Sometimes I talk better with horses than with people." To Pollack's surprise, in one particularly tricky scene, Redford refused the stunt double and insisted on riding Let's Merge down the traffic of the Strip at rush hour. "Secretly I think it was his biggest buzz," says Pollack. "Very symbolic on a personal level, and a little malevolent, since it screwed up traffic and the business of the town for half a day."

Fonda became Redford's anchor, a presence to keep him focused when, he admits, "there were mornings I didn't want to get out of bed. I was not a pleasant person to be around for that movie. Sydney said I behaved like an uncooperative bastard, and he was right. I didn't want press around, for instance. [The critic] Gene Siskel sneaked on the set, and I told Sydney, 'I will not act while he's here, period.' I was in a dark place. I later apologized to him. But we forged through it together, as I always performed for him as an actor."

With weather holdups during the southern Utah portion of the shoot in January and February, the $11.2 million budget overran by $1.3 million. Never missing a marketing moment, Ray Stark circulated the story that $300,000 had been spent filming forty-three takes of the key moment, when Sonny and Hallie kiss. "I justified it as our reward," said Pollack. "We'd been through a mountain of scripts and finally we got the magic." For Pollack, a lover of heyday Tracy-Hepburn, utter redemption was in the kiss. "Bob and Jane should be proud. That's the moment they joined the big leagues, in my book."

It seemed extraordinary after the million and one script deviations that *The Electric Horseman* would calmly find its place as a simple old-fashioned romantic comedy. But that's how it fared. At various stages all of the participants had prophesied doom for it, but it sidled out into the marketplace between *Moonraker* and *Apocalypse Now* in the winter of 1979 and took in a very respectable $60 million. To almost all reviewers it was an anachronism, but no less welcome for that. Roger Ebert in the *Chicago Sun-Times* summed up Pollack's triumph of instinct when he likened it to Capra's *It Happened One Night* and the other Golden Era romances. The relationship between Fonda and Redford, it turned out, was exactly like Hepburn and Bogart's in *The African Queen,* another movie about a mismatched pair sharing the rigors of life on the run. "Both Redford and Fonda have associated themselves with a lot of issues in this movie," wrote Ebert, listing the evils of corporate conglomeration, the preservation of wildlands, respect for animals, the phoniness of commercialism, and the pack instincts of TV journalists, among others. "But although this movie is filled with messages, it's not a message movie. The characters and plot seem to tap-dance past the serious stuff and concentrate on human relationships."

For Ebert, as for many critics, Pollack's strength was in "orchestrating" the Redford-Fonda chemistry. Like the directors of Bogart, Hepburn, Gable, Colbert and others, said Ebert, Pollack understood "that if you have the right boy and the right girl, all you have to do is stay out of the way of the horse."

The success of the movie, however, did little to mend the rift between actor and director. Many observed "the formula" at work—where Pollack relied heavily on the romantic cipher—and, given Redford's radical mindset, predicted a further breach.

"Dad wanted to direct movies to express his own way of telling a story, without any compromise," says Jamie. "He really wanted to get away from Sydney for a while." Still, while angling for his own directorial debut, he was amenable to acting in another film for another director.

Three years before, as he immersed himself in Native American issues for *The Outlaw Trail,* Redford had been prompted by author-activist Peter Matthiessen to follow the case of Leonard Peltier, a thirty-two-year-old Sioux on the Pine Ridge Reservation in South Dakota. The charges against Peltier arose from the deaths of two FBI agents and one Native American shot during an incident of public disorder in Oglala. Peltier claimed his innocence, and the evidence against him, as Matthiessen demonstrated, was tenuous. But in April 1977, Peltier was found guilty and sentenced to two consecutive life terms. Fonda and Brando were among Peltier's supporters, but Redford virtually adopted the case as his own. He met Peltier in prison, campaigned for his pardon, even took the matter to the White House, where successive presidents considered, but rejected, a pardon. "You start to look twice at the institutions you take for granted," says Redford. "It's a healthy state of mind to reach. It's not enough to drive a car, you ought to know something of what makes the car go." The possibility of a gross miscarriage of justice in Peltier's case started a train of inquiry that was echoed in a script from producer Ron Silverman that landed in Redford's hands during *The Electric Horseman.*

Brubaker, based on the writings of Arkansas prison reformer Thomas O. Murton, portrayed a corrupt justice system. Murton's story was every bit as sinister as Peltier's. Appointed by Governor Winthrop Rockefeller to revamp Arkansas's jails in the 1960s, Murton posed as a prisoner at Tucker Prison Farm and unearthed scandalous abuses and the covered-up murders of three inmates. As the bodies were disinterred, Murton demanded full disclosure in the national media. Instead, he was vilified and fired. His subsequent memoir, *Accomplices to the Crime,* attracted sympathetic attention, but it was ten years before Silverman acquired rights to the book and sealed a deal with Twentieth Century–Fox, with Bob Rafelson, Jack Nicholson's friend and business partner, directing.

In hindsight, the odds seemed against *Brubaker* succeeding. All the principals—producers, screenwriters and director—had variable, television-oriented careers. Silverman's background was in series like *Stoney Burke* and *The Wild Wild West.* Screenwriters W. D. Richter and Arthur Ross were also television writers, though Richter had done well with John Badham's recent adaptation of *Dracula.* Rafelson was, perhaps, the most controversial component. He had cocreated *The Monkees,* and he developed the Monkees' movie *Head,* which he directed. Rafelson admitted to having made *Head* heavily under the influence of LSD and in homage to the French New Wave, which was the film form he most admired. "I liked that complete disrespect for the film itself," he said, "the idea of handling it roughly and not aiming for perfect lighting." Though *Head* failed, Rafelson's follow-up with Nicholson, *Five Easy Pieces,* won four Academy Award nominations. But he was still widely regarded as a wild card.

Two more different artists, two more different Hollywood outsiders, than Redford and Rafelson would be hard to conjure. Redford is polite about their disagreements. In his version, Rafelson was working on a deep and probing script. At the same time, Redford was refining his own deep and probing interpretation. When, just five days after the completion of *The Electric Horseman,* Redford arrived on location in Columbus, Ohio, however, there were immediate problems. Rafelson had not, for starters, fully decided on casting. Key roles were still unfilled with only days to go until the start of shooting. The set itself, built inside an old state prison, was overmodified and all but unusable. Murton expressed the belief that the screenplay showed evidence of "creative folk [who have been] smoking pot." Redford felt that Rafelson was absorbed in "hip effect" and his own volatile ego, which was upsetting to the studio. "He was behaving like a martinet, which was not comfortable for anyone."

Redford stepped away from confrontation with Rafelson by preparing for the Brubaker character in his own way. He found himself internalizing more than usual. "It was an interesting place. My marriage was gone, despite my and Lola's attempts to save it. When things are failing, you examine them. So I was dissecting human behavior and thinking about social disorder and making connections. This was a fascinating place to work from in terms of relating to Murton's experience. I liked it that Brubaker was written as a gray character. I always liked that twilight area in projecting heroism, and there was some personal truth that felt hard earned on this one."

In widely reported accounts, Rafelson decked a senior Fox executive who was summoned to Columbus one week after shooting commenced to determine why the movie was already several days behind schedule. Other reports suggest Redford sought Rafelson's removal and asked Paul Newman to recommend a replacement. What is clear is that Newman suggested Stuart Rosenberg, the mild-mannered director of *Cool Hand Luke,* who had also directed Redford for television in *The Defenders.* Newman believed "Stuart was a far better bet for *Brubaker,* because his field of excellence was psychology. He was good at close-quarters stuff like prison dramas, that much we all knew." Redford welcomed Rosenberg and remembers him as a kindly man: "And he had the kind of sound temperament that I thought could salvage this from the brink, since the actors were starting to mutiny."

Rosenberg flew to Columbus on a borrowed Warners jet, shut down the production for ten days and barricaded himself in a nearby Holiday Inn with the script and a stack of notebooks. "I was absolutely appalled," he said. "There was an out-of-control atmosphere. I looked at what Rafelson shot and I couldn't, and wouldn't, use it. Everything he did was against my style, and some of it seemed plain dumb. For instance, he sliced the roof off the location—which was a *real prison*—to facilitate studio arc lighting. I thought, What a complete, stupid waste of money! To find *the real thing,* then try to turn it into a Hollywood studio! That alone multiplied my problems because it restricted me from shooting any wide shots. I also hated much of the script, which was open-ended. Bob says the character was gray. He wasn't—he was battleship gray. Dull. I wanted a poignant ending to the story, and Redford also wanted some reward for the audience who had to sit through a grim morality tale. First I thought of getting out of there. [There were] just too many problems. All this would take so much time to fix, but Fox gave me ten days." Rosenberg's biggest headache was what he called "despair" among the cast. "I had to take each of them aside in my hotel suite and sit them down to shore up their confidence. Then I was landed with the problem of Bob's contract, which had the notorious 'star clause.' The schedule had to be twelve weeks. If I went a day past that, the penalties were so huge as to make the movie commercially impossible. I thought about it. Then I decided I liked what this movie was trying to say. So we started . . . running like sprinters."

Rosenberg had known about the Murton book for ten years. "But I always doubted that it would see the light of day as a movie, since it was so critical of our prison system. After *All the President's Men,* Redford engendered trust. People knew he wouldn't shortchange them, that he'd 'do a Bob Woodward' and get to the bottom of things. So I felt that Bob was entitled to a measure of respect, since it was happening because he put his name behind it. Murton was also in no doubt. But it also put me on my guard, because it's not good for a director to be too respectful of actors. A director must lead."

The man Rosenberg remembered from *The Defenders* was much changed. Redford was, said Rosenberg, "a mess of contradictions, both calm and convulsive"—which was unsurprising, given the disarray of his personal life. "I can't say a word against him as an artist," says Rosenberg. "To me, he was very like Paul in his approach. He did not openly intellectualize as he went along, as Paul often didn't. It was all done in private, beforehand. He carefully prepared every movement, every line, its meaning and the play-out. He invented a lot himself, as all good actors do, which means he takes responsibility for what happens up on the screen, just like Paul did. And the director's contribution? I would say to him, 'Bob, this isn't working because the rhythm seems wrong.' Just that. And he, like Paul, would take it on himself to go back out on the floor and find this elusive rhythm, without any big, heart-wrenching analysis. That, and simply that, is what makes a good actor. I experienced the same with Myrna Loy, Barbara Stanwyck and Charles Boyer. They were all good actors. Over the years, in all the movies I directed, I learned one thing: that stardom is defined by intuition. Stars are not 'directed.' They possess an intuition for the audience response that is beyond the likes of me, or anyone else who calls themselves a director. They have some hotline to a greater intelligence, however you attribute that. I observed that neither Barbara Stanwyck nor Robert Redford really thought things through. Their gift was their intuition."

Miraculously, Rosenberg brought *Brubaker* in just three weeks over time, though the overrun meant the budget was shot. Redford liked what he saw of the rushes, but he was distracted. Even as he wrapped the last days in Ohio, he had Alvin Sargent's finished script for *Ordinary People,* the movie he would at last direct, in his hand. "I offered to help him with it," said Rosenberg, "but he said no thanks. He was in a rush to move on."

On a bright winter's afternoon, Stan and Mary Alice Collins waited at the bottom of the black run of Grizzly Bowl at Sundance, the snowy canyon winds whipping at their faces. Redford and Lola were up top, ready to go. As ever, Bob was first off the mark, slaloming off dramatically. Jerry Hill, the Sundance mountain manager, watched him go. Redford had learned to ski for *Downhill Racer* and never gave up the sport. "He was more showy than expert," says Hill, who has watched thousands of skiers over fifty years. But the appeal for Redford was more than spartan exercise. It was the love for the mountain that had him out all summer carefully cutting back the weed aspens and preparing the runs with Jamie, so that they could ski on a pristine surface at the start of every season.

This morning, Stan Collins was reveling in Redford's relaxation. "I missed the old Bob," says Collins. "In New York in the old days we played tennis in Central Park a couple of times a week and talked away the worries of the world. When he got his own court at Sundance, we played a lot. Then it became sporadic. There were always flights to catch and movie locations."

Stan watched the Redfords reach the end of the ski run. A table had been reserved at the Grill Room for dinner. Soft-shell crabs had been flown in, and he was looking forward to catching up. "But then someone came and said there was an urgent call for Bob. Hendler was calling from L.A., Hollywood business. Bob told Lola and the rest of us to go ahead for dinner, that he'd catch up later." Collins remembers the shadow crossing Lola's eyes. "She just looked at him and said, 'You know, Bob. Do what you have to do. Don't worry about us. We'll do what we need to do.' The meaning," says Collins, "was obvious."

"I admit it," says Redford, "I miscalculated the effects of fame and work. It took a toll, a hell of a toll, on Lola and the family. I thought I could handle it. I thought I had the recipe. But I was wrong. No matter how focused you feel you are, the distractions and deviations are too many. It was kind of a shock, I think, to all the family, to realize we'd moved on."

Redford shared with no one the extent of his domestic breakdown, but it disturbed him and, though he had doggedly avoided therapy, he felt the pressing need for objective analysis. In his view, the marriage had been good for fifteen years, but he and Lola had changed as individuals. Still, they tried to address the changes and rebuild. They'd tried a trial separation, which didn't work, and a recommitment, which didn't work, either. "Bob was born to be alone," believed Michael Ritchie. "Guilt was a real problem for me," Redford says now, reflecting on his priorities during the marriage. "Where did I fail, because I was certain *I did fail.* And why?"

At this emotionally intense time, the wheels started turning on his first film as a director, *Ordinary People.*

As far back as 1975 Redford had told Pollack that he wanted to direct. Pollack considered it "inevitable. He had to do it, because he had a visual sense all of his own." Professionally he seemed in prime position. But despite the money he had helped make for Warners, Columbia and Fox, and the many well-disposed influential friends, no one was especially keen on the idea of him as director of *Ordinary People*, a story considered dour. Finally just one—Bluhdorn's new protégé at Paramount, Barry Diller—welcomed the project. "I wasn't crazy about *Ordinary People,*" said Pollack. "I thought he chose a hard first subject, because it was entirely about emotion, so it was dependent on great directing of actors, of which he had no experience. Something more pictorially sumptuous, I thought, would have been right for his debut."

But Redford entertained no doubts. "I probably started as a director in the fifties," he says. "I was a magpie. I collected bits and pieces of life observations. A line from a book here, a character in conversation there, a piece of music, a childhood remembrance." Sure enough, elements of experience and observation, from the Pachelbel music first encountered in Big Sur to the North Shore Chicagoans he shared rooms with at the University of Colorado, populated his vision of Judith Guest's *Ordinary People* from the moment he read the novel in galley form. "It was a flood of stuff I couldn't stop, like I had been storing it all my life for this moment," he remembers.

Guest's novel is the story of the Jarretts, tax attorney Calvin and his homemaker wife, Beth, and their high school jock son, Conrad, who live in the elegant Chicago suburb of Lake Forest. Everything is tautly ordered but the family is in trauma, attempting to fix itself after the accidental death by drowning of older son Buck, for which Conrad blames himself and over which he has attempted suicide. Against Beth's wishes, Calvin supports Conrad's psychiatric therapy, where he attempts to come to terms with deeply divided feelings about his mother. "She'll never forgive me for getting blood all over the bathroom floor," Conrad tells his shrink.

Alvin Sargent had spent a year on the first draft but, says Redford, had trouble relating to the characters. "To him, the people in Guest's book were boring and transparent. But I found them intriguing. I remembered hitchhiking to a wedding in Lake Forest with a friend back in 1958. We went to a place full of immensely rich people drenched in ennui whose main concern was the status of their tax returns. That was the life in that part of Chicago. These were the Chicagoans whose lives I wanted to look inside." To egg on Sargent, Redford drove him to Lake Forest: "I dragged him to some parties to let him meet these people. I told him, 'Look at these people. Look at how seamless the façade is. Go past it. It's the hidden text that will lift the movie, not specifically the dialogue.' "

The more Redford dove into the script, the more he shut off his own self-analytical urges. "I knew I was headed for therapy, but I decided to postpone it till after the film. I didn't want to corrupt my read of the Jarretts, the analysis that I would put into the mouth of the psychiatrist Berger, by importing new analytical voices. I had a view of this family, of where it fell down through lack of talking, plain and simple, and I wanted to portray that on-screen, I suppose, as a kind of observational comment about the state of marriage in America at the end of the twentieth century."

Gary Hendler was brokering what would be one of his last deals for his client. While Diller himself was flexible, Michael Eisner, Diller's second in command, was insisting that Redford also star in the movie. "They got me over the coals," says Redford, "because they knew how badly I wanted to direct. But I refused point-blank to even consider acting in this film. I knew exactly what I wanted on-screen and I told Gary to hold out."

Hendler did. Eisner, according to his autobiography, was emphatic that if this gift of trust was to be given to Redford, an untried director, he would have to work for guild minimum wage. Hendler wanted a deal commensurate with what Redford was receiving as an actor. "I did not want to accept a high fee," says Redford. "My line was, 'Yes, I'd earned the best fees as an actor because I proved my worth. I had not proved anything as a director.' So I insisted on Gary backing off. I said, 'Whatever the standard first director's fee is, that's what I want.' " Hendler had been asking for $750,000. Now he accepted $30,000. When the movie scored, Diller chose to pay an unsolicited bonus of $750,000. Eisner lamented this payment, judging it "hardly worth it, since Redford never made another movie for us."

The casting of *Ordinary People* was a constant preoccupation throughout *Brubaker*. Redford entered the process with a clear picture in his mind: he wanted Gene Hackman for Calvin Jarrett, Mary Tyler Moore for Beth and Richard Dreyfuss for the psychiatrist. Little of this went as planned. Dreyfuss, when Redford called, confessed he was going through a nervous breakdown and was therefore incapacitated. Eisner, whose nature was to be intrusive, wanted Lee Remick for Beth, and Judd Hirsch, whom Shauna thought of as the ideal replacement for Dreyfuss, was tied up on the television series *Taxi,* with only eight days off in the foreseeable future. Redford dug in his heels, attempting to persuade Hackman and continuing to push for Moore. Slowly a new picture came into view. As a potential replacement to play the psychiatrist, Redford interviewed Donald Sutherland. "But suddenly Donald told me straight: 'I want to play the father.' I was more than surprised, but I was also very touched by his directness. He wasn't iffy. He just laid it out and in that instant convinced me." Sutherland became Calvin, which prompted Redford to go back to Hirsch. "I just felt it was too important not to lose authenticity in the casting, so I called up Judd, avoiding the agents, since they always mess things up, and made a proposal. My idea was if I could reschedule the work in such a way that all the psychiatrist scenes were done together over several days, like a minimovie within a movie, I could finish with Judd in a very short period of time and get him back to *Taxi.* Judd didn't hesitate. He loved the part and he said, 'Yes, I'll do it.' "

The biggest casting problem was Conrad. "We literally went around the country, trying places like the Louisville Rep, trying Los Angeles, San Francisco, the high schools." Finally Redford's publicist, Lois Smith, sent him a hazy videotape copy of a movie called *Friendly Fire* in which Tim Hutton, the nineteen-year-old son of the actor James Hutton, who had died of cancer four months previously, appeared briefly. "From the high school roundup, I'd already cast Elizabeth McGovern to play the kid's girlfriend," says Redford. "In fact, she was the first person I'd cast: she was so fresh and unaffected. Then I called in Tim, who was like his father, whom I knew—gangly, sensitive and inquisitive about human behavior. The minute I got Liz and Tim to read a scene together—pow! That was it. They took it out the window! I knew I'd have to reel them in for the movie, but I knew it was chemistry I could work with."

Hutton was aided, undeniably, by the new emotions of his recent loss. "He opened up a lot, which was helpful for both of us," says Redford. "But it was also dangerous ground, that no-man's-land between the director-actor engagement and personal interrelating. I was wary of transgressing. There was another factor. Many people considered the role of Conrad to be the heart of the piece. That wasn't true. I felt the key was Beth. Berger, the psychiatrist, was the bridge. But Beth was the ailment. To understand what Conrad was going through, we had to experience the distress of this damaged woman. More than anyone, we had to cast Beth right."

Pollack had strongly recommended Jane Fonda for the role. Redford thought different. For several months, whenever he walked on the shore beside his new L.A. base at Trancas Beach, near Malibu, he'd see Mary Tyler Moore, the actress who dominated comedy television through the 1970s with her eponymous ABC show, walking in the opposite direction. Hers was the only light entertainment he watched on TV through the seventies, and he liked her elegance. "She really barely acknowledged me," he says. "But I got to thinking what great, bright-eyed style she had and wondering about her own dark side."

Moore vaguely recalled a fleeting hello, but, she says, she "tended to avoid his eyes. All I ever saw of him were his shoes." Her respect for Redford's privacy was enhanced by her own shyness. "Neither of us, I learned, were social types. I was going through a period of major change. My comedy years were over. My marriage to [television executive] Grant Tinker was on the slide, and I was in a state of forced reevaluation." Over the next three years would come divorce, the accidental shooting death of her depressed son, Richie, the suicide of her younger sister, Ann, and the serious illnesses of both her parents. Redford knew nothing of Moore's problems but instructed his agent to call her agent, John Gaines.

Moore recalls her first meeting with Redford at the Wildwood office newly sited on the Paramount lot as a square dance. "It was all very formal, and I had to pinch myself to remember that this was *the* Robert Redford. Then something I hadn't expected occurred. He said, without apology, that he was concerned that my fame as TV's Mary Richards, whom he enjoyed, would destroy believability for the Beth role." Moore had read Guest's novel the month it appeared and wanted the role because it touched her personal experience. The key relationship in her own life was an unresolved one with a remote and commanding father. "I thought, Well, okay, we're off to a good start, because he has no trouble about being honest."

After the first interview, Moore heard nothing for a month. Then the unlikeliest opportunity came up to replace Tom Conti in the long-running Broadway hit *Whose Life Is It Anyway?* Gaines suggested Moore for the part, and Manny Azenberg, a good friend of Redford's since his Broadway days, endorsed her. Gaines's strategy, says Moore, was brilliant: "There was no doubt that Bob was interested in me. After that first interview he left me in a state of hope. But the reality was that he had Eisner to appease, and why would Paramount buy me? John Gaines said, 'Look, if

Azenberg takes you, there will be this visible belief in you as a serious actor. You will be proving your credentials by taking on the legitimate stage.' For me, of course, it was a lot of pressure. *Ordinary People* would come just before *Whose Life Is It Anyway?* Was I tenacious enough for all that? Could I deliver for *Ordinary People* in the first place? But I had faith in myself. I was deeply inside myself at that time, which was the right place to be. I felt, If Redford can just go that final mile, I can handle it."

Azenberg's judgment impressed Redford. After more reflection, he confirmed Moore's casting as Beth. Moore had little time to "organize the terrors" before flying with her assistant and hairdresser to Chicago, where they moved into a rented property in Lake Forest that would form the hub of production. Bit by bit Redford learned about the chaos in Moore's personal life: that her time in Lake Forest represented her first serious split with Tinker and the terminus of her marriage; that she had recently begun her first affair; and that her mind-set was both euphoric and depressed. "I didn't doubt Mary's strength as a woman and an actress," says Redford. "It was an advantage because I was attempting to project a character that I'd never seen in movies. I'd known many women like Beth in real life, people who cannot connect with their emotions. But only in real life. I felt we had new ground to cross."

Having studied so many directors up close, Redford knew that his point of entry to directing was to stay close to his actors. "I felt confident among actors. I felt I could relate in terms of reassurance and creating the positivity in the environment an actor needs." A week of rehearsals began, in theater fashion, with the actors seated in a circle, with scripts in their laps.

Sutherland, whose headlining career had begun with Altman's *M*A*S*H,* expected the momentary uncertainties of a first-time director but found Redford clearheaded and diametrically unlike Pakula, who had directed him on *Klute:* "Bob totally handed trust to the actor. He'd learned that himself, the need for space for the actor to find the role. I knew what I wanted to do with Jarrett, which is not to say he didn't. He did. But he gave me room."

For Moore, the process was like working with a master engineer. "We walked through it with the utmost detail. There was time to investigate the role, and then to let it fly. He restricted nothing. The only direction he gave me, other than the gentle shaping of the character, was about my mannerisms. There were gestures that hung over from [her television character] Mary Richards: the hand slapping the thigh, the raised hand jabbing in emphasis of a line, the snap-quick turn of the head."

Tim Hutton, who had researched his role by reading books in the Children in Crisis series and by attending group therapy sessions at a mental institution under an assumed name, believed he benefited best from daily walks with Redford in which the topics varied from cinematographic objectives to Hutton's struggle to overcome his father's death. "Bob understood everything," said Hutton. "It's hard to explain how secure you feel working with someone who knows your struggle and who knows how to help." In Moore's view, Hutton's comfort reflected the deeply personal connection Redford felt with the story. "We talked a lot about family. He gradually became open about his relationship with his father and how it impacted on him. He told me straight that he had great difficulty with his father's judgments and attitude to him. There was no acrimony. There was a loving acceptance, but, as in my own case, I got the impression that there was also a desire to resolve that part of his emotional life once and for all. I suspected there was something of his father, in his eyes, in Beth."

In the eyes of Marcella Scott, Redford had "never divested himself of the need to impress Charlie. They seemed bound together by destiny." In 1979, Charlie retired from Standard Oil to settle permanently in a large, timbered house overlooking San Francisco Bay. They wrote and talked often, but Redford admits to ongoing sparring: "I didn't visit him during *The Candidate* [filmed in nearby Marin County] and he resisted visiting Sundance for the longest time. When I finally arranged it for him, he complained about the altitude. I accepted that we were not of the same cut. But forgiveness wasn't the issue. Understanding was. He was a man bent out of shape by being exiled as a teenager, a man with self-worth problems, perhaps. But a good man."

Alan Pakula, the eternal analyst, adamantly believed Redford was engaging in some subtle personal transference with *Ordinary People.* "When I read it, I said, Oh, I get it. The novel is about parental tyranny. The catalyst, the character causing the dysfunction, is the mother. Bob is moving some furniture here. He is co-opting the novel's dysfunctional family for his father's or his own and investigating himself at a critical time." Redford is emphatic that both Pakula and Moore were wrong. "It had nothing to do with my father or his or my family. These were simply types of people I'd met, people whose lives were sequestered in privilege and made you wonder, What goes on beneath that veneer?"

Redford had made a decision back in 1962 as an actor never to get too caught up in the position of key lights or other technical markers during production. Now, as filming started, suddenly those technicalities were of paramount importance to him as a director. John Bailey, the young camera assistant from *Downhill Racer*, had graduated to cinematographer and was standing in front of him asking bewildering questions: "Do you want a Baby Junior on this, or a seventy-five . . . ?" Redford was frustrated. In his head, he already had the movie. It had come together first on paper, then while he drove around the North Shore looking for landscapes. He had instructed Phillip Bennett and Mike Riva, the art directors, about the empty lawns, trimmed topiary and stern houses he wanted. The landscape was in his mind, physically and spiritually. "But I got frustrated talking with John and the technicians, because I couldn't articulate it. Finally, I found myself tearing off strips of paper and drawing stick figures with light angles. Then it became easy, because I could literally 'paint' the movie. We went from there to the point that I created the storyboards, and John worked from them. It became a question of capturing that painted frame."

For all the participants, the unhesitating control Redford exercised over the production was impressive. To Donald Sutherland, such "mean-ass economy in direction" was extraordinary for a first-timer, even a little discomfiting: "He didn't say a lot but he was very specific when he did comment, and I discovered that what he said was almost always correct. Every time he suggested a different way of doing something, suddenly the words and the scene came out right." The trick of empowerment by inviting limitless improvisation, the trick first gifted to him by Mike Nichols, was passed on to all. Mary Tyler Moore found it joyous, but exhausting. "He allowed us to improvise whenever we wanted to. We knew what each scene was. His direction was, 'Try what feels good.' And if I felt something was only so-so and wanted another shot at it, he'd say, 'Try it whatever way.' " Moore averaged, she estimates, three or four takes per scene. "Paradoxically it felt tight, like whittling down a piece of wood to get to the point."

The precision with which Redford "saw" the Jarretts' world, Moore contends, is revealed in the one instance of multiple varied takes, in a solitary scene where Beth puts a cake in the refrigerator. Moore skipped over the scenes in read-throughs, but Redford had other thoughts about it. "It was about behavior," says Redford. "I wanted to capture this woman in an unobserved moment and see her rhythm, how she copes, how she handles things. It was about her fastidious way, her uptightness, her weakness." Moore experienced it as pure hell. "It was the bane of the production, and we tried every few days, every time we had a kitchen scene, to reshoot it. The scene had no dialogue. It was just me, as Beth, holding a cake with a circle of cherries around the top, looking at it, then adjusting the cherries and slipping the cake into the fridge. All I ever heard from Bob was, 'Mary, maybe we can try that cake scene again.' In the end, we shot it about twenty-five times, but still it didn't make it through to the final cut. I felt exhausted, naked, frustrated by that scene. I never understood while it was going on exactly what Bob was looking for. Later, I did. It was manifest in the book and in Alvin's screenplay and in the talks Bob and I had. What he was looking for was what the entire quest of the movie was for him: he was looking to capture the soul of Beth Jarrett in an unguarded moment. I felt he achieved that in the end."

The bleakness of the story was the main challenge for Redford. The title, he decided, wasn't ironic. There was truth in the irreconcilable conflict of trauma survival and disabling guilt. No answers were posited. Berger, the psychiatrist, probes Conrad's depression, but the critical resolution, which, in the visual reenactment, confronts Conrad with the flashback of his brother's drowning, fixes nothing in any practical sense; instead, Conrad is obliged to accept a continuum: that what has occurred is irreversible and will rebound onward, affecting not just his life, but the lives of his parents, especially Beth, who abandons her family at the end of the story. "What I wanted was to deal with people who have concerns they cannot handle because they cannot define them," says Redford. "I was trying to say this is what happened, this is how it is, accept it. To achieve that, we tuned in to the finest twitches of the performances. A face that reacts in a scene saying, 'I know what this is about' is miles away from the look that says, 'I cannot comprehend this.' The actor's gesture is minimal, but everything is in the tiniest inflection. That's what we sought."

Of enormous importance, says Redford, was the decision to base the production on Chicago's North Shore, away from Hollywood. It allowed for intimacy and independence, two critical elements of his debut. Several people, including Diller and Pollack, had suggested they visit the location to consult, but he had said no. Three months later, convening with editor Jeff Kanew at Paramount to view the first assembly, Redford felt immensely satisfied with his decision. Stuart Rosenberg, an early viewer of the finished product, quite liked the movie. Sydney Pollack, for whom Redford organized a private screening, liked it, too, but disliked the depiction of Beth. To Redford he said plainly, "The woman doesn't work"—which, says Redford, might as well have been, "The movie doesn't work." Pollack believed Moore was "clumpy and obvious" and unable to rise above her Mary Richards image. Says Redford, "He felt I'd made a grievous error of judgment casting her. I was hurt, but I had belief. I knew I had a good cut; it worked beautifully with the Pachelbel. I finished the movie and then I headed for the hills."

In January 1979, during the edit, Betty Webb, his grade school sweetheart, now a New Age counselor, visited with Bill Coomber's wife, Lucrecia, and found "a vastly changed man." Her memory was of the bright-eyed competitor, suave and determined to best any competition. He was now soft-spoken, even "subdued." Redford, in fact, judged it otherwise. "There'd been a long buildup of emotional issues. By the time I had locked down *Ordinary People,* which carried its own high toll, I was dumb with tiredness."

"After *Ordinary People,* his Hollywood world became more accessible to us kids," says Shauna, who, at that point, was studying art at the University of Colorado at Boulder. "Previously he had kept us away from it. Now the boundary came down. It was as if, with the movie, he'd at last expressed his true art and that Hollywood was finally a positive thing." But Amy, just ten, still found an obstacle in the relentlessness of her father's fame: "It just got bigger and more demanding. I was arts oriented, too, and I wanted to work close to him. But with the time pressures on him, it was hard to get enough personal time." Within a few years, teenage Amy would break ranks, shave half her head, stud her ears with rings and flee to England to study acting "and objectify things for myself, to get a grip on real life and real people." Stan Collins saw Redford struggle to hold his family together. "But it wasn't like it used to be. They were a great family. He and Lola were terrific, affectionate people. They were incapacitated, though, by lack of time."

Redford lamented the obligations of work and felt that "[Lola and I] were fulfilling our goals and, at the same time, measuring the distance between us." When Lola enrolled at Goddard College in Vermont to restart her education and begin building an independent life—a situation that coincided with *Ordinary People*—the sense of finality was unavoidable.

In the spring, with *The Electric Horseman* playing to receptive audiences and *Brubaker* set for a nationwide summer opening, Redford tried to balance himself by taking a road trip, exactly as he'd often done throughout the fifties and sixties. Supping with the kids in Denver, he decided to rent a car to drive solo to New York. "I wanted to recover normal human reality because *Ordinary People* brought me to that place. But there was no meeting the common man. There was just meeting the fan, the woman with the autograph book, the guy who knew the guy who knew your cousin, the endless handshakes, like I was one of those guys who walked on the moon."

In high summer *Ordinary People* opened with a showcase western premiere in Provo. Mary Tyler Moore and Tim Hutton were among Redford's guests at Sundance for the weekend. Moore, battling the ravages of incipient alcoholism, stayed at the A-frame, which was now a guest lodge under the shadow of the Big House. Moore just wanted to sleep but "could not believe the social schedule Bob set up for us. It was worse than any movie call sheet. It was horse riding at 9:00 a.m. Swimming at 11:00 a.m. Tennis at 1:00 p.m. Go, go, go. I couldn't keep up. It was worrying. I wondered, How the hell does he keep this pace?"

Ordinary People had been made for $6 million and generated receipts of $115 million, an astonishing success by any criteria. Pauline Kael continued to disapprove of Redford's work, chastising the director's emotional absence and the mood of "suburban suffocation," an extraordinary indictment, given the subject matter. But Jack Kroll in *Newsweek* applauded direction that was "clean and clear in style, drenched with seriousness and sensitivity." And Vincent Canby in *The New York Times* welcomed a film "so good, so full of first-rate feeling, that it would be presumptuous for a critic to re-edit it." The awards followed. By January 1981 *Ordinary People* was the acknowledged movie of the year, winning an award from the Directors Guild and snagging British Academy of Film and Television Arts nominations and, ultimately, six Academy Award nominations, among them for best director and best picture, contesting Polanski's *Tess*, David Lynch's *The Elephant Man* and Scorsese's *Raging Bull*.

"When I saw the awards trail beginning, I caved in," says Redford. "I just didn't want it. What I was doing was about personal art, about exploring myself and my audience. I was very proud of the film but I did not desire accolades. It sounds churlish, but I was sated on accolades. There are only so many times you want to be told, 'This is the best thing since *Gone With the Wind*' or 'You are the best leading man since Moses.' I thought, Screw this! and disappeared."

After attending a benefit at the Northwestern Hospital Institute of Psychiatry in Chicago, an invitation that arose from the new friendships he formed making *Ordinary People,* Redford joined the Brokaws for a long-scheduled six-day skiing trip across Colorado, Utah and Idaho. "I was in terrible shape, drained and emotional from the movie and the end of my marriage. The ironies were terrible. My family had been there from the start. They'd suffered so much waiting for me to do what I wanted to do. And then came the big fulfillment . . . and then *this.*"

At Sun Valley in Idaho the depression fogged his thinking. "I was skiing harder and faster, and I pitched myself against this impossible run, going all the way, from top to bottom. I skied it too fast and crashed, a full three-hundred-and-sixty-degree tumble."

He smashed his nose and collarbone and suffered multiple lacerations and a severe head wound. Semiconscious, he refused to go down the mountain on the first-aid toboggan and insisted—"stupidly"—on skiing down. Transferred comatose by ambulance to the hospital in Sun Valley, he remembers being wheeled into X-ray, passing out, then waking up to the sight of a pretty nurse gabbling about the announcement on the radio that *Ordinary People* was a hot favorite for six Academy Awards. "She was excited. She wasn't interested in my injuries anymore. It was that icon thing. And then those questions started: 'What's Mary Tyler Moore really like?' "

As soon as he recovered and could travel, he left for a soul retreat, a Native American festival in New Oraibi, Arizona, to which he had been invited. Two nights later he was in a Hopi kiva, bandaged up like a mummy, for the Powamu winter solstice bean dance. Still in pain, he found the environment once again restorative in the familiar Zen way. Without any conscious effort, it seemed, the company, the chanting, the talk elevated him to what he calls "a transcendental state of release that brought me away from the pain and anxieties of the world. I lost all the confusion and negativity of my thinking. It was like before, that feeling of going beyond 'the now' to a higher place. Next thing I knew, I was mellowed out and feeling well again. I thought, This is where I need to be, this place of roots. I need to work my way back here."

In March, Redford agreed to attend the fifty-third Academy Awards ceremony. Norman Jewison produced a running homage called "Film Is Forever" that punctuated the evening with memories from Gish to Gable and a tribute to Henry Fonda, which was presented by Redford. Duly, the awards came, to Hutton for best supporting actor (winning over Judd Hirsch, also nominated), to Sargent for best adapted screenplay, to Redford as best director, and for best picture. Mary Tyler Moore was nominated in the leading actress category, and though she lost to Sissy Spacek for *Coal Miner's Daughter,* she felt "vindicated." Redford took his award from Lillian Gish but found himself "weirdly unmoved. Probably it had to do with the cynicism I'd shared with the guys at the CU frat house, watching the Academy Awards on TV and making fun of the pomposity. When my turn came, I was thinking, So this is it! The big night." The acceptance speech for best picture was unscripted and longer than he intended: "I just didn't think I was going to see this, but I'm no less grateful. I would like to express my debt to the directors I've worked with in the past, for what I've learned from them, consciously and unconsciously. And I couldn't go much further without expressing what for me is the greatest gratitude, and that keys around the word 'trust.' I really am grateful for the trust I received from this terrific cast—Mary, Donald, Tim, Judd and Liz. I love them, and appreciate their love, too."

Within days he was in therapy, considering his future. "People consult therapists for the inevitable questions," says Redford, "and most boil down to, 'What have I done wrong?' I was no different." Twenty years later he would find a better perspective on the failure of his marriage in the writings of the social philosopher James Hillman. In *The Soul's Code,* Hillman implies that the tendency to cherish family and children is a smoke screen that denies the true responsibility of fulfilling one's own destiny, which is the key to all balance in existence. Citing appalling statistics regarding the abuse of children globally, Hillman talks of "a fatherless culture with dysfunctional children." In Hillman's writings, Redford would find a rationale for what he calls "the drift" of his life. Jamie, in a better position than most to evaluate, would later find "a thorough enlightenment" in Hillman. "My father, like everyone else, had a capacity for self-absolving denial," says Jamie. "But there's no denying that, if he did err as a parent, he erred for 'the calling.' What he got from Hillman was an understanding that intellectually endorsed what he was and how he was." Redford insists that the therapy was no palliative: "I was prepared to take criticism. You have to, to get enough out of it to move forward." Carol Rossen believes the therapy was "not to recover what was lost, but to reconcile himself to the losses incurred and those to come."

What was certain was that he had embarked on a new road, emerging from the straitjacket of superstardom with a grand new plan in mind.

PART FOUR

Canyon Keeper

We shall not cease from exploration
And the end of all our exploring
Will be to arrive where we started
And know the place for the first time.
T. S. Eliot, *Four Quartets*

18

Sundance

Several of the directors who worked with Redford recognized the barrier he had crossed with *Ordinary People* and speculated about his prospects. Most insightful was Michael Ritchie, who, despite his disappointment at being overlooked for *All the President's Men,* continued to cheer his old friend as a film formalist in the European tradition, "more interested in signs and ideas within a movie than plots and actors." The summary shone a light on Redford's direction. In the resolution of therapy, Redford himself saw his career as parallel tracks, starting from the same point, but serving separate aims. The acting drew on primitive instinct, with the economy of verbalism and gesture that Robert Pirsig noted, and achieved a solid audience connection. The directing, half hewn in projects like *Downhill Racer* and now fully formed, reflected an urge to break new ground. He did not see himself as European influenced, nor did he favor heavy intellectualization of his work. He liked Truffaut's work but was skeptical of Godard and much of the neorealist and New Wave work. All this made him a generalist; he didn't like to label his endeavor. But it was clear that anarchic ambition was at work. Some aspect of contemporary cinema rankled, and he found himself straining for another approach, another perspective.

Out of such an instinct, in the heady months of the creation of *Ordinary People,* the transition from Sundance the resort to Sundance the arts laboratory was made. One minor incident, says Redford, set the wheels in motion. Attracted as he was to experimental work, he was interested in the student films shown at the low-key United States Film and Video Festival staged in Salt Lake City by the Utah Film Commission since 1976. Created by his brother-in-law Sterling Van Wagenen and commission chairman John Earle, the festival was supported by Warners' vice president Mark Rosenberg, by director George Romero and by the actress

Katharine Ross. In 1978, Redford accepted the invitation to become honorary chairman, seeing his function, as with similar posts, as that of being a media magnet. But sitting in a tiny theater off Temple Square watching a 16 mm road movie called *The Whole Shootin' Match* by Texan Eagle Pennell, Redford had an epiphany. "I got to thinking, No one else is going to see this little gem. It seemed a crime to me. I imagined myself in Pennell's shoes, the way I'd felt all those years ago in a freezing apartment in Florence. At the time Wildwood was dug into setting up *Ordinary People,* with all our resources and contacts working for us. I decided, There is an inequity. This guy needs some help."

He invited Sterling Van Wagenen to Sundance to discuss a radical idea. Sterling recalls being surprised by the summons. He had had little contact with Redford beyond get-togethers at the Van Wagenen family home on Center Street during the sixties but had, he says, grown up idolizing his brother-in-law while remaining mostly distant from the film business. In his youth, says Van Wagenen, "film was for me *War of the Worlds* and *The Day the Earth Stood Still.*" In the early seventies, Van Wagenen encountered two formative influences: critic George Steiner and the British theater director Jonathan Miller. At Brigham Young University, Van Wagenen read Steiner's *Language and Silence,* which postulated the value of art in politics. Shortly after, in his early twenties, he fell into the job of assistant to Miller, who was directing a production of *Richard II* at the Los Angeles Music Center. Chafing from the narrow-mindedness of the local culture, says Van Wagenen, he was transformed in Los Angeles. He decided on a career in the arts in Utah, which led to his cofounding the film and video festival with Earle.

As Van Wagenen drove his little Beetle to Redford's office at the base of Timpanogos, he imagined chitchat about festival selections. Instead, Redford bluntly suggested a plan to merge the festival with his own half-defined "arts community," perhaps like Yaddo, the famous Saratoga Springs colony that had nurtured writers like John Cheever, Truman Capote and scores of Pulitzer winners. Redford was highly enthused, says Van Wagenen, envisioning a new horizon, with opportunities to drag Hollywood into Utah and stir up support for local writers and out-of-state students who wanted to tell stories on film, but lacked resources. Van Wagenen suggested that the model not be Yaddo, but George White's Eugene O'Neill Theater Retreat in Connecticut, where new and traditional plays were experimentally performed and critiqued by visiting dramaturges for the benefit of writers, directors and actors. "But I don't take credit," says Van Wagenen. "Bob knew what he wanted. He said, 'That's it, that's exactly how it should begin. Now we know what we want to build, let's get on and just do it.' "

The first objective, said Redford, was National Endowment for the Arts backing, and this was swiftly achieved with a $25,000 grant to fund an exploratory workshop in April 1979, just twelve weeks after completion of *Ordinary People.* This was followed by seminars in October and November, which were attended by Cathy Wyler, the daughter of director William Wyler, representing the NEA; Orion's vice president Mike Medavoy; United Artists vice president Claire Townsend; Howard Klein of the Ford Foundation; Czech filmmaker and ex–American Film Institute tutor Frank Daniel; Native American director Larry Littlebird and filmmakers Annick Smith, Victor Nunez, Robert Geller, Moctesuma Esparza and Sydney Pollack. Also attending were former congressman Wayne Owens; Redford's legal counsel Reg Gipson; Redford's constant personal assistant since *Three Days of the Condor,* Robbi Miller; and theater executive George White himself. "It was a very adventurous collection of people," says Van Wagenen, "and the composition of that team suggests Bob's outlook. It was he and he alone who mustered those heavyweight names. I certainly couldn't have done it. And he had a future game all mapped out in his mind. The NEA was for artistic credibility. Medavoy and Townsend were business credibility. The filmmakers were the think tank. George White was the great old sage. It was very sweetly tuned."

Redford felt himself rejuvenated by the new project. He attributes the fluidity of the organizational setup to Van Wagenen; Van Wagenen says it was Redford who sat in the NEA offices in Washington to make the pleas, who took the minutes of the meetings, who made the late-night phone calls to secure essential supporters, including cash investors. The financial champions, says Van Wagenen, were the NEA's Brian Doherty, Wall Streeter Dan Lufkin and Augie Busch of the Anheuser-Busch Brewery, all of whom contributed to the $100,000 seed capital. Redford personally contributed $100,000 a year over the next several years, "primarily to keep the doors open," says Reg Gipson, who contends the arrangement was "extremely fragile, living on the edge of a precipice really, in terms of a commonsense business plan."

The new Sundance Institute board, handpicked by Redford, included Christopher Dodd, later chairman of the Democratic Party and a U.S. senator; Marjorie Benton of UNICEF and Save the Children; Bill Bradley; Frank Daniel; filmmaker Saul Bass and Gipson. Under their guidance an innovative schooling program was designed, to commence in the summer of 1981. The object of this program was not to launch a rival or remodeled film festival, but to develop a George White–style summer lab for aspirant filmmakers, who could potentially take their work to the screens of the U.S. Film and Video Festival, and beyond. Admission to the lab would be a selection process from script submissions, headed by Frank Daniel. Successful candidates would then visit Sundance and rehearse and film excerpts of their work under the supervision of volunteer established actors, directors and technicians. The work would be analyzed, debated, refined and reshot over several days.

"The success of this format was entirely dependent on the quality of what we called creative and technical advisers," says Redford, who immediately sought the involvement of a host of friends and associates from film and theater, including Morgan Freeman, whom he'd met on *Brubaker,* Robert Duvall, Karl Malden, cinematographer Caleb Deschanel and writer Waldo Salt.

"It was footslog," says Reg Gipson, "not at all the overnight success some people have said. Bob was personally knocking on doors begging favors for a long, long time." Celebrity had rewarded him with positions in various boardrooms, among them the Museum of Modern Art's. At a MoMA benefit he targeted potential supporters. Actor Hume Cronyn recalls being buttonholed by Redford. "He told me this fanciful story of how he wanted to create a film and theater group in the Southwest that would change contemporary movies," said Cronyn. "I didn't believe a word of it, but I was smitten." Thereafter, Cronyn volunteered for the regulation six years on the board, all the time working also as an adviser, a role he kept till the last years of his life.

Michelle Satter, introduced to Redford by George White, was a Bostonian in her twenties who had organized outdoor festivals for her hometown Institute of Contemporary Arts. Initially she was invited to conduct a study of marketing and distribution, a gesture, she says, that comprehensively shows Redford's long-term vision. "It seemed crazy back then, because we were all newcomers with no product of any kind to distribute. I wondered was I wasting my time, but the energy generated by Bob was seductive. He led, we followed." Satter became lab director.

The first Sundance Institute lab took place over the month of June 1981, with a budget of $160,000 cobbled together from the NEA, Orion, Time Warner, the Ford Foundation, the Marjorie Benton Foundation, and Irene Diamond of the Diamond Foundation. By the standard that would shortly develop, it was primitive, just a handful of young tyros debating scripts in the mountain meadows with a bunch of seasoned pros, with the accent as much on theater—on account of the access to the on-site open-air theater—as film. Redford saw the immediate value of the process. "Half of the submissions were Third World themes. I'd seen so many minority films fail because of lack of finessing. Instantly, before our eyes, we saw how expert tutoring could address that. It was an issue of promoting confidence in aspiring filmmakers, as much as teaching technique." But his main preoccupation was the frantic assessment of so many new alliances, and a rear-guard fight to silence the dissenters. "I never talked as much as I did that summer," he says. Gary Hendler, for one, was deeply suspicious of the venture, believing it to be a wasteful indulgence. "The trouble with Bob," he complained to Gipson, "is that he only listens to himself."

Shortly after the first lab, Brent Beck asked for a meeting with Redford in the log cabin administrative annex a short walk from the main meeting hall.

"It won't work," he told Redford.

"Why?"

Beck slid across the desk the receipts of the two-week lab, which was serviced entirely by resort catering and accommodation. "Because, the way it is, almost none of these people, advisers or benefactors, are paying guests. So every time you convene a planning meeting, or a lab, it'll put a terrible strain on resources."

"So?"

"We're still a business, Bob. It's the bottom line that counts."

Redford glanced at the receipts and pushed them back.

"It will work," he told Beck.

At the time, Pollack reported himself uplifted. "The spirit of Sundance reminds me of my early experiences, when I was constantly turned on," he told a visiting journalist. "I'm refreshing myself." Like Redford, he also believed the Sundance Institute would work—but under one condition. "Utah is a beautiful place," he later said, "but there were obstacles beyond finance. The canyon is an hour by road from the Salt Lake City airport, and a long way from anywhere else. Those students and advisers would keep coming—but only if there was a hit product, something people could point to and say, 'That's different, and that came out of Sundance.' "

The formation of the institute took place against a background of new political upheaval. Ronald Reagan was in office, with a huge mandate, and Carter was out. Redford needed to make new connections, find new financial angles to further his concomitant environmental goals. He decided that the institute must embody a sister activist agency, and to this end he met with Gary Beer, a point man for his friend Ted Wilson, who had expertise in out-of-state PAC environmental groups. Redford and Beer clicked fast. "His style was against the grain," says Redford. "Immediately I thought, This is energy I can work with. We're in new territory here, and we need people who are ready to go against the tide." In time, Redford would see his choice of Beer as a mistake. Though Beer was unquestionably skilled at raising money, he had not, in Redford's view, the true sensitivity to the arts and environment that Sundance needed. For the moment, though, the glove fit. Born in New York and based in Washington, D.C., Beer knew Utah life inside out, having previously consulted for both the State of Utah and Governor Scott Matheson. "I was inured to the conservatism of Utahans," says Beer, "which put me ahead of the game in Redford's eyes. So we hit the ground running with this ambitious new Institute for Resource Management that would parallel the arts group under the Sundance Institute banner."

Redford had already engaged Hope Moore, a Carter ally from the Department of the Interior, as his environmental adviser. By the time Beer joined, Moore had in place a tentative graduate program for environmental studies at the University of Washington, a template educational scheme that Redford hoped would spread across the country's campuses. Beer saw it was doomed, through lack of maintenance funds. "All Bob had achieved amounted to establishing a community of like-minded people. This was crucial, obviously. But it was nothing without money to spread the word."

Beer relocated to Utah and worked alongside Van Wagenen, who welcomed a national operator with savvy instincts and solid pragmatism. For Beer, Van Wagenen was a family insider who could help him to a better understanding of his new boss. What emerged for all was a rapid growth in development that unfolded with the grace of good chess playing. "It wasn't straightforward," says Beer. "It was learn as you go. I discovered about Bob that he wasn't the radical he professed himself to be. On the contrary, he, too, was a pragmatist. He'd gone to war with Southern Cal Edison and ended up winning over Howard Allen. Once, Allen was his sworn enemy. By the time the Kaiparowits row was over, Allen was in Bob's camp. He'd been reeducated. From that, Bob learned the benefits of diplomacy. Howard Allen was welcomed into the Sundance family, which was a stroke of genius, because he opened up access to the corporate community, which got a lot of things moving for me."

The IRM was officially launched in the fall of 1982. Robert Wood, Carter's secretary of housing and urban development, was chairman. Wayne Owens, Ted Wilson, Stewart Udall and Howard Allen were among the principals. Chris Dodd and California congressman George Miller, straddling action committees, joined Beer in fund-raising duties.

Redford spent the year sharpening his political game. In April, he was on the campaign trail with Ted Wilson, who challenged Orrin Hatch for the Utah Senate seat. For three months, says Wilson, Redford sidelined all his arts work in order to accompany him on the stump. "He was the lifeblood of my campaign," says Wilson. "Hatch had the fiscal advantage, raising $4 million, against my $1 million. But most of what I raised was thanks to Bob. He drove it, and he didn't do it from behind a desk. He did it just like those scenes in *The Candidate,* joining me at street-corner rallies in places like Ogden and Provo. He was tireless." When they traveled together, says Wilson, all they did was scheme. "His objective was symbiosis," says Wilson. "Central to my politics was environmental review and new control mechanisms for the energy industry. Bob saw my election essentially as a tool for his own aims." Though Wilson failed in his bid, he saw Redford's objective harden: "He told me, 'At some point soon there will be a conservation crisis. As a nation we'll be forced to face the consequences of bad energy policies. We need a better information system to get ready for that day.' There's no two ways about it: he was visionary regarding energy and environment."

The previous spring, the National Committee for Air Quality had filed a shocking impact report that triggered marathon congressional debates about the enforcement of environmental laws. Then the NRDC launched the first coordinated scheme of legal actions against industrial polluters under its own Citizen National Enforcement Program. Redford joined the battle, seeking meetings with energy companies, landowners and local authorities all across the Southwest.

By 1982 America was deep in recession, with unemployment above 10 percent and interest rates sky-high. Beer observed Redford extend himself even at this time of economic downturn, digging deep into his own pockets, working with Indiana congressman Phil Sharp, another environmentalist, and drifting away from the world of movies and art. In his only major magazine interview of the era, Redford told journalist George Haddad-Garcia that he might direct another film, might star in two more.

But in truth the grip of the movies was unshakable. It was a calling to do with storytelling and polemic, with making people ruminate and infer and choose. It pressed upon him all the time, in his long insomniac nights of obsessive reading and now in the Sundance Institute, with the student labs bustling with activity at the end of his garden. After months of finance meetings and political rallies he found himself, once again, lured back to a movie. The previous year Barry Levinson, director of the recent *Diner,* had come to assist at the June lab and asked Redford, in return, to consider a role in his follow-up project. Sharing a flight to Los Angeles after a second lab session, Redford suggested Levinson forget the work he was developing and look instead at a script by Roger Towne, based on Bernard Malamud's 1952 novel, *The Natural.*

Redford had never forgotten the joy Tiger and Charlie found in baseball when he was a small child, or his own teenage fascination with Ted Williams, the left-handed (like himself) Boston Red Sox great. "I loved his individualism," says Redford. "He had no time for the media. His business was hitting, period. When I watched Ted, I saw a man with a mission." Redford's occasional fantasy of portraying Williams in a movie came alive when he read Towne's adaptation. Over the years he had poo-pooed the baseball movies he'd seen. None, not Gary Cooper as Lou Gehrig in *The Pride of the Yankees* nor James Stewart in *The Stratton Story,* touched him at all. "Because I was a baseball player, I saw all the flaws, none worse than Tony Perkins in Alan [Pakula] and Bob's [Mulligan] *Fear Strikes Out,* which was a poor depiction of the Red Sox's Jimmy Piersall." Apart from technical inaccuracies, no baseball movie had ever reflected the grandeur of the game for him. The Towne script, however, was onto something new.

Redford believed Malamud's source novel had a Swiftian dimension. It told the story of Roy Hobbs, a gifted midwestern kid who heads off to Chicago to try out for the Cubs, armed with Wonderboy, the bat he carved from a tree felled by lightning. En route he is seduced by Harriet, a strange siren who distracts him with tales and fables, then insanely shoots him. Recovered fifteen years later, Hobbs emerges from the shadows to become the star player of the New York Knights and win his choice of ladies. At this point, Malamud's fable about the corruption of heroes took a new turn in Towne's hands. In the novel, Hobbs falls for another venal woman, Memo Paris, niece of the team manager, and takes a bribe to throw the game of the season. But Towne introduced redemption in the angelic Iris, Hobbs's childhood sweetheart, who helps him overcome his injuries to right things.

Primarily based on the bizarre true-life story of Eddie Waitkus, the Philadelphia Phillies player whose career was cut short when he was shot by a crazed woman who then jumped out of a window, the novel also drew material from the 1919 World Series Black Sox scandal, where eight members of the Chicago White Sox threw games. On top of this, Malamud referenced an encyclopedia of fabled yarns, from the Fisher King to Orestes. Redford found the sources fascinating, "because I was convinced it was the only way to tell the Big Story of baseball. You could make a movie that would follow all the rules and maneuvers, but it would miss the symbolic scale of it all. Malamud's achievement, enhanced by Towne, was to introduce the mythic aspect."

Baltimore-born Levinson had evolved from television comedy writing in Los Angeles to scriptwriting for Mel Brooks's *Silent Movie* and *High Anxiety* to the semiautobiographical *Diner.* He, too, found the mythology of *The Natural* appealing. For *Diner,* he had abandoned conventional narrative to tell his story through vignettes. The originality of Towne's approach, which emphasized Malamud's fancy, was, to him, hypnotic: "First of all, I was attracted by Bob's personal attachment. Secondly, I am a huge baseball fan, just like Bob. But more than anything, I was won over by Malamud's story and Towne's development of it. It was simply one of the best things I'd ever read. Towne took this intricate tale and turned it into an edifying story about goodness. Bob didn't have to convince me. I said, 'Yes, yes, this will do.' "

A flood of creative ideas flowed between actor and director. Redford decided, as an homage, to adopt Ted Williams's number, 9. It was also decided that the photography by cinematographer Caleb Deschanel would take its cue from a character in the novel, Judge Banner, who refers to people in terms of darkness and light. The opposing female figures, the gunwoman Harriet and the bighearted Iris, would be depicted in darkness and iridescence, respectively. Hobbs's childhood would be shown in a two-color sepia-like palette that would emphasize the pale greens and burnt yellows of a summery Midwest. These conceptualizations were planned in detail with Redford and carefully hand-drawn before a foot of film was shot. "What Bob and I wanted from the movie was lightness and irony," says Levinson, "though most of the critics eventually chose to see it as a serious, even grim, piece of work."

Through June 1983 Redford prepared for the movie with a rigorous fitness routine that included weeks of batting practice with a team of semi-pro players. He phoned Ted Williams, who was fishing in Nova Scotia and missed his call. Williams would later affectionately acknowledge Redford's homage and send him signed memorabilia. "It was the best place to be," says Redford, "full of childhood dreaming and hardball playing. After my long absence, I was ready for a good movie."

The Natural would fulfill the first part of a two-picture deal that Gary Hendler had brokered for him with Columbia two years before. But Hendler was no longer Redford's legal counsel—he was the president of a new movie company, TriStar, a partnership between divisions of Columbia, HBO and CBS, which had inherited *The Natural.* The men took a walk on the beach at Malibu to discuss Hendler's new role. They had been together for sixteen years, and Redford was happy to credit his friend with enormous help in building his career and holding on to Sundance. But he had doubts about Hendler's ability to move into moviemaking. "It seemed to me a no-win scenario for him," says Redford. "He was being asked to run a studio with no practical knowledge, and that, to my thinking, had to be the role of the fall guy." Hendler wanted Redford's blessing of support and, reluctantly, Redford gave it. "But it was a lousy decision by me. Gary had the look of trouble in his eyes and I feared he was headed for disaster. I felt a loyalty to him that if that's what he wanted, I felt that's what he should get to do. But it got awkward when this new role he played put unwanted pressure on me at the worst time."

Redford was in Buffalo, in upstate New York, on August 1, just settling into the first scenes of *The Natural,* when he got a call from a distressed Shauna in Boulder. She was at the apartment that Redford had recently purchased for her near the CU campus and had just been told that her boyfriend, a twenty-two-year-old fellow student, Sidney Lee Wells, whose mother owned the apartment block, was dead. Shauna and Wells had been close for months, even contemplating marriage. Wells had been shot in the back of the head. His body was found just a few doors down from Shauna's place, in the apartment of Thayne Smika, a delinquent renter who owed several hundred dollars of back rent. Redford tried to comfort Shauna but she was, he says, "convulsed with confusion, in a terrible state." Jamie, also attending CU, comforted his sister while Redford rented a jet, picked up Lola and flew to Denver, arriving at the apartment within hours. Inevitable gossip surrounded the killing. Allegations of cocaine trading involving Wells were made, but the police suspected the murder occurred when Wells confronted Smika for payment of the rent. Smika would be arrested on suspicion of the murder but later released when prosecutors deemed the evidence against him too circumstantial. Four years later Smika would disappear, evading charges against him of forgery and theft, unrelated to the murder. The lack of closure in Wells's death would be a terrible burden on the family for years to come.

The Redford family attended Wells's funeral at the Christ Congregational Church in Longmont, Colorado. The atmosphere there was hysterical, with British tabloids paying locals to climb trees, the better to get photographs of the mourners. Redford, who had hired bodyguards, was sickened by the mêlée. "He was always somewhat retiring, but he became reclusive after that," said Alan Pakula. "I often wondered was it some natural paranoid response, some recognition that he and his family were higher-profile targets than the rest of us."

Redford returned to Levinson's location a week later in a tense mood. "My concentration, obviously, was dented. I was thinking of my daughter's dilemma, not any fictional scenario." The tragedy of the early part of *The Natural,* where Hobbs loses his career to the assault of a maniac, was intensified by the personal strain. At War Memorial Stadium in Buffalo, Redford had to face a gallery of hundreds and pretend to play ball. "It was the hardest thing in the world, with those worries on my back," he says, "but experience kicks in. You blank things and find the zone. That worked, because it was what Roy Hobbs was doing with Wonderboy, overcoming his troubles to win the big game for the Knights. The movie was about overcoming adversity, about the power of self-belief."

The cast, over whom Redford had approval, was a source of strength. Glenn Close, playing Iris, became a good friend and would later join the board of the Sundance Institute. Kim Basinger, cast as the seductress Memo Paris, also became a close companion, and for a while they were inseparable. "She was a blessing," says Redford. "I needed supporters and that was a lucky set for me. There was a lot of love going around."

From Levinson's point of view, Redford's vulnerability was both a challenge and an asset. "We needed each other, because there was an awful lot of stuff in that movie—the mythology, the poetry, the history, the humor. I like to talk. Bob sometimes likes to talk. And, boy, did we have a lot to talk about." The biggest challenge was the story's time span, which obliged Redford to portray Hobbs as a teenager and an aging player. "I wasn't concerned about the wide age issue," says Levinson. "But I was bothered by his batting. You cannot fake a great batter. We wanted 'the natural' and there must have been some anxiety for him because the word went out that he was Bob the Jock. There was apprehension. People laid bets. But we needn't have worried. Soon as he hit the field, he was sizzling. He took scores of pitches and lined them into the outfield and hit several three-hundred-footers into the right-field stands. He didn't just look the part of the ace. When push came to shove, he delivered Ted Williams."

Of some concern to Redford was the warmth he was conveying as Hobbs, who, in Towne's script, is impressively lovable. "I reviewed my work of the seventies and found I'd begun to come across on-screen as cold, something I hadn't intended," says Redford. "I decided this was the time to fix it." For *The Natural* he sought openness and innocence and was encouraged by Levinson's wry take on the world. "The trick really was Barry's spin on the humor. He was a comedy writer who started with Marty Feldman and Brooks, so he had a grin going on all the time. That carried into Hobbs. He said, 'Let's not be crease browed about this. We're looking to leave the audience with a smile on its face. It's a fun tale.' "

There were different kinds of complex challenges for Gary Hendler. *The Natural* was to be his big chance, the test of TriStar's marketing. Levinson and Redford both felt the sharp edge of Hendler's nervous impatience. "It was heartbreaking," says Redford, "because suddenly he was in charge of having to figure out the studio logo and come up with production schedules and deal with not just one star ego, but many, many star egos. He tried to deal with it valiantly, but all the time he was ill. He'd always suffered from stomach ulcers. When things went wrong, it was his stomach that gave in first. It was pushed into the background for a long time, but bit by bit we discovered the illness was more serious, that he had developed stomach cancer and was fighting that as well."

In the spring of 1984, Redford and Levinson found themselves burning the midnight oil for a rushed print to satisfy Hendler's too-hasty distribution schedule. "It made no sense," says Levinson, "because we'd spent $20 million making *The Natural* look so good, and here was this early completion deadline just to get in theaters to fit a summer social calendar."

The first cut, a three-and-a-half-hour assembly that included a subplot centering on actor Michael Madsen, quickly bit the dust. "We had so many elements so well balanced," says Levinson. "Randy Newman's Americana music was spot-on. Mel Bourne gave us a wonderful design look. But then Hendler gave us a put-up-or-shut-up date, and we stupidly caved in. He pressured us to death, and we let the movie go without it ever being properly finished." What doubly upset Redford and Levinson was

Hendler's last-minute decision to use a second-rate picture, *Where the Boys Are '84,* as the TriStar flagship instead. "I don't think there was malice of any kind in it," says Redford, "just terrible misjudgment, which arose from Gary's inexperience. The problem was, he was being pressured by higher-ups and gave in to that. He could have rationalized it with TriStar with greater strategy. But he was inexperienced and he didn't see the long view, so we all lost out."

When *The Natural* opened in May, just as TriStar had demanded, business was slack, and though it made its money back and garnered reasonable reviews, it seemed a hollow victory. For Levinson it left a sour taste "because there was a better version available"; for Redford it was "worthy, something I'm proud of." Nevertheless, its fate represented a downturn for Redford, if only in Hollywood icon terms. Alan Pakula thought it was a miscalculation. "He hadn't been on-screen as an actor for five years [*sic*]. His intellectual strengths were proved in *All the President's Men* and *Ordinary People.* My belief was that he needed something far grittier, more believable, than *The Natural.* I thought he was at a crossroads, winning that Academy Award. There was never a better time for him to turn to the classics, or roughen up. But he took the soft option." George Roy Hill felt the film was "vaporous."

The fact that Redford did his job as well as he did in the midst of Shauna's trauma was an achievement. But the squabbles about distribution that followed mitigated all sense of accomplishment. The relationship with Hendler from this point on was never better than awkward. They shared one more movie transaction, but within two years, as Redford predicted, Hendler lost control of TriStar. He was replaced and slipped into semiretirement, dying of cancer five years later.

Depressed and anxious as Shauna still was, Redford sought to distract her by involving her in prep work for a project that had been offered to him as potential director, but that Sydney Pollack had inherited. *Out of Africa,* based on Danish novelist Karen Blixen's memoirs, would be set in Kenya, and already he and Pollack had started their routine of fireside conversations to build the movie, in which he would star. As Christmas approached, he took Shauna with him to Africa. For months he had been corresponding with the paleoanthropologist Richard Leakey, who shared an interest in conservation. "I knew Shauna hadn't allowed herself to grieve," Redford remembers. "The shock was still in her system. She needed distance and she needed something to absorb her intellect. So I called Leakey and asked him to help out." In response, Leakey asked them to join an archaeological dig at Lake Turkana on the Ethiopian border. The trip helped them both recover.

But back in the United States in March, while Redford was returning from an institute board meeting, he received a call telling him Shauna had been involved in a serious car accident outside Provo. As she drove in darkness, her Bronco had run off Interstate 215 and plunged into the Jordan River, where she was trapped in the car. Only the heroic acts of four passersby who dove into the freezing waters in which Shauna's car was fully submerged saved her life. Press reports called Shauna "continually depressed," an understatement to those close to her. "It was the nightmare I dreaded," says Redford, "but she got through it, she got the help she needed. Lola, everyone, did their best."

Those who knew both Pollack and Redford felt the latter's success with *Ordinary People* created a new tension between the men, relieved to some degree by Pollack's success just a year or so later with *Tootsie*, a movie he also appeared in alongside Dustin Hoffman and which was nominated for ten Oscars. In Paul Newman's opinion, "those guys were in hot competition, no doubt about it." In Redford's view, though, Pollack was different from him, a deft traditionalist whose terrific skill was making serious subjects popular. He could deal diplomatically with the studios and was a master of patience, tact, organization. Redford felt himself edgier, attracted as much to whimsy as experiment and never content to repeat the formula. Some, like the actress Carlin Glynn, who served as adviser at the Sundance June lab tutorials, believed the spiritual differences of the friends opened a chasm. Each wanted elements of the other's expertise—Redford with directing, Pollack with acting—but found no common language of shared endeavor beyond their initial roles, with Redford acting and Pollack behind the camera. "I think it made for some cynicism," says Glynn. "They were buddies, but Sydney would not shy away from belittling Bob in front of people. I recall his attendance at one of the Sundance labs, addressing some students alongside Bob. Bob mispronounced some word, and Sydney was happy to correct him in front of the crowd, which I thought was unnecessary. They had this close connection, but it really started to strain."

For both men, the odds were against a comfortable ride on *Out of Africa.* There was disorder in Redford's career. Directing *Ordinary People* seemed to confuse his attitude toward himself as an actor. During 1981, he had been offered a role in *The Verdict,* a courtroom drama written by David Mamet that Sidney Lumet was to direct. Lumet, who had employed Redford long ago in *The Iceman Cometh,* was appalled by the actor's requests for six rewrites. The part required Redford to play a drunken lawyer hustling his way from one low-life client to the next, until he finally finds a case that offers salvation. Redford's aim with the rewrites, said Lumet, was to "eliminate the unpleasant side of the character, trying to make him more lovable so the audience would 'identify' with him." This, said Lumet, was "a misdirected cliché of movie-writing." After a year of procrastination, Richard Zanuck and Fox gave the role to Newman, who won an Academy Award nomination for it. "I don't concede it was about striving for the cliché," says Redford. "I just found the character unrelatable to me at that time." Before *Out of Africa* emerged, there were prospective projects with political satirist Garry Trudeau and with Tom McGuane, projects based on the Leonard Peltier case and the story of Irish nationalist hero Michael Collins—but few moved to the polished-script phase, let alone production planning. Only one, John Nichols's magic realist novel *The Milagro Beanfield War,* truly roused him, but he thought this could be a future directing project, and, anyway, the rights belonged to someone else.

Sensing career momentum slipping away and Wildwood teetering on the edge of extinction, Redford changed agents, signing with Mike Ovitz, who was in the process of setting up Creative Artists Agency, based on the Lew Wasserman–MCA model. Redford was wary of Ovitz, a failed law student who had started in the mailroom at William Morris, but he was respectful of Ovitz's chutzpah. In less than ten years Ovitz had established a client list of 675 leading players, covering all aspects of entertainment. He also admired Ovitz's CAA game plan, which was to sweeten the Wasserman technique by prepackaging movies in their entirety—concept, script, actors, all key creative personnel—and selling them to the studios. When they talked, Ovitz laid out his vision. He would not only remold Redford's acting career, but reboot Wildwood. *Out of Africa* became his first contractual coup.

Ovitz negotiated for Redford a fee of $6.5 million plus 10 percent of the gross, the actor's best terms since *A Bridge Too Far.* Some opined that Pollack was jealous that his own deal lagged far behind, but nothing was discussed between the men, who embarked on the project, says Redford, as equals.

The history of the project was convoluted. Blixen, who wrote novels under the name of Isak Dinesen, led the life of a coffee planter in colonial Africa. Orson Welles, David Lean and Nic Roeg had variously tried to mount a film about her life and romances, and a script, partly based on the memoir *Out of Africa,* had been in circulation since 1975. But it was Judith Thurman's 1982 biography, which uncovered Blixen's unhappy marriage and her strange love affair with Denys Finch Hatton, that mobilized the studios. Universal acquired the rights and, having sounded out Redford as a possible director, contracted Pollack. Pollack read Thurman's biography and loved it: "I thought it was feminist and unusual. I also saw the pictures unfolding in my mind of a landscape no one knew. I'd never visited Kenya, where the story was set. I knew David Lean's Africa, but this was completely different and therein was the excitement." Pollack made a handshake arrangement with Redford to star as Finch Hatton and commissioned a screenplay from Kurt Luedtke, the Brown-educated former editor of the *Detroit Free Press,* who had recently written *Absence of Malice* for him.

After the comedy of *Tootsie* Pollack was looking for something cerebral. "Apart from the obvious incongruity of the Jewish guy from South Bend, Indiana, tackling the life story of a Danish baroness among the Kikuyu and Somali tribesmen, there were a couple of big pluses from an adaptation point of view. Blixen's memoirs were not narrative in any film sense, so we could speculate a lot. Her autobiographical writings were very self-analytical, which allowed us accurately into her heart and soul. And, of course, there was the bigness of the landscape, which created an extraordinary background for storytelling. It's the kind of setting that amplifies everything, so you get power like a Shakespearean sonnet that seems small and yet has huge, huge resonance. I told Kurt, 'We're not into social history here, but every bit of it will tell the British colonial African story.' " Redford saw the risks of this kind of contextual storytelling. Referencing McCarthyism was one thing, but this was remote alien territory. "It didn't faze me. I was as stimulated as Sydney. But I saw that risk of 'America abroad' films. Foreign culture has been historically difficult for American filmmakers. There's often that 'John Wayne abroad' shallowness, which is the problem of one culture misinterpreting the subtleties of another. I thought the redeeming factor might be a damn good love story, which Sydney was so good at."

The character of Karen Blixen intrigued Redford. Born into wealth, she had been spurned by her first love, but settled for his brother, Bror von Blixen-Finecke, who extravagantly invested her money in a plantation on the inhospitable slopes of the Ngong Hills near Nairobi. Bror hunted game while Karen dallied with Finch Hatton, another hunter who used the coffee plantation as a base between safaris. When Bror and Karen divorced, Finch Hatton refused marriage and died shortly thereafter in a plane crash. The intrigue in Blixen's story centers on Finch Hatton's true nature. According to Thurman's biography, the evidence suggests Karen and Finch Hatton never made it to the bedroom; Blixen's personal writings suggest otherwise, and there is evidence that she miscarried his child. Redford welcomed this ambiguity: "Firstly, it gives me, the actor, a wide range of possibilities in playing out the fantasy. But it's also dynamic because the presence of Finch Hatton, historically and otherwise, becomes mystery incarnate. I thought he could be an interesting subject to portray."

Pollack wasn't troubled by the blank canvas. "Blixen hardly mentions Denys [in *Out of Africa,* published in 1937], but Kurt gathered enough from Judith and from another book by Errol Trzebinski on Finch Hatton to build this great, fated romance," he said. To play Blixen, Pollack considered a variety of actresses. In the sixties, there had been talk of Greta Garbo playing the role, and Pollack felt that a strongly sexual actress was vital. When Meryl Streep was proposed by Universal, he demurred. Streep was brilliant, but not, he felt, sexy enough. The decision was reversed when Streep insisted on an interview and showed up in a low-cut blouse and a push-up bra. "I really needed no convincing," he said. "She was our national treasure, and when we met, I understood that of course she could ooze sex when she chose to." Streep's involvement, too, was a further inducement for Redford. "It was always going to be the woman's story. The bottom line was her suffering. She was a pioneer as much as Jeremiah Johnson. The hardship she endured, trying to manage a thousand native workers, struggling against the economic and cultural odds, was too much. But she never gave up. She was sustained with the hope of this phantom lover, Denys, to keep her going. Meryl found the role very touching, very worthwhile."

Not everyone was equally confident about Redford playing Finch Hatton, the archetypal Englishman. The son of the thirteenth earl of Winchilsea, Finch Hatton was educated at Eton and Oxford and had served in the military in Egypt but was essentially a man of leisure, most comfortable sipping port on safari with the Prince of Wales. The leap for Redford was difficult, not least with the accent. But he resolved from the start to immerse himself in the Britishness. "I knew I could do it. I worked with a voice coach in London called Joan Washington. I worked it. It was good.

I was clear about how I wanted to play the character, and I understood Sydney was, too. I understood, as we began, that we were on the same page." Pollack, though, had others to answer to. "They all came up with the same beef," said Pollack, speaking of executives' response. " 'What about the accent?' My feeling was, It's a small concern. It won't matter. What does matter is we are getting a great star who generates electricity by the power of his presence. He is also a fine actor."

During the first days of filming at Mbogani, Blixen's first home near the Ngong Hills, Pollack took Redford aside. Redford recalls him saying, "Bob, I've just had a call from Frank Price [Universal's studio head], who says you won't be accepted as an Englishman, that it will confuse audiences. So we have to drop it." Redford pleaded his case, but was overruled. "From that point on, I began to struggle with the part," says Redford. "It's basic psychology. You have your approach. It works. You're on your way. And then the rug is pulled from under you. It damaged the process."

Though some crew members claimed Streep and Redford didn't get along, Redford is adamant that, in fact, their chemistry bore him up when some frustration with Pollack affected him. "She and I hit it off big time. Not only did we get along, we probably got along too well. It caused ripples. We liked to talk. We'd be off camera, between takes, taking it easy. We had a sense of humor in common. But Sydney didn't like that. He would break it up. It bothered him that I was connecting with her in some way that didn't fit his picture of me, or of us as a team. That wasn't easy to deal with, because I felt I was in a vise and I became resentful."

After *Tootsie,* says Redford, he believed that, if anything, their relationship might improve. "Till then, all his successes were movies in which I starred. I felt good that he'd got some important individual success. I thought our friendship would be the better for it. But it wasn't. He seemed to want more control than ever, and I wanted to be controlled less."

Pollack denied that. He claimed instead that the logistics of this, the most unwieldy production he'd ever attempted, diverted him from his usual close collaboration with Redford. "It was $31 million of pure hell," Pollack recalled. "We were very far from home, very reliant on the good offices of people we didn't know. We were importing animals, importing fake bone-stretched ears for the natives, marshaling giraffes, buffaloes, you name it." Peace Corps volunteers, expat students and tourists beefed up the legions of extras. "We had so many people problems, because the white extras were harder to find in big numbers. But it was worse than that. There was also a lot of local misunderstanding, that we were shooting a colonial story about two people who, today, would be judged as racist. With all those nuisances, I gave Bob my best."

Still, some cast members observed Redford retract. He avoided social contact, buried himself in books and newspapers, disappeared for days on end. "I was making this romantic movie, which required the most delicate emotions," says Redford, "and at the same time I was on the phone negotiating a divorce settlement and the dissolution of my former life with lawyers."

He was also beginning to have serious second thoughts about how Sydney wanted Finch Hatton portrayed. A number of memorable scenes, paramount among them the famous hair washing beside the hippo watering hole, conveyed the best of Hollywood magic. "As an actor inside that moment, there is an awareness of specialness," says Redford. "But there were issues. Sydney, I always felt, was afraid to express sex in an open, liberal way. He wanted to stay inside the safety boundary. But I always wanted to push it. I felt that a great electrical sexuality can be achieved in touch, in looks, in the caress. Meryl, of course, got that. She was nervous of the hippos, because they're territorial and we were in their space. But she gave a hell of a sensuality to that scene, and the movie gave me great joy in those times."

As Redford strove to project apt Englishness of manner opposite Streep's sharply Danish Blixen, Pollack pushed him to "reduce, reduce, reduce." Redford interpreted this as Pollack falling back on the easy option, substituting Redford the romantic icon for a properly realized characterization. In his view, Streep was "encouraged to fly," while he was restrained: "I felt I was a symbol, not a character." By the time the filming ended, Redford and Pollack were hardly talking.

In truth, Redford's iconography was the director's best asset. In what would end up to be a long, digressive two-and-a-half-hour movie, it is Redford's quixotic Finch Hatton—not Streep's virtuosity—that dominates. Once Finch Hatton begins courting Blixen, insistently inviting her to join him as he scouts for a camp base in the Mara for his soon-to-be safari tourists, a dull drama becomes engaging.

The southwestern premiere benefit for the Sundance Institute was staged at Redford's behest in Provo a week before Christmas 1985. Already there was talk of awards. The box office boomed, grossing $250 million—surpassing Redford's best earner to date, *The Sting*—and, duly, the Academy Award nominations came in copious measure, equaling those for Steven Spielberg's contender, *The Color Purple.* Pollack went on to win best director, and the movie won best film and five other awards.

The movie's one casualty was Redford. Not only was he overlooked on the awards circuit, but the critics were unkind. Pauline Kael once again singled him out: "He seems adrift, lost in another movie, and Pollack treats him with unseemly reverence." David Denby was harsh, too: "He is so far out of his league that at first one feels sorry for him. But only at first. Whether he can't do it, or won't do it, we're disgusted with him by the end." Vincent Canby in *The New York Times* understood the heart of the problem: "It's not Mr. Redford's fault. There is no role for him to act."

Mike Ovitz felt he had a radical recipe for recovery. The package Ovitz put together with his clients, director Ivan Reitman and *Top Gun* writers Jim Cash and Jack Epps Jr., was a fluffy thriller called *Legal Eagles,* which he urgently pressed on Redford. Alan Pakula, when he heard it, cringed: "It was light entertainment. I think Mike believed Bob should get back to *Barefoot in the Park,* which, given how Bob had strived to evolve, was ridiculous." Reitman, a Czech-born Canadian and an alumnus of the *Saturday Night Live* comedy coterie, had produced the crossover comedy *Animal House* in 1978. His directorial successes with *Meatballs* and *Stripes* should have served fair warning: they defined the coarse comedy Redford hated. "When I thought movie comedy, I thought Capra, Wilder, Cary Grant, Tracy and Hepburn," says Redford. "And when I wanted alternative comedy, I went for George Carlin. But I hated where 'hip' comedy went in the seventies. It was a terrible cycle. When I took on *Legal Eagles,* I didn't look into the people or the style closely enough. I just felt I should be open to Mike's advice."

Reitman's original choices for his *Legal Eagles* leads were Bill Murray, whom he'd discovered for *SNL,* and Dustin Hoffman. But their unavailability, said Ovitz, was Redford's opportunity. This was also Ovitz's golden moment. "Mike needed name players and neon lights to lift his own career and I walked into it. And it kind of made sense at the time. Reitman had just had a major success with *Ghostbusters,* so he was hot. And . . . it had to be something I could chill out with."

The script had started life as a documentary project about the battle over the estate of the artist Mark Rothko. What it had become was jokey fiction about rising district attorney Tom Logan's romantic attachment to a defense lawyer whose sexy client is accused of stealing a famous work of art by her father. The best part of the project for Redford was the financial deal Ovitz made: $8 million up front—most of which, one way or the other, went right into the institute projects. "But the script was the worry," says Redford. "It was a patchwork of clichés from any number of TV legal dramas and caper movies, and I should have been wiser." Debra Winger became his love interest, with Daryl Hannah, Terence Stamp and Brian Dennehy supporting.

Despite Redford's obvious marquee value, Reitman worried about his appropriateness for the role of Logan. As soon as they started, though, he says, he was won over. "I had very little sense of who Redford is. He is known as a fine, upstanding man who has a strong social conscience, which was great for the part of an assistant district attorney. But I was wondering where the comedy would come from. In time, he started telling me stories about himself, about his sense of humor, about his now-and-then bemusement, about his clumsiness." The redrafted version of Logan was a divorced man with a teenage daughter who skips lightly through life's trials. In Reitman's eyes, he would be "a kind of Spencer Tracy sparking off Debra's tough, sassy Kate Hepburn." Redford embraced this with open arms "because it gave me something concrete to hook up to, something to shape these very unreal lives."

But it was plot, not character, that drove *Legal Eagles,* and no amount of redrafting could salvage it. When the sexy client, played by Hannah, comes to Logan's apartment in the middle of the night and gives a silly performance-art recital to a cacophony of cracking fire, bells and whistles, then asks him rather aimlessly how he feels, Logan responds, "Uncomfortable." That, says Redford, encapsulates his escalating emotion during what he increasingly saw as a no-hope production.

Legal Eagles offended Debra Winger, a CAA client like Redford, because she felt Ovitz's "packaging" mania removed all integrity and opportunity. After filming, Winger split with CAA, vowing never to work with Ovitz again. The movie opened with the usual summer vacation razzle-dazzle in June 1986, was slaughtered by critics, made its money back and faded away.

19

One America?

In the disarray of failures—of marriage, friendships and films—one constant remained for Redford: Sundance. Here the ground stayed beneath his feet and the frontier air unfailingly reminded him that all was still possible, that endurance was what mattered most.

When he was away making movies, he was dependent on his sidemen at Sundance. Sterling Van Wagenen proved the most reliably staunch, and his job was to manage an entity in constant flux. There seemed no end to the inflow of youthful talent, and Sundance grew, aided by benefactors like Irene Diamond, whose foundation injected an annual $150,000 for the first couple of years. When Sundance began, Redford's alleged vision was simply for an arts retreat in the mountains where novice filmmakers could be tutored toward making new movies. By the mid-eighties, Sundance had expanded beyond the two-week June lab to encompass a producers' program, a screenwriters' lab, and a dance and theater workshop styled by Merce Cunningham, Michael Kidd and Twyla Tharp. Van Wagenen helped mold these labs but maintained a close focus on the showcasing of films in the shape of the U.S. Film and Video Festival, which had shifted from Salt Lake City to Park City in 1981, then surrendered its operation entirely to Sundance management in 1985. Both Redford and Van Wagenen recognized in the film festival the shopwindow to the world that might elevate the canyon-based arts experiment to something of wider significance. Both collaborated on refining it, and Redford came up with the notion of moving it from September to January ski season, the more to signify its uniqueness.

Redford's declared aim with Sundance was independence for the artist and the avoidance of commercialism. And yet there were painful, obvious paradoxes at play. Sundance, the mother ship resort, was a commercial entity on whose survival the institute depended. Also, the survival and viability of the experimenting artists depended on finding recognition beyond the idyllic glades of the canyon. Wasn't the composition of the infrastructure itself, embodying as it now did an established festival forum, the ideal route for widening the lab artists' audience? Sterling Van Wagenen thought so and felt many of Sundance's woes—a lack of media support, the constant cash flow crises—were curable by the simple expedient of entering into all-out production.

"It was an issue of linearity," says Van Wagenen. "We were coaching independent-thinking young filmmakers to make films, and at the same time we had a presentation forum up the road at Park City. There was no contradiction, in my mind, for anyone in the Sundance fraternity to get involved in actually making films." Redford's absence while preparing for *Out of Africa* and Van Wagenen's impatience would cause the first serious philosophical rift to unhinge Sundance, the effects of which are still felt today.

Under pressure from Van Wagenen, Redford agreed to commit to *Desert Bloom,* a first feature by a newcomer, Eugene Corr, honed in script at the labs, then coproduced by Sundance with funding from Columbia and launched at the festival. Redford knew nothing about Corr, other than that he had directed some long-forgotten PBS drama. *Desert Bloom* was an extremely ambitious film in that it strung a woman's emotional life story together from a series of vignettes, but it also reached beyond, searching for some parallel symbolism between the woman's blooming in a coming-of-age fated romance and the blooming of mushroom clouds in the fifties at Las Vegas bomb test sites, the locale of the story.

All this new development came courtesy of the Production Fund, an executive innovation funded to the tune of $1 million by the NEA, about which Redford maintained the highest suspicions. "There was a philosophical tension," admits Van Wagenen, "between the radicals and the conventionally minded. Bob was a rebel. But the NEA and the Ford Foundation wanted a conventional board, with logical strategies. Gary Beer, acting as business 'brain,' felt the same. To us, the Sundance Production Fund made perfect sense. But Bob was ambivalent, so from my perspective he was green-lighting things and at the same time undermining them with equivocality."

Redford thought Corr's movie was awful. "Corr had talent," he says. "He wrote a very nice script, but he had no experience to make a full-blown feature. After the first two days he handed the movie over to his assistant director. He couldn't watch the dailies." Redford prepared himself for confrontation with Van Wagenen and Beer. "I felt we were overextending at a cost to the filmmakers, and ourselves," he says. "The central principle of Sundance was to give the aspirant filmmakers room to explore and develop their ideas. It was not supposed to be about generating box office. I called up Sterling and told him, 'I have concerns. The institute is a lab, not a preproduction office.' But he was thinking differently."

Van Wagenen was also shepherding a second feature for Sundance, *The Trip to Bountiful,* which was to be directed by Pete Masterson. This was an immaculate Horton Foote script about an elderly woman's determined scheme to escape senile immobility and return to the homeland of her youthful bliss in Bountiful, Texas. It moved forward nimbly with Van Wagenen producing. Both movies would premiere at the 1986 Sundance Film Festival. They faced polar fates. *Desert Bloom* was recut and lambasted. *Bountiful* went on to win a best actress Academy Award for its star, Geraldine Page. That, however, did not please Redford. Resurfacing after *Legal Eagles,* he found a Sundance that felt disembodied and dangerously off-kilter. Recently, the programs had been run by Susan Lacey, of whom he was wary and who supported Van Wagenen's view of Sundance as a production entity. In one Sundance staffer's view, "Bob came back from Africa to discover that Sundance under Sterling, Lacey and Beer was a different business altogether. The accent was not on the students and the debates in the meadows. The accent was on Hollywood production, and the speed with which Lacey and Van Wagenen were pushing this forward."

Yet another Sundance production was already in progress, this time Van Wagenen's version of *The Giant Joshua,* a fictional story based on a dissertation about Mormon polygamy by Maurine Whipple originally published in 1941 and developed by John and Denise Earle. Van Wagenen's initial idea was to produce the movie, with Redford directing. It was clear the dynamic had changed between Van Wagenen and Redford, though, at first, few words were spoken. "I was trying to build a new ethos in those June labs," says Redford. "But we were in danger of becoming an assembly line."

Briefly, Redford went along with the board, endorsing the founding of a new company poised between Wildwood and the Sundance Production Fund, called North Fork Productions, specifically designed to make small-budget movies with Garth Drabinsky, chairman of Cineplex Odeon, an exhibitor with fifteen hundred screens at his disposal. Van Wagenen then announced his plan to direct *The Giant Joshua* himself. The entire process slammed to a dead stop. Van Wagenen felt he had been hijacked. "Bob took the reins from me, without any apology. I was all set, and then suddenly I found myself doing other assigned work."

There were certain things Redford could not compromise on. "He didn't set up the institute to make money," said Hume Cronyn. "I asked him one day, 'How would you like people to remember Sundance in a hundred years?' And he told me, 'Like Walden Pond. A place where some kid, some student, came up with a great idea that changed some lives.' "

Redford used his boardroom-majority prerogative and canceled the Production Fund. Preserving Sundance, he decided, meant doing it his way.

Within Redford's grasp was a project that corralled many of his interests. *The Milagro Beanfield War* was a magic realist novel, the first part of John Nichols's New Mexico trilogy about Hispanic life, myth and history, that exemplified the sanctity of place and the importance of avoiding the machinations of big business. Redford had first encountered it in the seventies, at the time of its publication. Ever since, it had haunted him. Before *Out of Africa,* he had driven impulsively to Taos, where Nichols lived, and discovered that Mocte Esparza, one of the Sundance labs' greatest supporters, owned the rights. Redford approached Esparza and they made a handshake deal to coproduce the film.

Redford admired all the distinctive oddities of *Milagro* (Spanish for "miracle"). Here was a David and Goliath story, where a humble farmer poaches a big developer's lands to access life-sustaining water and, in doing so, stirs an entire community to resist the behemoths. Here, too, was a yarn of ecological wisdom that rang loudly for Redford in the din of Reagan's trickle-down economics, which nudged free enterprise toward an unlegislated free-for-all. Here also was a story of cultural uniqueness, populated with poets and ghosts, all in service of the mythic themes of right and wrong. It seemed like a sparkling expression of Sundance-like ambition.

For Berkeley-born Nichols, the journey to *Milagro* began when he experienced "a conversion to humanist values" during a hiking trip in Guatemala in the sixties. The result was an evangelistic belief that national redemption lay in "securing the integrity of southwestern culture as a foundation for common ethics." Out of this epiphany, the New Mexico trilogy and *Milagro* were born. Nichols and Redford had much in common, including being inspired by the Sangre de Cristo Mountains, where the trilogy was set. Redford felt "an anthropological contact" with them, and a feeling of rightness. "That landscape brought me back to the long, long ago and all those lost wisdoms. You cannot be there and not feel the need to reevaluate. Nichols felt it. I felt it."

Nichols's experience with film was a staggered one. In 1966, at the age of twenty-five, he published a college romance, *The Sterile Cuckoo,* which was made into a movie by Alan Pakula. By the late sixties, he says, he had run dry, his writing suffused with political rage. He exiled himself to New Mexico "because [it] seemed to resemble a colonial country where political struggle could be as clearly focused as it was in four-fifths of the rest of the world." The five hundred pages of *The Milagro Beanfield War,* written over the winter of 1972, was a manifesto that said institutional power begets misery. Over the next five years, a number of players, including CBS, Tony Bill, Dustin Hoffman and Al Pacino, were attached, but the movie failed to take off. The trip wire, says Redford, was its panoramic scope, since the novel had two hundred characters. "But Mocte and I saw it more simply. It could never have been the huge production with the multicharacter viewpoints that John tried. It had to be a reduced ensemble piece cast with Hispanics. Mocte was wary about giving it to me, but when I showed him *Ordinary People,* he said, 'Fine, it's yours.' "

Esparza started the auditions, interviewing two thousand Hispanic actors and videotaping the best one hundred. Nichols's seventh draft of the script, reworked from the single viewpoint of the central character, the impoverished, agitating farmer Joe Mondragon, still did not please Redford. To hone it, he called David Ward, *The Sting*'s writer, whose career had progressed into directing and producing. Ward fashioned a Capraesque story of the homespun hero who takes on the fat cats; Mr. Smith here became a Chicano. "But there was also," says Ward, "the magical realism of the angel Coyote counseling Amarante, the village elder. Amarante says, 'People have forgotten how to speak to angels,' and that summed up the second strand, that greater forces were at work here than small farmers, big developers, lawyers and sheriffs. That's what I took hold of: the double strand. And that's how, finally, the *Milagro* movie began to work." Ten years down the line Ward found Redford more committed than ever. "I was intrigued to see how he had changed, because ten years at the top is ten years in a madhouse. But he was the same, even more so. He was the perfectionist. Social life, family life, everything came second. He was there 200 percent."

Just before his final business separation from Redford, Gary Hendler negotiated a last great deal with Universal for *The Milagro Beanfield War,* delivering a $10 million budget, which was negotiable upward should Redford agree to star in the movie. Redford demurred, insisting that nothing should detract from Hispanic heroes and the integrity of a provincial fable. To appease the studio, he offered compensatory bankable costars in the non-Hispanic roles. But his first choice, Melanie Griffith, whom he thought ideal for Flossie Devine, the seductress wife of Mondragon's land developer bête noire, refused even to audition. "I made an approach but lines got tangled and she probably thought, Who needs that arrogant bastard?" says Redford. Griffith, to her credit, rethought the invitation and agreed to meet at Wildwood's new Rockefeller Center suite, not to audition, she says, but for a one-on-one get-together. Recovering from a bout of drug dependency, she was unsure of herself but, says Redford, disarmingly honest. "We clicked. She was kooky and wild but very full of originality."

Original, too, was the idea to cast Christopher Walken as Kyril Montana, the agent assigned to end the bean field dispute. Redford's thinking was that "this would be a great chance for him to play against type. Because, if you take away the zany haircuts and the weirdness he likes to portray, he's quite WASPish. I wrote to him, explaining, and he responded. So we had casting that pleased Universal over one layer of the movie, and that gave us time to tackle the trickier Hispanic casting."

As Esparza screened his audition tapes, Redford was aware of "subcultural aspects one needed to be careful of. The Hollywood style of generalized ethnicity often destroys movies, but compromises are essential. What I wanted to do was minimize compromise. The challenge was that the pool of talent is so small and diffuse." Seventy-four-year-old Mexican Carlos Riquelme was cast as the oracle Amarante, and Brazilian Sonia Braga ideally fit the role of Chicana activist Ruby. Rubén Blades, the Panamanian salsa songwriter and actor, who wasn't summoned, took the initiative: "The word was out. I knew Redford was having trouble casting the movie. So I went up to him unannounced and said, 'Hey, compadre, how is the lay of the land? You want to do this movie right? Then you want me.' " Blades was cast as Sheriff Bernabe Montoya, the bridge between the warring factions.

The main role of Joe Mondragon remained elusive. Redford considered comedian Cheech Marin, then Edward James Olmos, a relative unknown, and rejected him because of age. Neither seemed fresh or young enough.

Finally Chick Vennera, a Broadway actor hungry for a movie break, arrived at Wildwood's Los Angeles office, recommended by producer Chuck Mulvehill. "Chuck's reasoning," says Vennera, "was that they'd looked everywhere else, so why not me? I wasn't Chicano, but I had Argentinean family and a definite Spanish affinity." Vennera read for Esparza, then went back to his motel. Four hours later he was called back to meet Redford. He read from the Ward script and knew instantly he had cracked it. "I'd done my homework, hanging out in border bars with a tape recorder to get the idiom and the accent. I was confident, fluid."

Filming commenced on what was scheduled as a ten-week shoot in August 1986. Originally, Redford wanted to shoot at Plaza del Cerro, a neighborhood of the town of Chimayo and the location of what is reputed to be the last surviving fortified Spanish plaza in North America. Ironically, the local folk resisted, objecting to any suggestion of commercialization. So the production moved to Truchas, New Mexico, forty miles from the unit base at Santa Fe, and higher in the Sangre de Cristo Mountains. "We had to rewrite the entire production schedule," says Redford. "We were forced to forget Chimayo and shoot it all in the mountains, but that ended up an advantage because all along I'd visualized a bleak, vivid horizon throughout the movie and that was available at the higher elevation."

Casting and location delays put pressure on Redford's schedule. Unlike on *Ordinary People,* he conducted no formal rehearsals. In Vennera's view, Redford "modeled" the movie, frame by frame, with cinematographer Robbie Greenberg. "It was the most extraordinary experience. I had a voice coach, Julie Adams, to keep the Chicano dialect straight, but beyond that artificiality Bob had us work like an improv exercise. We just did what we did as he moved the cameras around us and strategically placed this incredible natural light. A lot of directors will shoot five or six takes to cover themselves. Bob shot a very high ratio for entirely different reasons. He would say, 'Hey, Chick, try this scene that way.' And when I did it, he'd say, 'D'you want to try it your own way now?' That's a luxury actors don't often get. What it did was pump up the actors' esteem. It loaded the whole thing with a new level of emotion. And confidence. I suddenly understood why *Ordinary People* won an Academy Award. I saw that Bob had *a vision,* but within that he was so at ease as to allow everybody to contribute theirs."

The many start-up delays had pushed the shoot into December, a time of heavy seasonal snows in the mountains. The fact that many interiors scheduled for Chimayo had to be replaced with outdoor scenes intensified the problems. "Journalists started writing that there were wasteful delays," says Redford, "that I was doing my usual late shows, all those hoary clichés. But it was garbage. We were going well until the snows stopped us. We couldn't get continuity, we couldn't replace some of the interiors, so we put a nine-month hold on production to wait for the weather."

Redford planned to use the hiatus to spend time in Utah reasserting control over and streamlining Sundance. In Van Wagenen's eyes, Redford "resumed the tiller and let us know he was driving the boat." All production discussion was swept aside in favor of building expansion. New meeting rooms for lab students were already under way, as was a screening theater, partially funded by Hume Cronyn and his wife, Jessica Tandy, and named by them for Cronyn's friend and idol, Joe Mankiewicz. Alongside these was added a state-of-the-art film-editing suite, complete with Sony BVP-330s and broadcast-quality tape decks, equipment comparable with the best Hollywood had to offer and on which Redford would edit *The Milagro Beanfield War*. The other major expansion was the commissioning of thirty-seven new cottages along the aspen-clad southern flank of the central resort base, a critical rental revenue generator, in Brent Beck's opinion, since the rival Park City was draining away vacationers "and in that way undermining the solidity Bob needed for his Sundance vision to take hold."

Redford's greatest ally in this redesign was an old friend, local artist Mary Whitesides. Recently separated from her husband, she became his partner in the creation of a unified style for the new workshops and cottages. Whitesides had already established the Sundance interiors, working with her design partner, Nancy Maynard. Shortly after, *Architectural Digest* would commend their perspicacity: "Everything is natural. Nothing is precious, although a sense of fragility comes from the bouquets of dried wildflowers, the antique quilts and wicker and the Indian artifacts." Redford says, "What we wanted was to express a curatorial sensibility. It was a celebration of tradition. The tables we used were made by craftspeople in Santa Fe. The rawhide-and-iron table lamps were made by local blacksmiths. The plan was to extend this idea so that the resort would become a showcase for western artisanship and tribal folklore."

"[Mary] was the rock," says Brent Beck. "She understood Bob's passion, and she was there to encourage him. They worked very closely. Both Mary's and Bob's fingerprints were in every sheltered porch, every fabric, every fireplace, every bar of soap. He was conceptual; she was in the detail. For example, even though he was southwestern, he wanted to be different.

He wanted a European style. He claimed the Europeans understood use of space in a way Americans didn't. She converted that into an un-American spatial design, with wide, pitched ceilings, cozy nook firesides and intimate bedrooms with the biggest, softest beds. What they both produced was totally original, and it helped him pull back together a feeling of Sundance rooted in his heart."

Jamie sees Whitesides as a savior, no less: "She was among the most sensitive people I've ever met, and her protective affection for him changed him. It was as significant as that. Till then, since the marriage breakdown, his female relationships were fickle. She was a solid friend, and her presence at that time boosted Sundance to the next level."

In the fall of 1987 Redford returned eagerly to Truchas and resumed *Milagro.* The pressure was renewed. Members of the crew dropped out. He wasn't getting the performances he'd hoped for. "A couple of loose performances can throw a movie off," says Redford, "and here I failed. I saw more in characters like Mondragon than I was able to realize on-screen, to my great regret." He began a romance with Sonia Braga. She was thirty-six, tagged in the tabloids as the queen of Brazilian soaps but, in fact, a distinguished actress with quality roles behind her in Manuel Puig's arcane *Kiss of the Spider Woman* and Bruno Barreto's *Dona Flor and Her Two Husbands.* "Some magic obviously happened," says Vennera, for whose child Braga babysat, "and I think it came because of Bob's isolation. He had very few friends on location. Tom Brokaw joined us for a few days, and he was a jogging companion. Bernie [Pollack] and Gary [Liddiard] took lunches with him. But he was basically a loner, a sensitive soul, and my wife and I saw that he needed a woman's company."

The romance hit the headlines in May 1988 when, returning from a film festival trip to the Soviet Union, Redford met with Braga at Cannes, where his movie featured out of competition at the annual festival. By August they were in *Newsweek* and *People,* pictured at the Nostros Awards for Hispanic Achievement, where Redford conceded, "So, the secret's out?"

Milagro premiered in the United States in March. It barely covered its costs and suffered the loud disdain of critics like David Denby, who derided its muddled story line about "picturesque Chicanos." Roger Ebert's review diagnosed some of the problems. The movie, said Ebert, was a wonderful fable, "but the problem is, some of the people in the story know it's a fable and others do not. This causes an uncertainty that runs all through the film, making it hard to weigh some scenes against others. There are characters who seem to belong in an angry documentary . . .

and then there are characters who seem to come from a more fanciful time."

Redford consoled himself in the activism that was ever present but never fully integrated. Ted Wilson had been wrong in his belief that politics would swallow him up. But Redford never let up, staying in touch politically, investigating PACs and keeping a hand in EDF and NRDC initiatives. "It was hard to hang in there politically or spiritually [in the time of Reagan], but it was harder to quit," he says. "The realities spat in your face. Yes, Reaganomics created a boom. But the poor suffered. After Reagan crushed PATCO [the air traffic controllers' union], labor rights fell apart. The old industrial infrastructure gave way to the growing service sector, but there was no proper labor protection movement left. There were no safety nets for the poor, for the environment, for anyone. Anyone with a heart watched all this tragedy play out against the backdrop of ballyhoo about the Soviet 'evil empire,' and just went crazy. More than a hundred people in the Reagan administration eventually stood trial for corruption. But the media dumbed down to meet the sleaze. I felt the national fault lines were wider than ever, and I wanted to do my bit to bridge them."

"I knew he would get more involved," says former senator Bill Bradley, a close friend since his days with the New York Knickerbockers basketball team, "because he was outraged by national policy. Apart from the budget deficit and the racial and poverty bias, there was a terrible acceptance of environmental abuse. As a senator, obviously, it was my job to address this mess. But Bob was every bit as responsive. It got to the point where he said enough is enough. He took off the gloves and got back in the ring."

The Institute for Resource Management (IRM) was Redford's instrument of attack. Entirely of his own design, he convened a series of eco-conferences coordinated with NRDC's Citizen National Enforcement Program. At first Washington and the media shrugged them off. But the 1984 program that became known as the Bering Sea Accord changed that. Redford and his associate Paul Parker brought together representatives of nineteen oil companies, among them Standard Oil, Conoco and Texaco, along with conservation representatives from Alaska, for four sessions over a ten-month period to resolve a twenty-year debate over offshore oil drilling. The conservationists wanted to maintain the world's richest salmon grounds, which were also home to endangered species of whales, walrus and seals. The oil companies wanted to mine what is regarded as America's greatest untapped reserve. In the session staged on a boat in Morro Bay in late summer, the energy industry in effect stood down—temporarily—agreeing to conduct further research. Terry Minger, whom Redford had met on the *Outlaw Trail* ride, now an IRM executive, believed a miracle had been accomplished: "And the achievement was Redford's. IRM's function was to come to these conferences as a neutral body, which erred, if it erred, on the side of the environmentalists. Bob had learned from Kaiparowits, and he earned the trust of the industrialists by showing himself to be a rationalist first of all. He accepted that jobs and the economy were of supreme importance. He knew it was counterproductive to insult the other side. So instead he promoted exchange of information, education, understanding." The stand-down might not last forever, but the new research studies each side agreed on appeased everyone. Max Pitcher, vice president of exploration for Conoco, was effusive in his praise for Redford's ingenious moderation: "His message to both sides was, 'Don't be intractable. We have problems we must resolve as partners.' He lit the way for shared decision making."

At the following Canyon de Chelly conference, representatives of the Navajo Nation and the energy companies argued the development of the Southwest. Once again, the combatants were at first mutually unsympathetic. Redford took center stage, said Minger, doubly passionate because of his kinship with Native Americans. In his opening speech he pleaded for "balance in the inevitable land exploitation of a development-orientated society." Peterson Zah, the Navajo chairman and an IRM board member, responded with an angry recital of the damage already done: there were fifty million acres of Indian land in America; in the West, most were already scarred, with no less than three major generating stations and a dozen coal mines in the Canyon de Chelly reservation alone. "Labor benefits apart," said Zah, "there is a dilemma for us Indians if we continue to think this way about ourselves." According to Navajo legend, said Zah, humanity rose from the land and air around it: "Their skin from the red earth, their teeth from the white corn, their hair from the black thundercloud." Redford found Zah's speech "emotionally moving and intellectually motivating." Some weeks before, he'd met Wallace Stegner, his favorite western author, at an Ansel Adams exhibition in San Francisco. Stegner and Adams and Zah were calling attention to the same thing: that our nature, and our destiny, are defined by the environment that bred us and how we maintain it. "Occupying the planet seemed to me to be about stewardship," says Redford. "More and more I felt education was the tool to bring a workable peace to the rival factions. And roundtable talk in a depoliticized atmosphere was the place to start."

The notion for a major global warming summit to crown the IRM's work came in November 1987, during the last phase of making *Milagro,* while Redford was attending the Denver Symposium on Clean Air. Redford was riveted by a slide show about the buildup of carbon dioxide in the atmosphere presented by John Firor of the National Center for Atmospheric Research. The point was made that global warming was second only to nuclear holocaust as an imminent annihilatory threat. "I hadn't registered the phrase 'greenhouse effect' before," says Redford. "It suddenly struck me that *no one* was getting this message. The planet was in trouble, and we were arguing Republican versus Democratic policies. Someone needed to say, 'Hey, pay attention!' " Minger, newly elected president of the IRM, sat with Redford at the symposium. "He was keen to raise our international profile," said Minger. "Human survival seemed a good place to start."

Redford had recently accepted an invitation from the Moscow U.S. Information Agency for a movie retrospective to be hosted by the Tashkent Film Festival. In advance of the trip he took the opportunity to write to the U.S.S.R. Academy of Sciences in his role as IRM chairman, requesting an international conference on environmental change. Global warming was, of course, of concern for some scientists in Moscow. The national policy of *uskorenie,* or accelerated industrialization, paralleled America's thirst for corporate mergers and industrial expansion through the eighties and created the same kinds of pollution problems. Since the days of Benjamin Franklin, the Russian Academy of Sciences had exchanged information with American scientists, but the cold war put an end to that. Still, for more than twenty years, a sector of the Soviet scientific community had continued to research pollutants. In 1968 the Nobel laureate Andrei Sakharov appealed for a "law of geohygiene" to save the planet from "the poison of industrial pollutants produced in the United States and the U.S.S.R." Early in 1987 a minisummit in the form of a teleconference initiated by Roald Sagdeev of the Russian Space Research Institute, together with *Apollo 9* astronaut Rusty Schweickart and Walter Orr Roberts, the founder of the Colorado-based National Center for Atmospheric Research, opened the door for a new channel of bilateral exchange, which created an opportunity for Sundance. "To my surprise," says Redford, "the cooperation was immediate. This was the eve of the collapse of the Soviet bloc. Gorbachev was in power, but we had no way then of knowing how compliant he would be. We knew whispers about Russian democracy in the making, but that was all. Reagan still viewed the Soviets as the evil empire. But Gorbachev was lowering the drawbridge. It was he who facilitated ease of passage for us. Once we had the nod, the walls came down."

Redford was invited to cochair a workshop on global warming with the academy, which he did en route to Cannes for the festival showing of *Milagro.* Terry Minger, accompanying him, was astonished by the Soviets' openness. "It wasn't a hard sell at all," said Minger. "There was a great willingness to reverse the damage of *uskorenie.* We found friends there." During the Moscow workshop an agreement was signed for Sundance to host the first major climate change summit, christened Greenhouse Glasnost, the following summer. The speed of events, from perestroika to the Sundance symposium, said Minger, was extraordinary.

Back in New York, Redford employed what NRDC founding director John Adams calls "that old riverboat charisma" to draw together luminaries from all the relevant political, industrial and scientific fields for the symposium. Sagdeev, Schweickart and Roberts, the pioneers, were joined by Cecil Andrus, Howard Allen, astronomer Carl Sagan, U.S.S.R. consul general Valentin Kamenev, U.N. World Federation president Maurice Strong, Frederic Krupp and Michael Oppenheimer of the EDF and Richard Morgenstern of the EPA. Also among the seventy-member discussion panel were Susan Eisenhower, Bill Bradley, Stewart Udall, Rhode Island congresswoman Claudine Schneider and Adams. "It was an amazing feat of diplomacy," says Adams, "in which Bob applied every trick of his iconography and every social and political skill to bring so many different people to the same table. He had boundless energy and marvelous ideas. I still shake my head in admiration at the memory of Carl Sagan strolling in the woods with Garry Trudeau and a gaggle of Soviet scientists and arguing world survival. What a rainbow of talents, and exactly the right cross section of power brokers to redress the situation."

The coordination of the event absorbed three months of Sundance time, nudging aside film labs and tourist hikes. But the summit itself, says Bill Bradley, proved "the sort of democratic powerhouse that D.C. would be jealous of, probably was." There were lectures, debates, science shows, one-on-one lunches and suppers with translators running late into the nights. Out of it all came an open letter to Gorbachev—now, seemingly overnight, the leader of a neodemocracy—and George H. W. Bush, Reagan's successor as president. The heart of the letter was an appeal to both nations to formulate a shared global warming policy: "The U.S.A. and the U.S.S.R. are the two largest producers of greenhouse gases. The U.S.S.R. and the U.S.A. are also the two principal sources of the world's scientific knowledge which can be employed to restrain emissions." Both nations were asked to commit to "(1) the promotion of nonpolluting technologies, (2) the phasing out of chlorofluorocarbon emissions before 2000, (3) the reduction of worldwide deforestation, and (4) the initiation of a series of joint national educational programs."

The Sundance symposium foreshadowed the premier U.N. Earth Summit, held in Rio de Janeiro in June 1992. Major participants like Bradley and Adams imagined a breakthrough. "After all," says Bradley, "we as a community had time to look at the research and check the statistics. We had the evidence by then of how the planet was suffering." But when the time came, under Bush administration policy, the United States joined the Rio summit and, says Bradley, "sat on its hands." Ironically—inexcusably, says Adams—the Sundance debaters had virtually no representation. "No one in the current administration was too much interested, so we were elbowed out of position." For Al Gore, an ambitious senator not yet embarked upon a career in conservation, the Rio summit was "a disaster for America, and for the planet." Global pollution control, whether the United States liked it or not, *was* in the offing. But, though Sundance and the Rio summit requested legislated assurances of reduction in carbon dioxide emissions from all the leading nations, the United States' refusal to commit was a backward step, said Gore, in which America was setting a dangerous precedent of renewed isolation.

"I was exhilarated by the symposium and shattered by the play-out," says Redford. "You could say we achieved everything, and nothing. Rio proved that people everywhere were concerned. The old nonsense about it coming down to a battle of clean environment versus jobs no longer stood. There were economic statistics that showed no substantial conflict. What was needed was new thinking. We presented a new forum at the symposium and people listened. The science community wanted it. The diplomats wanted it. But government let us down."

"I was upset for Bob," says Adams, "because he shone a light and the politicians didn't care. He had spent a decade trying to bring academics, government officials and environmentalists together. In a wise world the IRM would have evolved into the president's permanent counsel. That never happened. Instead, it was ignored, squeezed, forgotten."

The IRM's demise became an issue of debate among the Sundance staffers and beyond. Many felt relieved that Redford was freeing himself from institutional politics and moving back toward film. Van Wagenen believed "it was best, because he lived, breathed and ate movies. He was a film artist before he was anything, and when he wasn't making films, he was uptight, a fish out of water." Indeed, Adams recognized as much and saw the cause of the IRM's failure in Redford himself: "The greatest asset of the IRM was his mind, and his intuition for deal making. But a part of his psyche was elsewhere, and he handed the power over to Minger and others. What the IRM needed as a fixture was a political tactician who could work both sides to fuse the middle. I believed Bob was that man. He had years of experience in the tough arena of show business, and he was masterly at resolving disputes. I finally thought, Politics' loss is the movie world's gain."

20

Beyond Hurricane Country

The students still came, the programs were ongoing, but Sundance was for most of the country largely invisible.

The entire operation, Redford came to believe, needed better, more effective, more widespread branding; with that, the indispensable media exposure would follow. A new approach was called for. "I knew I was scattered," says Redford. "I knew I was fair game for those who accused me of being a dabbler or stretching too far. But I was never offended by failure. In fact, risk was the lodestar."

The Production Fund may have failed and political forums may not have raised awareness enough, but in 1989 a modestly budgeted movie made by a twenty-five-year-old southerner would accomplish what Redford hoped for, electrifying the January film festival and propelling Sundance to the media center stage. At the beginning of the eighties, according to lab student and NYU film school graduate Tom DiCillo, New Yorkers viewed Sundance, labs and festival, as the home of the granolafest. "Before I first came there," says DiCillo, who was a cameraman for Jim Jarmusch, another lab attendee, "we laughed about Sundance. We associated it with boring pastorals about 'going home' and 'returning to the land.' " But there was far more to Sundance "product" than Utahan ideals or the mild, bucolic movies Van Wagenen had pursued. Redford saw this problem of recognition as deep-rooted. For many, it was hard to distinguish the labs, where the works in progress were nurtured with advisers, from the festival, where a committee selected new movies from far and wide to reflect the Sundance aspiration of diversity. Sometimes the lab projects grew into finished features with no help from Sundance beyond the script phase; these were often premiered at the festival. At other times the festival films were outside productions, with no prior association. The very first lab, in 1981, generated *El Norte,* a story about Guatemalan immigrants cowritten by Gregory Nava and Anna Thomas, which won a festival premiere and critical admiration on its cinema release two years later; *Three Thousand,* workshopped by Jonathan Lawton in 1988, would shortly metamorphose into the popular studio hit *Pretty Woman.* These successes strengthened Redford's belief in a new-style infrastructure for movie development. "The granola idea was anathema to me," says Redford. "I recognized where our earliest endeavors might have been misread, but the deduction was wrong. What I wanted in the labs was experiment. What I sought in the festival was variety."

The head of the selection committee for the remodeled film festival was Geoff Gilmore, the former head of the UCLA Film and Television Archive's programming department. For him, there was no "standard" Sundance festival movie: "We decided to go for the broadest range, ideological, marginal, countercultural, whatever. The charm, in fact, is that we decided we wanted no real definition other than newness. The idea was, Let us take down the barriers and bring an alternative stream of movies to the public."

For the 1989 festival, Gilmore chose Atlanta-born newcomer Steven Soderbergh's *sex, lies, and videotape,* a movie with a shoestring budget written in eight days and shot in thirty, about marital relationships and voyeurism. It won the audience prize and, crucially, distribution from the new marketing lion Miramax and would go on to win its writer-director a Palme d'Or at Cannes and an Academy Award nomination. "It wasn't something I personally connected with," said Sundance adviser Hume Cronyn, "but I saw how it was perfect for spotlighting the Sundance Bob wanted. The truth remained that the Sundance the board of governors imagined and the one Bob wanted weren't the same thing. Soderbergh's approach was radical, and that was Bob's kind of Sundance." Radical, Redford knew, wasn't sufficient. Sundance offerings must connect with the widest audience if the breakthrough of media acknowledgment was to happen. Soderbergh proved the perfect bridge.

The achievement for Soderbergh—and Sundance—was sizable. By the end of the eighties, cinema was in lockstep with the growth of technology, dominated by *Batman* and its look-alikes. There were still plenty of thoughtful movies about, including, in 1989, *Driving Miss Daisy* and *Dead Poets Society.* But *sex, lies, and videotape* employed Godardesque innovation, seeking, as Godard would seek, to film life—"to discover life in film, and discover film in life"—by using the homemade confessional newly available in the domestic video age. It was intimate; it was original. The movie was made for $3 million, without studio backing, and delivered via Sundance and Miramax to the kind of mass audience only available to big studio productions. Prizes apart, it earned almost $25 million, validating Sundance's pledge of experimentation. Soderbergh, in Roger Ebert's description, became "the poster boy for Sundance."

Victory was snatched from the jaws of defeat. The moneymen like Gary Beer and Brent Beck, whose job it was to balance the books, had felt Sundance was teetering on bankruptcy. Said Beer: "It was only a matter of time before major packages of land and development went up for sale because, to put it simply, Bob had us ridiculously overcommitted." To their credit, Beck and Beer had moved to solve the Sundance financial crisis by introducing a mail-order Sundance catalog. "To be honest, it took no great ingenuity," says Beck. "Sundance was known as a southwestern endeavor, and to most of our visitors Bob was still the Sundance Kid. Trading on the design paraphernalia that he and Mary Whitesides conceived was a no-brainer." Shortly before the breakthrough festival, the Sundance mail-order catalog was born, advertised first statewide, then nationally. Its launch in September 1989 cost $500,000, and though it provided vital new credit lines, it took four years to turn a profit.

The Soderbergh film brought the desired press attention, but also scrutiny. Redford was forced to face up to accusations of poor managerial skills. According to anonymous sources interviewed for a *Premiere* magazine story, indecision was Redford's main failing. The replacement of program director Susan Lacey by Tom Wilhite, formerly of Disney, led to division within the boardroom. One staffer recalled, "Wilhite was Bob's man, and those of us who were at the coal face for years felt neglected. We were just overlooked about his appointment, or the initiatives. Sundance was supposed to be about democracy and cooperative art, but that's not how it looked to us." To add insult to injury, Redford then interfered with Wilhite's new initiatives and awarded money to established writers who'd decided to change careers, moving, say, from television to film writing, without consulting anyone. "People started to wonder was Redford in control at all," said the staffer. Cinda Holt, a senior administrator, felt Redford's personal control was positive and vital but, at the same time, his distractions with projects like *Milagro* and the unending political activism weighed against a stable future.

The distractions would only continue, despite Redford's best intentions. The pattern was already established by now. Activism and film had to be parts of his life. Even as Holt and others were raising their concerns, he was producing a documentary about Yosemite with Van Wagenen and director-photographer Jon Else and, at last, a version of the Leonard Peltier story, called *Incident at Oglala,* with Michael Apted directing. Hume Cronyn spoke with the nascent mutineers but was unsympathetic. "I didn't agree with all his choices, but the way I saw it, Bob was assembling a delicate picture puzzle at Sundance. That required momentum and great dexterity. Remember, there was no independent cinema movement then. There was just the Hollywood way, then some crazy guys making little movies out in the boondocks. Bob was pioneering, he was laying the ground for a whole new cultural movement, and there was no map for that. He just played it day by day, doing the best he could." Cronyn especially admired the efforts of Redford, Gilmore and lab director Michelle Satter to extend the awareness of alternative moviemaking to the Latin and Far Eastern markets, persuading Gabriel García Márquez to convene a special lab for South American filmmakers and organizing a mini Sundance Film Festival in Tokyo. "But it was exhausting work for such a small-scale setup. I remember meeting Bob out jogging one morning, and he looked like an old man, so drained. I said all the platitudes and I invited him down to my home in the Bahamas, because I knew he needed time out, but he was just too busy."

Among the distractions was the decline in Jamie's health. Though Jamie had effectively diagnosed himself, the years of inaccurate treatment for his ulcerative colitis—where the body attacks the lining of the large intestine—had created other problems. His first major health collapse had occurred in 1981, shortly after *Ordinary People.* His body went into spasms and he suffered crippling arthritic-like pain that had him bedridden for days. But this wasn't an aggressive colitis attack, as diagnosed, and it would take many more years before the true extent of his illness became known. By the late eighties Jamie had abandoned hopes of a career in rock music because of his constant collapses. He had decided to return to his studies and move with his CU girlfriend, Kyle Smith, to Chicago, where he would study at Northwestern University Graduate School. "While I was transferring from my doctor in Utah to one in Chicago," says Jamie, "I was given a newly detailed series of tests, which included liver function. The result was black-and-white. The doctor came out and said to me, 'You have an end-term liver disease. But the good news is, you can get a transplant.' " It emerged that the wrong drugs prescribed over so many years had aggravated an underlying chronic liver ailment, and permanent liver damage had been done.

At the time, Jamie was in remission, suffering no symptoms. "So I backed off. I told Dad, 'I'll fix it my way, don't worry.' And I tried, I really tried. I tried acupuncture, herbs, every sort of quack cure." Redford took great joy in the fact that family life was stabilizing. In 1986 Shauna had finally emerged from the shadows of Sidney Wells's murder to marry the new man in her life, Eric Schlosser, the journalist son of Herb Schlosser, president of NBC. Jamie married Kyle in June 1988, shortly before his planned transfer to Northwestern. But soon afterward he collapsed and was hospitalized. "The Jesuit chaplain visited me at the hospital and asked my views on life and death," says Jamie. "That was *the* moment. It suddenly hit me: I'm really ill. I can die at any moment." Bothered by the insensitivity of the Jesuit, Jamie set out on a three-month exploration of faith, visiting dozens of churches and spiritual centers. He found sanctuary, temporarily, with the Unitarians. "There were limitations to what Dad could provide, and the Unitarians filled the void. I was different from my father. I was a believer in chaos theory. Dad was a believer in benevolent fate. I remember flying from Vegas to Utah with him during *The Electric Horseman.* We had time totally alone on the mountain then. Suddenly I understood that he viewed that tranquillity as a God-given thing. He had a superstitious religious outlook that was half Indian, half Christian. All of his life was a meditation on the interpretation of *the signs.* If he thought about some old friend and then the next day that friend called, he believed it was purposeful fate. I was not like that. I saw the mountain as nature, nothing with an agenda. Dad had 'belief' in a way I didn't, and the Unitarians, who believe in no afterlife, helped me accept the roll of the dice, the bare, pragmatic realities."

Amy describes her father's response to Jamie's illness as "that stubborn old mechanism of 'You cannot succumb to the false mythologies—it's *all* about winning.' " Redford concedes this might be true but adds, "I could not imagine the loss of Jamie, and wouldn't tolerate the concept. I was proud of him as a fighter. At his weakest moment I sat by his bedside and held his hand and told him, 'There's all sorts of *right* things I should say. But let me just cut to it: you have to get this devil off your back. You know that? You have to beat it.' "

Redford paused to reevaluate the allotment of his time. For the moment, the world of formal politics had lost its luster. There was progress on environmental reform: Wayne Owens was back in Congress after a twelve-year hiatus and was beginning to work the wilderness initiatives they'd long discussed; Bruce Babbitt, the Democrats' torchbearer since Gary Hart fell out of the 1988 presidential race, was another new friend with a strong, hopeful reformist slant. But Ted Wilson believed a fire had gone out in his friend: "[Bob] was upset by the ignominious outcome of Gary Hart's campaign, because he'd supported him very actively. On top of that was the disappointment of the IRM. All of it had a cumulative effect and movies seemed to be a far safer bet."

But the movies were far from a safe bet in the wake of *Legal Eagles* and *The Milagro Beanfield War*. For a decade Redford had off and on given the appearance of being bored and disinterested. Now he was forced to remind himself of the continuing importance of his maintaining a high profile to help Sundance. What he still had going for him was his working relationship with Mike Ovitz. And Ovitz had ideas, principal of which was packaging Redford with Spielberg. Spielberg was in an unassailable position, having raked in fortunes with successive megahits over fifteen years and won three Oscars. His latest nostalgic notion was to remake the 1943 Spencer Tracy movie *A Guy Named Joe,* a love story set among firefighters in national parks. Spielberg and Redford met at Spielberg's home, which was filled with amusement park items like gumball machines and arcade games, and watched the Victor Fleming–directed film in the den. But Redford was uncomfortable and found "no reason to remake a movie that was pretty average to begin with." (The movie was finally made by Spielberg, retitled *Always,* and starring Richard Dreyfuss.) An alternative was offered by Disney. Frank Wells, now Disney's president and chief operating officer under chairman Michael Eisner, liked and trusted Redford and let it be known he wanted him under contract. Maybe Wildwood could nominate some mutually interesting projects that would unite Redford and Disney?

Redford's hesitation reflected his recognition of the importance of choosing the right project after such a lengthy fallow period, but also his awareness of the changes in cinema. Soderbergh's breakthrough seemed a signal moment not just for Sundance, but for moviemaking in general. By the end of the eighties, the status quo as it existed in the twenties still prevailed. The industry still functioned as an elite club, whose membership was never more than twenty-five thousand. The eight major studios (Columbia, Disney, MGM/UA, Orion, Paramount, Twentieth Century–Fox, Universal and Warners) still monopolized distribution and the box office, their takings amounting to 80 percent of all movie earnings. Their required packaging and slick marketing-cum-distribution had become far more expensive. Gary Lucchesi, the new president of Paramount, defined the working model: for the average movie, $3 to $7 million was spent on the star name, about $2 million on the director and $1 on the script. Then untold millions were invested in marketing. When the humorist Art Buchwald sued Paramount for the theft of an idea that became Eddie Murphy's *Coming to America,* Paramount argued that the movie, even though it had earned $350 million, had yet to show a profit. Such profligate extravagance was bound to run aground, and it did when reform-minded David Puttnam became Columbia's chairman and refused to support the overweight Warren Beatty movie *Ishtar.* Puttnam further offended Ovitz by stating emphatically that his studio would no longer have anything to do with star packages. By the dawn of the new decade, Ovitz's brief shining moment was past and studios were in the process of redefining themselves. Disney, under Wells and Eisner—who imported Jeffrey Katzenberg from Paramount to manage the movie and TV divisions—was now, unthinkably, earning its way with a fair smattering of R-rated movies, such as Paul Mazursky's *Down and Out in Beverly Hills.* "It was a different playing field then," says Redford. "Home video loosened it up, and investigative journalism shook out the fat cats, as when Begelman was busted for fiddling his clients' checks. What we had in the early nineties was a jerky period of culture growth that meant more was possible in the mainstream than had been for years."

Briefly Redford contemplated Manny Azenberg's offer of a return to Broadway in Arthur Miller's *The Crucible,* which, wrote Azenberg, "[Mike] Nichols believes you should do, and has agreed to direct for virtually nothing." When Redford finally refused, Azenberg came up with the idea of Redford and Pollack in *The Odd Couple.* "I don't recall that as anything other than a joke," says Redford.

Redford found himself having supper again with Pollack and discussing a new project, the Universal-funded *Havana,* to be set in Batista-era Cuba. Jamie, who, among the family, was closest to the Pollacks, was stunned by what he called "the volte-face," believing the friendship had "irrevocably ended with the breach of trust during *Out of Africa.*" Alan Pakula saw things differently: "No one 'read' Bob like Sydney. The eighties had not been great for Bob. The world was different. So maybe the call of the familiar was the attraction."

Pollack had fallen in love with Cuba when he first visited with Mary Hemingway in 1978. "I was struck by every aspect of it," said Pollack.

"The architecture. The climate. The people. The danger. The hope. I saw immediately what Hemingway got out of it, and I imagined what it must have been like while he was there and the future was up for grabs." The script, originally commissioned from Judith Rascoe, grew in fits and starts over the next ten years and was finished by David Rayfiel. "Think 1950s, an all-American fast-talking gambler falling in love with a Communist gangster's moll in the political turmoil of the Caribbean, with Sydney directing," says Rayfiel. "It *had to* be Bob." Carlin Glynn, still a regular participant in the Sundance labs, doubted that Redford and Pollack could patch up their differences. Pollack's commitment to Sundance, beyond his ownership of a house in the canyon tract, had now diminished to nothing. His life was fully absorbed in mainstream Hollywood, with the offices of his development company, Mirage, shifting from one studio lot to another. "It became quite a mysterious alliance [between Redford and Pollack]," says Glynn. "And the kind of films each wanted to make were just different. To attempt another collaboration at that point seemed like the craziest folly."

Redford's desire to repair the friendship equaled his need to rebuild his career—and his need to fortify Sundance. "I had an affection for Sydney that never waned. I also admired his creative skills and appreciated what he gave to me in those twenty years of good collaboration." At the end of the eighties, the gift Pollack bore was an intriguing demi-hero called Jack Weil in a psychologically involving romance. In Rascoe's plot, inveterate, expert gambler Weil heads for Cuba in the last days of the Batista regime, befriending Roberta (Lena Olin), the wife of rebel leader Dr. Arturo Duran (Raul Julia), on the Key West ferry. The country is about to fall to the revolutionaries, and Weil's guess is that the high rollers will hit the casinos for one last big game. This, he reckons, is his last chance for a big score. His efforts are compromised by his passion for Roberta, which becomes a dangerous involvement when Duran mysteriously disappears. The love story evolves into suspense, building to a bittersweet finale that echoes Cuba's fate.

For Pollack (and, later, several critics) Weil was a quasi Finch Hatton, another adventurer inured to true human engagement—perhaps, indeed, an opportunity to "correct" Finch Hatton. Redford saw something entirely different. His identification with Weil, he says, was his strongest since the Jeremiah Johnson character. "No role is strictly autobiographical, but you transfer your ethos and experience. Weil was one of my more interesting characters because I related to his personal journey. He goes to Cuba looking out only for himself. Then he meets Roberta and attachment comes into it. One learns that there is no true state of independence. You can be as rebellious as you like, but finally you conform in order to survive, or to help those you love survive. Weil was fascinating because he made a snap decision to adjust his belief system. He was a man at the end of a long journey acknowledging the limits of his dream and facing up. It resonated personally."

Little of the old-style collaboration accompanied this, their seventh movie together, but Redford threw himself heartily into it, believing that the movie also had "something to say about the tragedy of Cuba." Pollack said, "We were bound by a belief that a huge part of Latin culture is lost to Americans. This movie isn't overt social commentary in any way, but I like to think most of my movies shot against political events stimulate productive discussion. I think Bob and I liked where we started on *Havana*."

The movie was filmed partly in Key West, mostly in Santo Domingo in the Dominican Republic. Redford loved the foreign location for its richness, verdantly opposite but not unlike the New Mexico of *Milagro*, where he'd just taken a long-term lease on a hideaway home. The location calmed the tensions between the men, if only because its remoteness isolated them from the irritations of routine life. For a while they bonded as of old, hanging out together with Pollack's brother, Bernie, exploring the hill town bars and flying to and from locations in Pollack's plane. Under the surface, though, the scars of *Out of Africa* festered. Michael Ritchie believed that the reforged union was doomed by the men's recent histories.

Havana became an overlong (almost six-month) shoot that *The Washington Post* blamed on "overstudied" plotting. In classic Pollack style, the script was being constantly reworked by Rayfiel, but it could not, said Michael Ritchie, get away from the fact that it was really a rehashed and uncredited *Casablanca*. "It was quite brazen, actually. In *Casablanca* Bogey is nuts about the sexy Swede, Ingrid Bergman, who's married to the underground leader Paul Henreid. In *Havana* it's Bob mad about the sexy Swede, Lena Olin, who's married to the rebel leader played by Raul Julia. Even the musical atmospherics are copied, with *Casablanca*'s Dooley Wilson replaced by vintage Sinatra. I think the hard laboring was caused by Sydney and his writers striving too hard." Redford blames the shadow of *Out of Africa*. "I think that movie set the bar too high, in Sydney's mind. He was trying hard, too hard, to make *Havana* something it couldn't be."

Redford had wanted Jane Fonda to play Robe
on Olin, who had come to prominence in *The*
Being and *Enemies: A Love Story.* In Redford's view
sented "a perfect foil" to leaven his creation of
it turned out, Olin's Scandinavian theater-train
often against his loose, shoot-from-the-hip, part-
is not to say she wasn't a fine actress."

Pollack contended that the friendship stayed
tions over Redford's work habits grew. "It was n
lem this time, but his refusal to *do the homework*
Jack Weil's dexterity with cards was essential. So
groom him and I begged him to practice. But he
or two was all he'd put in. His attitude was, 'I c
been playing poker for forty years!' "

Redford insists he did the homework. "But we
I, too, was a director, and I sometimes saw the s
that, and maybe it caused tensions. Also, I was
trolling my relationship with the leading actress,
of Africa. I was comfortable in my own space."

In the judgment of many, Redford insidiously
that *Havana* became his. Alongside the other R
tions it stands alone in mood and inflection,
individualism stamped clearly throughout. The
the moral values, the societal judgments, the v
his. David Rayfiel states that Redford had sma
input, adding depth to characters beyond his c
but he had a vision of its tone, and Sydney didr

The handful of wry lines written by Rayfiel as
among Redford's favorites. Weil saves Roberta's
from the coming revolution. He returns alon
scene he walks down to the ocean in a bleak su
a new decade," he says in voice-over. "I'm doir
not the same. I sit with my back to the wall, wat
know who's going to walk in. Somebody blow
cane country." The strife of existence and the
mands, says Redford, are what *Havana* is abo
area so rare in Hollywood films. When Jack W
stitutes one dream for another. First he's a h

Eberts. Redford had taken Eberts's advice that a James Bond–type franchise was possible, optioned all the books for Wildwood and, with Eberts, made a funding deal with Columbia. The deal also involved complex product placement sponsorship for shortfall funding, where individual commodities are promoted by being featured in the movies. It was hardly worth the bother. Errol Morris, maker of the award-winning indie *The Thin Blue Line,* was assigned to direct the first movie, and Lou Diamond Phillips was cast as Officer Jim Chee. The decision to shoot entirely within the Navajo and Hopi reservations of Arizona for authenticity immediately mired the production. There were accusations of cynical cost cutting by engaging lowest-salaried extras and exploiting Native American resources without payment. Redford was forced to interrupt work on *Havana* to intervene. "But his real mistake," says Wildwood producer Patrick Markey, a friend of Redford's since *Brubaker,* "was that he didn't insist on actually directing the movie himself. Bob had the Indian sensibilities; Errol did not. I tried to fire Errol in the first week, because his attitude to the Native Americans was all wrong. We got sunk, financially, morally, in every way, because of Errol's patronizing attitude. We called in Bob because we had to rebuild faith quickly before we lost the extras, the backgrounds, everything."

Joyce Deep was summoned to stem the rebellion. Her reward was an invitation to join what Redford now decided was Sundance's "second team," whose environmental crusade, locally and nationally, would go on. "I checked him out," says Deep, "and I judged him to be a brilliant national cultural asset who was really, worryingly disorganized. The reason I joined was his energy, which reminded me of Mike Dukakis's. He was very holistic, very universal in his approach to culture and politics. I understood quickly that he was overcommitted with the movies and what he then called 'the Sundance entities.' It was a complicated situation that covered national environmental awareness, local energy issues in Utah, fund-raising for his nonprofit arts institute and all the other bits and pieces of commercial endeavor in retail catalogs, farm produce, the resort, et cetera. It seemed unmanageable, but he wanted help to simplify it. There was no grand plan. It was all in motion. He asked me how I saw it, and I said, 'It's all about reprioritization.' He liked that. We agreed that was a great place to start."

The employment of Deep, Ted Wilson felt, cast the mold for all future activism. "He basically said, 'From now on I'll fight the battles by proxy.

I'll support the key congressional movers, I'll debate in the op-eds, but I'll do it at one point remove. Stop thinking of me as an elective candidate. I'm a moviemaker.' " Redford was supporting NRDC's campaign to block Congress from exempting nuclear reactors from the provisions of the Clean Air Act, activism that brought him close to Julie Mack, another new assignee. Mack was the prime organizer of the Utah Clean Air Coalition, which he had joined in the highway-planning dispute. She became his environmental spokesperson, aligning Sundance with the newly formed Utah Wilderness Coalition to help draft a Citizens' Proposal Bill, to counteract a wilderness-limiting Republican proposal that was in the offing. Logan-born Mack professed herself "shocked" by Redford's preparedness for the fight. "When I came for the job interview, he was disorganized. There was a fat file of issues spilling onto the floor. But he had done his research. He didn't want to be a figurehead. He wanted to be in the action, anatomizing the legislation, analyzing the court judgments, dismembering government. He would constantly cite his belief in grassroots political action. He would say, 'The little fight is as important as the heavyweight bout. We can't let precedent steamroll the people. We have to rewrite legislation.' He made it very clear to me and Joyce that this was a new, fighting Sundance."

Stormy waters lay ahead. Within months, Weil was gone. A major investigative feature by Peter Biskind in *Premiere* magazine charged Beer with mismanagement and Redford with naïve neglect. According to Biskind, Sundance, in Redford's absence, had become a fiscally compromised embarrassment. Wilhite, said Biskind, failed because, despite innovative creativity, he didn't click with Redford. Weil did, but, wrote Biskind, she failed because she followed Beer's example of rudderless extravagance. According to Gary Burr, resort manager Brent Beck's assistant, Beer "charged the institute for flowers and catering expenses for parties," incurring entertainment bills of $200 to $300 per night, two or three nights a week. His expenses often approached $20,000 monthly, said Burr. "By the time the summer [programs] came around, there wasn't enough money for [the institute] to pay for food and housing. Gary didn't understand that he was working for a nonprofit, and that the people around him were working for almost nothing."

"I never abused the institute finances," says Beer in his defense. "But I was the sitting target because, after Sterling Van Wagenen, I came to oversee all the different areas at the same time. That was one hell of a juggling act, and I defy anyone to string together all the different cultures of L.A., the studios, the Beltway, the politicos, the trust funds—and *not* spend money. Also, whatever I did, I did with Bob's and [lawyer] Reg Gipson's full support." Gipson believes that "blaming Gary was cheap and mean-spirited, because there were so many complicated aspects concerning the seeking of grants, pursuing benefactors, forging friendships with studios, and generally building up a machine that empowered independent film-making. Biskind may have forgotten that we were dealing here with something no one had ever attempted before." One of Biskind's sharpest swipes was at Redford, who, he claimed, maneuvered undeserved tax relief against resort expenses. Redford admits only to "some really dumb errors of judgment in the power I entrusted in people. There's no question that there were mistakes, but they weren't of the sinister caliber that was implied. They were mistakes of inexperience, maybe of overambition." Still, the core indictment was a cruel one: that Redford couldn't or wouldn't run Sundance himself and, in the words of an anonymous staffer, "wouldn't let anyone else run it either." Redford doesn't disagree: "Much was true, and it was painful for me as the years unfolded and the true nature of some of my senior management people emerged and the skeletons came out of the cupboards. Our problem was the relative size of Sundance. It was not a little arts colony by the Provo River. It was always meant to reach out, and by the nineties, with the festival booming, we had affiliates in Cuba, Russia and Japan. That's a lot of people moving in a lot of directions at the same time, and that means it's going to be hard to keep track. I made a mistake with Gary Beer because he worked for his own interests. He didn't relate to the junior staffers, and I saw the rifts, but ignored them. I also made a mistake with Reg Gipson, whom I allowed too much latitude."

As public scrutiny of Sundance went on, Redford redrew the lines. Among Wilhite's innovations was the Great Movie Music symposium, a black-tie fund-raiser staged at Lincoln Center that mustered many of Hollywood's scoring luminaries and their families and supporters. It raised $600,000, with Redford hosting. Redford canceled subsequent fund-raisers, proving to some that Biskind was right in his accusation of "schizophrenic leadership." In Redford's mind he was reestablishing the tactical position he had taken back in 1981, when the institute began. "I told Gary, 'Do not use me as the flag carrier in this way. I will help. I will meet people and state our case. But I do not want to become the calling card. If the institute's principles are good enough, it is destined to work. If not, so be it. So no more black-ties.' "

The first planning meeting for the embryonic Sundance Institute and arts center, near Redford's home in Provo Canyon. Redford is fourth from left, with brother-in-law Sterling Van Wagenen seated, looking up at him. *(Courtesy of Robert Redford/Sundance Institute)*

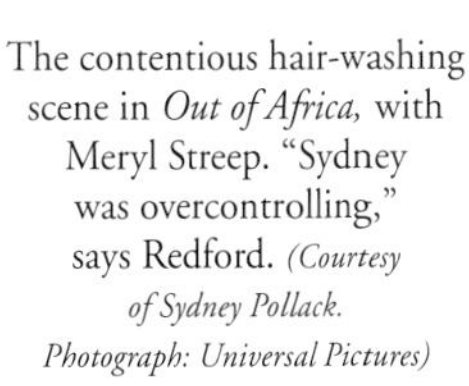

The contentious hair-washing scene in *Out of Africa,* with Meryl Streep. "Sydney was overcontrolling," says Redford. *(Courtesy of Sydney Pollack. Photograph: Universal Pictures)*

Chatting with Sterling Van Wagenen, the Sundance Institute's first director. Their friendship would falter over which films to support in the mid-1980s. *(Courtesy of Robert Redford/ Sundance archive)*

Base Camp, Sundance, today. "It's about creative exploration in the open air," says Redford. *(Ree Ward Callan/Sundance archive)*

Redford during a June lab week at Sundance. "A lot of talking, a lot of sharing, a lot of experimentation." *(Courtesy of Robert Redford/Sundance archive)*

Directing for the first time: *Ordinary People,* with Timothy Hutton and Mary Tyler Moore, in Chicago, 1980 *(Courtesy of Robert Redford/ Wildwood Enterprises)*

With Barry Levinson, director of *The Natural,* 1984 *(Courtesy of Robert Redford)*

Receiving the Academy Award for directing *Ordinary People,* 1981 *(Courtesy of Robert Redford)*

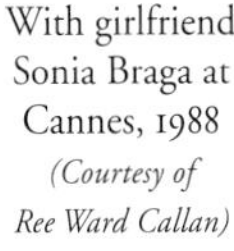

With girlfriend Sonia Braga at Cannes, 1988 *(Courtesy of Ree Ward Callan)*

Greenhouse Glasnost, an international initiative, was mounted at Sundance with the Soviet Academy of Sciences, to raise awareness of global warming and environmental risk, in 1989. *(Courtesy of Robert Redford/Sundance archive)*

On the set of Sydney Pollack's *Havana,* with Lena Olin, 1990
(Courtesy of Robert Redford. Photograph: Universal Pictures)

With Brad Pitt and Craig Sheffer in *A River Runs Through It,* 1992. It was a film Redford had a deep feeling for.
(Courtesy of Robert Redford/Wildwood Enterprises)

Directing Rob Morrow and Martin Scorsese in *Quiz Show,* one of Redford's most acclaimed films, 1995
(Courtesy of Robert Redford/Wildwood Enterprises)

Working with Kristin Scott Thomas on location in Montana for *The Horse Whisperer,* 1998. Redford preferred the far longer version to the one that was released.
(Courtesy of Robert Redford/ Wildwood Enterprises)

Golf in Georgia, with Matt Damon and Will Smith, on location for *The Legend of Bagger Vance,* 2000. Redford was always a fine athlete.
(Courtesy of Robert Redford/Wildwood Enterprises)

The Last Castle, filming in Tennessee, during the spring of 2001
(Courtesy of Robert Redford. Photograph: DreamWorks SKG)

With Brad Pitt
in Tony Scott's
Spy Game, 2001
*(Courtesy of Robert Redford.
Photograph: Universal Pictures)*

Directing Meryl Streep and Tom Cruise in *Lions for Lambs* (2007),
a film Redford saw as a stimulant for debate about social responsibility
(Courtesy of Robert Redford/Wildwood Enterprises. Photograph: United Artists Pictures)

Playing his age with dignity
and distinction in the ill-fated
An Unfinished Life, British
Columbia, Canada, 2005
*(Courtesy of Robert Redford.
Photograph: Miramax Pictures)*

The director
(Courtesy of Robert Redford/Wildwood Enterprises)

After he received his lifetime achievement Academy Award, in the company of Barbra Streisand, 2002
(Courtesy of Robert Redford)

An unending political passion: with candidate Ted Wilson, following the results of his state senate race. Salt Lake City, November 1982
(Courtesy of Robert Redford/Sundance archive)

A recent contemplative moment
(Courtesy of Robert Redford/Sundance archive)

With Sibylle Szaggars—Bylle—
on vacation in 2008.
They would marry in 2009.
*(Shauna Redford Schlosser,
Sundance archive)*

Family show: Jamie and daughter, Lena, accompany Bylle and Bob to the opening of Bylle's art exhibition in Sonoma, 2007.
*(Sundance archive/*Sonoma *magazine)*

The consolation of moviemaking remained impervious. For several years Redford had been circling one project, an adaptation of Norman Maclean's elegiac novella *A River Runs Through It.* Its resonance of times past, of the joy and dilemma of family and the mystery of origins, lured him first in 1981. Now it assumed an urgent relevance, and by a series of fortuitous events, the rights came his way.

Maclean, a University of Chicago professor, published the pithy, part-autobiographical book shortly after his retirement in the 1970s. In 1981, while visiting Tom McGuane in Montana, Redford found himself debating the authenticity of the concept of the western. "We were discussing the essence of the western experience—living it, as opposed to loving it," says Redford. "We started talking about authors who caught the truth: A. B. Guthrie, Vardis Fisher, Wallace Stegner. Then Tom told me about this amazing little story by a retired professor. He said, 'Trust me, read it, it's the real thing.' " Redford says he was overcome by the last line in the book: "I am haunted by waters." "I thought, Whoa, this cuts to the heart all right. This connects environment, family and the immutable nature of destiny. This is the western *I* want to see."

In the mid-eighties, Redford invited the reclusive Maclean, who still lived in Chicago, to Sundance to discuss a possible adaptation, but before he could conclude a deal, the rights were snatched from him by Annick Smith, a lab student who'd established a homestead ranch in Montana's Blackfoot River Valley, the locale of *A River Runs Through It.* Smith developed her adaptation at Sundance but failed to win studio backing. Others before her had tried to mount this film, including the actor William Hurt. When Smith's option lapsed, Redford stepped in.

Redford kept up a constant correspondence with Maclean and visited Chicago repeatedly. "I was fatalistic. Norman was idiosyncratic. If his views and my views corresponded, then it would work. I confronted him like that. I said, 'I will tell you what I'd like to do, and you tell me straight if you like my thinking or not. When it comes down to it, I'll give you the draft script. If you dislike whatever it is I want to shoot, you be the decider: you pull the plug. If you say stop, I'll stop.' "

Ovitz could find no studio backing for the project. Wildwood persisted, with Redford funding development from his own pocket. Redford had chosen as the screenwriter the relatively inexperienced Richard Friedenberg, who had written a moving script for a James Garner television movie called *Promise* that Redford liked. When Redford had first sent Friedenberg a copy of Maclean's book, the screenwriter's response was negative: "The piece was just 104 pages long, and there was no story," says Friedenberg. "It was lyrical, with a clunky 55-page section about fly-fishing in the middle. I told Redford, 'Jews don't fly-fish.' "

A rapid correspondence began between Friedenberg and Redford. But Friedenberg refused to sign a contract. "Because I had been in situations where promises were made, and then I, the writer, could not deliver. There were other issues. I understood this book had immense appeal for Bob, but he is primarily a visual person. His concepts seemed entirely visual. I worried about that. But then I accept, as the screenwriter, my responsibility is to find the story line. So that is how we progressed. The deal was, I would go off, meet Maclean, research and invent some film story line that reflected the book."

Maclean was in his eighties and ailing. But Friedenberg's friendship with Maclean's daughter, Jean, established the bridge of understanding between author and adapter. "The old boy was in the last days of his life, so I'd ask the questions and Jean would communicate them and then write down Norman's answers," says Friedenberg. "What I got in Montana was the feel for the period. But talking with Jean in Chicago, I saw the dichotomies between the book and the reality. The thing was, Norman left out a lot. It was in those gaps I found the invisible story Bob wanted."

A River Runs Through It is a short generational history of the Macleans leading to the rite-of-passage boyhood story of Norman and his failed attempt to save his self-destructive brother, Paul. Friedenberg discovered that Maclean's sweetheart, later wife, Jessie, a central character in the story, was not the uptight Scot that Maclean described; in Friedenberg's definition, she was "a flapper, more like wild boy Paul than straight-and-narrow Norman." This liberated Friedenberg's fictionalizing of the Maclean family story and allowed him, after three years and numerous drafts, to write a filmable narrative. "The breakthrough came on the plane to Montana," remembers Friedenberg, "after I'd learned all about Jessie from Jean. I saw that the problem of the novella was the balance between the competing brothers who reflect different values in a changing world. In the book, Norman is in his thirties, and he describes the tussles with his father and his brother, Paul. But because he is recounting events, he himself never matures as a character. It is all told from the thirty-year-old perspective. What I realized was, I had to find a Norman *who grows.* What I did was fix on the moment he returns from college, intending to join the Forestry Service, and discovers his younger brother has somehow assumed seniority as the star journalist and general high achiever in his absence. So the elder became the younger and the movie dynamic of raw competitiveness was set up."

Friedenberg wrote a ten-page summary in longhand and mailed it to Wildwood. Redford immediately had a personal connection with Friedenberg's blueprint: here was an essay about the interconnectedness of all things, rooted in the competitive growth of complementary boys growing into manhood under the direction of a piously misdirected father, a Montana yarn that might have been the Westwood tale of himself, Coomber and Charlie. "You only had to see the passion he put into it to know that there were private elements of Bob's autobiography there, too," says Friedenberg.

The recent box office and Academy Award success of the low-key film *Driving Miss Daisy,* the brainchild of his old boss Richard Zanuck and his wife, Lili Fini Zanuck, gave Redford hope. But every major studio turned down the film and Redford was forced to turn to an old friend, producer Jake Eberts. For two years Friedenberg had been roughing it, living on bare expenses from Wildwood. Then Eberts dove in. "I had no trouble saying, 'Sure,' " says Eberts. "I grew up fly-fishing in Quebec, I loved the story, I loved Bob's work on *Ordinary People.* We had a short meeting, that's all it took. Then I went out to look for the $10 million to get us going." The studios were still saying no. Hume Cronyn recalled the apathy surrounding the film-in-preparation. "I met a bigwig from Paramount at the Wyndham [Hotel, Cronyn's home in New York] who told me Redford had lost it," said Cronyn. " 'He's finished,' the guy said. 'The activism has burned his brain. This is a goddamn movie about trout.' I knew what this guy meant, but I saw it the other way. *A River Runs Through It* was like *The Old Man and the Sea.* It was contemplative. It was as much an experiment as anything anyone was doing at the June labs."

Redford wouldn't give in. He began casting and told his Wildwood coproducer Patrick Markey to find locations to duplicate Missoula, Montana. For a moment, it seemed a deal with Sherry Lansing at Fox would work out—but Lansing withdrew. "I was going to do it one way or the other," says Redford. "Even if that meant funding it from my own pocket. I told Markey, 'Press on!' "

Redford says he conceived the movie in consultation with the Maclean family and Friedenberg "in spasms, like I painted in Paris thirty-five years before." For the key job of cinematographer he chose forty-five-year-old Frenchman Philippe Rousselot, who had won two Césars, the French equivalent of the Academy Award. Rousselot had worked with Eric Rohmer before making his first English-language movie, the heavily stylized *Diva.* Redford admired his use of light, exemplified in John Boorman's lush woodland-set *The Emerald Forest.* "That whole notion of interconnected nature required the most subtle control of light between sky, forest and water. Rousselot was fresh to America then, and very focused. The time was right to utilize him."

Tom Skerritt was called on to fill the role of the Presbyterian minister father of the Maclean boys. But the boys were harder to come by. At one point, the Bridges brothers, Jeff and Beau, were considered, then a wide array of actors, including Ethan Hawke, were auditioned. Redford's vision for the boys was rigid. "I didn't want stars. I wanted great intelligence and sensitivity." Late in the day Brad Pitt showed up. Pitt, then primarily a television actor, had just scored on the big screen in Ridley Scott's *Thelma and Louise.* "I thought he looked the part, but he didn't convince me," says Redford. "He also carried a heavy dose of attitude, which put me off." According to Pitt, he was rejected outright but went on to demonstrate the kind of bullish intransigence Redford himself had shown with people like Mike Nichols. "I would not accept no," says Pitt. "I'd been tracking this project for months. I said to Bob, 'Look, I want to have another reading.' So I called up a buddy, Dermot Mulroney, and we decided to take the two scenes I'd auditioned with and make a minimovie, complete with sound track." Mulroney's wife, Catherine Keener, who had starred in Pitt's just completed indie movie, *Johnny Suede,* directed by Sundance alumnus Tom DiCillo, acted in the demo. Melissa Etheridge contributed the music. Redford says, "Brad may have shown me some show reel, but I'd made my mind up anyway. I cast Craig Sheffer, because he looked right and he wanted that role of Norman badly. I thought Brad would balance him well, playing Paul. There was a stance about Brad I liked. He acts tough, like he has to face down the world and all its ills. But inside I saw he is a sensitive person who craves approval, like the character Paul." British actresses Emily Lloyd and Brenda Blethyn were cast as Norman's sweetheart, Jessie, and Clara Maclean, the boys' mother. Apart from admiring their individual qualities—Lloyd had just completed David Leland's accomplished *Wish You Were Here,* and Blethyn was fast becoming a fixture in British art house film—Redford saw anthropological accuracy in the women's casting: "There is a definite quality in the Britishness that rubs sharply against rural Americana, but complements it. It's a prissy arrogance that's part of the Puritan in the American heart. I got two contrasting aspects of that in Emily and Brenda: the teenage rebel and the convention-bound patrician."

On April 2, 1991, during preproduction in Livingston, Montana, news came that Charlie Redford had died of heart failure in his home at Tiburon, after a long bout with Alzheimer's. Only three months before, Redford had become a grandfather when Shauna and Eric's daughter, Michaela, was born, "an occasion of the greatest joy," he says. More than ever the issues of family and duty and human responsibility preoccupied him. "From our deepening conversations I knew a lot of his own life was in *River*," says Friedenberg. "We talked over some key issues. Communication had always been a problem within his family, especially communication with his father. A similar separation existed with Norman and Paul and their father—though Bob said the reverend reminded him more of his grandfather, whose attitude to his son was to chastise a wrongdoing by imposing a silence. After his father's death the issue of scripting the silences became emphatic. We started to actually create dead spaces, which made problems for the actors, particularly Craig Sheffer, who could not understand the lack of a verbalized philosophy for his Norman character. He persisted in complaining—a lot. He would sit in the wings writing his own eloquent speeches for Norman, and it was maddening for Bob because he just didn't get it. He didn't get Bob. It was only later, when he saw the movie finished and screened at the Toronto Film Festival, that he took us aside and said, 'Shit! What was I trying to do? *Now* I get it.' "

Redford had made his peace with Charlie, after a fashion. Through the late eighties they exchanged letters constantly, always barbed and full of wit, but increasingly affectionate. Redford bought his father a giant television for his new home; Charlie responded with a clever memo about his failing eyesight. Redford offered Charlie the use of his house at Trancas Beach, invited him to Utah, asked him to share Thanksgiving at a rented house in Weston, Connecticut. But Charlie was still his father's son, still oppressed by the austerity from Westerly, still scared. Family friend Marcella Scott saw rivalry till the end.

With Bill Coomber at his side, just like old times, Redford took the wheel of his Porsche to drive from Los Angeles to San Francisco for the funeral service in Mill Valley. Coomber found his stepbrother much changed: "I felt he was a lot edgier, maybe less in control of his temperament." Coomber also felt "profound sadness" for Redford's loss in never achieving insight or intimacy with Helen, Charlie's wife. For his part, Redford found the trip "just priceless time together. That long drive allowed us to review the years, because I had seen so little of him. It was strange, driving north to my dad's funeral, because it was a road trip into both our past lives. Lots of memories. Seminal moments. The need to escape as teenagers. The madness in Westwood. The crazy hot-rodding in the Valley. The bust-ups, the breakdowns. A lot of misunderstanding was patched up. We were brothers again, tighter than ever."

When *River* started shooting six weeks later, around Livingston and Big Timber, Montana, Redford told Patrick Markey, "The movie's already done in my head." Markey recalls, "He was sizzling. It was the sweetest filming experience I've ever had. It poured out of him, and there was no indication of the paucity of the source material. Instead, it felt like he was compressing a saga comparable with Flaubert or Proust into this immaculate vignette. Rousselot didn't lead it visually, Bob did. He was onto every fiber of it. The sound. The costuming. The accents. The attitude of people. Everything."

"The absence of a studio deal didn't slow us down," Friedenberg says. "There was not much tension at all." According to Friedenberg, the one errant aspect was Pitt's and Sheffer's tendency to drop in anachronistic improvisations and challenge Redford's subtleties.

Central to the book was its fishing location, the 130-mile-long Blackfoot River, which wound from the Lewis and Clark Mountains to its intersection with the Clark Fork River near Missoula. For hundreds of years the Blackfoot Indians called the waterway the River on the Road to the Buffalo, and Maclean, as a child, revered it. But Markey found it unusable. "The headwaters were orange and toxic because an old mine, the Mike Horse, had caved into it fifteen years ago. All the residue zinc, lead and cadmium poured down, year after year. It was ruined, and the fish Maclean hunted, the cutthroat, rainbow, bull and brown trout, were mostly gone. Bob was sickened by it." Markey moved the fly-fishing scenes to the Gallatin and Yellowstone rivers. Redford was immediately receptive to the local chapter of Trout Unlimited, which sought assistance for an awareness campaign about local pollution. "Bob sidetracked once again," says Markey. "It was, 'How the hell do we celebrate the sanctity of heritage in this film when the Blackfoot is a cesspool?' It came right into the middle of his agenda, and he offered to join fund-raisers for National Fish and Wildlife and the American Rivers association, which had the Blackfoot registered as one of the ten most endangered waterways. It wasn't nostalgia. He worried all the time about what he called 'capturing the past.' The loss of the Blackfoot proved his point, and he worried that the movie would not articulate itself properly, that it would not be enough, ecologically speaking."

In the early screenplays, a voice-over narration by Norman, introducing and interspersed throughout the story, was included. But as the editing began, the voice-over caused problems, exacerbated by Redford's temporary distraction. Strained finances dictated that he interrupt production to accept a big-budget movie, *Sneakers,* that Ovitz had put together. In consequence, he was in San Francisco working on the thriller when he should have been on *River.* Editors often cut from the director's notes, but here the process failed. The first editor was fired, having cut the movie, says Friedenberg, "in far too modern a way." Another editor, Bob Estrin, had been summoned to recut at the Lantana facilities in Santa Monica. "I almost lost the movie," says Redford, "and that's the price for not paying attention. When I saw the assembly footage, I was horrified. We had drifted too far away from what Maclean wanted. Richard had written an invented opening speech that just felt wrong. I wanted *Norman's* words, because that was where the magic was. We scrapped the narration we'd started with and began a brand-new edit." Also abandoned was Elmer Bernstein's entire sound track, which Redford felt too "standard." Instead, Mark Isham was recruited to create something nostalgic and evocative.

For the new voice-overs, Redford asked Wallace Stegner, among others, to try reading the substitute lyrical narration, which was mostly Maclean's. "I came close with Wally, but he read flat," says Redford. In the end he opted to voice it himself, "because it felt comfortable. I knew how Norman sounded, I knew his way, I became Norman. So I introduced the story, and filled the gaps, keeping the reflective tone. Norman had died in 1990, but I sent demos to the Maclean family, who approved. It got to feel very good then, like we were pleasing the old ghost."

For Sheila Andrews, Redford's friend from high school, this new movie was nothing less than encyclopedic. "I felt *A River Runs Through It* was his meditation on American values beyond *Jeremiah Johnson* or *All the President's Men* or anything else," she said. One early line of Norman's narration—"It is those we live with and love and should know who elude us"—explained a great deal for Alan Pakula. "I read an article that said that what he and Sydney had in common was that both liked to make the kind of movies they'd enjoyed watching as they grew up. But *River* was unlike anything Bob saw, or anything Sydney could have made. Brad [Pitt] speculated that Bob was trying to outdo what Sydney had done with *Out of Africa,* that it was arty competition. But of course it wasn't. There had been plenty of romantic biopics like *Out of Africa* before. There had never been a movie like *River.* It wasn't autobiography, but it was a unique meditation about heartland Americanism that grew from his and Maclean's experiences. It was also an amazingly delicate construct that deserved the award nominations, and then some. It ticked all the boxes of all-time classic."

Within twenty-four hours of the completion of editing of *A River Runs Through It,* Jake Eberts had sealed a distribution deal with Columbia. Thereafter, the movie's marketing was cofunded by his own company, Allied Filmmakers, an affiliate of Pathe that had started five years before with Sean Connery's *The Name of the Rose.* "The point is, we remained independent," says Eberts. "My objective had been to preserve Bob's vision, as Bob's was to preserve Norman's. It was undiluted, which is all he wanted."

Ovitz had made a good deal for Redford on *Sneakers:* $8 million against 10 percent of the gross, which was $2 million more than current hotshot Sylvester Stallone was earning. All the usual perks and sidebars were in the contract, including the critically important casting approvals. But Redford was still unhappy. He confided his unease to one of CAA's rising stars, Bryan Lourd. "He talked to me confidentially," says Lourd. "He didn't want to go the direction Mike was pushing him. He said he wanted significant movies, not significant checks, as a priority. There were changes in the zeitgeist and he acknowledged that and was ready to play to that, which all intelligent performers must do, but he also wanted to keep his attention on the long term. He wanted a substantial body of work to look back on."

Making *Sneakers* for ten weeks on the Universal back lot, in Simi Valley and around San Francisco was no great strain. *River* had brightened him greatly. Things were going well with Kathy O'Rear. Bernie Pollack considered him "unusually cheerful." Redford also found himself comfortable with the director, Phil Alden Robinson. There was also the element of fun. The tricky conspiracy plot helped educate Redford about the computer age. And though much play was made in the press of the fact that the story line was skewed toward the new, youthful pinup River Phoenix, Redford ignored the barbs. "You have to keep reminding yourself you are not working for the critics."

Forty-two-year-old Robinson, whose modest baseball movie *Field of Dreams* had done so well, shared the kind of devotion to script that endeared him to his lead actor. The cover of the script given to Redford read, "Based on 27 man-years of drafts by Phil Alden Robinson, Walter F. Parkes and Lawrence Lasker." It was Parkes and Lasker who'd pitched to Universal the notion of "a high-tech *Dirty Dozen*" as a follow-up to their 1983 computer-age *War Games;* but it was Robinson who, he says, "went on to write the forty million plot variations." Robinson first saw himself as the screenwriter of the project only and refused Parkes's initial entreaties to direct *Sneakers,* despite the career boost of *Field of Dreams.* According to Parkes, "we finagled Phil, and as soon as we had him, it seemed, we got Redford. Then Redford was the magnet for the other big hitters like Sidney Poitier and Ben Kingsley who came aboard."

The story line was unashamed Hitchcockian MacGuffin territory, involving National Security Agency infiltration that recalled *Three Days of the Condor.* Redford's role was computer genius Martin Bishop (a name that references two of the CIA men listed as victims in *Condor*), whose electronic analysis team is tricked into stealing a mysterious black box that they subsequently learn has the power to breach all encrypted national security systems worldwide. What appears to be a story of NSA perfidy emerges as a grudge war between Redford's Bishop and his college-days competitor, the devious Cosmo, played by Ben Kingsley.

"My way of enjoying the role was hooking in to the whole issue of privacy in this information age," says Redford. "Bishop's team can get into anyone's files. Not long before, I learned I'd been investigated by the Treasury Department and the LAPD. That blew me away. Treasury checked me out for six months because I went to Cuba to visit García Márquez for the Sundance Latin American program. In the case of the LAPD investigation, the best bet is they saw the Leonard Peltier film [Apted's *Incident at Oglala*] and figured I was undercover with American Indian Movement radicals. All of it was paranoid nonsense, of course, but it made me think: this is Orwell's Big Brother in the making. We are in a society now that has hidden cameras in malls, at banks, at drugstores. We have computers on our desks that are as much windows into our lives as windows on the world. People can hack into our personal information. Our credit cards are routinely stolen. Our Social Security numbers are traded. *Sneakers* reminds us to pay attention to all this new technology."

Redford worked from October through February, with breaks to wrap the edit of *A River Runs Through It* and ski with the family at Christmas. Frustrated as he was by the lightness of the subject, he was thankful for a movie that felt effortlessly sweet, especially because of Robinson's humor and the kinship of ensemble acting. He found River Phoenix a gentle, respectful student; Dan Aykroyd (playing the gadgets wizard Mother) "all mischief and treason"; Poitier, Kingsley and Mary McDonnell, playing the love interest, stimulating dinner companions. The best moments, though, were the days in San Francisco when he found time to visit with Amy, who was attending San Francisco State University, studying film. In the last five years Amy's interest in movies had grown through internships at the June labs. She had also spent time in London, where she'd started acting. Of the Redford children, friends say, Amy was most effusive in either applauding or criticizing her father. "She wasn't good at phony politeness," says a Sundance staffer. "In fact, she went punk, adopting a punk look with a punk attitude. When she addressed you directly, you tended to listen." When Redford visited, says Amy, she was unimpressed by his description of *Sneakers:* "I told him he should be acting more and starring less."

Universal's summer testing of a rough cut of *Sneakers* yielded such positive results that the release planned for Christmas was moved up to September. Decent reviews followed, and a satisfying gross: $51.5 million in the United States alone, a return doubled worldwide.

The success did not dissuade Redford from breaking with Ovitz. "From the beginning I never really trusted him," says Redford. "But I thought he was smart and shrewd in a tough business. I also thought that having someone represent you in so savage an environment who actually loves to do what you hate doing—that is, deal chasing—was a boon." But, as he had told Lourd, he had grown uncomfortable with the direction in which Ovitz was nudging him.

A number of projects Redford liked had died on the vine: a George Washington biopic; a morality tale about the rain forest that he discussed with Spielberg, who "got the visuals, but couldn't get the subtext of the story"; a romantic comedy, *The President Elopes,* which Penny Marshall developed. Worryingly, none caught fire and he redoubled his efforts to find a script that would engage him and properly contrast *River.*

Lourd now gave Redford an Amy Holden Jones script he had under development with new Paramount chairperson Sherry Lansing for his clients Demi Moore and Woody Harrelson. It was based on New York journalist Jack Engelhard's hard-edged novel *Indecent Proposal,* with a flagrantly sexual theme. "It wasn't drafted with Bob at all in mind," says Lourd. "But he told me he was a risk taker, and I had an inkling this was just sufficiently outrageous for him."

Redford recalls reading the script in one sitting and being alternately engaged, surprised and amused by it. The role proposed to him was of a middle-aged billionaire intent on buying sex with a married young woman on a weekend in Vegas. "My gut did the talking," Redford says. "Finally, it was fun and it was *now.* I didn't ask for anyone's opinions. I called Lourd and said, 'Yeah, it will work.' " Lourd, together with his agent partner David "Doc" O'Connor, takes credit for revitalizing Redford's career in the nineties. "Unquestionably he needed to find the new-generation audience," says Lourd. "He was *the* megastar of the seventies, but tempus fugit and all that. It is the eighteen- to twenty-five-year-olds who pay for the tickets. Bob had to shake up that market, and I knew putting him with Woody, who was huge from the TV series *Cheers,* and Demi, who was very hot, would open up that new audience for him."

Before the filming commenced, there was some irate discussion about the alterations to the source material. Engelhard, who viewed himself as a political conservative, felt his work was being distorted. He later deplored the choice of Redford: "The billionaire in my novel is not Robert Redford, but an Arab sheik. The husband is a Jewish speechwriter and the wife is a Grace Kelly type. So the novel, obviously, has many layers, political, religious, cultural, which Hollywood won't touch." English director Adrian Lyne reshaped the essence and under his supervision the Engelhard novel retained its Faustian theme but became less a study of cultural differences than of sexual role-play. Lyne, who began his career directing shorts in Britain fourteen years before, had stunningly captured the social fallout of sexual liberalism in *Fatal Attraction,* his fourth movie, which was nominated for six Academy Awards, earned $450 million and was labeled by *Time* "the zeitgeist hit of the decade." One of his follow-ups, *Jacob's Ladder,* about madness, comprehensively showed his grasp of deviant psychology. "The genius of Lyne was his timing," says Lourd. "*Fatal Attraction* was the postfeminist, post–*Fear of Flying* kickback. *Indecent Proposal* cautioned against the sex-and-wealth 'me me me' nineties." Redford's enthusiasm was for "this nexus of energies, the morality tale, the timing, the subtexts." Redford knew he was catching a wave. In 1992 Paul Verhoeven's *Basic Instinct* ingeniously blended Russ Meyer with *Dynasty;* Lyne's *Indecent Proposal* had the same populist targeting, and was as illuminating of the insatiable urges of twenty-four-hour Las Vegas as *Peyton Place* once was of New England's deceptive serenity.

In the movie, David (Harrelson) and Diana Murphy (Moore), lovers since high school, run out of money building their Santa Monica dream home and try to recoup at the gaming tables; they fail. Entrepreneur John Gage (Redford) then offers David a million dollars for a night in bed with Diana. In the novel, the characters are shady. In the film, Diana is the dewy-eyed happily married wife who falls for her seducer. David in turn becomes the conscience-stricken sinner, a characterization that owes something to Richard Gere's role in *Pretty Woman.* "Of course this was perverse heroism," says Redford. "But it worked as great entertainment in the Reagan era, when everything was about the cash and the cost and, it seemed, everyone was playing dirty."

In October 1992, the week *Indecent Proposal* wrapped in Las Vegas, *A River Runs Through It* premiered at the Ziegfeld in New York as another benefit for NRDC. A month before, Redford had joined the Maclean family for "a very moving and gratifying" American Rivers benefit screening at Bozeman, Montana. Of all Redford's movies, only a handful enjoyed such unanimous critical praise, exemplified by Richard Schickel's review in *Time,* in which he wrote that the movie scored "because [Redford] has rigorously maintained the understated tone of a book that never plea-bargains, never asks outright for sympathy or understanding, yet ultimately, powerfully, elicits both."

Six months later, *Indecent Proposal* opened nationwide on a maximum-distribution twenty-five hundred screens and raced around the world, earning more than $260 million, Redford's greatest moneymaker to date. His nineties rebirth had come after a thirty-year career of determined variety, experiment and invention. He had proved again his imagination and durability as he straddled the art house and middlebrow markets. He was back at the epicenter.

21

Delivering the Moment

Redford's attitude toward his children had always been one of tough love. Financial indulgence, he believed, suffocated the families of the rich. He would give each of his children a home and beyond that nothing other than trust, care and emotional support. After an interrupted period of study in Chicago, Jamie and Kyle returned to make a home in Denver, where their son, Dylan Larson, was born and from where Jamie pursued the life of a writer independently, working under the guidance of Josh Donner, a William Morris agent. It was while he was drafting a soon-to-be-abandoned sci-fi version of *The Odyssey* for Universal that the call came from the University of Nebraska Medical Center, a hospital renowned for its treatment of liver disease, reporting the availability of a suitable liver for transplant. Redford was in New York, in the final days of preparing a new film, *Quiz Show.* He left the production and joined Jamie to fly to Nebraska. En route Redford told Jamie he wanted him to write the next Tony Hillerman movie for Wildwood. "It was such a boost," says Jamie, "because his attitude had always been one of promoting self-sufficiency. On that flight he changed. He knew I was at my lowest, that there were so few people for me to lean on, and he gave me this gesture of hope, something to hang in for."

Though *Quiz Show* was a fragile project that had almost slipped from his grip on several occasions, Redford felt he should delay it for one year. "My son's well-being obviously came first. I sat by his bed and reassured him. I told him, 'I'll be there, hell or high water.' But Jamie made the decision. 'Get on with the movie,' he told me. 'Do what you were put here for, and let me do what I have to do.' "

Jamie's first operation, an eight-hour procedure, seemed to be a success, but his recovery was hampered by a faulty valve in the new liver. Each Friday night after shooting in New York, Redford took a plane to Omaha. "I knew the operation didn't work," says Jamie. "Your body tells you. The blood tests were coming back okay, but something *felt* wrong." On the day Jamie was due for release from the hospital, an ultrasound test showed a thrombosis on the hepatic artery, a condition that suggested fatal atrophy of the bile ducts. It was dealt with surgically. Jamie was again registered for a nationwide liver search. For the next three days, says Redford, Jamie was "out of it, but steady." There followed, says Redford, twelve of the worst weeks of both their lives. Finally, over the Fourth of July weekend, a replacement liver was located. "People often asked me about the value of celebrity in such a situation," says Jamie. "They say, 'I'm sure Robert Redford gets to pull strings.' But it's not true. My father was 100 percent involved. He consulted on every aspect of the surgeries. He never stopped talking with the consultants. But that's as far as it went. Celebrity can't help in the life-and-death department." The constant tension brought father and son closer than they'd been since their days together in Europe. "At times like those you review your life experience," says Jamie. "I saw both my parents as being loving supporters. My mother was the nurturer of my youth. My father was sometimes absent, but always there in spirit. At the time of my operations, the roles reversed. My mother would have been there for anything I asked: she never let me down. But in the crisis it was my dad who oversaw it all. He needed to do that. I saw it clearly. It was not a case of redeeming himself or making up for anything. It was just his time to bat had come, and he was there."

The instant Jamie opened his eyes after the second liver transplant, he knew the surgery had worked. "It was a beautiful dawning, like someone turning on the sunshine again. Just a feeling of, *Yes, this is right! This is how I have been waiting to feel all my life.*" The recovery, though, was complicated by recurring ulcerative colitis, which resulted in the removal of Jamie's colon. It wasn't until October of the following year that he was healthy enough to resume an active lifestyle, exercising, traveling, writing to deadlines for Wildwood. Redford felt "an unspeakable relief, one of the truly great moments of my life."

Hume Cronyn believed Redford was "hardened" by the crisis, but Redford contends that the opposite was true, that he came more than ever to cherish life and found new depths of love within family that he'd hoped would also extend to friendships like Pollack's. For Cronyn, Redford had become reclusive: "He let friends slip away; he stopped returning calls." Jamie says no: "He was, and is, a snob in one sense only: he must receive something intellectually or spiritually from a friendship. I think his hurt at that time was that friends for both of us were thin on the ground. Some serious rethinking began. When you're at death's door, you reevaluate things like love and truth."

The notion of truth, subjective and empirical, had been an intellectual preoccupation for as long as Redford could remember, and it was the appeal that lay behind his pursuit of *Quiz Show.* Richard Friedenberg contends that *A River Runs Through It* triumphed not as a homily but because it revolved around the absolute truth of who Redford really was: "It wasn't the story. It was this guy on horseback resolving his personal issues of purpose and survival within the universe of a movie." Carol Rossen believes Redford is someone who feels compelled to contribute to public life, while remaining committed to the isolated, reflective existence that centered on the verities. "Truth is his big hang-up in life," she says. Film after film of his reflected a pursuit of the question: "What is wrong with this picture?" *Quiz Show* would be his sharpest commentary so far on "the truth" of national values.

Indecent Proposal opened doors for him, and he parlayed that into a deal with Jeff Katzenberg at Disney to acquire *Quiz Show,* a project that had been developed by Barry Levinson and Sundance hero Steven Soderbergh at TriStar, then abandoned when stars Richard Dreyfuss and Tim Robbins dropped out. Based on a nonfiction book by Richard Goodwin called *Remembering America: A Voice from the Sixties, Quiz Show* was an account of the NBC game-fixing scandals of the late fifties. Redford felt a personal connection. He had once been a contestant on Merv Griffin's *Play Your Hunch,* where the promised fee of $75 morphed into fishing gear and he had been forced to identify himself as a painter, rather than the actor he had already become. Redford had watched Charles Van Doren's performances on the *Twenty One* quiz show throughout 1958 and tried to believe his assertion of innocence. "I wanted to go on believing, but the Merv Griffin show straightened me out," says Redford. "As a nation, we didn't pay enough attention, and the fact was, we were experiencing a fundamental breach in morality." Redford quotes social theorist Neil Postman's argument for the two ways in which cultures can corrupt: they can be prison cultures in the Orwellian model or burlesques in the Huxleian prophecy. In a world dominated by technologies, Huxley said, spiritual devastation is likely to come from the enemy with the smiling face. "When a population is distracted by trivia," wrote Postman in *Amusing Ourselves to Death,* "when cultural life is redefined as a perpetual round of entertainments, when serious public conversation becomes a form of baby talk, when, in short, a people become an audience and their public business a vaudeville act, then a nation finds itself at risk. Culture death is a real possibility."

Redford engaged former *Washington Post* critic Paul Attanasio to write a new screenplay. Goodwin was a congressional investigator who had drawn the details of his book from public records. To this, Attanasio and Redford added characters from Redford's New York television experiences, transforming MCA agents into CBS executives. "They were interchangeable. I'd met enough Ray Starks in my time to know. It was all a machine dictated by profit, and it was immoral. Maybe television was always like that. Maybe the voracity of it, the volume of airtime to fill, dictated it. But at the time of the *Twenty One* scandal, something sordid was unveiled. Bizarrely, people accepted it. Maybe the sinning was in the pact the viewers made with the program makers. The people wanted these shows, and they wanted heroes like Van Doren, and maybe they didn't care that they were being lied to. My take on the project was as a reminder of our choice at that moment in national life to say, 'Hey, this is what we did, this is the deal we made, and this is how we are. We accept venality; we are not too interested in honesty or decency, only in rhetoric.' "

As Redford prepared *Quiz Show,* he was drawn into a controversy. In 1987, the NEA had been castigated when it contributed $75,000 to the Southeastern Center for Contemporary Art, in whose gallery New York photographer Andres Serrano displayed his "Piss Christ," a photograph of a crucifix in a jar of urine. The religious right's complaints were nothing compared with the storm accompanying the following year's retrospective at Washington's Corcoran Gallery of Art of photographer Robert Mapplethorpe's work, which featured 170 studies, mostly of flowers, with five explicit images that celebrated his gay lifestyle exhibited in a secondary, screened-off area. Despite the overwhelmingly positive reviews, the show was suddenly deemed improper and withdrawn. Senator Jesse Helms was the main objector, and he went on to propose a censorship amendment to the NEA's charter. Subsequently, Congressman Philip Crane took up the fight, introducing bills in 1992 and 1993 to abolish the NEA that so incensed Wallace Stegner that he turned down the National Medal of Arts in protest of "political control." Redford dove into the fray. "Like Wally, I found it impossible not to speak out. What we were witnessing was an attempt to restrict freedom of speech. The arts were always the forum for discovery. The problem with Helms and the do-gooders is they induce stagnancy. Cultural stagnancy reinforces prejudice and imbalance. The job of the arts is to challenge that."

Redford debated where he could but he poured his rage most forcefully into *Quiz Show,* a film studded with invective but mounted with the most meticulous control. To play Charles Van Doren, Redford chose the British actor Ralph Fiennes; for Herbie Stempel, the avaricious contestant who blows the whistle, he cast John Turturro; for investigator Dick Goodwin he cast Rob Morrow; Barry Levinson and Martin Scorsese were cast, "mischievously," says Levinson, as voices of reason. For the role of the poet Mark Van Doren, Charles's father, Redford wanted Paul Scofield, who had retired from theater several years before. In the eyes of some, Redford was wryly toying with stereotypes in the storytelling and the casting. "It felt biased," says Jeremy Larner. "In the script Stempel becomes the sweaty shylock, a miserable human being who betrays himself and everyone else for money and celebrity. It's anti-Jewish." Michael Ritchie strongly disagreed, believing that of all Redford's movies, this was the one laden with irony. Redford also refutes the bias: "It was historically accurate. Jeremy missed the point completely. If I was targeting anyone, it was those executives." The real Herbert Stempel, still living in Brooklyn at the time of the movie's release in the fall of 1994, publicly reiterated that the movie was "not a fraud."

Filmed by cinematographer Michael Ballhaus, *Quiz Show* has the glazed beauty of a fifties commercial, where mechanical objects and furniture—the sparkling Chrysler 300 the Goodwin character covets, the art deco architecture—vie to outshine the performers, and everyone (except Stempel) is immaculately tailored and coiffed. There is, too, a breathless Steadicam pace to the drama that serves to replicate "live" television. This was a style markedly different from the slow-resolving rhythms of *A River Runs Through It* and bears witness to Redford's range as a director.

Redford knew he had a good movie in the can long before the edit. Having resisted video playback on location until then, he now relied heavily on it to check performances on a day-by-day basis. "But my style of directing remained exactly the same: give the actors their space, try it your way, try it theirs." Fiennes, Morrow and Turturro all went on record praising what Morrow expressed as the "joy of working with a generous director who knows what you're doing because he's done it himself."

When the movie was released in September, it created a furor. Retired prosecuting attorney Joseph Stone, who, in real life, had led the Manhattan DA's office investigation, objected. In his view, Redford was as venal as *Twenty One*'s producers, offering up "a trumped-up, scaled-down, pandering mishmash of half-truths, fabrication, distortion, omission and character assassination." The fact that Stone had been the first man to expose the quiz show scandals but was not named in the film, said Stempel, may have upset the retired lawyer. But, insisted Stempel, "I am essentially the fuse that lit the dynamite. If I feel comfortable with the [honesty of the] movie, there's no reason he shouldn't."

Redford's only regret was that he couldn't persuade the Van Doren family to cooperate with the movie. William Goldman in *Premiere* compared his former friend's offering with the other Oscar contenders that year—*Pulp Fiction, Forrest Gump, Four Weddings and a Funeral* and *The Shawshank Redemption*—and damned Redford with faintest praise: "[It] did wonderfully with what it had. It's what it didn't have that bothered me." The view, to some, had a self-canceling transparency.

Redford was nearing sixty, a little weary of the boardroom vying at Sundance, a little ill at ease in his domestic arrangement with Kathy O'Rear. More and more—ironically—he sought retreat from Utah itself and spent more time with his children in their various homes. With them, he says, he felt anchored and challenged in equal measure. To the tune of the title song from *Jesus Christ Superstar,* the kids had redrafted the lyric:

Double R Superstar,
Who in the hell do you think you are?

He found this amusing, not least because the incisive wit showed they knew what he knew: it was time to fundamentally reassess himself. Not long after *Quiz Show* he agreed to appear on *Inside the Actors Studio.* He told his audience of three hundred mostly film students (and also Paul Newman and Arthur Penn) that his greatest regret was not learning to play a musical instrument and that, while he would like a reunion movie with Newman or Streisand, he didn't favor sequels. "I was thinking of this theory I developed," says Redford. "It's called *taking responsibility for a talent.* I came to accept that a large audience wanted to see me as this representational romantic character of some moral standing. I concluded there was a rightness in that." Once, Jack Kroll of *Newsweek* wrote that he'd liked *The Electric Horseman* and admired the whole attractive, lovable heroic icon business. "Kroll ended his feature saying Jane and I were fine actors, and then he added, 'Wouldn't it be wonderful to see what these two people could bring to roles of bad character?' That pissed me off.

Three years later Jack Kroll did a personal interview with me and I said, 'Can we go off record?' And he was a nice man and said, 'Sure.' Then I laid it out for him. I told him what he said was bordering on the unethical. The implication was that I was in some way shortchanging people because I played heroes. I told him, 'You want me to play the psycho? I did that in my apprenticeship, did it for years. An actor learns by experiment. I have been there and back. Now I play the hero, but one who has earned whatever he has to give by way of some sacrifice, some study. If you want me to play the Arnold Schwarzenegger hero, I cannot do that. I cannot be the stuntman. But I can do the guy in *Electric Horseman,* I can do Jack Weil. There's no disgrace in playing to your strengths.' "

After *Quiz Show,* says Bryan Lourd, "he confused me utterly, because he was marching to a different drum. The projects that seemed right he avoided. For example, because he wanted to stretch and because he liked to sing, he told me he wanted to do *Phantom of the Opera.* Andrew Lloyd Webber was interested in meeting him. But then every time I tried to set up the meeting, Bob cried off. I'd say, 'You need to meet him, to sing for him.' And all he'd do was say, 'Sure, no problem at all.' But he just wouldn't see it through." The only project that came close to realization was *The Hot Zone,* a story of runaway viruses that might wipe out life on earth, based on a book by Richard Preston. "I got the impression that he was more interested in the documentary, social value of the story line, and not entertainment," says Lourd. "And that was the abiding mood: he accepted his position as an iconic pinup and he wanted to stretch but his course was undefined."

Bit by bit Redford came to accept that the dilemma within himself was best resolved by making movies that played to his core audience while reserving formal experiment for Sundance and its programs. Accordingly, Lourd tried to encourage the new, entrenched relationship with Disney and its affiliates. After the death of Walt Disney and some lean years, the company under Michael Eisner was building new amusement parks worldwide that complemented its new movies. During the first five years of Eisner's reign, the studio's audience share had grown from 3 percent to 20 percent. In 1992, Eisner welcomed Joe Roth, the cofounder of Morgan Creek, under the Disney umbrella with a newly created division, Caravan Pictures, and the following spring Disney bought Miramax, the indie distribution company of brothers Harvey and Bob Weinstein, for $60 million. Lourd felt Redford had a double advantage at Disney, since Frank Wells, who was still very much part of the management equation, was so fond of the actor. Indeed, late in March 1994, as *Quiz Show* began filming, Wells had invited Redford to join a helicopter ski trip in Nevada. Redford had to decline the invitation and thus was spared the tragedy that followed. Flying home on April 3, the helicopter carrying Wells and his party crashed into a mountainside, killing all on board. The death of Wells created a feud at Disney when Eisner refused to give the vacated executive post to next-in-line Jeffrey Katzenberg. After a flurry of lawsuits, Katzenberg quit Disney to join Steven Spielberg and David Geffen in the founding of DreamWorks SKG. One of Katzenberg's last projects within the Disney organization, Jon Avnet's *Up Close and Personal,* was offered to Redford. He accepted.

The movie was featherweight but its antecedents were intriguing. It was based on the life of Jessica Savitch, a television broadcaster briefly famous for her rise at NBC at a time when men dominated the news. Drug addiction unhinged her and she came unglued on air during a live prime-time broadcast in 1983. Fired from the network, Savitch drowned shortly after in a bizarre car accident in New Hope, Pennsylvania. The rights to Alanna Nash's 1988 oral biography *Golden Girl* were acquired by John Foreman, the producing partner of Paul Newman, who commissioned John Gregory Dunne to develop a script for Katzenberg. According to Dunne in his memoir, what ensued was a nightmare of greed and whim in La-La Land. From the start, said Dunne, Disney wanted the real-life characters reinvented. Neither Savitch, a bisexual who had had an interracial affair, nor her abusive mentor, Ron Kershaw, were deemed palatable. Dunne and his wife, Joan Didion, who also contributed, quit the project after a dozen dead-end drafts. Thereafter *Up Close and Personal* languished until Foreman died in 1993 and a team at Touchstone, a Disney division, gave the project to producer Scott Rudin, who brought Dunne and Didion back on board. But Rudin's subsequent choice of Avnet as director—and the further *fifteen* rewrites—wore everyone down. What Dunne described was a phalanx of subliterate boors attempting to justify executive salaries by ascribing dramatic gravitas to what was a pulp story line about a long-in-the-tooth TV news hack playing Henry Higgins to a sexy pseudo-Savitch wannabe. The pragmatic Rudin was remorseless, said Dunne. For the umpteenth "fine-tuned" draft he instructed Dunne and Didion: "Deliver the moment. . . . We need a stronger credit sequence, use the bookend frame, we have a POV deficit, we want another beat here, deliver the moment, stretch it out, this is clunky . . . cut all the Washington chat in the S&L scene, but save her line, 'Get the fuck out of my shot,' it's who she is, lose the Taco Bell sequence, it's OTN [for 'on the nose'] or OTT [for 'over the top'], split the first newsroom sequence, do it over two days, deliver the moment . . . deliver the moment. . . ."

Avnet, fresh from the Academy Award–nominated *Fried Green Tomatoes,* cast Michelle Pfeiffer as the newsgirl and delivered the umpteenth script in preparation to Redford. "I chose not to be cynical," says Avnet. "There's no shame in creating a smash hit. Entertainment need not negate intelligence. *It's a Wonderful Life,* for example, is very calculated and incredibly schmaltzy, but it is also now regarded as a masterpiece." Avnet's first major work, *The Burning Bed,* made for television and starring Farrah Fawcett, was superficially racy but about battered women. "That's the prime example of what's possible in so-called pedestrian Hollywood," says Avnet. "What was *The Burning Bed*? Just another movie of the week. But the hidden text was loaded. It generated one hundred thousand telephone calls from battered women, it changed the national vernacular, it brought the issue to the table. Fellini did it, too, in *La Strada.* R. D. Laing had a patient who wanted to commit suicide and decided not to after seeing *La Strada.* That makes for a political achievement. This is what so-called simple entertainment can do."

Rudin saw no hidden layers in *Up Close and Personal:* "It's about two movie stars," he repeatedly reminded Dunne. In the end, there was no mixed-up Savitch, or shadowy Ron Kershaw. Instead, Pfeiffer and Redford signed on unconditionally to play sexy Tally Atwater and her wise, sexy old-hand mentor Warren Justice.

Fried Green Tomatoes had wonderful wit, most memorable in the scene depicting the mutual lesbian passions of two lead characters in a food fight. No such subtlety inspired Avnet in *Up Close and Personal,* which played out as a media age *My Fair Lady.* In the final act, Tally earns her network stripes by broadcasting live from inside a prison during a murderous riot, with Warren Justice coaching her by radio. "It's the great showdown," says Avnet, "the gunfight scene, the rite of passage, the big seduction all rolled into one. Michelle knew what I wanted to achieve, as did Bob. It was old-style movie drama."

Based in Miami and Philadelphia, with interiors at Culver City, the movie was shot over seventy-seven days in the summer of 1995. "Bob engaged all the way," says Avnet, "from our first meeting with John and Joan at his home in Connecticut until the last day and the wrap. He was a full collaborator, even suggesting the music montage. He loved Michelle, who brought her family along to location, as I brought my son, Jake.

Sometimes he had his kids and his grandkids along. He was at home with us, because we were this band of strolling players and this was his natural habitat."

Redford's profound enjoyment in *Up Close and Personal* amounted to a new mission statement. "Not everything need be *War and Peace*," he says. "I lost no sleep over it." The box office returns crowned his instincts: more than $100 million. He was, once again, at sixty, an uncompromised romantic idol. But that, as ever, turned out to be the salve, not the be-all.

After *Ordinary People,* Redford stated emphatically that he would never appear in a movie he directed. But in the flux of middle-age self-challenge, he reversed this decision and suddenly decided to direct himself in a movie for the first time. The Disney relationship was rosy, and with substantial new hits behind him, brokering the premium deal was straightforward. He chose *The Horse Whisperer,* an as-yet-unreleased novel by new English author Nicholas Evans, which had been hotly auctioned at the October 1994 Frankfurt Book Fair. Wildwood's development chief, Rachel Pfeffer, acquired the rights, believing the blend of romance with a western setting ideal for Redford, whom George Roy Hill had once described as "the natural-born saddlebum." In Evans's novel, Tom Booker, the horse whisperer, is part Zen master, part equine doctor. Romance between Booker and hard-nosed Manhattan businesswoman Annie Maclean begins when Booker tries to help Annie's daughter, Grace, who has been maimed in a riding accident that also severely injured her horse, Pilgrim. In the book, the emotionally frozen Annie becomes pregnant, leaving many unanswered questions. Redford liked the book but disliked the overly melodramatic ending. "My immediate thought was that it would work as a movie if the romance simmered and came close to the boil, but then the Booker character and the woman are stranded by moral dilemma," says Redford.

Readying *The Horse Whisperer*—with Eric Roth, the screenwriter of *Forrest Gump,* drafting the script—Redford decamped to a rented Italianate stucco villa in the foothills of Mount St. Helena at Calistoga, California, an hour north of San Francisco and close to George Lucas's Skywalker Ranch in Marin County, where he intended to do the postproduction work. He was at the end of his romance with Kathy O'Rear and the start of a new relationship with a Hamburg-born expressionist artist,

Sibylle Szaggars. Bylle was in her mid-thirties, dark haired and adept at riding and skiing. She had worked for the Andrew Lloyd Webber organization in London and New York before deciding to pursue her own art out west. They'd met at Sundance, where she stayed while absorbing the southwestern environment for her work. "The relationship with Kathy ended because they were just too different," says a family friend. "Kathy worked like a miner to keep it going, sending him daily letters and sermons, and trying to keep up. But their lives weren't in harmony. She was spending time with her mother in Florida, where her father was very ill; he was elsewhere." Bylle's nature, the same friend observes, was closer to his. "She's a true artist, literate, humorous and active. But the key is, she puts no pressure on him. She's not a woman who sits around waiting for his call. She gets on with her painting and her life, and he loves that sense of freedom she provides."

At too few times throughout his life had he enjoyed domesticity. Now he slipped into a happy routine, shipping in his favorite furniture and his portable sauna, which stood on the tiled terrace overlooking the mountain where Robert Louis Stevenson and Fanny Osbourne had honeymooned in a shack a hundred years before. Bylle pitched in in the kitchen, her dog, Max, always at her heels. Their life in Napa County, she says, was relaxed in a way it could not have been in Los Angeles, Utah or New York. They hiked together, took daily five-mile jogs and read. Jamie, recovering well from his transplant and beginning to write for Wildwood, was in the process of moving to nearby Fairfax. More than ever father and son spent time together, often walking on the beach at Bodega Bay. "I saw my father sharpen up in a way he hadn't done in quite a time," says Jamie. "He had been diffuse. I feel in the middle nineties his purpose became clearer to him. The inner conflicts were less, and Bylle was a positive force in calming him. He worked out hard for *The Horse Whisperer* because he was anxious about the difficulty of directing and starring and fusing all the elements he wanted. He knew he had to be in top physical form."

The one disturbance in his routine was the weekly trip to L.A.—a town he had come to loathe—for casting meetings. He met with Emma Thompson, hoping to interest her in the female lead. "The British do austerity better than any American. The concept I had was to portray Annie as a version of Tina Brown of *Vanity Fair,* with a little of the visible brittleness of Margaret Thatcher." Thompson turned down the part, citing personal problems. His next choice was Kristin Scott Thomas, whom he'd first spotted as the woman secretly in love with Hugh Grant in *Four Weddings and a Funeral.* Redford wanted "an actor who could instantly relate dignity" to play Annie's husband, the romantic competitor to Booker, and chose Australian Sam Neill. Hardest to cast was Grace, the preteen accident victim. Working with casting coordinator Michelle Hartley, he finally decided on fifteen-year-old New Yorker Scarlett Johansson, who had just completed her first lead in Lisa Krueger's modest indie film about foster home runaways, *Manny and Lo.*

Then Eric Roth's script arrived. "It didn't work at all," says Redford. "I wanted to pull the plug. I became unsure of the story. What I was seeking was a fable about faith and redemption, not a story about a sexually frustrated woman." He tried Roth again. "What I wanted to do was for us both to fly to Montana and check out the location because I felt it should 'speak' in this script, as it had in *A River Runs Through It.* I wanted Roth with me, to write as we went, but he wouldn't play ball." Disney dithered, threatening to withdraw should Redford delay any further, but, as ever, he followed his instincts, funding the development personally for the next five months and assigning Richard LaGravenese, who had contributed to Clint Eastwood's *The Bridges of Madison County,* to take over the writing. LaGravenese had attended the Sundance labs as an adviser, and Redford thought highly of him.

By April 1997 Redford was racing against the melting snows in Albany, New York, to begin filming the road accident in which Grace and Pilgrim are injured. Previously, since *Ordinary People,* he had used his own drawings to denote scenes as he visualized them for the cinematographer. On *The Horse Whisperer* he spent hundreds of hours scribbling and collaborating with two storyboard artists and with cinematographer Bob Richardson, famous for his work with Oliver Stone and his inventive use of light. "For the New York part of the movie," says Redford, "I wanted a very congested and disharmonious visual sense that reflected Annie's heart. For Big Sky Montana I wanted Frederic Remington." What this translated to, daringly, was a movie that would be presented in two screen aspect ratios: the New York scenes in standard 1.85:1 ratio, and the Montana sequences widened to a 2.35:1 ratio. There was also a conscious decision, shared with LaGravenese, Richardson and editor Tom Rolf—who had edited *Sneakers*—to create a "novelistic" pace to the drama. The notion in part came from the casting of highly lyrical actors like Dianne Wiest, who played Booker's sister. "Actors like Wiest have extraordinary power," says Redford. "The timbre of their voice carries meaning. I wanted this film to take its time so that the audience could find those small pleasures. I also wanted the audience to slow down to the pace of the West so that the journey made by Grace and especially Annie from Manhattan to Montana is a temporal experience."

The filming spanned the rest of the year. Wiest and Scott Thomas were fine, as was young Ty Hillman, a local find, playing Booker's nephew. Johansson was a "complete natural," says Redford. "A real talent, though she acted by the numbers."

Directing himself, however, proved a bigger challenge than he'd imagined. "Your judgments move to another level. There is absolutely no way you can properly balance your performance, other than by intuition." On-location video playback was of limited help. "Yes, it was valuable to be able to try something, then go to the monitor and evaluate. But it was an experience like no other I'd had. I was not sociable during *The Horse Whisperer.* I cut off and was dependent on Bylle as my lifeline to the real world."

Throughout the movie Redford was most impressed by Scott Thomas. There was just one, late problem. LaGravenese's revision had removed the pregnancy and melodrama of Evans's book and used Redford's idea of restraint and redemption. Through Booker's calm and guidance, Grace's confidence is restored and, in the parallel story line, the slow-burning attraction between easterner and westerner turns into full-on love. At the end, Annie finally faces separation from Booker, as she must return to her family and her life in New York. "Kristin was strong," says Redford. "She was often very poignant, and I told her how much it meant, how well she'd read Annie. But then came the goodbye, where the two of them studiously avoid the Big Love Scene. It is a heartrending moment that required Kristin to break down and weep, but she couldn't get it. She tried. She struggled with the text and the reasons. But it wouldn't work in her head."

Watching her unease, Redford called her aside. "What's going on?" he asked her.

Scott Thomas was shuffling notes in her hand. "I don't know why I'm leaving. I mean, my character is confusing here. Why am I doing this?"

"I found myself looking her straight in the eye," Redford recalls, "and saying, maybe a little sternly, 'You're doing it because it's the end of the movie and you have to do it.' "

The economy of words epitomized Redford's trust in good actors. The tears came on cue.

At one point during preproduction, walking at Bodega Bay, Jamie had queried his father's involvement in the film, sparing any niceties. "Why are you doing this crap?" Jamie asked, reminding his father of the work he personally most admired, work like *Jeremiah Johnson,* which seemed courageous, encoded, loaded with worth by comparison. "I interpreted that as the biggest challenge," says Redford, "because there's no question about the facile nature of screen romances, or the seduction of the old Disney way. It was a bit of a minefield. But I promised him I was aiming for something more stratified and purist. I said, 'It won't be playful. It won't be sexy. But it'll try to tell a great story with feeling.' "

Some believe another, deeper stream fed the movie: that Redford, fully acknowledging Pollack's skill with love stories and his contribution to Redford's romantic iconography, wanted to demonstrate his individual worth. "If that was true," said Hume Cronyn, "it was a big plus. The jock in Bob never died. And competition is a great incentive."

According to *Vanity Fair,* Joe Roth, the new chairman of Walt Disney Studios, wept when he saw the first half hour of the movie, claiming it indicated one of the most emotional pictures he'd ever seen. Half a year later, with the movie running four months behind schedule, word came from Burbank that Roth disliked the Montana sequences and judged the film overlong and tedious. At Disney's request, Redford engaged two extra editors, Hank Corwin and Freeman Davies, known respectively for Oliver Stone movies and MTV work, to radically recut it down from four hours.

The best part of the postproduction, says Redford, was his decision to install editing facilities in the basement at Calistoga, far from Burbank. "It saved my sanity because I could be upstairs and hit a hot idea, then run down to the basement and insert it." Still, Tom Rolf often found Redford struggling for objectivity: "Of course, it wasn't easy with Roth on his back, but that's the way of Hollywood. His trouble was with his own scenes mostly, the ones where he was on-screen, carrying the drama. I would see an obvious moment to cut in some sequence, and he'd say, 'No, no, no, there must be a better cutting point for me.' He was impossible to please. He was very critical of his own performance and he sweated blood on it."

To satisfy Disney, fifty minutes of cuts were made, but the film still came in at almost three hours. Redford sought more cuts, and Rolf steered him to an early hospital scene, which, said Rolf, ran long. Rolf proposed to cut what he deemed an unnecessary verbal exchange where a doctor tells Annie that Grace has had half her leg amputated. Once the information is related, said Rolf, the scene is over. Redford objected. When the doctor delivers his line, LaGravenese scripted Annie's response as "Which leg?" Rolf says, "I said to Bob, 'Please, it's redundant. We can save three minutes here.' "

Redford refused emphatically. "For me it was the Chekhovian element," he says. "The obvious cut was the commercial way. But Chekhov would always present the surprise beat, the wrong reaction that drove right to the heart of the meaning. So I said to Tom, 'To hell with Disney. To hell with time fixations. Do it this way.' "

By Christmas, assembly work on the film had shifted to Skywalker. Tom Newman had started scoring the music; the final vocal dubbing was in train at Todd-AO in Los Angeles. Then, in March, the marketers flew to northern California with their distribution projections and pasteup designs for billboards to be used as far away as Sydney and Tokyo. Predictably, the template poster featured a smoky close-up of Booker and Annie poised for a kiss. Redford would have none of it. "I'm trying to present this as a story of some metaphysical power," he told the ten-man team gathered around a boardroom table at Skywalker. "I don't want the cliché."

Redford came out of the Disney meeting furious—and very significantly troubled. "I was expected to do *Oprah Winfrey* and *Larry King* and *Barbara Walters* and bang the drum all over the planet. I saw the 'me' they wanted to package, the commodity. I said, 'No, I don't wish to do this again. It's a story, a movie story, that's all. Let the audience decide its value. Take it or leave it.' "

The Horse Whisperer had cost $80 million, making it the biggest budget Redford had handled for a directorial feature. His slice was $10 million, with a 10 percent profit share. When the movie opened in May 1998—with a galloping horse dominating the poster—its success around the world was instant. It made its money back in eight weeks and went on to gross more than $120 million.

But the damage was done with Roth. "I heard he hated it," says Redford. "But he never had the guts to confront me directly." Calls went unanswered, and it became clear that Lourd's dream of a multipicture deal with Disney was dead.

What was most significant about the play-out of *The Horse Whisperer*, however, was the intransigence of Redford's marketing response. Much as he conceded to the nobility of playing iconic heroes, and to the public's expectation of him, his greater need was newness and discovery. His nature was always stoutly independent. And there is a paradox in the fundamental ideals we associate with individuality. We expect the individual to remain faithful to their essential character, but we also expect rebellious renewal. Redford conformed: he was ready for change again.

22

The Edge

Studio connections would come and go, but the resolution of independence was permanent. So, too, was Sundance, in Redford's mind. But that commitment would be put to the test once again.

Sundance's finances had, ironically, been at their most fragile since the start of the nineties. The exponential growth of the entities (defined as arts, corporate and activist departments) following the 1989 film festival breakthrough looked good on paper, but the greater exposure meant greater demands on resources. The Sundance Institute, the arts lab beating heart of the empire, began the decade $1 million in debt. The regular benefactors—including Paul Newman, David Puttnam, Vidal Sassoon, Jake Eberts, Irene Diamond and Hume Cronyn—could not fund all that needed to be done to keep the pace. Brent Beck and Gary Beer's retail catalog, now largely in the design hands of Shauna, proved a cash-flow asset, but much more was needed. By the mid-nineties, with the institute budget in excess of $5 million yearly, much was dependent on the film festival. In 1995, 30 percent of the institute's budget was covered by the festival receipts, but still there was a colossal deficit.

In 1994 Redford came up with a possible solution, conceiving the idea of a dedicated Sundance television cable channel that would present alternative moviemaking to a wider audience. The concept seemed a natural one, piggybacking on a communication phenomenon that had taken wing since the deregulation of the television industry in 1972. Cable was originally a modest business, devised to relay over-the-air broadcasts to inaccessible areas. By the mid-nineties almost half of all householders across the country were cable subscribers. Redford entrusted Beer to build a partnership with Showtime (a division of CBS), Universal Studios (part of NBC Universal) and an international cofunder, Polygram Filmed Entertainment.

The aim was to start in big, sophisticated markets like New York, then expand into other urban areas where cable thrived, until gradually a national coverage was achieved. The initial target audience was four million, projected to grow to fifteen million. The Independent Film Channel, however, beat Sundance to the starting gate by a substantial lead. IFC was a sister channel to "cable's cultural powerhouse" Bravo and started transmitting in September 1994 with an advisory board that included Martin Scorsese, Jim Jarmusch, Steven Soderbergh and Spike Lee. Sundance Cable got going eighteen months later, promising a similar bill of uncensored alternative viewing, with an accent on Sundance festival films and documentaries. "But it was a heartbreaker," says Redford. "We were well capable of moving faster, but the executive expertise was sloppy, and the window of opportunity was missed." Sundance Cable, nevertheless, pushed on, launching to three million households in February 1996, with Nora Ryan of Showtime as titular head and Dalton Delan of the Travel Channel in charge. "We had all the tools to take on the IFC," says Redford. "Beyond that, it was just a question of sales drive and determination."

There was also financial scope, it was decided, in Sundance movie theaters. Redford remembered from his childhood a picture house he loved, the Aero on Santa Monica Boulevard, where he'd seen *The Fallen Sparrow* with his uncle David. In the early nineties, its fading art deco splendor prompted him to purchase the site and restore the building to its former grandeur. This set in motion another underwriting plan. "What I imagined was, again, the alternative experience," says Redford. "What we had was the characterless multiplex, the same in Seattle as in Orlando. I thought of a different setup, where each exhibition arena would serve two purposes. First, it would culturally reflect its location in every way, in the building design, the building components, the local history. Second, it would offer integrated facilities that promoted independent filmmaking at the most basic level. For example, a library unit, an equipment rental space, even an advisory desk." He hoped this vision of Sundance Cinema Centers could expand internationally. In meetings with the key players in the Sundance family—Geoff Gilmore and Nicole Guillemet (overseers of the film festival) and Ken Brecher and Michelle Satter (overseers of institute and labs respectively) and international programs director Patricia Boero—a potential map of global Sundance Cinema Centers was drawn up, stretching from Cuba to China. To partner this extraordinary venture, Redford signed a deal with Richard A. Smith, chairman of General Cinema, the eighth-largest chain of theaters in the country.

Meanwhile, the day-to-day struggle to keep afloat went on. Ostensibly, Gary Beer was directing overall business operations for the multientity Sundance Group, as it was now known, but it was Redford who made the decisions, halving the administrative budget to $2.7 million and pressing all his business contacts for more support. Broadway designer Ian Calderon, serving as a Sundance business adviser, persuaded Sony to contribute gratis equipment to the labs, so that student filmmakers would have the best available new technology. Other contributions came from SegaSoft and Panavision, and new funding came from the Cissy Patterson Trust and the Edward John Noble Foundation.

All the time, says Redford, he was aware of his failings as a manager: "I tended to be disorganized and too spontaneous," he says, "and I also trusted too much." He became concerned at this time that crucial initiatives were being mishandled within the group. Failings in the actualization of the cable scheme and the cinema centers initiative sounded the alarm, but then Redford discovered troubling aspects of the deal making. The finger pointed to Gary Beer, who, as one staffer put it, "tended to operate as a one-man band." Redford was particularly bothered that the cable deal allowed Beer to cash in his Sundance shares at any time. Arguments ensued, then Beer resigned "by mutual agreement." In his place Redford installed Bob Freeman, who had helped create the sports-themed restaurant franchise ESPN Zone. To join him in a retooled management, Redford also appointed Gordon Bowen, a Madison Avenue adman responsible for the redesign of American Express and Coca-Cola, with responsibility to rebrand Sundance. Shortly after, as part of the executive shake-up, the team managing the new cable channel was replaced by Tom Harbeck, former creative linchpin of Nickelodeon.

There was still, stubbornly, a perception problem about Sundance and what it truly represented. The oft-expressed, easy-target obloquy "purveyors of granola film" was fueled by the rebels of Sundance themselves. In June 1990 Quentin Tarantino had arrived at the labs to workshop *Reservoir Dogs* with adviser Steve Buscemi. Eighteen months later, as a favor, festival director Geoff Gilmore rushed the late-delivered movie into festival competition. When it failed to win the grand jury prize, Tarantino left town declaring Sundance a waste of time. "They were liberal in the worst sense," he was reported saying. "When [the competition] was over I stormed out. It was a slightly less dramatic version of, Fuck off!" On its later release *Reservoir Dogs* was much honored as the movie that reclaimed the spirit of film noir for America. But no credit went to Sundance.

Sterling Van Wagenen was vehement about what he saw as a built-in contradictory dilemma. "When the summer labs started in 1981, the sanctity of the independent artist was written in stone. In those early meetings we were surrounded by Victor Nunez, Moctesuma Esparza, Larry Littlebird and Annick Smith, all of whom had very strong opinions and were protective of the notion of liberal thinking and freedom. It was a place for radicals. Those people were weeded out over the years. At my last Sundance board meeting, which was held in a conference room at CAA in Beverly Hills, Joe Roth was sitting on one side of me, and Mike Ovitz on the other. When I looked around, there were no independent filmmakers in the room at all." Hume Cronyn said, "The problem centers on the word 'independent.' Bob always stated that he wanted to create opportunity for new voices, some paradigm that allowed others to speak, as it were. This was about equal opportunity arts. But those new artists are looking for the wide audience, too, and they often become absorbed in the mainstream. So 'granola' only means 'organic' and 'new.' What happens afterward, after these new independent voices break out, is nothing to do with Sundance, or its identity."

Sundance was still, unquestionably, a lure for those with fresh ideas. By the mid-nineties, the institute (now distinguished as the nonprofit kernel of the group) operated eight separate creative workshops, covering tuition in all areas of filmmaking, with the June writer-director labs attracting more than a thousand applicants yearly. The ten-day for-profit film festival had become a national cultural reference point, a place, wrote Richard Zoglin in *Time,* where "festivalgoers complain about overcrowded screenings" and distributors like Samuel Goldwyn Films, Sony Pictures Classics and Fine Line flocked, following Miramax's trail, to buy "a selection of offerings from Latin and Native American filmmakers." But it was all still, despite Van Wagenen's suggestion, *independent* film, conceived away from studio patronage, nurtured with altruistic aim and made available in the most democratic of forums.

Redford still saw perceptual difficulties with his core determination for Sundance: to create opportunity for artists. "I saw the problem of my personal fame and the association with what attempted to be an egalitarian colony. I began to wonder was that problem ever answerable. Was it best, in order to get a night's sleep, just to step out of the equation?" In his journal he wrote: "How can I express what Sundance is? I seem to have found something in taking the value of the old, and integrating it in the new. A third eye for a new third way. But it's a sonofabicth to make people get it.

I have to get it so clear that I can pass it down as an axiom. A word. An icon. An acorn."

Whatever the criticisms, whatever the difficulties, the public had a stubborn appetite for Sundance. "People wanted it," says Gordon Bowen. "Bob always spoke of inclusiveness, of the validity of a forum that allowed all American filmmakers a good chance. He wasn't overly political or philosophical, and that's what brought so many people in. Marginalized people, minorities, whoever, could have a shot at it. One forum for all. Speaking as a product promoter, I thought this is noble, decent and secure."

Security, though, was the real problem. After two years, Redford was depressed to learn the Sundance Channel was reaching just six million subscribers, compared with the IFC's ten million–plus. He was losing ground. A series of emergency task force workshops was arranged to review the overall executive management of the group. Initially, it looked hopeful. Progress with the cinema centers seemed assured. Building was already under way at the University of Pennsylvania and in Portland, San Francisco, Dallas and Boston. Sites in Europe, China and Cuba had been visited, surveyed and short-listed. Media reportage was positive, even enthused.

But at a time of millennial recession, when yet another severe stock market tumble chilled the world, four of the six leading movie exhibitors went out of business. In the summer of 2000, to Redford's astonishment, General Cinema Corporation, the partners in the Sundance chain, filed for Chapter 11. Within a short time, Bowen, Harbeck and Freeman were gone. Sundance was, again, in executive free fall.

In November 1998, shortly after completing a new political thriller, *The Devil's Own,* with Brad Pitt in Ireland, Alan Pakula died in a car accident near Melville, New York. Redford was upset by the news, doubly so because he'd just returned from a visit to another dear friend, the environmentalist Margaret Owings, who lay dying at her home at Big Sur. He wrote an emotional eulogy for Pakula in *Time.* Just weeks before, Pakula had mused on his old collaborator's durability. Sundance, Pakula opined, was a kind of Camelot that "has worked long enough for people to start debating independence in filmmaking, which in itself validates it." And yet, he felt, Redford's most enduring creation must be his screen persona. "He has disappointed me at times, and yet, in terms of a romantic icon, no one holds a candle to him. He assumed Clark Gable's crown, and they will both be remembered for the complexity under the surface. They were glamorous, but there was always the threat that romance is dangerous."

But Redford's screen persona, if it was to be solely encapsulated in *The Horse Whisperer,* provided a personal conundrum. He was in his sixties when he romanced Kristin Scott Thomas, almost twenty-five years his junior, on the screen. And while it is true that "the contract" the heroic star makes with his audience is often forgiving, his basic adventurous nature railed against stagnation. Few Hollywood actors maintain bankability into their late sixties. Those that have—Jack Nicholson, Clint Eastwood, Sean Connery—endure because they embrace old age. The extraordinary potency of Redford's romantic image, however, complicated the transition.

George Roy Hill, confined to his Upper East Side apartment in the late stages of Parkinson's disease, hadn't spoken to Redford in years but was aware of the inevitable changes he faced. For him, Redford's career as an actor divided in two: he was the buckskin saddlebum, a part of his nature that grew from the Texas frontier; the other part arose from his friendship with Pollack, a probing Jewish sobriety that extracted the seductive Casanova from what Hill called "troubled" Irishness. "Everyone wants to be Irish in Hollywood," said Hill, "because it connotes Shaw and Joyce and that long, tormented history of suffering and alienation. Nowadays they're even calling Jack Nicholson an Irishman. But Bob's Irishness, as remote as it is, springs from the genuine well of despair. He has trouble balancing himself in the world." Reflecting on his work over the years, Hill concluded: "There's a lack of resolution that makes Redford special. It's summed up in that final scene in *The Candidate,* his best picture, where, after the shenanigans of the election, McKay says, 'What do we do now?' That *question* is in Bob." For Hill, the way forward for Redford in his sixties was "to turn inward, and give voice to some of that turmoil we've only seen glimpses of."

At the turn of the century, Redford seemed ready for transformation. He was in contact with Robert Pirsig, whose *Zen and the Art of Motorcycle Maintenance,* a personal account of recovery from a nervous breakdown on a road trip with his son, deeply touched Redford. He found it "familiar" in the best sense and had met with Pirsig years before in an attempt to mount a movie based on the book. Pakula had wondered if Redford's seemingly exotic desire to make the movie wasn't unfulfilled remedial family work. Redford thought not. It was, he insists, a desire to connect with "the freedom inherent in the surrender to insanity, or the insanity inherent in freedom." Pirsig invited Redford to join him on the road in a battered old Cadillac. Redford imagined the delights of immersing in Pirsig's spiritual adventures and finding out more about the "energetic facts" of true awareness poached from Carlos Castaneda's Yaqui guru, Don Juan Matus, that Pirsig so obsessively beat the drum about. But Redford was tied up with Sundance business, and the Pirsig connection slipped.

At that moment, serendipitously, Jake Eberts arrived with the outline of a novel called *The Legend of Bagger Vance.* In Eberts's recollection the novel "somehow seemed important. I found myself flying to L.A. to see Bob with a sense of urgent purpose." An arrangement to meet at Redford's beach house was made, but with a flight delay and heavy traffic, Eberts arrived at Trancas Beach in a sweat, running late. "I was wired, and when Bob saw the state I was in, he offered to find me a change of T-shirt. I thought, That's it, then. Knowing him, I've lost my window. He'll start taking calls and answering faxes and I can forget *Bagger Vance.*"

Eberts offered to read the outline there and then to Redford, and within the space of one page, he saw the change in Redford. "He switched off the fax and phone and settled in. 'I like this,' he told me, and I knew my instinct was right: that he was waiting for a movie like this, something mystical and fresh, to take him in a new direction."

Steven Pressfield's novel *The Legend of Bagger Vance* was attractive to Redford in part because of its subject matter, golf. He had started playing golf while caddying at the Bel Air Club in 1948 and at one time played to scratch. Recently, as part of his rehabilitation, Jamie had taken to the game, and since he and his father were near neighbors in northern California, it seemed an ideal way of sharing time. But the greatest draw was the philosophical symbolism of the story, which amounted to nothing less than a midlife confessional, laying out the values that dictated all his choices.

Redford had recently discovered analyst James Hillman's *The Soul's Code,* with its theory of benevolent destiny. According to Jamie, *Bagger Vance*—the fictional story of a gifted golfer who loses his swing—"echoed" Hillman. "It was obvious Dad was crossing a bridge, in terms of his self-definition," says Jamie. "And *Bagger Vance* was an expression of that."

In keeping with his desire to explore new collaborations, Redford commissioned former psychiatrist Jeremy Leven to draft the screenplay and assigned design to Stuart Craig, whose work on movies like *Gandhi* and *Mary Reilly* impressed him. With Leven, he emphasized that this was a movie of metaphors; when he met Craig, he told him, "I want an exaggerated sense of reality. I want the golfing greens to be greener and the 1920s setting to be fairy-tale." His casting notions swung like a pendulum. First, wildly, he thought of playing the title role himself or costarring with golf adepts like Jack Nicholson or Sean Connery. But Connery and Nicholson, like himself, were past sixty and far from the youthful presences in Pressfield's novel. He switched to the idea of Morgan Freeman as Bagger, the golfing mystic, and Brad Pitt as the story's troubled hero, Rannulph Junuh. Both men turned him down. Eberts landed DreamWorks as the funder, and though Redford found enthusiasm and support from Katzenberg, the studio nudged the movie toward the casting of Matt Damon as Junuh and Will Smith as a younger, racier Bagger Vance. (Damon had never held a golf club, but a tutor took care of that.)

Superficially, Leven's *Bagger Vance* became a romance. Set in the Depression-era Deep South, it tells the tale of war-traumatized Junuh trying to break a perennial bender by helping his former sweetheart, Adele, who is striving to save the town's economy. She has inherited her father's golf course and wants to stage a tournament hosting golf legends Walter Hagen and Bobby Jones. For the tournament to go ahead, Junuh, once the district's great sports hope, must participate, but he cannot recapture the rhythm of his famous swing. The mysterious caddie Bagger Vance arrives from nowhere and, with Adele's loving coaching, guides Junuh back into the zone.

But the romance, says Redford, was merely the hook. Of most value was the morality fable. For Pressfield, the original inspiration was mysticism in the form of the Mahabharata, as summarized in the Bhagavad Gita: Rannulph Junuh, or R. Junuh, is Arjuna, the mythical character who refuses to fight for possession of the kingdom that is rightfully his, since he believes war is wasteful. Lord Krishna lectures him on duty, explaining who Arjuna truly is, who God is, and how one finds peace and meaning in conflict.

In Redford's interpretation the mysticism was secondary to a hero's story. It was, says Redford, drawn from the Jungian well, and from elements of Joseph Campbell's *The Hero with a Thousand Faces,* which illuminates the interweaving of all cultural mythologies and proposes the importance of the retelling of tales to reinforce our sense of common spiritual purpose. "Given that we have abandoned myth in our culture," says Redford, "it seemed like the right time to offer this compendium. I had a sense that the way we receive information is faulty. Too much that comes into our heads—from the daily media, mostly—is redundant. Do we really *need* to know such a huge amount of detail about the minutiae of every event in every country? *Bagger Vance* was about remembering who we are and this shared spiritual journey we're on."

As with so many script developments over the years, Redford's perfectionist vision slowed the process. Leven drafted and redrafted but was replaced by LaGravenese, since his divided attention on another directorial project irritated Redford. "Bob was really authoring himself," says Eberts, "but that's his style. He is the ghostwriter, don't doubt it." Script finally in hand, Rachel Portman, an English composer, was engaged to produce the lushly nostalgic sound track. Michael Ballhaus, the cinematographer of *Quiz Show,* was, untypically, hired again. South African Charlize Theron, whom Redford had liked in *The Astronaut's Wife,* was cast as Adele. For Theron, *Bagger Vance* had a special resonance. Her own life story was about recovering the groove. Her father had run a very successful business as a road builder. When he died, the banks descended, recalling loans. Only her mother's tenacity, says Theron, regained the family's solvency. "I related to *Bagger Vance,*" said Theron. "[I had] an emotional connection with the characters and with their predicament." Jack Lemmon, professing himself retired, was lured back as the elderly narrator recalling Junuh's grand moment. Says Redford, "As a director, you are looking for actors that are tonal, like paints on a palette. You need them to complement and set off each other. I didn't get all the right people on *Bagger,* but I got enough to make a go of it."

There was optimism in the air in the summer of 1999 as *Bagger Vance* shooting got under way in Savannah, Georgia. "He'd proven a lot commercially with *The Horse Whisperer,*" says Jake Eberts, "and we were feeling he was going from strength to strength."

When the movie wrapped at Christmas, Redford was satisfied. He stayed alone in Utah as the year 2000 dawned, in the Big House, reading Carlos Baker's *Emerson Among the Eccentrics.* Throughout his life, he learned, Emerson carried a compass. The miracle of its magnetic needle, wrote Baker, bore witness to the divine spirit of nature. "I like," said Emerson, "to hold the visible god in my hand." Redford found the notion of palpable metaphor intriguing. It recalled for him his instinctive aspiration in all his ambitious work. "I tried not to overanalyze any movie of mine or anyone else's, and generally self-important cinema annoys me. But there's no question that there's such a thing as 'serious cinema.' Seriousness, as Leonard Cohen says, is deeply agreeable to the human spirit. So there's a validity to movies of ambition, movies that say something. Concept and realization may not marry, of course. Movies fail. But the trying is legitimate. I didn't always stretch with my work, but when I did, it was in hope of generating other ideas—in the audience, as in myself. Observation, commentary, polemic—all seem to me fairly within the remit of modern cinema. And it's healthy to stretch." Such was the reasoning behind *Bagger Vance.*

Bagger Vance was announced for a June 2000 release, but when Walter Parkes, the studio executive, saw the proposed final cut, it was pulled at the last minute. Reportedly, Parkes was less than delighted with its two hours–plus of sunset golf courses, mellow whimsy and rambling voice-overs. "Parkes couldn't make sense of it," says a Sundance staffer. "The trouble was, as the cliché goes, no one knows nothing in Hollywood. They all admired *A River Runs Through It.* But it didn't make the money *The Horse Whisperer* made. *Bagger Vance* was visually akin to *River,* so there was wariness. Also, to be truthful, DreamWorks' big hits that summer were *Gladiator* and *Cast Away,* two big, starry, showy melodramas. They wanted more of the same from Bob, not a morality tale."

In November 2000, DreamWorks finally authorized the release of *Bagger Vance.* The movie previewed in New York the day America cast its vote in the Bush-Gore election. It was not an auspicious day for Redford in any respect. The size of the movie's failure was considerable. Routinely reviewed as a disappointment, it earned just $30 million, against a production cost of $60 million. *Gladiator,* by comparison, earned half a billion dollars.

When Redford visited Bali and Java with Bylle a few weeks before the opening of *Bagger Vance,* with Sundance's business problems heavy on his mind, he wrote in his diary: "A strange thing. I have huge-scaled symmetrical thoughts of an order not like me, complete, formal and philosophical—and negative. So much negative energy pouring out of me, day and night, it feels like torture. Yet what sustains me is the faith that this is process."

The fact that he had produced a movie so full of mystical whimsy and hopeful philosophy—and one so personally revelatory—and the fact that it had been so resoundingly rejected drove him freshly and deeper into self-analysis. As reflected in the controversy of the disputed national election result, America too was going through a time of great uncertainty and self-questioning. Hurt as he was by the rejection of the movie, he was heartened by this national urge for reevaluation.

The Clinton era in general had been good for him, and the National

Medal of Arts, presented to him by the president at a White House ceremony in May 1999, seemed as much an acknowledgment of his constant conservation work as of Sundance and some durable films. The two campaigns he participated in during the Clinton era, though—the ones he took most pride in—had delivered mixed results.

The expanded highway dispute with the Utah Department of Transportation that had absorbed a hefty amount of his spare time since the seventies seemed resolved when, with Governor Calvin Rampton's intervention, the proposed six lanes were reduced to four. Sundance then suggested further truncation to an environmentally friendly new two-lane road that would be serviced with picnic areas and scenic hike routes built by Redford. Sundance's environmental spokesperson, Julie Mack, felt victory was in sight, that the defacement of the canyon was uppermost in the minds of all locals. But Redford always underestimated local opposition to him and the reality that, for many, he was still an interloper imposing personal priorities. Beyond the ring of resort properties buffering what Gary Beer called "the little kingdom" were three hundred acres of privately owned lands run by eight independent property owner associations amassed under the North Fork Property Owners Council. "They'd always argued with Sundance," says Beer, "starting with rows about who got the first use of the community plows when everyone was snowed in each January. Their position was that they frankly didn't care that Bob's resort had brought a little cash into the local economy each winter season and each summer lab season. They weren't interested in the small fry and they certainly didn't want talk of conservation. They just wanted to make good and invite all and every developer into the area."

The conservationist Utah Coalition's lawyers, partly funded by Redford, lost to the UDOT in the Salt Lake courts. The widened four-lane highway that would allow a heavier volume of cross-state traffic was authorized and, within weeks, construction began. According to Mack, the evidence of serious environmental damage was immediate. Landslide pollution poisoned much of the Provo River stock, and sections of the mountainside fringing the road became unstable and had to be harnessed with permanent, unprepossessing steel buttresses. "It was a case of what happens when you start unraveling a ball of string," says Mack. "It might have been worse, with a six-lane highway and wider land reclaim, but it was still upsetting for everyone interested in land protection."

But there were successes, too. Under Clinton, Republicans in Congress had advanced a bill that proposed the limiting of wilderness in Utah to just 1.8 million acres of Bureau of Land Management–preserved lands. President Clinton had vetoed it. Redford, Mack and Joyce Deep, serving the Utah Coalition, worked with Wayne Owens and Bill Bradley on an alternative Citizens' Proposal Bill calling for 5.7 million wilderness acres. Even the most loyal of Sundance staffers—people like mountain manager Jerry Hill—had their doubts about Redford's goals: "I saw the coalition's viewpoint but the bottom line was our employment and our survival. Preservation was fine. Still, we, and our children, needed to be able to utilize this landscape as needs be." But Ted Wilson, a Mormon, agreed with Redford, feeling it was a moral responsibility that had religious echoes, a land tithing comparable with the Mormons' culture of tithing income. Redford won this round and the bill finally signed into law by Clinton effectively endorsed unspecified expanded wilderness.

Joyce Deep's respect for Redford's vision and tenacity grew. But among his executive staff there was greater dissent. He was often regarded as a difficult, sometimes intimidating presence. "You knew his wrath," said one staffer, "and you always tried to avoid his company if you were on the wrong side of a discussion." But Deep defended the kind of obstinancy needed to match the challenges he had set himself. "He could be a pain in the ass," she says, "because it was often hard, say, writing a speech for him, to please him in the details. He also was not known for dishing out massive praise. But he was a fighter, with the best. And he was modest, too modest, in situations like the wilderness challenge. He wanted to credit the coalition, but his personal achievement was huge. His style was to get his hands dirty, and he did most of it out of the media glare. When he wanted [California senator] Dianne Feinstein on our side, he just got in his car and drove right up to her home in San Francisco on a Sunday morning and knocked on her door: 'Can I talk with you about these bills? We need you on our side.' Feinstein became one of the great voices of the conservationists, and that was thanks to him, though few people knew it."

When President Clinton inaugurated a new national park in the Escalante Red Rocks—at 1.7 million acres, the biggest new national easement since Teddy Roosevelt's day—Redford was standing proudly beside him on the Grand Canyon podium, though, says John Adams, he'd made it clear that he bore no special allegiance to any one party. "Though he'd done so much for us at the NRDC, we didn't regard him as 'our own' because he resisted labels. He felt he wanted to address the causes that felt right, and be unimpeded by partisanship of any kind." Redford liked the

Clintons, admired the president's work, especially in race relations, and concluded "his centrist policy is probably right, for now at any rate."

Through 1998 and 1999 Redford continued to be sporadically involved in elective politics. He supported twenty-three candidates in congressional elections. Only six of the candidates for whom he made radio commercials or speeches failed to win a seat. In the presidential stakes, however, he was not so lucky. Bill Bradley's aborted run for the presidency saddened him. But he continued to support the League of Conservation Voters and strategized "a better, effective awareness of environmental threat issues by taking a state-by-state approach, candidate by candidate, rather than lobbying for change at the top."

Joyce Deep saw the obsessive nature of his strategizing, but as she got to know him better, she also saw that everything was secondary to his love of cinema. "He'd talk shop, politically speaking, for hours," she says. "If [a political story] was dominating the headlines, he was first in with a point of view—never gossipy, but intellectually probing. Still, there was always the shadow of some creative project. You'd want a meeting to discuss someone's congressional campaign, and he'd be looking at his watch. There was always some Wildwood imperative, just one more script to read."

In the aftermath of the collapse of the would-be Sundance Cinema Centers and the poor showing for *Bagger Vance,* Redford was depressed. Bylle took him home to Hamburg to distract and revive him. With Sundance teetering again, she suggested an independent review of Redford's finances, corporate and personal.

For years he had entrusted his investments and property purchases totally to Reg Gipson. Gipson had become a family friend, always with a smile on his face and a kind word. The two men had a natural kinship that made time in each other's company—whether in Gipson's Corporate Management Group offices on Avenue of the Stars in Los Angeles or in Calistoga or Utah—joyful. "I'd never really paid attention," says Redford. "Reg handed me summary sheets of my outgoings and I asked no questions." There were sensitive areas, on reflection, where Redford should have asked questions. He did not, for example, query the stock purchases advised by Gipson's brother's brokerage in New York, or the details of the six major mortgages on properties stretching across the country, from

Manhattan to Trancas Beach. "I would go out, make a movie and call Reg and say, 'I like New Mexico. Buy me a property, or take a lease.' " Now, when the review results were in, Redford was staggered by the accumulated exposure of his mortgages and the size of his personal debts. He saw the error of his ways.

Immediately, he instructed Gipson to sell off all his properties except in Utah. He was, he admits, "tailspinning." His film business lawyer since the seventies—originally backing up Hendler and at the fore since Hendler's demise—was the esteemed, expensive Barry Tyerman. Redford consulted Tyerman, passing on Gipson's records. The men met in Tyerman's office in Century Park in Los Angeles. Redford recalls Tyerman's sharp intake of breath. "You need to declare bankruptcy," said Tyerman.

Redford knew the wisdom of Tyerman's expertise but could not bring himself to accede. His track record of stubbornness and winning—from defying Paramount over *Blue* to helping defeat the Republicans' rollback wilderness initiative—bore him up. "Of course I probably should have taken Barry's advice and laid down my hand. But that would mean walking away from Sundance. That was never going to happen."

Redford rolled up his sleeves once again.

23

The Actor in Transit

The original design of the Sundance Group was radically modified, out of necessity. A new, edgier version of Sundance Productions, headed up by former MGM executive Jeff Kleeman and capitalizing on the marquee value of the Redford connection to produce movies made either independently or under the auspices of South Fork Pictures, a Wildwood-allied company managed by Michael Nozik, was launched. It coproduced a number of Sundance-developed features, such as Ed Burns's *She's the One,* with the urgent goal of buttressing Sundance's finances.

It wasn't to be. And neither was the salvation package that hung on Microsoft's cofounder Paul Allen's Vulcan Productions, the seemingly perfect cash-rich partner to plug the gap left by the collapse of General Cinema. With Allen's cash, Redford intended to buy out his cable partners and rid himself of what he saw as "the boardroom compromises" that dogged the institute's history. He came close, but Vivendi, the French conglomerate, undercut him, purchasing Universal (the Sundance channel's co-owners) and, says Redford, scared Allen off.

Being tested as never before, Redford relied on his quirky attributes of self-sufficiency, instinctive reasoning and sheer will to keep him on track. "He was never good at self-pity," says Jamie. "Because he was a man of action, every crisis he saw, in the Chinese way, as an opportunity. So, perversely, he was wildly motivated when things hit the bottom."

Redford saw the remedy as a mixture of introducing new blood and, at the same time, reinstating old concepts. He retained a Salt Lake City adviser, lawyer Tom Jolley, and two young accountants, Kyle Pexton and Tye Davis, who immediately took charge and redirected his energies. Within a very short time, new initiatives for the Sundance Institute were announced to steer it back to its arts-purist roots. These included the establishment of the International Documentary Fund, a scheme to underwrite fifty indie documentaries over five years for the Sundance Channel, aided by $4.5 million in grants from the Open Society Institute.

But the best efforts of Jolley, Pexton and Davis couldn't counter the damage of years of financial overreaching. In 2002 Bruce Willard, founder and president of the apparel catalog The Territory Ahead, acquired a controlling 50 percent share of the Sundance catalog in a deal that replenished Redford's personal wealth, and, therefore, stabilized Sundance. Two years later, Willard and Redford sold the company to Boston-based Webster Capital and New York–based ACI Capital for close to $40 million. Willard disposed of all his shares, but Redford maintained a nominal 3 percent, less as an investment than a fingerprint.

How painful was this surrender for Redford? "It cut him up because of the unavoidable suggestion that a key component was gone," said one longtime staffer. "Sundance had been growing its branches over the years. This was the first to truly go." Redford insists, "It was a necessary reordering, that's all. Over the years, Shauna, myself and others built a very individual and unique western profile in the retail trade, and we continue to take pride in that. It's out there, it goes on, and I am still a part of the Sundance catalog and always will be, so the 'acorn' pertains."

What lay ahead was a continuing erosion and a fight that he knew could only be engaged in by maintaining the high public profile that launched Sundance in the first place. Reasoning the importance of his mission, he decided, was easy. Emerson spoke of a nation in terms of "conscience keepers," and that was a concept that still sat well with him. Bob Woodward, who had stayed in touch with him, believes that "conscience" is the word that underlies *All the President's Men* and so many of Redford's other ambitious works. It also, Woodward believes, lies at the heart of his Sundance experimentation and, further back, at the heart of his decision in the sixties to acquire and preserve the Sundance canyon: "He had a problem about profligate use of land and indifference, and that never stopped." Though he was most comfortable domestically now in northern California, the canyon—and the colony it bred—continued to embody his raison d'être. "I hated this continual firefighting. But then what worthwhile cause is easy?" says Redford. "I knew I had to persevere in order to finance Sundance, and that came down to persevering as an actor and an artist."

Out of the threatened bankruptcy came renewed vigor to experiment and extend. The next film he took on, *Spy Game,* seemed at first a backward step. It was originally developed by Dutch director Mike van Diem and producer Douglas Wick and inherited by *Enemy of the State* director Tony Scott. The attraction for Redford was Scott's dazzling son et lumière reputation and by Michael Frost Beckner's electric script, which bore distinct tones of Wick's all-time favorite movie, *Three Days of the Condor.* Markedly in the stylized contemporary thriller fashion, which borrowed an MTV sensibility of equal emphasis on rock music and flash editing, the movie represented a distinct step into the youth market, a pleasing act of appeasement to Lourd and CAA.

Beckner's script, revised with David Arata, was set in 1991 and dealt with two generations of CIA field operatives, moving forward and backward over sixteen years of subterfuge in Vietnam, Berlin, Beirut and China. Superficially a buddy story, *Spy Game* distinguished itself as a condensed history of recent American foreign policy, enshrining a critique of institutional amorality. That naturally pleased the man who had created *All the President's Men.* Redford's role was CIA veteran Nathan Muir, who, on his last day at Langley, learns that his protégé, "Boy Scout" Bishop, played by Brad Pitt, has been incarcerated in a Chinese prison under sentence of death. Intercut with long Redford monologues that unveil the sacrificing of his friend, the movie ticks down toward Bishop's hour of execution.

Filming *Spy Game* presented substantial logistical problems. To convey the variations of time and place, Scott used archive black-and-white reversal film stock that intensifies colors, digital video, differing gauges of standard film and vintage cameras. Redford's work, from late November through January 2001, mainly involved location shooting in Morocco, followed by the Langley CIA interiors staged at Shepperton Studios, outside London. Originally, the Beirut sequences were scheduled for Tel Aviv and Haifa. "But we had troublesome incidents in Israel," said Scott. "There was a firebomb thrown at our hotel, and then it reached a crisis point when someone was killed and dumped on the steps. We cut our losses and looked elsewhere to duplicate Beirut." The troubles were heightened by the fact that Pitt had signed on for Steven Soderbergh's *Ocean's Eleven,* which was due to commence directly after Christmas. "We were hemmed in [by Pitt's dates]," said Scott, "so there was a stopwatch on us all the time. But Bob understood the pressures on Brad, and he never complained."

Forbearance required an emotional adjustment by Redford. A decade before, he had effectively started Brad Pitt's career. Now it was Pitt in the spotlight, and it was Pitt's minders and agents who dictated scheduling and the mood on the set. Redford could grin and bear it, though he did chafe at Pitt's insistence on a closed set, with no interruptions or visitors. Pitt himself was courteous, announcing to the media that he'd committed to the picture "basically because Bob was aboard" and expressing warm friendship to Redford throughout. "I wasn't, obviously, resentful," says Redford. "I fully understood the rules of the game and I acknowledged how hard it is to retain balance in the kind of promotional frenzy Brad was experiencing. I'd been there. I knew the territory. Now it was his moment. So I sat it out when I had to."

Shooting shifted to Casablanca. For Redford, this was the best news. Just the previous year he had promised Bylle a long vacation in Morocco. As he expected, he felt an affinity for the local culture and threw himself into learning as much as he could about it. "We can't bury our heads in the ground about foreign cultures," he says, "and I took this opportunity to observe and learn with enthusiasm." The urge to understand Arab life, says Redford, was exactly equal to the drive to experience Europe in the fifties. "I found I connected comfortably with the setting," says Redford, "the same way I connected with the Hispanic people, or the people of the Celtic Isles."

A surprising ebullience about moviemaking returned to Redford during *Spy Game.* The breakneck speed of the movie gave him energy. He lamented the fact that, because he was sixty-four, the insurance underwriters limited the helicopter battle sequences in which he could appear. "I did some stuff regardless," he says, "and it was new to me, a real adrenaline blast. The insurers were pulling their hair out, because it was all dangerous, low-level flying, with explosions going off right and left. I loved it."

Redford fit in easily with this new, teen-targeted movie dynamic that demanded texturally variant story lines, an astonishing array of visuals and an average shot duration of 2.6 seconds. "It was a new film language, but it was also a case of the more things change, the more they remain the same. You can set off a million firecrackers, but if you don't have a story to tell and capable actors to relate it, you have nothing but smoke."

Redford's effortless command was highlighted because of its juxtaposition to Pitt's hip, crinkly eyed posturings. "Robert Redford has been around for so long," wrote Edward Guthmann in the *San Francisco Chronicle,* "and has diversified his talents to such an extent—director, environmentalist, indie film guru—that one forgets what a strong and persuasive actor he can be. . . . There's a texture, a dimension to him now that wasn't there before—not only in his weather-beaten face and lumpy hands, but in the way he holds himself and regards the world; in the way he commits himself to this role and doesn't balk at playing the cynical, callous and dishonest aspects of his character."

Spy Game may not have been *Zen and the Art of Motorcycle Maintenance,* Jamie observed, but the central device of the mentor-protégé—what Scott called "the father-son story"—provided what he sought: a chance to essay the bonds of fractured kinship and the difficult business of fixing things.

A career marker was noted by many. Rita Kempley of *The Washington Post* wrote that the film helped Redford "regain the dignity he threw away as Demi Moore's billionaire john in *Indecent Proposal.*" But if CAA imagined such success would plant him firmly in the youth market like, say, Mel Gibson, they were wrong. For a follow-up, Redford quickly opted for a script by thirty-eight-year-old Israeli-born former radio journalist Rod Lurie, who had recently appeared on the front page of *Variety* with his controversial political sleeper, *The Contender,* about a campaign to humiliate a female vice presidential candidate, starring Joan Allen. That movie had been modestly funded by DreamWorks to the tune of $9 million but, after a slow start during the summer, crossed the $100 million earnings mark.

As a journalist broadcasting on KABC talk radio in Los Angeles, Lurie had a reputation as an outspoken leftist who was occasionally barred from press screenings and Republican get-togethers. Redford was flattered that Lurie credited *All the President's Men* as his greatest artistic inspiration. With West Point and a career as a broadcaster behind him, Lurie had started as a filmmaker in 1998 with a half-hour short, *Four Second Delay,* which won the Special Jury Prize at the Deauville American Film Festival. It portrayed a radio call-in show galvanized when a listener threatens to kill hostages unless the on-air interviewee, Bob Woodward, confesses the identity of Deep Throat. Lurie followed this with his feature debut, the one-set *Deterrence,* a political meditation in which the president is forced to a nuclear showdown with Iraq from the isolation of a remote, snow-bound diner. "He was obviously smart," says Redford, "and he was very ballsy. He appeared to have an interesting slant on human behavior, and he also had in his hands a great script. I thought it would be good because he was a younger voice, a new-ideas man to work with."

The men first met in Redford's hotel suite in London shortly before

Christmas. "All we talked about was *All the President's Men,*" says Lurie. "And then he agreed to a second meeting on the next day, and on the next day all we talked about was *Quiz Show.*" They exchanged views on national politics and Hollywood politics. Lurie had, he told Redford, wrestled with DreamWorks over a project to follow *The Contender,* a dilemma Redford well related to. His intention was to film only his own stories, but then DreamWorks gave him "The Castle," the script by David Scarpa and Graham Yost that interested Redford. Redford overcame a personal momentary hesitation. The experience with DreamWorks on *Bagger Vance* rankled, but an undamaged admiration for Katzenberg still existed.

Redford's fascination was with the role of Lieutenant General Irwin, a disgraced career soldier who tackles institutional evil wrought by the governor of the jail to which he's confined. "I thought the role was a little like *Brubaker,*" says Lurie, "and a little of many of the idealist roles he'd played. But it was also new ground. It was taxing because it required him to face new situations he'd never depicted on-screen, like playing the family man."

Redford found the script's metaphor engrossing. "I liked that it analyzed the relationship between honor and leadership," he says. He also had fresh ground to explore as an actor: "In the movie Irwin dies. I'd never portrayed death on-screen in a movie, and the actor in me said, It's about time!"

In February 2001 shooting commenced at the movie's sole location, the disused Tennessee state penitentiary that had once housed James Earl Ray, the assassin of Martin Luther King Jr. By now the movie was retitled *The Last Castle,* to avoid confusion with a low-budget Australian comedy just released. Lurie felt "privileged," he says, to have Redford walk out into the prison yard on that freezing winter's morning. He wasn't the only one enamored of Redford. On the day he arrived, says Lurie, the assembled cast and crew, numbering a hundred, "fell into a kind of reverential awe." James Gandolfini of television's *The Sopranos* was cast as Colonel Winter, the prison governor who first welcomes the once-esteemed Irwin, then, after months of provocative challenge to his authority, grows to hate him. "Jim was critical," says Lurie, "because the story needed a huge character to stand up to Irwin, who I knew would assume even greater weight with Redford in charge." Redford enjoyed the heavyweight opposition: "Years before, I remember sensing my game rise when I faced Jason Robards in

The Iceman Cometh. Great actors move you. *The Last Castle* had moments of the great two-hander, moments when you looked at Jim and didn't know what was coming. Those are the moments that excite the actor."

Chess framed *The Last Castle.* "It was really very precise," says Lurie, "because it's evenhanded. Irwin arrives in a dignified glory, his battlefield reputation preceding him. The inmates bow to his status. But they're scared of Winter. Little by little Winter's jealousy of Irwin changes the attitude of the inmates. He bullies them, and he makes mistakes humiliating Irwin in front of them, and finally the inmates' loyalty to Irwin transforms to a frenzy of revolt, the object of which is to capture the prison flag and fly it in the upside-down position that signals distress, meaning that Winter is the monster and injustice rules the prison. So the movie becomes, literally, 'Your move, my move,' to capture the king."

The Last Castle brought out Redford's most ambitious acting performance in thirty years. Lurie felt all Redford's history—the activism, the rebelliousness, the independence—pour out of him. "Bob never ceased to remind us how much he despised institutional thuggery," says Lurie. In one sequence, Irwin pulls a young inmate, Aguilar, played by Clifton Collins, in line, showing him how to properly salute. "It took fifteen takes to get a decent salute out of Bob," says Lurie. The best he could muster, preserved on film, seems more an act of offense than any three-star gesture. "In all those little details he was giving us who he was, what he stood for, how he regards misused authority."

During April, Redford got to play his big death scene. He'd done it before on television, and died offscreen in *Out of Africa* and *The Great Waldo Pepper,* but he says, "when I squared up, it was tougher and more emotionally draining than I'd imagined." The unease arose from the recent deaths of close friends like Margaret Owings and Pakula; on his mind, too, were the recent close shaves he'd personally experienced. Not long before, he'd survived a motorcycle skid on a bend of the Alpine Loop that sent him off the precipice, a genuine brush with death. Later, a chartered Learjet he took with Bylle and her dog, Max, back to Santa Rosa from New Mexico lost both of its engines for nine minutes. The plane lost twenty-one thousand feet in altitude. Redford recalls the panic in the cockpit and the mechanical process of locking his seat belt "with the absolute certainty it was all over. What I felt was the inevitable: Shit, how simple! Someone fits a plug wrong and—*pow!*—we end like this. And then I felt the strangest thing: a mix of anger, fear, resolve . . . and optimism. We were heading toward the ground and it all dispelled in, *Hell, I'm not ready to go! There's too much to do!*" At eighteen thousand feet, the engines kicked in and the pilots brought the jet down safely in Las Vegas. When everyone hit the bar for a whiskey, says Redford, the atmosphere was strangely serene. "Because you are so humbled by the enormousness of chance, and by your fragility. You are drinking whiskey with your boots on the good earth solely because destiny says so. You personally did nothing to alter the situation. Destiny made its mind up."

Playing the death scene, where Winter snatches a pistol and shoots Irwin in a riot, Redford employed a Method-like sense memory: "That one little scene exhausted me. So many thoughts—indeed, a lifetime's personal losses—crammed into two minutes. Irwin raises the flag, takes the bullet, slumps, pushes away the doctor who rushes to help him and just blinks to acknowledge the moment, that he has done his duty, he has liberated the men and delivered the whole point of the story, which is that great moral leadership cannot be quashed. So much to say in one flash of time."

In the first drafts, there were no women in *The Last Castle*. Then Lurie's script doctor, Bill Nicholson, introduced a scene where Rosalie, Irwin's daughter, visits him in prison, and the family dimension opens. Robin Wright Penn was cast as Rosalie. "A couple of years before," says Lurie, "Robin would have been Redford's love interest. Now she was his kid, sitting opposite him, reminding him of his vintage." Lurie found Redford's sudden acceptance of the scene deeply moving. "I think it was the best-acted scene in the movie, maybe one of his best-ever acting moments. So much was going down in that scene. It was a ritual exchange, the termination of one kind of history, the beginning of another."

With an October 2001 release planned, David Sameth, the marketer at DreamWorks, prepared artwork for trade ads showing the upside-down distress flag. The movie tested well, and in September, Lurie was in Hollywood, working with composer Jerry Goldsmith on the sound track theme for Irwin. During the second week in September, Redford was in New York for important Sundance Channel meetings, which ended earlier than scheduled, allowing him to fly back west on September 10. On September 11, United 93, the early morning flight from Newark to San Francisco that he normally favored, was hijacked by al-Qaida and crashed in Pennsylvania within an hour of the World Trade Center attack. Amy, now an off-Broadway actress living on the Lower East Side, a mile and a half from the towers, was in New York that day, as was Shauna and her family, who lived on the Upper East Side. Neither could be reached. It took a full day of frantic calls to confirm their safety.

One could argue that a movie about the anatomizing of truth, morality, honor and leadership never seemed so vital but, given the heightened emotion of the nation in crisis, muddled responses seemed inevitable. *The Washington Post,* reviewing the film a month after 9/11, complained of a movie that "hits us over the head with symbolism" without probing that symbolism, a manifestly self-canceling criticism, in the eyes of some. Michael Atkinson in *The Village Voice* excoriated the film for fudging the issue of freedom and employing "the *Cool Hand Luke* paradigm [reshaped as] an inane recruitment ad."

On the phone to Terry Lawson of the *Detroit Free Press,* Redford wondered about the appropriateness of releasing the movie at that time, but found himself reconciled. Driving from Los Angeles to Utah, he said, he'd encountered a billboard with the defiant flag—DreamWorks had abandoned the upside-down flag in its marketing and put the flag right side up, in a show of support and defiance triggered by 9/11—and questioned its use in promotion. "But, on the other hand, you think, What could be more relevant?"

Redford's antipathy toward the government, however, remained clear in letters he wrote to the *Los Angeles Times* and interviews conducted on National Public Radio, a forum he much admired. On the surface he appeared conciliatory: "We have to hope there are some smart minds holding court right now, and we have to support them and believe in ourselves as a country and a people and as *an idea.*" But he was still, as *Rolling Stone* had labeled him just twelve days before 9/11, a "hot dissident"; if the Bush administration had a list of enemies, said *Rolling Stone,* Redford hovered near the top of it. Wary of appearing unpatriotic, he was still cautioning about the risk of public manipulation in crises: "As the country pulls together we can run dangerously close to a kind of jingoism that eliminates other aspects of democracy, like free speech." He opposed the extension of the war from Afghanistan into Iraq, he said, but was keen that the challanges at home were not forgotten. "Another symbol of patriotism is the land and how we feel about it. Preservation of the environment should be part of our national defense. We can develop alternative energy measures, including conservation, to end our dependence on oil."

As for all thinking people, 9/11 prompted a self-evaluation in which politics played merely a part. Hollywood's response, Redford felt, was critical. In the Sundance spring catalog, for which he still wrote introductory notes, he'd advised against apathy toward Hollywood, lobbying his readers "to demand something from our communications outlets other than values of entertainment and cosmetics." In an interview with *The Salt Lake Tribune* he expanded: "My gut says that, for a period of time, there will be a reaction that will have Hollywood minding its business, because it doesn't want to get on the wrong side. But that's not to say that, once the dust clears, [it won't] come back, because violence sells. Hollywood has been lax in accepting some social responsibility for its product. It's not that we should all be making church films, but when you're going to make a film that [will] have a harsh impact and is going to touch on a negative part of our society, you have to be prepared to take responsibility." *The Boston Globe*'s Sam Allis asked Redford to assess the distance between himself and blockbuster Hollywood. His truth, said Redford, was different: "It is the plight of the individual who has come up against the effects of the current state of things. What has always driven [my truth] is the humane side of the problems that society forces on us, the struggle to remain humane against the tide of crushing elements."

Time magazine, though, summed up an identity dilemma Redford still faced. While he was keen to redefine essences, it was happy to keep judging him by the iconography he had once embraced. Its focus was less on political relevance than *The Last Castle*'s disastrous box office performance. "Most critics have declared it a stinker," wrote Jess Cagle, who then promptly cited Redford's failure to win over the youth market, as Michael Douglas and Harrison Ford had so resoundingly done.

In spite of the naysayers there was joyful reorientation the following March, in 2002, when Redford's peers bestowed on him an honorary Academy Award, marking a lifetime contribution to cinema. Sidney Poitier was honored the same evening. Redford's citation noted his achievements as "actor, director, producer, creator of Sundance and inspiration to independent and innovative filmmakers everywhere." Redford took great pride in this moment "because it reconciled my two worlds—the independent cinema and my acting."

Though Sundance celebrated the indie movie, his career had mostly been a thing apart. In its day, *Downhill Racer* exemplified the glory of experiment with a Bolex camera and duct tape, but he had steered clear of small movies. Now there seemed a need to pare back the indulgences and remember what it was to be starting out with a script, and not a marketer, calling the shots. To this end, Michael Nozik found *The Clearing,* a modest effort being mounted by a small production company, to be directed by Pieter Jan Brugge, a friend of Alan Pakula's who had been nominated for an Academy Award for producing the tobacco industry exposé *The Insider.* The Dutch-born Brugge, who had earned his fine arts degree at the American Film Institute, where he was sponsored by the Dutch Ministry of Culture, had no experience of directing. Funded by Thousand Words Productions, he'd written a script with novelist Justin Haythe, based on the true story of the abduction of an industrialist in Holland in the eighties, which he'd then brought to Sundance. With Redford's commitment, Fox Searchlight, a specialist division of Twentieth Century–Fox pledged to new filmmakers, which had developed close links with the institute, underwrote the budget of $9.5 million, allowing Redford a nominal fee.

Redford's long-stated preference was for "the gray area of human experience" in characters who were restrained, not extreme. But *The Clearing* postulated the most extreme situation. The story centers on Wayne Hayes, a wealthy car tycoon, married with two grown children, who is abducted from the suburban Pittsburgh estate of his seemingly tranquil American dream and dragged by his abductor, a disgruntled former employee named Arnold Mack, into the woods. As the narrative follows Hayes's attempts to rationalize with and calm his abductor, his wife, Eileen, is simultaneously learning that her husband has a mistress and a secret life.

"Personally it was a horrendous shoot," says Redford, "because I am claustrophobic, and I spent almost all that film climbing hills in the woods of North Carolina in handcuffs. There was so little money, ergo so little time, and therefore I was always wearing those damned cuffs. It freaked me out, which made achieving the tension easy." Redford liked working with Willem Dafoe (the abductor), and especially Helen Mirren (Eileen), whom he regards as one of the greatest women performers around. "And [the writers] made a good go of that script—good lines, a good reality." The best of it, said Redford, was its warm morality. Eileen truly loves her husband. "He is a man who needs to be appreciated, and that gets harder as he gets older," she says. That line resonates when Wayne escapes Mack but, succumbing to guilt and the moral order, willfully allows himself to be shot.

Redford had never presented any of his own movies at the Sundance Film Festival. But Geoff Gilmore knew *The Clearing* was perfect for a screening in January 2003. It felt right. Redford resisted, says Gilmore, telling Nozik, "They'll [the critics] rip me apart. They'll call it incest."

Gilmore confronted Redford and told him, "Look, I want it for the festival because I think it's the kind of film we should have, and the fact that you're in it basically says you're contributing to the very thing you created. It's as simple as that."

Ruthe Stein, writing about the film in the *San Francisco Chronicle,* welcomed Redford's stretch: "In his late 60s, with the effect of his time outdoors etched on his face, he's no longer the pretty boy he once was. Far from hiding this, he seems to relish it, as if it's liberated him as an actor. . . . With ageism a constant issue in Hollywood, Redford should be applauded for his attitude as well as for hitting a bull's-eye." Stephen Hunter in *The Washington Post* noted "an anti-vanity film," and doffed his hat to the marker Redford had set down: "This spirit of honesty cxtends to the character himself," wrote Hunter, "which, far from being the heroic Redford of yore, is shown to have been inadequate and far from heroic."

There was an unquestionable maturation, a coming-to-terms quality, about Redford's work since *The Last Castle*. His next choice made clear a consolidation. The project was *An Unfinished Life,* a Miramax movie to be directed by Lasse Hallström, whose wife, Lena Olin, Redford had remained friendly with since *Havana.* Hallström was known for his work with the Swedish pop group ABBA, but his transfer to American film introduced a unique talent who could straddle art house and pop cinema appeal. The screenplay for *An Unfinished Life,* written by Mark and Virginia Spragg, was developed by Kelliann Ladd's company as a project for Paul Newman but inherited by Disney in its acquisition of Miramax. Its first director, Redford learned, was Mark Rydell. When he dropped out, Walter Salles, the Brazilian director, and Robert Altman vied, but Hallström won out. Miramax's choice of female lead was Jennifer Lopez, a singer they believed was destined for movie stardom.

Redford loved the role on offer because, he says, it was unlike anything he'd ever played. He was to be down-at-the-heels, ornery, bitter and "rich in overt desperation"—another role of extremes. He would play Einar Gilkyson, a farmer in his mid-sixties living off the land in remote Wyoming, where he tends to his lifelong friend, Mitch, played by Morgan Freeman, who is incapacitated following a bear attack. Einar's spiritual crisis is his inability to recover from the death of his son, whose widow, Jean, played by Lopez, seeks refuge with him from an abusive boyfriend. Einar's world is upended. As Mitch wrestles with his hatred of the bear who destroyed his life, Einar faces the reality of what he has become—that his existence is numbed by the stultifying effect of blaming Jean for his son's loss. For Hallström the film was "about things going wrong in the universe, and how the universe has to right itself." For Redford it was about forgiveness and personal evolution.

The movie started filming the last week of April 2003 in Kamloops, British Columbia. "I didn't really direct Bob," says Hallström. "I got to witness him working." It seemed clear that Redford was in the process of remodeling his image to striking effect. If *The Clearing* was an admission of age, *An Unfinished Life* wallowed in the damage and detritus of time. From the first frames, where Einar starts the daily drudgery, milking the cow and preparing medication for his bedridden friend, to the last, where he scares off Jean's abusive boyfriend and makes his peace with the new family he has found, Redford seemed experimentally fresh. There was nothing familiar about the performance. What emerged, for those who knew him, was a completely untypical self-revelation. Redford had, said Pollack, "always cherished the theory of keeping something back from the audience." Here, searching for the essence of late-life despair, he laid it all out. The script helped. The words were written for him. But it was Redford, not Einar, who grumbled incessantly in a chronic, half-audible inner dialogue; it was Redford whose empathy with animals and landscape brought the light to his face; it was Redford who struggled to pass a compliment; it was Redford who expressed devotional love with a mere shrug.

An Unfinished Life deserved recognition—for some, even merited the best actor Academy Award he had never scored—but it was not destined to succeed. Hampered by oversentimentality—and by the Weinsteins' second thoughts about Lopez's talent, which induced ridiculous pressures on Hallström to "shoot more of the damned bear"—the movie was lost in a maze of boardroom bickering. When Disney acquired Miramax ten years before, the Weinsteins were small change. Then Miramax grew powerfully as a production entity, turning out multiple award-winners like *The English Patient* and *Chicago* and contributing 40 percent of the studio's output by 2003. But it had never been a comfortable partnership. Michael Eisner never really hit it off with the Weinsteins, and throughout there had been disputes, the most damning of which was Eisner's refusal to back the Weinsteins in making the *Lord of the Rings* series, which was picked up so triumphantly by New Line Cinema.

At Christmas 2003, when *An Unfinished Life* was due for release, the Weinsteins' contract with Disney was up for renewal and, inevitably, under debate. It was announced instead that the movie would open the Cannes Film Festival in May. When that was canceled, it was to be the major holiday release of Christmas 2004. The delay reflected a contractual tug-of-war. By the time Eisner parted ways with the Weinsteins, *An Unfinished Life* was all but forgotten.

And so one of Redford's most important movies, a careful template for his late-life work, dribbled onto screens in September 2005. There was no marketing, and reviewers mostly dismissed it. Kirk Honeycutt in *The Hollywood Reporter* wrote, unfairly for many, that "the film never realizes its dramatic potential, choosing to take predictable story paths with obvious characters." Pete Travers in *Rolling Stone* acknowledged the skillful rapport between Freeman and Redford but hated the "drag-ass solemnity." And *Variety* disliked both the movie and Redford, "who seems to be putting his own laconic spin on a part that feels like it was written for Clint Eastwood."

Was Redford's performance so lacking? The question is vital, because the barrier he'd reached—age—he'd met with awareness, energy and the highest ambition. Writer Walter Kirn's observation at the time of *The Horse Whisperer* provides the plausible answer to negative reviews. Great stars like De Niro and Pacino, said Kirn, are the sum total of the roles they've played, "but Redford stands for the industry itself, in all its California dreaminess." As such, no variation of the gilded icon was permissible. Sydney Pollack, estranged from his old sparring partner since the filming of *Havana,* spoke of the difficulty of separating "acting" from "megastardom": "It's an impossible conundrum because that kind of stardom has invested the actor with the audience's preconceived needs. Look at Elvis. He was this phenomenon who satisfied everyone's dream of rebellion, and then he settled down to make cozy movies. He was never forgiven. Take Stallone. He tried comedy and he made a good fist of it, but they threw it out. Take Woody [Allen]. He's allowed to make a certain kind of movie, but dare he move out of the box? Same with a star like Bob. It's a deal with the devil. He will always be thirty, blond, perfection. There will be moments when smart critics will cut through it, but even the best of them want the idealized actor. They want the continuance, because no one wants the death of fantasy, no one can stand too much reality."

Redford's personal realities, however, were unavoidable.

24

Jeremiah's Way

Tom Jolley and the young Salt Lake City accountants proved a godsend, but they couldn't reverse the damage of years of less than efficient managerial control at Sundance and the overhiring and overspending that arose from bad deputizing. Redford accepted their verdicts with aplomb, but he was adamant about the importance of preserving Sundance.

In May, shortly after the delayed release of *An Unfinished Life,* he announced the relaunch of the Sundance Cinema Centers, this time in partnership with Paul Richardson and Bert Manzari, described by *The Hollywood Reporter* as "stalwarts of the independent theater chain business for more than thirty years." On its heels came another IRM-style venture, the Sundance U.S. Conference of Mayors Summit, staged with the United Nations–funded International Council for Local Environmental Initiatives, for the purpose of reactivating debate about global warming. The conference, attended by forty-five mayors, was a success, but its collateral value was as an expression of Redford's never-say-die stubbornness in the face of overwhelming doubt. A twelve-step resolution committed 170 cities to a new pact for pollution reduction independent of national policy, and Redford again felt stimulated, even optimistic.

Sundance, however, needed more than initiatives. It needed cash. A quick fix offered itself in Paramount's animated *Charlotte's Web,* a version of E. B. White's children's classic directed by Gary Winick, which Redford did as a favor to Winick and in which he lent his voice as the ornery Ike the Horse. The movie was useful, but it was the project he wanted to do next that he thought could earn him big dollars. *Lions for Lambs* was written by Matthew Carnahan, brother of Joe Carnahan, the director of the successful cop thriller *Narc,* and originated with Paula Wagner, the long-term production associate of Tom Cruise. In 2005, Cruise's life and career had taken a turn with marriage to Katie Holmes and a series of ill-judged promotional appearances that allegedly offended the executive of his old studio, Paramount, and caused the termination of his contract. Cruise and Wagner's partnership with Paramount had lasted fourteen years and spanned several major blockbusters. In November 2006 it was announced that they had become effective controllers of the relaunched United Artists, a studio division of MGM that had served only as a boutique name since its collapse in the early nineties. In its new incarnation, MGM remained majority owner, but Cruise and Wagner took control of development and the creative rebirth of a studio that had been made famous ninety years before as a venture partnership between Charlie Chaplin, Mary Pickford, Douglas Fairbanks and D. W. Griffith.

The two projects the new UA planned to relaunch with were the wartime *Valkyrie,* which would star Tom Cruise, and Carnahan's *Lions for Lambs,* which Lourd proposed to Redford to direct and star in. Redford had great incentive to make *Lions for Lambs* work because he knew that a successful outcome could well lead to further codevelopments with UA, even a formal business partnership.

Lions for Lambs was about the war in Afghanistan or, more specifically, the national mood relating to American involvement in a foreign conflict that seemed to many not much different from Asian engagements of old. Redford was to play an idealistic West Coast professor, Stephen Malley, who attempts to motivate a college student slacker, whom Carnahan based on himself. The story also traced the fate of two of Malley's motivated students who join the U.S. Army and enter the conflict in Afghanistan. In a parallel plotline, a Republican senator and presidential hopeful attempts to persuade a leading female journalist to whitewash a questionable military strategy against the Taliban.

"I thought it was massively challenging," says Redford, "because it could so easily slip into leftist bias, and that would defeat its purpose. Malley's mission is to encourage social engagement in his students. It calls for talk before action. It's about learning as much as teaching, but it couldn't be preachy. It's about morality, but it can't be moralistic. Because of the divisive nature of Bush's war on terror, I thought it was timely. As a director, I emphatically *wasn't* taking sides. I didn't want to say this or that is right or wrong. I just felt *Lions for Lambs* could provoke a meaningful wider discussion."

Redford envisaged Meryl Streep for the journalist Janine Roth and Denzel Washington for the Republican senator Irving. Streep jumped at the part. But Cruise became Irving. "You roll with these things," says Redford, "and of greater concern to me was the small budget—$35 million—and the short time frame, since our deal was to have the movie ready for a grand UA launch by Christmas 2007."

Troubles rained down. First, no major soundstage was available in Hollywood, so production was based at "a utility barn" at Ren-Mar Studios on Cahuenga Boulevard. Since extensive Afghanistan action scenes were required and the budget would allow no foreign locations, complex snow-machine work was sited at sunny Rocky Peak Park in Simi Valley. Then came eighteen-hour days "shuffling and reshuffling pages like card sharks." Some people thought Cruise was unprepared. He did not interact well with Streep and Cruise and Redford seemed to be on different wavelengths. Cruise was on record saying his interest in the project revolved around Redford, whose work he had followed joyfully since *Ordinary People.* But Redford struggled with his costar's approach. "At one point he brought in some neoconservative foreign policy advisers, among them Robert Kagan, whom I thought were inappropriate," says Redford. "I called him on it, saying, 'Wait a second, Tom. This is not the way I want to do this, and certainly not with these people in my eye line.' " Cruise backed off. The delays went on. "It got to the point where we had to deploy cards with the lines written on them," says a crew member. "Meryl lost interest. She started playing with her BlackBerry. Bob freaked. It became very, very tense."

Lions for Lambs stumbled through to make its deadline and opened, as promised, in November 2007. The previews did not go well. After the first screening in New York, Fox News reported that neither Streep nor Redford accompanied Cruise to the Museum of the Moving Image, where he was being honored that night. Observers read between the lines.

Ironically, the film incited some of the most impassioned reviews of Redford's recent career. Critic Amy Biancolli in the *Houston Chronicle* called it Redford's "bravest" film, and *The Hollywood Reporter* agreed that it "raises many important questions." But these plaudits were challenged by savage reviews deriding "pompous-assery" and "preachiness."

Redford considered the failure his and his alone, and lamented the fact that the movie grossed just $63 million worldwide, rendering a loss, taking marketing costs into consideration, estimated by *The New York Times* of about $50 million. Shortly after, with *Valkyrie* running late, Wagner announced the termination of her association with UA, and Redford's hope for some continuing production relationship was dead.

In May 2008 the bombshell came when the Sundance Channel was sold. The channel, in terms of audience numbers, sponsorship investment and its documentary production slate, was never healthier. Surpassing the projections made twelve years before, almost thirty million homes were now served, but its sacrifice was inevitable. It was the bitterest pill to accept that the purchaser was Rainbow Media, the programming subsidiary of Cablevision, owners of the Independent Film Channel. Redford's 6 percent share gave him $30 million. In the acquisition announcement, Josh Sapan, CEO of Rainbow, praised Sundance's record of achievement without acknowledging what media analysts predicted: that Sundance and the IFC would probably be merged in the coming years.

Wounded but uncowed, Redford stayed on as creative adviser to the Sundance Channel, retaining an office alongside its chief executive at Penn Plaza in New York. He immediately began to work toward a series of short films designed for mobile phone users. "I don't intend to rescind any of the policy we started out with," he said defiantly. "Sundance Channel was conceived to preserve experiment and diversity, and that's what it will continue to do."

Behind the bravado was a deep hurt. Sundance as defined just ten years before was no longer viable. "But he told us," said one staffer, "it's about evolution. We go forward with Sundance and remember our purpose: stewardship of independence, the same old acorn."

There was, of course, much for Redford to be thankful for. His personal life was never so serene, his fulfillment rich in interacting with his children and grandchildren, whose legions swelled to five when Amy and her husband, Denver-born CalArts theater director Matt August, had a daughter, Eden Hart, in August 2008. Old wounds, too, seemed healed. Lola's new life was based around Lake Champlain in Charlotte, Vermont, from where she ran Clio Inc., a media-based "virtual corporation" designed to pursue environmental and sociological activism, with her new husband, George Burrill. Part of each year she spent in New Zealand, but Redford often dined with her, enjoying, says Jamie, "the most pleasant relationship imaginable."

There was a special joy in seeing the creative growth among his loved ones. Shauna was no longer involved with the catalog or Sundance, but she continued painting and resided in Connecticut with her husband, Eric Schlosser, whose books *Fast Food Nation* and *Reefer Madness* became classroom staples and earned him the moniker of the new Upton Sinclair. Jamie's screenwriting was thriving, with two script credits for the Hillerman Indian detective stories, now funded by PBS, under his belt and a directorial feature debut with *Spin,* a small-budget movie about a Latino family that starred Rubén Blades and was well received. Amy was also on the road to a significant film career, moving from acting roles in mainstream television series like *Sex and the City* to her own directorial start, *The Guitar,* described by festival director Geoff Gilmore as "a whimsical fairy tale," which premiered at the 2008 Sundance Film Festival. Redford "stood back and relished" all this, and was especially moved by the progress of Bylle, whose art rapidly evolved, veering through southwestern and Arabic themes to coalesce in Miró-like dream imagery that won the attention of IMG Artists, the adventurous management group whose concert and exhibition festivals would provide a global forum for her. "I had a skepticism about American expressionist art since CU," says Redford. "But Bylle's experiments changed my perspective. It reminds me how not all problems respond to linearity. The abstract viewpoint, the lateral thought, the *poetry,* is often the way to resolution."

The serenity was dented by losses: Pakula, Michael Ritchie, George Roy Hill and Stuart Rosenberg all passed away over a short period. Then came news that Paul Newman and Sydney Pollack were in advanced stages of terminal cancer.

For years he'd been trying to revive collaboration with Newman, and he'd come closest just recently, in optioning Bill Bryson's sunny memoir, *A Walk in the Woods,* about the author's trek with an ornery old buddy along the Appalachian Trail. Newman loved the idea, and the film was already alive in Redford's mind, was even penciled in for a 2009 shoot. Friendship between the men had never wavered. They had a spontaneous mutual empathy, a love of sports and the arts. Humor kept it moving. Throughout its thirty-five-plus-year span they kept in touch, usually visiting each other in Connecticut, at Newman's home in Westport. Newman's pleasure in his children's charity work and the initiatives that launched his Committee Encouraging Corporate Philanthropy (CECP) was as meaningful to him as Sundance was to Redford, but they never ceased taunting each other's self-seriousness. Throughout the years, the jokes were so endless they'd become ingrained. Once, Newman wrote to ask Redford to include his daughter's boyfriend's hemp-woven western shirts in the Sundance catalog. "Sure," Redford wrote back. "On the assumption that, if they don't work as fashion, they can be smoked." When Newman's Own, the internationally marketed sauces and other food products whose profits went to the Hole in the Wall children's charity, took off, Redford sharpened the gibes. In a scene in *The Milagro Beanfield War,* a shopper in the background asks the clerk for Newman's Own salad dressing. "That's no good," says the storekeeper. "Try something else."

Even in the grip of terminal illness, Newman remained ambitious. Keen on *A Walk in the Woods,* he also wanted to direct for the stage for the first time, and his production of *Of Mice and Men* was under way at the Westport Country Playhouse when he passed away on September 26. Redford saw him six weeks before he died. He had recovered well from a long bout of chemotherapy at Sloan-Kettering and was at peace. "It was tough. He was frail. But we'd had such a joyous shared experience and his spirit was so strong that it was hard to be sad about it. I was pleased. He was pleased. It was a calm adieu."

Making his peace with Sydney, though, was never going to be easy. Their history was too intense, their achievements over forty years too intricately interlinked. Living in Pacific Palisades, Pollack had been working nonstop until *The Interpreter,* his 2005 movie with Nicole Kidman. He hadn't visited Sundance for several years but maintained an interest in indie film and was preproducing a drama for HBO about the Bush-Gore presidential election when stomach cancer was diagnosed. He resigned from the movie, *Recount,* and Redford heard of his illness through the children, Becky and Rachel, who had stayed very close friends with Shauna and Amy. Redford phoned the Pollacks' home and spoke to Claire, his wife, but the requested callback from Sydney never came. Finally, Redford "just got in the car and drove over and said, 'Hey, what's going on?' " The reunion was awkward. Pollack was upbeat, even exuberant. But there was no talk of the past.

"Sydney knew what lay ahead and had settled his mind on dealing with it, and I was just content that we were able to spend some time," says Redford, "and to let him know how thankful I was for the friendship and the work."

In June, at the private memorial service for Pollack at an aviation hangar in Santa Monica, Redford carefully prepared notes for his eulogy. Dustin Hoffman was there, along with Al Pacino, George Clooney, Harrison Ford and a throng of leading Hollywood figures reflective of Pollack's achievement. Redford found himself divided. He'd once written to Carol Rossen that L.A. remained forever uncomfortable for him, "still and always the gorilla in the living room." Now, surrounded by the faces that emblematized the L.A. Pollack loved, he felt depressed by the gap between them. "I've no doubt [the depression] was in response to the special nature of our friendship. It's hard to summarize such a complicated and devoted friendship in a handful of words, and it's hard to share it."

In the end, bobbing on a sea of emotions, he cast away his notes and improvised. He told the gathered friends and family, "I think a part of you dies when someone you love dies."

It was, of course, finally about film, just film. The relative failure of the recent films he most cared about, *An Unfinished Life* and *Lions for Lambs,* was, in the greater scheme of things, unimportant. His movies had cumulatively earned almost $1 billion and he was still acknowledged, as he was at the millennium when *Life* selected him as a symbol of grace and glamour for the twentieth century. Reflecting on his oeuvre, he decided that *Jeremiah Johnson* was his favorite movie, because it was all about continuing. Johnson suffers the slings and arrows, but is uncowed. In the same spirit, he would go on, choosing two new movie projects that sprang from his interests in sports and society. With *Lions for Lambs* coproducer Tracy Falco, a recent executive appointee at Universal, he agreed to develop a film based on the story of the first African American Major League Baseball player, Jackie Robinson, in which he would play the Brooklyn Dodgers general manager, Branch Rickey. Given the new accent on national integration that came with Barack Obama's election as president in 2008, the subject felt timely. But superseding it came *The Conspirator,* a script about the assassination of Abraham Lincoln that crucially examined the role of John Wilkes Booth's alleged collaborator Mary Surratt whose state execution, along with three other coconspirators, remains controversial. Redford's film, finally greenlighted as a new directorial venture in the spring of 2010, was designed less as a historical piece than a polemic. Bob Woodward was thankful for his stubborn engagement with social issues in his films. "The gift he brought to me and Carl and *All the President's Men* was the gift of an observer. He had a skill to hover above the project and cut to the key elements with amazing acuity," says Woodward. "That degree of analytical skill enhances everything he does, and we need it in all divisions of our society."

It was this observational obsession that ultimately explains his appetite for storytelling and his ongoing quest for characters to play. As with Chaucer and Dickens, who charted their worlds with scorn and affection in equal measure, his urge remained to shine a light on his own. "I could never stop acting," he told Jamie, "because it would be like removing curiosity and, to me, that would be like removing life itself." Acting and stardom, of course, were different matters. Acting he was compelled to; stardom was a gift, something to be grateful for, and proud of. Proud not in vainglory, but because he knew what he'd achieved in transferring its power into something concretely separate—Sundance—where others could engage and experiment with their own art. What remained, beyond the challenge of age, was the problem of how to hold on to the magical province he had created.

The Sundance Group, in its high-flight ambition, was dead. But the Sundance Institute, the arts principle, was intact—though still under threat because of the failure of the business umbrella. Redford remained committed to restoring its vitality and was heartened when Bylle's art opened a door. IMG Artists was launching an inaugural California version of its well-established Tuscan Sun Festival. The IMG format combined concerts performed by the world's most acclaimed musical artists with literary, culinary and visual art exhibitions. Barrett Wissman, IMG Artists' chief executive, wanted to showcase Bylle's work as a local artist. Wissman met Redford and told him of his plans to explore cross-cultural events globally. Already there were Sun Festivals in Asia and Europe, and Wissman saw an important new opportunity in the Middle East, where Sheikh Zayed bin Sultan al-Nahayan of the United Arab Emirates was developing Abu Dhabi with unprecedented focus on the arts. Wissman suggested bringing Sundance to Abu Dhabi, which was an idea that immediately appealed to Redford's vision of constant evolution. In July, the sheikh sent his private Gulfstream jet to collect Redford for a visit to his desert kingdom. There Redford proposed the Middle Eastern Sundance Institute. Several prominent Sundance board members opposed Redford's plan, but he was adamant: "Sundance was always about risk and exploration. I saw this as a wonderful opportunity to engage new voices across the globe and I determined to pursue it."

Redford dismisses the idea of involvement in Middle East politics but acknowledges the potency of film emerging from the nexus of modern Arabia. He was well aware of the contrary opinions of the Emirates' society, aware of the implications of association with a cultural tradition infamous for its downgrading of women, where, even today, women are airbrushed from newspaper photographs. "Articulating opinions, disseminating, debating: that's what film is about for me. Today the whole region of the Middle East is the crucible. Much of the future—all our futures—will be decided in this area."

Back in the Sundance boardroom, skepticism prevailed, and Redford buckled down for a fight. "My sense is that the resistance will go on. Sundance needs nourishment."

Sundance, of course, was more than an arts principle. It was a place. In his diary, speculating on the importance of the canyon, he wrote: "For years I searched for a religious concept that would fit. Nothing ever did. All concepts, even though momentarily satisfying, fell victim to resistance. And resistance became reality. Then, some thirty years ago, I realized it had been underfoot all the while: it was nature. It contains no politics and no corruption of power. It is constant."

Not long before, to consecrate its continuance, Redford had instructed Julie Mack to survey all the Sundance holdings, which spread over more than six thousand acres of meadow oakbrush, chokecherry and aspen forest, to define a conservation easement of almost one thousand acres, which would be the Redford Family Nature and Wildlife Preserve, entrusted to the nation in perpetuity. This symbolic gesture, perceived as a tax break maneuver by the cynical, was as solid a marker as the Promontory Summit transcontinental railroad golden spike. At the dedication ceremony held at the high vantage of Smith Corner, Jamie told the assembled friends and supporters: "I know that I speak for my sisters when I say that of all the things [my father] provided to us, the most important are these values of conservation. We hope to carry them and pass them on to our children. Any of you who knew me as a teenager, tearing up the canyon on my motorcycle, putting my guitar amp on the deck, trying to see if people could hear me across the other side of the mountain, might have wondered what was going to happen to these lands. Well, I'm here to tell you some good news: nothing is going to happen to them, absolutely nothing other than what geological time and nature have in store."

The fact that the family's affection for Sundance had never wavered was the source of greatest pride of all to Redford. Shauna visited less, but her heart was still there. Jamie had a voice in management, always ready to engage in boardroom disputes and come down on the side of continuance. Amy spent Christmas in the A-frame with Matt and her new baby. "So much of our childhood and, I suppose, our shared dreams are in this place," says Amy. "My memories are ones of compassion and unity and all that could be achieved by staying in harmony with the elements. But it has changed. Once, Sundance was a place of meditation and retreat. Now it is the forefront of a mission."

Growing up, Jamie says, his father often seemed to him like a spirit tethered by the longest, thinnest thread to planet Earth. Still, in the force of his tenacity, he had become Jamie's greatest influence: "In my darkest days on the transplant waiting list anticipating death, my father's courage kept me going." Ironically, Jamie was now his father's role model. "I love all my children equally, but Jamie has carried me forward," says Redford. "I write to him when I'm in distress. I tell him my woes and he shows me the way. His journey has been farther than any of ours. He's seen more of the darkness and more of the light."

In July 2009 Redford married Bylle in a quiet ceremony at the Louis C. Jacob Hotel in Hamburg, confounding those who believed he would never settle. The union is tighter and more secure than any he has enjoyed in his life, but in many ways the doubters are right. Redford remains peripatetic, shifting with the seasons from New York to Santa Fe, from Sundance to St. Helena. Jamie remains in Fairfax, where they often meet. "I try to slow him down," says Jamie. "I tell him to go back to Sundance, that that's his destiny, that's the final frontier."

Redford well knows it, and to recognize a frontier, as Heidegger says, is to have gone beyond it.

Acknowledgments

It is impossible to adequately thank the many people who gave this book life. What started as a modest project became a ten-year one, reflective of the broad ground covered. Patience and belief became the cornerstones I depended on, and I am grateful to those who stayed true.

I could not have written the book without the input of my children, Corey Callan and Paris Callan, both drama and film students who will, I've no doubt, make their marks. Corey's wisdom and scholarship color every page (especially the annotations). Paris was an equally ingenious adviser, giving me insight and understanding from the beaches of Oahu to the darkest nights in Dublin. I was a distracted father far too often during these years, and I wrap my thanks in sincerest apology. The next one, I promise, will be easier.

The initiator of the book died before it saw the light of day. Susan Hill was an exceptional editor. She was also a loved friend. We worked together on three books, but that was the least of it. It was her conviction that Robert Redford was undervalued, and I hope herein I've answered some of her questions about him. Another key contributor who passed away during the writing was the author Francis Xavier Feighan, the best buddy, who took me around the San Fernando Valley of Redford's boyhood. I'm indebted to him for establishing the network of contacts in Los Angeles and for supplying the linguistic riddles (words were his thing) that made his in-the-field reports so joyfully sustaining. Francis conducted a number of important interviews for this book and opened thirty years of his movie files to me. I miss our afternoons at Jerry's Deli on Ventura Boulevard.

Thanks to William Armstrong for green-lighting this work to begin with and for publishing my work for so many years. Thanks, also, to the writers John McGahern, Brian Clemens and Anthony Shaffer, who variously edited me, encouraged me and pushed me onward. Also to Philip Hinchcliffe and Chris Menaul, who grounded me in London way back and opened the drama doors at the BBC and elsewhere that were foundational in building this book. I also must acknowledge the early directors of my own dramas, Briann MacLochlainn, Michael O'Herlihy and Martin Campbell, who taught me most of what I know about filmmaking.

Since research for this book spanned two continents, my appreciation goes to a number of people on both sides of the Atlantic who built the bridges. Where I could, I visited every homestead, grave site or movie studio, the better to understand my subject's journey. Gerald M. Cruthers and Marilyn Cruthers worked tirelessly in Connecticut and Rhode Island to assemble genealogical details and catalog all the residences of the New England Redfords. In Austin and San Marcos, Peggy Tombs scoured the Texan history. At the same time, Karen Cook and Judith Moore worked in Scotland, Birmingham and Manchester, tracing the Redfords of yore. In England, Michael Herbert, deputy registrar of the Manchester Register Office, was immensely helpful. In Los Angeles, Sheila Winston and Lisa Thornberg provided further document research and support and transport when I and my family were in town. In Carlisle, Pennsylvania, John J. Slonaker, chief of the Historical Reference Branch at the Department of the Army, was very helpful. Orla McEvoy, Lia O'Sullivan, Emer Ghee, Shirely Connell, Jeni McConnell, Paul Melrose, Colette Colfer, Catherine Barry and Fiona O'Dwyer collated library research and made sense of a mountain of often contradictory files, spanning centuries. In Utah, I relied on the Trojans of Sundance, often Jean Bair Davis. Also at Sundance, Michelle Satter, Mike Washburn, Nicole Guillemet, Geoff Gilmore and Joyce Deep were greatly supportive. I owe a special thanks to Julie Mack for her determination to explain the workings of Utah life and politics, and for making me feel welcome.

The Los Angeles participants were crucial. Marcella Scott Krisel, a close friend of Martha and Charlie Redford's from the Santa Monica days, was the first person to introduce me to the Redfords' old neighborhood. Carol Eve Rossen was a sound navigator over transatlantic midnight phone calls. I am also indebted to Bill and Lucrecia Coomber, Pat Ader, Lala Brady, George Menard, Vivian Christensen, Margaret Mitchell Clayton, Nina Gallagher, Steve Bernhardt, Jan and Bob and Tom Holman Peterson, Bill Chertok, Jim Collis, Kit Andrews, Sheila Andrews, Joanne Ward, Betty Webb, Tissie Keissig, Terry Drinkwater, Dave Ryan, Dave Stein, Don Leonard, Robert Nairin, Bill Van Atta, Alan Jackson, Andy Dowdy and Cal Vincent. Bob Brigham, Dick Guttman, Jack and Frances Stovall, Lionel Krisel and Bob Enrietto of the Hawaii Film Commission were also supportive. Shirley Story Ackroyd opened the doors for us in Van Nuys. Thereafter, at Van Nuys High School, I must thank Diane Sharrer. Judy Anderson at Laser Disc Association supplied me with transcripts of Paul Newman's commentaries on *Butch Cassidy and the Sundance Kid,* which were useful. At Wildwood Enterprises in Los Angeles, the patient and fastidious Donna Kail kept it all moving in Los Angeles, and Sarah Mendleson and—especially—Connie Wethington kept me smiling.

In New York, Meg McSweeney of the American Academy of Dramatic Arts went beyond the call of duty as archivist and prompter, and I'm thankful for our friendship. The former president of the academy, George Cuttingham, also assisted in analyzing the academy's history and Redford's tenure. At the Shubert Archive, Mark E. Schwartz supplied many documents. Martha Wilson, Garson Kanin's assistant, was also hugely supportive. Also in New York I was helped by the late Harryetta Peterka, Kevin Scott and Dale Zaklad at the Museum of Radio and Television (now the Paley Center for Media), and the great theatrical sleuth, Jay Stein. At *Architectural Digest,* Josie Haskin kindly supplied copies of the 1975 layout of the Redfords' Fifth Avenue home. At the Pratt Institute in Brooklyn, the academic advisement director, Beverly Warmath, was a terrific help. Donaldson Brown and Carla Cogan of Wildwood's New York office were kind and efficient at every turn. I wish to make a special note of Ginny Burns Kelly. The time I spent with her in New York and the stories she shared were inspirational.

In London, this marathon work was nurtured at various stages by Helen Gummer,

Allegra Houston, Ian Chapman and Ian Macmillan. It was Jeremy Trevathan who saw the need for an American center of operations and introduced Knopf into the equation.

In all, I met, interviewed and corresponded with more than three hundred players in Robert Redford's world. They gave me courtesy, debate, hospitality, memorabilia and time. Among them, I express special appreciation to Sydney Pollack (who took time out from shooting a movie at Paramount to open his script files and assist me), George Roy Hill (who provided a day of unforgettable reminiscences in his New York home), Michael Ritchie, Barbra Streisand, Alan J. Pakula ("the shrink"), Jane Fonda (thank you, Jan), Arthur Penn, Bob Woodward, Stuart Rosenberg, Hume Cronyn, Paul Newman (special thanks to Dorese, in Paul Newman's office), Paul Burke, Tom Skerritt, Mike Connors, Patrick Markey, John Saxon, Sondra Lee, Jack Clayton, Liam Clancy, Julie Harris, Bradford Dillman, Hugh Hall, Mary Tyler Moore, Barry Levinson, Chick Vennera, Mike Nichols, Jeremy Larner, David Ward, Stephanie Phillips, Mike Dowd, Mike Frankfurt, Steve Frankfurt, Richard Altman, Michael Phillips, Julia Phillips, Garson Kanin, Tom DiCillo, Ken Brecher, Brent Beck, Fae Beck, Alex Beck, Jerry Hill, Mike Moder, Gary Beer, Richard Friedenberg, John Landis, David Cronenberg, Frank R. Pierson, Jeremy Kagan, Reg Gipson, Stuart Craig, Karen Tenkhoff, Susan Harmon, Hank Corwin, Tom Rolf, Freeman Davies, Thomas Newman, Gavin Lambert, Dan Melnick, Walter Coblenz, Chris Soldel, Manny Azenberg, Bryan Lourd, James Grady, Joanna Lumley, Gordon Bowen, Bob Crawford, Marion Dougherty, Harry Mastrogeorge, John Pierce, Pete Masterson, Carlin Masterson, John Adams of the Natural Resources Defense Council, Michael Nozik, Damon Pennington, Rubén Blades, Richard Ayres, Jack Brendlinger, Stan Collins, Mary Alice Collins, Conrad Hall, Cynthia Burke, David Rayfiel, Bernie Pollack, Gary Liddiard, Bunny Parker, Ian Calderon, Sherman Labby, Richard Schickel, Sterling Van Wagenen, Wayne Van Wagenen, Bill Bradley, Ted Wilson, George Peppard, James Coburn, Monique James, Rob Morrow, Debbie Slyne, Michael J. Reilly, Lou Marks, Marjorie Bird, Buddy Hoffman, Ben Young, Jo Sanchez, Robert Altman, Leslie Halliwell, Eric Gertz, Richard Brooks, Ron Greene, Jake Eberts, Ed Brown, Michael Daves, Bill Carver, Joan Claybrook, Jon Avnet, Ted Zachary, Rod Taylor, Penny Fuller and Yoko Ono.

Among the libraries and records offices consulted or visited were the Mugar Memorial Library at Boston University; the Connecticut State Library in Hartford; the Rhode Island Historical Society in Providence; the Manchester Central Library in England; the Manchester Register Office in Spinningfields; the General Register Office for Scotland in Edinburgh; the Foundation for Ancient Research and Mormon Studies in Provo, Utah; the Margaret Herrick Library of the Academy of Motion Picture Arts and Sciences in Los Angeles; the library of the Museum of Television and Radio (now the Paley Center for Media) in New York City; the archive at the Pratt Institute in Brooklyn; the library of the British Film Institute in London; the archive of the University of Colorado at Boulder (thank you, Jeannine Malmsberry and library technician Marty Conner Covey); the Federal Archives Library in Fort Worth, Texas; and Trinity College Library Dublin.

Also in Ireland, I must thank the ever-supportive Trina Stalley, Professor Roger Stalley, Professor Kevin Rockett of Trinity College's drama, film and music department, Trinity College provost John Hegarty, Ian Condy (thank you for those overnight deliveries of New York newspapers), Dr. John Kelly, Shay Hennessy, Ray McGovern, Sean Simon, my inspirational sister, Jeannette and Jim Kearney, my great brothers Eamonn and Ron Callan and the wonderful Mae Ward, a special lady we loved who sadly passed away just before completion of this work. I must not forget Antony and Jay Worrall Thompson, who egged me on endlessly, or my business partner and friend, Olivier Capt (and Alma). Also, transcendently, Brian Wilson.

The nature of this book was accumulative as much as evaluative. Two leading players kept control of the flying pieces. They are Lois Smith of PMK, who introduced me to Robert Redford and was the project's manager from its earliest days, and Wendy Hopkins, Redford's Utah assistant, who fielded every query, promise and complaint and supplied mountains of FedEx packages to nourish me. I came to regard Wendy as my field guide.

Robert Redford was a gracious host. His generosity goes without saying, but his trust was the greater gift. Because of him, I had the opportunity to talk with Jamie Redford, Shauna Redford Schlosser, Amy Hart Redford and Sibylle Szaggars, and their candid insights proved invaluable.

For safe navigation of this book to its home between Knopf covers, I thank Sonny Mehta. I'm also indebted to the great Jonathan Segal, who honed a quarter of a million words into a manageable text and never ceased challenging me to go one better. Jon's support, vision and skill are deeply appreciated.

Finally, a word of gratitude to my father, Michael Callan, a supreme storyteller and historian, whom we also lost just weeks before the publication of this work. His appetite for education and his example of tireless labor drive my life. My dear mother, Margaret Feeney (whose favorite movie heroine, like Robert Redford's, was Greer Garson), followed every stage of the setup of this work with a passion, but sadly passed before we made it into print also. The heart of this work belongs to both of them. The rest is in the hands of my constant muse and collaborator, Ree Ward Callan, and the undefeatable Corey Wilson Callan and Paris Callan. We crossed some oceans.

Notes and Sources

Since this is Robert Redford's life story, I have attempted to allow him to speak for himself. To that end, several interviews, formal and informal, were conducted over fourteen years, commencing in March 1995. Sessions took place in Sundance, Utah; Marin County, California; Los Angeles; New York; and Dublin, Ireland. Apart from formal taped sessions, we met often for lunches and dinners. Redford kindly commented on various aspects of this work in progress and introduced me to members of his family and to friends, business partners and co-workers. In all, more than three hundred participants in the Robert Redford story were interviewed.

The primary research source, beyond interviews and visiting with Redford during the production for his movies, was his own jottings. An ardent scribbler, he keeps a bound notebook in his briefcase and constantly writes down observations, reflections and literary snippets that come his way. He started keeping a diary in Los Angeles in 1957 and, irregularly since, has filled several volumes of reminiscences. These take the form of short essays, which are occasionally little more than illustrated doodles. Throughout, though, there are fragments of detailed self-analysis and seminal notions of new projects. The early diaries, called "Varwood" and "The German Diary," are housed in the Mugar Memorial Library at Boston University. Other journals, including "Redford Musings," dating from the 1970s, are at the Sundance archive in Utah. Redford's well-dispersed drawings and paintings dating from 1954 have now been gathered and cataloged at the Corporate Management Group offices in Los Angeles.

Additionally, the Sundance archive turned over to me Redford's correspondence files from the 1960s onward. Meticulously kept, they record his communications with individuals as diverse as Richard Leakey, Bill Bradley and Mort Sahl. Also supplied and referenced were the screenplays of the Wildwood-produced films, kept at the Sundance archive.

The late Sydney Pollack graciously allowed me access to his script library at Mirage, his production company, housed at Paramount Studios. There I had the chance to read his personal shooting versions of the seven movies he made with Redford, together with his preparatory notes and correspondence with David Rayfiel, Dalton Trumbo, Errol Trzebinski and others.

George Roy Hill wrote my letter of introduction to the Margaret Herrick Library at the Academy of Motion Picture Arts and Sciences in Los Angeles, where his papers are lodged. The Hill archive includes versions of his scripts and correspondence, which are revealing about his casting process and authorial views.

Redford's acting school, the American Academy of Dramatic Arts, gave me access to the archive files relating to his schooling there in 1957–59. These include his workshop assessments.

Other documents were supplied by Emerson Junior High School and Van Nuys High School in Los Angeles, the Pratt Institute in Brooklyn, and the Sundance Institute in Los Angeles.

Wayne Van Wagenen of Provo, Utah, supplied me with a large file of clippings and family memorabilia relating to the Redford and Van Wagenen families, including genealogical papers.

Civic, business and marriage records were gathered in five separate areas: Scotland, Manchester, Rhode Island, Texas and Los Angeles.

I have refrained from citing reviews where I have used just a short quotation to convey the general critical reception to a particular film or play.

All major written and published materials referred to are listed in the bibliography.

Introduction *America Is the Girl*

xii *"people need the chance to see":* Robert Redford, "Search for Common Ground," *Harvard Business Review,* May–June 1987, 108.

xii *"This rustic Xanadu and the ideals behind [it]":* Walter Kirn, "The Two Hollywoods," *The New York Times Magazine,* November 16, 1997.

xiv *"a subtle blend of Owen Wister's Trampas":* Laurence Luckinbill, "Oh, You Sundance Kid!" *Esquire,* October 1970, 160.

1. *West*

3 *"our Manifest Destiny":* Thomas R. Hietala, *Manifest Design: American Exceptionalism and Empire* (Ithaca, N.Y.: Cornell University Press, 2003), 255.

3 *California, especially, inspired heaven:* James Kirby Martin et al., eds., *America and Its People* (New York: HarperCollins College, 1993), 432.

4 *"California college girls are larger":* Timothy White, *The Nearest Faraway Place: Brian Wilson, the Beach Boys, and the Southern California Experience* (New York: Henry Holt, 1994), 8.

4 *as the Dust Bowl casualties came west:* Ibid., 55.

4 *It wasn't unusual, if you were born:* Interview with George Menard, March 26, 1995.

5 *the Redfords, Saxon in origin, had split:* Civic record documents, Manchester Central Library, including marriage of Peter Redford and Ann Mellor, July 17, 1820 (Public Record no. 44); Peter, son of Peter and Alice Redford, baptized May 20, 1792 (Public Record no. 18); Peter Radford [adapted to Redford] married Alice Burrow September 16, 1787 (Public Record no. 38). Occupation: muslin weaver. Other children of Peter and Alice include Ann, their firstborn, who was baptized twice at Salford Christ Church (King Street Bible Christian) and Manchester Cathedral. Other Redfords (and Radfords) indicate Catholic baptism services. Pre-1850, all signed documents by Redfords and marital partners are marked with an *X,* representing their signature.

5 *Henry Redford, a merchant who became:* James Alexander Manning, ed., *The Lives*

of the Speakers of the House of Commons, from the Time of King Edward III to Queen Victoria (London: G. Willis, 1851), 211.

6 *In 1849, Presbyterian Elisha Redford married:* Elisha Redford (1827–1904) Civic Record, Manchester, 1850. Elisha Redford born November 9, 1827, Manchester, England. Father Peter Redford, born, Manchester, England; mother Anne Bradshaw, born, Manchester, England. Elisha's wife is listed as Ann McCreery [*sic*]. From Stonington, Rhode Island Register (Stonington Deaths, January–June, 1907 [*sic*], Vol. P).

6 *By century's end, Elisha was not much better off:* Last Will and Testament of Elisha Redford, dated May 4, 1874. District of Stonington Probate Court. Book 36, page 288.

7 *While the Harts drifted, the Greens built:* Untitled documents in the Federal Archives Library, Forth Worth, Texas.

7 *Along with three partners, he founded:* Ibid. State Representative Libby Linebarger wrote to Robert Redford on September 25, 1990: "One of the counties I represent is Hayes County, a beautiful area along the eastern base of the Texas Hill Country. . . . A resident of Hayes County and former state representative, Bob Barton, has been doing a great deal of research on Hayes County's earliest settlers and discovered that you are the great-great-grandson of two of Hayes County's earliest settlers and Democratic elected officials." On December 17, Redford responded: "Believe it or not, my knowledge of family history is limited. No one really ever gave it to me. Only a man named Eddie Gresin (Green) of San Marcos has kept me at all informed."

8 *His father, John Gabriel, was a traveling salesman:* Genealogy from Missouri Records office, Travis County Records, Austin City Directory, Department of Commerce and Labor: twelfth national census June 1900; fourteenth national census, 1920, etc. Descendants of George Green and Pate-Green ancestor chart established by Peggy Blackmore Tombs, Marble Falls, Texas.

8 *It was the unlikeliest of marriages:* Travis County Records Office. Vol. 17, page 503. Certificate of marriage, April 30, 1913, Hayes County. Miss Sallie Green to Mr. Archibald W. Hart.

8 *Tot was dwarfish beside:* Interview with George Menard, March 26, 1995.

9 *Rooted in Texas after their 1913 marriage:* Travis County Deeds Records Register. Several property acquisitions, starting with Vol. 270, page 451: between F. J. Compte and Archibald Hart and Sallie P. Hart, recorded August 31, 1915, for purchase of Lot No. (12) and the west one-half of Lot No. 13 in the Block No. 30 of Travis Heights, a subdivision . . . Later purchases to Vol. 594, dated September 1, 1938 (for tract No. 3 in Ridgetop).

9 *Tot's relationship with Mary P. Robinson:* Travis County Records. Criminal District Court No 45, 324, dated June term A.D. 1928. *A.W. Hart vs. Sallie P. Hart.*

9 *Elisha was dead by then:* Death certificate. Elisha Redford of 25 Noyes Avenue, Stonington. Age, 76. Occupation: Jack-spinner. January 22, 1904.

9 *Charles had become a deadbeat:* Advertisement in *Westerly Directory,* circa 1908. "Westerly Band. Concerts, Parades and Picnics Attended. Chas. Redford: Leader, 54 High Street, Westerly, R.I." Death certificate. Charles Redford of 19 Daniels Street, Pawtucket, Rhode Island. Age, 67. Occupation: Insurance agent. April 9, 1918.

10 *the year the Marx Brothers:* Jack Benny and Joan Benny, *Sunday Nights at Seven* (New York: Random House, 1992), 34.

10 *In 1911 Tiger married:* International Genealogical Index for Ireland, 1992 edition: Taylor family tree research conducted by Judith Moore, B.A., A.L.A., Family Histories, Flixton, Manchester. Lena Taylor, daughter of Henry and Mary Taylor, née Tucker; Henry son of John Taylor and Elizabeth Girvin, Kircubbin, Co. Down, Ireland.

12 *She joined the glee club:* Martha Hart Redford's scrapbooks. Sundance archive, Utah.

13 *After high school graduation, Martha enrolled: Spin-Drift,* the annual of Santa Monica Junior College, 1934. ("Charlie Redford led the Corsairs batters . . ." p. 85; Martha Hart and Charles Redford, pictured, among the seven-person Student Body Commission.) Copies, *The Samojac,* weekly newsletter, Santa Monica Junior College, 1933–34.

13 *"Charlie was living at the corner house":* Interview with Marcella Scott Krisel, November 20, 1995.

14 *At Christmas he sent her a card:* Martha Hart Redford's scrapbooks, Sundance archive.

14 *Charlie and Menard decided to join the CCC:* Interview with George Menard, March 26, 1995.

14 *Martha fell ill:* Interview with Margaret Mitchell, October 16, 1995.

14 *Beyond Charlie and the doctors:* Interview with Marcella Scott Krisel, November 20, 1995.

15 *On the evening of August 18:* Birth Certificate No. 9191. Local Register No. 501. August 18, 1936. Charles Robert Redford Jr., born to Charles Robert Redford, 1471 So. Bedford Street, Los Angeles, aged 21, and Martha Woodruff Hart, aged 22. Born at 8.02 p.m. At Santa Monica Hospital.

15 *she sent out frilled blue cards:* Martha Hart Redford's scrapbooks, Sundance archive.

2. *Two Americas*

16 *the work programs of the New Deal:* James Kirby Martin et al., eds., *America and Its People* (New York: HarperCollins College, 1993), 832–58.

16 *The pleasure piers, stretching from Venice:* Fred E. Bastem, *Santa Monica Bay* (Los Angeles: General Publishing Group, 1997), 122.

16 *pushing beachfront prices past:* Ibid., 182.

16 *for Charlie, Martha and the baby, economic security:* Interview with Vivian Knudson Christensen, October 29, 1995.

17 *Though single-minded, Martha embraced:* Interview with Margaret Mitchell, October 16, 1995.

17 *Many friends found it remarkable:* Interviews with Marcella Scott Krisel, January 15, 1996, and Margaret Mitchell, October 16, 1995.

17 *a $3,000 mortgage:* Interview with George Menard, February 9, 1996.

20 *as director Alan Pakula believed:* Interview with Alan J. Pakula, May 8, 1997.

21 *Studying accountancy part-time:* Interview with Marcella Scott Krisel, January 15, 1996.

21 *Redford's bond with David:* Interview with George Menard, February 9, 1996.

23 *Betty Webb saw Bobby Redford as a loner:* Interview with Betty Webb, November 19, 1996.

24 *Throughout 1942 and 1943 Japanese bombing scares:* Bastem, *Santa Monica Bay,* 182.

24 *David was a sergeant in the Third Army:* After Action Report, Third Army, August 1, 1944–May 9, 1945. Staff Section, Volume 11. Unclassified, dated 10/29/1984. Includes Top Secret letter from Headquarters, Third United States Army, APO 403, dated January 1, 1945, signed by Brigadier General Hobart R. Gray, Chief of Staff, detailing special ops, including "(d.) Continue to hold present line, including Saarlautern bridge-head, withdrawing only on Army order . . . by command of Lieutenant General Patton." U.S. Army Military History Institute, PA. Also letter from the American Battle Monuments Commission, Washington, D.C., regarding final resting place of 1SGT David G. Redford 39157314, April 10, 1997.

3. *Krazy in Brentwood*

26 *Charlie particularly was wary of national paranoia:* Interview with George Menard, February 9, 1996.

26 *Douglas aircraft manufacturing had boomed:* Fred E. Bastem, *Santa Monica Bay* (Los Angeles: General Publishing Group, 1997), 181.

31 *The previous year, HUAC had forced Rossen:* Interview with Carol Rossen, December 2, 1997.

32 *Coomber remembers their first meeting:* Interview with Bill Coomber, July 7, 1995.

32 *Her fortune came from her father:* Interview with Elizabeth "Lala" Brady, September 30, 1996.

33 *In the Emerson school newspaper: The Emersonian,* dated September 1949.

4. *East of Eden*

36 *Back home the adventuring with Coomber:* Interview with Bill Coomber, July 7, 1995.

37 *In November the Redfords moved to the Valley:* Interview with Kathleen "Kitty" Andrews, March 4, 1996.

37 *Kitty knew Redford was slipping away:* Ibid.

38 *Charlie continued to believe his son's:* Interview with George Menard, March 26, 1995.

39 *Redford started out brooding and isolated:* Interview with Jack Brendlinger, April 14, 1998.

39 *Redford's insularity swung to extroversion:* Interview with Pat Ader, January 22, 1997.

43 *In May 1955, Martha died:* Certificate of Death No. 6253. Martha W. Redford, May 2, 1955, 1:30 p.m. At St. Joseph's Hospital, 501 South Buena Vista Street, Burbank, Los Angeles. Cause of death: Unnoted. Signed by physician, John M. Thomson, who lists he has been treating her for seven days. Burial: Forest Lawn Memorial Park.

5. *Behind the Mirror*

44 *In November, Lena died:* Certificate of death No. 18734. Lena Taylor Redford, died November 1, 1955, aged seventy years.

45 *In Manhattan, they bought round-trip tourist-class tickets:* Interview with Jack Brendlinger, May 28, 1997.

47 *There, for $40, they rented a Moorish villa:* Diary journal, Robert Redford Papers, Mugar Memorial Library, Boston University.

47 *In October the friends returned to Paris:* Interview with Jack Brendlinger, May 28, 1997.

50 *They arrived back in the United States:* Diary journal, Robert Redford Papers, Mugar Memorial Library, Boston University.

50 *On his first sight of New York . . . Miller wrote:* Henry Miller, *The Air-Conditioned Nightmare* (New York: New Directions Publishing, 1970), 12.

51 *Here, instantly, Redford's mood changed:* In "Varwood," a journal of his stay at the apartment complex in the summer of 1957, twenty-seven pages, dated 1958, Robert Redford Papers, Mugar Memorial Library, Boston University.

52 *"Our relationship got off to a better start":* Lola Redford interview, *Provo Herald,* April 13, 1971.

53 *One of the Provo roommates didn't approve:* Interview with Jack Brendlinger, May 28, 1997.

53 *On May 3, he had written off:* Letter on file, from Robert Redford, May 3, 1957. Sundance archive.

53 *Redford and Brendlinger were evicted:* Interview with Jack Brendlinger, May 28, 1997.

53 *"Kindly look with favor upon my stepson":* Letter to the American Academy of Dramatic Arts from Helen Redford, dated August 1, 1957. Sundance archive.

53 *On September 1 he mailed the requested check:* Letter on file, from Robert Redford, September 1, 1957. Sundance archive.

6. *At the Academy*

57 *The graduate course was a two-year program:* Interview with Harry Mastrogeorge, April 18, 1999.

59 *Francis Lettin, the senior rehearsal instructor:* Documents on file, archive of the American Academy of Dramatic Arts, fall 1957.

60 *Ginny Burns and another close friend:* Interview with Ginny Burns Kelly, September 9, 1995.

60 *Both sides of her family:* Interview with Wayne Van Wagenen, January 30, 1998. Also documents on the Van Wagenen genealogy, supplied by Wayne Van Wagenen, including the diary of his great-grandfather H. N. McBride, recounting events in the mid-nineteenth century and dated 1923.

61 *The speech teacher insisted he:* Documents on file, archive of the American Academy of Dramatic Arts, fall 1957.

62 *Redford continued to cling to his fine arts interests:* Interview with Ginny Burns Kelly, September 9, 1995.

62 *Summer was coming, and Redford contacted Charlie:* Interview with Bill Coomber, July 7, 1995.
63 *"facing what [Bob and I] knew would be":* Lola Redford interview, *Provo Herald,* April 13, 1971.
63 *Among the new friends at the Mormon Manhattan ward functions:* Interview with Stan Collins, June 10, 1996.
65 *Redford played Creon in a classicist style:* Interview with Richard Altman, February 14, 1998.

7. *Graduation*

66 *The writer David Rayfiel:* Interview with David Rayfiel, March 11, 1998.
67 *MCA started as a modest Chicago management company:* Frank Rose, *The Agency: William Morris and the Hidden History of Show Business* (New York: HarperBusiness, 1995), 76.
68 *Around this time, Mike Thoma also recommended him:* Interview with Harry Mastrogeorge, April 18, 1999.
70 *But he was dismayed that:* Interview with Ginny Burns Kelly, September 9, 1995.
72 *The funeral service was attended:* Interview with Ginny Burns Kelly, November 22, 1995. Certificate of Death. Scott Anthony Redford Cert No. 156–59 124826. Date of death: November 17, 1959. Aged 2 1/2 months. Cause of death: Bronchopneumonia. Bureau of Vital Records. Department of Health, New York.
72 *Close to 80 percent of all homes:* Norman L. Rosenberg and Emily S. Rosenberg, *In Our Times: America Since World War II* (Englewood Cliffs, N.J.: Prentice-Hall, 1976), 83.
73 *NBC offered Redford a part:* Interview with Monique James, April 26, 1996.
74 Playhouse 90, *which had been running on CBS:* Gordon F. Sander, *Serling: The Rise and Twilight of Television's Last Angry Man* (New York: Dutton, 1992), 160.

8. *The New Frontier*

77 *The problem was that Sidney Lumet:* Interview with Marion Dougherty, October 14, 1996.
78 *Set in 1912,* Iceman *deals:* Arthur Gelb and Barbara Gelb, *O'Neill* (New York: Harper and Brothers, 1968), 871–79.
78 *"[O'Neill] did not feel":* Ibid., 831–32.
78 *Redford would write in his eulogy: Time,* January 8, 2001.
79 *Harryetta Peterka, a friend from AADA, remembered Herman Shumlin:* Interview with Harryetta Peterka, September 16, 1995.
86 *Saxon admits that he angled to:* Interview with John Saxon, January 9, 1996.
87 *on an afternoon when he was visiting Monique James:* Interview with Monique James, April 26, 1996.
88 *They end up gamboling in bed:* Norma Krasna, *Sunday in New York* (New York: Random House, 1962), 114.
89 *The ebullience was short-lived:* Interview with Sondra Lee, May 2, 1996.
90 *Pollack was still in Los Angeles:* Interview with Sydney Pollack, September 1, 1995.
90 *The high-volume work . . . rolled in:* Interview with Monique James, April 26, 1996.

9. *Big Pictures*

96 *At producer Arnold Saint Subber's house:* Interview with Mike Nichols, August 20, 1997.

97 *Simon, a fluid and prolific writer:* Neil Simon, *Rewrites: A Memoir* (New York: Simon & Schuster, 1998), 39.

97 *"Corie: You can't even walk into a candy store":* Neil Simon, *Barefoot in the Park* (New York: Random House, 1964), 93.

98 *The stresses caused by this relationship:* Elizabeth Ashley, *Actress* (New York: Evans, 1978), 19–31.

100 *Ashley's affair with Peppard:* Ibid., 19.

102 *The fifties, as the film historian:* Leslie Halliwell and Philip Purser, *Halliwell's Television Companion* (London: Granada, 1982), xii.

103 *something Robert Shaw was reluctant to agree to:* Interview with Mike Connors, July 6, 1995.

10. *Child's Play*

108 "For we wrestle not against flesh and blood": From the unpublished screenplay "Inside Daisy Clover" by Gavin Lambert.

108 *The movie, written for Wood:* Interview with Gavin Lambert, October 18, 1996.

111 *One incident during filming:* Warren G. Harris, *Natalie and R.J.: Hollywood's Star-Crossed Lovers* (New York: Doubleday, 1988), 136.

115 *Rosenberg reluctantly called Spiegel:* Interview with Arthur Penn, October 11, 1996.

115 *Jane Fonda . . . was curious about Redford:* Interview with Jane Fonda, February 19, 1999.

119 This Property Is Condemned, *meanwhile, was in development hell:* Interview with Sydney Pollack, September 1, 1995.

123 *The Andalusian coast Redford opted for:* William Sansom, "The Great Game of Getting Away from It All," *Life,* April 1960.

123 *Shauna had enrolled:* Interview with Shauna Redford Schlosser, June 3, 1998.

125 *In July, Stan Collins received a postcard:* Interview with Stan Collins, June 14, 1996.

127 *Peer Oppenheimer, a journalist he'd met:* Peer J. Oppenheimer, "The Hide-and-Seek Life of Robert Redford," *Family Weekly,* August 20, 1967.

127 *Talk of westerns filled his evenings:* Interview with Sydney Pollack, September 1, 1995.

11. *Toward Concord*

130 *It earned $9 million:* John Douglas Eames, *The Paramount Story* (London: Octopus, 1985), 256.

130 *Paramount's wrath seemed inevitable:* Interview with Mike Frankfurt, May 14, 1996.

131 *The record profits of $20 million:* Eames, *The Paramount Story,* 115.

133 *In his memoirs, Polanski wrote:* Roman Polanski, *Roman* (London: Pan, 1982), 282.

135 *Sitting on the perimeter fence:* Interview with Mike Frankfurt, May 14, 1996.

136 *On August 5, 1968, in a press conference:* "Film Star, 4 Others Buy Timp Haven Ski Resort," *Salt Lake Tribune,* business section, August 6, 1968, 18.

137 *By 1940, of the 477 movies released:* Edward Buscombe, ed., *The BFI Companion to the Western* (London: Andre Deutsch, 1988), 47–53.

137 *The story's significance, as Harry Lawton wrote:* Harry W. Lawton, *Tell Them Willie Boy Is Here* (New York: Award, 1970), 8.

138 *An article in* Variety *criticized:* Byro, review of *Tell Them Willie Boy Is Here, Variety,* October 19, 1969. Excerpted in James Spada, *The Films of Robert Redford* (Secaucus, N.J.: Citadel Press, 1984), 132.

141 *"He was tough—from a poor part of town":* James Salter, *Burning the Days: Recollection* (New York: Random House, 1997), 234.

141 *Salter's treatment, dated September 1967:* Robert Redford Papers, Mugar Memorial Library, Boston University. Redford has scribbled on the front page, "First project under new banner 'Wildwood Productions.' "

143 *CMA was an outgrowth of MCA:* Interview with Stephanie Phillips, July 20, 1996.

146 *But film historian Andrew Horton, later evaluating his oeuvre:* Andrew Horton, *The Films of George Roy Hill* (Irvington, N.Y.: Columbia University Press, 1984), xiv.

147 *Humor, on which the simple, linear story:* Interview with Paul Newman, June 10, 1996.

12. *Fame*

158 *The back injury at the end of filming:* Interview with Marcella Scott Krisel, November 6, 1997.

161 *Redford took pride in his business sense:* Interview with Mike Frankfurt, May 14, 1996.

161 *Redford assigned Wayne, Lola's brother:* Interview with Wayne Van Wagenen, January 30, 1998.

163 *When they started out, Hendler was:* Interview with Reg Gipson, September 15, 1995.

166 *The epilogue of Eastman's original draft:* Charles Eastman, *Little Fauss and Big Halsy* (New York: Noonday Press, 1970), 160.

166 *"Somewhere is Halsy, somewhere is Little":* Ibid., 161.

166 *In the fall of 1970, Paramount complained:* Letter to Gary Hendler from Mike Frankfurt, dated October 5, 1970, recording Stanley Jaffe's complaints against Redford. Sundance archive.

13. *Two and a Half Careers*

169 *Pollack and Calley decided to shoot:* Interview with Sydney Pollack, February 15, 2002.

171 *Milius's script had been gutted:* Sydney Pollack's script and notes on file, Mirage Productions, Paramount Studios, California.

172 *The writer Robert Pirsig has observed:* Robert M. Pirsig, *Lila: An Inquiry into Morals* (London: Black Swan, 1992), 55.

173 *As postproduction finished, Lola and the kids:* Interview with Mike Shinderling, February 9, 1998.

174 *For months he had been observing:* Interview with Julie Mack, June 20, 1996. This dispute stretched into the 1990s. Continuing highway dispute: "Canyon Group Doesn't Want Four Lanes," *Provo Herald,* May 21, 1986; "School Board Joins Provo Citizens in Possible Suing of UDOT," *Provo Herald,* May 28, 1986; Statement Submitted by Robert Redford on the Supplemental Environmental Impact Statement for the Provo Canyon Road, June 11, 1987; Utah Department of Transportation Draft Agenda for Utah Transport Commission, May 18, 1993, sent to Appel & Mattson, law offices (representing objection lobby); Draft letter to Governor Michael O. Leavitt regarding Highway 189, with notes by Redford, May 11, 1994; "UDOT Asked to Delay Project," *The Salt Lake Tribune,* December 5, 1995.

176 *George Roy Hill was keen to adapt:* Interview with George Roy Hill, September 4, 1995.

179 *Six years before, Louella Parsons had allowed him:* Louella O. Parsons, "Barefoot Boy Comes Home," *New York Journal American,* May 30, 1965.

179 *Laurence Luckinbill, writing for* Esquire: Laurence Luckinbill, "Oh, You Sundance Kid!" *Esquire,* October 1970, 160.

183 *Jerry Brown came to believe:* Interview with Jeremy Larner, September 7, 1995.

185 *Ritchie, whose capacity for intellectual theorizing:* Interview with Michael Ritchie, September 4, 1995.

187 *Carlson herself admitted to "schizophrenic" feelings:* Bruce Bahrenburg, *Filming "The Candidate"* (New York: Warner, 1972), 94.

188 *Robert Penn Warren once wrote:* Ernest Hemingway, *A Farewell to Arms,* with an introduction by Robert Penn Warren (New York: Charles Scribner's Sons, 1929), viii.

188 *In 1968 Tiger died of heart failure:* Obituary in *The New London* (*Conn.*) *Day,* February 29, 1968: "Waterford. Charles Elisha Redford, formerly of 35 Summer Street, died Wednesday at Waterford Convalescent Hospital. . . . He was the grandfather of actor Robert Redford. . . . Burial will be at River Bend Cemetery, Westerly."

188 *There was the well-circulated magazine report:* "A California Hippie Claims, 'Robert Redford Is My Husband!' " *Movie Life,* August 1970.

14. *Idols*

190 *Stark commissioned an original script:* Arthur Laurents, *Original Story By: A Memoir of Broadway and Hollywood* (New York: Alfred A. Knopf, 2000), 264.

191 *In his memoirs Laurents reports:* Ibid., 269.

192 *Worst of all, said Pollack, Laurents had not:* Interview with Sydney Pollack, September 1, 1995.

192 *In a detailed correspondence, Trumbo analyzed:* Correspondence from Dalton Trumbo to Sydney Pollack, undated, appended to the script of *The Way We Were* in Sydney Pollack's script files at Mirage Productions, Paramount Studios, Los Angeles.

192 *"The reason I have been so hung up on Hayden's book":* Letter from Sydney Pollack to Dalton Trumbo, undated, appended to the script of *The Way We Were* in Sydney Pollack's script files at Mirage Productions, Paramount Studios, Los Angeles.

194 *"Katie: Doesn't it make you angry":* From the unpublished screenplay *The Way We Were,* by Arthur Laurents.

195 *"I just loved working with him":* Letter to the author from Barbra Streisand, August 2, 1996.

198 *It had started in October 1970:* Interview with David Ward, November 8, 1997.

200 *George Roy Hill stormed into the office:* Interview with George Roy Hill, June 12, 1995.

202 *Four lawsuits were launched against* The Sting: Interview with David Ward, November 8, 1997.

203 *Evans wanted to gift the famous role:* Robert Evans, *The Kid Stays in the Picture* (New York: Hyperion, 1994), 237.

205 *Clayton's vision for the movie was specific:* Neil Sinyard, *Jack Clayton* (Manchester: Manchester University Press, 2000), 144.

206 *Clayton wrote in his preparatory notes:* Ibid., 146.

207 *Bruce Bahrenburg, a writer:* Bruce Bahrenburg, *Filming "The Great Gatsby"* (New York: Berkley Medallion, 1974), 248.

209 *"Ultimately," said Farrow, "[it] was a victim":* Mia Farrow, *What Falls Away* (New York: Doubleday, 1997), 174.

15. *Watergate*

211 *CAN's progress, says administrator Cynthia Burke:* Interview with Cynthia Burke (Cynthia Stein during CAN era), August 28, 1998. Copies of CAN newsletters, undated, six- to eight-page features include, in issue 2, "All About Breads," "Home Eco" (on recycling); in issue 7, "Cleaning Products: Good Clean Fun?" "A Note on Aerosols"; in issue 13, "The Over the Counter Drug Culture," "CAN's (Condensed) Drug Dictionary." All features uncredited.

212 *In 1972, Adams asked Ayres:* Interview with Richard Ayres, October 18, 1997.

215 *After a period of friction with Hill:* Letter from George Roy Hill to Bill Goldman, undated but appears to be July 1973: "Bill, I am in the process of outlining the script changes. . . . I think it is unrealistic to think we could ever work together again as we once did." George Roy Hill Papers, Margaret Herrick Library, Academy of Motion Picture Arts and Sciences, Los Angeles.

215 *Hill's notebooks attest to great ambition:* Documents regarding *The Great Waldo Pepper,* unpaginated and undated, George Roy Hill Papers, Margaret Herrick Library, Academy of Motion Picture Arts and Sciences, Los Angeles.

217 *Lindsey's comments provoked the often impulsive Hill:* Letter from William H. Honan, Arts and Leisure Editor, *The New York Times,* to H. H. Martin, Universal Pictures, dated June 18, 1976: "Regarding Robert Lindsey's May 30th article . . . I think we're perfectly in the clear on 'Waldo.' " George Roy Hill Papers, Margaret Herrick Library, Academy of Motion Picture Arts and Sciences, Los Angeles.

217 *The sixteen-point addendum to his* Waldo *contract:* Copy of contract, George Roy Hill Papers, Margaret Herrick Library, Academy of Motion Picture Arts and Sciences, Los Angeles.

219 *Goldman was offended that:* Bernstein Interview with Bob Woodward, January 18, 2009.

219 *In the weeks that followed, Redford and Pakula:* Interview with Alan J. Pakula, April 9, 1996.

223 *Redford felt he was focused:* Interview with Sydney Pollack, September 1, 1995.

230 *Hal Holbrook and others spoke of:* Interview with Carol Rossen, December 29, 1998.

16. *Out of Acting*

237 *"It was my first major conservation issue":* Robert Redford, "Duel for the West," *USA Weekend,* November 3–5, 1995, an article summarizing Redford's philosophy about the overdevelopment of the Utah wilderness. Also, a fifty-page paper, "Marketability of Coal from Andalex Resources' Proposed Smoky Hollow Coal Mine," prepared for Grand Canyon Trust by John Duffied and Chris Neher, Bioeconomics Inc., and Arnold Silverman, University of Montana, May 20, 1995, which includes current and historical trends in Utah coal production.

240 *"It was as if some supernatural force":* Letter from Robert Redford to Dan Arensmeier, June 17, 1978. Sundance archive.

242 *"Education was the answer":* "NRDC 1970–1990—Twenty Years Defending the Environment: A Report" (New York: NRDC, 1990); Colum F. Lynch, "Global Warning," *The Amicus Journal* (a publication of the Natural Resources Defense Council), spring 1996; "25 Years of the Environment," anniversary edition, winter 1996.

242 *In Ford's last days in office:* Interview with Joyce Deep, September 16, 1995.

245 *In 1978 he laid it out:* Robert Redford, interview with Daniel Geery, *Los Angeles Herald Examiner,* January 30, 1978.

247 *Diamond Fork Ranch, became the base:* From 1974 approximately a hundred mares were bred and traded yearly. The breeding operation ceased in 1983, and the ranch was sold in 1996. Thereafter, the nearby Charleston Ranch was purchased for crop cultivation. It comprised thirty-one acres and cultivated black-tipped wheat, amaranth, sunflowers, sweet Annie, Indian corn, larkspur, Rocky Mountain penstemon, poppies, twelve varieties of grasses, thirty varieties of herbs, field greens, carrots, squash and onions. Much of the produce was used in the kitchens of the Sundance resort. Information: Sundance archive.

247 *The American League for Industry and Vital Energy was quick: Southern Utah News,* April 22, 1976.

251 *"We've had three decades of lousy noisefests":* Interview with Joseph E. Levine conducted by Francis Feighan, circa September 1976.

252 *Levine sweated like a workhorse:* Ibid.

252 *Goldman overcame the inherent dramatic weakness:* William Goldman, *Adventures in the Screen Trade* (New York: Warner, 1983), 282.

254 *incited Mobil Oil to place:* "Musings of an Oil Person," *The New York Times,* May 11, 1978.

256 *"Wildwood stationery lies fallow":* From "Redford Musings," a notebook in the Sundance archive.

17. *Painted Frames*

258 *even dictionaries listed him under words:* The online *New Oxford American Dictionary* defines "idol" as "an image or representation of a god used as an object of worship; a person or thing that is greatly admired, loved, or revered: *movie idol Robert Redford.*"

259 *Later Steve Bernhardt, Redford's old friend:* Interview with Steve Bernhardt, July 2, 1997.

261 *At one point, Rayfiel sent:* Among notes appended to the script for *The Electric Horseman,* in Sydney Pollack's script library at Mirage Productions, Paramount Studios, Los Angeles.

261 *"The present version is too encumbered":* Note on discarded script draft of *The Electric Horseman* in Sydney Pollack's script files at Mirage Productions, Paramount Studios, Los Angeles.

261 *"When I was a kid":* Handwritten notes by Sydney Pollack, appended to the script of *The Electric Horseman* in Sydney Pollack's script files at Mirage Productions, Paramount Studios, Los Angeles.

263 *Never missing a marketing moment:* Ray Stark interview with Sydney Pollack, September 1, 1995.

264 *Redford had been prompted by author-activist Peter Matthiessen: Premiere,* April 1992, 29.

264 *Murton's story was every bit as sinister:* Thomas O. Murton and Joe Hyams, *Accomplices to the Crime: The Arkansas Prison Scandal* (New York: Grove Press, 1969).

265 *Rafelson admitted to having made* Head: Interview with Stephen Farber, *The New York Times,* Arts section, February 16, 1997.

265 *"I liked that complete disrespect":* Interview with Bob Rafelson, online at www.filmfestivals.com/cannes98/starsus7.htm.

266 *In widely reported accounts, Rafelson decked a senior Fox executive:* Interview with Stuart Rosenberg, June 7, 2000.

268 *On a bright winter's afternoon, Stan and Mary Alice Collins:* Interview with Stan Collins, June 1, 1996.

270 *Eisner, according to his autobiography:* Michael Eisner, *Work in Progress: Risking Failure, Surviving Success* (New York: Hyperion, 1999), 94–95, 102.

272 *Moore heard nothing for a month:* Interview with Mary Tyler Moore, September 21, 1996.

274 *"Bob understood everything":* Ivan Butler, interview with Tim Hutton, *Films and Filming* 331 (April 1982).

275 *To Donald Sutherland, such "mean-ass economy":* Interview with Donald Sutherland, conducted by Francis Feighan, August 1981.

278 *Moore, battling the ravages of incipient alcoholism:* Interview with Mary Tyler Moore, September 26, 1996.

280 *"I just didn't think I was going to see this, but I'm no less grateful":* Text of Robert Redford's Academy Award acceptance speech from March 31, 1981, transcribed in *Red Book,* a fanzine published by Trudy Hoffman, June 1981.

280 *In* The Soul's Code, *Hillman implies:* James Hillman, *The Soul's Code: In Search of Character and Calling* (New York: Warner, 1997).

18. *Sundance*

286 *Michelle Satter, introduced to Redford:* Interview with Michelle Satter, June 19, 1996.

286 *The first Sundance Institute lab took place:* Sundance Institute literature, including "Sundance June 1982 Program," with an introduction by Redford and Frank Daniel and a full listing of advisers and sponsors (board of trustees: Redford,

Robert "Reg" Gipson, Saul Bass, Marjorie Benton, Ian Calderon, Ian Cumming, Frank Daniel, Moctesuma Esparza, Robert Geller, Dr. Robert Gray, Alan Jacobs, Howard Klein, Karl Malden, Mary McFadden, John McMillian, Mike Medavoy, Victor Nunez, Wayne Owens, Sydney Pollack, Annick Smith, Anthony Thomopoulos, Claire Townsend, Robert Townsend and George White); also "Sundance Institute Filmmakers and Screenwriters Laboratory, May 29–June 27, 1996," with an introduction by Redford and a full listing of advisers and sponsors (board of trustees: Redford, Gary Beer, Glenn Close, Jake Eberts, Ted Field, Carlos Fuentes, Robert E. Gipson, George Gund, Steven Haft, Michael Kuhn, Pat Mitchell, Michael Ovitz, Sydney Pollack, Tom Rothman, Bradford Smith, Brandon Tartikoff, Denzel Washington, Alonzo Watson Jr., Richard Weinberg, Walter Weisman, James Wiatt, Hume Cronyn [emeritus], Irene Diamond [emeritus], George White [emeritus], Sundance archive.

The selection process for the first lab was by invitation from the first set of creative and technical advisers. Only one person, Claire Townsend, made the project selections, though this process was altered in years to come. The advisers were Victor Nunez (director of *Gal Young 'Un*), Alan Jacobs (former director of the Association of Independent Video and Filmmakers), George White, Claire Townsend (vice president for production at Twentieth Century–Fox), Robert Geller (PBS producer), Moctesuma Esparza (producer of *La Raza*), Frank Daniel (chairman of the film division of Columbia University's School of the Arts), Sterling Van Wagenen and Robert Redford.

Of the ten projects chosen in the first year, records of nine remain on file. After the first year, projects were chosen from a wider pool of random submissions, which, within ten years, numbered in the thousands. Among the first season's projects were *El Norte* (Gregory Nava and Anna Thomas), *Learning to Fall* (Ann Beattie), *St. Elmo's Fire* (David Shicklele), *The Giant Joshua* (John and Denise Earle), *The Trials of Daniel Boone* (Steve Wax and Steve Channing), *The Man Who Killed the Deer* (Larry Littlebird), *Ghost Dancers* (Barry Pritchard), *Gestation in the Tombs* (Pablo Figueroa), and *South Bronx Drama* (Jon Alpert).

286 *By the standard that would shortly develop:* Interview with Robert Redford, June 9, 1999. The theater lab program was always of equal importance in Redford's eyes. "I'm so glad I was in theater in the fifties, in that fading era when it was all about storytelling and bodies in the space," he says. "You learn so much about telling the tale, and that's critical, of course, for movies. At Sundance, I saw theater workshopping as a key activity. It bled into the film work, and that was as I wanted it."

The theater labs, running through July of each year, became very productive. Over a five-year period at the start of the millennium, twenty-five projects nurtured at the July labs went into full theatrical production across the country, including Tony Kushner's *Angels in America.*

287 *"The trouble with Bob":* Interview with Reg Gipson, September 16, 1995.

287 *Shortly after the first lab, Brent Beck:* Interview with Brent Beck, September 11, 1995.

287 *At the time, Pollack reported himself uplifted:* Gerald Peary, "Sundance," *American Film,* October 1981, 47–51.

288 *Redford had already engaged Hope Moore:* Interview with Gary Beer, October 18, 1995.

289 *The IRM was officially launched:* John Aloysius Farrell, "Westernizing with Robert Redford," *The Denver Post Magazine,* December 1, 1985.

291 *A flood of creative ideas flowed:* Interview with Barry Levinson, March 6, 1999.

292 *Wells had been shot in the back of the head:* Kirk Mitchell, "Celebrity Link Drew Global Attention to Killing," *The Denver Post,* March 16, 2008.

296 *Only the heroic acts of four passersby: Provo Herald,* March 9, 1985.

297 *Redford's aim with the rewrites:* Sidney Lumet, *Making Movies* (New York: Vintage, 1996), 39.

298 *But it was Judith Thurman's 1982 biography:* Judith Thurman, *Isak Dinesen: The Life of a Storyteller* (New York: St. Martin's Press, 1982).

299 *Blixen's personal writings suggest otherwise:* Isak Dinesen, *Letters from Africa 1914–1931,* ed. Frans Lasson (Chicago: University of Chicago Press, 1981), 103–430.

299 *Kurt gathered enough from Judith:* Errol Trzebinski, *Silence Will Speak: A Study of the Life of Denys Finch Hatton and His Relationship with Karen Blixen* (Chicago: University of Chicago Press, 1985).

303 *Reitman worried about his appropriateness:* Interview with Ivan Reitman, conducted by Francis Feighan, June 1988.

19. *One America?*

306 *Recently, the programs had been run by Susan Lacey:* Interview with Sterling Van Wagenen, September 29, 1997.

307 *For Berkeley-born Nichols, the journey to* Milagro: John Nichols, *A Fragile Beauty* (Salt Lake City: Peregrine Smith Books, 1987), 1.

311 *New meeting rooms for lab students:* Interview with Ian Calderon, June 17, 1996.

311 *Redford's greatest ally in this redesign:* Interview with Jamie Redford, December 16, 1998.

314 *At the following Canyon de Chelly conference: The New York Times,* June 25, 1984.

317 *"The U.S.A and the U.S.S.R. are the two largest producers":* Draft of IRM statement, unsigned, marked "as delivered," dated 1988. Sundance archive.

317 *The Sundance symposium foreshadowed:* Interview with Bill Bradley, July 2, 1997.

318 *The IRM's demise became an issue of debate:* Interview with Gary Beer, October 18, 1995.

20. *Beyond Hurricane Country*

320 *"to discover life in film":* Elizabeth Ezra, ed., *European Cinema* (New York: Oxford University Press, 2004), 169.

321 *According to anonymous sources interviewed:* Peter Biskind, "Robert Redford and the Unfulfilled Promise of the Sundance Institute," *Premiere,* February 1991. Aljean Harmetz, "Sundance Film Festival Veers from Mainstream," *The New York Times,* January 17, 1991.

322 *Though Jamie had effectively diagnosed himself:* Interview with Jamie Redford, April 2, 1998.

324 *The industry still functioned as an elite club:* Ron Base and David Haslam, *The Movies of the Eighties* (London: Macdonald, 1990), 207.

325 *"[Mike] Nichols believes you should do":* Letter from Manny Azenberg, date illegible. Sundance archive.

331 *A major investigative feature:* Biskind, "Robert Redford and the Unfulfilled Promise."

333 *Ovitz could find no studio backing:* Interview with Jake Eberts, March 22, 1998.

337 *Charlie responded with a clever memo:* Letter from Charles Redford to Robert Redford, November 26, 1988, Sundance archive.

341 *It was Parkes and Lasker who'd pitched:* Interview with Phil Alden Robinson, conducted by Francis Feighan, January 1993.

343 *"The billionaire in my novel":* Jack Engelhard interviewed by Greg Sheffield, NewsBuster.org, published online March 23, 2006.

21. *Delivering the Moment*

347 *"When a population is distracted by trivia":* Neil Postman, *Amusing Ourselves to Death* (London: William Heinemann, 1985), 161.

349 *Retired prosecuting attorney Joseph Stone: New York Post,* March 8, 1995.

351 *During the first five years of Eisner's reign:* Ron Base and David Haslam, *The Movies of the Eighties* (London: Macdonald, 1990), 220.

352 *According to Dunne in his memoir:* John Gregory Dunne, *Monster: Living Off the Big Screen* (New York: Random House, 1997), 31–32.

354 *After* Ordinary People, *Redford stated emphatically:* Sue Clarke, "The Redford Conference," *Photoplay,* August 1976.

22. *The Edge*

361 *By the mid-nineties almost half of all householders:* www.marketingcharts.com.

362 *IFC was a sister channel:* Rainbow Media Holdings LLC, a subsidiary of Cablevision, the current owners of the Sundance Channel (since May 2008), originally owned Bravo, as well as the Independent Film Channel. In 2002 Rainbow sold Bravo to NBC (now NBC Universal) for $1.25 billion. Rainbow Media Web site.

363 *"They were liberal in the worst sense":* Peter Biskind, *Down and Dirty Pictures: Miramax, Sundance, and the Rise of Independent Film* (New York: Simon & Schuster, 2004), 121.

364 *By the mid-nineties, the institute:* Interview with Michelle Satter, June 18, 1996.

365 *He wrote an emotional eulogy: Time,* November 21, 1998.

369 *"Seriousness, as Leonard Cohen says": Songs from the Life of Leonard Cohen,* BBC video documentary. Produced by Debbie Geller. Directed by John Archer (BBC Enterprises, 1988).

371 *Sundance then suggested further truncation:* Interview with Julie Mack, April 12, 1998.

371 *Under Clinton, Republicans in Congress:* HR 1745, proposing the protection of 1.8 million acres. The opposing green coalition's proposed HR 1500 (protecting 5.7 million acres) was supported by Redford. League of Conservation Voters circular to the United States Senate, by Deb Callahan, President, March 13, 1996, regarding opposition to S 884, the Utah Public Lands Management Act, a precursor to HR 1745, *Deseret News,* September 29, 1995.

372 *When President Clinton inaugurated a new national park:* Bill Clinton, *My Life* (New York: Alfred A. Knopf, 2002), 888; "President Protects Utah Lands," *USA Today,* September 20, 1996.

23. *The Actor in Transit*

379 *Lurie had a reputation as an outspoken leftist:* Bernard Weinraub, "Press: Hollywood Still Directs Its Coverage," *The New York Times,* June 1, 1992.

383 *On the phone to Terry Lawson:* Article by Terry Lawson in the *Detroit Free Press,* October 19, 2001.

383 *Redford's antipathy toward the government:* Op-ed by Robert Redford, *Los Angeles Times,* December 2, 2002, endorsing Vote Solar's activities.

383 *if the Bush administration had:* "Annual Hot List," *Rolling Stone,* August 30, 2001.

387 *Miramax grew powerfully as a production entity:* Peter Biskind, *Down and Dirty Pictures: Miramax, Sundance, and the Rise of Independent Film* (New York: Simon & Schuster, 2004), 189–95; Laura M. Holson, "How the Tumultuous Marriage of Miramax and Disney Failed," *The New York Times,* March 6, 2005.

388 *Writer Walter Kirn's observation:* Walter Kirn, "The Two Hollywoods," *The New York Times Magazine,* November 16, 1997.

24. *Jeremiah's Way*

389 *he announced the relaunch of the Sundance Cinema Centers: The Hollywood Reporter,* August 1, 2006.

389 *On its heels came another IRM-style venture:* Debra DeHaney-Howard, "Mayors Discuss Climate Protection Solutions at Sundance Summit," *U.S. Mayor Newspaper,* November 20, 2006.

392 *In May 2008 the bombshell came:* Brian Stelter, "Cablevision Unit Buys Sundance Channel," *The New York Times,* May 8, 2008; Jacques Steinberg, "Redford Is to Keep His Mark on Channel," *The New York Times,* July 1, 2008.

392 *His personal life was never so serene:* Interview with Amy Redford, January 14, 2009.

395 *His movies had cumulatively earned almost $1 billion:* Calculated from figures posted on boxofficemojo.com.

Bibliography

The editions listed are those referred to during the preparation of this book.

Acocella, Joan. *Willa Cather and the Politics of Criticism.* Lincoln: University of Nebraska Press, 2000.

Anderson, Kent. *Television Fraud: The History and Implications of the Quiz Show Scandals.* New York: Greenwood Press, 1979.

Ashley, Elizabeth. *Actress.* New York: Evans, 1978.

Attanasio, Paul. "Quiz Show." Screenplay based on *Remembering America: A Voice from the Sixties* by Richard Goodwin. Unpublished screenplay. Sundance archive.

Bahrenburg, Bruce. *Filming "The Candidate."* New York: Warner, 1972.

———. *Filming "The Great Gatsby."* New York: Berkley Medallion, 1974.

Baker, Carlos. *Emerson Among the Eccentrics: A Group Portrait.* New York: Viking, 1996.

Base, Ron, and David Haslam. *The Movies of the Eighties.* London: Macdonald, 1990.

Basten, Fred E. *Santa Monica Bay.* Los Angeles: General Publishing Group, 1997.

Beauchamp, Cari, and Henri Behar. *Hollywood on the Riviera.* New York: Morrow, 1992.

Bergon, Frank, ed. *The Wilderness Reader.* New York: New American Library, 1980.

Berlo, Janet Catherine, and Ruth B. Phillips. *Native North American Art.* New York: Oxford University Press, 1998.

Bernstein, Walter. *Inside Out: A Memoir of the Blacklist.* New York: Alfred A. Knopf, 1996.

Beschloss, Michael R., ed. *Taking Charge: The Johnson White House Tapes, 1963–1964* New York: Simon & Schuster, 1997.

Biskind, Peter. *Down and Dirty Pictures: Miramax, Sundance, and the Rise of Independent Film.* New York: Simon & Schuster, 2004.

Boddy, William. *Fifties Television: The Industry and Its Critics.* Urbana: University of Illinois Press, 1990.

Bordwell, David. *The Classical Hollywood Cinema: Film Style and Mode of Production to 1960.* New York: Columbia University Press, 1985.

Bourne, Peter G. *Jimmy Carter.* New York: Scribner, 1997.

Bowden, Charles, and Jack Dykinga. *Stone Canyons of the Colorado Plateau.* With a foreword by Robert Redford. New York: Harry N. Abrams, 1996.

Bradlee, Ben. *A Good Life: Newspapering and Other Adventures.* New York: Simon & Schuster, 1996.

Brando, Marlon. *Brando: Songs My Mother Taught Me.* London: Century, 1994.

Brown, Dee. *When the Century Was Young: A Writer's Notebook.* Little Rock, Ark.: August House, 1993.

Brown, Jared. *Alan J. Pakula: His Films and His Life.* New York: Backstage Books, 2005.

Bruck, Connie. *When Hollywood Had a King: The Reign of Lew Wasserman, Who Leveraged Talent into Power and Influence.* New York: Random House, 2003.

Buhle, Paul, and Dave Wagner. *A Very Dangerous Citizen: Abraham Lincoln Polonsky and the Hollywood Left.* Berkeley: University of California Press, 2001.

Buscombe, Edward, ed. *The BFI Companion to the Western.* London: Andre Deutsch, 1988.

Campbell, Joseph. *The Hero with a Thousand Faces.* 2nd ed. Princeton, N.J.: Princeton University Press, 1968.

Carnahan, Matthew. "Lions for Lambs." Unpublished screenplay. Sundance archive.

Carson, Rachel. *Silent Spring.* London: Penguin, 1991.

Clinch, Minty. *Robert Redford.* London: New English Library, 1990.

Clinton, Bill. *My Life.* New York: Alfred A. Knopf, 2004.

Cook, David A. *A History of Narrative Film.* 4th ed. New York: Norton, 2004.

Cowley, Julian, ed. *The Great Gatsby.* York Notes Advanced. London: Longman/York Press, 1998.

Denenberg, R. V. *Understanding American Politics.* London: Fontana, 1976.

Dick, Bernard F. *Engulfed: The Death of Paramount Pictures and the Birth of Corporate Hollywood.* Lexington: University Press of Kentucky, 2001.

Dinesen, Isak. *Letters from Africa 1914–1931.* Edited by Frans Lasson. Chicago: University of Chicago Press, 1984.

———. *Out of Africa.* New York: Modern Library, 1992.

Downing, David. *Robert Redford.* London: W. H. Allen, 1977.

Dunne, John Gregory. *Monster: Living Off the Big Screen.* New York: Random House, 1997.

Eames, John Douglas. *The Paramount Story.* London: Octopus, 1985.

Eastman, Charles. *Little Fauss and Big Halsy.* New York: Noonday Press, 1970.

Eberts, Jake, and Terry Ilott. *My Indecision Is Final: Rise and Fall of Goldcrest Films.* London: Faber and Faber, 1990.

Eisner, Michael. *Work in Progress: Risking Failure, Surviving Success.* New York: Hyperion, 1999.

Emery, Fred. *Watergate.* New York: Touchstone, 1995.

Evans, Nicholas. *The Horse Whisperer.* New York: Dell, 1995.

Evans, Robert. *The Kid Stays in the Picture.* New York: Hyperion, 1994.

Farrow, Mia. *What Falls Away.* New York: Doubleday, 1997.

Fisher, Vardis. *Mountain Man: A Novel of Male and Female in the Early American West.* Boise, Idaho: Opal Laurel Holmes, 1972.

Fitzgerald, F. Scott. *The Great Gatsby.* Edited and with an introduction by Matthew J. Bruccoli. New York: Scribners, 1991.

Fonda, Jane. *My Life So Far.* New York: Random House, 2005.

Foote, Horton. *Collected Plays.* Vol. 2. Hanover, N.H.: Smith and Kraus, 1996.

Fraser-Cavassoni, Natasha. *Sam Spiegel.* New York: Simon & Schuster, 2003.

Friedenberg, Richard. "A River Runs Through It." Unpublished screenplay based on the novella by Norman Maclean. Sundance archive.

Friedenberg, Richard, and Robert Redford. *A River Runs Through It: Bringing a Classic to the Screen.* Livingston, Mont.: Clark City Press, 1992.

Gabel, Shainee, and Kristin Hahn. *Anthem: An American Road Story.* New York: Avon, 1997.

Gelb, Arthur, and Barbara Gelb. *O'Neill.* With an introduction by Brooks Atkinson. New York: Harper and Brothers, 1962.

Goldman, William. *Adventures in the Screen Trade.* New York: Warner, 1983.

———. *Butch Cassidy and the Sundance Kid: The Screenplay.* New York: Dell, 1969.

———. *The Season: A Candid Look at Broadway.* New York: Harcourt, Brace and World, 1969.

Goldman, William, and George Roy Hill. *The Great Waldo Pepper: The Screenplay.* New York: Dell, 1975.

Gomery, Douglas. *The Hollywood Studio System: A History.* London: British Film Institute, 2008.

Goodwin, Richard N. *Remembering America: A Voice from the Sixties.* New York: Little Brown, 1988.

Gore, Al. *Earth in the Balance: Forging a New Common Purpose.* London: Earthscan, 1992.

Graham, Katharine. *Personal History.* New York: Random House, 1998.

Greene, Ray. *Hollywood Migraine: The Inside Story of a Decade in Film.* Dublin: Merlin, 2000.

Griffiths, Trevor R., and Carole Woodis. *Theatre Guide.* London: Bloomsbury, 1988.

Grobel, Lawrence. *Conversations with Marlon Brando.* London: Bloomsbury, 1991.

Guest, Judith. *Ordinary People.* New York: Viking, 1976.

Hall, Oakley. *The Downhill Racers.* New York: Viking Press, 1963.

Halliwell, Leslie, and Philip Purser. *Halliwell's Television Companion.* London: Granada, 1982.

Hansen, Frantz Leander. *The Aristocratic Universe of Karen Blixen: Destiny and the Denial of Fate.* Brighton: Sussex Academic Press, 2003.

Harris, Mark. *Pictures at a Revolution: Five Movies and the Birth of the New Hollywood.* London: Penguin, 2009.

Harris, Warren G. *Natalie and R.J.: Hollywood's Star-Crossed Lovers.* New York: Doubleday, 1988.

Harrison, William, and W. D. Richter. *Brubaker.* A novelization by William Harrison. New York: Ballantine, 1980.

Hathaway, J. Bourge, and Robert Alan Clayton. *Quiet Pride: Ageless Wisdom of the American West.* Hillsboro, Ore.: First Glance Books, 1992.

Haynes, Williams. *Stonington Chronology, 1649–1976.* Chester, Conn.: Pequot Press/Stonington Historical Society, 1976.

Hemingway, Ernest. *A Farewell to Arms.* With an introduction by Robert Penn Warren. New York: Charles Scribner's Sons, 1929.

Hershberger, Mary. *Jane Fonda's War: A Political Biography of an Antiwar Icon.* New York: New Press, 2005.

Hietala, Thomas R. *Manifest Design: American Exceptionalism and Empire.* Ithaca, N.Y.: Cornell University Press, 2003.

Hillman, James. *The Soul's Code: In Search of Character and Calling.* New York: Warner, 1997.

Hilms, Michele. *The Television History Book.* London: British Film Institute, 2008.

Hoffman, Basil. *Acting: And How to Be Good at It.* With an introduction by Sydney Pollack. Los Angeles: Ingenuity Press, 2006.

Horton, Andrew. *The Films of George Roy Hill.* Rev. ed. With a foreword by Paul Newman. Jefferson, N.C.: McFarland, 2005.

Hughes, Robert. *Culture of Complaint: The Fraying of America.* New York: Oxford, 1993.

Jenkins, Henry. *Convergence Culture: Where Old and New Media Collide.* Rev. ed. New York: New York University Press, 2008.

Johnstone, Iain. *The Arnhem Report: A Bridge Too Far.* London: Star, 1977.

———. *Dustin Hoffman.* London: Hippocrene Books, 1984.

———. *Tom Cruise: All the World's a Stage.* London: Hodder and Stoughton, 2007.

Kael, Pauline. *I Lost It at the Movies.* London: Marion Boyars, 1994.

Krisel, Marcella. *The Sound of Symbols.* Self-published, 1974.

LaGravenese, Richard. "The Horse Whisperer." Unpublished screenplay based on the novel by Nicholas Evans. Sundance archive.

Lambert, Gavin. *Inside Daisy Clover.* London: Serpent's Tail, 1996.

———. *Natalie Wood.* New York: Back Stage Books, 2005.

Larner, Jeremy. *Nobody Knows: Reflections on the McCarthy Campaign of 1968.* Ontario: Macmillan, 1970.

Laurents, Arthur. *Original Story By: A Memoir of Broadway and Hollywood.* New York: Alfred A. Knopf, 2000.

———. *The Way We Were.* New York: Harper and Row, 1972.

Lawton, Harry. *Tell Them Willie Boy Is Here.* New York: Award, 1970. First published in 1960 as *Willie Boy: A Desert Manhunt* by Paisano Press.

Leon, Michèle. *Sydney Pollack.* Paris: Pygmalion, 1991.

Leonelli, Elisha. *Robert Redford and the American West.* Philadelphia: Xlibris, 2007.

Leven, Jeremy. "The Legend of Bagger Vance." Unpublished screenplay based on the novel by Steven Pressfield. Sundance archive.

Levine, Carole. *Provoking Democracy: Why We Need the Arts.* Malden, Mass.: Wiley-Blackwell, 2007.

Litwak, Mark. *Reel Power: The Struggle for Influence and Success in the New Hollywood.* New York: Morrow, 1986.

Lumet, Sidney. *Making Movies.* New York: Vintage, 1996.

Maclean, Norman. *A River Runs Through It.* Chicago: University of Chicago Press, 1976.

Mair, George. *The Barry Diller Story: The Life and Times of America's Greatest Entertainment Mogul.* New York: Wiley, 1997.

Malamud, Bernard. *The Natural.* New York: Avon, 1980.

Mamet, David. *Bambi vs. Godzilla: On the Nature, Purpose, and Practice of the Film Business.* New York: Simon & Schuster, 2008.

Martin, James Kirby, Randy Roberts, Steven Mintz, Linda O. McMurry and James Jones, eds. *America and Its People.* New York: HarperCollins College, 1993.

McDowall, Roddy. *Double Exposure.* New York: Delacorte, 1966.

McKay, David. *American Politics and Society.* Oxford: Blackwell, 1995.

McPherson, Robert S. *Navajo Land, Navajo Culture: The Utah Experience in the Twentieth Century.* Norman: University of Oklahoma Press, 2003.

Meyer, Janet L. *Sydney Pollack: A Critical Filmography.* Jefferson, N.C.: McFarland, 2008.

Miller, Henry. *The Colossus of Maroussi.* London: Secker and Warburg, 1942.

Monanco, James. *American Film Now: The People, the Power, the Money, the Movies.* New York: New American Library, 1979.

Moore, Mary Tyler. *After All.* New York: Putnam, 1995.

Morgan, Ted. *Reds: McCarthyism in Twentieth-Century America.* New York: Random House, 2003.

Murton, Thomas O. *The Dilemma of Prison Reform.* New York: Irvington, 1982.

Murton, Thomas O., and Joe Hyams. *Accomplices to the Crime: The Arkansas Prison Scandal.* New York: Grove Press, 1969.

Nash, Alanna. *Golden Girl: The Story of Jessica Savitch.* New York: Dutton, 1988.

Newman, Paul, and A. E. Hotchner. *In Pursuit of the Common Good: Twenty-five Years of Improving the World, One Bottle of Salad Dressing at a Time.* New York: Doubleday, 2005.

Nibley, Hugh W. *Brigham Young on the Environment.* Provo, Utah: FARMS, 1972.

Nichols, John. *A Fragile Beauty.* Salt Lake City: Peregrine Smith Books, 1987.

———. *The Milagro Beanfield War.* New York: Ballantine, 1976.

Nichols, John, and David Ward. "The Milagro Beanfield War." Unpublished screenplay based on the novel by John Nichols. Sundance archive.

Nickens, Christopher, and Karen Swenson. *The Films of Barbra Streisand.* New York: Citadel Press, 2000.

O'Brien, Daniel. *Paul Newman.* London: Faber and Faber, 2004.

Olsen, Larry Dean. *Outdoor Survival Skills.* With a foreword by Robert Redford. Provo, Utah: Brigham Young University Press, 1974.

Owings, Margaret Wentworth. *Voice from the Sea.* With an introduction by Jane Goodall. Monterey, Calif.: Monterey Bay Aquarium Press, 1998.

Page, Suzanne, with Jake Page. *A Celebration of Being: Photographs of the Hopi and Navajo.* With an introduction by Robert Redford. Flagstaff, Ariz.: Northland, 1989.

Pfaff, Eugene E., Jr., and Mark Emerson. *Meryl Streep: A Critical Biography.* Jefferson, N.C.: McFarland, 1987.

Pfeiffer, Bruce Brooks. *Frank Lloyd Wright: Taliesin West.* New York: ADA Editions, 2002.

Pipkin, Turn, and Marshall Frech, eds. *Barton Springs Eternal: The Soul of a City.* Austin, Tex.: Softshoe, 1993.

Pirsig, Robert M. *Lila: An Inquiry into Morals.* London: Black Swan, 1992.

———. *Zen and the Art of Motorcycle Maintenance.* London: Bodley Head, 1974.

Postman, Neil. *Amusing Ourselves to Death.* London: Heinemann, 1985.

Pressfield, Steven. *The Legend of Bagger Vance: A Novel of Golf and the Game of Life.* New York: Morrow, 1995.

Ran, Ronald, and Luigi Scorcia. *Acting Teachers of America: A Vital Tradition.* With a foreword by J. Michael Miller. New York: Allworth Press, 2007.

Redford, Robert. *The Outlaw Trail: A Journey Through Time.* New York: Grosset and Dunlap, 1978.

———. "Search for Common Ground." *Harvard Business Review* (May–June 1987): 108.

Rhode, Eric. *A History of the Cinema: From Its Origins to 1970.* London: Penguin, 1976.

Ritchie, Michael. *Please Stand By: A Prehistory of Television.* New York: Overlook Press, 1995.

Rose, Frank. *The Agency.* New York: Harper Business, 1995.

Rosenberg, Norman L., and Emily S. Rosenberg, *In Our Times: America Since World War II.* Englewood Cliffs, N.J.: Prentice Hall, 1976.

Rossen, Carol. *Counterpunch.* New York: Dutton, 1988.

Sahl, Mort. *Heartland.* New York: Harcourt Brace Jovanovich, 1976.

Salter, James. *Burning the Days: Recollection.* New York: Random House, 1997.

Sander, Gordon F. *Serling: The Rise and Twilight of Television's Last Angry Man.* New York: Dutton, 1992.

Santopietro, Tom. *The Importance of Being Barbra: The Brilliant, Tumultuous Career of Barbra Streisand.* New York: Thomas Dunne Books, 2006.

Sargent, Alvin. "Ordinary People." Unpublished screenplay based on the novel by Judith Guest. Sundance archive.

Sarris, Andrew. *The American Cinema: Directors and Directions 1929–1968.* New York: Da Capo Press, 1996.

Saunders, Dave. *Direct Cinema: Observational Documentary and the Politics of the Sixties.* New York: Wallflower Press, 2007.

Schatz, Thomas. *The Genius of the System: Hollywood Filmmaking in the Studio Era.* New York: Pantheon, 1989.

Schickel, Richard. *The Disney Version: The Life, Times, Art and Commerce of Walt Disney.* New York: Simon & Schuster, 1972.

Schlossmacher, Heidrun M. "Reinventing the Past: The Films Directed by Robert Redford." Master's thesis, Rutgers, The State University of New Jersey–Newark, 1998. By permission of Sundance archive.

Simon, Neil. *Rewrites: A Memoir.* New York: Simon & Schuster, 1998.

Sinyard, Neil. *Jack Clayton.* Manchester: Manchester University Press, 2000.

Smith, Lori. *Party in a Box: The Story of the Sundance Film Festival.* Salt Lake City: Gibbs Smith, 1999.

Soderbergh, Steven. *Steven Soderbergh: Interviews.* Edited by Anthony Kaufman. Conversations with Filmmakers Series. Jackson: University Press of Mississippi, 2002.

Spada, James. *The Films of Robert Redford.* Secaucus, N.J.: Citadel Press, 1984.

Spoto, Donald. *Camerado: Hollywood and the American Man.* New York: New American Library, 1978.

Stegner, Wallace. *Mormon Country.* Lincoln, Neb.: Bison, 1981.

———. *A Sense of Place.* Read by the author. Minocqua, Wisc.: NorthWord Audio Press, 1986.

Stephanson, Anders. *Manifest Destiny: American Expansion and the Empire of Right.* New York: Hill and Wang, 1996.

Stern, Stewart. *No Tricks in My Pockets: Paul Newman Directs.* New York: Grove Weidenfeld, 1989.

Streisand, Barbra, et al. *Inside the Actors Studio: Barbra Streisand.* DVD. Universal Music Group, 2004.

Thompson, David, ed. *Levinson on Levinson.* London: Faber and Faber, 1992.

Thompson, David. *"Have You Seen . . . ?": A Personal Introduction to 1,000 Films.* New York: Alfred A. Knopf, 2008.

Thorp, Raymond W., and Robert Bunker. *Crow Killer: The Saga of Liver-Eating Johnson.* Bloomington: Indiana University Press, 1958.

Thurman, Judith. *Isak Dinesen: The Life of a Storyteller.* New York: St. Martin's Press, 1982.

Tichler, Rosemarie, and Barry Jay Kaplan. *Actors at Work.* With a foreword by Mike Nichols. New York: Faber and Faber/Farrar, Straus and Giroux, 2007.

Trzebinski, Errol. *Silence Will Speak: A Study of the Life of Denys Finch Hatton and His Relationship with Karen Blixen.* Chicago: University of Chicago Press, 1985.

Turner, Geoffrey. *Indians of North America.* New York: Sterling, 1992.

Udall, Stewart L. *The Quiet Crisis.* New York: Holt, Rinehart and Winston, 1965.

Watson, Steven. *The Birth of the Beat Generation.* With an afterword by Robert Creeley. New York: Pantheon, 1998.

Woodward, Bob. *The Secret Man: The Story of Deep Throat.* New York: Simon & Schuster, 2006.

Woodward, Bob, and Carl Bernstein. *All the President's Men.* 2nd ed. New York: Simon & Schuster, 1994.

———. *The Final Days.* New York: Simon & Schuster, 2005.

Zuckerman, Andrew. *Wisdom: 50 Unique and Original Portraits.* New York: Abrams, 2008.

Filmography

Films as Actor and/or Director

War Hunt (United Artists, 1962)

Directed by Denis Sanders. Produced by Terry Sanders. Coproducers: Denis Sanders and Noel Black. Written by Stanford Whitore. Music: Bud Shank. Cinematography: Ted D. McCord. Editor: John Hoffman. Art director: Edgar Lansbury. Production company: T-D Enterprises.

With John Saxon, Sydney Pollack, Charles Aidman, Tommy Matsude, Gavin MacLeod, Anthony Ray, Tom Skerritt, William Challee, Nancy Hseuh and Robert Redford (as Private Roy Loomis).

Situation Hopeless . . . but Not Serious (Paramount, 1965)

Directed by Gottfried Reinhardt. Produced by Gottfried Reinhardt. Assistant producer: Jose De Villaverde. Written by Jan Lustig and Silvia Reinhardt. Based on the novel *The Hiding Place* by Robert Shaw. Music: Harold Byrne. Cinematography: Kurt Hasse. Editor: Walter Boos. Art directors: Werner Achmann, Herbert Strabel and Rolf Zehetbauer. Production company: Castle Productions.

With Alec Guinness, Mike Connors, Paul Dahlke, Frank Wolff, Mady Rahl, Anita Höfer, Elisabeth von Molo and Robert Redford (as Captain Hank Wilson).

Inside Daisy Clover (Warner Bros., 1965)

Directed by Robert Mulligan. Produced by Alan J. Pakula. Written by Gavin Lambert. Based on his novel. Music: André Previn. Cinematography: Charles Lang. Editor: Aaron Stell. Production designer: Robert Clatworthy. Costumers: Edith Head (for Natalie Wood) and Bill Thomas. Production company: Warner Bros.

With Natalie Wood, Christopher Plummer, Robert Redford (as Wade Lewis), Roddy McDowall, Ruth Gordon, Katharine Bard, Peter Helm, Betty Harford, John Hale, Harold Gould, Ottola Nesmith and Edna Holland.

The Chase (Columbia, 1966)

Directed by Arthur Penn. Produced by Sam Spiegel. Written by Horton Foote and Lillian Hellman. Based on the play by Horton Foote. Music: John Barry. Cinematography: Joseph LaShelle and Robert Surtees (uncredited). Editor: Gene Milford. Production designer: Richard Day. Costumer: Donfeld. Production company: Horizon Films/Lone Star.

With Marlon Brando, Jane Fonda, Robert Redford (as Charlie "Bubber" Reeves), E. G. Marshall, Angie Dickinson, Janice Rule, Miriam Hopkins, Martha Hyer, Richard Bradford, Robert Duvall, James Fox, Diana Hyland, Henry Hill, Jocelyn Brando, Katherine Walsh, Lori Martin, Marc Seaton, Paul Williams, Malcolm Atterbury, Nydia Westman, Joel Fluellen, Steve Ihnat, Maurice Manson, Bruce Cabot, Steve Whittaker, Pamela Curran and Ken Renard.

This Property Is Condemned (Paramount, 1966)

Directed by Sydney Pollack. Produced by Ray Stark and John Houseman. Written by Tennessee Williams, Francis Ford Coppola, Fred Coe, Edith R. Sommer and David Rayfiel. Music: Kenyon Hopkins. Cinematography: James Wong Howe. Editor: Adrienne Fazan. Production designer: Stephen B. Grimes. Costumer: Edith Head. Production company: Seven Arts.

With Natalie Wood, Robert Redford (as Owen Legate), Charles Bronson, Kate Reid, Mary Badham, Alan Baxter, Robert Blake, Dabney Coleman, John Harding, Ray Hemphill, Brett Pearson, Jon Provost, Robert Random, Quintin Sondergaard, Mike Steen, Bruce Watson, Ralph Roberts and Nick Stuart.

Barefoot in the Park (Paramount, 1967)

Directed by Gene Saks. Produced by Hal B. Wallis. Executive producer: Joseph H. Hazen. Associate producer: Paul Nathan. Written by Neil Simon. Based on his play. Music: Neal Hefti. Cinematography: Joseph LaShelle. Editor: William A. Lyon. Art directors: Hal Pereira and Walter H. Tyler. Costumer: Edith Head. Production company: Nancy Enterprises Inc.

With Robert Redford (as Paul Bratter), Jane Fonda, Charles Boyer, Mildred Natwick, Herb Edelman, Mabel Albertson, Fritz Feld, James Stone, Ted Hartley, Billie Bird, Paul E. Burns, John Indrisano and Doris Roberts.

Tell Them Willie Boy Is Here (Universal, 1969)

Directed by Abraham Polonsky. Produced by Jennings Lang and Philip A. Waxman. Written by Abraham Polonsky. Based on the book by Harry Lawton. Music: Dave Grusin. Cinematography: Conrad Hall. Editor: Melvin Shapiro. Art directors: Henry Bumstead and Alexander Golitzen. Costumer: Edith Head. Production company: Universal.

With Robert Redford (as Deputy Sheriff Christopher "Coop" Cooper), Katharine Ross, Robert Blake, Susan Clark, Barry Sullivan, John Vernon, Charles Aidman, Charles McGraw, Shelly Novack, Robert Lipton, Lloyd Gough, Ned Romero, John Wheeler, Erik Holland, Garry Walberg, Jerry Velasco, George Tyne, Lee de Broux, Wayne Sutherlin, Jerome Raphael, Lou Frizzell, Mikel Angel, Johnny Coons, Everett Creach, John Daheim, Robert Dulaine, Kenneth Holzman, John Hudkins, Spencer Lyons, Steve Shemayne and Stanley Torres.

Butch Cassidy and the Sundance Kid (Twentieth Century–Fox, 1969)

Directed by George Roy Hill. Produced by John Foreman. Executive producers: Paul Monash and Paul Newman. Written by William Goldman. Music: Burt Bacharach. Cinematography: Conrad Hall. Editors: John C. Howard and Richard C. Meyer.

Art directors: Philip M. Jeffries and Jack Martin Smith. Production company: Twentieth Century–Fox/Campanile Productions.

With Paul Newman, Robert Redford (as the Sundance Kid), Katharine Ross, Strother Martin, Henry Jones, Jeff Corey, George Furth, Cloris Leachman, Ted Cassidy, Kenneth Mars, Donnelly Rhodes, Jody Gilbert, Timothy Scott, Don Keefer, Charles Dierkop, Pancho Córdova, Nelson Olmsted, Paul Bryar, Sam Elliott, Charles Akins, Eric Sinclair, José Chávez and Percy Helton.

Downhill Racer (Paramount, 1969)

Directed by Michael Ritchie. Produced by Richard Gregson. Written by James Salter. Based on the novel by Oakley Hall. Music: Kenyon Hopkins. Cinematography: Brian Probyn. Editor: Richard A. Harris. Art director: Ian Whittaker. Costumer: Cynthia May. Production company: Wildwood Enterprises.

With Robert Redford (as David Chappellet), Gene Hackman, Camilla Sparv, Joe Jay Jalbert, Tom J. Kirk, Dabney Coleman, Jim McMullan, Oren Stevens, Karl Michael Vogler, Rip McManus, Jerry Dexter, Kenneth Kirk, Arnold Alpiger, Jack Ballard, Robert Brendlin, Carole Carle, Kathleen Crowley, Harald Dietl, Christian Doerman, Michael Gempart, Rudi Gertsch, Walter Gnilka, Werner Heyking, Robin Hutton-Potts, Noam Pitlik, Pete Rohr, James Sandoe, Harald Schreiber, Heini Schuler, Alexander Stampfer, Walter Stroud, Ulrike von Zerboni, Eddie Waldburger and Marco Walli.

Little Fauss and Big Halsy (Paramount, 1970)

Directed by Sidney J. Furie. Produced by Albert S. Ruddy. Executive producers: Brad Dexter and Gray Frederickson. Written by Charles Eastman. Music: Carl Perkins. Cinematography: Ralph Woolsey. Editor: Argyle Nelson Jr. Art director: Lawrence G. Paull. Production company: Alfan.

With Robert Redford (as Halsy Knox), Michael J. Pollard, Lauren Hutton, Noah Beery Jr., Lucille Benson, Ray Ballard, Linda Gaye Scott, Erin O'Reilly, Ben Archibek, Sharmagne Leland-St. John and Beverly Yissar.

The Hot Rock (Twentieth Century–Fox, 1972)

Directed by Peter Yates. Produced by Hal Landers and Bobby Roberts. Written by William Goldman. Based on the novel by Donald E. Westlake. Music: Quincy Jones. Cinematography: Edward R. Brown. Editor: Alixe Gordin. Production designer: John Robert Lloyd. Costumer: Ruth Morley. Production company: Landers-Roberts Productions.

With Robert Redford (as John Dortmunder), George Segal, Ron Leibman, Paul Sand, Moses Gunn, William Redfield, Topo Swope, Charlotte Rae, Graham Jarvis, Harry Bellaver, Seth Allen, Robert Levine, Lee Wallace, Robert Weil, Lynne Gordon, Grania O'Malley, Fred Cook, Mark Dawson, Gilbert Lewis, George Bartenieff, Ed Bernard, Charles White, Christopher Guest, Zero Mostel, Burt Richards and Arnold Williams.

Jeremiah Johnson (Warner Bros., 1972)

Directed by Sydney Pollack. Produced by Joe Wizan. Associate producers: John R. Coonan and Mike Moder. Written by John Milius and Edward Anhalt. Adapted from the story "Crow Killer" by Robert Bunker and Raymond W. Thorp. Based on *Mountain Man* by Vardis Fisher. Additional writing (uncredited) by David Rayfiel.

Music: Tim McIntire and John Rubinstein. Cinematography: Duke Callaghan. Editor: Thomas Stanford. Art director: Ted Haworth. Costumer: Wesley Jeffries. Costume supervisor (uncredited): Bernie Pollack. Production company: Sanford.

With Robert Redford (as Jeremiah Johnson), Will Geer, Delle Bolton, Josh Albee, Joaquín Martínez, Allyn Ann McLerie, Stefan Gierasch, Richard Angarola, Paul Benedict, Charles Tyner, Jack Colvin, Matt Clark and Tanya Tucker.

The Candidate (Warner Bros., 1972)

Directed by Michael Ritchie. Produced by Walter Coblenz. Associate producer: Nelson Rising. Written by Jeremy Larner. Music: John Rubinstein. Cinematography: John Korty and Victor J. Kemper. Editors: Robert Estrin and Richard A. Harris. Production designer: Gene Callahan. Costumer: Patricia Norris. Production company: Redford-Ritchie Productions.

With Robert Redford (as Bill McKay), Peter Boyle, Melvyn Douglas, Don Porter, Allen Garfield, Karen Carlson, Quinn K. Redeker, Morgan Upton, Michael Lerner, Kenneth Tobey, Chris Prey, Joe Miksak, Jenny Sullivan, Tom Dahlgren, Gerald Hiken, Jason Goodrow, Robert De Anda, Robert Goldsby, Mike Barnicle, Lois Foraker, David Moody, George Meyer, Dudley Knight, Fred L. Van Amburg, Richard Bergholtz, Jesse Birnbaum, Ken Cory, Alan Cranston, Judy Fayard, Leslie Allen, Mark Anger, Gene S. Cantamessa, Broderick Crawford, Susan Demott, Maury Green, Cedrick Hardman, Pat Harrington Jr., Hubert H. Humphrey, Lu Hurley, Ken Jones, Walter Krabien, Grover Lewis, Garry Liddiard, George McGovern, Terry McGovern, Robert Moretti, Harvey Orkin, Dick Poston, Rollin Post, Nelson Rising, Elsie Ritchie, Howard K. Smith, Bill Stout, Barry Sullivan, John V. Tunney, Jesse M. Unruh, Jerome Waldie, Ward Wardman, Dick Whittington, Natalie Wood, Sam Yorty, Bruce Chesse, Lee Stanley, Stanley Tretick and Mike Wallace.

The Way We Were (Columbia, 1973)

Directed by Sydney Pollack. Produced by Ray Stark. Written by Arthur Laurents. Additional writing by David Rayfiel (uncredited). Music: Marvin Hamlisch. Cinematography: Harry Stradling Jr. Editor: John F. Burnett. Production designer: Stephen B. Grimes. Costumers: Dorothy Jeakins and Moss Mabry. Costume supervisor (uncredited): Bernie Pollack. Production company: Rastar.

With Barbra Streisand, Robert Redford (as Hubbell Gardner), Bradford Dillman, Lois Chiles, Patrick O'Neal, Viveca Lindfors, Allyn Ann McLerie, Murray Hamilton, Herb Edelman, Diana Ewing, Sally Kirkland, Marcia Mae Jones, Don Keefer, George Gaynes, Eric Boles, Barbara Peterson, Roy Jenson, Brendan Kelly, James Woods, Constance Forslund, Robert Gerringer, Susan Blakely, Edward Power, Susanne Zenor and Dan Seymour.

The Sting (Universal, 1973)

Academy Award nomination: Best Actor

Academy Award: Best Picture

Directed by George Roy Hill. Produced by Tony Bill, Michael Phillips and Julia Phillips. Associate producer: Robert L. Crawford. Written by David Ward. Music: Scott Joplin. Cinematography: Robert Surtees. Editor: William Reynolds. Art director: Henry Bumstead. Costumer: Edith Head. Production company: Zanuck-Brown Productions.

With Paul Newman, Robert Redford (as Johnny Hooker), Robert Shaw, Charles Durning, Ray Walston, Eileen Brennan, Harold Gould, John Heffernan, Dana Elcar, Jack Kehoe, Dimitra Arliss, Robert Earl Jones, James Sloyan, Charles Dierkop, Lee Paul, Sally Kirkland, Avon Long, Arch Johnson, Ed Bakey, Brad Sullivan, John Quade, Larry D. Mann, Leonard Barr, Paulene Myers, Joe Tornatore, Jack Collins, Tom Spratley, Kenneth O'Brien, Ken Sansom, Ta-Tanisha and Billy Benedict.

The Great Gatsby (Paramount, 1974)

Directed by Jack Clayton. Produced by David Merrick. Written by Francis Ford Coppola. Based on the novel by F. Scott Fitzgerald. Music: Nelson Riddle. Cinematography: Douglas Slocombe. Editor: Tom Priestley. Production designer: John Box. Costumer: Theoni V. Aldredge. Production company: Newdon Productions.

With Robert Redford (as Jay Gatsby), Mia Farrow, Bruce Dern, Karen Black, Scott Wilson, Sam Waterston, Lois Chiles, Howard Da Silva, Roberts Blossom, Edward Herrmann, Elliott Sullivan, Arthur Hughes, Kathryn Leigh Scott, Beth Porter, Paul Tamarin, John Devlin, Patsy Kensit, Marjorie Wildes, Blain Fairman, Bob Sherman, Norman Chancer, Regina Baff, Janet Arters, Louise Arters, Sammy Smith, Brooke Adams (uncredited) and Tom Ewell (uncredited).

Three Days of the Condor (Warner Bros., 1975)

Directed by Sydney Pollack. Produced by Stanley Schneider. Executive producer: Dino De Laurentiis. Written by Lorenzo Semple Jr. Based on the novel by James Grady. Music: Dave Grusin. Cinematography: Owen Roizman. Editor: Don Guidice. Production designer: Stephen B. Grimes. Costumers: Theoni V. Aldredge and Joseph G. Aulisi. Production companies: Dino De Laurentiis Productions and Wildwood Enterprises.

With Robert Redford (as Joseph Turner), Faye Dunaway, Cliff Robertson, Max von Sydow, John Houseman, Addison Powell, Walter McGinn, Tina Chen, Michael Kane, Don McHenry, Michael B. Miller, Jess Osuna, Dino Narrizano, Helen Stenborg, Patrick Gorman, Hansford Rowe, Carlin Glynn, Hank Garrett, Arthur French, Jay Devlin, Frank Savino, Robert Phalen, John Randolph Jones, Garrison Phillips, Lee Steele, Ed Crowley, John Connell, Norman Bush, James Keane, Ed Setrakian, Myron Natwick, Michael Prince, Carol Gustafson, Sal Schillizzi, Harmon William, David Bowman, Eileen Gordon, Robert Dahdah, Steve Bonino, Jennifer Rose, David Allen, Glenn Ferguson, Paul Dwyer, Marian Swan, Dorothi Fox and Ernest Harden Jr.

The Great Waldo Pepper (Universal, 1975)

Directed by George Roy Hill. Produced by George Roy Hill. Associate producer: Robert Crawford. Written by William Goldman. Based on a story by George Roy Hill. Music: Henry Mancini. Cinematography: Robert Surtees. Editor: William Reynolds. Art director: Henry Bumstead. Costumer: Edith Head. Production company: Jennings Lang.

With Robert Redford (as Waldo Pepper), Bo Svenson, Bo Brundin, Susan Sarandon, Geoffrey Lewis, Edward Herrmann, Philip Bruns, Roderick Cook, Kelly Jean Peters, Margot Kidder, Scott Newman, James S. Appleby, Patrick W. Henderson Jr., James N. Harrell, Elma Aicklen, Deborah Knapp, John A. Zee, John Reilly, Jack Manning, Joe Billings, Lawrence P. Casey, Greg Martin and Art Scholl.

All the President's Men (Warner Bros., 1976)

Directed by Alan J. Pakula. Produced by Walter Coblenz. Written by William Goldman. Based on the book by Bob Woodward and Carl Bernstein. Music: David Shire. Cinematography: Gordon Willis. Editor: Robert L. Wolfe. Production designer: George Jenkins. Production company: Wildwood Enterprises.

With Dustin Hoffman, Robert Redford (as Bob Woodward), Jack Warden, Martin Balsam, Hal Holbrook, Jason Robards, Jane Alexander, Meredith Baxter, Ned Beatty, Stephen Collins, Penny Fuller, John McMartin, Robert Walden, Frank Wills, F. Murray Abraham, David Arkin, Henry Calvert, Dominic Chianese, Bryan Clark, Nicolas Coster, Lindsay Crouse, Valerie Curtin, Gene Dynarski, Nate Esformes, Ron Hale, Richard Herd, Polly Holliday, James Karen, Paul Lambert, Frank Latimore, Gene Lindsey, Anthony Mannino, Allyn Ann McLerie, James Murtaugh, John O'Leary, Jess Osuna, Neva Patterson, George Pentecost, Penny Peyser, Joshua Shelley, Sloane Shelton, Lelan Smith, Jaye Stewart, Ralph Williams, George Wyner, Leroy Aarons, Donnlynn Bennett, Stanley Bennett Clay, Carol Coggin, Laurence Covington, John Devlin, John Furlong, Sidney Ganis, Amy Grossman, Cynthia Herbst, Basil Hoffman, Mark Holtzman, Jamie Smith-Jackson, Barbara Lipsky and Doug Llewelyn.

A Bridge Too Far (United Artists, 1977)

Directed by Richard Attenborough. Produced by Joseph E. Levine and Richard P. Levine. Written by William Goldman. Based on the book by Cornelius Ryan. Music: John Addison. Cinematography: Geoffrey Unsworth. Editor: Antony Gibbs. Production designer: Terence Marsh. Costumer: Anthony Mendleson. Production company: Joseph E. Levine Productions.

With Dirk Bogarde, James Caan, Michael Caine, Sean Connery, Edward Fox, Elliott Gould, Gene Hackman, Anthony Hopkins, Hardy Kruger, Ryan O'Neal, Laurence Olivier, Robert Redford (as Major Cook), Maximilian Schell, Liv Ullmann, Denholm Elliott, Peter Faber, Christopher Good, Frank Grimes, Jeremy Kemp, Wolfgang Preiss, Nicholas Campbell, Paul Copley, Donald Douglas, Keith Drinkel, Colin Farrell, Richard Kane, Walter Kohut, Paul Maxwell, Stephen Moore, Donald Pickering, Gerald Sim, Mary Smithuysen, John Stride, Siem Vroom, Eric Van't Wout, Marlies van Alcmaer, Alun Armstrong, David Auker, Michael Bangerter, Hartmut Becker, Hans von Borsody, Michael Byrne, Michael Graham Cox, Hans Croiset, Lex van Delden, Garrick Hagon, Geoffrey Hinsliff, John Judd, Stanley Lebor, Barry McCarthy, Anthony Milner, Anthony Pullen Shaw, John Ratzenberger, John Salthouse, Peter Settelen, Chris Williams, Fred Williams, Josephine Peeper, Hary Ditson, Erik Chitty, David English, Brian Hawksley, Norman Gregory, Michael Wolf, Sean Mathias, Tim Beekman, Edward Seckerson, Tom van Beek, Bertus Botterman, Henny Alma, Ray Jewers, John Peel, Ben Cross, Hilary Minster, Ben Howard, Johan te Slaa, Georgette Reyevski, Pieter Groenier, Adrienne Kleiweg, Peter Gordon, Arthur Hill, Brian Gwaspari, Stephen Rayment, Timothy Morand, James Wardroper, Neil Kennedy, Jonathan Hackett, Jack Galloway, Milton Cadman, Toby Salaman, Philip Raymond, Myles Reithermann, John Morton, Patrick Ryecart, Dick Rienstra, Ian Liston, Paul Rattee, Mark Sheridan, George Innes, Niall Padden and Michael Graves.

The Electric Horseman (Columbia, 1979)

Directed by Sydney Pollack. Produced by Ray Stark. Written by Robert Garland. Additional writing by David Rayfiel (uncredited). Based on a story by Shelly Burton and Paul Gaer. Music: Dave Grusin. Cinematography: Owen Roizman. Editor: Sheldon Kahn. Production designer: Stephen B. Grimes. Costumer: Bernie Pollack. Production companies: Rastar and Wildwood Enterprises.

With Robert Redford (as Norman "Sonny" Steele), Jane Fonda, Valerie Perrine, Willie Nelson, John Saxon, Nicolas Coster, Allan Arbus, Wilford Brimley, Will Hare, Basil Hoffman, Timothy Scott, James Sikking, James Kline, Frank Speiser, Quinn K. Redeker, Lois Hamilton, Sarah Harris, Tasha Zemrus, James Novak, Deborah L. Maxwell, Michele Heyeden, Robin Timm, Patricia Blair, Gary M. Fox, Richard Perlmutter, Carol Eileen Montgomery, Theresa Ann Dent, Perry Sheehan Adair, Sarge Allen, Gary Liddiard and Sydney Pollack.

Brubaker (Twentieth Century–Fox, 1980)

Directed by Stuart Rosenberg. Produced by Ron Silverman. Written by W. D. Richter and Arthur A. Ross. Based on the books by Thomas O. Murton and Joe Hyams. Music: Lalo Schifrin. Cinematography: Bruno Nuytten. Editor: Robert Brown. Production designer: J. Michael Riva. Costumers: Tom Bronson and Bernie Pollack. Production company: Twentieth Century–Fox.

With Robert Redford (as Henry Brubaker), Yaphet Kotto, Jane Alexander, Murray Hamilton, David Keith, Morgan Freeman, Matt Clark, Tim McIntire, Richard Ward, John Van Ness, M. Emmet Walsh, Albert Salmi, Linda Haynes, Everett McGill, Val Avery, Ron Frazier, David Harris, Joe Spinell, James Keane, Konrad Sheehan, Ray Poole, Nathan George, Don Blakely, Lee Richardson, John McMartin, Alex Brown, John Chappell, Brent Jennings, Harry Groener, William Newman, Noble Willingham, Wilford Brimley, Jane Cecil, Ebbe Roe Smith, Young Hwa Han, Vic Polizos, Jack O'Leary, James Dukas and J. C. Quinn.

Ordinary People (Paramount, 1980)
Academy Award: Best Director

Directed by Robert Redford. Produced by Ronald L. Schwary. Written by Alvin Sargent. Additional writing by Nancy Dowd (uncredited). Based on the novel by Judith Guest. Music: Marvin Hamlisch. Theme: Johann Pachelbel. Cinematography: John Bailey. Editor: Jeff Kanew. Art directors: Phillip Bennett and J. Michael Riva. Costumer: Bernie Pollack. Production companies: Wildwood Enterprises and Paramount.

With Donald Sutherland, Mary Tyler Moore, Judd Hirsch, Timothy Hutton, M. Emmet Walsh, Elizabeth McGovern, Dinah Manoff, Frederic Lehne, James Sikking, Basil Hoffman, Scott Doebler, Quinn K. Redeker, Mariclare Costello, Meg Mundy, Elizabeth Hubbard, Adam Baldwin, Richard Whiting, Carl DiTomasso, Tim Clarke, Ken Dishner, Lisa Smyth, Ann Eggert, Randall Robbins, Cynthia Baker, John Stimpson, Liz Kinney, Rudy Hornish, Clarissa Downey, Cynthia Burke, Jane Alderman, Paul Preston, Gustave Lachenauer, Marilyn Rockafellow, Don Billett, Ronald Solomon, Virginia Long, Paula Segal, Estelle Meyers, Stuart Shiff, Rose Wool, Douglas Kinney, Constance Addington, Edwin Bederman, Bobby Coyne, Michael Creadon, Steven Hirsch, Allison Caine, Randy De Troit and Michael T. Weiss.

The Natural (TriStar, 1984)

Directed by Barry Levinson. Produced by Mark Johnson. Executive producers: Roger Towne and Philip M. Breen. Written by Roger Towne and Phil Dusenberry. Based on the novel by Bernard Malamud. Music: Randy Newman. Cinematography:

Caleb Deschanel. Editor: Stu Linder. Production designers: Mel Bourne and Angelo P. Graham. Costumers: Gloria Gresham and Bernie Pollack. Production companies: Delphi II Productions and TriStar Pictures.

With Robert Redford (as Roy Hobbs), Glenn Close, Kim Basinger, Wilford Brimley, Barbara Hershey, Robert Prosky, Richard Farnsworth, Joe Don Baker, John Finnegan, Alan Fudge, Paul Sullivan Jr., Rachel Hall, Robert Rich III, Michael Madsen, Jon Van Ness, Mickey Treanor, George Wilkosz, Anthony J. Ferrara, Philip Mankowski, Danny Aiello III, Joe Castellano, Eddie Cipot, Ken Grassano, Robert Kalaf, Barry Kivel, Steve Kronovet, James Meyer, Mike Starr, Sam Green, Martin Grey, Joseph Mosso, Richard Oliveri, Laurence Couzens, Duke McGuire, Stephen Poliachik, Kevin Lester, Joseph Charboneau, Robert Rudnick, Ken Kamholz and James Mohr.

Out of Africa (Universal, 1985)
Academy Award: Best Picture
Directed by Sydney Pollack. Produced by Sydney Pollack. Coproducer: Terence Clegg. Executive producer: Kim Jorgensen. Written by Kurt Luedtke. Based on the books *Isak Dinesen: The Life of a Storyteller* by Judith Thurman and *Silence Will Speak* by Errol Trzebinski and on *Out of Africa, Shadows on the Grass* and *Letters from Africa* by Isak Dinesen. Music: John Barry. Cinematography: David Watkin. Editors: Pembroke J. Herring, Sheldon Kahn, Fredric Steinkamp and William Steinkamp. Production designer: Stephen B. Grimes. Costumer: Milena Canonero. Production company: Mirage Entertainment.

With Meryl Streep, Robert Redford (as Denys Finch Hatton), Klaus Maria Brandauer, Michael Kitchen, Malick Bowens, Joseph Thiaka, Stephen Kinyanjui, Michael Gough, Suzanna Hamilton, Rachel Kempson, Graham Crowden, Leslie Phillips, Mike Bugara, Shane Rimmer, Job Seda, Mohammed Umar, Donal McCann, Kenneth Mason, Tristram Jellinek, Stephen B. Grimes, Annabel Maule, Benny Young, Sbish Trzebinski, Allaudin Qureshi, Niven Boyd, Iman, Peter Strong, Abdulla Sunado, Amanda Parkin, Muriel Gross, Ann Palmer and Keith Pearson.

Legal Eagles (Universal, 1986)
Directed by Ivan Reitman. Produced by Ivan Reitman. Executive producers: Michael C. Gross and Joe Medjuck. Written by Jim Cash and Jack Epps Jr. Story by Jim Cash, Jack Epps Jr. and Ivan Reitman. Music: Elmer Bernstein. Cinematography: László Kovács. Editors: William Gordean, Pembroke Herring and Sheldon Kahn. Production designer: John DeCuir Jr. Costumers: Bernie Pollack and Albert Wolsky. Production companies: Mirage Entertainment and Northern Lights Entertainment.

With Robert Redford (as Tom Logan), Debra Winger, Daryl Hannah, Brian Dennehy, Terence Stamp, Steven Hill, David Clennon, John McMartin, Jennifer Dundas, Roscoe Lee Browne, Christine Baranski, Sara Botsford, David Hart, James Hurdle, Gary Howard Klar, Christian Clemenson, Bart Burns, Bruce French, Lynn Hamilton, Paul Jabara, Chevi Colton, Annie Abbott, Kristine Sutherland and Everett Quinton.

The Milagro Beanfield War (Universal, 1988)
Directed by Robert Redford. Produced by Robert Redford and Moctesuma Esparza. Executive producer: Gary J. Hendler. Written by John Nichols and David S. Ward. Based on the novel by John Nichols. Music: Dave Grusin. Cinematography: Robbie Greenberg. Editors: Dede Allen and Jim Miller. Production designer: Joe Aubel and

Thomas Roysden. Costumer: Bernie Pollack. Production companies: Esparza and Wildwood Enterprises.

With Rubén Blades, Richard Bradford, Sonia Braga, Julie Carmen, James Gammon, Melanie Griffith, John Heard, Carlos Riquelme, Daniel Stern, Chick Vennera, Christopher Walken, Freddy Fender, Tony Genaro, Jerry Hardin, Ronald G. Joseph, Mario Arrambide, Robert Carricart, Alberto Morin, Federico Roberto, Natividad Vacío, Eloy Vigil, Trinidad Silva, Consuelo Luz, Mike Gomez, Olga Merediz, Leandro Cordova, Eva Cantu, Astrea Romero, Donald Salazar, Reynaldo Cantu, Alfredo Romero, Arnold Berns and Cipriano Vigil.

Havana (Universal, 1990)

Directed by Sydney Pollack. Produced by Sydney Pollack and Richard Roth. Executive producer: Ronald L. Schwary. Written by Judith Rascoe and David Rayfiel. Music: Dave Grusin. Cinematography: Owen Roizman. Editors: Fredric Steinkamp and William Steinkamp. Production designer: Terence Marsh. Costumer: Bernie Pollack. Production company: Mirage Entertainment.

With Robert Redford (as Jack Weil), Lena Olin, Raul Julia (uncredited), Alan Arkin, Tomas Milian, Daniel Davis, Tony Plana, Betsy Brantley, Lise Cutter, Richard Farnsworth, Mark Rydell, Vasek Simek, Fred Asparagus, Richard Portnow, Dion Anderson, Carmine Caridi, James Medina, Joe Lala, Salvador Levy, Bernie Pollack, Owen Roizman, Victor Rivers, Alex Ganster, René Monclova, Miguel Ángel Suárez, Segundo Tarrau, Félix Germán, Giovanna Bonnelly, David Jose Rodriguez, Franklin Rodríguez, Hugh Kelly, Karen Russell, David Gibson, Adriano González and Raúl Rosado.

Sneakers (Universal, 1992)

Directed by Phil Alden Robinson. Produced by Lawrence Lasker and Walter F. Parkes. Executive producer: Lindsley Parsons Jr. Written by Phil Alden Robinson, Lawrence Lasker and Walter F. Parkes. Music: James Horner. Cinematography: John Lindley. Editor: Tom Rolf. Production designer: Patrizia von Brandenstein. Costumer: Bernie Pollack. Production company: Universal.

With Robert Redford (as Martin Bishop), Sidney Poitier, David Strathairn, Dan Aykroyd, River Phoenix, Bodhi Elfman, Denise Dowse, Hanyee, Timothy Busfield, Eddie Jones, Time Winters, Mary McDonnell, Jun Asai, Donal Logue, George Hearn, Lee Garlington, John Shepard, Ellaraino, Shayna Hollinquist, Dayna Hollinquist, Jacqueline Brand, Julie Gigante, Victoria Miskolczy, David Speltz, Leslie Hardy, Amy Benedict and James Earl Jones.

A River Runs Through It (Columbia, 1992)

Directed by Robert Redford. Produced by Robert Redford, Amalia Mato and Patrick Markey. Executive producer: Jake Eberts. Coproducers: Barbara Maltby, Annick Smith and William Kittredge. Written by Richard Friedenberg. Based on a story by Norman Maclean. Music: Mark Isham. Cinematography: Philippe Rousselot. Editors: Robert Estrin and Lynzee Klingman. Production designer: Jon Hutman. Costumers: Kathy O'Rear, Bernie Pollack and Reese Spensley (uncredited). Production company: Allied Filmmakers.

With Craig Sheffer, Brad Pitt, Tom Skerritt, Brenda Blethyn, Emily Lloyd, Edie McClurg, Stephen Shellen, Vann Gravage, Nicole Burdette, Susan Traylor, Michael

Cudlitz, Rob Cox, Buck Simmonds, Fred Oakland, David Creamer, Madonna Reubens, John Reubens, Arnold Richardson, MacIntyre Dixon, William Hootkins, Al Richardson, Jess Schwidde, Chuck Adamson, Rex Kendall, Jack Kroll, Martina Kreidl, Noah Snyder, Margot Kiser, Philip A. Braun, Tracy Mayfield, Anne Merren, Chuck Tweed, Prudence Johnson, D. Gorton, Lincoln Quesenberry, Hawk Forssell, Jim Dunkin, Jacob Snyder, Don Jeffery, Cecily Johnson, Caleb Shiff and Robert Redford (uncredited, as the narrator).

Indecent Proposal (Paramount, 1993)

Directed by Adrian Lyne. Produced by Sherry Lansing. Coproducer: Michael Tadross. Executive producers: Alex Gartner and Tom Schulman. Written by Jack Engelhard and Amy Holden Jones. Based on the book by Jack Engelhard. Music: John Barry. Cinematography: Howard Atherton. Editor: Joe Hutshing. Art director: Gae Buckley. Production designer: Mel Bourne. Costumers: Beatrix Aruna Pasztor, Bernie Pollack and Bobbie Read. Production company: Paramount.

With Robert Redford (as John Gage), Demi Moore, Woody Harrelson, Seymour Cassel, Oliver Platt, Billy Bob Thornton, Rip Taylor, Billy Connolly, Joel Brooks, Pierre Epstein, Danny Zorn, Kevin West, Pamela Holt, Tommy Bush, Mariclare Costello, Curt Odle, Jedda Jones, Myra J., Edwonda White, James Migliore, Nicholas Georgiade, Ritamarie Kelly, Sam Micco, Jospeh Ruskin, Joe La Due, Ben W. Fluker, Carleen Sbordone, Toru Nagai, Steven Dean, Frankie J. Allison, Dana Williams, David Cousin, Catlyn Day, Irene Olga López, Dru Davis, Rudy E. Morrison, Richard Livingston, Joe Bays, David Rees, Françoise Bush, Elizabeth Gardner, Art Cabrera, Israel Juarbe, Lydia Nicole, Iqbal Theba, Maurice Sherbanee, Yasemin Baytok, Elsa Raven, Matthew Barry, Chi Muoi Lo, Art Chudabala, Michelle O'Brien, Hilary Reynolds, Rebecca Howard, Selma Archerd, Katherine Pope, Jerome Rosenfeld, Nancy Thom, Robert "Bobby Z" Zajonc, Alan D. Purwin, Harold A. Katinszky, Neil Looy, Robert T. Convey, Bruce H. Redding, Sheena Easton and Herbie Hancock.

Quiz Show (Buena Vista, 1994)

Academy Award nomination: Best Director

Directed by Robert Redford. Produced by Michael Jacobs, Michael Nozik, Julian Krainin and Robert Redford. Coproducers: Richard N. Goodwin, Jeff McCracken and Gail Mutrux. Executive producers: Richard Dreyfuss, Judith James and Frederick Zollo. Associate producer: Susan Moore. Written by Paul Attanasio. Based on the book by Richard N. Goodwin. Music: Mark Isham. Cinematography: Michael Ballhaus. Editor: Stu Linder. Production designer: Jon Hutman. Costumer: Kathy O'Rear. Production companies: Hollywood Pictures, Wildwood Enterprises and Baltimore Pictures.

With John Turturro, Rob Morrow, Ralph Fiennes, Paul Scofield, David Paymer, Hank Azaria, Christopher McDonald, Johann Carlo, Elizabeth Wilson, Allan Rich, Mira Sorvino, George Martin, Paul Guilfoyle, Griffin Dunne, Michael Mantell, Byrone Jennings, Ben Shenkman, Timothy Busfield, Jack Gilpin, Bruce Altman, Martin Scorsese, Joseph Blaire, Ernie Sabella, Barry Levinson, Debra Monk, Mario Cantone, Timothy Britten Parker, Grace Phillips, Jerry Grayson, Scott Lucy, Matt Keeslar, Ron Scott Bertozzi, Harriet Sansom Harris, Mary Shultz, Dave Wilson, Robert Caminiti, Eddie Korbich, Joseph Attanasio, Katherine Turturro and Ethan Hawke (uncredited).

Up Close and Personal (Buena Vista, 1996)

Directed by Jon Avnet. Produced by Jon Avnet, Jordan Kerner and David Nicksay. Executive producers: John Foreman and Ed Hookstratten. Written by Joan Didion and John Gregory Dunne. Suggested by the book *Golden Girl: The Story of Jessica Savitch,* written by Alanna Nash. Music: Thomas Newman. Cinematography: Karl Walter Lindenlaub. Editor: Debra Neil-Fisher. Production designer: Jeremy Conway. Costumer: Albert Wolsky. Production companies: Cinergi Pictures Entertainment and Touchstone Pictures.

With Robert Redford (as Warren Justice), Michelle Pfeiffer, Stockard Channing, Joe Mantegna, Kate Nelligan, Glenn Plummer, James Rebhorn, Scott Bryce, Raymond Cruz, Dedee Pfeiffer, Miguel Sandoval, Noble Willingham, James Karen, Brian Markinson, Michael Laskin, Robert Keith Watson, Lily Nicksay, Joanna Sanchez, Daniel Zacapa, Heidi Swedberg, Fern Buchner, Miguel Pérez, Nicholas Cascone, Kenneth Fuchs, Julie Foreman, Edwina Moore, Patti David Suarez, Marc Macaulay, Mary Elizabeth Sheridan and Marian Lamb Bechtelheimer.

The Horse Whisperer (Buena Vista, 1998)

Directed by Robert Redford. Produced by Robert Redford and Patrick Markey. Associate producer: Karen Tenkhoff. Coproducer: Joseph Reidy. Written by Eric Roth and Richard LaGravenese. Based on the novel by Nicholas Evans. Music: Thomas Newman. Cinematography: Robert Richardson. Editors: Tom Rolf, Hank Corwin and Freeman Davies. Production designer: Jon Hutman. Costumers: Bernie Pollack and Judy L. Ruskin. Production companies: Wildwood Enterprises and Touchstone Pictures.

With Robert Redford (as Tom Booker), Kristin Scott Thomas, Sam Neill, Dianne Wiest, Scarlett Johansson, Chris Cooper, Cherry Jones, Ty Hillman, Kate Bosworth, Austin Schwarz, Dustin Schwarz, Jeanette Nolan, Steve Frye, Don Edwards, Jessalyn Gilsig, William "Buddy" Bird, John Hogarty, Michel Lalonde, C. J. Byrnes, Kathy Baldwin Keenan, Allison Moorer, George Sack Jr., Kellee Sweeney, Stephen Pearlman, Joelle Carter, Sunny Chae, Anne Joyce, Tara Sobeck, Kristy Ann Servidio, Marie Engle, Curt Pate, Steven Brian Conard and Tammy Pate.

The Legend of Bagger Vance (DreamWorks, 2000)

Directed by Robert Redford. Produced by Jake Eberts, Robert Redford and Michael Nozik. Executive producer: Karen Tenkhoff. Coproducers: Chris Brigham and Joseph P. Reidy. Written by Jeremy Leven. Additional writing: Jamie Redford (uncredited). Based on the novel by Steven Pressfield. Music: Rachel Portman. Cinematography: Michael Ballhaus. Editor: Hank Corwin. Production designer: Stuart Craig. Costumer: Judianna Makovsky. Production companies: Wildwood Enterprises, Allied Filmmakers and Epsilon Pictures.

With Will Smith, Matt Damon, Charlize Theron, Bruce McGill, Joel Gretsch, J. Michael Moncreif, Lane Smith, Peter Gerety, Michael O'Neill, Thomas J. Ryan, Trip Hamilton, Dermot Crowley, Harve Presnell, Danny Nelson, Bob Penny, Michael McCarty, Carrie Preston, Turner Green, Blake King, Andrea Powell, John Bennes, Jonathan Green, Shane Brown, J. Don Ferguson, E. Roger Mitchell and Jack Lemmon (uncredited).

Spy Game (Universal, 2001)

Directed by Tony Scott. Produced by Marc Abraham, Douglas Wick and Stephanie Antosca. Executive producers: Armyan Bernstein, Thomas A. Bliss, James W. Skotchdopole and Iain Smith. Written by Michael Frost Beckner and David Arata. Based on the story by Michael Frost Beckner. Music: Ryeland Allison and Harry Gregson-Williams. Cinematography: Dan Mindel. Editor: Christian Wagner. Production designer: Norris Spencer. Costumer: Louise Frogley. Production companies: October Pictures, Beacon Communications, Red Wagon Productions and Zaltman Film.

With Robert Redford (as Nathan D. Muir), Brad Pitt, Catherine McCormack, Stephen Dillane, Larry Bryggman, Marianne Jean-Baptiste, Matthew Marsh, Todd Boyce, Michael Paul Chan, Garrick Hagon, Andrew Grainger, Bill Buell, Colin Stinton, Ted Maynard, Tom Hodgkins, Rufus Wright, Demetri Goritsas, Quinn Collins, Sam Scudder, David Hemmings, James Aubrey and Charlotte Rampling.

The Last Castle (DreamWorks, 2001)

Directed by Rod Lurie. Produced by Robert Lawrence. Executive producer: Don Zepfel. Written by David Scarpa and Graham Yost. Based on the story by David Scarpa. Music: Jerry Goldsmith. Cinematography: Shelly Johnson. Editors: Michael Jablow and Kevin Stitt. Production designer: Kirk M. Petruccelli. Costumer: Ha Nguyen. Production companies: DreamWorks SKG and Robert Lawrence Productions Inc.

With Robert Redford (as Lieutenant General Eugene Irwin), James Gandolfini, Mark Ruffalo, Steve Burton, Delroy Lindo, Paul Calderon, Samuel Ball, Jeremy Childs, Clifton Collins Jr., George W. Scott, Brian Goodman, Michael Irby, Frank Military, Maurice Bullard, Nick Kokich, David Alford, Dean Hall, Peg Allen, Rick Vito, Forrest D. Bradford, Scott Michael, Dean Miller, Kristen Shaw, Michael Davis, Joe Keenan, David Chattam, James Jerome Thomas, Mary Jean McAdams and Robin Wright Penn (uncredited).

The Clearing (Fox Searchlight, 2004)

Directed by Pieter Jan Brugge. Produced by Pieter Jan Brugge, Jonah Smith and Palmer West. Associate producer: Jawal Nga. Written by Justin Haythe. Based on the story by Pieter Jan Brugge and Justin Haythe. Music: Craig Armstrong. Cinematography: Denis Lenoir. Editor: Kevin Tent. Production designer: Chris Gorak. Costumer: Florence-Isabelle Megginson. Production companies: Fox Searchlight, Thousand Words, Wildwood Enterprises and Mediastream Dritte Film.

With Robert Redford (as Wayne Hayes), Helen Mirren, Willem Dafoe, Alessandro Nivola, Matt Craven, Melissa Sagemiller, Wendy Crewson, Larry Pine, Diane Scarwid, Elizabeth Ruscio, Gwen McGee, Sarah Koskoff, Graciela Marin, Mike Pniewski, Geoff McKnight, Tom Arcuragi, Audrey Wasilewski, Peter Gannon, Jacqi Loewy, Matt Miller, Mark Emery Moore, Joel Nunley and Ted Manson.

An Unfinished Life (Miramax, 2005)

Directed by Lasse Hallström. Produced by Kelliann Ladd and Alan Ladd Jr. Coproducer: Su Armstrong. Executive producers: Graham King, Meryl Poster, Michelle Raimo, Matthew Rhodes, Joe Roth, Mark Rydell, Bob Weinstein and Harvey Weinstein. Written by Mark Spragg and Virginia Korus Spragg. Music: Deborah Lurie. Cinematography: Oliver Stapleton. Editor: Andrew Mondshein. Production designer: David Gropman. Costumer: Tish Monaghan. Production companies: Initial Entertainment Group, Revolution Studios, Miramax Films, Persistent Entertainment, Laddy Company and Kalis Productions.

With Robert Redford (as Einar Gilkyson), Jennifer Lopez, Morgan Freeman, Josh Lucas, Damian Lewis, Camryn Manheim, Becca Gardner, Lynda Boyd, Rob Hayter, P. Lynn Johnson, Byron Lucas, Trevor Moss, R. Nelson Brown, Dillard Brinson, Jason Diablo, Sean J. Dory, Bryan Korenberg, Bonnie Barton, Danielle Dunn-Morris, Jill Tead, Jayne Dancose, Ken Camroux-Taylor, Sandra Polson, Dale Kipling and Bart the Bear.

Charlotte's Web (Paramount, 2006)
Part-animated movie

Directed by Gary Winick. Produced by Jordan Kerner. Coproducer: Tony Winley. Executive producers: Edgar Bronfman Sr., Paul Neesan, Julia Pistor and Bernie Williams. Written by Susannah Grant and Karey Kirkpatrick. Adaptation by Earl Hamner Jr. Based on the book by E. B. White. Music: Danny Elfman. Cinematography: Seamus McGarvey. Editors: Susan Littenberg and Sabrina Pilsco. Production designer: Stuart Wurtzel. Production companies: Walden Media, Nickelodeon Movies, Kerner Entertainment and Sandman Studios.

With Julia Roberts, Dakota Fanning, Steve Buscemi, Dominic Scott Kay, John Cleese, Oprah Winfrey, Cedric the Entertainer, Kathy Bates, Reba McEntire, André Benjamin, Thomas Haden Church, Beau Bridges and Robert Redford (as the voice of Ike).

Lions for Lambs (MGM-UA, 2007)

Directed by Robert Redford. Produced by Matthew Michael Carnahan, Andrew Hauptman, Tracy Falco and Robert Redford. Associate producer: William Holderman. Written by Matthew Michael Carnahan. Music: Mark Isham. Cinematography: Philippe Rousselot. Editor: Joe Hutshing. Production designer: Jan Roelfs. Production companies: United Artists, Cruise-Wagner Productions, Wildwood, Andell Entertainment and Brat Na Pont Productions.

With Robert Redford (as Professor Stephen Malley), Meryl Streep, Tom Cruise, Michael Peña, Andrew Garfield, Peter Berg, Kevin Dunn, Derek Luke, Larry Bates, Christopher May, David Pease, Heidi Janson, Christopher Carley, George Back, Kristy Wu, Bo Brown, Josh Zuckerman, Samantha Carro, Christopher Jordan, Angela Stefanelli, John Brently Reynolds, Paula Rhodes, Muna Otaru, Clay Wilcox, Sarayu Rao, Amanda Loncar, Richard Burns, Kevin Collins, Candace Moon, Chris Hoffman, Louise Linton, Jennifer Sommerfield, Wynonna Smith, Babar Peerzada, Wade Harlan, Paul Adams and Michael Peoples.

The Conspirator (Lionsgate, 2011)

Directed by Robert Redford. Produced by Brian Peter Falk, Bill Holderman, Robert Redford, Greg Shapiro, Robert Stone and Webster Stone. Executive producer: Jeremiah Samuels. Written by Gregory Bernstein and James D. Solomon. Cinematography: Newton Thomas Sigel. Editor: Craig McKay. Production designer: Kalina Ivanov. Production company: American Film Company/ Wildwood Enterprises.

With Norman Reedus, Alexis Bledel, James McAvoy, Justin Long, Evan Rachel Wood, Robin Wright, Johnny Simmons, Danny Huston, Kevin Kline, Jonathan Groff, Toby Kebbell, Tom Wilkinson, James Badge Dale, Stephen Root and Colm Meaney.

Additional Films and Television Productions as Executive Producer or Producer (*)

The Solar Film (Warner Bros., 1980)
Directed by Saul and Elaine Bass (animation)

Promised Land (Vestron, 1987)
Directed by Michael Hoffman

Some Girls (MGM, 1988)
Directed by Michael Hoffman

The Dark Wind (Carolco, 1991)
Directed by Errol Morris

*Incident at Oglala: The Leonard Peltier Story** (Miramax, 1992)
Directed by Michael Apted

*The American President** (Columbia, 1995)
Directed by Rob Reiner

She's the One (Twentieth Century–Fox, 1996)
Directed by Edward Burns

*A Civil Action** (Paramount, 1998)
Directed by Steven Zaillian

Slums of Beverly Hills (Fox Searchlight, 1998)
Directed by Tamara Jenkins

No Looking Back (Gramercy, 1998)
Directed by Edward Burns

Love in the Time of Money (ContentFilm, 2002)
Directed by Peter Mattei

Skinwalkers (PBS, 2002)
Directed by Chris Eyre

People I Know (Miramax, 2002)
Directed by Daniel Algrant

Coyote Waits (PBS, 2003)
Directed by Jan Egleson

The Motorcycle Diaries (Focus Features, 2004)
Directed by Walter Salles

A Thief of Time (PBS, 2004)
Directed by Chris Eyre

The Unforeseen (Sundance Channel, 2007)
Directed by Laura Dunn

Iconoclasts (Sundance Channel, 2005–2008)
Directed by Joe Berlinger and Bruce Sinofksy (five episodes)

Principal Television Performances

Armstrong Circle Theatre (1959)
Episode: "Berlin: City with a Short Fuse"
As Private Benjamin Peebles

Maverick (1960)
Episode: "The Iron Hand"
As Jimmy Coleman

The Deputy (1960)
Episode: "Last Gunfight"
As Burt Johnson

Hallmark Hall of Fame (1960)
Episode: "Captain Brassbound's Conversion"
As Blue Jacket

Playhouse 90 (1960)
Episode: "In the Presence of Mine Enemies"
As Sergeant Lott

Tate (1960)
Episodes: "The Bounty Hunter" and "Comanche Scalps"
As John Torsett and Tad Dundee

Moment of Fear (1960)
Episode: "The Golden Deed"
As "Stranger"

Perry Mason (1960)
Episode: "The Case of the Treacherous Toupee"
As Dick Hart

Play of the Week (1960)
Episode: "The Iceman Cometh" (in three parts)
As Don Parritt

Naked City (1961)
Episode: "Tombstone for a Derelict"
As Baldwin

The Americans (1961)
Episode: "The Coward"
As George Harrod

Whispering Smith (1961)
Episode: "The Grudge"
As Johnny Gates

Route 66 (1961)
Episode: "First-Class Mouliak"
As Janosh

Bus Stop (1961)
Episode: "The Covering Darkness"
As Art Ellison

The New Breed (1961)
Episode: "Ladykiller"
As the Hitchhiker

Alfred Hitchcock Presents (1961)
Episode: "The Right Kind of Medicine"
As Charlie Marx

The Twilight Zone (1962)
Episode: "Nothing in the Dark"
As Harold Beldon

Dr. Kildare (1962)
Episode: "The Burning Sky"
As Mark Hadley

Alcoa Premiere (1962)
Episode: "The Voice of Charlie Pont"
As George Laurents

The Alfred Hitchcock Hour (1962)
Episode: "A Piece of the Action"
As Chuck Marsden

The Untouchables (1963)
Episode: "Snowball"
As Jackson Emmit Parker

The Alfred Hitchcock Hour (1963)
Episode: "A Tangled Web"
As David Chesterman

The Dick Powell Show (1963)
Episode: "The Last of the Big Spenders"
As Nick Oakland

Breaking Point (1963)
Episode: "Bird and Snake"
As Roger Morton

The Virginian (1963)
Episode: "The Evil That Men Do"
As Matthew Cordell

The Defenders (1964)
Episode: "The Siege"
As Gary Degan

Theater Performances

Tall Story by Julius Epstein (Belasco Theatre, New York, 1959)
Directed by Herman Shumlin
As Basketball Player

Tiger at the Gates by Jean Anouilh (Bucks County Playhouse, Pennsylvania, 1959)
Directed by Mike Ellis
As Paris

The Highest Tree by Dore Schary (Longacre Theatre, New York, 1959)
Directed by Dore Schary
As the son

Little Moon of Alban by James Costigan (Longacre Theatre, New York, 1960)
Directed by Herman Shumlin
As Dennis Walsh

Sunday in New York by Norman Krasna (Cort Theatre, New York, 1961–62)
Directed by Garson Kanin
As Mike Mitchell

Barefoot in the Park by Neil Simon (Biltmore Theatre, New York, 1963–64)
Directed by Mike Nichols
As Paul Bratter

Index

A Note on the Author

MICHAEL FEENEY CALLAN is the author of a collection of short stories, for which he won the Hennessy Literary Award, two novels, and several plays, as well as biographies of Anthony Hopkins, Richard Harris, Julie Christie, and Sean Connery. He has worked for the BBC, Ireland's Ardmore Studios, and PBS as a writer, producer, and director of television dramas and documentaries. He lives in Dublin.